PEARSON CUSTOM LIBRARY

Management 3200
Operations Management

PEARSON

ISBN 10: 0-558-23342-2
ISBN 13: 978-0-558-23342-6

PEARSON

Table of Contents

Operations and Productivity

Outline

Learning Objectives

When you complete this selection you should be able to

1. Define operations management
2. Explain the distinction between goods and services
3. Explain the difference between production and productivity
4. Compute single-factor productivity
5. Compute multifactor productivity
6. Identify the critical variables in enhancing productivity

Operations Management at Hard Rock Cafe

Operations managers throughout the world are producing products every day to provide for the well-being of society. These products take on a multitude of forms. They may be washing machines at Whirlpool, motion pictures at Dreamworks, rides at Disney World, or food at Hard Rock Cafe. These firms produce thousands of complex products every day—to be delivered as the customer ordered them, when the customers wants them, and where the customer wants them. Hard Rock does this for over 35 million guests worldwide every year. This is a challenging task, and the operations manager's job, whether at Whirlpool, Dreamworks, Disney, or Hard Rock, is demanding.

Orlando-based Hard Rock Cafe opened its first restaurant in London in 1971, making it over 35 years old and the granddaddy of theme restaurants. Although other theme restaurants have come and gone, Hard Rock is still going strong, with 121 restaurants in more than 40 countries—and new restaurants opening each year. Hard Rock made its name with rock music memorabilia, having started when Eric Clapton, a regular customer, marked his favorite bar stool by hanging his guitar on the wall in the London cafe. Now Hard Rock has millions of dollars invested in memorabilia. To keep customers coming back time and again, Hard Rock creates value in the form of good food and entertainment.

The operations managers at Hard Rock Cafe at Universal Studios in Orlando provide more than

Hard Rock Café

3,500 custom products, in this case meals, every day. These products are designed, tested, and then analyzed for cost of ingredients, labor requirements, and customer satisfaction. On approval, menu items are put into production—and then only if the ingredients are available from qualified suppliers. The production process, from receiving, to cold storage, to grilling or baking or frying, and a dozen other steps, is designed and maintained to yield a quality

▶ *Operations managers are interested in the attractiveness of the layout, but they must be sure that the facility contributes to the efficient movement of people and material with the necessary controls to ensure that proper portions are served.*

Hard Rock Café

▲ Lots of work goes into designing, testing, and costing meals. Then suppliers deliver quality products on time, every time, for well-trained cooks to prepare quality meals. But none of that matters unless an enthusiastic wait staff, such as the one shown here, is doing its job.

◄ Hard Rock Cafe in Orlando, Florida, prepares over 3,500 meals each day. Seating over 1,500 people, it is one of the largest restaurants in the world. But Hard Rock's operations managers serve the hot food hot and the cold food cold.

◄ Efficient kitchen layouts, motivated personnel, tight schedules, and the right ingredients at the right place at the right time are required to delight the customer.

meal. Operations managers, using the best people they can recruit and train, also prepare effective employee schedules and design efficient layouts.

Managers who successfully design and deliver goods and services throughout the world understand operations. In this text, we look not only at how Hard Rock's managers create value but also how operations managers in other services, as well as in manufacturing, do so. Operations management is demanding, challenging, and exciting. It affects our lives every day. Ultimately, operations managers determine how well we live.

Video 1.1

Operations Management
at Hard Rock

Operations management (OM) is a discipline that applies to restaurants like Hard Rock Cafe as well as to factories like Sony, Ford, and Whirlpool. The techniques of OM apply throughout the world to virtually all productive enterprises. It doesn't matter if the application is in an office, a hospital, a restaurant, a department store, or a factory—the production of goods and services requires operations management. And the *efficient* production of goods and services requires effective applications of the concepts, tools, and techniques of OM.

In this selection, we first define *operations management*, explaining its heritage and exploring the exciting role operations managers play in a huge variety of businesses. Then we discuss production and productivity in both goods- and service-producing firms. This is followed by a discussion of operations in the service sector and the challenge of managing an effective production system.

WHAT IS OPERATIONS MANAGEMENT?

Learning Objective

1. Define operations management

Production
The creation of goods and services.

Operations management (OM)
Activities that relate to the creation of goods and services through the transformation of inputs to outputs.

Production is the creation of goods and services. **Operations management (OM)** is the set of activities that creates value in the form of goods and services by transforming inputs into outputs. Activities creating goods and services take place in all organizations. In manufacturing firms, the production activities that create goods are usually quite obvious. In them, we can see the creation of a tangible product such as a Sony TV or a Harley-Davidson motorcycle.

In an organization that does not create a tangible good or product, the production function may be less obvious. We often call these activities *services*. The services may be "hidden" from the public and even from the customer. The product may take such forms as the transfer of funds from a savings account to a checking account, the transplant of a liver, the filling of an empty seat on an airplane, or the education of a student. Regardless of whether the end product is a good or service, the production activities that go on in the organization are often referred to as operations, or *operations management*.

ORGANIZING TO PRODUCE GOODS AND SERVICES

To create goods and services, all organizations perform three functions (see Figure 1). These functions are the necessary ingredients not only for production but also for an organization's survival. They are:

1. *Marketing*, which generates the demand, or at least takes the order for a product or service (nothing happens until there is a sale).
2. *Production/operations*, which creates the product.
3. *Finance/accounting*, which tracks how well the organization is doing, pays the bills, and collects the money.

Universities, churches or synagogues, and businesses all perform these functions. Even a volunteer group such as the Boy Scouts of America is organized to perform these three basic functions. Figure 1 shows how a bank, an airline, and a manufacturing firm organize themselves to perform these functions. The blue-shaded areas of Figure 1 show the operations functions in these firms.

WHY STUDY OM?

We study OM for four reasons:

1. OM is one of the three major functions of any organization, and it is integrally related to all the other business functions. All organizations market (sell), finance (account), and produce (operate), and it is important to know how the OM activity functions. Therefore, we study *how people organize themselves for productive enterprise*.
2. We study OM because we want to know *how goods and services are produced*. The production function is the segment of our society that creates the products and services we use.
3. We study OM to *understand what operations managers do*. By understanding what these managers do, you can develop the skills necessary to become such a manager. This will help you explore the numerous and lucrative career opportunities in OM.

4. We study OM *because it is such a costly part of an organization.* A large percentage of the revenue of most firms is spent in the OM function. Indeed, OM provides a major opportunity for an organization to improve its profitability and enhance its service to society. Example 1 considers how a firm might increase its profitability via the production function.

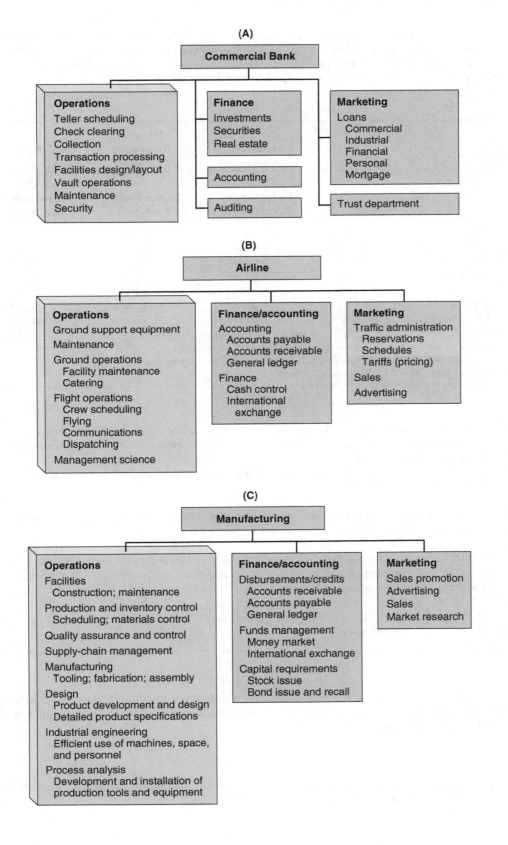

◄ **Figure 1**

Organization Charts for Two Service Organizations and One Manufacturing Organization

(A) A bank, (B) an airline, and (C) a manufacturing organization. The blue areas are OM activities.

(A)

Commercial Bank

Operations
Teller scheduling
Check clearing
Collection
Transaction processing
Facilities design/layout
Vault operations
Maintenance
Security

Finance
Investments
Securities
Real estate

Accounting

Auditing

Marketing
Loans
  Commercial
  Industrial
  Financial
  Personal
  Mortgage

Trust department

(B)

Airline

Operations
Ground support equipment

Maintenance

Ground operations
  Facility maintenance
  Catering

Flight operations
  Crew scheduling
  Flying
  Communications
  Dispatching

Management science

Finance/accounting
Accounting
  Accounts payable
  Accounts receivable
  General ledger

Finance
  Cash control
  International
    exchange

Marketing
Traffic administration
  Reservations
  Schedules
  Tariffs (pricing)

Sales

Advertising

(C)

Manufacturing

Operations
Facilities
  Construction; maintenance
Production and inventory control
  Scheduling; materials control
Quality assurance and control
Supply-chain management
Manufacturing
  Tooling; fabrication; assembly
Design
  Product development and design
  Detailed product specifications
Industrial engineering
  Efficient use of machines, space,
  and personnel
Process analysis
  Development and installation of
  production tools and equipment

Finance/accounting
Disbursements/credits
  Accounts receivable
  Accounts payable
  General ledger
Funds management
  Money market
  International exchange
Capital requirements
  Stock issue
  Bond issue and recall

Marketing
Sales promotion
Advertising
Sales
Market research

EXAMPLE 1

Examining the options for increasing contribution

Fisher Technologies is a small firm that must double its dollar contribution to fixed cost and profit in order to be profitable enough to purchase the next generation of production equipment. Management has determined that if the firm fails to increase contribution, its bank will not make the loan and the equipment cannot be purchased. If the firm cannot purchase the equipment, the limitations of the old equipment will force Fisher to go out of business and, in doing so, put its employees out of work and discontinue producing goods and services for its customers.

Approach: Table 1 shows a simple profit-and-loss statement and three strategic options (marketing, finance/accounting, and operations) for the firm. The first option is a *marketing option*, where good marketing management may increase sales by 50%. By increasing sales by 50%, contribution will in turn increase 71%. But increasing sales 50% may be difficult; it may even be impossible.

▶ **Table 1**

Options for Increasing Contribution

	Current	Marketing Option[a] Increase Sales Revenue 50%	Finance/ Accounting Option[b] Reduce Finance Costs 50%	OM Option[c] Reduce Production Costs 20%
Sales	$100,000	$150,000	$100,000	$100,000
Costs of goods	−80,000	−120,000	−80,000	−64,000
Gross margin	20,000	30,000	20,000	36,000
Finance costs	− 6,000	− 6,000	− 3,000	− 6,000
Subtotal	14,000	24,000	17,000	30,000
Taxes at 25%	− 3,500	− 6,000	− 4,250	− 7,500
Contribution[d]	$ 10,500	$ 18,000	$ 12,750	$ 22,500

[a]Increasing sales 50% increases contribution by $7,500, or 71% (7,500/10,500).
[b]Reducing finance costs 50% increases contribution by $2,250, or 21% (2,250/10,500).
[c]Reducing production costs 20% increases contribution by $12,000, or 114% (12,000/10,500).
[d]Contribution to fixed cost (excluding finance costs) and profit.

The second option is a *finance/accounting option*, where finance costs are cut in half through good financial management. But even a reduction of 50% is still inadequate for generating the necessary increase in contribution. Contribution is increased by only 21%.

The third option is an *OM option*, where management reduces production costs by 20% and increases contribution by 114%.

Solution: Given the conditions of our brief example, Fisher Technologies has increased contribution from $10,500 to $22,500. It may now have a bank willing to lend it additional funds.

Insight: The OM option not only yields the greatest improvement in contribution but also may be the only feasible option. Increasing sales by 50% and decreasing finance cost by 50% may both be virtually impossible. Reducing operations cost by 20% may be difficult but feasible.

Learning exercise: What is the impact of only a 15% decrease in costs in the OM option? [Answer: A $19,500 contribution.]

Example 1 underscores the importance of an effective operations activity of a firm. Development of increasingly effective operations is the approach taken by many companies as they face growing global competition.[1]

[1]See related discussion in Michael Hammer, "Deep Change: How Operational Innovation Can Transform Your Company," *Harvard Business Review* 82, no. 4 (2004): 85–93.

WHAT OPERATIONS MANAGERS DO

All good managers perform the basic functions of the management process. The **management process** consists of *planning*, *organizing*, *staffing*, *leading*, and *controlling*. Operations managers apply this management process to the decisions they make in the OM function. The 10 major decisions of OM are shown in Table 2. Successfully addressing each of these decisions requires planning, organizing, staffing, leading, and controlling. Typical issues relevant to these decisions and the chapter where each is discussed are also shown.

How This Book Is Organized

The 10 decisions shown in Table 2 are activities required of operations managers. The ability to make good decisions in these areas and allocate resources to ensure their effective execution goes a long way toward an efficient operations function. The text is structured around these 10 decisions. Throughout the book, we discuss the issues and tools that help managers make these 10 decisions. We also consider the impact that these decisions can have on the firm's strategy and productivity.

Where Are the OM Jobs?   How does one get started on a career in operations? The 10 OM decisions identified in Table 2 are made by individuals who work in the disciplines shown in the blue areas of Figure 1. Competent business students who know their accounting, statistics, finance, and OM have an opportunity to assume entry-level positions in all of these areas. As you read this text, identify disciplines that can assist you in making these decisions. Then take courses in those areas. The more background an OM student has in accounting, statistics, information systems, and mathematics, the more job opportunities will be available. About 40% of *all* jobs are in OM. Figure 2 shows some recent job opportunities.

Management process
The application of planning, organizing, staffing, leading, and controlling to the achievement of objectives.

Ten OM Strategy Decisions

Design of Goods and Services

Managing Quality

Process Strategy

Location Strategies

Layout Strategies

Human Resources

Supply Chain Management

Inventory Management

Scheduling

Maintenance

◀ **Table 2**

Ten Critical Decisions of Operations Management

Ten Decision Areas	Issues	Chapter(s)
Design of goods and services	What good or service should we offer? How should we design these products?	5
Managing quality	How do we define the quality? Who is responsible for quality?	6, Supplement 6
Process and capacity design	What process and what capacity will these products require? What equipment and technology is necessary for these processes?	7, Supplement 7
Location strategy	Where should we put the facility? On what criteria should we base the location decision?	8
Layout strategy	How should we arrange the facility? How large must the facility be to meet our plan?	9
Human resources and job design	How do we provide a reasonable work environment? How much can we expect our employees to produce?	10, Supplement 10
Supply chain management	Should we make or buy this component? Who are our suppliers and who can integrate into our e-commerce program?	11, Supplement 11
Inventory, material requirements planning, and JIT (just-in-time)	How much inventory of each item should we have? When do we reorder?	12, 14, 16
Intermediate and short-term scheduling	Are we better off keeping people on the payroll during slowdowns? Which job do we perform next?	13, 15
Maintenance	Who is responsible for maintenance? When do we do maintenance?	17

PLANT MANAGER

Division of Fortune 1000 company seeks plant manager for plant located in the upper Hudson Valley area. This plant manufactures loading dock equipment for commercial markets. The candidate must be experienced in plant management including expertise in production planning, purchasing, and inventory management. Good written and oral communication skills are a must along with excellent understanding of and application skills in managing people.

Operations Analyst

Expanding national coffee shop; top 10 "Best Places to Work" wants junior level systems analyst to join our excellent store improvement team. Business or I.E. degree, work methods, labor standards, ergonomics, cost accounting knowledge a plus. This is a hands on job and excellent opportunity for team player with good people skills. West Coast location. Some travel required.

Quality Manager

Several openings exist in our small package processing facilities in the Northeast, Florida, and Southern California for quality managers. These highly visible positions require extensive use of statistical tools to monitor all aspects of service timeliness and workload measurement. The work involves (1) a combination of hands-on applications and detailed analysis using databases and spreadsheets, (2) process audits to identify areas for improvement, and (3) management of implementation of changes. Positions involve night hours and weekends. Send resume.

Supply Chain Manager and Planner

Responsibilities entail negotiating contracts and establishing long-term relationships with suppliers. We will rely on the selected candidate to maintain accuracy in the purchasing system, invoices, and product returns. A bachelor's degree and up to 2 years related experience are required. Working knowledge of MRP, ability to use feedback to master scheduling and suppliers and consolidate orders for best price and delivery are necessary. Proficiency in all PC Windows applications, particularly Excel and Word, is essential. Knowledge of Oracle business system I is a plus. Effective verbal and written communication skills are essential.

Process Improvement Consultants

An expanding consulting firm is seeking consultants to design and implement lean production and cycle time reduction plans in both service and manufacturing processes. Our firm is currently working with an international bank to improve its back office operations, as well as with several manufacturing firms. A business degree required; APICS certification a plus.

▲ **Figure 2** **Many Opportunities Exist for Operations Managers**

THE HERITAGE OF OPERATIONS MANAGEMENT

The field of OM is relatively young, but its history is rich and interesting. Our lives and the OM discipline have been enhanced by the innovations and contributions of numerous individuals. We now introduce a few of these people, and we provide a summary of significant events in operations management in Figure 3.

Eli Whitney (1800) is credited for the early popularization of interchangeable parts, which was achieved through standardization and quality control. Through a contract he signed with the U.S. government for 10,000 muskets, he was able to command a premium price because of their interchangeable parts.

Frederick W. Taylor (1881), known as the father of scientific management, contributed to personnel selection, planning and scheduling, motion study, and the now popular field of ergonomics. One of his major contributions was his belief that management should be much more resourceful and aggressive in the improvement of work methods. Taylor and his colleagues, Henry L. Gantt and Frank and Lillian Gilbreth, were among the first to systematically seek the best way to produce.

Another of Taylor's contributions was the belief that management should assume more responsibility for:

1. Matching employees to the right job.
2. Providing the proper training.
3. Providing proper work methods and tools.
4. Establishing legitimate incentives for work to be accomplished.

Taylor revolutionized manufacturing: his scientific approach to the analysis of daily work and the tools of industry frequently increased productivity 400%.

Charles Sorensen towed an automobile chassis on a rope over his shoulders through the Ford plant while others added parts.

By 1913, Henry Ford and Charles Sorensen combined what they knew about standardized parts with the quasi-assembly lines of the meatpacking and mail-order industries and added the revolutionary concept of the assembly line, where men stood still and material moved.[2]

Quality control is another historically significant contribution to the field of OM. Walter Shewhart (1924) combined his knowledge of statistics with the need for quality control and provided the foundations for statistical sampling in quality control. W. Edwards Deming (1950)

[2]Jay Heizer, "Determining Responsibility for the Development of the Moving Assembly Line," *Journal of Management History* 4, no. 2 (1998): 94–103.

Customization Focus

**Mass Customization Era
1995–2010**
Globalization
Internet/E-Commerce
Enterprise Resource Planning
Learning Organization
International Quality Standards
Finite Scheduling
Supply Chain Management
Mass Customization
Build-to-Order

Quality Focus

Cost Focus

**Early Concepts
1776–1880**
Labor Specialization
    (Smith, Babbage)
Standardized Parts (Whitney)

**Scientific Management Era
1880–1910**
Gantt Charts (Gantt)
Motion & Time Studies
    (Gilbreth)
Process Analysis (Taylor)
Queuing Theory (Erlang)

**Mass Production Era
1910–1980**
Moving Assembly Line
    (Ford/Sorensen)
Statistical Sampling
    (Shewhart)
Economic Order
    Quantity (Harris)
Linear Programming
    PERT/CPM (DuPont)
Material Requirements
    Planning

**Lean Production Era
1980–1995**
Just-in-Time
Computer-Aided Design
Electronic Data Interchange
Total Quality Management
Baldrige Award
Empowerment
Kanbans

▲ **Figure 3** **Significant Events in Operations Management**

believed, as did Frederick Taylor, that management must do more to improve the work environment and processes so that quality can be improved.

Operations management will continue to progress with contributions from other disciplines, including *industrial engineering* and *management science*. These disciplines, along with statistics, management, and economics, contribute to improved models and decision making.

Innovations from the *physical sciences* (biology, anatomy, chemistry, physics) have also contributed to advances in OM. These innovations include new adhesives, faster integrated circuits, gamma rays to sanitize food products, and higher-quality glass for LCD and plasma TVs. Innovation in products and processes often depends on advances in the physical sciences.

Especially important contributions to OM have come from *information technology*, which we define as the systematic processing of data to yield information. Information technology—with wireless links, Internet, and e-commerce—is reducing costs and accelerating communication.

Decisions in operations management require individuals who are well versed in management science, in information technology, and often in one of the biological or physical sciences. In this textbook, we look at the diverse ways a student can prepare for a career in operations management.

OPERATIONS IN THE SERVICE SECTOR

Manufacturers produce a tangible product, while service products are often intangible. But many products are a combination of a good and a service, which complicates the definition of a service. Even the U.S. government has trouble generating a consistent definition. Because definitions vary, much of the data and statistics generated about the service sector are inconsistent. However, we define **services** as including repair and maintenance, government, food and

Services
Economic activities that typically produce an intangible product (such as education, entertainment, lodging, government, financial, and health services).

lodging, transportation, insurance, trade, financial, real estate, education, legal, medical, entertainment, and other professional occupations.[3]

Differences between Goods and Services

Let's examine some of the differences between goods and services:

- Services are usually *intangible* (for example, your purchase of a ride in an empty airline seat between two cities) as opposed to a tangible good.
- Services are often *produced and consumed simultaneously*; there is no stored inventory. For instance, the beauty salon produces a haircut that is "consumed" simultaneously, or the doctor produces an operation that is "consumed" as it is produced. We have not yet figured out how to inventory haircuts or appendectomies.
- Services are often *unique*. Your mix of financial coverage, such as investments and insurance policies, may not be the same as anyone else's, just as the medical procedure or a haircut produced for you is not exactly like anyone else's.
- Services have *high customer interaction*. Services are often difficult to standardize, automate, and make as efficient as we would like because customer interaction demands uniqueness. In fact, in many cases this uniqueness is what the customer is paying for; therefore, the operations manager must ensure that the product is designed (i.e., customized) so that it can be delivered in the required unique manner.
- Services have *inconsistent product definition*. Product definition may be rigorous, as in the case of an auto insurance policy, but inconsistent because policyholders change cars and mature.
- Services are often *knowledge based*, as in the case of educational, medical, and legal services, and therefore hard to automate.
- Services are frequently *dispersed*. Dispersion occurs because services are frequently brought to the client/customer via a local office, a retail outlet, or even a house call.

Table 3 indicates some additional differences between goods and services that affect OM decisions. Although service products are different from goods, the operations function continues to transform resources into products. Indeed, the activities of the operations function are often very similar for both goods and services. For instance, both goods and services must have quality standards established, and both must be designed and processed on a schedule in a facility where human resources are employed.

Having made the distinction between goods and services, we should point out that in many cases, the distinction is not clear-cut. In reality, almost all services and almost all goods are a mixture of a service and a tangible product. Even services such as consulting may require a tangible report. Similarly, the sale of most goods includes a service. For instance, many products have the service components of financing and delivery (e.g., automobile sales). Many also require after-sale training and maintenance (e.g., office copiers and machinery). "Service" activ-

► Table 3

Differences between Goods and Services

Attributes of Goods (tangible product)	Attributes of Services (intangible product)
Product can be resold.	Reselling a service is unusual.
Product can be inventoried.	Many services cannot be inventoried.
Some aspects of quality are measurable.	Many aspects of quality are difficult to measure.
Selling is distinct from production.	Selling is often a part of the service.
Product is transportable.	Provider, not product, is often transportable.
Site of facility is important for cost.	Site of facility is important for customer contact.
Often easy to automate.	Service is often difficult to automate.
Revenue is generated primarily from the tangible product.	Revenue is generated primarily from the intangible services.

[3]This definition is similar to the categories used by the U.S. Bureau of Labor Statistics.

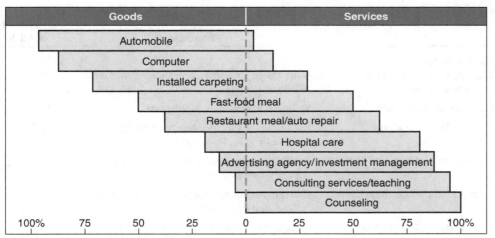

◄ **Figure 4**

Most Goods Contain a Service, and Most Services Contain a Good

ities may also be an integral part of production. Human resource activities, logistics, accounting, training, field service, and repair are all service activities, but they take place within a manufacturing organization.

When a tangible product is *not* included in the service, we may call it a **pure service**. Although there are not very many pure services, in some instances counseling may be an example. Figure 4 shows the range of *services* in a product. The range is extensive and shows the pervasiveness of service activities.

Pure service
A service that does not include a tangible product.

Growth of Services

Services now constitute the largest economic sector in postindustrial societies. Until about 1900, most Americans were employed in agriculture. Increased agricultural productivity allowed people to leave the farm and seek employment in the city. Similarly, manufacturing employment has decreased somewhat in the last 25 years. The changes in manufacturing and service employment, in millions, are shown in Figure 5(a). Interestingly, as Figure 5(b)

▼ **Figure 5** Development of the Service Economy and Manufacturing Productivity

Sources: U.S. Bureau of Labor Statistics; Federal Reserve Board, Industrial Production and Capacity Utilization (2003); Statistical Abstract of the United States (2005).

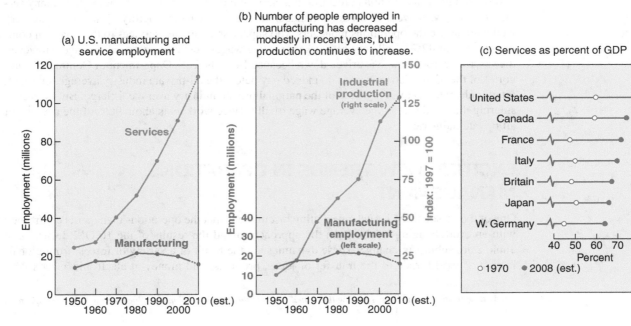

► **Table 4**

Examples of Organizations in Each Sector

Source: Statistical Abstract of the United States (2007), Table 606 and Bureau of Labor Statistics, 2007.

Sector	Example	Percent of All Jobs
Service Sector		
Education, Legal, Medical, and other services	Notre Dame University, San Diego Zoo, Arnold Palmer Hospital	25.5 ⎤
Trade (retail, wholesale)	Walgreen's, Wal-Mart, Nordstrom	15.1 ⎥
Utilities, Transportation	Pacific Gas & Electric, American Airlines, Santa Fe R.R., Roadway Express	5.2 ⎥
Professional and Business Services	Snelling and Snelling, Waste Management, Inc., Pitney-Bowes	10.1 ⎬ 78.6
Finance, Information, Real Estate	Citicorp, American Express, Prudential, Aetna, Trammell Crow, EDS, IBM	9.6 ⎥
Food, Lodging, Entertainment	Olive Garden, Hard Rock Cafe, Motel 6, Hilton Hotels, Walt Disney, Paramount Pictures	8.5 ⎥
Public Administration	U.S., State of Alabama, Cook County	4.6 ⎦
Manufacturing Sector	General Electric, Ford, U.S. Steel, Intel	11.5
Construction Sector	Bechtel, McDermott	7.9
Agriculture	King Ranch	1.6
Mining Sector	Homestake Mining	.4
Grand Total		100.0

Service sector

The segment of the economy that includes trade, financial, lodging, education, legal, medical, and other professional occupations.

indicates, while the *number* of people employed in manufacturing has held relatively steady since 1950, each person is now producing about 20 times more than in 1950. Services became the dominant employer in the early 1920s, with manufacturing employment peaking at about 32% in 1950. The huge productivity increases in agriculture and manufacturing have allowed more of our economic resources to be devoted to services, as shown in Figure 5(c). Consequently, much of the world can now enjoy the pleasures of education, health services, entertainment, and myriad other things that we call services. Examples of firms and percentage of employment in the U.S. **service sector** are shown in Table 4. Table 4 also provides employment percentages for the nonservice sectors of manufacturing, construction, agriculture, and mining on the bottom four lines.

Service Pay

Although there is a common perception that service industries are low paying, in fact, many service jobs pay very well. Operations managers in the maintenance facility of an airline are very well paid, as are the operations managers who supervise computer services to the financial community. About 42% of all service workers receive wages above the national average. However, the service-sector average is driven down because 14 of the U.S. Department of Commerce categories of the 33 service industries do indeed pay below the all-private industry average. Of these, retail trade, which pays only 61% of the national private industry average, is large. But even considering the retail sector, the average wage of all service workers is about 96% of the average of all private industries.[4]

EXCITING NEW TRENDS IN OPERATIONS MANAGEMENT

One of the reasons OM is such an exciting discipline is that the operations manager is confronted with an ever-changing world. Both the approach to and the results of the 10 OM decisions in Table 2 are subject to change. These dynamics are the result of a variety of forces, from globalization of world trade to the transfer of ideas, products, and money at electronic speeds. The

[4]Herbert Stein and Murray Foss, *The New Illustrated Guide to the American Economy* (Washington, DC: The AIE Press, 1995): 30.

Past		Causes		Future
Local or national focus	→	*Reliable worldwide communication and transportation networks*	→	Global focus, moving production offshore
Batch (large) shipments	→	*Short product life cycles and cost of capital put pressure on reducing inventory*	→	Just-in-time performance
Low-bid purchasing	→	*Supply chain competition requires that suppliers be engaged in a focus on the end customer*	→	Supply-chain partners, collaboration, alliances, outsourcing
Lengthy product development	→	*Shorter life cycles, Internet, rapid international communication, computer-aided design, and international collaboration*	→	Rapid product development, alliances, collaborative designs
Standardized products	→	*Affluence and worldwide markets; increasingly flexible production processes*	→	Mass customization with added emphasis on quality
Job specialization	→	*Changing sociocultural milieu; increasingly a knowledge and information society*	→	Empowered employees, teams, and lean production
Low-cost focus	→	*Environmental issues, ISO 14000, increasing disposal costs*	→	Environmentally sensitive production, green manufacturing, recycled materials, remanufacturing
Ethics not at forefront	→	*Businesses operate more openly; public and global review of ethics; opposition to child labor, bribery, pollution*	→	High ethical standards and social responsibility expected

▲ **Figure 6** Changing Challenges for the Operations Manager

direction now being taken by OM—where it has been and where it is going—is shown in Figure 6. We now introduce some of the challenges shown in Figure 6:

- *Global focus:* The rapid decline in communication and transportation costs has made markets global. At the same time, resources in the form of capital, materials, talent, and labor have also become global. Contributing to this rapid globalization are countries throughout the world that are vying for economic growth and industrialization. Operations managers are responding with innovations that generate and move ideas, production, and finished goods rapidly.
- *Just-in-time performance:* Vast financial resources are committed to inventory, making it costly. Inventory also impedes response to rapid changes in the marketplace. Operations managers are viciously cutting inventories at every level, from raw materials to finished goods.
- *Supply chain partnering:* Shorter product life cycles, driven by demanding customers, as well as rapid changes in material and processes, require suppliers to be more in tune with the needs of the end user. And because suppliers often have unique expertise, operations managers are outsourcing and building long-term partnerships with critical players in the supply chain.
- *Rapid product development:* Rapid international communication of news, entertainment, and lifestyles is dramatically chopping away at the life span of products. Operations managers are responding with management structures and technology that are faster and alliances (partners) that are more effective.
- *Mass customization:* Once managers begin to recognize the world as the marketplace, then the individual differences become quite obvious. Cultural differences, compounded by individual differences, in a world where consumers are increasingly aware of innovation and options, places substantial pressure on firms to respond. Operations managers are responding with production processes that are flexible enough to cater to individual whims of consumers. The goal is to produce customized products, whenever and wherever needed.

- *Empowered employees:* The knowledge explosion and a more technical workplace have combined to require more competence at the workplace. Operations managers are responding by moving more decision making to the individual worker.
- *Environmentally sensitive production:* The operation manager's continuing battle to improve productivity is increasingly concerned with designing products and processes that are environmentally friendly. That means designing products that are biodegradable, or automobile components that can be reused or recycled, or making packaging more efficient.
- *Ethics:* Operations managers are taking their place in the continuing challenge to enhance ethical behavior.

These and many more topics that are part of the exciting challenges to operations managers are discussed in this text.

THE PRODUCTIVITY CHALLENGE

Productivity

The ratio of outputs (goods and services) divided by one or more inputs (such as labor, capital, or management).

The creation of goods and services requires changing resources into goods and services. The more efficiently we make this change, the more productive we are and the more value is added to the good or service provided. **Productivity** is the ratio of outputs (goods and services) divided by the inputs (resources, such as labor and capital) (see Figure 7). The operations manager's job is to enhance (improve) this ratio of outputs to inputs. Improving productivity means improving efficiency.[5]

This improvement can be achieved in two ways: reducing inputs while keeping output constant or increasing output while keeping inputs constant. Both represent an improvement in productivity. In an economic sense, inputs are labor, capital, and management, which are integrated into a production system. Management creates this production system, which provides the conversion of inputs to outputs. Outputs are goods and services, including such diverse items as guns, butter, education, improved judicial systems, and ski resorts. *Production* is the making of goods and services. High production may imply only that more people are working and that employment levels are high (low unemployment), but it does not imply high *productivity*.

Learning Objective

3. Explain the difference between production and productivity

Measurement of productivity is an excellent way to evaluate a country's ability to provide an improving standard of living for its people. *Only through increases in productivity can the standard of living improve.* Moreover, only through increases in productivity can labor, capital, and management receive additional payments. If returns to labor, capital, or management are increased without increased productivity, prices rise. On the other hand, downward pressure is placed on prices when productivity increases, because more is being produced with the same resources.

The benefits of increased productivity are illustrated in the *OM in Action* box "Improving Productivity at Starbucks."

▶ **Figure 7**

The Economic System Adds Value by Transforming Inputs to Outputs

An effective feedback loop evaluates process performance against a plan or standard. It also evaluates customer satisfaction and sends signals to managers controlling the inputs and process.

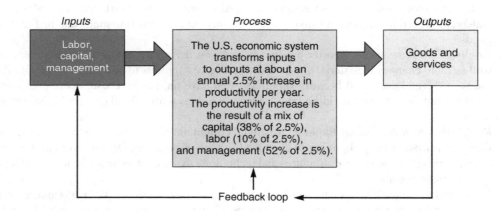

[5]*Efficiency* means doing the job well—with a minimum of resources and waste. Note the distinction between being *efficient*, which implies doing the job well, and *effective*, which means doing the right thing. A job well done—say, by applying the 10 decisions of operations management—helps us be *efficient*; developing and using the correct strategy helps us be *effective*.

OM in Action   Improving Productivity at Starbucks

"This is a game of seconds . . . " says Silva Peterson, whom Starbucks has put in charge of saving seconds. Her team of 10 analysts is constantly asking themselves: "How can we shave time off this?"

Peterson's analysis suggested that there were some obvious opportunities. First, stop requiring signatures on credit-card purchases under $25. This sliced 8 seconds off the transaction time at the cash register.

Then analysts noticed that Starbucks's largest cold beverage, the Venti size, required two bending and digging motions to scoop up enough ice. The scoop was too small. Redesign of the scoop provided the proper amount in one motion and cut 14 seconds off the average time of one minute.

Third were new espresso machines; with the push of a button, the machines grind coffee beans and brew. This

Marc Asnin, CORBIS-NY

allowed the server, called a "barista" in Starbucks's vocabulary, to do other things. The savings: about 12 seconds per espresso shot.

As a result, operations improvements at Starbucks outlets have increased the average yearly volume by nearly $200,000, to about $940,000 in the past 6 years. This is a 27% improvement in productivity—about 4.5% per year. In the service industry, a 4.5% per year increase is very tasty.

Sources: The Wall Street Journal (April 12, 2005): B2:B7; *Knight Ridder Tribune Business News* (July 25, 2003):1; **www.finfacts.com**, October 6, 2005.

For well over a century (from about 1869), the U.S. has been able to increase productivity at an average rate of almost 2.5% per year. Such growth has doubled U.S. wealth every 30 years. The manufacturing sector, although a decreasing portion of the U.S. economy, has recently seen annual productivity increases exceeding 4%, and the service sector, with increases of almost 1%, has also shown some improvement. The combination has moved U.S. annual productivity growth in this early part of the 21st century slightly above the 2.5% range for the economy as a whole.[6]

In this selection, we examine how to improve productivity through the operations function. Productivity is a significant issue for the world and one that the operations manager is uniquely qualified to address.

Video 1.2

The Transformation Process at Regal Marine

Productivity Measurement

The measurement of productivity can be quite direct. Such is the case when productivity is measured by labor-hours per ton of a specific type of steel. Although labor-hours is a common measure of input, other measures such as capital (dollars invested), materials (tons of ore), or energy (kilowatts of electricity) can be used.[7] An example of this can be summarized in the following equation:

$$\text{Productivity} = \frac{\text{Units produced}}{\text{Input used}} \qquad (1)$$

For example, if units produced = 1,000 and labor-hours used is 250, then:

$$\text{Productivity} = \frac{\text{Units produced}}{\text{Labor-hours used}} = \frac{1,000}{250} = 4 \text{ units per labor-hour}$$

The use of just one resource input to measure productivity, as shown in Equation (1), is known as **single-factor productivity**. However, a broader view of productivity is **multifactor productivity**, which includes all inputs (e.g., capital, labor, material, energy). Multifactor productivity is also known as *total factor productivity*. Multifactor productivity is calculated by combining the input units as shown here:

$$\text{Productivity} = \frac{\text{Output}}{\text{Labor} + \text{Material} + \text{Energy} + \text{Capital} + \text{Miscellaneous}} \qquad (2)$$

Learning Objective

4. Compute single-factor productivity

Single-factor productivity
Indicates the ratio of one resource (input) to the goods and services produced (outputs).

Multifactor productivity
Indicates the ratio of many or all resources (inputs) to the goods and services produced (outputs).

---

[6]According to the *Statistical Abstract of the United States*, non-farm business sector productivity increase for 1995 was 0.9%; 1996, 2.5%; 1997, 2.0%; 1998, 2.6%; 1999, 2.4%; 2000, 2.9%; 2001, 1.1%; 2002, 4.8%; (see Table 633). Productivity increase for 2003, 4.5%; 2004, 4.0%; 2005, 2.9%; and 2006, 1.6% (U.S. Dept. of Labor, April 2007). **www.bls.gov/newsreleases/archives**.

[7]The quality and time period are assumed to remain constant.

To aid in the computation of multifactor productivity, the individual inputs (the denominator) can be expressed in dollars and summed as shown in Example 2.

EXAMPLE 2

Computing single- and multifactor gains in productivity

Collins Title wants to evaluate its labor and multifactor productivity with a new computerized title-search system. The company has a staff of four, each working 8 hours per day (for a payroll cost of $640/day) and overhead expenses of $400 per day. Collins processes and closes on 8 titles each day. The new computerized title-search system will allow the processing of 14 titles per day. Although the staff, their work hours, and pay are the same, the overhead expenses are now $800 per day.

Approach: Collins uses Equation (1) to compute labor productivity and Equation (2) to compute multifactor productivity.

Solution:

$$\text{Labor productivity with the old system: } \frac{8 \text{ titles per day}}{32 \text{ labor-hours}} = .25 \text{ titles per labor-hour}$$

$$\text{Labor productivity with the new system: } \frac{14 \text{ titles per day}}{32 \text{ labor-hours}} = .4375 \text{ titles per labor-hour}$$

$$\text{Multifactor productivity with the old system: } \frac{8 \text{ titles per day}}{\$640 + 400} = .0077 \text{ titles per dollar}$$

$$\text{Multifactor productivity with the new system: } \frac{14 \text{ titles per day}}{\$640 + 800} = .0097 \text{ titles per dollar}$$

Learning Objective

5. Compute multifactor productivity

Labor productivity has increased from .25 to .4375. The change is .4375/.25 = 1.75, or a 75% increase in labor productivity. Multifactor productivity has increased from .0077 to .0097. This change is .0097/.0077 = 1.26, or a 26% increase in multifactor productivity.

Insight: Both the labor (single-factor) and multifactor productivity measures show an increase in productivity. However, the multifactor measure provides a better picture of the increase because it includes all the costs connected with the increase in output.

Learning exercise: If the overhead goes to $960 (rather than $800), what is the multifactor productivity? [Answer: .00875.]

Related problems: 1, 2, 5, 6, 7, 8, 9, 11, 12, 14, 15

Use of productivity measures aids managers in determining how well they are doing. But results from the two measures can be expected to vary. If labor productivity growth is entirely the result of capital spending, measuring just labor distorts the results. Multifactor productivity is usually better, but more complicated. Labor productivity is the more popular measure. The multifactor-productivity measures provide better information about the trade-offs among factors, but substantial measurement problems remain. Some of these measurement problems are listed here:

1. *Quality* may change while the quantity of inputs and outputs remains constant. Compare an HDTV of this decade with a black-and-white TV of the 1950s. Both are TVs, but few people would deny that the quality has improved. The unit of measure—a TV—is the same, but the quality has changed.

2. *External elements*[8] may cause an increase or a decrease in productivity for which the system under study may not be directly responsible. A more reliable electric power service may greatly improve production, thereby improving the firm's productivity because of this support system rather than because of managerial decisions made within the firm.

3. *Precise units of measure* may be lacking. Not all automobiles require the same inputs: Some cars are subcompacts, others are 911 Turbo Porsches.

 Video 1.3

Productivity at Whirlpool

Productivity measurement is particularly difficult in the service sector, where the end product can be hard to define. For example, economic statistics ignore the quality of your haircut, the outcome of a court case, or service at a retail store. In some cases, adjustments are made for the quality of the product sold but *not* the quality of the sales presentation or the advantage of a

[8]These are exogenous variables—that is, variables outside the system under study that influence it.

broader product selection. Productivity measurements require specific inputs and outputs, but a free economy is producing worth—what people want—which includes convenience, speed, and safety. Traditional measures of outputs may be a very poor measure of these other measures of worth. Note the quality-measurement problems in a law office, where each case is different, altering the accuracy of the measure "cases per labor-hour" or "cases per employee."

Productivity Variables

As we saw in Figure 7, productivity increases are dependent on three **productivity variables**:

1. *Labor*, which contributes about 10% of the annual increase.
2. *Capital*, which contributes about 38% of the annual increase.
3. *Management*, which contributes about 52% of the annual increase.

These three factors are critical to improved productivity. They represent the broad areas in which managers can take action to improve productivity.[9]

Productivity variables
The three factors critical to productivity improvement—labor, capital, and the art and science of management.

Labor Improvement in the contribution of labor to productivity is the result of a healthier, better-educated, and better-nourished labor force. Some increase may also be attributed to a shorter workweek. Historically, about 10% of the annual improvement in productivity is attributed to improvement in the quality of labor. Three key variables for improved labor productivity are:

1. Basic education appropriate for an effective labor force.
2. Diet of the labor force.
3. Social overhead that makes labor available, such as transportation and sanitation.

Learning Objective

6. Identify the critical variables in enhancing productivity

Illiteracy and poor diets are a major impediment to productivity, costing countries up to 20% of their productivity.[10] Infrastructure that yields clean drinking water and sanitation is also an opportunity for improved productivity, as well as an opportunity for better health, in much of the world.

In developed nations, the challenge becomes *maintaining and enhancing the skills of labor* in the midst of rapidly expanding technology and knowledge. Recent data suggest that the average American 17-year-old knows significantly less mathematics than the average Japanese at the same age, and about half cannot answer the questions in Figure 8. Moreover, more than 38% of American job applicants tested for basic skills were deficient in reading, writing, or math.[11]

Overcoming shortcomings in the quality of labor while other countries have a better labor force is a major challenge. Perhaps improvements can be found not only through increasing competence of labor but also via *better utilized labor with a stronger commitment*. Training, motivation, team building, and the human resource strategies discussed in further Chapter, as well as improved education, may be among the many techniques that will contribute to increased labor productivity. Improvements in labor productivity are possible; however, they can be expected to be increasingly difficult and expensive.

Many American high schools exceed a 50% dropout rate in spite of offering a wide variety of programs.

Between 20% and 30% of U.S. workers lack the basic skills they need for their current jobs.
(Source: Nan Stone, Harvard Business Review.)

6 yds	
	4 yds

What is the area of this rectangle?

_____ 4 square yds
_____ 6 square yds
_____ 10 square yds
_____ 20 square yds
_____ 24 square yds

If $9y + 3 = 6y + 15$ then $y =$

_____ 1   _____ 4
_____ 2   _____ 6

Which of the following is true about 84% of 100?

_____ It is greater than 100
_____ It is less than 100
_____ It is equal to 100

◀ **Figure 8**

About Half of the 17-Year-Olds in the U.S. Cannot Correctly Answer Questions of This Type

[9]The percentages are from Herbert Stein and Murray Foss, *The New Illustrated Guide to the American Economy* (Washington, DC: AIE Press, 1995): 67.

[10]See report by Christopher Wanjek, "Food at Work: Workplace Solutions for Malnutrition, Obesity, and Chronic Diseases," *International Labor Office*, 2005.

[11]"Can't Read, Can't Count," *Scientific American* (October 2001): 24; and "Economic Time Bomb: U.S. Teens are Among Worst at Math," *The Wall Street Journal* (December 7, 2004):B1.

Capital   Human beings are tool-using animals. Capital investment provides those tools. Capital investment has increased in the U.S. every year except during a few very severe recession periods. Annual capital investment in the U.S. has increased at an annual rate of 1.5% after allowances for depreciation.

Inflation and taxes increase the cost of capital, making capital investment increasingly expensive. When the capital invested per employee drops, we can expect a drop in productivity. Using labor rather than capital may reduce unemployment in the short run, but it also makes economies less productive and therefore lowers wages in the long run. Capital investment is often a necessary, but seldom a sufficient ingredient in the battle for increased productivity.

The trade-off between capital and labor is continually in flux. The higher the interest rate, the more projects requiring capital are "squeezed out": they are not pursued because the potential return on investment for a given risk has been reduced. Managers adjust their investment plans to changes in capital cost.

Management   Management is a factor of production and an economic resource. Management is responsible for ensuring that labor and capital are effectively used to increase productivity. Management accounts for over half of the annual increase in productivity. This increase includes improvements made through the use of knowledge and the application of technology.

Knowledge society
A society in which much of the labor force has migrated from manual work to work based on knowledge.

Using knowledge and technology is critical in postindustrial societies. Consequently, postindustrial societies are also known as knowledge societies. **Knowledge societies** are those in which much of the labor force has migrated from manual work to technical and information-processing tasks requiring ongoing education. The required education and training are important high-cost items that are the responsibility of operations managers as they build organizations and workforces. The expanding knowledge base of contemporary society requires that managers use *technology and knowledge effectively.*

More effective use of capital also contributes to productivity. It falls to the operations manager, as a productivity catalyst, to select the best new capital investments as well as to improve the productivity of existing investments.

The productivity challenge is difficult. A country cannot be a world-class competitor with second-class inputs. Poorly educated labor, inadequate capital, and dated technology are second-class inputs. High productivity and high-quality outputs require high-quality inputs, including good operations managers.

▼ *The effective use of capital often means finding the proper trade-off between investment in capital assets (automation, left) and human assets (a manual process, right). While there are risks connected with any investment, the cost of capital and physical investments is fairly clear-cut, but the cost of employees has many hidden costs including fringe benefits, social insurance, and legal constraints on hiring, employment, and termination.*

TEK Image/Photo Researchers, Inc.

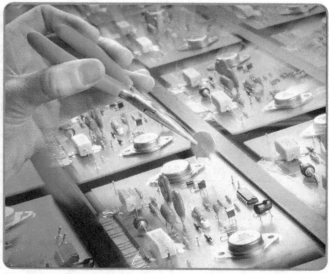

John McLean, Photo Researchers, Inc.

◀ *Siemens, the multi-billion-dollar German conglomerate, has long been known for its apprentice programs in its home country. Because education is often the key to efficient operations in a technological society, Siemens has spread its apprentice-training programs to its U.S. plants. These programs are laying the foundation for the highly skilled workforce that is essential for global competitiveness.*

Siemens AG

Productivity and the Service Sector

The service sector provides a special challenge to the accurate measurement of productivity and productivity improvement. The traditional analytical framework of economic theory is based primarily on goods-producing activities. Consequently, most published economic data relate to goods production. But the data do indicate that, as our contemporary service economy has increased in size, we have had slower growth in productivity.

Productivity of the service sector has proven difficult to improve because service-sector work is:

1. Typically labor-intensive (for example, counseling, teaching).
2. Frequently focused on unique individual attributes or desires (for example, investment advice).
3. Often an intellectual task performed by professionals (for example, medical diagnosis).
4. Often difficult to mechanize and automate (for example, a haircut).
5. Often difficult to evaluate for quality (for example, performance of a law firm).

The more intellectual and personal the task, the more difficult it is to achieve increases in productivity. Low-productivity improvement in the service sector is also attributable to the growth of low-productivity activities in the service sector. These include activities not previously a part of the measured economy, such as child care, food preparation, house cleaning, and laundry service. These activities have moved out of the home and into the measured economy as more and more women have joined the workforce. Inclusion of these activities has probably resulted in lower measured productivity for the service sector, although, in fact, actual productivity has probably increased because these activities are now more efficiently produced than previously.[12]

However, in spite of the difficulty of improving productivity in the service sector, improvements are being made. And this text presents a multitude of ways to make these improvements. Indeed, what can be done when management pays attention to how work actually gets done is astonishing![13]

Although the evidence indicates that all industrialized countries have the same problem with service productivity, the U.S. remains the world leader in overall productivity *and* service productivity. Retailing is twice as productive in the U.S. as in Japan, where laws protect shopkeepers from discount chains. The U.S. telephone industry is at least twice as productive as Germany's. The U.S. banking system is also 33% more efficient than Germany's banking oligopolies. However, because productivity is central to the operations manager's job and because the service sector is so large, we take special note in this text of how to improve productivity in the service sector. (See, for instance, the *OM in Action* box "Taco Bell Improves Productivity to Lower Costs.")

[12]Allen Sinai and Zaharo Sofianou, "The Service Economy—Productivity Growth Issues" (CSI Washington, DC), *The Service Economy* (January 1992): 11–16.

[13]These conclusions are not unique. See the work of Michael van Biema and Bruce Greenwald, "Managing Our Way to Higher Service-Sector Productivity," *Harvard Business Review* 75, no. 4 (July–August 1997): 89.

Taco Bell Improves Productivity to Lower Costs

Founded in 1962 by Glenn Bell, Taco Bell is seeking competitive advantage via low cost. Like many other services, Taco Bell increasingly relies on its operations function to improve productivity and reduce cost.

First, it revised its menu and designed meals that were easy to prepare. Taco Bell then shifted a substantial portion of food preparation to suppliers who could perform food processing more efficiently than a stand-alone restaurant. Ground beef is now precooked prior to arrival and then reheated, as are many dishes that arrive in plastic boil bags for easy sanitary reheating. Similarly, tortillas arrive already fried and onions prediced. Efficient layout and automation has cut to 8 seconds the time needed to prepare tacos and burritos and has cut time in the drive-thru lines by one minute.

These advances have been combined with training and empowerment to increase the span of management from one supervisor for 5 restaurants to one supervisor for 30 or more.

Operations managers at Taco Bell believe they have cut in-store labor by 15 hours per day and reduced floor space by more than 50%. The result is a store that can handle twice the volume with half the labor. Effective operations management has resulted in productivity increases that support Taco Bell's low-cost strategy. Taco Bell is now the fast-food low-cost leader and has a 73% share of the Mexican fast-food market.

Sources: Jackie Hueter and William Swart, *Interfaces* (January–February 1998): 75–91; and *Nation's Restaurant News* (August 15, 2005):68–70.

ETHICS AND SOCIAL RESPONSIBILITY

Operations managers are subjected to constant changes and challenges. The systems they build to convert resources into goods and services are complex. The physical and social environment changes, as do laws and values. These changes present a variety of challenges that come from the conflicting perspectives of stakeholders such as customers, distributors, suppliers, owners, lenders, and employees. These stakeholders, as well as government agencies at various levels, require constant monitoring and thoughtful responses.

Identifying ethical and socially responsible responses while building productive systems is not always clear-cut. Among the many ethical challenges facing operations managers are:

- Efficiently developing and producing safe, quality products.
- Maintaining a clean environment.
- Providing a safe workplace.
- Honoring community commitments.

Managers must do all of this in an ethical and socially responsible way while meeting the demands of the marketplace. If operations managers have a *moral awareness and focus on increasing productivity* in a system where all stakeholders have a voice, then many of the ethical challenges will be successfully addressed. The organization will use fewer resources, the employees will be committed, the market will be satisfied, and the ethical climate will be enhanced. Throughout this text, we note a variety of ways in which operations managers can take ethical and socially responsible actions to successfully address these challenges. We also end each chapter with an *Ethical Dilemma* exercise.

Summary

Operations, marketing, and finance/accounting are the three functions basic to all organizations. The operations function creates goods and services. Much of the progress of operations management has been made in the twentieth century, but since the beginning of time, humankind has been attempting to improve its material well-being. Operations managers are key players in the battle for improved productivity.

However, as societies become increasingly affluent, more of their resources are devoted to services. In the U.S., more than three-quarters of the workforce is employed in the service sector. Productivity improvements are difficult to achieve, but operations managers are the primary vehicle for making improvements.

Key Terms

Production
Operations management (OM)
Management process
Services

Pure service
Service sector
Productivity
Single-factor productivity

Multifactor productivity
Productivity variables
Knowledge society

Solved Problems

Virtual Office Hours help is available on Student DVD.

Solved Problem 1

Productivity can be measured in a variety of ways, such as by labor, capital, energy, material usage, and so on. At Modern Lumber, Inc., Art Binley, president and producer of apple crates sold to growers, has been able, with his current equipment, to produce 240 crates per 100 logs. He currently purchases 100 logs per day, and each log requires 3 labor-hours to process. He believes that he can hire a professional buyer who can buy a better-quality log at the same cost. If this is the case, he can increase his production to 260 crates per 100 logs. His labor-hours will increase by 8 hours per day.

What will be the impact on productivity (measured in crates per labor-hour) if the buyer is hired?

Solution

(a)
$$\text{Current labor productivity} = \frac{240 \text{ crates}}{100 \text{ logs} \times 3 \text{ hours/log}}$$
$$= \frac{240}{300}$$
$$= .8 \text{ crates per labor-hour}$$

(b)
$$\begin{aligned}\text{Labor productivity} \\ \text{with buyer}\end{aligned} = \frac{260 \text{ crates}}{(100 \text{ logs} \times 3 \text{ hours/log}) + 8 \text{ hours}}$$
$$= \frac{260}{308}$$
$$= .844 \text{ crates per labor-hour}$$

Using current productivity (.80 from [a]) as a base, the increase will be 5.5% (.844/.8 = 1.055, or a 5.5% increase).

Solved Problem 2

Art Binley has decided to look at his productivity from a multifactor (total factor productivity) perspective (refer to Solved Problem 1). To do so, he has determined his labor, capital, energy, and material usage and decided to use dollars as the common denominator. His total labor-hours are now 300 per day and will increase to 308 per day. His capital and energy costs will remain constant at $350 and $150 per day, respectively. Material costs for the 100 logs per day are $1,000 and will remain the same. Because he pays an average of $10 per hour (with fringes), Binley determines his productivity increase as follows:

Solution

	Current System		System with Professional Buyer	
Labor:	300 hrs. @ $10 =	$3,000	308 hrs. @ $10 =	$3,080
Material:	100 logs/day	1,000		1,000
Capital:		350		350
Energy:		150		150
Total Cost:		$4,500		$4,580

Multifactor productivity of current system:
= 240 crates/4,500 = .0533 crates/dollar

Multifactor productivity of proposed system:
= 260 crates/4,580 = .0568 crates/dollar

Using current productivity (.0533) as a base, the increase will be .066. That is, .0568/.0533 = 1.066, or a 6.6% increase.

Self-Test

- **Before taking the self-test**, *refer to the learning objectives listed at the beginning of the selection and the key terms listed at the end of the selection.*
- *Use the key at the back of the text to* **correct** *your answers.*
- **Restudy** *pages that correspond to any questions you answered incorrectly or material you feel uncertain about.*

1. OM jobs constitute what percentage of all jobs?
   a) 20%
   b) 35%
   c) 18%
   d) 40%

2. Productivity increases when:
   a) inputs increase while outputs remain the same.
   b) inputs decrease while outputs remain the same.
   c) outputs decrease while inputs remain the same.
   d) inputs and outputs increase proportionately.
   e) inputs increase at the same rate as outputs.

3. The capital investment each year in the U.S. usually:
   a) decreases.
   b) remains constant.
   c) increases.
   d) decreases unless favorably taxed.
   e) is very cyclical.

4. Productivity increases each year in the U.S. are the result of three factors:
   a) labor, capital, management
   b) engineering, labor, capital
   c) engineering, capital, quality control
   d) engineering, labor, data processing
   e) engineering, capital, data processing

5. Which appears to provide the best opportunity for increases in productivity?
   a) labor
   b) capital
   c) management
   d) engineering

6. When returns to labor, capital, or management are increased without increased productivity, prices:
   a) rise.
   b) fall.
   c) stay the same.
   d) unable to determine.

7. Problems in the measurement of productivity include:
   a) the unknown effect of external elements.
   b) the absence of precise units of measure.
   c) the effects of quality over time.
   d) all of the above.

8. The person who introduced standardized, interchangeable parts was:
   a) Eli Whitney.
   b) Henry Ford.
   c) Adam Smith.
   d) W. Edwards Deming.
   e) Frederick W. Taylor.

Internet and Student CD-ROM/DVD Exercises

Visit our Companion Web site or use your student CD-ROM/DVD to help with material in this chapter.

 On Our Companion Web site, www.prenhall.com/heizer
- Self-Study Quizzes
- Practice Problems
- Virtual Company Tour
- Power Point Lecture

 On Your Student CD-ROM
- Practice Problems
- POM for Windows

On Your Student DVD
- Video Clips and Video Case
- Virtual Office Hours for Solved Problems

Discussion Questions

1. Why should one study operations management?
2. Identify four people who have contributed to the theory and techniques of operations management.
3. Briefly describe the contributions of the four individuals identified in the preceding question.
4. Figure 1 outlines the operations, finance/accounting, and marketing functions of three organizations. Prepare a chart similar to Figure 1 outlining the same functions for one of the following:
   (a) a newspaper
   (b) a drugstore
   (c) a college library
   (d) a summer camp
   (e) a small costume-jewelry factory
5. Answer question 4 for some other organization, perhaps an organization where you have worked.
6. What are the three basic functions of a firm?
7. Name the 10 decision areas of operations management.
8. Name four areas that are significant to improving labor productivity.
9. The U.S., and indeed much of the world, has been described as a "knowledge society." How does this affect productivity measurement and the comparison of productivity between the U.S. and other countries?
10. What are the measurement problems that occur when one attempts to measure productivity?
11. Mass customization and rapid product development were identified as current trends in modern manufacturing operations. What is the relationship, if any, between these trends? Can you cite any examples?
12. What are the five reasons productivity is difficult to improve in the service sector?
13. Describe some of the actions taken by Taco Bell to increase productivity that have resulted in Taco Bell's ability to serve "twice the volume with half the labor."

Ethical Dilemma

Major corporations with overseas subcontractors (such as Ikea in Bangladesh, Unilever in India, and Nike in China) have been criticized, often with substantial negative publicity, when children as young as 10 have been found working in the subcontractor's facilities. The standard response is to perform an audit and then enhance controls so it does not happen again. In one such case, a 10-year-old was terminated. Shortly thereafter, the family, without the 10-year-old's contribution to the family income, lost its modest home, and the 10-year-old was left to scrounge in the local dump for scraps of metal. Was the decision to hire the 10-year-old ethical? Was the decision to terminate the 10-year-old ethical?

Problems*

• **1** John Lucy makes wooden boxes in which to ship motorcycles. John and his three employees invest a total of 40 hours per day making the 120 boxes.
a) What is their productivity?
b) John and his employees have discussed redesigning the process to improve efficiency. If they can increase the rate to 125 per day, what will be their new productivity?
c) What will be their percentage *increase* in productivity and percentage change? Px

• **2** Riverside Metal Works produces cast bronze valves on a 10-person assembly line. On a recent day, 160 valves were produced during an 8-hour shift. Calculate the labor productivity of the line. Px

• **3** This year, Benson, Inc., will produce 57,600 hot water heaters at its plant in Yulee, Florida, in order to meet expected global demand. To accomplish this, each laborer at the Yulee plant will work 160 hours per month. If the labor productivity at the plant is 0.15 hot water heaters per labor hour, how many laborers are employed at the plant?

• **4** As a library or Internet assignment, find the U.S. productivity rate (increase) last year for the (a) national economy, (b) manufacturing sector, and (c) service sector.

• **5** Lori produces "Final Exam Care Packages" for resale by her sorority. She is currently working a total of 5 hours per day to produce 100 care packages.
a) What is Lori's productivity?
b) Lori thinks that by redesigning the package, she can increase her total productivity to 133 care packages per day. What will be her new productivity?
c) What will be the percentage increase in productivity if Lori makes the change? Px

•• **6** Eric Johnson makes billiard balls in his New England plant. With recent increases in his costs, he has a newfound interest in efficiency. Eric is interested in determining the productivity of his organization. He would like to know if his organization is maintaining the manufacturing average of 3% increase in productivity. He has the following data representing a month from last year and an equivalent month this year:

	Last Year	Now
Units produced	1,000	1,000
Labor (hours)	300	275
Resin (pounds)	50	45
Capital invested ($)	10,000	11,000
Energy (BTU)	3,000	2,850

*Note: Px means the problem may be solved with POM for Windows and/or Excel OM.

Show the productivity percentage change for each category and then determine the improvement for labor-hours, the typical standard for comparison. Px

•• **7** Eric Johnson (using data from Problem 6) determines his costs to be as follows:
• *Labor:* $10 per hour
• *Resin:* $5 per pound
• *Capital expense:* 1% per month of investment
• *Energy:* $.50 per BTU.
Show the percent change in productivity for one month last year versus one month this year, on a multifactor basis with dollars as the common denominator. Px

• **8** Kleen Karpet cleaned 65 rugs in October, consuming the following resources:

Labor:	520 hours at $13 per hour
Solvent:	100 gallons at $5 per gallon
Machine rental:	20 days at $50 per day

a) What is the labor productivity per dollar?
b) What is the multifactor productivity? Px

•• **9** David Upton is president of Upton Manufacturing, a producer of Go-Kart tires. Upton makes 1,000 tires per day with the following resources:

Labor:	400 hours per day @ $12.50 per hour
Raw material:	20,000 pounds per day @ $1 per pound
Energy:	$5,000 per day
Capital:	$10,000 per day

a) What is the labor productivity per labor-hour for these tires at Upton Manufacturing?
b) What is the multifactor productivity for these tires at Upton Manufacturing?
c) What is the percent change in multifactor productivity if Upton can reduce the energy bill by $1,000 per day without cutting production or changing any other inputs? Px

•• **10** Sawyer's, a local bakery, is worried about increased costs—particularly energy. Last year's records can provide a fairly good estimate of the parameters for this year. Judy Sawyer, the owner, does not believe things have changed much, but she did invest an additional $3,000 for modifications to the bakery's ovens to make them more energy-efficient. The modifications were supposed to make the ovens at least 15% more efficient. Sawyer has asked you to check the energy savings of the new ovens and also to look over other measures of the bakery's productivity to see if the

23

Andreas Buck/Das Fotoarchiv, Peter Arnold, Inc.

modifications were beneficial. You have the following data to work with:

	Last Year	Now
Production (dozen)	1,500	1,500
Labor (hours)	350	325
Capital investment ($)	15,000	18,000
Energy (BTU)	3,000	2,750

•• **11** Cunningham Performance Auto, Inc., modifies 375 autos per year. The manager, Peter Cunningham, is interested in obtaining a measure of overall performance. He has asked you to provide him with a multifactor measure of last year's performance as a benchmark for future comparison. You have assembled the following data. Resource inputs were: labor, 10,000 hours; 500 suspension and engine modification kits; and energy, 100,000 kilowatthours. Average labor cost last year was $20 per hour, kits cost $1,000 each, and energy costs were $3 per kilowatt-hour. What do you tell Mr. Cunningham? **Px**

•• **12** Lake Charles Seafood makes 500 wooden packing boxes for fresh seafood per day, working in two 10-hour shifts. Due to increased demand, plant managers have decided to operate three 8-hour shifts instead. The plant is now able to produce 650 boxes per day. Calculate the company's productivity before the change in work rules and after the change. What is the percent increase in productivity? **Px**

•••• **13** Charles Lackey operates a bakery in Idaho Falls, Idaho. Because of its excellent product and excellent location, demand has increased by 25% in the last year. On far too many occasions, customers have not been able to purchase the bread of their choice. Because of the size of the store, no new ovens can be added. At a staff meeting, one employee suggested ways to load the ovens differently so that more loaves of bread can be baked at one time. This new process will require that the ovens be loaded by hand, requiring additional manpower. This is the only thing to be changed. If the bakery makes 1,500 loaves per month with a labor productivity of 2.344 loaves per labor-hour, how many workers will Lackey need to add? (*Hint:* Each worker works 160 hours per month.)

•• **14** Refer to Problem 13. The pay will be $8 per hour for employees. Charles Lackey can also improve the yield by purchasing a new blender. The new blender will mean an increase in his investment. This added investment has a cost of $100 per month, but he will achieve the same output (an increase to 1,875) as the change in labor hours. Which is the better decision?
a) Show the productivity change, in loaves per dollar, with an increase in labor cost (from 640 to 800 hours).
b) Show the new productivity, in loaves per dollar, with only an increase in investment ($100 per month more).
c) Show the percent productivity change for labor and investment.

•••• **15** Refer to Problems 13 and 14. If Charles Lackey's utility costs remain constant at $500 per month, labor at $8 per hour, and cost of ingredients at $0.35 per loaf, but Charles does not purchase the blender suggested in Problem 14, what will the productivity of the bakery be? What will be the percent increase or decrease?

•• **16** In December, General Motors produced 6,600 customized vans at its plant in Detroit. The labor productivity at this plant is known to have been 0.10 vans per labor-hour during that month. If 300 laborers were employed at the plant that month, how many hours did the average laborer work that month?

•• **17** Natalie Attired runs a small job shop where garments are made. The job shop employs eight workers. Each worker is paid $10 per hour. During the first week of March, each worker worked 45 hours. Together, they produced a batch of 132 garments. Of these garments, 52 were "seconds" (meaning that they were flawed). The seconds were sold for $90 each at a factory outlet store. The remaining 80 garments were sold to retail outlets at a price of $198 per garment. What was the labor productivity, in dollars per labor-hour, at this job shop during the first week of March?

Case Studies

National Air Express

National Air is a competitive air-express firm with offices around the country. Frank Smith, the Chattanooga, Tennessee, station manager, is preparing his quarterly budget report, which will be presented at the Southeast regional meeting next week. He is very concerned about adding capital expense to the operation when business has not increased appreciably. This has been the worst first quarter he can remember: snowstorms, earthquakes, and bitter cold. He has asked Martha Lewis, field services supervisor, to help him review the available data and offer possible solutions.

Service Methods
National Air offers door-to-door overnight air-express delivery within the U.S. Smith and Lewis manage a fleet of 24 trucks to handle freight in the Chattanooga area. Routes are assigned by area, usually delineated by zip code boundaries, major streets, or key geographical features, such as the Tennessee River. Pickups are generally handled between 3:00 P.M. and 6:00 P.M., Monday through Friday. Driver routes are a combination of regularly scheduled daily stops and pickups that the customer calls in as needed. These call-in pickups are dis-

patched by radio to the driver. Most call-in customers want as late a pickup as possible, just before closing (usually at 5:00 P.M.).

When the driver arrives at each pickup location, he or she provides supplies as necessary (an envelope or box if requested) and must receive a completed air waybill for each package. Because the industry is extremely competitive, a professional, courteous driver is essential to retaining customers. Therefore, Smith has always been concerned that drivers not rush a customer to complete his or her package and paperwork.

Budget Considerations

Smith and Lewis have found that they have been unable to meet their customers' requests for a scheduled pickup on many occasions in the past quarter. Although, on average, drivers are not handling any more business, they are unable on some days to arrive at each location on time. Smith does not think he can justify increasing costs by $1,200 per week for additional trucks and drivers while productivity (measured in shipments per truck/day) has remained flat. The company has established itself as the low-cost operator in the industry but has at the same time committed itself to offering quality service and value for its customers.

Discussion Questions

1. Is the productivity measure of shipments per day per truck still useful? Are there alternatives that might be effective?
2. What, if anything, can be done to reduce the daily variability in pickup call-ins? Can the driver be expected to be at several locations at once at 5:00 P.M.?
3. How should package pickup performance be measured? Are standards useful in an environment that is affected by the weather, traffic, and other random variables? Are other companies having similar problems?

Source: Adapted from a case by Phil Pugliese under the supervision of Professor Marilyn M. Helms, University of Tennessee at Chattanooga. Reprinted by permission.

Zychol Chemicals Corporation

Bob Richards, the production manager of Zychol Chemicals, in Houston, Texas, is preparing his quarterly report, which is to include a productivity analysis for his department. One of the inputs is production data prepared by Sharon Walford, his operations analyst. The report, which she gave him this morning, showed the following:

	2006	2007
Production (units)	4,500	6,000
Raw material used (barrels of petroleum by-products)	700	900
Labor hours	22,000	28,000
Capital cost applied to the department ($)	$375,000	$620,000

Bob knew that his labor cost per hour had increased from an average of $13 per hour to an average of $14 per hour, primarily due to a move by management to become more competitive with a new company that had just opened a plant in the area. He also knew that his average cost per barrel of raw material had increased from $320 to $360. He was concerned about the accounting procedures that increased his capital cost from

$375,000 to $620,000, but earlier discussions with his boss suggested that there was nothing that could be done about that allocation.

Bob wondered if his productivity had increased at all. He called Sharon into the office and conveyed the above information to her and asked her to prepare this part of the report.

Discussion Questions

1. Prepare the productivity part of the report for Mr. Richards. He probably expects some analysis of productivity inputs for all factors, as well as a multifactor analysis for both years with the change in productivity (up or down) and the amount noted.
2. The producer price index had increased from 120 to 125, and this fact seemed to indicate to Mr. Richards that his costs were too high. What do you tell him are the implications of this change in the producer price index?
3. Management's expectation for departments such as Mr. Richards's is an annual productivity increase of 5%. Did he reach this goal?

Source: Professor Hank Maddux III, Sam Houston State University.

Hard Rock Cafe: Operations Management in Services

Video Case

In its 37 years of existence, Hard Rock has grown from a modest London pub to a global power managing 121 cafes, 5 hotels, casinos, live music venues, and a huge annual Rockfest concert. This puts Hard Rock firmly in the service industry—a sector that employs over 75% of the people in the U.S. Hard Rock moved its world headquarters to Orlando, Florida, in 1988 and has expanded to more than 40 locations throughout the U.S., serving over 100,000 meals each day. Hard Rock chefs are modifying the menu from classic American—burgers and chicken wings—to include higher-end items such as stuffed veal chops and lobster tails. Just as taste in music changes over time, so does Hard Rock Cafe, with new menus, layouts, memorabilia, services, and strategies.

At Orlando's Universal Studios, a traditional tourist destination, Hard Rock Cafe serves over 3,500 meals each day. The cafe employs about 400 people. Most are employed in the restaurant, but some work in the retail shop. Retail is now a standard and increasingly prominent feature in Hard Rock Cafes (since close to 48% of revenue comes from this source). Cafe employees include kitchen and wait staff, hostesses, and bartenders. Hard Rock employees are not only competent in their job skills but are also passionate about music and have engaging personalities. Cafe staff is scheduled down to 15-minute intervals to meet seasonal and daily demand changes in the tourist environment of Orlando. Surveys are done on a regular basis to evaluate quality of food and service at the cafe.

Scores are rated on a 1 to 7 scale, and if the score is not a 7, the food or service is a failure.

Hard Rock is adding a new emphasis on live music and is redesigning its restaurants to accommodate the changing tastes. Since Eric Clapton hung his guitar on the wall to mark his favorite bar stool, Hard Rock has become the world's leading collector and exhibitor of rock 'n' roll memorabilia, with changing exhibits at its cafes throughout the world. The collection includes 1,000's of pieces, valued at $40 million. In keeping with the times, Hard Rock also maintains a Web site, **www.hardrock.com**, which receives over 100,000 hits per week, and a weekly cable television program on VH-1. Hard Rock's brand recognition, at 92%, is one of the highest in the world.

Discussion Questions*

1. From your knowledge of restaurants, from the video, from the *Global Company Profile* that opens this chapter, and from the case itself, identify how each of the 10 decisions of operations management is applied at Hard Rock Cafe.

2. How would you determine the productivity of the kitchen staff and wait staff at Hard Rock?

3. How are the 10 decisions of OM different when applied to the operations manager of a service operation such as Hard Rock versus an automobile company such as Ford Motor Company?

*You may wish to play this video case on your DVD before addressing these questions.

Additional Case Study

Harvard has selected this Harvard Business School case to accompany this chapter:

harvardbusinessonline.hbsp.harvard.edu

- **Taco Bell Corp.** (#692-058): Illustrates the power of breakthrough thinking in a service industry.

Bibliography

Deo, Balbinder S., and Doug Strong. "Cost: The Ultimate Measure of Productivity." *Industrial Management* 42, no. 3 (May–June 2000): 20–23.

Dewan, Sanjeev. "Information Technology and Productivity: Evidence from Country-Level Data." *Management Science* 46, no. 4 (April 2000): 548–562.

Hounshell, D. A. *From the American System to Mass Production 1800–1932: The Development of Manufacturing.* Baltimore: Johns Hopkins University Press, 1985.

Lewis, William W., *The Power of Productivity.* Chicago: University of Chicago Press, 2004.

Sahay, B. S. "Multi-factor Productivity Measurement Model for Service Organization." *International Journal of*

Productivity and Performance Management 54, no. 1–2 (2005):7–23.

Tangen, S. "Demystifying Productivity and Performance." *International Journal of Productivity and Performance Measurement* 54, no. 1–2 (2005):34–47.

Taylor, F. W. *The Principles of Scientific Management.* New York: Harper & Brothers, 1911.

van Biema, Michael, and Bruce Greenwald. "Managing Our Way to Higher Service-Sector Productivity." *Harvard Business Review* 75, no. 4 (July–August 1997): 87–95.

Wrege, C. D. *Frederick W. Taylor, the Father of Scientific Management: Myth and Reality.* Homewood, IL: Business One Irwin, 1991.

Internet Resources

American Productivity and Quality Center: **www.apqc.org**

American Statistical Association (ASA) offers business and economics DataLinks, a searchable index of statistical data: **www.econ-datalinks.org**

Economics and Statistics Administration: **www.esa.doc.gov**

Federal Statistics: **www.fedstats.gov**

National Bureau of Economic Research: **www.nber.org**

U.S. Bureau of Labor Statistics: **stats.bls.gov**

U.S. Census Bureau: **www.census.gov**

Solutions to Even Numbered Problems

2 2 valves/hr.

4 Varies by site and source.

6 Productivity of labor: 9.3%
   Productivity of resin: 11.1%
   Productivity of capital: −10.0%
   Productivity of energy: 6.1%

8 (a) .0096 rugs/labor-dollar
   (b) .00787 rugs/dollar

10 Productivity of capital dropped; labor and energy productivity increased.

12 Before: 25 boxes/hr.
    After: 27.08 boxes/hr.
    Increase: 8.3%

14 (a) .293 loaves/dollar
    (b) .359 loaves/dollar
    (c) Labor change: 0%; Investment change: 22.5%

16 220 hours per laborer; 66,000 labor hours

Solutions to Self Test

1. d; 2. b; 3. c; 4. a; 5. c; 6. a; 7. d, 8. a.

Operations Strategy in a Global Environment

Outline

Learning Objectives

When you complete this selection you should be able to

1. Define mission and strategy
2. Identify and explain three strategic
   approaches to competitive advantage
3. Identify and define the 10 decisions of
   operations management
4. Identify five OM strategy insights
   provided by PIMS research
5. Identify and explain four global
   operations strategy options

Global Company Profile: Boeing

Boeing's Global Strategy Yields Competitive Advantage

Boeing's strategy for its 787 Dreamliner is unique from both an engineering and global perspective.

The Dreamliner incorporates the latest in a wide range of aerospace technologies, from airframe and engine design to superlightweight titanium graphite laminate, carbon fiber and epoxy, and composites. Another innovation is the electronic monitoring system that allows the airplane to report maintenance requirements to ground-based computer systems. Boeing has also worked with General Electric and Rolls-Royce to develop more efficient engines. The advances in engine technology contribute as much as 8% of the increased fuel/payload efficiency of the new airplane, representing a nearly two-generation jump in technology.

Boeing Commercial Airplane Group

▲ With the 787's state-of-the-art design, more spacious interior, and global suppliers, Boeing has garnered record sales worldwide.

Some of the International Suppliers of Boeing 787 Components

Latecoere	France	Passenger doors
Labinel	France	Wiring
Dassault	France	Design and PLM software
Messier-Bugatti	France	Electric brakes
Thales	France	Electrical power conversion system and integrated standby flight display
Messier-Dowty	France	Landing gear structure
Diehl	Germany	Interior lighting
Cobham	UK	Fuel pumps and valves
Rolls-Royce	UK	Engines
Smiths Aerospace	UK	Central computer system
BAE Systems	UK	Electronics
Alenia Aeronautica	Italy	Upper center fuselage and horizontal stabilizer
Toray Industries	Japan	Carbon fiber for wing and tail units
Fuji Heavy Industries	Japan	Center wing box
Kawasaki Heavy Industries	Japan	Forward fuselage, fixed sections of wing, landing gear wheel well
Teijin Seiki	Japan	Hydraulic actuators
Mitsubishi Heavy Industries	Japan	Wing box
Chengdu Aircraft Group	China	Rudder
Hafei Aviation	China	Parts
Korean Airlines	South Korea	Wingtips
Saab	Sweden	Cargo and access doors

This state-of-the-art Boeing 787 is also *global*. Led by Boeing at its Everett, Washington, facility, an international team of aerospace companies developed the airplane. New technologies, new design, new manufacturing processes, and committed international suppliers are helping Boeing and its partners achieve unprecedented levels of performance in design, manufacture, and operation.

The 787 is global with a range of 8,300 miles. And it is global because it is being built across the world. With a huge financial risk of over $5 billion, Boeing needed partners. The global nature of both technology and the aircraft market meant finding exceptional developers and suppliers, wherever they might be. It also meant finding firms willing to step up to the risk associated with a very expensive new product. These partners not only spread the risk but also bring commitment to the table. Countries that have a stake in the 787 are more likely to buy from Boeing than from the European competitor Airbus Industries.

Boeing teamed with more than 20 international systems suppliers to develop technologies and design concepts for the 787. Boeing found its 787 partners in over a dozen countries; a few of them are shown in the table on the left.

The Japanese companies Toray, Teijin Seiki, Fuji, Kawasaki, and Mitsubishi are producing over 35% of the project, providing whole composite fuselage sections. Italy's Alenia Aeronautica is building an additional 10% of the plane.

Many U.S. companies, including Crane Aerospace, Fairchild Controls, Goodrich, General Dynamics, Hamilton Sundstrand, Honeywell, Moog, Parker Hannifin, Rockwell Collins, Vought Aircraft, and Triumph Group are also suppliers. Boeing has 70% to 80% of the Dreamliner built by other companies. And even some of the portion built by Boeing is produced at Boeing facilities outside the U.S., in Australia and Canada.

The global Dreamliner is efficient, has a global range, and is made from components produced around the world. The result: a state-of-the-art airplane reflecting the global nature of business in the 21st century and one of the fastest-selling commercial jets in history.

Boeing Commercial Airplane Group

▲ *Boeing's collaborative technology enables a "virtual workspace" that allows engineers on the 787, including partners in Australia, Japan, Italy, Canada and across the United States, to make concurrent design changes to the airplane in real time. Designing, building, and testing the 787 digitally before production reduced design errors and improved production efficiencies.*

◄ *Components from Boeing's worldwide supply chain come together on an assembly line in Everett, Washington. Although components come from throughout the world, about 35% of the 787 structure comes from Japanese companies.*

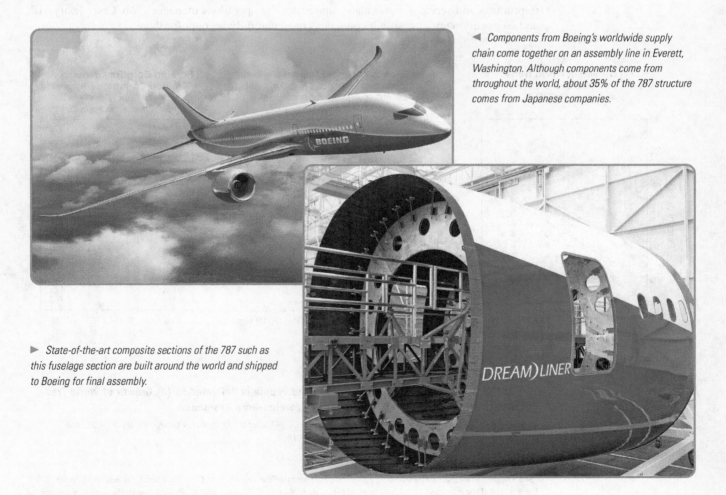

► *State-of-the-art composite sections of the 787 such as this fuselage section are built around the world and shipped to Boeing for final assembly.*

Today's operations manager must have a global view of operations strategy. Since the early 1990s, nearly 3 billion people in developing countries have overcome the cultural, religious, ethnic, and political barriers that constrain productivity and are now players on the global economic stage. As these barriers disappear, simultaneous advances are being made in technology, reliable shipping, and cheap communication. The unsurprising result is the growth of world trade, global capital markets, and the international movement of people; see Figure 1(a), (b), and (c). This means: increasing economic integration and interdependence of countries—in a word, globalization.[1] In response, organizations are hastily extending their operations globally with innovative strategies. For instance:

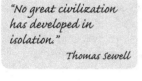

"No great civilization has developed in isolation."

Thomas Sewell

- Boeing is competitive because both its sales and production are worldwide.
- Italy's Benetton moves inventory to stores around the world faster than its competition by building flexibility into design, production, and distribution.
- Sony purchases components from suppliers in Thailand, Malaysia, and elsewhere around the world for assembly in its electronic products.
- Volvo, considered a Swedish company, is controlled by a U.S. company, Ford. But the current Volvo S40 is built in Belgium on a platform shared with the Mazda 3 (built in Japan) and the Ford Focus (built and sold in Europe.)
- China's Haier (pronounced "higher") is now producing compact refrigerators (it has one-third of the U.S. market) and refrigerated wine cabinets (it has half of the U.S. market) in South Carolina.

Globalization means that domestic production and exporting may no longer be a viable business model; local production and exporting no longer guarantee success or even survival. There are new standards of global competitiveness that impact quality, variety, customization, convenience, timeliness, and cost. The globalization of strategy contributes efficiency and adds value to products and services, but it also complicates the operations manager's job. Complexity, risk and competition are intensified; companies must carefully account for them.

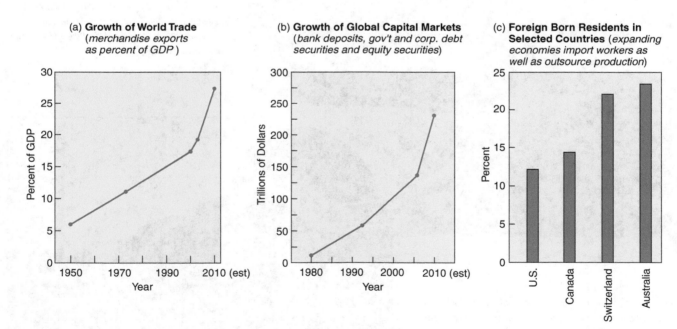

▲ **Figure 1** Movement of Goods, Capital, and People is Reflected in (a) Growth of World Trade, (b) Growth of Global Capital Markets, and (c) Foreign-Born Residents

Sources: Federal Reserve Bank of Dallas (May–June 2006) and (July–August 2005); *McKinsey Quarterly* (July 26, 2006); and Organization for Economic Cooperation and Development (OECD).

[1]See Thomas Friedman's *The World Is Flat: A Brief History of the Twenty-first Century*, Farrar, Straus, and Giroux, 2005, for his stimulating discussion of how new players, new playing field, and new processes ensure the rapid expansion of globalization.

A GLOBAL VIEW OF OPERATIONS

We have identified six reasons domestic business operations decide to change to some form of international operation. They are:

1. Reduce costs (labor, taxes, tariffs, etc.).
2. Improve supply chain.
3. Provide better goods and services.
4. Understand markets.
5. Learn to improve operations.
6. Attract and retain global talent.

Let us examine, in turn, each of the six reasons.

Reduce Costs Many international operations seek to take advantage of the tangible opportunities to reduce their costs. Foreign locations with lower wages can help lower both direct and indirect costs. (See the *OM in Action* box "U.S. Cartoon Production at Home in Manila.") Less stringent government regulations on a wide variety of operation practices (e.g., environmental control, health and safety, etc.) reduce costs. Opportunities to cut the cost of taxes and tariffs also encourage foreign operations. In Mexico, the creation of **maquiladoras** (free trade zones) allows manufacturers to cut their costs of taxation by paying only on the value added by Mexican workers. If a U.S. manufacturer, such as GM, brings a $500 engine to a maquiladora operation for assembly work costing $25, tariff duties will be charged only on the $25 of work performed in Mexico.

Shifting low-skilled jobs to another country has several potential advantages. First, and most obviously, the firm may reduce costs. Second, moving the lower skilled jobs to a lower cost location frees higher cost workers for more valuable tasks. Third, reducing wage costs allows the savings to be invested in improved products and facilities (and the retraining of existing workers, if necessary) at the home location. The impact of this approach is shown in the *OM in Action* box "Going Global to Compete."

Trade agreements have also helped reduce tariffs and thereby reduce the cost of operating facilities in foreign countries. The **World Trade Organization (WTO)** has helped reduce tariffs from 40% in 1940 to less than 3% today. Another important trade agreement is the **North American Free Trade Agreement (NAFTA)**. NAFTA seeks to phase out all trade and tariff barriers among Canada, Mexico, and the U.S. Other trade agreements that are accelerating global trade include APEC (the Pacific Rim countries), SEATO (Australia, New Zealand, Japan, Hong Kong, South Korea, New Guinea, and Chile), and MERCOSUR (Argentina, Brazil, Paraguay, and Uruguay).

Maquiladoras
Mexican factories located along the U.S.–Mexico border that receive preferential tariff treatment.

World Trade Organization (WTO)
An international organization that promotes world trade by lowering barriers to the free flow of goods across borders.

NAFTA
A free trade agreement between Canada, Mexico, and the U.S.

OM in Action U.S. Cartoon Production at Home in Manila

Fred Flintstone is not from Bedrock. He is actually from Manila, capital of the Philippines. So are Tom and Jerry, Aladdin, and Donald Duck. More than 90% of American television cartoons are produced in Asia and India, with the Philippines leading the way. With their natural advantage of English as an official language and a strong familiarity with U.S. culture, animation companies in Manila now employ more than 1,700 people. Filipinos think Western, and "you need to have a group of artists that can understand the humor that goes with it," says Bill Dennis, a Hanna-Barbera executive.

Major studios like Disney, Marvel, Warner Brothers, and Hanna-Barbera send *storyboards*—cartoon action

Neal Peters Collection

outlines—and voice tracks to the Philippines. Artists there draw, paint, and film about 20,000 sketches for a 30-minute episode. The cost of $130,000 to produce an episode in the Philippines compares with $160,000 in Korea and $500,000 in the U.S.

Sources: The New York Times (February 26, 2004): A29; and *The Wall Street Journal* (August 9, 2005): D8.

European Union (EU)
A European trade group that has 27 member states.

Another trading group is the **European Union (EU)**.[2] The European Union has reduced trade barriers among the participating European nations through standardization and a common currency, the euro. However, this major U.S. trading partner, with 490 million people, is also placing some of the world's most restrictive conditions on products sold in the EU. Everything from recycling standards to automobile bumpers to hormone-free farm products must meet EU standards, complicating international trade.

Improve the Supply Chain   The supply chain can often be improved by locating facilities in countries where unique resources are available. These resources may be expertise, labor, or raw material. For example, auto-styling studios from throughout the world are migrating to the auto mecca of southern California to ensure the necessary expertise in contemporary auto design. Similarly, world athletic shoe production has migrated from South Korea to Guangzhou, China: this location takes advantage of the low-cost labor and production competence in a city where 40,000 people work making athletic shoes for the world. And a perfume essence manufacturer wants a presence in Grasse, France, where much of the world's perfume essences are prepared from the flowers of the Mediterranean.

Provide Better Goods and Services   Although the characteristics of goods and services can be objective and measurable (e.g., number of on-time deliveries), they can also be subjective and less measurable (e.g., sensitivity to culture). We need an ever better understanding of differences in culture and of the way business is handled in different countries. Improved understanding as the result of a local presence permits firms to customize products and services to meet unique cultural needs in foreign markets.

Another reason for international operations is to reduce response time to meet customers' changing product and service requirements. Customers who purchase goods and services from U.S. firms are increasingly located in foreign countries. Providing them with quick and adequate service is often improved by locating facilities in their home countries.

Understand Markets   Because international operations require interaction with foreign customers, suppliers, and other competitive businesses, international firms inevitably learn about opportunities for new products and services. Europe led the way with cell phone innovations, and now the Japanese lead with the latest cell phone fads. Knowledge of these markets not only helps firms understand where the market is going but also helps firms diversify their customer base, add production flexibility, and smooth the business cycle.

OM in Action   Going Global to Compete

Banking giant Wachovia Corp. of Charlotte, North Carolina, has inked a $1.1 billion deal with India's Genpact to outsource finance and accounting jobs. Wachovia has also handed over administration of its human resources programs to Illinois-based Hewitt Associates. This is "what we need to do to become a great customer-relationship company," says Wachovia executive P. J. Sidebottom. The expected cost savings of $600 million to $1 billion over the next three years will be invested in the U.S. to boost the core banking business. These investments will be made in new ATMs, branches, and personnel.

Similarly, Dana Corp. of Toledo, Ohio, is also taking a global approach. Dana established a joint venture with Cardanes S.A. to produce truck transmissions in Queretaro, Mexico. Then Dana switched 288 U.S. employees in its Jonesboro, Arkansas, plant from producing truck transmissions at breakeven to axle production at a profit. Productivity is up in Jonesboro, and the Mexican joint venture is making money. Employees in both Jonesboro and Queretaro, as well as stockholders, came out ahead on the move. Dana is also moving operations to China, India, Eastern Europe, and South America.

Resourceful organizations like Wachovia and Dana use a global perspective to become more efficient, which allows them to develop new products, retrain employees, and invest in new plant and equipment.

Sources: Business Week (January 30, 2006): 50–64; *Forbes* (May 8, 2006): 58; and **www.dana.com/news/**.

---

[2]The 27 members of the European Union (EU) as of 2007 were Austria, Belgium, Bulgaria, Cyprus, Czech Republic, Denmark, Estonia, Finland, France, Germany, Greece, Hungary, Ireland, Italy, Latvia, Lithuania, Luxembourg, Malta, the Netherlands, Poland, Portugal, Romania, Slovakia, Slovenia, Spain, Sweden, United Kingdom: not all have adopted the Euro.

◀ *A worldwide strategy places added burdens on operations management. Because of economic and lifestyle differences, designers must target products to each market. For instance, clothes washers sold in northern countries must spin-dry clothes much better than those in warmer climates, where consumers are likely to line-dry them. Similarly, as shown here, Whirlpool refrigerators sold in Bangkok are manufactured in bright colors because they are often put in living rooms.*

Kraipit Phanvut, SIPA Press

Another reason to go into foreign markets is the opportunity to expand the *life cycle* (i.e., stages a product goes through) of an existing product. While some products in the U.S. are in a "mature" stage of their product life cycle, they may represent state-of-the-art products in less developed countries. For example, the U.S. market for personal computers could be characterized as "mature" but as in the "introductory" stage in many developing countries, such as Albania, Vietnam, and Myanmar (Burma).

Learn to Improve Operations   Learning does not take place in isolation. Firms serve themselves and their customers well when they remain open to the free flow of ideas. For example, GM found that it could improve operations by jointly building and running, with the Japanese, an auto assembly plant in San Jose, California. This strategy allows GM to contribute its capital and knowledge of U.S. labor and environmental laws while the Japanese contribute production and inventory ideas. GM also used its employees and experts from Japan to help design its U.S. Saturn plant around production ideas from Japan. Similarly, operations managers have improved equipment and layout by learning from the ergonomic competence of the Scandinavians.

Attract and Retain Global Talent   Global organizations can attract and retain better employees by offering more employment opportunities. They need people in all functional areas and areas of expertise worldwide. Global firms can recruit and retain good employees because they provide both greater growth opportunities and insulation against unemployment during times of economic downturn. During economic downturns in one country or continent, a global firm has the means to relocate unneeded personnel to more prosperous locations. Global organizations also provide incentives for people who like to travel or take vacations in foreign countries.

So, to recap, successfully achieving a competitive advantage in our shrinking world means maximizing all of the possible opportunities, from tangible to intangible, that international operations can offer.

Cultural and Ethical Issues

One of the great challenges as operations go global is reconciling differences in social and cultural behavior. With issues ranging from bribery, to child labor, to the environment, managers sometimes do not know how to respond when operating in a different culture. What one country's culture deems acceptable may be considered unacceptable or illegal in another.

In the last decade, changes in international laws, agreements, and codes of conduct have been applied to define ethical behavior among managers around the world. The World Trade Organization, for example, helps to make uniform the protection of both governments and industries from foreign firms that engage in unethical conduct. Even on issues where significant differences between cultures exist, as in the area of bribery or the protection of intellectual property, global uniformity is slowly being accepted by most nations.

Globalization may take us to the floating factory: A six-person crew will take a factory from port to port to obtain the best market, material, labor, and tax advantages. The service industry, by way of the floating resort (the cruise ship), already provides such an example.

"The ethics of the world market are very clear. Manufacturers will move wherever it is cheapest or most convenient to their interests."

Carlos Arias Macelli, owner of a Guatemala plant that supplies JCPenney

In spite of cultural and ethical differences, we live in a period of extraordinary mobility of capital, information, goods, and even people. We can expect this to continue. The financial sector, the telecommunications sector, and the logistics infrastructure of the world are healthy institutions that foster efficient and effective use of capital, information, and goods. Globalization, with all its opportunities and risks, is here and will continue. It must be embraced as managers develop their missions and strategies.

DEVELOPING MISSIONS AND STRATEGIES

An effective operations management effort must have a *mission* so it knows where it is going and a *strategy* so it knows how to get there. This is the case for a small or domestic organization, as well as a large international organization.

Mission

Mission
The purpose or rationale for an organization's existence.

Economic success, indeed survival, is the result of identifying missions to satisfy a customer's needs and wants. We define the organization's **mission** as its purpose—what it will contribute to society. Mission statements provide boundaries and focus for organizations and the concept around which the firm can rally. The mission states the rationale for the organization's existence. Developing a good strategy is difficult, but it is much easier if the mission has been well defined. Figure 2 provides examples of mission statements.

Once an organization's mission has been decided, each functional area within the firm determines its supporting mission. By *functional area* we mean the major disciplines required by the firm, such as marketing, finance/accounting, and production/operations. Missions for each function are developed to support the firm's overall mission. Then within that function lower-level supporting missions are established for the OM functions. Figure 3 provides such a hierarchy of sample missions.

► **Figure 2**

Mission Statements for Four Organizations

Sources: Annual reports: courtesy of FedEx and Merck; Hard Rock Cafe: *Employee Handbook.* Arnold Palmer Hospital.

FedEx
FedEx is committed to our People-Service-Profit philosophy. We will produce outstanding financial returns by providing totally reliable, competitively superior, global air–ground transportation of high-priority goods and documents that require rapid, time-certain delivery. Equally important, positive control of each package will be maintained utilizing real time electronic tracking and tracing systems. A complete record of each shipment and delivery will be presented with our request for payment. We will be helpful, courteous, and professional to each other and the public. We will strive to have a completely satisfied customer at the end of each transaction.
Merck
The mission of Merck is to provide society with superior products and services—innovations and solutions that improve the quality of life and satisfy customer needs—to provide employees with meaningful work and advancement opportunities and investors with a superior rate of return.
Hard Rock Cafe
Our Mission: To spread the spirit of Rock 'n' Roll by delivering an exceptional entertainment and dining experience. We are committed to being an important, contributing member of our community and offering the Hard Rock family a fun, healthy, and nurturing work environment while ensuring our long-term success.
Arnold Palmer Hospital
Arnold Palmer Hospital is a healing environment providing family-centered care with compassion, comfort and respect ... when it matters most.

Sample Company Mission	
To manufacture and service an innovative, growing, and profitable worldwide microwave communications business that exceeds our customers' expectations.	

Sample Operations Management Mission	
To produce products consistent with the company's mission as the worldwide low-cost manufacturer.	

Sample OM Department Missions	
Product design	To design and produce products and services with outstanding quality and inherent customer value.
Quality management	To attain the exceptional value that is consistent with our company mission and marketing objectives by close attention to design, procurement, production, and field service opportunities.
Process design	To determine and design or produce the production process and equipment that will be compatible with low-cost product, high quality, and a good quality of work life at economical cost.
Location	To locate, design, and build efficient and economical facilities that will yield high value to the company, its employees, and the community.
Layout design	To achieve, through skill, imagination, and resourcefulness in layout and work methods, production effectiveness and efficiency while supporting a high quality of work life.
Human resources	To provide a good quality of work life, with well-designed, safe, rewarding jobs, stable employment, and equitable pay, in exchange for outstanding individual contribution from employees at all levels.
Supply-chain management	To collaborate with suppliers to develop innovative products from stable, effective, and efficient sources of supply.
Inventory	To achieve low investment in inventory consistent with high customer service levels and high facility utilization.
Scheduling	To achieve high levels of throughput and timely customer delivery through effective scheduling.
Maintenance	To achieve high utilization of facilities and equipment by effective preventive maintenance and prompt repair of facilities and equipment.

◄ **Figure 3**

Sample Missions for a Company, the Operations Function, and Major OM Departments

Strategy

With the mission established, strategy and its implementation can begin. **Strategy** is an organization's action plan to achieve the mission. Each functional area has a strategy for achieving its mission and for helping the organization reach the overall mission. These strategies exploit opportunities and strengths, neutralize threats, and avoid weaknesses. In the following sections we will describe how strategies are developed and implemented.

Firms achieve missions in three conceptual ways: (1) differentiation, (2) cost leadership, and (3) response.[3] This means operations managers are called on to deliver goods and services that are (1) *better*, or at least different, (2) *cheaper*, and (3) more *responsive*. Operations managers translate these *strategic concepts* into tangible tasks to be accomplished. Any one or combination

Strategy
How an organization expects to achieve its missions and goals.

Learning Objective

2. Identify and explain three strategic approaches to competitive advantage

[3]See related discussion in Michael E. Porter, *Competitive Strategy: Techniques for Analyzing Industries and Competitors* (New York: The Free Press, 1980). Also see Donald C. Hambrick and James W. Fredrickson, "Are You Sure You Have a Strategy?" *Academy of Management Executive* 15, no. 4 (November 2001): 48–59.

Video 2.1

Operations Strategy at Regal Marine

of these three strategic concepts can generate a system that has a unique advantage over competitors. For example, Hunter Fan has differentiated itself as a premier maker of quality ceiling fans that lower heating and cooling costs for its customers. Nucor Steel, on the other hand, satisfies customers by being the lowest-cost steel producer in the world. And Dell achieves rapid response by building personal computers with each customer's requested software in a matter of hours.

Clearly, strategies differ. And each strategy puts different demands on operations management. Hunter Fan's strategy is one of *differentiating* itself via quality from others in the industry. Nucor focuses on value at *low cost*, and Dell's dominant strategy is quick, reliable *response*.

ACHIEVING COMPETITIVE ADVANTAGE THROUGH OPERATIONS

Competitive advantage
The creation of a unique advantage over competitors.

Each of the three strategies provides an opportunity for operations managers to achieve competitive advantage. **Competitive advantage** implies the creation of a system that has a unique advantage over competitors. The idea is to create customer value in an efficient and sustainable way. Pure forms of these strategies may exist, but operations managers will more likely be called on to implement some combination of them. Let us briefly look at how managers achieve competitive advantage via *differentiation*, *low cost*, and *response*.

Competing on Differentiation

Safeskin Corporation is number one in latex exam gloves because it has differentiated itself and its products. It did so by producing gloves that were designed to prevent allergic reactions about which doctors were complaining. When other glove makers caught up, Safeskin developed hypoallergenic gloves. Then it added texture to its gloves. Then it developed a synthetic disposable glove for those allergic to latex—always staying ahead of the competition. Safeskin's strategy is to develop a reputation for designing and producing reliable state-of-the-art gloves, thereby differentiating itself.

Differentiation
Distinguishing the offerings of an organization in a way that the customer perceives as adding value.

Differentiation is concerned with providing *uniqueness*. A firm's opportunities for creating uniqueness are not located within a particular function or activity but can arise in virtually everything the firm does. Moreover, because most products include some service, and most services include some product, the opportunities for creating this uniqueness are limited only by imagination. Indeed, **differentiation** should be thought of as going beyond both physical characteristics and service attributes to encompass everything about the product or service that influences the value that the customers derive from it. Therefore, effective operations managers assist in defining everything about a product or service that will influence the potential value to the customer. This may be the convenience of a broad product line, product features, or a service related to the product. Such services can manifest themselves through convenience (location of distribution centers, stores, or branches), training, product delivery and installation, or repair and maintenance services.

Experience differentiation
Engaging the customer with a product through imaginative use of the five senses, so the customer "experiences" the product.

In the service sector, one option for extending product differentiation is through an *experience*. Differentiation by experience in services is a manifestation of the growing "experience economy."[4] The idea of **experience differentiation** is to engage the customer—to use people's five senses so they become immersed, or even an active participant, in the product. Disney does this with the Magic Kingdom. People no longer just go on a ride; they are immersed in the Magic Kingdom—surrounded by a dynamic visual and sound experience that complements the physical ride. Some rides further engage the customer by having them steer the ride or shoot targets or villains.

Theme restaurants, such as Hard Rock Cafe, likewise differentiate themselves by providing an "experience." Hard Rock engages the customer with classic rock music, big-screen rock videos, memorabilia, and staff who can tell stories. In many instances, a full-time guide is available to explain the displays, and there is always a convenient retail store so the guest can take home a tangible part of the experience. The result is a "dining experience" rather than just a

Video 2.2

Hard Rock's Global Strategy

---

[4]For an engaging book on the experience economy, see Joseph Pine II and James H. Gilmore, *The Experience Economy*, (Boston: Harvard Business School Press, 1999). Also see Leonard L. Berry, Lewis P. Carbone, and Stephan H. Haeckel, "Managing the Total Customer Experience," *MIT Sloan Management Review* (spring 2002): 85–90.

meal. In a less dramatic way, your local supermarket delivers an experience when it provides music and the aroma of freshly baked bread, and when it has samples for you to taste.

Competing on Cost

Southwest Airlines has been a consistent moneymaker while other U.S. airlines have lost billions. Southwest has done this by fulfilling a need for low-cost and short-hop flights. Its operations strategy has included use of secondary airports and terminals, first-come, first-served seating, few fare options, smaller crews flying more hours, snacks-only or no-meal flights, and no downtown ticket offices.

Additionally, and less obviously, Southwest has very effectively matched capacity to demand and effectively utilized this capacity. It has done this by designing a route structure that matches the capacity of its Boeing 737, the only plane in its fleet. Second, it achieves more air miles than other airlines through faster turnarounds—its planes are on the ground less.

One driver of a low-cost strategy is a facility that is effectively utilized. Southwest and others with low-cost strategies understand this and utilize resources effectively. Identifying the optimum size (and investment) allows firms to spread overhead costs, providing a cost advantage. For instance, Wal-Mart continues to pursue its low-cost strategy with superstores, open 24 hours a day. For 20 years, it has successfully grabbed market share. Wal-Mart has driven down store overhead costs, shrinkage, and distribution costs. Its rapid transportation of goods, reduced warehousing costs, and direct shipment from manufacturers have resulted in high inventory turnover and made it a low-cost leader. Franz Colruyt, as discussed in the *OM in Action* box, is also winning with a low-cost strategy.

Low-cost leadership entails achieving maximum *value* as defined by your customer. It requires examining each of the 10 OM decisions in a relentless effort to drive down costs while meeting customer expectations of value. A low-cost strategy does *not* imply low value or low quality.

Low-cost leadership
Achieving maximum value as perceived by the customer.

Competing on Response

The third strategy option is response. Response is often thought of as *flexible* response, but it also refers to *reliable* and *quick* response. Indeed, we define **response** as including the entire range of values related to timely product development and delivery, as well as reliable scheduling and flexible performance.

Response
A set of values related to rapid, flexible, and reliable performance.

OM in Action   Low-Cost Strategy Wins at Franz Colruyt

Belgian discount food retailer Franz Colruyt NV is so obsessed with cutting costs that there are no shopping bags at its checkout counters, the lighting at its stores is dimmed to save money on electricity, and employees clock out when they go on 5-minute coffee breaks. And to keep costs down at the company's spartan headquarters on the outskirts of Brussels, employees don't have voice mail on their phones. Instead, two receptionists take messages for nearly 1,000 staffers. The messages are bellowed out every few minutes from loudspeakers peppered throughout the building.

This same approach is evident at all 160 of Colruyt's shopping outlets, which are converted factory warehouses, movie theaters, or garages, with black concrete floors, exposed electrical wires, metal shelves, and discarded boxes strewn about. There is no background music (estimated annual cost saving: 2 million euros or $2.5 million), nor are there bags for packing groceries (estimated annual cost saving: 5 million euros). And all the store's freezers have doors, so the company can save about 3 million euros a year on electricity for refrigeration.

The company also employs a team of 30 "work simplifiers"—in Colruyt jargon—whose job is to come up with new ways to improve productivity. One recently discovered that 5 seconds could be shaved from every minute it takes customers to check out if they paid at a separate station from where groceries are scanned, so that when one customer steps away from the scanner, another can step up right away.

Chief Executive Rene De Wit says Colruyt's strategy is simple: cut costs at every turn and undersell your competitors. In an industry where margins of 1% to 2% are typical, Colruyt's cost cutting is so effective that a profit margin of 6.5% dwarfs those of rivals.

A low-cost strategy places significant demands on operations management, but Franz Colruyt, like Wal-Mart, makes it work.

Sources: The Wall Street Journal (September 22, 2003): R3, R7; and *DC Velocity* (September 2004): 38–40.

▶ *Response strategy wins orders at Super Fast Pizza. Using a wireless connection, orders are transmitted to $20,000 kitchens in vans. The driver, who works solo, receives a printed order, goes to the kitchen area, pulls premade pizzas from the cooler, and places them in the oven— it takes about 1 minute. The driver then delivers the pizza—sometimes even arriving before the pizza is ready.*

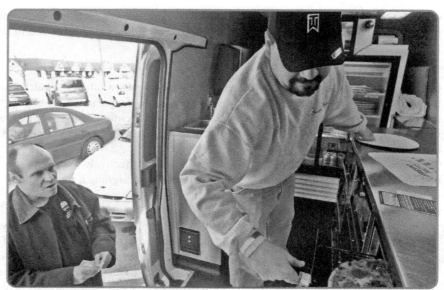

AP Wide World Photos

Flexible response may be thought of as the ability to match changes in a marketplace where design innovations and volumes fluctuate substantially.

Hewlett-Packard is an exceptional example of a firm that has demonstrated flexibility in both design and volume changes in the volatile world of personal computers. HP's products often have a life cycle of months, and volume and cost changes during that brief life cycle are dramatic. However, HP has been successful at institutionalizing the ability to change products and volume to respond to dramatic changes in product design and costs—thus building a *sustainable competitive advantage*.

The second aspect of response is the *reliability* of scheduling. One way the German machine industry has maintained its competitiveness despite having the world's highest labor costs is through reliable response. This response manifests itself in reliable scheduling. German machine firms have meaningful schedules—and they perform to these schedules. Moreover, the results of these schedules are communicated to the customer and the customer can, in turn, rely on them. Consequently, the competitive advantage generated through reliable response has value to the end customer.

The third aspect of response is *quickness*. Johnson Electric, discussed in the *OM in Action* box, competes on speed—speed in design, production, and delivery. Whether it is a production

OM in Action   Response Strategy at Hong Kong's Johnson Electric

Patrick Wang, managing director of Johnson Electric Holdings, Ltd., walks through his Hong Kong headquarters with a micromotor in his hand. This tiny motor, about twice the size of his thumb, powers a Dodge Viper power door lock. Although most people have never heard of Johnson Electric, we all have several of its micromotors nearby. This is because Johnson is the world's leading producer of micromotors for cordless tools, household appliances (such as coffee grinders and food processors), personal care items (such as hair dryers and electric shavers), and cars. A luxury Mercedes, with its headlight wipers, power windows, power seat adjustments, and power side mirrors, may use 50 Johnson micromotors.

Like all truly global businesses, Johnson spends liberally on communications to tie together its global network of factories, R&D facilities, and design centers. For example, Johnson Electric installed a $20 million videoconfer-

encing system that allows engineers in Cleveland, Ohio, and Stuttgart, Germany, to monitor trial production of their micromotors in China.

Johnson's first strength is speed in product development, speed in production, and speed in delivering—13 million motors a month, mostly assembled in China but delivered throughout the world. Its second strength is the ability to stay close to its customers. Johnson has design and technical centers scattered across the U.S., Europe, and Japan. "The physical limitations of the past are gone" when it comes to deciding where to locate a new center, says Patrick Wang. "Customers talk to us where they feel most comfortable, but products are made where they are most competitive."

Sources: Hoover's Company Records (January 1, 2006): 58682; Far Eastern Economic Review (May 16, 2002): 44–45; and The Economist (June 22, 1996): 65.

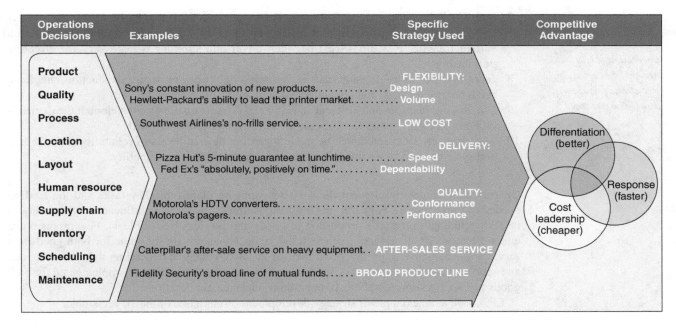

▲ **Figure 4**   Operations Management's Contribution to Strategy

system at Johnson Electric, a lunch delivered in 15 minutes at Bennigan's, or customized pagers delivered in three days from Motorola, the operations manager who develops systems that respond quickly can have a competitive advantage.

In practice, these three *concepts* —differentiation, low cost, and response—are often implemented via the six *specific strategies* shown in Figure 4: (1) flexibility in design and volume, (2) low cost, (3) delivery, (4) quality, (5) after-sales service, and (6) a broad product line. Through these six specific strategies, OM can increase productivity and generate a sustainable competitive advantage. Proper implementation of the following decisions by operations managers will allow these strategies to be achieved.

TEN STRATEGIC OM DECISIONS

Differentiation, low cost, and response can be achieved when managers make effective decisions in 10 areas of OM. These are collectively known as **operations decisions**. The 10 decisions of OM that support missions and implement strategies follow:

1. *Goods and service design:* Designing goods and services defines much of the transformation process. Costs, quality, and human resource decisions are often determined by design decisions. Designs usually determine the lower limits of cost and the upper limits of quality.
2. *Quality:* The customer's quality expectations must be determined and policies and procedures established to identify and achieve that quality.
3. *Process and capacity design:* Process options are available for products and services. Process decisions commit management to specific technology, quality, human resource use, and maintenance. These expenses and capital commitments determine much of the firm's basic cost structure.
4. *Location selection:* Facility location decisions for both manufacturing and service organizations may determine the firm's ultimate success. Errors made at this juncture may overwhelm other efficiencies.
5. *Layout design:* Material flows, capacity needs, personnel levels, technology decisions, and inventory requirements influence layout.
6. *Human resources and job design:* People are an integral and expensive part of the total system design. Therefore, the quality of work life provided, the talent and skills required, and their costs must be determined.

> *"In the future, there will be just two kinds of firms: those who disrupt their markets and those who don't survive the assault."*
>
> *Professor Richard D'Aveni, author of Hypercompetition*

Learning Objective

3. Identify and define the 10 decisions of operations management

Operations decisions
The strategic decisions of OM are goods and service design, quality, process design, location selection, layout design, human resources and job design, supply chain management, inventory, scheduling, and maintenance.

7. *Supply chain management:* These decisions determine what is to be made and what is to be purchased. Consideration is also given to quality, delivery, and innovation, all at a satisfactory price. Mutual trust between buyer and supplier is necessary for effective purchasing.

8. *Inventory:* Inventory decisions can be optimized only when customer satisfaction, suppliers, production schedules, and human resource planning are considered.

9. *Scheduling:* Feasible and efficient schedules of production must be developed; the demands on human resources and facilities must be determined and controlled.

10. *Maintenance:* Decisions must be made regarding desired levels of reliability and stability, and systems must be established to maintain that reliability and stability.

> "Operations is typically thought of as an execution of strategy; for us it is the strategy."
>
> *Joe R. Lee,*
> *Former chairman of*
> *Darden Restaurants*

Operations managers implement these 10 decisions by identifying key tasks and the staffing needed to achieve them. However, the implementation of decisions is influenced by a variety of issues, including a product's proportion of goods and services (see Table 1). Few products are either all goods or all services. Although the 10 decisions remain the same for both goods and services, their relative importance and method of implementation depend on this ratio of goods and services. Throughout this text, we discuss how strategy is selected and implemented for both goods and services through these 10 operations management decisions.

Let's look at an example of strategy development through one of the 10 decisions.

EXAMPLE 1

Strategy development

Pierre Alexander has just completed chef school and is ready to open his own restaurant. After examining both the external environment and his prospective strengths and weaknesses, he makes a decision on the mission for his restaurant, which he defines as "To provide outstanding French fine dining for the people of Chicago."

Approach: Alexander's supporting operations strategy is to ignore the options of *cost leadership* and *quick response* and focus on *differentiation.* Consequently, his operations strategy requires him to evaluate product designs (menus and meals) and selection of process, layout, and location. He must also evaluate the human resources, suppliers, inventory, scheduling, and maintenance that will support his mission and a differentiation strategy.

Solution: Examining just one of these 10 decisions, *process design,* requires that Alexander consider the issues presented in the following figure.

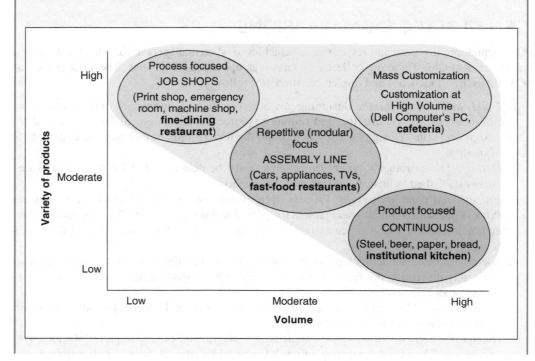

The first option is to operate in the lower right corner of the preceding figure, where he could produce high volumes of food with a limited variety, much as in an institutional kitchen. Such a process could produce large volumes of standard items such as baked goods and mashed potatoes prepared with state-of-the-art automated equipment. Alexander concludes that this is not an acceptable process option.

Alternatively, he can move to the middle of the figure, where he could produce more variety and lower volumes. Here he would have less automation and use prepared modular components for meals, much as a fast-food restaurant does. Again, he deems such process designs inappropriate for his mission.

Another option is to move to the upper right corner and produce a high volume of customized meals, but neither Alexander nor anyone else knows how to do this with gourmet meals.

Finally, Alexander can design a process that operates in the upper left corner of the figure, which requires little automation but lends itself to high variety. This process option suggests that he build an extremely flexible kitchen suitable for a wide variety of custom meals catering to the whims of each customer. With little automation, such a process would be suitable for a huge variety. This process strategy will support his mission and desired product differentiation. Only with a process such as this can he provide the fine French-style gourmet dining that he has in mind.

Insight: By considering the options inherent in each of the 10 OM decisions, managers—Alexander, in this case—can make decisions that support the mission.

Learning exercise: If Alexander's mission were to offer less expensive meals and reduce the variety offered but still do so with a French flair, what might his process strategy be? [Answer: Alexander might try a repetitive (modular) strategy and mimic the La Madeleine cafeteria-style restaurants.]

▼ **Table 1** The Differences Between Goods and Services Influence How the 10 Operations Management Decisions Are Applied

Operations Decisions	Goods	Services
Goods and service design	Product is usually tangible.	Product is not tangible. A new range of product attributes—a smile.
Quality	Many objective quality standards.	Many subjective quality standards—nice color.
Process and capacity design	Customer is not involved in most of the process.	Customer may be directly involved in the process—a haircut.
		Capacity must match demand to avoid lost sales—customers often avoid waiting.
Location selection	May need to be near raw materials or labor force.	May need to be near customer—car rental.
Layout design	Layout can enhance production efficiency.	Can enhance product as well as production—layout of a fine-dining restaurant.
Human resources and job design	Workforce focused on technical skills. Labor standards can be consistent. Output-based wage system possible.	Direct workforce usually needs to be able to interact well with customer—bank teller. Labor standards vary depending on customer requirements—legal cases.
Supply chain management	Supply chain relationships critical to final product.	Supply chain relationships important but may not be critical
Inventory	Raw materials, work-in-process, and finished goods may be inventoried.	Most services cannot be stored; so other ways must be found to accommodate fluctuations in demand—can't store haircuts.
Scheduling	Ability to inventory may allow leveling of production rates.	Often concerned with meeting the customer's immediate schedule with human resources.
Maintenance	Maintenance is often preventive and takes place at the production site.	Maintenance is often "repair" and takes place at the customer's site.

▼ **Table 2** Operations Strategies of Two Drug Companies

	Brand Name Drugs, Inc.	Generic Drug Corp.
Competitive Advantage	**Product Differentiation**	**Low Cost**
Product Selection and Design	Heavy R&D investment; extensive labs; focus on development in a broad range of drug categories	Low R&D investment; focus on development of generic drugs
Quality	Quality is major priority, standards exceed regulatory requirements	Meets regulatory requirements on a country-by-country basis as necessary
Process	Product and modular production process; tries to have long product runs in specialized facilities; builds capacity ahead of demand	Process focused; general production processes; "jobshop" approach, short-run production; focus on high utilization
Location	Still located in city where it was founded	Recently moved to low-tax, low-labor-cost environment
Layout	Layout supports automated product-focused production	Layout supports process-focused "job shop" practices
Human Resources	Hire the best; nationwide searches	Very experienced top executives provide direction; other personnel paid below industry average
Supply Chain	Long-term supplier relationships	Tends to purchase competitively to find bargains
Inventory	Maintains high finished goods inventory primarily to ensure all demands are met	Process focus drives up work-in-process inventory; finished goods inventory tends to be low
Scheduling	Centralized production planning	Many short-run products complicate scheduling
Maintenance	Highly trained staff; extensive parts inventory	Highly trained staff to meet changing demands

The 10 decisions of operations management are implemented in ways that provide competitive advantage, not just for fine-dining restaurants, but for all the goods and services that enrich our lives. How this might be done for two drug companies, one seeking a competitive advantage via differentiation, and the other via low cost, is shown in Table 2.

ISSUES IN OPERATIONS STRATEGY

Once a firm has formed a mission, developing and implementing a specific strategy requires that the operations manager consider a number of issues. We will examine these issues in three ways. First, we look at what *research* tells us about effective operations management strategies. Second, we identify some of the *preconditions* to developing effective OM strategy. Third, we look at the *dynamics* of OM strategy development.

Research

PIMS

A program established in cooperation with GE to identify characteristics of high-return-on-investment firms.

Strategic insight has been provided by the findings of the Strategic Planning Institute.[5] Its **PIMS** program (profit impact of market strategy) was established in cooperation with the General Electric Corporation. PIMS has collected nearly 100 data items from about 3,000 cooperating organizations. Using the data collected and high *return on investment* (ROI)[6] as a measure of success, PIMS has been able to identify some characteristics of high-ROI firms. Among those characteristics that affect strategic OM decisions are:

Learning Objective

4. Identify five OM strategy insights provided by PIMS research

1. High product quality (relative to the competition).
2. High capacity utilization.
3. High operating efficiency (the ratio of expected to actual employee productivity).
4. Low investment intensity (the amount of capital required to produce a dollar of sales).
5. Low direct cost per unit (relative to the competition).

[5]See B. Leavy, "Assessing Your Strategic Alternatives," *Strategy and Leadership* (2003): 29, or R. D. Buzzel and B. T. Gale, *The PIMS Principles* (New York: The Free Press, 1987).
[6]Like other performance measures, *return on investment* (ROI) has limitations, including sensitivity to the business cycle, depreciation policies and schedules, book value (goodwill), and transfer pricing.

These five findings support a high return on investment and should therefore be considered as an organization develops a strategy. In the analysis of a firm's relative strengths and weaknesses, these characteristics can be measured and evaluated. The specific strategic approaches suggested earlier, in Figure 4, indicate where an operations manager may want to go, but without achieving the five characteristics of firms with a high return on investment, that journey may not be successful.

Another research study indicates the significant role that OM can play in competitive strategy. When a wide mix of 248 businesses were asked to evaluate the importance of 32 categories in obtaining a sustainable competitive advantage, 28% of the categories selected fell under operations management. When quality/service is added, the total goes to 44%. The study supports the major role OM strategy plays in developing a competitive advantage.[7]

Preconditions

Before establishing and attempting to implement a strategy, the operations manager needs to understand that the firm is operating in an open system in which a multitude of factors exists. These factors influence strategy development and execution. The more thorough the analysis and understanding of both the external and internal factors, the more the likelihood of success. Although the list of factors to be considered is extensive, at a minimum it entails an understanding of:

1. Strengths and weaknesses of competitors, as well as possible new entrants into the market, substitute products, and commitment of suppliers and distributors.
2. Current and prospective environmental, technological, legal, and economic issues.
3. Product life cycle, which may dictate the limitations of operations strategy.
4. Resources available within the firm and within the OM function.
5. Integration of the OM strategy with the company's strategy and other functional areas.

> *"To the Japanese, strategy is so dynamic as to be thought of as 'accommodation' or 'adaptive persistence.'"*
> *Richard Pascale, MIT Sloan Management Review*

Dynamics

Strategies change for two reasons. First, strategy is dynamic because of *changes within the organization*. All areas of the firm are subject to change. Changes may occur in a variety of areas, including personnel, finance, technology, and product life. All may make a difference in an organization's strengths and weaknesses and therefore its strategy. Figure 5 shows possible change in both overall strategy and OM strategy during the product's life. For instance, as a product moves from introduction to growth, product and process design typically move from development to stability. As the product moves to the growth stage, forecasting and capacity planning become issues.

Strategy is also dynamic because of *changes in the environment*.[8] Boeing provides an example, in the opening *Global Company Profile* in this chapter, of how strategy must change as the environment changes. Its strategies, like many OM strategies, are increasingly global. Microsoft also had to adapt quickly to a changing environment. Microsoft's shift in strategy was caused by changing customer demand, security, and the Internet. Microsoft moved from operating systems to office products, to Internet service provider, and now to an integrator of computers and television.

STRATEGY DEVELOPMENT AND IMPLEMENTATION

Once firms understand the issues involved in developing an effective strategy, they evaluate their internal strengths and weaknesses as well as the opportunities and threats of the environment. This is known as **SWOT analysis** (for *S*trengths, *W*eaknesses, *O*pportunities, and *T*hreats). Beginning with SWOT analyses, firms position themselves, through their strategy, to have a competitive advantage. The firm may have excellent design skills or great talent at identifying outstanding locations. However, the firm may recognize limitations of its manufacturing process or in finding good suppliers. The idea is to maximize opportunities and minimize threats in the environment while maximizing the advantages of the organization's strengths and minimizing the weaknesses. Any preconceived ideas about mission are then reevaluated to ensure they are consistent with the SWOT analysis. Subsequently, a strategy for achieving the mission is developed. This strategy is continually evaluated against the value provided customers and competi-

SWOT analysis
A method of determining internal strengths and weaknesses and external opportunities and threats.

---

[7]See David A. Aaker, "Creating a Sustainable Competitive Advantage," *California Management Review* (winter 1989): 91–106.
[8]Anita M. McGahan, "How Industries Change," *Harvard Business Review* 82, no. 10 (October 11, 2004): 87–94.

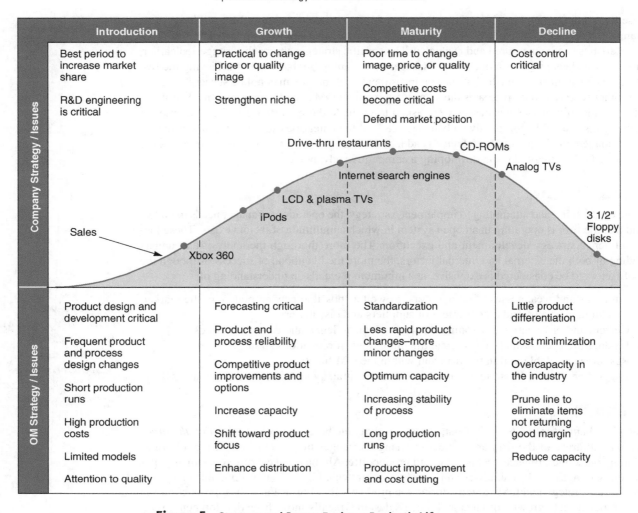

	Introduction	Growth	Maturity	Decline
Company Strategy / Issues	Best period to increase market share R&D engineering is critical	Practical to change price or quality image Strengthen niche	Poor time to change image, price, or quality Competitive costs become critical Defend market position	Cost control critical
OM Strategy / Issues	Product design and development critical Frequent product and process design changes Short production runs High production costs Limited models Attention to quality	Forecasting critical Product and process reliability Competitive product improvements and options Increase capacity Shift toward product focus Enhance distribution	Standardization Less rapid product changes–more minor changes Optimum capacity Increasing stability of process Long production runs Product improvement and cost cutting	Little product differentiation Cost minimization Overcapacity in the industry Prune line to eliminate items not returning good margin Reduce capacity

Curve labels: Sales, Xbox 360, iPods, LCD & plasma TVs, Internet search engines, Drive-thru restaurants, CD-ROMs, Analog TVs, 3 1/2" Floppy disks

▲ **Figure 5** **Strategy and Issues During a Product's Life**

tive realities. The process is shown in Figure 6. From this process critical success factors are identified.

Critical Success Factors and Core Competencies

Critical success factors (CSFs)

Activities or factors that are *key* to achieving competitive advantage.

Because no firm does everything exceptionally well, a successful strategy requires determining the firm's critical success factors and core competencies. **Critical success factors (CSFs)** are those activities that are necessary for a firm to achieve its goals. Critical success factors can be so significant that a firm must get them right to survive in the industry. A CSF for McDonald's, for example,

► **Figure 6**

Strategy Development Process

Environmental Analysis
Identify the strengths, weaknesses, opportunities, and threats.
Understand the environment, customers, industry, and competitors.

Determine Corporate Mission
State the reason for the firm's existence and identify the value it wishes to create.

Form a Strategy
Build a competitive advantage, such as low price, design or volume flexibility, quality, quick delivery, dependability, after-sale services, or broad product lines.

◄ *Honda's core competence is the design and manufacture of gas-powered engines. This competence has allowed Honda to become a leader in the design and manufacture of a wide range of gas-powered products. Tens of millions of these products are produced and shipped around the world.*

www.HondaNews.com

is layout. Without a play area, an effective drive-thru, and an efficient kitchen, McDonald's cannot be successful. CSFs are often necessary, but not sufficient for competitive advantage. On the other hand, **core competencies** are the set of unique skills, talents, and capabilities that a firm does at a world-class standard. They allow a firm to set itself apart and develop a competitive advantage. Organizations that prosper identify their core competencies and nurture them. While McDonald's CSFs may include layout, its core competency may be consistency and quality. Honda Motors's core competence is gas-powered engines—engines for automobiles, motorcycles, lawn mowers, generators, snow blowers, and more. The idea is to build CSFs and core competencies that provide a competitive advantage and support a successful strategy and mission. A core competence may be a subset of CSFs or a combination of CSFs. The operations manager begins this inquiry by asking:

Core competencies
A set of skills, talents, and activities that a firm does particularly well.

- "What tasks must be done particularly well for a given strategy to succeed?"
- "Which activities will help the OM function provide a competitive advantage?"
- "Which elements contain the highest likelihood of failure, and which require additional commitment of managerial, monetary, technological, and human resources?"

Only by identifying and strengthening critical success factors and core competencies can an organization achieve sustainable competitive advantage.

In this text we focus on the 10 OM decisions that typically include the CSFs. Potential CSFs for marketing, finance, and operations are shown in Figure 7. The 10 operations management

◄ **Figure 7**

Implement Strategy by Identifying and Executing Critical Success Factors and Supporting the Core Competence

Support a Core Competence and Implement Strategy by Identifying and Executing the Critical Success Factors in the Functional Areas

Marketing	Finance/Accounting	Operations
Service	Leverage	
Distribution	Cost of capital	
Promotion	Working capital	
Price	Receivables	
Channels of distribution	Payables	
Product positioning (image, functions)	Financial control	
	Lines of credit	

Decisions	Sample Options	Chapter
Product	Customized or standardized	5
Quality	Define customer expectations and how to achieve them	6,S6
Process	Facility design, capacity	7,S7
Location	Near supplier or near customer	8
Layout	Work cells or assembly line	9
Human resource	Specialized or enriched jobs	10,S10
Supply chain	Single or multiple suppliers	11,S11
Inventory	When to reorder; how much to keep on hand	12,14,16
Schedule	Stable or fluctuating production rate	13,15
Maintenance	Repair as required or preventive maintenance	17

decisions we develop in this text provide an excellent initial checklist for determining CSFs and identifying core competencies within the operations function. For instance, the 10 decisions, related CSFs, and core competencies can allow a firm to differentiate its product or service. That differentiation may be via a core competence of innovation and new products, where the CSFs are product design and speed to market, as is the case for 3M and Rubbermaid. Similarly, differentiation may be via quality, where the core competence is institutionalizing quality, as at Toyota. Differentiation may also be via maintenance, where the CSFs are product reliability and after-sale service, as is the case at IBM and Canon.

Activity map

A graphical link of competitive advantage, CSFs, and supporting activities.

Whatever the CSFs and core competences, they must be supported by the related activities. One approach to identifying the activities is an **activity map**, which links competitive advantage, CSFs, and supporting activities. For example, Figure 8 shows how Southwest Airlines, whose core competence is operations, built a set of integrated activities to support its low-cost competitive advantage. Notice how the CSFs support operations and in turn are supported by other activities.[9] The activities fit together and reinforce each other. And the better they fit and reinforce each other, the more sustainable the competitive advantage. By focusing on enhancing its core competence and CSFs with a supporting set of activities, Southwest Airlines has become one of the great airline success stories.

Build and Staff the Organization

The operations manager's job is a three-step process. Once a strategy and critical success factors have been identified, the second step is to group the necessary activities into an organizational structure. The third step is to staff it with personnel who will get the job done. The manager

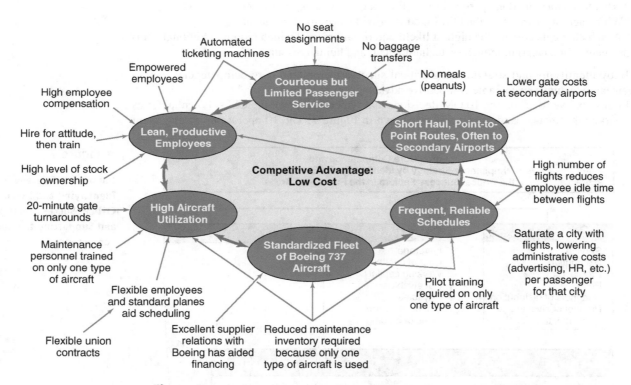

▲ **Figure 8** **Activity Mapping of Southwest Airlines's Low-Cost Competitive Advantage**

To achieve a low-cost competitive advantage, Southwest has identified a number of critical success factors (connected by red arrows) and support activities (shown by blue arrows). As this figure indicates, a low-cost advantage is highly dependent on a very well run operations function.

[9]Michael E. Porter and C. Roland Christensen, "What Is Strategy?" *Harvard Business Review* (November–December 1996): 61–75.

works with subordinate managers to build plans, budgets, and programs that will successfully implement strategies that achieve missions. Firms tackle this organization of the operations function in a variety of ways.

Integrate OM with Other Activities

The organization of the operations function and its relationship to other parts of the organization vary with the OM mission. Moreover, the operations function is most likely to be successful when the operations strategy is integrated with other functional areas of the firm, such as marketing, finance, information technology, and human resources. In this way, all of the areas support the company's objectives. For example, short-term scheduling in the airline industry is dominated by volatile customer travel patterns. Day-of-week preference, holidays, seasonality, college schedules, and so on, all play a role in changing flight schedules. Consequently, airline scheduling, although an OM activity, can be a part of marketing. Effective scheduling in the trucking industry is reflected in the amount of time trucks travel loaded. However, scheduling of trucks requires information from delivery and pickup points, drivers, and other parts of the organization. When the OM function results in effective scheduling in the air passenger and commercial trucking industries, a competitive advantage can exist.

The operations manager provides a means of transforming inputs into outputs. The transformations may be in terms of storage, transportation, manufacturing, dissemination of information, and utility of the product or service. *The operations manager's job is to implement an OM strategy, provide competitive advantage, and increase productivity.*

> *"The manufacturing business of tomorrow will not be run by financial executives, marketers, or lawyers inexperienced in manufacturing, as so many U.S. companies are today."*
>
> *Peter Drucker*

GLOBAL OPERATIONS STRATEGY OPTIONS

As we suggested early in this chapter, many operations strategies now require an international dimension. We tend to call a firm with an international dimension an international business or a multinational corporation. An **international business** is any firm that engages in international trade or investment. This is a very broad category and is the opposite of a domestic, or local, firm.

A **multinational corporation (MNC)** is a firm with *extensive* international business involvement. MNCs buy resources, create goods or services, and sell goods or services in a variety of countries. The term *multinational corporation* applies to most of the world's large, well-known businesses. Certainly IBM is a good example of an MNC. It imports electronics components to the U.S. from over 50 countries, exports computers to over 130 countries, has facilities in 45 countries, and earns more than half its sales and profits abroad.

Operations managers of international and multinational firms approach global opportunities with one of four operations strategies: *international*, *multidomestic*, *global*, and *transnational* (see Figure 9). The matrix of Figure 9 has a vertical axis of cost reduction and a horizontal axis of local responsiveness. Local responsiveness implies quick response and/or the differentiation necessary for the local market. The operations manager must know how to position the firm in this matrix. Let us briefly examine each of the four strategies.

International business
A firm that engages in cross-border transactions.

Multinational corporation (MNC)
A firm that has extensive involvement in international business, owning or controlling facilities in more than one country.

International Strategy

An **international strategy** uses exports and licenses to penetrate the global arena. As Figure 9 suggests, the international strategy is the least advantageous, with little local responsiveness and little cost advantage. There is little responsiveness because we are exporting or licensing a good from the home country. And the cost advantages may be few because we are using the existing production process at some distance from the new market. However, an international strategy is often the easiest, as exports can require little change in existing operations, and licensing agreements often leave much of the risk to the licensee.

International strategy
A strategy in which global markets are penetrated using exports and licenses.

Multidomestic Strategy

The **multidomestic strategy** has decentralized authority with substantial autonomy at each business. Organizationally these are typically subsidiaries, franchises, or joint ventures with substantial independence. The advantage of this strategy is maximizing a competitive response for the

Multidomestic strategy
A strategy in which operating decisions are decentralized to each country to enhance local responsiveness.

▶ **Figure 9**

Four International Operations Strategies

Sources: See a similar presentation in M. Hitt, R. D. Ireland, and R. E. Hoskisson, *Strategic Management, Competitiveness and Globalization,* 6th ed. (Cincinnati: Southwestern College Publishing, 2006).

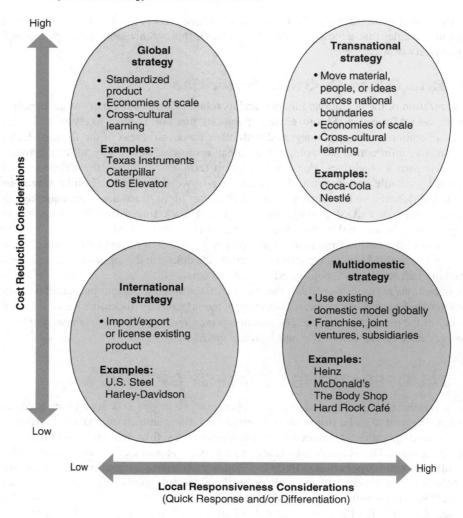

5. Identify and explain four global operations strategy options

local market; however, the strategy has little or no cost advantage. Many food producers, such as Heinz, use a multidomestic strategy to accommodate local tastes because global integration of the production process is not critical. The concept is one of "we were successful in the home market, let's export the management talent and processes, not necessarily the product, to accommodate another market." McDonald's is operating primarily as a multidomestic, which gives it the local responsiveness needed to modify its menu country by country. McDonald's can then serve beer in Germany, wine in France, McHuevo (poached egg hamburger) in Uruguay, and hamburgers without beef in India. With over 2,000 restaurants in Japan and a presence of more than a generation, the average Japanese family thinks Japan invented McDonald's. Interestingly, McDonald's prefers to call itself *multilocal*.[10]

Global Strategy

Global strategy

A strategy in which operating decisions are centralized and headquarters coordinates the standardization and learning between facilities.

A **global strategy** has a high degree of centralization, with headquarters coordinating the organization to seek out standardization and learning between plants, thus generating economies of scale. This strategy is appropriate when the strategic focus is cost reduction but has little to recommend it when the demand for local responsiveness is high. Caterpillar, the world leader in earth-moving equipment, and Texas Instruments, a world leader in semiconductors, pursue global strategies. Caterpillar and Texas Instruments find this strategy advantageous because the end products are similar throughout the world. Earth-moving equipment is the same in Nigeria as

[10]James L. Watson, ed., *Golden Arches East: McDonald's in East Asia* (Stanford University Press, 1997): 12. *Note:* McDonald's also operates with some of the advantages of a global organization. By using very similar product lines throughout the world, McDonald's obtains some of the standardization advantages of a global strategy. However, it manages to retain the advantages of a multidomestic strategy.

▲ *In a continuing fierce worldwide battle, both Komatsu and Caterpillar seek global advantage in the heavy equipment market. As Komatsu (left) moved west to the UK, Caterpillar (right) moved east, with 13 facilities and joint ventures in China. Both firms are building equipment throughout the world as cost and logistics dictate. Their global strategies allow production to move as markets, risk, and exchange rates dictate.*

in Iowa, which allows Caterpillar to have individual factories focus on a limited line of products to be shipped worldwide. This results in economies of scale and learning within each facility. A global strategy also allows Texas Instruments to build optimum-size plants with similar process and to then maximize learning by aggressive communication between plants. The result is an effective cost reduction advantage for Texas Instruments.

Transnational Strategy

A **transnational strategy** exploits the economies of scale and learning, as well as pressure for responsiveness, by recognizing that core competence does not reside in just the "home" country but can exist anywhere in the organization. *Transnational* describes a condition in which material, people, and ideas cross—or *transgress*—national boundaries. These firms have the potential to pursue all three operations strategies (i.e., differentiation, low cost, and response). Such firms can be thought of as "world companies" whose country identity is not as important as its interdependent network of worldwide operations. Key activities in a transnational company are neither centralized in the parent company nor decentralized so that each subsidiary can carry out its own tasks on a local basis. Instead, the resources and activities are dispersed, but specialized, so as to be both efficient and flexible in an interdependent network. Nestlé is a good example of such a company. Although it is legally Swiss, 95% of its assets are held and 98% of its sales are made outside Switzerland. Fewer than 10% of its workers are Swiss. Similarly, service firms such as Asea Brown Boveri (an engineering firm that is Swedish but headquartered in Switzerland), Reuters (a news agency), Bertelsmann (a publisher), and Citicorp (a banking corporation) can be viewed as transnationals. We can expect the national identities of these transnationals to continue to fade.

Transnational strategy
A strategy that combines the benefits of global-scale efficiencies with the benefits of local responsiveness.

Summary

Global operations provide an increase in both the challenges and opportunities for operations managers. Although the task is challenging, operations managers can and do improve productivity. They can build and manage OM functions that contribute in a significant way to competitiveness. Organizations identify their strengths and weaknesses. They then develop effective missions and strategies that account for these strengths and weaknesses and complement the opportunities and threats in the environment. If this procedure is performed well, the organization can have competitive advantage through some combination of product differentiation, low cost, and response. This competitive advantage is often achieved via a move to international, multidomestic, global, or transnational strategies.

Effective use of resources, whether domestic or international, is the responsibility of the professional manager, and professional managers are among the few in our society who *can* achieve this performance. The challenge is great, and the rewards to the manager and to society substantial.

Key Terms

Maquiladoras
World Trade Organization (WTO)
North American Free Trade Agreement (NAFTA)
European Union (EU)
Mission
Strategy
Competitive advantage

Differentiation
Experience differentiation
Low-cost leadership
Response
Operations decisions
PIMS
SWOT analysis
Critical success factors

Core competencies
Activity map
International business
Multinational corporation (MNC)
International strategy
Multidomestic strategy
Global strategy
Transnational strategy

Solved Problem

 Virtual Office Hours help is available on Student DVD.

Solved Problem 1

Strategy at Pirelli SpA The global tire industry continues to consolidate. Michelin buys Goodrich and Uniroyal and builds plants throughout the world. Bridgestone buys Firestone, expands its research budget, and focuses on world markets. Goodyear spends almost 4% of its sales revenue on research. These three aggressive firms have come to dominate the world tire market, with total market share approaching 60%. And the German tire maker Continental AG has strengthened its position as fourth in the world, with a dominant presence in Germany. Against this formidable array, the old-line Italian tire company Pirelli SpA found it difficult to respond effectively. Although Pirelli still had 5% of the market, it was losing millions a year while the competition was getting stronger. Tires are a tough, competitive business that rewards companies having strong market shares and long production runs. Pirelli has some strengths: an outstanding reputation for excellent high-performance tires and an innovative manufacturing function.

Use a SWOT analysis to establish a feasible strategy for Pirelli.

Solution

First, find an opportunity in the world tire market that avoids the threat of the mass-market onslaught by the big three tire makers. Second, utilize the internal marketing strength represented by Pirelli's strong brand name and history of winning World Rally Championships. Third, maximize the internal innovative capabilities of the operations function.

To achieve these goals, Pirelli made a strategic shift out of low-margin standard tires and into higher-margin performance tires. Pirelli established deals with luxury brands Jaguar, BMW, Maserati, Ferrari, Bentley, and Lotus Elise and established itself as a provider of a large share of tires on new Porsches, S-class Mercedes, and Saabs. As a result, more than 70% of the company's tire production is now high-performance tires. People are willing to pay a premium for Pirellis.

The operations function continued to focus its design efforts on performance tires and developing a system of modular tire manufacture that allows much faster switching between models. This modular system, combined with investments in new manufacturing flexibility, has driven batch sizes down to as small as 150 to 200, making small-lot performance tires economically feasible. Manufacturing innovations at Pirelli have streamlined the production process, moving it from a 14-step process to a 3-step process. A threat from the big three going after the performance market remains, but Pirelli has bypassed its weakness of having a small market share. The firm now has a presence in 120 countries and sales exceeding $3.5 billion.

Sources: Just Auto (September 2005): 8–14; *Hoover's Company Records* (October 15, 2005): 41369; and *Frankfurter Allgemeine Zeitung* (February 11, 2002): 5.

Discussion Questions

1. Based on the descriptions and analyses in this chapter, would Boeing be better described as a global firm or a transnational firm? Discuss.
2. List six reasons to internationalize operations.
3. Coca-Cola is called a global product. Does this mean that Coca-Cola is formulated in the same way throughout the world? Discuss.
4. Define *mission*.
5. Define *strategy*.
6. Describe how an organization's *mission* and *strategy* have different purposes.
7. Identify the mission and strategy of your automobile repair garage. What are the manifestations of the 10 OM decisions at the garage? That is, how is each of the 10 decisions accomplished?
8. As a library or Internet assignment, identify the mission of a firm and the strategy that supports that mission.
9. How does an OM strategy change during a product's life cycle?
10. There are three primary ways to achieve competitive advantage. Provide an example, not included in the text, of each. Support your choices.
11. Describe PIMS's five characteristics of high-return-on-investment (ROI) firms.
12. Given the discussion of Southwest Airlines in the text, define an *operations* strategy for that firm.
13. How must an operations strategy integrate with marketing and accounting?

Self-Test

- *Before taking the self-test*, refer to the learning objectives listed at the beginning of the selection and the key terms listed at the end of the selection.
- Use the key at the back of the text to **correct** your answers.
- *Restudy* pages that correspond to any questions you answered incorrectly or material you feel uncertain about.

1. Among the ways for a firm to effectively use its OM function to yield competitive advantage are:
a) rapid design changes.
b) speed of delivery.
c) maintain a variety of product options.
d) all of the above.

2. A mission statement is beneficial to an organization because it:
a) is a statement of the organization's economic purpose.
b) provides a basis for the organization's culture.
c) identifies important constituencies.
d) establishes a basis for strategy formulation.
e) ensures profitability.

3. A strategy is:
a) a functional area of the firm.
b) the purpose for which an organization is established.
c) the goal that is to be achieved.
d) an action plan to achieve a mission.
e) a critical success factor.

4. The PIMS program developed a number of criteria that were based on evaluating firms who did well at:
a) profitability.
b) sustained sales growth.
c) achieving their mission.

d) high return on investments.
e) establishing goals.

5. Which of the following are not characteristics of high return-on-investment firms?
a) high variety of product options
b) high product quality relative to the competition
c) high capacity utilization
d) low investment intensity
e) all are characteristic of high ROI firms

6. A company that is organized across international boundaries with decentralized authority and substantial autonomy at each business via subsidiaries, franchises, or joint ventures has:
a) a global strategy.
b) a transnational strategy.
c) an international straetgy.
d) a multidomestic strategy.
e) a regional strategy.

7. The relatively few activities that make a difference between a firm having and not having a competitive advantage are known as:
a) activity maps.
b) SWOT.
c) critical success factors.
d) global profile.
e) response strategy.

8. The three strategic approaches to competitive advantage are _____, _____, and _____.

Internet and Student CD-ROM/DVD Exercises

Visit our Companion Web site or use your student CD-ROM/DVD to help with material in this chapter.

 On Our Companion Web site,
www.prenhall.com/heizer
- Self-Study Quizzes
- Practice Problems
- Virtual Company Tour
- Internet Case
- Power Point Lecture

On Your Student CD-ROM
- Practice Problems

On Your Student DVD
- Video Clips and Video Cases
- Virtual Office Hours for Solved Problem

Ethical Dilemma

As a manufacturer of athletic shoes whose image, indeed performance, is widely regarded as socially responsible, you find your costs increasing. Traditionally, your athletic shoes have been made in Indonesia and South Korea. Although the ease of doing business in those countries has been improving, wage rates have also been increasing. The labor-cost differential between your present suppliers and a contractor who will get the shoes made in China now exceeds $1 per pair. Your sales next year are projected to be 10 million pairs, and

your analysis suggests that this cost differential is not offset by any other tangible costs; you face only the political risk and potential damage to your commitment to social responsibility. Thus, this $1 per pair savings should flow directly to your bottom line. There is no doubt that the Chinese government engages in censorship, remains repressive, and is a long way from a democracy. Moreover, you will have little or no control over working conditions, sexual harassment, and pollution. What do you do and on what basis do you make your decision?

Problems

• 1 The text provides three primary ways—strategic approaches (differentiation, cost, and response)—for achieving competitive advantage. Provide an example of each not given in the text. Support your choices. (*Hint:* Note the examples provided in the text.)

•• 2 Within the food service industry (restaurants that serve meals to customers, but not just fast food), find examples of firms that have sustained competitive advantage by competing on the basis of (1) cost leadership, (2) response, and (3) differentiation. Cite one example in each category; provide a sentence or two in support of each choice. Do not use fast-food chains for all categories. (*Hint:* A "99¢ menu" is very easily copied and is not a good source of sustained advantage.)

•• 3 Browse through *The Wall Street Journal*, the financial section of a daily paper, or read business news online. Seek articles that constrain manufacturing innovation and productivity—workers aren't allowed to do this, workers are not or cannot be trained to do that, this technology is not allowed, this material cannot be handled by workers, and so forth. Be prepared to share your articles in class discussion.

•• 4 Match the product with the proper parent company and country in the table below:

Product	Parent Company	Country
Arrow Shirts	a. Volkswagen	1. France
Braun Household Appliances	b. Bidermann International	2. Great Britain
Lotus Autos	c. Bridgestone	3. Germany
Firestone Tires	d. Campbell Soup	4. Japan
Godiva Chocolate	e. Credit Lyonnais	5. U.S.
Häagen-Daz Ice Cream (USA)	f. Ford Motor Company	6. Switzerland
Jaguar Autos	g. Procter & Gamble	7. Malaysia
MGM Movies	h. Michelin	
Lamborghini Autos	i. Nestlé	
Goodrich Tires	j. Proton	
Alpo Pet Foods		

••• 5 Identify how changes within an organization affect the OM strategy for a company. For instance, discuss what impact the following internal factors might have on OM strategy:
a) Maturing of a product.
b) Technology innovation in the manufacturing process.
c) Changes in laptop computer design that move disk drives from CD-ROM drives to DVD drives.

••• 6 Identify how changes in the external environment affect the OM strategy for a company. For instance, discuss what impact the following external factors might have on OM strategy:
a) Major increases in oil prices.
b) Water- and air-quality legislation.
c) Fewer young prospective employees entering the labor market.

d) Inflation versus stable prices.
e) Legislation moving health insurance from a pretax benefit to taxable income.

•• 7 Develop a ranking for corruption in the following countries: Mexico, Turkey, Denmark, the U.S., Taiwan, Brazil, and another country of your choice. (*Hint:* See sources such as *Transparency International*, *Asia Pacific Management News*, and *The Economist*.)

•• 8 Develop a ranking for competitiveness and/or business environment for Britain, Singapore, the U.S., Hong Kong, and Italy. (*Hint:* See the *Global Competitive Report*, *World Economic Forum*, Geneva, and *The Economist*.)

Case Studies

Minit-Lube

A substantial market exists for automobile tune-ups, oil changes, and lubrication service for more than 200 million cars on U.S. roads. Some of this demand is filled by full-service auto dealerships, some by Sears and Firestone, and some by other tire/service dealers. However, Minit-Lube, Mobil-Lube, Jiffy-Lube and others have also developed strategies to accommodate this opportunity.

Minit-Lube stations perform oil changes, lubrication, and interior cleaning in a spotless environment. The buildings are clean, painted white, and often surrounded by neatly trimmed landscaping. To facilitate fast service, cars can be driven through three abreast. At Minit-Lube, the customer is greeted by service representatives who are graduates of Minit-Lube U. The Minit-Lube school is not unlike McDonald's Hamburger University near Chicago or Holiday Inn's training school in Memphis. The greeter takes the order, which typically includes fluid checks (oil, water, brake fluid, transmission fluid, differential grease) and the necessary lubrication, as well as filter changes for air and oil. Service personnel in neat uniforms then move into action. The standard three-person team has one person checking fluid levels under the hood, another assigned interior vacuuming and window cleaning, and the third in the garage pit, removing the oil filter, draining the oil, checking the differential and transmission, and lubricating as necessary. Precise task assignments and good training are designed to move the car into and out of the bay in 10 minutes. The idea is to charge no more, and hopefully less, than gas stations, automotive repair chains, and auto dealers, while providing better service.

Discussion Questions

1. What constitutes the mission of Minit-Lube?
2. How does the Minit-Lube operations strategy provide competitive advantage? (*Hint:* Evaluate how Minit-Lube's traditional competitors perform the 10 decisions of operations management vs. how Minit-Lube performs them.)
3. Is it likely that Minit-Lube has increased productivity over its more traditional competitors? Why? How would we measure productivity in this industry?

Strategy at Regal Marine

Video Case

Regal Marine, one of the U.S.'s 10 largest power-boat manufacturers, achieves its mission—providing luxury performance boats to customers worldwide—using the strategy of differentiation. It differentiates its products through constant innovation, unique features, and high quality. Increasing sales at the Orlando, Florida, family-owned firm suggest that the strategy is working.

As a quality boat manufacturer, Regal Marine starts with continuous innovation, as reflected in computer-aided design (CAD), high-quality molds, and close tolerances that are controlled through both defect charts and rigorous visual inspection. In-house quality is not enough, however. Because a product is only as good as the parts put into it, Regal has established close ties with a large number of its suppliers to ensure both flexibility and perfect parts. With the help of these suppliers, Regal can profitably produce a product line of 22 boats, ranging from the $14,000 19-foot boat to the $500,000 44-foot Commodore yacht.

"We build boats," says VP Tim Kuck, "but we're really in the 'fun' business. Our competition includes not only 300 other boat, canoe, and yacht manufacturers in our $17 billion industry, but home theaters, the Internet, and all kinds of alternative family enter-tainment." Fortunately for Regal, with the strong economy and the repeal of the boat luxury tax on its side, it has been paying down debt and increasing market share.

Regal has also joined with scores of other independent boat makers in the American Boat Builders Association. Through economies of scale in procurement, Regal is able to navigate against billion-dollar competitor Brunswick (makers of the Sea Ray and Bayliner brands). The *Global Company Profile* featuring Regal Marine provides further background on Regal and its strategy.

Discussion Questions*

1. State Regal Marine's mission in your own words.
2. Identify the strengths, weaknesses, opportunities, and threats that are relevant to the strategy of Regal Marine.
3. How would you define Regal's strategy?
4. How would each of the 10 operations management decisions apply to operations decision making at Regal Marine?

*You may wish to play this video case on your DVD before addressing these questions.

Hard Rock Cafe's Global Strategy

Video Case

Hard Rock is bringing the concept of the "experience economy" to its cafe operation. The strategy is to incorporate a unique "experience" into its operations. This innovation is somewhat akin to mass customization in manufacturing. At Hard Rock, the experience concept is to provide not only a custom meal from the menu but a dining event that includes a unique visual and sound experience not duplicated anywhere else in the world. This strategy is succeeding. Other theme restaurants have come and gone while Hard Rock continues to grow. As Professor C. Markides of the London Business School says, "The trick is not to play the game better than the competition, but to develop and play an altogether different game."* At Hard Rock, the different game is the experience game.

From the opening of its first cafe in London in 1971, during the British rock music explosion, Hard Rock has been serving food and rock music with equal enthusiasm. Hard Rock Cafe has 40 U.S. locations, about a dozen in Europe, and the remainder scattered throughout the world, from Bangkok and Beijing to Beirut. New construction, leases, and investment in remodeling are long term; so a global strategy means special consideration of political risk, currency risk, and social norms in a context of a brand fit. Although Hard Rock is one of the most recognized brands in the world, this does not mean its cafe is a natural everywhere. Special consideration must be given to the supply chain for the restaurant and its accompanying retail store. About 48% of a typical cafe's sales are from merchandise.

The Hard Rock Cafe business model is well defined, but because of various risk factors and differences in business practices and employment law, Hard Rock elects to franchise about half of its cafes. Social norms and preferences often suggest some tweaking of menus for local taste. For instance, Europeans, particularly the British, still have some fear of mad cow disease; therefore, Hard Rock is focusing less on hamburgers and beef and more on fish and lobster in its British cafes.

Because 70% of Hard Rock's guests are tourists, recent years have found it expanding to "destination" cities. While this has been a winning strategy for decades, allowing the firm to grow from 1 London cafe to 110 facilities in 41 countries, it has made Hard Rock susceptible to economic fluctuations that hit the tourist business hardest. So Hard Rock is signing a long-term lease for a new location in Nottingham, England, to join recently opened cafes in Manchester and Birmingham—cities that are not standard tourist destinations. At the same time, menus are being upgraded. Hopefully, repeat business from locals in these cities will smooth demand and make Hard Rock less dependent on tourists.

Discussion Questions†

1. Identify the strategy changes that have taken place at Hard Rock Cafe since its founding in 1971.

2. As Hard Rock Cafe has changed its strategy, how has its responses to some of the 10 decisions of OM changed?

3. Where does Hard Rock fit in the four international operations strategies outlined in Figure 9? Explain your answer.

*Constantinos Markides, "Strategic Innovation," *MIT Sloan Management Review* 38, no. 3 (spring 1997): 9.

†You may wish to play this video case on your DVD before addressing these questions.

Additional Case Studies

Internet Case Study: Visit our Companion Web site at **www.prenhall.com/heizer** *for this free case study:*
• **Motorola's Global Strategy:** Focuses on Motorola's international strategy.

Harvard has selected these Harvard Business School cases to accompany this chapter.

harvardbusinessonline.hbsp.harvard.edu

• **Eli Lilly and Co.: Manufacturing Process Technology Strategy—1991** (#692056): Manufacturing pursues comparative advantage in an industry where R&D is the primary competitive advantage.
• **Fresh Connections** (#600-022): Investigates how to structure operations to take advantage of the continued growth in the home meal replacement market.
• **Hitting the Wall: Nike and International Labor Practices** (#7000047): Nike must deal with a spate of alarmingly bad publicity regarding wages in developing countries.
• **Hewlett-Packard Singapore (A)** (#694035): Product development issues when source and recipients of knowledge are separated both geographically and culturally.
• **Komatsu Ltd.** (#398-016): Describes strategic and organizational transformations at Komatsu, a major Japan-based producer of construction equipment.
• **McDonald's Corp.** (#693028): Changing environment and competition forces McDonald's to rethink its operating strategy.
• **Southwest Airlines—1993 (A)** (#694023): Provides insight into Southwest's strategy, operations, marketing, and culture.
• **Toys "Я" Us Japan** (#796-077): Documents Toys "Я" Us difficulties as it enters the Japanese toy market.
• **Lenzing AG: Expanding in Indonesia** (#796-099): Presents the issues surrounding expansion in a foreign country.

Bibliography

Bhagwati, J. *In Defense of Globalization.* Oxford, UK: Oxford University Press, 2004.

Crotts, J. C., D. R. Dickson, and R. C. Ford. "Aligning Organizational Processes with Mission: The Case of Service Excellence." *Academy of Management Executive* 19, no. 3 (August 2005): 54–68.

Drucker, P. F. "The Emerging Theory of Manufacturing." *Harvard Business Review* 68, no. 3 (May–June 1990): 94–103.

Flynn, B. B., R. G. Schroeder, and E. J. Flynn. "World Class Manufacturing: An Investigation of Hayes and Wheelwright's Foundation." *Journal of Operations Management* 17, no. 3 (March 1999): 249–269.

Friedman, Thomas. *The World Is Flat: A Brief History of the Twenty-first Century.* New York: Farrar, Straus, and Giroux, 2005.

Greenwald, Bruce, and Judd Kahn. "All Strategy Is Local." *Harvard Business Review*, 83, no. 9 (September 2005): 94–104.

Kaplan, Robert S., and David P. Norton. *Strategy Maps.* Boston: Harvard Business School Publishing, 2003.

Luke, Royce D., Stephen L. Walston, and Patrick Michael Plummer. *Healthcare Strategy: In Pursuit of Competitive Advantage.* Chicago: Health Administration Press, 2003.

Porter, M. E. *The Competitive Advantage of Nations.* New York: The Free Press, 1990.

Wolf, Martin. *Why Globalization Works.* London: Yale University Press, 2004.

Womack, J. P., D. T. Jones, and D. Roos. *The Machine That Changed the World.* New York: Rawson Associates, 1990.

Internet Resources

Business Policy and Strategy, Division of the Academy of Management: **www.aom.pace.edu/bps**
European Union: **europa.eu.int/index_en.htm**
International Trade Administration: **www.ita.doc.gov**
Manufacturing Strategies, maintained at Cranfield University: **www.cranfield.ac.uk/som**

Transparency International maintains a Bribe Payers Perception Index (BPI) and a Corruption Perceptions Index: **www.transparency.de**, **www.globalcorruptionreport.org**
World Bank: **www.worldbank.org**
World Economic Forum: **www.weforum.org**
World Trade Organization: **www.wto.org**

Solutions to Even Numbered Problems

2 Cost leadership: Sodexho
   Response: a catering firm
   Differentiation: a fine-dining restaurant
4 The first few:
   Arrow; Bidermann International, France
   Braun; Procter & Gamble, U.S.
   Lotus Autos; Proton, Malaysia
   Firestone; Bridgestone, Japan
   Godiva; Campbell Soup, U.S.

6 Some general thoughts to get you going:
   (a) Energy costs change the cost structure of airlines.
   (b) Environmental constraints force changes in process technology (paint manufacturing and application) and product design (autos).
8 Look at current ranking at **www.weforum.org**.

Solutions to Self Test

1. d; **2.** a; **3.** d; **4.** d; **5.** a; **6.** d; **7.** c; **8.** differentiation, cost, response.

Forecasting

Outline

Learning Objectives

When you complete this selection you should be able to

1. Understand the three time horizons and which models apply for each
2. Explain when to use each of the four qualitative models
3. Apply the naive, moving average, exponential smoothing, and trend methods
4. Compute three measures of forecast accuracy
5. Develop seasonal indexes
6. Conduct a regression and correlation analysis
7. Use a tracking signal

Forecasting Provides a Competitive Advantage for Disney

When it comes to the world's most respected global brands, Walt Disney Parks & Resorts is a visible leader. Although the monarch of this magic kingdom is no man but a mouse—Mickey Mouse—it's CEO Robert Iger who daily manages the entertainment giant.

Disney's global portfolio includes Hong Kong Disneyland (opened 2005), Disneyland Paris (1992), and Tokyo Disneyland (1983). But it is Disney World (in Florida) and Disneyland (in California) that drive profits in this $32 billion corporation, which is ranked 54th in the *Fortune* 500 and 79th in the *Financial Times* Global 500.

Revenues at Disney are all about people—how many visit the parks and how they spend money while there. When Iger receives a daily report from his six theme parks in Orlando, the report contains only two numbers: the *forecast* of yesterday's attendance at the parks (Magic Kingdom, Epcot, Animal Kingdom, MGM Studios, Typhoon Lagoon, and Blizzard Beach) and the *actual* attendance. An error close to zero is expected. Iger takes his forecasts very seriously.

The forecasting team at Disney World doesn't just do a daily prediction, however, and Iger is not its only customer. The team also provides daily,

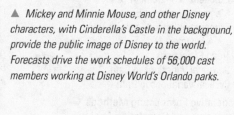

▲ *Mickey and Minnie Mouse, and other Disney characters, with Cinderella's Castle in the background, provide the public image of Disney to the world. Forecasts drive the work schedules of 56,000 cast members working at Disney World's Orlando parks.*

Kelly-Mooney Photography, Corbis/Bettmann

◄ *The giant sphere is the symbol of Epcot, one of Disney's six Orlando parks, for which forecasts of meals, lodging, entertainment, and transportation must be made. This Disney monorail moves guests among parks and the 20 hotels on the massive 47-square-mile property (about the size of San Francisco and twice the size of Manhattan).*

▶ A daily forecast of attendance is made by adjusting Disney's annual operating plan for weather forecasts, the previous day's crowds, conventions, and seasonal variations. One of the two water parks at Disney World, Typhoon Lagoon, is shown here.

Kevin Fleming, CORBIS-NY

Peter Cosgrove, AP Wide World Photos

◀ Forecasts are critical to making sure rides are not overcrowded. Disney is good at "managing demand" with techniques such as adding more street activities to reduce long lines for rides.

weekly, monthly, annual, and 5-year forecasts to the labor management, maintenance, operations, finance, and park scheduling departments. Forecasters use judgmental models, econometric models, moving-average models, and regression analysis.

With 20% of Disney World's customers coming from outside the United States, its economic model includes such variables as gross domestic product, cross-exchange rates, and arrivals into the U.S. Disney also uses 35 analysts and 70 field people to survey 1 million people each year. The surveys, administered to guests at the parks and its 20 hotels, to employees, and to travel industry professionals, examine future travel plans and experiences at the parks. This helps forecast not only attendance but behavior at each ride (e.g., how long people will wait, how many times they will ride). Inputs to the monthly forecasting model include airline specials, speeches by the chair of the Federal Reserve, and Wall Street trends. Disney even monitors 3,000 school districts inside and outside the U.S. for holiday/vacation schedules. With this approach, Disney's 5-year attendance forecast yields just a 5% error on average. Its annual forecasts have a 0% to 3% error.

Attendance forecasts for the parks drive a whole slew of management decisions. For example, capacity on any day can be increased by opening at 8 A.M. instead of the usual 9 A.M., by opening more shows or rides, by adding more food/beverage carts (9 million hamburgers and 50 million Cokes are sold per year!), and by bringing in more employees

Joe Raedle, Getty Images

▲ Disney uses characters such as Minnie Mouse to entertain customers when lines are forecast to be long. On slow days, Disney calls fewer cast members to work.

(called "cast members"). Cast members are scheduled in 15-minute intervals throughout the parks for flexibility. Demand can be managed by limiting the number of guests admitted to the parks, with the "fast pass" reservation system, and by shifting crowds from rides to more street parades.

At Disney, forecasting is a key driver in the company's success and competitive advantage.

Every day, managers like those at Disney make decisions without knowing what will happen in the future. They order inventory without knowing what sales will be, purchase new equipment despite uncertainty about demand for products, and make investments without knowing what profits will be. Managers are always trying to make better estimates of what will happen in the future in the face of uncertainty. Making good estimates is the main purpose of forecasting.

In this selection, we examine different types of forecasts and present a variety of forecasting models. Our purpose is to show that there are many ways for managers to forecast. We also provide an overview of business sales forecasting and describe how to prepare, monitor, and judge the accuracy of a forecast. Good forecasts are an *essential* part of efficient service and manufacturing operations.

WHAT IS FORECASTING?

Forecasting

The art and science of predicting future events.

Forecasting is the art and science of predicting future events. Forecasting may involve taking historical data and projecting them into the future with some sort of mathematical model. It may be a subjective or intuitive prediction. Or it may involve a combination of these—that is, a mathematical model adjusted by a manager's good judgment.

As we introduce different forecasting techniques in this selection, you will see that there is seldom one superior method. What works best in one firm under one set of conditions may be a complete disaster in another organization, or even in a different department of the same firm. In addition, you will see that there are limits as to what can be expected from forecasts. They are seldom, if ever, perfect. They are also costly and time-consuming to prepare and monitor.

Few businesses, however, can afford to avoid the process of forecasting by just waiting to see what happens and then taking their chances. Effective planning in both the short run and long run depends on a forecast of demand for the company's products.

Forecasting Time Horizons

Learning Objective

1. Understand the three time horizons and which models apply for each

A forecast is usually classified by the *future time horizon* that it covers. Time horizons fall into three categories:

1. *Short-range forecast:* This forecast has a time span of up to 1 year but is generally less than 3 months. It is used for planning purchasing, job scheduling, workforce levels, job assignments, and production levels.
2. *Medium-range forecast:* A medium-range, or intermediate, forecast generally spans from 3 months to 3 years. It is useful in sales planning, production planning and budgeting, cash budgeting, and analysis of various operating plans.
3. *Long-range forecast:* Generally 3 years or more in time span, long-range forecasts are used in planning for new products, capital expenditures, facility location or expansion, and research and development.

Medium and long-range forecasts are distinguished from short-range forecasts by three features:

1. First, intermediate and long-run forecasts *deal with more comprehensive issues* and support management decisions regarding planning and products, plants, and processes. Implementing some facility decisions, such as GM's decision to open a new Brazilian manufacturing plant, can take 5 to 8 years from inception to completion.
2. Second, short-term forecasting usually *employs different methodologies* than longer-term forecasting. Mathematical techniques, such as moving averages, exponential smoothing, and trend extrapolation (all of which we shall examine shortly), are common to short-run projections. Broader, *less* quantitative methods are useful in predicting such issues as whether a new product, like the optical disk recorder, should be introduced into a company's product line.
3. Finally, as you would expect, short-range forecasts *tend to be more accurate* than longer-range forecasts. Factors that influence demand change every day. Thus, as the time horizon lengthens, it is likely that forecast accuracy will diminish. It almost goes without saying, then, that sales forecasts must be updated regularly to maintain their value and integrity. After each sales period, forecasts should be reviewed and revised.

Our forecasting ability has improved, but it has been outpaced by an increasingly complex world economy.

The Influence of Product Life Cycle

Another factor to consider when developing sales forecasts, especially longer ones, is product life cycle. Products, and even services, do not sell at a constant level throughout their lives. Most successful products pass through four stages: (1) introduction, (2) growth, (3) maturity, and (4) decline.

Products in the first two stages of the life cycle (such as virtual reality and LCD TVs) need longer forecasts than those in the maturity and decline stages (such as $3\frac{1}{2}$" floppy disks and skateboards). Forecasts that reflect life cycle are useful in projecting different staffing levels, inventory levels, and factory capacity as the product passes from the first to the last stage.

TYPES OF FORECASTS

Organizations use three major types of forecasts in planning future operations:

1. **Economic forecasts** address the business cycle by predicting inflation rates, money supplies, housing starts, and other planning indicators.
2. **Technological forecasts** are concerned with rates of technological progress, which can result in the birth of exciting new products, requiring new plants and equipment.
3. **Demand forecasts** are projections of demand for a company's products or services. These forecasts, also called *sales forecasts*, drive a company's production, capacity, and scheduling systems and serve as inputs to financial, marketing, and personnel planning.

Economic and technological forecasting are specialized techniques that may fall outside the role of the operations manager. The emphasis in this book will therefore be on demand forecasting.

Economic forecasts
Planning indicators that are valuable in helping organizations prepare medium- to long-range forecasts.

Technological forecasts
Long-term forecasts concerned with the rates of technological progress.

Demand forecasts
Projections of a company's sales for each time period in the planning horizon.

THE STRATEGIC IMPORTANCE OF FORECASTING

Good forecasts are of critical importance in all aspects of a business: *The forecast is the only estimate of demand until actual demand becomes known.* Forecasts of demand therefore drive decisions in many areas. Let's look at the impact of product forecast on three activities: (1) human resources, (2) capacity, and (3) supply chain management.

Human Resources

Hiring, training, and laying off workers all depend on anticipated demand. If the human resources department must hire additional workers without warning, the amount of training declines and the quality of the workforce suffers. A large Louisiana chemical firm almost lost its biggest customer when a quick expansion to around-the-clock shifts led to a total breakdown in quality control on the second and third shifts.

Video 4.1

Forecasting at Hard Rock Cafe

Capacity

When capacity is inadequate, the resulting shortages can mean undependable delivery, loss of customers, and loss of market share. This is exactly what happened to Nabisco when it underestimated the huge demand for its new low-fat Snackwell Devil's Food Cookies. Even with production lines working overtime, Nabisco could not keep up with demand, and it lost customers. When excess capacity is built, on the other hand, costs can skyrocket.

Supply Chain Management

Good supplier relations and the ensuing price advantages for materials and parts depend on accurate forecasts. For example, auto manufacturers who want TRW Corp. to guarantee sufficient airbag capacity must provide accurate forecasts to justify TRW plant expansions. In the global marketplace, where expensive components for Boeing 787 jets are manufactured in dozens of countries, coordination driven by forecasts is critical. Scheduling transportation to Seattle for final assembly at the lowest possible cost means no last-minute surprises that can harm already-low profit margins.

SEVEN STEPS IN THE FORECASTING SYSTEM

Forecasting follows seven basic steps. We use Disney World, the focus of this selection's *Global Company Profile*, as an example of each step:

1. *Determine the use of the forecast:* Disney uses park attendance forecasts to drive staffing, opening times, ride availability, and food supplies.
2. *Select the items to be forecasted:* For Disney World, there are six main parks. A forecast of daily attendance at each is the main number that determines labor, maintenance, and scheduling.
3. *Determine the time horizon of the forecast:* Is it short, medium, or long term? Disney develops daily, weekly, monthly, annual, and 5-year forecasts.
4. *Select the forecasting model(s):* Disney uses a variety of statistical models that we shall discuss, including moving averages, econometrics, and regression analysis. It also employs judgmental, or nonquantitative, models.
5. *Gather the data needed to make the forecast:* Disney's forecasting team employs 35 analysts and 70 field personnel to survey 1 million people/businesses every year. It also uses a firm called Global Insights for travel industry forecasts and gathers data on exchange rates, arrivals into the U.S., airline specials, Wall Street trends, and school vacation schedules.
6. *Make the forecast.*
7. *Validate and implement the results:* At Disney, forecasts are reviewed daily at the highest levels to make sure that the model, assumptions, and data are valid. Error measures are applied; then the forecasts are used to schedule personnel down to 15-minute intervals.

These seven steps present a systematic way of initiating, designing, and implementing a forecasting system. When the system is to be used to generate forecasts regularly over time, data must be routinely collected. Then actual computations are usually made by computer.

Regardless of the system that firms like Disney use, each company faces several realities:

1. Forecasts are seldom perfect. This means that outside factors that we cannot predict or control often impact the forecast. Companies need to allow for this reality.
2. Most forecasting techniques assume that there is some underlying stability in the system. Consequently, some firms automate their predictions using computerized forecasting software, then closely monitor only the product items whose demand is erratic.
3. Both product family and aggregated forecasts are more accurate than individual product forecasts. Disney, for example, aggregates daily attendance forecasts by park. This approach helps balance the over- and underpredictions of each of the six attractions.

FORECASTING APPROACHES

There are two general approaches to forecasting, just as there are two ways to tackle all decision modeling. One is a quantitative analysis; the other is a qualitative approach. **Quantitative forecasts** use a variety of mathematical models that rely on historical data and/or causal variables to forecast demand. Subjective or **qualitative forecasts** incorporate such factors as the decision maker's intuition, emotions, personal experiences, and value system in reaching a forecast. Some firms use one approach and some use the other. In practice, a combination of the two is usually most effective.

Overview of Qualitative Methods

In this section, we consider four different *qualitative* forecasting techniques:

1. **Jury of executive opinion:** Under this method, the opinions of a group of high-level experts or managers, often in combination with statistical models, are pooled to arrive at a group estimate of demand. Bristol-Meyers Squibb Company, for example, uses 220 well-known research scientists as its jury of executive opinion to get a grasp on future trends in the world of medical research.
2. **Delphi method:** There are three different types of participants in the Delphi method: decision makers, staff personnel, and respondents. Decision makers usually consist of a group of

Quantitative forecasts
Forecasts that employ one or more mathematical models that rely on historical data and/or causal variables to forecast demand.

Qualitative forecasts
Forecasts that incorporate such factors as the decision maker's intuition, emotions, personal experiences, and value system.

Jury of executive opinion
A forecasting technique that takes the opinion of a small group of high-level managers and results in a group estimate of demand.

Delphi method
A forecasting technique using a group process that allows experts to make forecasts.

5 to 10 experts who will be making the actual forecast. Staff personnel assist decision makers by preparing, distributing, collecting, and summarizing a series of questionnaires and survey results. The respondents are a group of people, often located in different places, whose judgments are valued. This group provides inputs to the decision makers before the forecast is made.

2. Explain when to use each of the four qualitative models

The state of Alaska, for example, has used the Delphi method to develop its long-range economic forecast. An amazing 90% of the state's budget is derived from 1.5 million barrels of oil pumped daily through a pipeline at Prudhoe Bay. The large Delphi panel of experts had to represent all groups and opinions in the state and all geographic areas. Delphi was the perfect forecasting tool because panelist travel could be avoided. It also meant that leading Alaskans could participate because their schedules were not affected by meetings and distances.

3. **Sales force composite:** In this approach, each salesperson estimates what sales will be in his or her region. These forecasts are then reviewed to ensure that they are realistic. Then they are combined at the district and national levels to reach an overall forecast. A variation of this approach occurs at Lexus, where every quarter Lexus dealers have a "make meeting." At this meeting, they talk about what is selling, in what colors, and with what options, so the factory knows what to build.[1]

Sales force composite
A forecasting technique based on salespersons' estimates of expected sales.

4. **Consumer market survey:** This method solicits input from customers or potential customers regarding future purchasing plans. It can help not only in preparing a forecast but also in improving product design and planning for new products. The consumer market survey and sales force composite methods can, however, suffer from overly optimistic forecasts that arise from customer input. The 2001 crash of the telecommunication industry was the result of overexpansion to meet "explosive customer demand." Where did these data come from? Oplink Communications, a Nortel Networks supplier, says its "company forecasts over the last few years were based mainly on informal conversations with customers."[2]

Consumer market survey
A forecasting method that solicits input from customers or potential customers regarding future purchasing plans.

Overview of Quantitative Methods

Five quantitative forecasting methods, all of which use historical data, are described in this chapter. They fall into two categories:

1. Naive approach
2. Moving averages
3. Exponential smoothing
4. Trend projection
5. Linear regression

} **time-series models**

} **associative model**

Time-Series Models **Time-series** models predict on the assumption that the future is a function of the past. In other words, they look at what has happened over a period of time and use a series of past data to make a forecast. If we are predicting sales of lawn mowers, we use the past sales for lawn mowers to make the forecasts.

Time series
A forecasting technique that uses a series of past data points to make a forecast.

Associative Models Associative models, such as linear regression, incorporate the variables or factors that might influence the quantity being forecast. For example, an associative model for lawn mower sales might use factors such as new housing starts, advertising budget, and competitors' prices.

TIME-SERIES FORECASTING

A time series is based on a sequence of evenly spaced (weekly, monthly, quarterly, and so on) data points. Examples include weekly sales of Nike Air Jordans, quarterly earnings reports of Microsoft stock, daily shipments of Coors beer, and annual consumer price indices. Forecasting

---

[1]Jonathan Fahey, "The Lexus Nexus," *Forbes* (June 21, 2004): 68–70.
[2]"Lousy Sales Forecasts Helped Fuel the Telecom Mess," *The Wall Street Journal* (July 9, 2001): B1–B4.

time-series data implies that future values are predicted *only* from past values and that other variables, no matter how potentially valuable, may be ignored.

Decomposition of a Time Series

Analyzing time series means breaking down past data into components and then projecting them forward. A time series has four components:

1. *Trend* is the gradual upward or downward movement of the data over time. Changes in income, population, age distribution, or cultural views may account for movement in trend.
2. *Seasonality* is a data pattern that repeats itself after a period of days, weeks, months, or quarters. There are six common seasonality patterns:

Period of Pattern	"Season" Length	Number of "Seasons" in Pattern
Week	Day	7
Month	Week	$4-4\frac{1}{2}$
Month	Day	28–31
Year	Quarter	4
Year	Month	12
Year	Week	52

Restaurants and barber shops, for example, experience weekly seasons, with Saturday being the peak of business. See the *OM in Action* box "Forecasting at Olive Garden and Red Lobster." Beer distributors forecast yearly patterns, with monthly seasons. Three "seasons"—May, July, and September—each contain a big beer-drinking holiday.

3. *Cycles* are patterns in the data that occur every several years. They are usually tied into the business cycle and are of major importance in short-term business analysis and planning. Predicting business cycles is difficult because they may be affected by political events or by international turmoil.
4. *Random variations* are "blips" in the data caused by chance and unusual situations. They follow no discernible pattern, so they cannot be predicted.

Figure 1 illustrates a demand over a 4-year period. It shows the average, trend, seasonal components, and random variations around the demand curve. The average demand is the sum of the demand for each period divided by the number of data periods.

Naive Approach

The simplest way to forecast is to assume that demand in the next period will be equal to demand in the most recent period. In other words, if sales of a product—say, Nokia cell phones—were 68 units in January, we can forecast that February's sales will also be 68

▶ **Figure 1**

Product Demand Charted over 4 Years with a Growth Trend and Seasonality Indicated

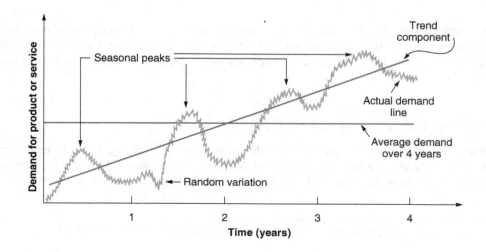

OM in Action   Forecasting at Olive Garden and Red Lobster

It's Friday night in the college town of Gainesville, Florida, and the local Olive Garden restaurant is humming. Customers may wait an average of 30 minutes for a table, but they can sample new wines and cheeses and admire scenic paintings of Italian villages on the restaurant's walls. Then comes dinner with portions so huge that many people take home a doggie bag. The typical bill: under $15 per person.

Crowds flock to the Darden restaurant chain's Olive Garden, Red Lobster, Seasons 52, and Bahama Breeze for value and consistency *and* they get it.

Every night, Darden's computers crank out forecasts that tell store managers what demand to anticipate the next day. The forecasting software generates a total meal forecast and breaks that down into specific menu items. The system tells a manager, for instance, that if 625 meals will be served the next day, "you will serve these items in these quantities. So before you go home, pull 25 pounds of shrimp and 30 pounds of crab out, and tell your operations

people to prepare 42 portion packs of chicken, 75 scampi dishes, 8 stuffed flounders, and so on." Managers often fine tune the quantities based on local conditions, such as weather or a convention, but they know what their customers are going to order.

By relying on demand history, the forecasting system has cut millions of dollars of waste out of the system. The forecast also reduces labor costs by providing the necessary information for improved scheduling. Labor costs decreased almost a full percent in the first year, translating in additional millions in savings for the Darden chain. In the low-margin restaurant business, every dollar counts.

Source: Interviews with Darden executives, 2006, 2007.

phones. Does this make any sense? It turns out that for some product lines, this **naive approach** is the most cost-effective and efficient objective forecasting model. At least it provides a starting point against which more sophisticated models that follow can be compared.

Naive approach
A forecasting technique that assumes demand in the next period is equal to demand in the most recent period.

Moving Averages

A **moving-average** forecast uses a number of historical actual data values to generate a forecast. Moving averages are useful *if we can assume that market demands will stay fairly steady over time*. A 4-month moving average is found by simply summing the demand during the past 4 months and dividing by 4. With each passing month, the most recent month's data are added to the sum of the previous 3 months' data, and the earliest month is dropped. This practice tends to smooth out short-term irregularities in the data series.

Mathematically, the simple moving average (which serves as an estimate of the next period's demand) is expressed as

$$\text{Moving average} = \frac{\Sigma \text{ Demand in previous } n \text{ periods}}{n} \qquad (1)$$

where n is the number of periods in the moving average—for example, 4, 5, or 6 months, respectively, for a 4-, 5-, or 6-period moving average.

Example 1 shows how moving averages are calculated.

Moving averages
A forecasting method that uses an average of the n most recent periods of data to forecast the next period.

Learning Objective

3. Apply the naive, moving average, exponential smoothing, and trend methods

---

Donna's Garden Supply wants a 3-month moving-average forecast, including a forecast for next January, for shed sales.

Approach: Storage shed sales are shown in the middle column of the table below. A 3-month moving average appears on the right.

EXAMPLE 1

Determining the moving average

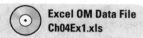

Month	Actual Shed Sales	3-Month Moving Average
January	10	
February	12	
March	13	
April	16	$(10 + 12 + 13)/3 = 11\frac{2}{3}$
May	19	$(12 + 13 + 16)/3 = 13\frac{2}{3}$
June	23	$(13 + 16 + 19)/3 = 16$
July	26	$(16 + 19 + 23)/3 = 19\frac{1}{3}$
August	30	$(19 + 23 + 26)/3 = 22\frac{2}{3}$
September	28	$(23 + 26 + 30)/3 = 26\frac{1}{3}$
October	18	$(26 + 30 + 28)/3 = 28$
November	16	$(30 + 28 + 18)/3 = 25\frac{1}{3}$
December	14	$(28 + 18 + 16)/3 = 20\frac{2}{3}$

Solution: The forecast for December is $20\frac{2}{3}$. To project the demand for sheds in the coming January, we sum the October, November, and December sales and divide by 3: January forecast = $(18 + 16 + 14)/3 = 16$.

Insight: Management now has a forecast that averages sales for the last 3 months. It is easy to use and understand.

Learning exercise: If actual sales in December were 18 (rather than 14), what is the new January forecast? [Answer: $17\frac{1}{3}$.]

Related problems: 1a, 2b, 5a, 6, 8a,b, 10a, 13b, 15, 47

When a detectable trend or pattern is present, *weights* can be used to place more emphasis on recent values. This practice makes forecasting techniques more responsive to changes because more recent periods may be more heavily weighted. Choice of weights is somewhat arbitrary because there is no set formula to determine them. Therefore, deciding which weights to use requires some experience. For example, if the latest month or period is weighted too heavily, the forecast may reflect a large unusual change in the demand or sales pattern too quickly.

A weighted moving average may be expressed mathematically as:

$$\text{Weighted moving average} = \frac{\Sigma\ (\text{Weight for period } n)(\text{Demand in period } n)}{\Sigma\ \text{Weights}} \tag{2}$$

Example 2 shows how to calculate a weighted moving average.

EXAMPLE 2

Determining the weighted moving average

Donna's Garden Supply (see Example 1) wants to forecast storage shed sales by weighting the past 3 months, with more weight given to recent data to make them more significant.

Approach: Assign more weight to recent data, as follows:

Weights Applied	Period
3	Last month
2	Two months ago
1	Three months ago
6	Sum of weights

$$\text{Forecast for this month} = \frac{3 \times \text{Sales last mo.} + 2 \times \text{Sales 2 mos. ago} + 1 \times \text{Sales 3 mos. ago}}{\text{Sum of the weights}}$$

Solution: The results of this weighted-average forecast are as follows:

Month	Actual Shed Sales	Three-Month Weighted Moving Average
January	10	
February	12	
March	13	
April	16	$[(3 \times 13) + (2 \times 12) + (10)]/6 = 12\frac{1}{6}$
May	19	$[(3 \times 16) + (2 \times 13) + (12)]/6 = 14\frac{1}{3}$
June	23	$[(3 \times 19) + (2 \times 16) + (13)]/6 = 17$
July	26	$[(3 \times 23) + (2 \times 19) + (16)]/6 = 20\frac{1}{2}$
August	30	$[(3 \times 26) + (2 \times 23) + (19)]/6 = 23\frac{5}{6}$
September	28	$[(3 \times 30) + (2 \times 26) + (23)]/6 = 27\frac{1}{2}$
October	18	$[(3 \times 28) + (2 \times 30) + (26)]/6 = 28\frac{1}{3}$
November	16	$[(3 \times 18) + (2 \times 28) + (30)]/6 = 23\frac{1}{3}$
December	14	$[(3 \times 16) + (2 \times 18) + (28)]/6 = 18\frac{2}{3}$

Insight: In this particular forecasting situation, you can see that more heavily weighting the latest month provides a much more accurate projection.

Learning exercise: If the assigned weights were 4, 2, and 1 (instead of 3, 2, and 1) what is the forecast for January's weighted moving average? [Answer: $15\frac{1}{7}$.]

Related problems: 1b, 2c, 5c, 6, 7, 10b

Both simple and weighted moving averages are effective in smoothing out sudden fluctuations in the demand pattern to provide stable estimates. Moving averages do, however, present three problems:

1. Increasing the size of *n* (the number of periods averaged) does smooth out fluctuations better, but it makes the method less sensitive to *real* changes in the data.
2. Moving averages cannot pick up trends very well. Because they are averages, they will always stay within past levels and will not predict changes to either higher or lower levels. That is, they *lag* the actual values.
3. Moving averages require extensive records of past data.

Figure 2, a plot of the data in Examples 1 and 2, illustrates the lag effect of the moving-average models. Note that both the moving-average and weighted-moving-average lines lag the actual demand. The weighted moving average, however, usually reacts more quickly to demand changes. Even in periods of downturn (see November and December), it more closely tracks the demand.

Data that are 20 years old may not be so useful. It is not always necessary to use all data.

Exponential Smoothing

Exponential smoothing is a sophisticated weighted-moving-average forecasting method that is still fairly easy to use. It involves very *little* record keeping of past data. The basic exponential smoothing formula can be shown as follows:

New forecast = Last period's forecast
+ α (Last period's actual demand − Last period's forecast)   (3)

Exponential smoothing
A weighted-moving-average forecasting technique in which data points are weighted by an exponential function.

► **Figure 2**

**Actual Demand vs.
Moving-Average and
Weighted-Moving-Average
Methods for Donna's
Garden Supply**

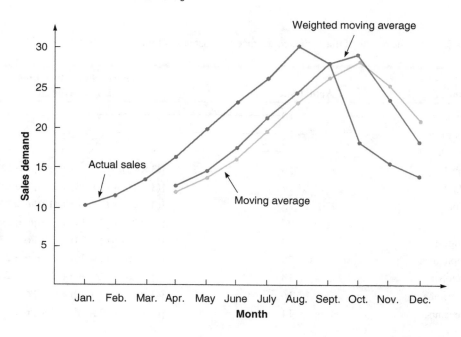

Smoothing constant

The weighting factor used in an
exponential smoothing forecast,
a number between 0 and 1.

where α is a weight, or **smoothing constant**, chosen by the forecaster, that has a value between 0 and 1. Equation (3) can also be written mathematically as:

$$F_t = F_{t-1} + \alpha(A_{t-1} - F_{t-1}) \tag{4}$$

where
  F_t = new forecast
  F_{t-1} = previous period's forecast
  α = smoothing (or weighting) constant ($0 \le \alpha \le 1$)
  A_{t-1} = previous period's actual demand

The concept is not complex. The latest estimate of demand is equal to the old estimate adjusted by a fraction of the difference between the last period's actual demand and the old estimate. Example 3 shows how to use exponential smoothing to derive a forecast.

EXAMPLE 3

Determining a
forecast via
exponential
smoothing

In January, a car dealer predicted February demand for 142 Ford Mustangs. Actual February demand was 153 autos. Using a smoothing constant chosen by management of $\alpha = .20$, the dealer wants to forecast March demand using the exponential smoothing model.

Approach: The exponential smoothing model in Equations 3 and 4 can be applied.

Solution: Substituting the sample data into the formula, we obtain:

New forecast (for March demand) $= 142 + .2(153 - 142) = 142 + 2.2$

$= 144.2$

Thus, the March demand forecast for Ford Mustangs is rounded to 144.

Insight: Using just two pieces of data, the forecast and the actual demand, plus a smoothing constant, we developed a forecast of 144 Ford Mustangs for March.

Learning exercise: If the smoothing constant is changed to .30, what is the new forecast? [Answer: 145.3]

Related problems: 1c, 3, 4, 5d, 6, 9d, 11, 12, 13a, 17, 18, 37, 43, 47, 49

The *smoothing constant*, α, is generally in the range from .05 to .50 for business applications. It can be changed to give more weight to recent data (when α is high) or more weight to past data (when α is low). When α reaches the extreme of 1.0, then in Equation (4), $F_t = 1.0A_{t-1}$. All the older values drop out, and the forecast becomes identical to the naive model mentioned earlier in this chapter. That is, the forecast for the next period is just the same as this period's demand.

The following table helps illustrate this concept. For example, when $\alpha = .5$, we can see that the new forecast is based almost entirely on demand in the last three or four periods. When $\alpha = .1$, the forecast places little weight on recent demand and takes many periods (about 19) of historical values into account.

	Weight Assigned to				
Smoothing Constant	Most Recent Period (α)	2nd Most Recent Period $\alpha(1 - \alpha)$	3rd Most Recent Period $\alpha(1 - \alpha)^2$	4th Most Recent Period $\alpha(1 - \alpha)^3$	5th Most Recent Period $\alpha(1 - \alpha)^4$
$\alpha = .1$	.1	.09	.081	.073	.066
$\alpha = .5$	.5	.25	.125	.063	.031

Selecting the Smoothing Constant   The exponential smoothing approach is easy to use, and it has been successfully applied in virtually every type of business. However, the appropriate value of the smoothing constant, α, can make the difference between an accurate forecast and an inaccurate forecast. High values of α are chosen when the underlying average is likely to change. Low values of α are used when the underlying average is fairly stable. In picking a value for the smoothing constant, the objective is to obtain the most accurate forecast.

Measuring Forecast Error

The overall accuracy of any forecasting model—moving average, exponential smoothing, or other—can be determined by comparing the forecasted values with the actual or observed values. If F_t denotes the forecast in period t, and A_t denotes the actual demand in period t, the *forecast error* (or deviation) is defined as:

$$\text{Forecast error} = \text{Actual demand} - \text{Forecast value}$$

$$= A_t - F_t$$

Several measures are used in practice to calculate the overall forecast error. These measures can be used to compare different forecasting models, as well as to monitor forecasts to ensure they are performing well. Three of the most popular measures are mean absolute deviation (MAD), mean squared error (MSE), and mean absolute percent error (MAPE). We now describe and give an example of each.

Mean Absolute Deviation   The first measure of the overall forecast error for a model is the **mean absolute deviation (MAD)**. This value is computed by taking the sum of the absolute values of the individual forecast errors and dividing by the number of periods of data (n):

$$\text{MAD} = \frac{\Sigma\, |\text{Actual} - \text{Forecast}|}{n} \qquad (5)$$

Mean absolute deviation (MAD)
A measure of the overall forecast error for a model.

Example 4 applies MAD, as a measure of overall forecast error, by testing two values of α.

During the past 8 quarters, the Port of Baltimore has unloaded large quantities of grain from ships. The port's operations manager wants to test the use of exponential smoothing to see how well the technique works in predicting tonnage unloaded. He guesses that the forecast of grain unloaded in the first quarter was 175 tons. Two values of α are to be examined: $\alpha = .10$ and $\alpha = .50$.

Approach: Compare the actual data with the data we forecast (using each of the two α values) and then find the absolute deviation and MADs.

EXAMPLE 4

Determining the mean absolute deviation (MAD)

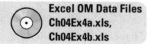
Solution: The following table shows the *detailed* calculations for $\alpha = .10$ only:

Quarter	Actual Tonnage Unloaded	Forecast with $\alpha = .10$	Forecast with $\alpha = .50$
1	180	175	175
2	168	$175.50 = 175.00 + .10(180 - 175)$	177.50
3	159	$174.75 = 175.50 + .10(168 - 175.50)$	172.75
4	175	$173.18 = 174.75 + .10(159 - 174.75)$	165.88
5	190	$173.36 = 173.18 + .10(175 - 173.18)$	170.44
6	205	$175.02 = 173.36 + .10(190 - 173.36)$	180.22
7	180	$178.02 = 175.02 + .10(205 - 175.02)$	192.61
8	182	$178.22 = 178.02 + .10(180 - 178.02)$	186.30
9	?	$178.59 = 178.22 + .10(182 - 178.22)$	184.15

To evaluate the accuracy of each smoothing constant, we can compute forecast errors in terms of absolute deviations and MADs:

Quarter	Actual Tonnage Unloaded	Forecast with $\alpha = .10$	Absolute Deviation for $\alpha = .10$	Forecast with $\alpha = .50$	Absolute Deviation for $\alpha = .50$
1	180	175	5.00	175	5.00
2	168	175.50	7.50	177.50	9.50
3	159	174.75	15.75	172.75	13.75
4	175	173.18	1.82	165.88	9.12
5	190	173.36	16.64	170.44	19.56
6	205	175.02	29.98	180.22	24.78
7	180	178.02	1.98	192.61	12.61
8	182	178.22	3.78	186.30	4.30
		Sum of absolute deviations:	82.45		98.62
	$\text{MAD} = \dfrac{\Sigma\lvert\text{Deviations}\rvert}{n}$		10.31		12.33

Insight: On the basis of this comparison of the two MADs, a smoothing constant of $\alpha = .10$ is preferred to $\alpha = .50$ because its MAD is smaller.

Learning exercise: If the smoothing constant is changed from $\alpha = .10$ to $\alpha = .20$, what is the new MAD? [Answer: 10.21.]

Related problems: 5b, 8c, 9c, 14, 23, 37a

Most computerized forecasting software includes a feature that automatically finds the smoothing constant with the lowest forecast error. Some software modifies the α value if errors become larger than acceptable.

Mean squared error (MSE)
The average of the squared differences between the forecasted and observed values.

Mean Squared Error   The **mean squared error (MSE)** is a second way of measuring overall forecast error. MSE is the average of the squared differences between the forecasted and observed values. Its formula is:

$$\text{MSE} = \frac{\Sigma(\text{Forecast errors})^2}{n} \tag{6}$$

Example 5 finds the MSE for the Port of Baltimore introduced in Example 4.

EXAMPLE 5

Determining the mean squared error (MSE)

The operations manager for the Port of Baltimore now wants to compute MSE for $\alpha = .10$.

Approach: Use the same forecast data for $\alpha = .10$ from Example 4, then compute the MSE using Equation (6).

Solution:

Quarter	Actual Tonnage Unloaded	Forecast for $\alpha = .10$	(Error)^2
1	180	175	$5^2 = 25$
2	168	175.50	$(-7.5)^2 = 56.25$
3	159	174.75	$(-15.75)^2 = 248.06$
4	175	173.18	$(1.82)^2 = 3.33$
5	190	173.36	$(16.64)^2 = 276.89$
6	205	175.02	$(29.98)^2 = 898.70$
7	180	178.02	$(1.98)^2 = 3.92$
8	182	178.22	$(3.78)^2 = 14.31$

Sum of errors squared = 1,526.46

$$MSE = \frac{\Sigma(\text{Forecast errors})^2}{n} = 1{,}526.54/8 = 190.8$$

Insight: Is this MSE = 190.8 good or bad? It all depends on the MSEs for other forecasting approaches. A low MSE is better because we want to minimize MSE. MSE exaggerates errors because it squares them.

Learning exercise: Find the MSE for $\alpha = .50$. [Answer: MSE = 195.24. The result indicates that $\alpha = .10$ is a better choice because we seek a lower MSE. Coincidentally, this is the same conclusion we reached using MAD in Example 4]

Related problems: 8d, 14, 20

A drawback of using the MSE is that it tends to accentuate large deviations due to the squared term. For example, if the forecast error for period 1 is twice as large as the error for period 2, the squared error in period 1 is four times as large as that for period 2. Hence, using MSE as the measure of forecast error typically indicates that we prefer to have several smaller deviations rather than even one large deviation.

Mean Absolute Percent Error A problem with both the MAD and MSE is that their values depend on the magnitude of the item being forecast. If the forecast item is measured in thousands, the MAD and MSE values can be very large. To avoid this problem, we can use the **mean absolute percent error (MAPE)**. This is computed as the average of the absolute difference between the forecasted and actual values, expressed as a percentage of the actual values. That is, if we have forecasted and actual values for n periods, the MAPE is calculated as:

$$MAPE = \frac{\sum_{i=1}^{n} 100 \left|\text{Actual}_i - \text{Forecast}_i\right|/\text{Actual}_i}{n} \quad (7)$$

Mean absolute percent error (MAPE)
The average of the absolute differences between the forecast and actual values, expressed as a percent of actual values.

Example 6 illustrates the calculations using the data from Examples 4 and 5.

EXAMPLE 6

Determining the
mean absolute
percent error (MAPE)

The Port of Baltimore wants to now calculate the MAPE when $\alpha = .10$.

Approach: Equation (7) is applied to the forecast data computed in Example 4.

Solution:

Quarter	Actual Tonnage Unloaded	Forecast for $\alpha = .10$	Absolute Percent Error 100 (|error|/actual)
1	180	175.00	100(5/180) = 2.78%
2	168	175.50	100(7.5/168) = 4.46%
3	159	174.75	100(15.75/159) = 9.90%
4	175	173.18	100(1.82/175) = 1.05%
5	190	173.36	100(16.64/190) = 8.76%
6	205	175.02	100(29.98/205) = 14.62%
7	180	178.02	100(1.98/180) = 1.10%
8	182	178.22	100(3.78/182) = 2.08%
			Sum of % errors = 44.75%

$$\text{MAPE} = \frac{\Sigma \text{ Absolute percent errors}}{n} = \frac{44.75\%}{8} = 5.59\%$$

Insight: MAPE expresses the error as a percent of the actual values, undistorted by a single large value.

Learning exercise: What is MAPE when α is .50? [Answer: MAPE = 6.75%. As was the case with MAD and MSE, the $\alpha = .1$ was preferable for this series of data.]

Related problems: 8e, 33c

The MAPE is perhaps the easiest measure to interpret. For example, a result that the MAPE is 6% is a clear statement that is not dependent on issues such as the magnitude of the input data.

Exponential Smoothing with Trend Adjustment

Simple exponential smoothing, the technique we just illustrated in Examples 3 to 6, is like any other moving-average technique: It fails to respond to trends. Other forecasting techniques that can deal with trends are certainly available. However, because exponential smoothing is such a popular modeling approach in business, let us look at it in more detail.

Here is why exponential smoothing must be modified when a trend is present. Assume that demand for our product or service has been increasing by 100 units per month and that we have been forecasting with $\alpha = 0.4$ in our exponential smoothing model. The following table shows a severe lag in the 2nd, 3rd, 4th, and 5th months, even when our initial estimate for month 1 is perfect:

Month	Actual Demand	Forecast for Month $T(F_T)$
1	100	$F_1 = 100$ (given)
2	200	$F_2 = F_1 + \alpha (A_1 - F_1) = 100 + .4(100 - 100) = 100$
3	300	$F_3 = F_2 + \alpha (A_2 - F_2) = 100 + .4(200 - 100) = 140$
4	400	$F_4 = F_3 + \alpha (A_3 - F_3) = 140 + .4(300 - 140) = 204$
5	500	$F_5 = F_4 + \alpha (A_4 - F_4) = 204 + .4(400 - 204) = 282$

To improve our forecast, let us illustrate a more complex exponential smoothing model, one that adjusts for trend. The idea is to compute an exponentially smoothed average of the data and then adjust for positive or negative lag in trend. The new formula is:

$$\text{Forecast including trend}(FIT_t) = \text{Exponentially smoothed forecast}(F_t) + \text{Exponentially smoothed trend}(T_t)$$

(8)

With trend-adjusted exponential smoothing, estimates for both the average and the trend are smoothed. This procedure requires two smoothing constants: α for the average and β for the trend. We then compute the average and trend each period:

$F_t = \alpha$(Actual demand last period) $+ (1 - \alpha)$(Forecast last period + Trend estimate last period)

or:

$$F_t = \alpha(A_{t-1}) + (1 - \alpha)(F_{t-1} + T_{t-1}) \tag{9}$$

$T_t = \beta$(Forecast this period − Forecast last period)
$+ (1 - \beta)$(Trend estimate last period)

or:

$$T_t = \beta(F_t - F_{t-1}) + (1 - \beta)T_{t-1} \tag{10}$$

where F_t = exponentially smoothed forecast of the data series in period t
T_t = exponentially smoothed trend in period t
A_t = actual demand in period t
α = smoothing constant for the average $(0 \le \alpha \le 1)$
β = smoothing constant for the trend $(0 \le \beta \le 1)$

So the three steps to compute a trend-adjusted forecast are:

Step 1: Compute F_t, the exponentially smoothed forecast for period t, using Equation (9).
Step 2: Compute the smoothed trend, T_t, using Equation (10).
Step 3: Calculate the forecast including trend, FIT_t, by the formula $FIT_t = F_t + T_t$.

Example 7 shows how to use trend-adjusted exponential smoothing.

A large Portland manufacturer wants to forecast demand for a piece of pollution-control equipment. A review of past sales, as shown below, indicates that an increasing trend is present:

Month (t)	Actual Demand (A_t)	Month (t)	Actual Demand (A_t)
1	12	6	21
2	17	7	31
3	20	8	28
4	19	9	36
5	24	10	?

Smoothing constants are assigned the values of $\alpha = .2$ and $\beta = .4$. The firm assumes the initial forecast for month 1 (F_1) was 11 units and the trend over that period (T_1) was 2 units.

Approach: A trend-adjusted exponential smoothing model, using Equations (9) and (10) and the three steps above, is employed.

Solution:

Step 1: Forecast for month 2:

$$F_2 = \alpha A_1 + (1-\alpha)(F_1 + T_1)$$
$$F_2 = (.2)(12) + (1-.2)(11+2)$$
$$= 2.4 + (.8)(13) = 2.4 + 10.4 = 12.8 \text{ units}$$

Step 2: Compute the trend in period 2:

$$T_2 = \beta(F_2 - F_1) + (1-\beta)T_1$$
$$= .4(12.8 - 11) + (1 - .4)(2)$$
$$= (.4)(1.8) + (.6)(2) = .72 + 1.2 = 1.92$$

Step 3: Compute the forecast including trend (FIT_t):

$$FIT_2 = F_2 + T_2$$
$$= 12.8 + 1.92$$
$$= 14.72 \text{ units}$$

EXAMPLE 7

Computing a trend-adjusted exponential smoothing forecast

 Active Model 4.3

Example 7 is further illustrated in Active Model 4.3 on the CD-ROM.

We will also do the same calculations for the third month:

Step 1. $F_3 = \alpha A_2 + (1 - \alpha)(F_2 + T_2) = (.2)(17) + (1 - .2)(12.8 + 1.92)$
$= 3.4 + (.8)(14.72) = 3.4 + 11.78 = 15.18$

Step 2. $T_3 = \beta(F_3 - F_2) + (1 - \beta)T_2 = (.4)(15.18 - 12.8) + (1 - .4)(1.92)$
$= (.4)(2.38) + (.6)(1.92) = .952 + 1.152 = 2.10$

Step 3. $FIT_3 = F_3 + T_3$
$= 15.18 + 2.10 = 17.28.$

Table 1 completes the forecasts for the 10-month period.

► **Table 1**

Forecast with $\alpha = .2$
and $\beta = .4$

Month	Actual Demand	Smoothed Forecast, F_t	Smoothed Trend, T_t	Forecast Including Trend FIT_t
1	12	11	2	13.00
2	17	12.80	1.92	14.72
3	20	15.18	2.10	17.28
4	19	17.82	2.32	20.14
5	24	19.91	2.23	22.14
6	21	22.51	2.38	24.89
7	31	24.11	2.07	26.18
8	28	27.14	2.45	29.59
9	36	29.28	2.32	31.60
10	—	32.48	2.68	35.16

Insight: Figure 3 compares actual demand (A_t) to an exponential smoothing forecast that includes trend (FIT_t). FIT picks up the trend in actual demand. A simple exponential smoothing model (like we saw in Examples 3 and 4) trails far behind.

► **Figure 3**

Exponential Smoothing with Trend-Adjustment Forecasts Compared to Actual Demand Data

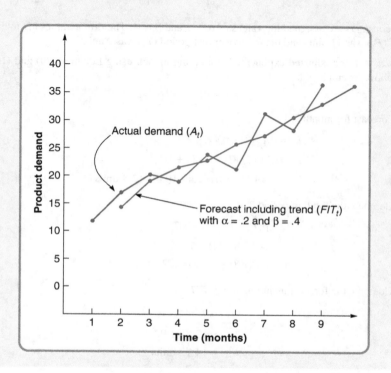

Learning exercise: Using the data for actual demand for the 9 months, compute the exponentially smoothed forecast *without* trend (using Equation (4) as we did earlier in Examples 3 and 4). Apply α = .2 and assume an initial forecast for month 1 of 11 units. Then plot the months 2–10 forecast values on Figure 3. What do you notice? [Answer: Month 10 forecast = 24.65. All the points are below and lag the trend-adjusted forecast.]

Related problems: 19, 20, 21, 22, 44

The value of the trend-smoothing constant, β, resembles the α constant because a high β is more responsive to recent changes in trend. A low β gives less weight to the most recent trends and tends to smooth out the present trend. Values of β can be found by the trial-and-error approach or by using sophisticated commercial forecasting software, with the MAD used as a measure of comparison.

Simple exponential smoothing is often referred to as *first-order smoothing*, and trend-adjusted smoothing is called *second-order*, or *double smoothing*. Other advanced exponential-smoothing models are also used, including seasonal-adjusted and triple smoothing.[3]

Trend Projections

The last time-series forecasting method we will discuss is **trend projection**. This technique fits a trend line to a series of historical data points and then projects the line into the future for medium to long-range forecasts. Several mathematical trend equations can be developed (for example, exponential and quadratic), but in this section, we will look at *linear* (straight-line) trends only.

Trend projection
A time-series forecasting method that fits a trend line to a series of historical data points and then projects the line into the future for forecasts.

If we decide to develop a linear trend line by a precise statistical method, we can apply the *least-squares method*. This approach results in a straight line that minimizes the sum of the squares of the vertical differences or deviations from the line to each of the actual observations. Figure 4 illustrates the least-squares approach.

A least-squares line is described in terms of its *y*-intercept (the height at which it intercepts the *y*-axis) and its slope (the angle of the line). If we can compute the *y*-intercept and slope, we can express the line with the following equation:

$$\hat{y} = a + bx \tag{11}$$

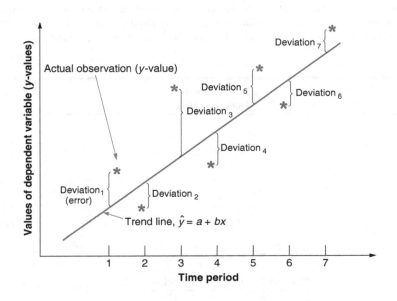

◀ **Figure 4**

The Least-Squares Method for Finding the Best-Fitting Straight Line, Where the Asterisks Are the Locations of the Seven Actual Observations or Data Points

[3]For more details, see D. Groebner, P. Shannon, P. Fry, and K. Smith, *Business Statistics*, 7th ed. (Upper Saddle River, NJ: Prentice Hall, 2008).

where $\hat{y}$ (called "y hat") = computed value of the variable to be predicted (called the *dependent variable*)

a = y-axis intercept

b = slope of the regression line (or the rate of change in y for given changes in x)

x = the independent variable (which in this case is *time*)

Statisticians have developed equations that we can use to find the values of a and b for any regression line. The slope b is found by:

$$b = \frac{\Sigma xy - n\bar{x}\bar{y}}{\Sigma x^2 - n\bar{x}^2}$$ (12)

where b = slope of the regression line
Σ = summation sign
x = known values of the independent variable
y = known values of the dependent variable
$\bar{x}$ = average of the x-values
$\bar{y}$ = average of the y-values
n = number of data points or observations

We can compute the y-intercept a as follows:

$$a = \bar{y} - b\bar{x}$$ (13)

Example 8 shows how to apply these concepts.

EXAMPLE 8

Forecasting with least squares

Excel OM Data File Ch04Ex8.xls

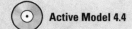

Active Model 4.4

Example 8 is further illustrated in Active Model 4.4 on the CD-ROM.

The demand for electric power at N.Y. Edison over the period 2001 to 2007 is shown in the following table, in megawatts. The firm wants to forecast 2008 demand by fitting a straight-line trend to these data.

Year	Electrical Power Demand	Year	Electrical Power Demand
2001	74	2005	105
2002	79	2006	142
2003	80	2007	122
2004	90		

Approach: With a series of data over time, we can minimize the computations by transforming the values of x (time) to simpler numbers. Thus, in this case, we can designate 2001 as year 1, 2002 as year 2, and so on. Then Equations (12) and (13) can be used to create the trend projection model.

Solution:

Year	Time Period (x)	Electric Power Demand (y)	x^2	xy
2001	1	74	1	74
2002	2	79	4	158
2003	3	80	9	240
2004	4	90	16	360
2005	5	105	25	525
2006	6	142	36	852
2007	7	122	49	854
	$\Sigma x = 28$	$\Sigma y = 692$	$\Sigma x^2 = 140$	$\Sigma xy = 3{,}063$

$$\bar{x} = \frac{\Sigma x}{n} = \frac{28}{7} = 4 \qquad \bar{y} = \frac{\Sigma y}{n} = \frac{692}{7} = 98.86$$

$$b = \frac{\Sigma xy - n\bar{x}\bar{y}}{\Sigma x^2 - n\bar{x}^2} = \frac{3{,}063 - (7)(4)(98.86)}{140 - (7)(4^2)} = \frac{295}{28} = 10.54$$

$$a = \bar{y} - b\bar{x} = 98.86 - 10.54(4) = 56.70$$

Thus, the least squares trend equation is $\hat{y} = 56.70 + 10.54x$. To project demand in 2008, we first denote the year 2008 in our new coding system as $x = 8$:

$$\text{Demand in } 2008 = 56.70 + 10.54(8)$$
$$= 141.02, \text{ or } 141 \text{ megawatts}$$

Insight: To evaluate the model, we plot both the historical demand and the trend line in Figure 5. In this case, we may wish to be cautious and try to understand the 2006 to 2007 swing in demand.

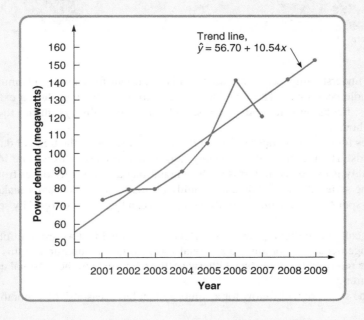

◀ **Figure 5**

Electrical Power and the Computed Trend Line

Learning exercise: Estimate demand for 2009. [Answer: 151.56 or 152 megawatts.]

Related problems: 6, 13c, 16, 25, 39, 49

Notes on the Use of the Least-Squares Method Using the least-squares method implies that we have met three requirements:

1. We always plot the data because least-squares data assume a linear relationship. If a curve appears to be present, curvilinear analysis is probably needed.
2. We do not predict time periods far beyond our given database. For example, if we have 20 months' worth of average prices of Microsoft stock, we can forecast only 3 or 4 months into the future. Forecasts beyond that have little statistical validity. Thus, you cannot take 5 years' worth of sales data and project 10 years into the future. The world is too uncertain.
3. Deviations around the least-squares line (see Figure 4) are assumed to be random. They are normally distributed, with most observations close to the line and only a smaller number farther out.

Seasonal Variations in Data

Seasonal variations in data are regular up-and-down movements in a time series that relate to recurring events such as weather or holidays. Demand for coal and fuel oil, for example, peaks during cold winter months. Demand for golf clubs or sunscreen may be highest in summer.

Seasonality may be applied to hourly, daily, weekly, monthly, or other recurring patterns. Fast-food restaurants experience *daily* surges at noon and again at 5 P.M. Movie theaters see higher demand on Friday and Saturday evenings. The post office, Toys "Я" Us, The Christmas Store, and Hallmark Card Shops also exhibit seasonal variation in customer traffic and sales.

Seasonal variations

Regular upward or downward movements in a time series that tie to recurring events.

Yamaha Motor Corp., USA

▶ Demand for many products is seasonal. Yamaha, the manufacturer of these jet skis and snowmobiles, produces products with complementary demands to address seasonal fluctuations.

Learning Objective

5. Develop seasonal indexes

Because John Deere understands seasonal variations in sales, it has been able to obtain 70% of its orders in advance of seasonal use (through price reductions and incentives such as 0% interest) so it can smooth production.

Similarly, understanding seasonal variations is important for capacity planning in organizations that handle peak loads. These include electric power companies during extreme cold and warm periods, banks on Friday afternoons, and buses and subways during the morning and evening rush hours.

Time-series forecasts like those in Example 8 involve reviewing the trend of data over a series of time periods. The presence of seasonality makes adjustments in trend-line forecasts necessary. Seasonality is expressed in terms of the amount that actual values differ from average values in the time series. Analyzing data in monthly or quarterly terms usually makes it easy for a statistician to spot seasonal patterns. Seasonal indices can then be developed by several common methods.

In what is called a *multiplicative seasonal model*, seasonal factors are multiplied by an estimate of average demand to produce a seasonal forecast. Our assumption in this section is that trend has been removed from the data. Otherwise, the magnitude of the seasonal data will be distorted by the trend.

Here are the steps we will follow for a company that has "seasons" of 1 month:

1. Find the *average historical demand each season* (or month in this case) by summing the demand for that month in each year and dividing by the number of years of data available. For example, if, in January, we have seen sales of 8, 6, and 10 over the past 3 years, average January demand equals $(8 + 6 + 10)/3 = 8$ units.
2. Compute the *average demand over all months* by dividing the total average annual demand by the number of seasons. For example, if the total average demand for a year is 120 units and there are 12 seasons (each month), the average monthly demand is $120/12 = 10$ units.
3. Compute a *seasonal index* for each season by dividing that month's actual historical demand (from step 1) by the average demand over all months (from step 2). For example, if the average historical January demand over the past 3 years is 8 units and the average demand over all months is 10 units, the seasonal index for January is $8/10 = .80$. Likewise, a seasonal index of 1.20 for February would mean that February's demand is 20% larger than the average demand over all months.
4. Estimate next year's total annual demand.
5. Divide this estimate of total annual demand by the number of seasons, then multiply it by the seasonal index for that month. This provides the *seasonal forecast*.

Example 9 illustrates this procedure as it computes seasonal indices from historical data.

EXAMPLE 9

Determining seasonal indices

A Des Moines distributor of Sony laptop computers wants to develop monthly indices for sales. Data from 2005–2007, by month, are available.

Approach: Follow the five steps listed above.

Solution:

Month	Demand 2005	Demand 2006	Demand 2007	Average 2005–2007 Demand	Average Monthly Demand[a]	Seasonal Index[b]
Jan.	80	85	105	90	94	.957 (= 90/94)
Feb.	70	85	85	80	94	.851 (= 80/94)
Mar.	80	93	82	85	94	.904 (= 85/94)
Apr.	90	95	115	100	94	1.064 (= 100/94)
May	113	125	131	123	94	1.309 (= 123/94)
June	110	115	120	115	94	1.223 (= 115/94)
July	100	102	113	105	94	1.117 (= 105/94)
Aug.	88	102	110	100	94	1.064 (= 100/94)
Sept.	85	90	95	90	94	.957 (= 90/94)
Oct.	77	78	85	80	94	.851 (= 80/94)
Nov.	75	82	83	80	94	.851 (= 80/94)
Dec.	82	78	80	80	94	.851 (= 80/94)

Total average annual demand = 1,128

[a]Average monthly demand $= \dfrac{1,128}{12 \text{ months}} = 94$.   [b]Seasonal index $= \dfrac{\text{Average 2005–2007 monthly demand}}{\text{Average monthly demand}}$.

If we expected the 2008 annual demand for computers to be 1,200 units, we would use these seasonal indices to forecast the monthly demand as follows:

Month	Demand	Month	Demand
Jan.	$\dfrac{1,200}{12} \times .957 = 96$	July	$\dfrac{1,200}{12} \times 1.117 = 112$
Feb.	$\dfrac{1,200}{12} \times .851 = 85$	Aug.	$\dfrac{1,200}{12} \times 1.064 = 106$
Mar.	$\dfrac{1,200}{12} \times .904 = 90$	Sept.	$\dfrac{1,200}{12} \times .957 = 96$
Apr.	$\dfrac{1,200}{12} \times 1.064 = 106$	Oct.	$\dfrac{1,200}{12} \times .851 = 85$
May	$\dfrac{1,200}{12} \times 1.309 = 131$	Nov.	$\dfrac{1,200}{12} \times .851 = 85$
June	$\dfrac{1,200}{12} \times 1.223 = 122$	Dec.	$\dfrac{1,200}{12} \times .851 = 85$

Insight: Think of these indices as percentages of average sales. The average sales (without seasonality) would be 94, but with seasonality, sales fluctuate from 85% to 131% of average.

Learning exercise: If 2008 annual demand is 1,150 laptops (instead of 1,200), what will the January, February, and March forecasts be? [Answer: 92, 82, and 87.]

Related problems: 27, 28

For simplicity, only 3 periods are used for each monthly index in the preceding example. Example 10 illustrates how indices that have already been prepared can be applied to adjust trend-line forecasts for seasonality.

San Diego Hospital wants to improve its forecasting by applying both trend and seasonal indices to 66 months of data it has collected. It will then forecast "patient-days" over the coming year.

Approach: A trend line is created; then monthly seasonal indices are computed. Finally, a multiplicative seasonal model is used to forecast months 67 to 78.

EXAMPLE 10

Applying both trend and seasonal indices

Solution: Using 66 months of adult inpatient hospital days, the following equation was computed:

$$\hat{y} = 8{,}090 + 21.5x$$

where
$\hat{y}$ = patient days
x = time, in months

Based on this model, which reflects only trend data, the hospital forecasts patient days for the next month (period 67) to be:

Patient days = 8,090 + (21.5)(67) = 9,530 (trend only)

While this model, as plotted in Figure 6, recognized the upward trend line in the demand for inpatient services, it ignored the seasonality that the administration knew to be present.

► **Figure 6**

Trend Data for San Diego Hospital

Source: From "Modern Methods Improve Hospital Forecasting" by W. E. Sterk and E. G. Shryock from *Healthcare Financial Management*, Vol. 41, no. 3, p. 97. Reprinted by permission of Healthcare Financial Management Association.

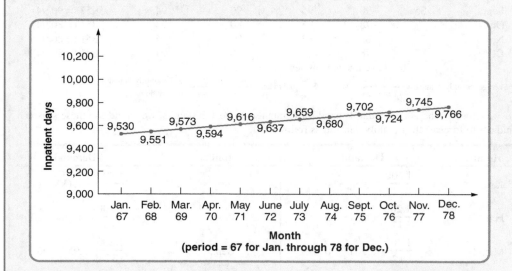

The following table provides seasonal indices based on the same 66 months. Such seasonal data, by the way, were found to be typical of hospitals nationwide.

Seasonality Indices for Adult Inpatient Days at San Diego Hospital

Month	Seasonality Index	Month	Seasonality Index
January	1.04	July	1.03
February	0.97	August	1.04
March	1.02	September	0.97
April	1.01	October	1.00
May	0.99	November	0.96
June	0.99	December	0.98

These seasonal indices are graphed in Figure 7. Note that January, March, July, and August seem to exhibit significantly higher patient days on average, while February, September, November, and December experience lower patient days.

However, neither the trend data nor the seasonal data alone provide a reasonable forecast for the hospital. Only when the hospital multiplied the trend-adjusted data times the appropriate seasonal index did it obtain good forecasts. Thus, for period 67 (January):

Patient days = (Trend-adjusted forecast) (Monthly seasonal index) = (9,530)(1.04) = 9,911

The patient days for each month are:

Period	67	68	69	70	71	72	73	74	75	76	77	78
Month	Jan.	Feb.	March	April	May	June	July	Aug.	Sept.	Oct.	Nov.	Dec.
Forecast with Trend & Seasonal	9,911	9,265	9,764	9,691	9,520	9,542	9,949	10,068	9,411	9,724	9,355	9,572

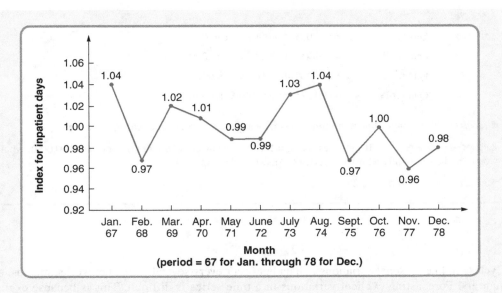

◀ **Figure 7**

Seasonal Index for San Diego Hospital

A graph showing the forecast that combines both trend and seasonality appears in Figure 8.

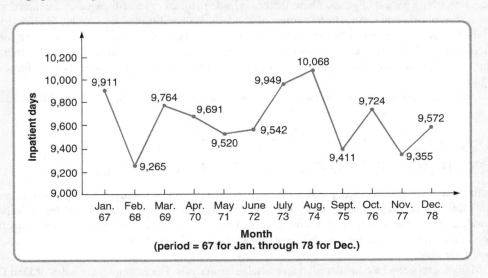

◀ **Figure 8**

Combined Trend and Seasonal Forecast

Insight: Notice that with trend only, the September forecast is 9,702, but with both trend and seasonal adjustments the forecast is 9,411. By combining trend and seasonal data the hospital was better able to forecast inpatient days and the related staffing and budgeting vital to effective operations.

Learning exercise: If the slope of the trend line for patient-days is 22.0 (rather than 21.5) and the index for December is .99 (instead of .98), what is the new forecast for December inpatient days? [Answer: 9,708.]

Related problems: 26, 29

Example 11 further illustrates seasonality for quarterly data at a department store.

EXAMPLE 11

Adjusting trend data with seasonal indices

Management at Davis's Department Store has used time-series regression to forecast retail sales for the next 4 quarters. Sales estimates are $100,000, $120,000, $140,000, and $160,000 for the respective quarters. Seasonal indices for the 4 quarters have been found to be 1.30, .90, .70, and 1.15, respectively.

Approach: To compute a seasonalized or adjusted sales forecast, we just multiply each seasonal index by the appropriate trend forecast:

$$\hat{y}_{seasonal} = \text{Index} \times \hat{y}_{trend\ forecast}$$

Solution: Quarter I: $\hat{y}_I = (1.30)(\$100,000) = \$130,000$

Quarter II: $\hat{y}_{II} = (.90)(\$120,000) = \$108,000$

Quarter III: $\hat{y}_{III} = (.70)(\$140,000) = \$98,000$

Quarter IV: $\hat{y}_{IV} = (1.15)(\$160,000) = \$184,000$

Insight: The straight-line trend forecast is now adjusted to reflect the seasonal changes.

Learning exercise: If the sales forecast for Quarter IV was 180,000 (rather than 160,000), what would be the seasonally adjusted forecast? [Answer: $207,000.]

Related problems: 26, 29

Cyclical Variations in Data

Cycles

Patterns in the data that occur every several years.

Cycles are like seasonal variations in data but occur every several *years*, not weeks, months, or quarters. Forecasting cyclical variations in a time series is difficult. This is because cycles include a wide variety of factors that cause the economy to go from recession to expansion to recession over a period of years. These factors include national or industrywide overexpansion in times of euphoria and contraction in times of concern. Demand forecasting cycles for individual products can also be driven by product life cycles—the stages products go through from introduction through decline. Life cycles exist for virtually all products; striking examples include floppy disks, video recorders, and the original Game Boy. We leave cyclical analysis to forecasting texts.

Developing associative techniques of variables that affect one another is our next topic.

ASSOCIATIVE FORECASTING METHODS: REGRESSION AND CORRELATION ANALYSIS

Unlike time-series forecasting, *associative forecasting* models usually consider *several* variables that are related to the quantity being predicted. Once these related variables have been found, a statistical model is built and used to forecast the item of interest. This approach is more powerful than the time-series methods that use only the historical values for the forecasted variable.

Linear-regression analysis

A straight-line mathematical model to describe the functional relationships between independent and dependent variables.

Many factors can be considered in an associative analysis. For example, the sales of Dell PCs may be related to Dell's advertising budget, the company's prices, competitors' prices and promotional strategies, and even the nation's economy and unemployment rates. In this case, PC sales would be called the *dependent variable*, and the other variables would be called *independent variables*. The manager's job is to develop *the best statistical relationship between PC sales and the independent variables*. The most common quantitative associative forecasting model is **linear-regression analysis**.

Learning Objective

6. Conduct a regression and correlation analysis

Using Regression Analysis for Forecasting

We can use the same mathematical model that we employed in the least squares method of trend projection to perform a linear-regression analysis. The dependent variables that we want to forecast will still be $\hat{y}$. But now the independent variable, x, need no longer be time. We use the equation:

$$\hat{y} = a + bx$$

where $\hat{y}$ = value of the dependent variable (in our example, sales)
a = y-axis intercept
b = slope of the regression line
x = independent variable

Example 12 shows how to use linear regression.

EXAMPLE 12

Computing a linear
regression equation

Nodel Construction Company renovates old homes in West Bloomfield, Michigan. Over time, the company has found that its dollar volume of renovation work is dependent on the West Bloomfield area payroll. Management wants to establish a mathematical relationship to help predict sales.

Approach: Nodel's VP of operations has prepared the following table, which lists company revenues and the amount of money earned by wage earners in West Bloomfield during the past 6 years:

**Excel OM Data File
Ch04Ex12.xls**

Nodel's Sales (in $ millions), y	Local Payroll (in $ billions), x	Nodel's Sales (in $ millions), y	Local Payroll (in $ billions), x
2.0	1	2.0	2
3.0	3	2.0	1
2.5	4	3.5	7

The VP needs to determine whether there is a straight-line (linear) relationship between area payroll and sales. He plots the known data on a scatter diagram:

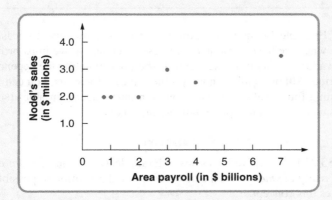

It appears from the six data points that there is a slight positive relationship between the independent variable (payroll) and the dependent variable (sales): As payroll increases, Nodel's sales tend to be higher.

Solution: We can find a mathematical equation by using the least-squares regression approach:

Sales, y	Payroll, x	x^2	xy
2.0	1	1	2.0
3.0	3	9	9.0
2.5	4	16	10.0
2.0	2	4	4.0
2.0	1	1	2.0
3.5	7	49	24.5
$\Sigma y = 15.0$	$\Sigma x = 18$	$\Sigma x^2 = 80$	$\Sigma xy = 51.5$

$$\bar{x} = \frac{\Sigma x}{6} = \frac{18}{6} = 3$$

$$\bar{y} = \frac{\Sigma y}{6} = \frac{15}{6} = 2.5$$

$$b = \frac{\Sigma xy - n\bar{x}\,\bar{y}}{\Sigma x^2 - n\bar{x}^2} = \frac{51.5 - (6)(3)(2.5)}{80 - (6)(3^2)} = .25$$

$$a = \bar{y} - b\bar{x} = 2.5 - (.25)(3) = 1.75$$

The estimated regression equation, therefore, is:

$$\hat{y} = 1.75 + .25x$$

or:

$$\text{Sales} = 1.75 + .25 \, (\text{payroll})$$

If the local chamber of commerce predicts that the West Bloomfield area payroll will be $6 billion next year, we can estimate sales for Nodel with the regression equation:

$$\text{Sales (in \$ millions)} = 1.75 + .25(6)$$
$$= 1.75 + 1.50 = 3.25$$

or:

$$\text{Sales} = \$3,250,000$$

Insight: Given our assumptions of a straight-line relationship between payroll and sales, we now have an indication of the slope of that relationship: Sales increases at the rate of a million dollars for every quarter billion dollars in the local payroll. This is because $b = .25$.

Learning exercise: What are Nodel's sales when the local payroll is $8 billion? [Answer: $3.75 million.]

Related problems: 24, 30, 31, 32, 33, 35, 38, 40, 41, 46, 48, 49

The final part of Example 12 shows a central weakness of associative forecasting methods like regression. Even when we have computed a regression equation, we must provide a forecast of the independent variable x—in this case, payroll—before estimating the dependent variable y for the next time period. Although this is not a problem for all forecasts, you can imagine the difficulty of determining future values of *some* common independent variables (such as unemployment rates, gross national product, price indices, and so on).

Standard Error of the Estimate

The forecast of $3,250,000 for Nodel's sales in Example 12 is called a *point estimate* of y. The point estimate is really the *mean*, or *expected value*, of a distribution of possible values of sales. Figure 9 illustrates this concept.

Standard error of the estimate

A measure of variability around the regression line—its standard deviation.

To measure the accuracy of the regression estimates, we must compute the **standard error of the estimate**, $S_{y,x}$. This computation is called the *standard deviation of the regression:* It measures the error from the dependent variable, y, to the regression line, rather than to the mean. Equation (14) is a similar expression to that found in most statistics books for computing the standard deviation of an arithmetic mean:

$$S_{y,x} = \sqrt{\frac{\Sigma(y - y_c)^2}{n - 2}} \tag{14}$$

where $y = y$-value of each data point
         y_c = computed value of the dependent variable, from the regression equation
         n = number of data points

▶ **Figure 9**

Distribution about the Point Estimate of $3.25 Million Sales

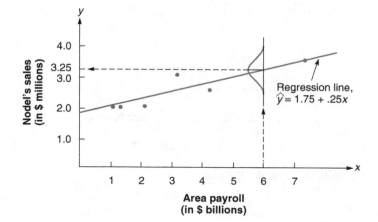

◄ *Glidden Paints' assembly lines fill thousands of cans per hour. To predict demand, the firm uses associative forecasting methods such as linear regression, with independent variables such as disposable personal income and GNP. Although housing starts would be a natural variable, Glidden found that it correlated poorly with past sales. It turns out that most Glidden paint is sold through retailers to customers who already own homes or businesses.*

ICI Paints

Equation (15) may look more complex, but it is actually an easier-to-use version of Equation (14). Both formulas provide the same answer and can be used in setting up prediction intervals around the point estimate.[4]

$$S_{y,x} = \sqrt{\frac{\Sigma y^2 - a\Sigma y - b\Sigma xy}{n-2}}$$ (15)

Example 13 shows how we would calculate the standard error of the estimate in Example 12.

EXAMPLE 13

Computing the standard error of the estimate

Nodel's VP of operations now wants to know the error associated with the regression line computed in Example 12.

Approach: Compute the standard error of the estimate, $S_{y,x}$, using Equation (15).

Solution: The only number we need that is not available to solve for $S_{y,x}$ is Σy^2. Some quick addition reveals $\Sigma y^2 = 39.5$. Therefore:

$$S_{y,x} = \sqrt{\frac{\Sigma y^2 - a\Sigma y - b\Sigma xy}{n-2}}$$
$$= \sqrt{\frac{39.5 - 1.75(15.0) - .25(51.5)}{6-2}}$$
$$= \sqrt{.09375} = .306 \text{ (in \$ millions)}$$

The standard error of the estimate is then $306,000 in sales.

Insight: The interpretation of the standard error of the estimate is similar to the standard deviation; namely, ±1 standard deviation = .6827. So there is a 68.27% chance of sales being ±$306,000 from the point estimate of $3,250,000.

Learning exercise: What is the probability sales will exceed $3,556,000? [Answer: About 16%.]

Related problems: 41e, 48b

Correlation Coefficients for Regression Lines

The regression equation is one way of expressing the nature of the relationship between two variables. Regression lines are not "cause-and-effect" relationships. They merely describe the relationships among variables. The regression equation shows how one variable relates to the value and changes in another variable.

Another way to evaluate the relationship between two variables is to compute the **coefficient of correlation**. This measure expresses the degree or strength of the linear relationship. Usually

Coefficient of correlation
A measure of the strength of the relationship between two variables.

---

[4]When the sample size is large ($n > 30$), the prediction interval value of y can be computed using normal tables. When the number of observations is small, the *t*-distribution is appropriate. See D. Groebner et al., *Business Statistics*, 7th ed. (Upper Saddle River, NJ: Prentice Hall, 2008).

► **Figure 10**

**Four Values of the
Correlation Coefficient**

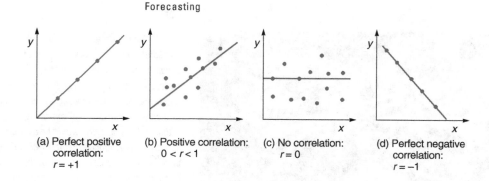

(a) Perfect positive
correlation:
$r = +1$

(b) Positive correlation:
$0 < r < 1$

(c) No correlation:
$r = 0$

(d) Perfect negative
correlation:
$r = -1$

identified as r, the coefficient of correlation can be any number between +1 and −1. Figure 10 illustrates what different values of r might look like.

To compute r, we use much of the same data needed earlier to calculate a and b for the regression line. The rather lengthy equation for r is:

$$r = \frac{n\Sigma xy - \Sigma x \Sigma y}{\sqrt{[n\Sigma x^2 - (\Sigma x)^2][n\Sigma y^2 - (\Sigma y)^2]}}$$

(16)

Example 14 shows how to calculate the coefficient of correlation for the data given in Examples 12 and 13.

EXAMPLE 14

Determining the coefficient of correlation

A high r doesn't always mean one variable will be a good predictor of the other. Skirt lengths and stock market prices may be correlated, but a rise in one doesn't mean the other will also go up.

In Example 12, we looked at the relationship between Nodel Construction Company's renovation sales and payroll in its hometown of West Bloomfield. The VP now wants to know the strength of the association between local payroll and sales.

Approach: We compute the r value using Equation 16. We need to first add one more column of calculations—for y^2.

Solution: The data, including the column for y^2 and the calculations, are shown here:

y	x	x^2	xy	y^2
2.0	1	1	2.0	4.0
3.0	3	9	9.0	9.0
2.5	4	16	10.0	6.25
2.0	2	4	4.0	4.0
2.0	1	1	2.0	4.0
3.5	7	49	24.5	12.25
$\Sigma y = 15.0$	$\Sigma x = 18$	$\Sigma x^2 = 80$	$\Sigma xy = 51.5$	$\Sigma y^2 = 39.5$

$$r = \frac{(6)(51.5) - (18)(15.0)}{\sqrt{[(6)(80) - (18)^2][(6)(39.5) - (15.0)^2]}}$$

$$= \frac{309 - 270}{\sqrt{(156)(12)}} = \frac{39}{\sqrt{1{,}872}}$$

$$= \frac{39}{43.3} = .901$$

Insight: This r of .901 appears to be a significant correlation and helps confirm the closeness of the relationship between the two variables.

Learning exercise: If the coefficient of correlation was −.901 rather than +.901, what would this tell you? [Answer: The negative correlation would tell you that as payroll went up, Nodel's sales went down—a rather unlikely occurrence that would suggest you recheck your math.]

Related problems: 24d, 35d, 38c, 41f, 48b

Although the coefficient of correlation is the measure most commonly used to describe the relationship between two variables, another measure does exist. It is called the **coefficient of determination** and is simply the square of the coefficient of correlation—namely, r^2. The value of r^2 will always be a positive number in the range $0 \le r^2 \le 1$. The coefficient of determination is the percent of variation in the dependent variable (y) that is explained by the regression equation. In Nodel's case, the value of r^2 is .81, indicating that 81% of the total variation is explained by the regression equation.

Coefficient of determination
A measure of the amount of variation in the dependent variable about its mean that is explained by the regression equation.

Multiple-Regression Analysis

Multiple regression is a practical extension of the simple regression model we just explored. It allows us to build a model with several independent variables instead of just one variable. For example, if Nodel Construction wanted to include average annual interest rates in its model for forecasting renovation sales, the proper equation would be:

$$\hat{y} = a + b_1 x_1 + b_2 x_2 \tag{17}$$

Multiple regression
An associative forecasting method with more than one independent variable.

where
$\hat{y}$ = dependent variable, sales
a = a constant, the y intercept
x_1 and x_2 = values of the two independent variables, area payroll and interest rates, respectively
b_1 and b_2 = coefficients for the two independent variables

The mathematics of multiple regression becomes quite complex (and is usually tackled by computer), so we leave the formulas for a, b_1, and b_2 to statistics textbooks. However, Example 15 shows how to interpret Equation (17) in forecasting Nodel's sales.

EXAMPLE 15

Using a multiple-regression equation

Nodel Construction wants to see the impact of a second independent variable, interest rates, on its sales.

Approach: The new multiple-regression line for Nodel Construction, calculated by computer software, is:

$$\hat{y} = 1.80 + .30x_1 - 5.0x_2$$

We also find that the new coefficient of correlation is .96, implying the inclusion of the variable x_2, interest rates, adds even more strength to the linear relationship.

Solution: We can now estimate Nodel's sales if we substitute values for next year's payroll and interest rate. If West Bloomfield's payroll will be $6 billion and the interest rate will be .12 (12%), sales will be forecast as:

$$\text{Sales (\$ millions)} = 1.80 + .30(6) - 5.0(.12)$$
$$= 1.8 + 1.8 - .6$$
$$= 3.00$$

or:

$$\text{Sales} = \$3,000,000$$

Insight: By using both variables, payroll and interest rates, Nodel now has a sales forecast of $3 million and a higher coefficient of correlation. This suggests a stronger relationship between the two variables and a more accurate estimate of sales.

Learning exercise: If interest rates were only 6%, what would be the sales forecast? [Answer: $3,300,000.]

Related problems: 34, 36

MONITORING AND CONTROLLING FORECASTS

Once a forecast has been completed, it should not be forgotten. No manager wants to be reminded that his or her forecast is horribly inaccurate, but a firm needs to determine why actual demand (or whatever variable is being examined) differed significantly from that projected.

If the forecaster is accurate, that individual usually makes sure that everyone is aware of his or her talents. Very seldom does one read articles in *Fortune*, *Forbes*, or *The Wall Street Journal*, however, about money managers who are consistently off by 25% in their stock market forecasts.

One way to monitor forecasts to ensure that they are performing well is to use a tracking signal. A **tracking signal** is a measurement of how well a forecast is predicting actual values. As forecasts are updated every week, month, or quarter, the newly available demand data are compared to the forecast values.

Tracking signal

A measurement of how well the forecast is predicting actual values.

The tracking signal is computed as the *running sum of the forecast errors (RSFE)* divided by the *mean absolute deviation (MAD)*:

$$\left(\begin{array}{c}\text{Tracking} \\ \text{signal}\end{array}\right) = \frac{\text{RSFE}}{\text{MAD}}$$

$$= \frac{\Sigma(\text{Actual demand in period } i - \text{Forecast demand in period } i)}{\text{MAD}} \quad (18)$$

where

$$\text{MAD} = \frac{\Sigma |\text{Actual} - \text{Forecast}|}{n}$$

as seen earlier in Equation (5).

Positive tracking signals indicate that demand is *greater* than forecast. *Negative* signals mean that demand is *less* than forecast. A good tracking signal—that is, one with a low RSFE—has about as much positive error as it has negative error. In other words, small deviations are okay, but positive and negative errors should balance one another so that the tracking signal centers closely around zero. A consistent tendency for forecasts to be greater or less than the actual values (that is, for a high RSFE) is called a **bias** error. Bias can occur if, for example, the wrong variables or trend line are used or if a seasonal index is misapplied.

Bias

A forecast that is consistently higher or consistently lower than actual values of a time series.

Once tracking signals are calculated, they are compared with predetermined control limits. When a tracking signal exceeds an upper or lower limit, there is a problem with the forecasting method, and management may want to reevaluate the way it forecasts demand. Figure 11 shows the graph of a tracking signal that is exceeding the range of acceptable variation. If the model being used is exponential smoothing, perhaps the smoothing constant needs to be readjusted.

How do firms decide what the upper and lower tracking limits should be? There is no single answer, but they try to find reasonable values—in other words, limits not so low as to be triggered with every small forecast error and not so high as to allow bad forecasts to be regularly overlooked. One MAD is equivalent to approximately .8 standard deviation, ±2 MADs = ±1.6 standard deviations, ±3 MADs = ±2.4 standard deviations, and ±4 MADs = ±3.2 standard deviations. This fact suggests that for a forecast to be "in control," 89% of the errors are expected to fall within ±2 MADs, 98% within ±3 MADs, or 99.9% within ±4 MADs.[5]

Learning Objective

7. Use a tracking signal

Example 16 shows how the tracking signal and RSFE can be computed.

▶ **Figure 11**

A Plot of Tracking Signals

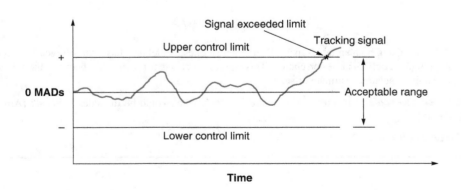

[5]To prove these three percentages to yourself, just set up a normal curve for ±1.6 standard deviations (*z*-values). Using the normal table in Appendix I, you find that the area under the curve is .89. This represents ±2 MADs. Likewise, ±3 MADs = ±2.4 standard deviations encompass 98% of the area, and so on for ±4 MADs.

EXAMPLE 16

Computing the
tracking signal
at Carlson Bakery

Carlson's Bakery wants to evaluate performance of its croissant forecast.

Approach: Develop a tracking signal for the forecast and see if it stays within acceptable limits, which we define as ±4 MADs.

Solution: Using the forecast and demand data for the last 6 quarters for croissant sales, we develop a tracking signal in the table below:

Quarter	Actual Demand	Forecast Demand	Error	RSFE	Absolute Forecast Error	Cumulative Absolute Forecast Error	MAD	Tracking Signal (RSFE/MAD)
1	90	100	−10	−10	10	10	10.0	−10/10 = −1
2	95	100	−5	−15	5	15	7.5	−15/7.5 = −2
3	115	100	+15	0	15	30	10.0	0/10 = 0
4	100	110	−10	−10	10	40	10.0	−10/10 = −1
5	125	110	+15	+5	15	55	11.0	+5/11 = +0.5
6	140	110	+30	+35	30	85	14.2	+35/14.2 = +2.5

$$\text{At the end of quarter 6, MAD} = \frac{\Sigma\,|\text{Forecast errors}|}{n} = \frac{85}{6} = 14.2$$

$$\text{and Tracking signal} = \frac{\text{RSFE}}{\text{MAD}} = \frac{35}{14.2} = 2.5 \text{ MADs}$$

Insight: Because the tracking signal drifted from −2 MAD to +2.5 MAD (between 1.6 and 2.0 standard deviations), we can conclude that it is within acceptable limits.

Learning exercise: If actual demand in quarter 6 was 130 (rather than 140), what would be the MAD and resulting tracking signal? [Answer: MAD for quarter 6 would be 12.5, and the tracking signal for period 6 would be 2 MADs.]

Related problems: 37, 45

Adaptive Smoothing

Adaptive forecasting refers to computer monitoring of tracking signals and self-adjustment if a signal passes a preset limit. For example, when applied to exponential smoothing, the α and β coefficients are first selected on the basis of values that minimize error forecasts and then adjusted accordingly whenever the computer notes an errant tracking signal. This process is called **adaptive smoothing**.

Adaptive smoothing
An approach to exponential smoothing forecasting in which the smoothing constant is automatically changed to keep errors to a minimum.

Focus Forecasting

Rather than adapt by choosing a smoothing constant, computers allow us to try a variety of forecasting models. Such an approach is called focus forecasting. **Focus forecasting** is based on two principles:

1. Sophisticated forecasting models are not always better than simple ones.
2. There is no single technique that should be used for all products or services.

Focus forecasting
Forecasting that tries a variety of computer models and selects the best one for a particular application.

Bernard Smith, inventory manager for American Hardware Supply, coined the term *focus forecasting*. Smith's job was to forecast quantities for 100,000 hardware products purchased by American's 21 buyers.[6] He found that buyers neither trusted nor understood the exponential smoothing model then in use. Instead, they used very simple approaches of their own. So Smith developed his new computerized system for selecting forecasting methods.

[6]Bernard T. Smith, *Focus Forecasting: Computer Techniques for Inventory Control* (Boston: CBI Publishing, 1978).

Smith chose seven forecasting methods to test. They ranged from the simple ones that buyers used (such as the naive approach) to statistical models. Every month, Smith applied the forecasts of all seven models to each item in stock. In these simulated trials, the forecast values were subtracted from the most recent actual demands, giving a simulated forecast error. The forecast method yielding the least error is selected by the computer, which then uses it to make next month's forecast. Although buyers still have an override capability, American Hardware finds that focus forecasting provides excellent results.

FORECASTING IN THE SERVICE SECTOR

Forecasting in the service sector presents some unusual challenges. A major technique in the retail sector is tracking demand by maintaining good short-term records. For instance, a barbershop catering to men expects peak flows on Fridays and Saturdays. Indeed, most barbershops are closed on Sunday and Monday, and many call in extra help on Friday and Saturday. A downtown restaurant, on the other hand, may need to track conventions and holidays for effective short-term forecasting. The *OM in Action* box "Forecasting at FedEx's Customer Service Center" provides an example of a major service-sector industry, the call center.

Specialty Retail Shops Specialty retail facilities, such as flower shops, may have other unusual demand patterns, and those patterns will differ depending on the holiday. When Valentine's Day falls on a weekend, for example, flowers can't be delivered to offices, and those romantically inclined are likely to celebrate with outings rather than flowers. If a holiday falls on a Monday, some of the celebration may also take place on the weekend, reducing flower sales. However, when Valentine's Day falls in midweek, busy midweek schedules often make flowers the optimal way to celebrate. Because flowers for Mother's Day are to be delivered on Saturday or Sunday, this holiday forecast varies less. Due to special demand patterns, many service firms maintain records of sales, noting not only the day of the week but also unusual events, including the weather, so that patterns and correlations that influence demand can be developed.

Fast-Food Restaurants Fast-food restaurants are well aware not only of weekly, daily, and hourly but even 15-minute variations in demands that influence sales. Therefore, detailed forecasts of demand are needed. Figure 12(a) shows the hourly forecast for a typical fast-food restau-

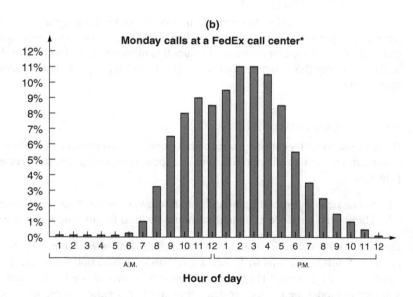

▲ **Figure 12** Forecasts Are Unique: Note the Variations Between (a) Hourly Sales at a Fast-Food Restaurant and (b) Hourly Call Volume at FedEx

*Based on historical data: see *Journal of Business Forecasting* (Winter 1999–2000): 6–11.

rant. Note the lunchtime and dinnertime peaks. This contrasts to the 10:30 A.M. and 4:30 P.M. peaks at FedEx's call center in Figure 12(b).

Firms like Taco Bell now use point-of-sale computers that track sales every quarter hour. Taco Bell found that a 6-week moving average was the forecasting technique that minimized its mean squared error (MSE) of these quarter-hour forecasts. Building this forecasting methodology into each of Taco Bell's 6,500 stores' computers, the model makes weekly projections of customer transactions. These in turn are used by store managers to schedule staff, who begin in 15-minute increments, not 1-hour blocks as in other industries. The forecasting model has been so successful that Taco Bell has increased customer service while documenting more than $50 million in labor cost savings in 4 years of use.[7]

Summary

Forecasts are a critical part of the operations manager's function. Demand forecasts drive a firm's production, capacity, and scheduling systems and affect the financial, marketing, and personnel planning functions.

There are a variety of qualitative and quantitative forecasting techniques. Qualitative approaches employ judgment, experience, intuition, and a host of other factors that are difficult to quantify. Quantitative forecasting uses historical data and causal, or associative, relations to project future demands. Table 2 summarizes the formulas we introduced in quantita-

tive forecasting. Forecast calculations are seldom performed by hand. Most operations managers turn to software packages such as Forecast PRO, SAP, tsMetrix, AFS, SAS, SPSS, or Excel.

No forecasting method is perfect under all conditions. And even once management has found a satisfactory approach, it must still monitor and control forecasts to make sure errors do not get out of hand. Forecasting can often be a very challenging, but rewarding, part of managing.

[7]J. Hueter and W. Swart, "An Integrated Labor Management System for Taco Bell," *Interfaces* 28, no. 1 (January-February 1998): 75–91.

▶ **Table 2**

Summary of Forecasting Formulas

Moving averages—forecasts based on an average of recent values

$$\text{Moving average} = \frac{\Sigma \text{ Demand in previous } n \text{ periods}}{n} \tag{1}$$

Weighted moving averages—a moving average with weights that vary

$$\text{Weighted moving average} = \frac{\Sigma \text{ (Weight for period } n)(\text{Demand in period } n)}{\Sigma \text{ Weights}} \tag{2}$$

Exponential smoothing—a moving average with weights following an exponential distribution

$$\text{New forecast} = \text{Last period's forecast} + \alpha \text{ (Last period's actual demand} - \text{Last period's forecast)} \tag{3}$$

$$F_t = F_{t-1} + \alpha(A_{t-1} - F_{t-1}) \tag{4}$$

Mean absolute deviation—a measure of overall forecast error

$$\text{MAD} = \Sigma \mid \text{Actual} - \text{Forecast} \mid /n = \frac{\Sigma \mid \text{Forecast Errors} \mid}{n} \tag{5}$$

Mean squared error—a second measure of forecast error

$$\text{MSE} = \frac{\Sigma(\text{Forecast errors})^2}{n} \tag{6}$$

Mean absolute percent error—a third measure of forecast error

$$\text{MAPE} = \frac{\sum_{i=1}^{n} 100 \mid \text{Actual}_i - \text{Forecast}_i \mid / \text{Actual}_i}{n} \tag{7}$$

Exponential smoothing with trend adjustment—an exponential smoothing model that can accommodate trend

$$\text{Forecast including trend}(FIT_t) = \text{Exponentially smoothed forecast}(F_t) + \text{Exponentially smoothed trend}(T_t) \tag{8}$$

$$F_t = \alpha(A_{t-1}) + (1 - \alpha)(F_{t-1} + T_{t-1}) \tag{9}$$

$$T_t = \beta(F_t - F_{t-1}) + (1 - \beta)T_{t-1} \tag{10}$$

Trend projection and regression analysis—fitting a trend line to historical data or a regression line to an independent variable

$$\hat{y} = a + bx \tag{11}$$

$$b = \frac{\Sigma xy - n\overline{x}\,\overline{y}}{\Sigma x^2 - n\overline{x}^2} \tag{12}$$

$$a = \overline{y} - b\overline{x} \tag{13}$$

Multiple regression analysis—a regression model with more than one independent (predicting) variable

$$\hat{y} = a + b_1 x_1 + b_2 x_2 + \quad + b_n x_n \tag{17}$$

Tracking signal—a measurement of how well the forecast is predicting actual values

$$\text{Tracking signal} = \frac{\text{RSFE}}{\text{MAD}} = \frac{\Sigma(\text{Actual demand in period } i - \text{Forecast demand in period } i)}{\text{MAD}} \tag{18}$$

Key Terms

Forecasting	Naive approach	Standard error of the estimate
Economic forecasts	Moving averages	Coefficient of correlation
Technological forecasts	Exponential smoothing	Coefficient of determination
Demand forecasts	Smoothing constant	Multiple regression
Quantitative forecasts	Mean absolute deviation (MAD)	Tracking signal
Qualitative forecasts	Mean squared error (MSE)	Bias
Jury of executive opinion	Mean absolute percent error (MAPE)	Adaptive smoothing
Delphi method	Trend projection	Focus forecasting
Sales force composite	Seasonal variations	
Consumer market survey	Cycles	
Time series	Linear-regression analysis	

Using Software in Forecasting

This section presents three ways to solve forecasting problems with computer software. First, you can create your own Excel spreadsheets to develop forecasts. Second, you can use the Excel OM software that comes with the text and is found on the student CD. Third, POM for Windows is another program that is located on the student CD.

Creating Your Own Excel Spreadsheets

Excel spreadsheets (and spreadsheets in general) are frequently used in forecasting. Exponential smoothing, trend analysis, and regression analysis (simple and multiple) are supported by built-in Excel functions.

Program 1 illustrates how to build an Excel forecast for the data in Example 8. The goal for N.Y. Edison is to create a trend analysis of the 2001–2007 data. Note that in cell D4 you can enter either = $B$16 + $B$17 * C4 *or* = TREND ($B$4: $B$10, $C$4:$C$10, C4).

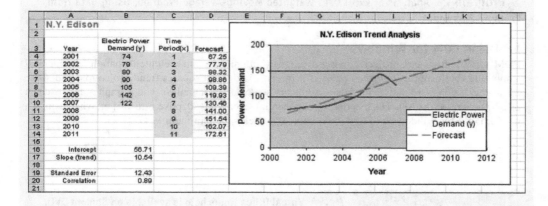

◄ **Program 1**

Using Excel to Develop Your Own Forecast with Data from Example 8

		Computations	
Value	**Cell**	**Excel Formula**	**Action**
Trend line column	D4	=$B$16+$B$17*C4	Copy to D5:D14
		(or =TREND($B$4:$B$10,$C$4:$C$10,C4))	
Intercept	B16	=INTERCEPT(B4:B10, C4:C10)	
Slope (trend)	B17	=SLOPE(B4:B10, C4:C10)	
Standard error	B19	=STEYX(B4:B10, C4:C10)	
Correlation	B20	=CORREL(B4:B10, C4:C10)	

As an alternative, you may want to experiment with Excel's built-in regression analysis. To do so, under the *Tools* menu bar selection choose *Data Analysis*, then *Regression*. Enter your *Y* and *X* data into two columns (say B and C). When the regression window appears, enter the *Y* and *X* ranges, then select *OK*. Excel offers several plots and tables to those interested in more rigorous analysis of regression problems.

X Using Excel OM

Excel OM's forecasting module has five components: (1) moving averages, (2) weighted moving averages, (3) exponential smoothing, (4) regression (with one variable only), and (5) decomposition. Excel OM's error analysis is much more complete than that available with the Excel add-in.

Program 2 illustrates Excel OM's input and output, using Example 2's weighted moving-average data.

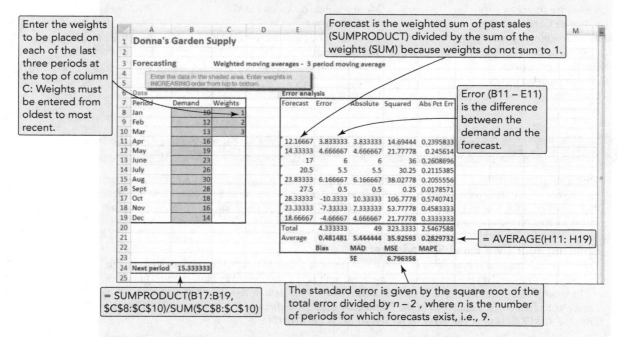

Enter the weights to be placed on each of the last three periods at the top of column C: Weights must be entered from oldest to most recent.

Forecast is the weighted sum of past sales (SUMPRODUCT) divided by the sum of the weights (SUM) because weights do not sum to 1.

Error (B11 – E11) is the difference between the demand and the forecast.

= SUMPRODUCT(B17:B19, $C$8:$C$10)/SUM($C$8:$C$10)

The standard error is given by the square root of the total error divided by $n - 2$, where n is the number of periods for which forecasts exist, i.e., 9.

= AVERAGE(H11: H19)

▲ **Program 2** Analysis of Excel OM's Weighted Moving-Average Program, Using Data from Example 2 as Input

P Using POM for Windows

POM for Windows can project moving averages (both simple and weighted), handle exponential smoothing (both simple and trend adjusted), forecast with least squares trend projection, and solve linear-regression (associative) models. A summary screen of error analysis and a graph of the data can also be generated. As a special example of exponential smoothing adaptive forecasting, when using an α of 0, POM for Windows will find the α value that yields the minimum MAD.

Solved Problems

Virtual Office Hours help is available on Student DVD.

Solved Problem 1

Sales of Volkswagen's popular Beetle have grown steadily at auto dealerships in Nevada during the past 5 years (see table below). The sales manager had predicted in 2002 that 2003 sales would be 410 VWs. Using exponential smoothing with a weight of $\alpha = .30$, develop forecasts for 2004 through 2008.

Year	Sales	Forecast
2003	450	410
2004	495	
2005	518	
2006	563	
2007	584	
2008	?	

solution

Year	Forecast
2003	410.0
2004	422.0 = 410 + .3 (450 – 410)
2005	443.9 = 422 + .3 (495 – 422)
2006	466.1 = 443.9 + .3 (518 – 443.9)
2007	495.2 = 466.1 + .3 (563 – 466.1)
2008	521.8 = 495.2 + .3 (584 – 495.2)

Solved Problem 2

In Example 7, we applied trend-adjusted exponential smoothing to forecast demand for a piece of pollution-control equipment for months 2 and 3 (out of 9 months of data provided). Let us now continue this process for month 4. We want to confirm the forecast for month 4 shown in Table 1 (p. 120) and Figure 3 (p. 120).

For month 4, $A_4 = 19$, with $\alpha = .2$, and $\beta = .4$

solution

$$F_4 = \alpha A_3 + (1-\alpha)(F_3 + T_3)$$
$$= (.2)(20) + (1-.2)(15.18 + 2.10)$$
$$= 4.0 + (.8)(17.28)$$
$$= 4.0 + 13.82$$
$$= 17.82$$
$$T_4 = \beta(F_4 - F_3) + (1-\beta)T_3$$
$$= (.4)(17.82 - 15.18) + (1-.4)(2.10)$$
$$= (.4)(2.64) + (.6)(2.10)$$
$$= 1.056 + 1.26$$
$$= 2.32$$
$$FIT_4 = 17.82 + 2.32$$
$$= 20.14$$

Solved Problem 3

Room registrations in the Toronto Towers Plaza Hotel have been recorded for the past 9 years. To project future occupancy, management would like to determine the mathematical trend of guest registration. This estimate will help the hotel determine whether future expansion will be needed. Given the following time-series data, develop a regression equation relating registrations to time (e.g., a trend equation). Then forecast 2009 registrations. Room registrations are in the thousands:

1999: 17   2000: 16   2001: 16   2002: 21   2003: 20
2004: 20   2005: 23   2006: 25   2007: 24

solution

Year	Transformed Year, x	Registrants, y (in thousands)	x^2	xy
1999	1	17	1	17
2000	2	16	4	32
2001	3	16	9	48
2002	4	21	16	84
2003	5	20	25	100
2004	6	20	36	120
2005	7	23	49	161
2006	8	25	64	200
2007	9	24	81	216
	$\Sigma x = 45$	$\Sigma y = 182$	$\Sigma x^2 = 285$	$\Sigma xy = 978$

$$b = \frac{\Sigma xy - n\bar{x}\bar{y}}{\Sigma x^2 = n\bar{x}^2} = \frac{978 - (9)(5)(20.22)}{285 - (9)(25)} = \frac{978 - 909.9}{285 - 225} = \frac{68.1}{60} = 1.135$$
$$a = \bar{y} - b\bar{x} = 20.22 - (1.135)(5) = 20.22 - 5.675 = 14.545$$
$$\hat{y}(\text{registrations}) = 14.545 + 1.135x$$

The projection of registrations in the year 2009 (which is $x = 11$ in the coding system used) is:

$$\hat{y} = 14.545 + (1.135)(11) = 27.03$$

or 27,030 guests in 2009

Solved Problem 4

Quarterly demand for Ford F150 pickups at a New York auto dealer is forecast with the equation:

$$\hat{y} = 10 + 3x$$

where x = quarters, and:

Quarter I of 2006	= 0
Quarter II of 2006	= 1
Quarter III of 2006	= 2
Quarter IV of 2006	= 3
Quarter I of 2007	= 4
	and so on

and:

$$\hat{y} = \text{quarterly demand}$$

The demand for trucks is seasonal, and the indices for Quarters I, II, III, and IV are 0.80, 1.00, 1.30, and 0.90, respectively. Forecast demand for each quarter of 2008. Then, seasonalize each forecast to adjust for quarterly variations.

solution

Quarter II of 2007 is coded $x = 5$; Quarter III of 2007, $x = 6$; and Quarter IV of 2007, $x = 7$. Hence, Quarter I of 2008 is coded $x = 8$; Quarter II, $x = 9$; and so on.

$$\hat{y}(2008 \text{ Quarter I}) = 10 + 3(8) = 34$$
$$\hat{y}(2008 \text{ Quarter II}) = 10 + 3(9) = 37$$
$$\hat{y}(2008 \text{ Quarter III}) = 10 + 3(10) = 40$$
$$\hat{y}(2008 \text{ Quarter IV}) = 10 + 3(11) = 43$$

Adjusted forecast = $(.80)(34) = 27.2$
Adjusted forecast = $(1.00)(37) = 37$
Adjusted forecast = $(1.30)(40) = 52$
Adjusted forecast = $(.90)(43) = 38.7$

Active Model Exercise

This active model, as well as the three others in this chapter, appears on your CD-ROM. It allows you to evaluate important elements of an exponential smoothing forecast.

▶ **Active Model 4.2**

Exponential Smoothing Using Data from Example 4

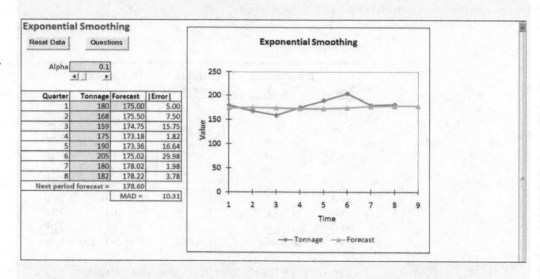

Questions

1. What happens to the graph when $\alpha = 0$?

2. What happens to the graph when $\alpha = 1$?

3. Generalize what happens to a forecast as alpha increases.

4. At what level of alpha is the mean absolute deviation (MAD) minimized?

Self-Test

- **Before taking the self-test**, refer to the learning objectives at the beginning of the chapter, the notes in the margins, and the glossary at the end of the selection.
- Use the key at the back of the selection to **correct** your answers.
- **Restudy** pages that correspond to any questions you answered incorrectly or material you feel uncertain about.

1. Forecasting time horizons include:
   a) long range
   b) medium range
   c) short range
   d) all of the above

2. Quantitative methods of forecasting include:
   a) sales force composite
   b) jury of executive opinion
   c) consumer market survey
   d) exponential smoothing
   e) all are quantitative methods

3. The method that considers the relationship between data and the variable being predicted is:
   a) exponential smoothing
   b) associative forecasting
   c) weighted moving average
   d) all of the above

4. Three popular measures of forecast accuracy are:
   a) total error, average error, and mean error
   b) average error, median error, and maximum error
   c) median error, minimum error, and maximum absolute error
   d) mean absolute error, mean squared error, and mean absolute percent error

5. In exponential smoothing, when the smoothing constant is high:
   a) more weight is placed on the more recent data
   b) less weight is placed on the more recent data
   c) the forecast will be a high number
   d) the forecast is a number between −1 and +1

6. With regard to a regression-based forecast, the *standard error of the estimate* gives a measure of:
   a) the overall accuracy of the forecast
   b) the time period for which the forecast is valid
   c) the time required to derive the forecast equation
   d) the maximum error of the forecast
   e) all of the above

7. The main difference between simple and multiple regression is _____.

8. The difference between a *moving average* model and an *exponential smoothing* model is that _____.

9. The purpose of drawing a scatter diagram is to _____.

Internet and Student CD-ROM/DVD Exercises

Visit our Companion Web site or use your student CD-ROM/DVD to help with material in this chapter.

 On Our Companion Web Site,
www.prenhall.com/heizer
- Self-Study Quizzes
- Practice Problems
- Virtual Company Tour
- Internet Case
- PowerPoint Lecture

On Your Student CD-ROM
- Practice Problems
- Active Model Exercises
- Excel OM
- Excel OM Data Files
- POM for Windows

On Your Student DVD
- Video Clip and Video Case
- Virtual Office Hours for Solved Problems

Discussion Questions

1. What is a qualitative forecasting model, and when is its use appropriate?
2. Identify and briefly describe the two general forecasting approaches.
3. Identify the three forecasting time horizons. State an approximate duration for each.
4. Briefly describe the steps that are used to develop a forecasting system.
5. A skeptical manager asks what medium-range forecasts can be used for. Give the manager three possible uses/purposes.
6. Explain why such forecasting devices as moving averages, weighted moving averages, and exponential smoothing are not well suited for data series that have trends.
7. What is the basic difference between a weighted moving average and exponential smoothing?

8. What three methods are used to determine the accuracy of any given forecasting method? How would you determine whether time-series regression or exponential smoothing is better in a specific application?
9. Research and briefly describe the Delphi technique. How would it be used by an employer you have worked for?
10. What is the primary difference between a time-series model and an associative model?
11. Define time series.
12. What effect does the value of the smoothing constant have on the weight given to the recent values?
13. Explain the value of seasonal indices in forecasting. How are seasonal patterns different from cyclical patterns?
14. Which forecasting technique can place the most emphasis on recent values? How does it do this?

15. In your own words, explain adaptive forecasting.
16. What is the purpose of a tracking signal?
17. Explain, in your own words, the meaning of the correlation coefficient. Discuss the meaning of a negative value of the correlation coefficient.
18. What is the difference between a dependent and an independent variable?

19. Give examples of industries that are affected by seasonality. Why would these businesses want to filter out seasonality?
20. Give examples of industries in which demand forecasting is dependent on the demand for other products.
21. What happens to the ability to forecast for periods farther into the future?

Ethical Dilemma

In 2006, the board of regents responsible for all public higher education funding in a large Midwestern state hired a consultant to develop a series of enrollment forecasting models, one for each college. These models used historical data and exponential smoothing to forecast the following year's enrollments. Based on the model, which included a smoothing constant (α) for each school, each college's budget was set by the board. The head of the board personally selected each smoothing constant, based on what she called her "gut reactions and political acumen."

What do you think the advantages and disadvantages of this system are? Answer from the perspective of (a) the board of regents and (b) the president of each college. How can this model be abused and what can be done to remove any biases? How can a *regression model* be used to produce results that favor one forecast over another?

Problems*

• **1** The following gives the number of pints of type A blood used at Woodlawn Hospital in the past 6 weeks:

Week Of	Pints Used
August 31	360
September 7	389
September 14	410
September 21	381
September 28	368
October 5	374

a) Forecast the demand for the week of October 12 using a 3-week moving average.
b) Use a 3-week weighted moving average, with weights of .1, .3, and .6, using .6 for the most recent week. Forecast demand for the week of October 12.
c) Compute the forecast for the week of October 12 using exponential smoothing with a forecast for August 31 of 360 and $\alpha = .2$. **Px**

•• **2**

Year	1	2	3	4	5	6	7	8	9	10	11
Demand	7	9	5	9	13	8	12	13	9	11	7

a) Plot the above data on a graph. Do you observe any trend, cycles, or random variations?
b) Starting in year 4 and going to year 12, forecast demand using a 3-year moving average. Plot your forecast on the same graph as the original data.
c) Starting in year 4 and going to year 12, forecast demand using a 3-year moving average with weights of .1, .3, and .6, using .6 for the most recent year. Plot this forecast on the same graph.
d) As you compare forecasts with the original data, which seems to give the better results? **Px**

Note: **Px** means the problem may be solved with POM for Windows and/or Excel OM.

• **3** Refer to Problem 2. Develop a forecast for years 2 through 12 using exponential smoothing with $\alpha = .4$ and a forecast for year 1 of 6. Plot your new forecast on a graph with the actual data and the naive forecast. Based on a visual inspection, which forecast is better? **Px**

• **4** A check-processing center uses exponential smoothing to forecast the number of incoming checks each month. The number of checks received in June was 40 million, while the forecast was 42 million. A smoothing constant of .2 is used.
a) What is the forecast for July?
b) If the center received 45 million checks in July, what would be the forecast for August?
c) Why might this be an inappropriate forecasting method for this situation? **Px**

•• **5** The Carbondale Hospital is considering the purchase of a new ambulance. The decision will rest partly on the anticipated mileage to be driven next year. The miles driven during the past 5 years are as follows:

Year	Mileage
1	3,000
2	4,000
3	3,400
4	3,800
5	3,700

a) Forecast the mileage for next year using a 2-year moving average.
b) Find the MAD based on the 2-year moving average forecast in part (a). (Hint: You will have only 3 years of matched data.)
c) Use a weighted 2-year moving average with weights of .4 and .6 to forecast next year's mileage. (The weight of .6 is for the most recent year.) What MAD results from using this approach to forecasting? (Hint: You will have only 3 years of matched data.)
d) Compute the forecast for year 6 using exponential smoothing, an initial forecast for year 1 of 3,000 miles, and $\alpha = .5$. **Px**

•• **6** The monthly sales for Telco Batteries, Inc., were as follows:

Month	Sales
January	20
February	21
March	15
April	14
May	13
June	16
July	17
August	18
September	20
October	20
November	21
December	23

a) Plot the monthly sales data.
b) Forecast January sales using each of the following:
   i) Naive method.
   ii) A 3-month moving average.
   iii) A 6-month weighted average using .1, .1, .1, .2, .2, and .3, with the heaviest weights applied to the most recent months.
   iv) Exponential smoothing using an $\alpha = .3$ and a September forecast of 18.
   v) A trend projection.
c) With the data given, which method would allow you to forecast next March's sales? PX

• **7** The actual demand for the patients at Omaha Emergency Medical Clinic for the first six weeks of this year follows:

Week	Actual No. of Patients
1	65
2	62
3	70
4	48
5	63
6	52

Clinic administrator Marc Schniederjans wants you to forecast patient demand at the clinic for week 7 by using this data. You decide to use a weighted moving average method to find this forecast. Your method uses four actual demand levels, with weights of 0.333 on the present period, 0.25 one period ago, 0.25 two periods ago, and 0.167 three periods ago.

What is the value of your forecast? PX

• **8** Daily high temperatures in St. Louis for the last week were as follows: 93, 94, 93, 95, 96, 88, 90 (yesterday).
a) Forecast the high temperature today, using a 3-day moving average.
b) Forecast the high temperature today, using a 2-day moving average.
c) Calculate the mean absolute deviation based on a 2-day moving average.
d) Compute the mean squared error for the 2-day moving average.
e) Calculate the mean absolute percent error for the 2-day moving average. PX

••• **9** Dell uses the CR5 chip in some of its laptop computers. The prices for the chip during the last 12 months were as follows:

Month	Price per Chip	Month	Price per Chip
January	$1.80	July	1.80
February	1.67	August	1.83
March	1.70	September	1.70
April	1.85	October	1.65
May	1.90	November	1.70
June	1.87	December	1.75

a) Use a 2-month moving average on all the data and plot the averages and the prices.
b) Use a 3-month moving average and add the 3-month plot to the graph created in part (a).
c) Which is better (using the mean absolute deviation): the 2-month average or the 3-month average?
d) Compute the forecasts for each month using exponential smoothing, with an initial forecast for January of $1.80. Use $\alpha = .1$, then $\alpha = .3$, and finally $\alpha = .5$. Using MAD, which α is the best? PX

•• **10** Data collected on the yearly registrations for a Six Sigma seminar at the Quality College are shown in the following table:

Year	1	2	3	4	5	6	7	8	9	10	11
Registrations (000)	4	6	4	5	10	8	7	9	12	14	15

a) Develop a 3-year moving average to forecast registrations from year 4 to year 12.
b) Estimate demand again for years 4 to 12 with a 3-year weighted moving average in which registrations in the most recent year are given a weight of 2, and registrations in the other 2 years are each given a weight of 1.
c) Graph the original data and the two forecasts. Which of the two forecasting methods seems better? PX

• **11** a) Use exponential smoothing with a smoothing constant of 0.3 to forecast the registrations at the seminar given in Problem 10. To begin the procedure, assume that the forecast for year 1 was 5,000 people signing up.

b) What is the MAD? PX

•• **12** Consider the following actual and forecast demand levels for Big Mac hamburgers at a local McDonald's restaurant:

Day	Actual Demand	Forecast Demand
Monday	88	88
Tuesday	72	88
Wednesday	68	84
Thursday	48	80
Friday		

The forecast for Monday was derived by observing Monday's demand level and setting Monday's forecast level equal to this demand level. Subsequent forecasts were derived by using exponential smoothing with a smoothing constant of 0.25. Using this exponential smoothing method, what is the forecast for Big Mac demand for Friday? PX

••• **13** As you can see in the following table, demand for heart transplant surgery at Washington General Hospital has increased steadily in the past few years:

Year	1	2	3	4	5	6
Heart Transplants	45	50	52	56	58	?

The director of medical services predicted 6 years ago that demand in year 1 would be 41 surgeries.

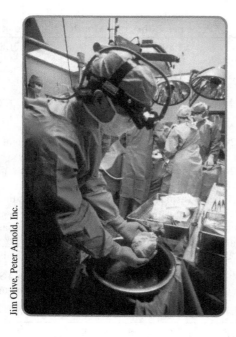

Jim Olive, Peter Arnold, Inc.

a) Use exponential smoothing, first with a smoothing constant of .6 and then with one of .9, to develop forecasts for years 2 through 6.
b) Use a 3-year moving average to forecast demand in years 4, 5, and 6.
c) Use the trend-projection method to forecast demand in years 1 through 6.
d) With MAD as the criterion, which of the four forecasting methods is best? **Px**

•• **14** Following are two weekly forecasts made by two different methods for the number of gallons of gasoline, in thousands, demanded at a local gasoline station. Also shown are actual demand levels, in thousands of gallons:

	Forecasts		
Week	Method 1	Method 2	Actual Demand
1	0.90	0.80	0.70
2	1.05	1.20	1.00
3	0.95	0.90	1.00
4	1.20	1.11	1.00

What are the MAD and MSE for each method?

• **15** Refer to Solved Problem 1 on page 139. Use a 3-year moving average to forecast the sales of Volkswagen Beetles in Nevada through 2008. What is the MAD? **Px**

• **16** Refer to Solved Problem 1. Using the trend projection method, develop a forecast for the sales of Volkswagen Beetles in Nevada through 2008. What is the MAD? **Px**

• **17** Refer to Solved Problem 1. Using smoothing constants of .6 and .9, develop forecasts for the sales of VW Beetles. What effect did the smoothing constant have on the forecast? Use MAD to determine which of the three smoothing constants (.3, .6, or .9) gives the most accurate forecast. **Px**

•••• **18** Consider the following actual (A_t) and forecast (F_t) demand levels for a product:

Time Period t	Actual Demand A_t	Forecast Demand F_t
1	50	50
2	42	50
3	56	48
4	46	50
5		

The first forecast, F_1, was derived by observing A_1 and setting F_1 equal to A_1. Subsequent forecasts were derived by exponential smoothing. Using the exponential smoothing method, find the forecast for time period 5. (Hint: You need to first find the smoothing constant, α.)

••• **19** Income at the law firm of Smith and Wesson for the period February to July was as follows:

Month	February	March	April	May	June	July
Income (in $ thousand)	70.0	68.5	64.8	71.7	71.3	72.8

Use trend-adjusted exponential smoothing to forecast the law firm's August income. Assume that the initial forecast for February is $65,000 and the initial trend adjustment is 0. The smoothing constants selected are $\alpha = .1$ and $\beta = .2$. **Px**

••• **20** Resolve Problem 19 with $\alpha = .1$ and $\beta = .8$. Using MSE, determine which smoothing constants provide a better forecast. **Px**

• **21** Refer to the trend-adjusted exponential smoothing illustration in Example 7. Using $\alpha = .2$ and $\beta = .4$, we forecast sales for 9 months, showing the detailed calculations for months 2 and 3. In Solved Problem 2, we continued the process for month 4.
In this problem, show your calculations for months 5 and 6 for F_t, T_t, and FIT_t. **Px**

• **22** Refer to Problem 21. Complete the trend-adjusted exponential-smoothing forecast computations for periods 7, 8, and 9. Confirm that your numbers for F_t, T_t, and FIT_t match those in Table 1. **Px**

•• **23** Sales of vegetable dehydrators at Bud Banis's discount department store in St. Louis over the past year are shown below. Management prepared a forecast using a combination of exponential smoothing and its collective judgment for the 4 months (March, April, May, and June of 2007):

Month	2006–2007 Unit Sales	Management's Forecast
July	100	
August	93	
September	96	
October	110	
November	124	
December	119	
January	92	
February	83	
March	101	120
April	96	114
May	89	110
June	108	108

a) Compute MAD and MAPE for management's technique.
b) Do management's results outperform (i.e., have smaller MAD and MAPE than) a naive forecast?
c) Which forecast do you recommend, based on lower forecast error?

•• 24 Howard Weiss, owner of a musical instrument distributorship, thinks that demand for bass drums may be related to the number of television appearances by the popular group Stone Temple Pilots during the previous month. Weiss has collected the data shown in the following table:

Demand for Bass Drums	3	6	7	5	10	7
Stone Temple Pilots' TV Appearances	3	4	7	6	8	5

a) Graph these data to see whether a linear equation might describe the relationship between the group's television shows and bass drum sales.
b) Use the least-squares regression method to derive a forecasting equation.
c) What is your estimate for bass drum sales if the Stone Temple Pilots performed on TV nine times last month?
d) What are the correlation coefficient (r) and the coefficient of determination (r^2) for this model, and what do they mean? **Px**

• 25 The following gives the number of accidents that occurred on Florida State Highway 101 during the last 4 months:

Month	Number of Accidents
January	30
February	40
March	60
April	90

Forecast the number of accidents that will occur in May, using least-squares regression to derive a trend equation. **Px**

• 26 In the past, Arup Mukherjee's tire dealership in Pensacola sold an average of 1,000 radials each year. In the past 2 years, 200 and 250, respectively, were sold in fall, 350 and 300 in winter, 150 and 165 in spring, and 300 and 285 in summer. With a major expansion planned, Mukherjee projects sales next year to increase to 1,200 radials. What will be the demand during each season?

•• 27 Mark Cotteleer owns a company that manufactures sailboats. Actual demand for Mark's sailboats during each season in 2004 through 2007 was as follows:

	Year			
Season	2004	2005	2006	2007
Winter	1,400	1,200	1,000	900
Spring	1,500	1,400	1,600	1,500
Summer	1,000	2,100	2,000	1,900
Fall	600	750	650	500

Mark has forecasted that annual demand for his sailboats in 2009 will equal 5,600 sailboats. Based on this data and the multiplicative seasonal model, what will the demand level be for Mark's sailboats in the spring of 2009?

•• 28 Attendance at Los Angeles's newest Disneylike attraction, Vacation World, has been as follows:

Quarter	Guests (in thousands)	Quarter	Guests (in thousands)
Winter '05	73	Summer '06	124
Spring '05	104	Fall '06	52
Summer '05	168	Winter '07	89
Fall '05	74	Spring '07	146
Winter '06	65	Summer '07	205
Spring '06	82	Fall '07	98

Compute seasonal indices using all of the data. **Px**

• 29 Central States Electric Company estimates its demand trend line (in millions of kilowatt hours) to be:

$$D = 77 + 0.43Q$$

where Q refers to the sequential quarter number and $Q = 1$ for winter 1984. In addition, the multiplicative seasonal factors are as follows:

Quarter	Factor (Index)
Winter	.8
Spring	1.1
Summer	1.4
Fall	.7

Forecast energy use for the four quarters of 2009, beginning with winter.

• 30 Brian Buckley has developed the following forecasting model:

$$\hat{y} = 36 + 4.3x$$

where $\hat{y}$ = demand for Aztec air conditioners and
         x = the outside temperature (°F)

a) Forecast demand for the Aztec when the temperature is 70°F.
b) What is demand when the temperature is 80°F?
c) What is demand when the temperature is 90°F? **Px**

•• 31 Coffee Palace's manager, Joe Felan, suspects that demand for mocha latte coffees depends on the price being charged. Based on historical observations, Joe has gathered the following data, which show the numbers of these coffees sold over six different price values:

Price	Number Sold
$2.70	760
$3.50	510
$2.00	980
$4.20	250
$3.10	320
$4.05	480

Using these data, how many mocha latte coffees would be forecast to be sold according to simple linear regression if the price per cup were $1.80? **Px**

101

• **32** The following data relate the sales figures of the bar in Marty and Polly Starr's small bed-and-breakfast inn in Marathon, Florida, to the number of guests registered that week:

Week	Guests	Bar Sales
1	16	$330
2	12	270
3	18	380
4	14	300

a) Perform a linear regression that relates bar sales to guests (not to time).
b) If the forecast is for 20 guests next week, what are the sales expected to be? **Px**

• **33** The number of transistors (in millions) made at a plant in Japan during the past 5 years follows:

Year	Transistors
1	140
2	160
3	190
4	200
5	210

a) Forecast the number of transistors to be made next year, using linear regression.
b) Compute the mean squared error (MSE) when using linear regression.
c) Compute the mean absolute percent error (MAPE). **Px**

• **34** The number of auto accidents in a certain region is related to the regional number of registered automobiles in thousands (X_1), alcoholic beverage sales in $10,000s (X_2), and rainfall in inches (X_3). Furthermore, the regression formula has been calculated as:

$$Y = a + b_1X_1 + b_2X_2 + b_3X_3$$

where Y = number of automobile accidents
$a = 7.5$
$b_1 = 3.5$
$b_2 = 4.5$
$b_3 = 2.5$

Calculate the expected number of automobile accidents under conditions a, b, and c:

	X_1	X_2	X_3
(a)	2	3	0
(b)	3	5	1
(c)	4	7	2

Px

•• **35** John Howard, a Mobile, Alabama, real estate developer, has devised a regression model to help determine residential housing prices in South Alabama. The model was developed using recent sales in a particular neighborhood. The price (Y) of the house is based on the size (square footage = X) of the house. The model is:

$$Y = 13,473 + 37.65X$$

The coefficient of correlation for the model is 0.63.
a) Use the model to predict the selling price of a house that is 1,860 square feet.

b) An 1,860-square-foot house recently sold for $95,000. Explain why this is not what the model predicted.
c) If you were going to use multiple regression to develop such a model, what other quantitative variables might you include?
d) What is the value of the coefficient of determination in this problem? **Px**

• **36** Accountants at the firm Michael Vest, CPAs, believed that several traveling executives were submitting unusually high travel vouchers when they returned from business trips. First, they took a sample of 200 vouchers submitted from the past year. Then they developed the following multiple-regression equation relating expected travel cost to number of days on the road (x_1) and distance traveled (x_2) in miles:

$$\hat{y} = \$90.00 + \$48.50x_1 + \$.40x_2$$

The coefficient of correlation computed was .68.
a) If Wanda Fennell returns from a 300-mile trip that took her out of town for 5 days, what is the expected amount she should claim as expenses?
b) Fennell submitted a reimbursement request for $685. What should the accountant do?
c) Should any other variables be included? Which ones? Why? **P**

•• **37** Sales of music stands at Johnny Ho's music store in Columbus, Ohio, over the past 10 weeks are shown in the table below. Forecast demand for each week, including week 10, using exponential smoothing with $\alpha = .5$ (initial forecast = 20):

Week	Demand	Week	Demand
1	20	6	29
2	21	7	36
3	28	8	22
4	37	9	25
5	25	10	28

a) Compute the MAD.
b) Compute the tracking signal. **Px**

•• **38** City government has collected the following data on annual sales tax collections and new car registrations:

Annual Sales Tax Collections (in millions)	1.0	1.4	1.9	2.0	1.8	2.1	2.3
New Car Registrations (in thousands)	10	12	15	16	14	17	20

Determine the following:
a) The least-squares regression equation.
b) Using the results of part (a), find the estimated sales tax collections if new car registrations total 22,000.
c) The coefficients of correlation and determination. **Px**

•• **39** Dr. Susan Sweeney, a Providence psychologist, specializes in treating patients who are agoraphobic (i.e., afraid to leave their homes). The following table indicates how many patients Dr. Sweeney has seen each year for the past 10 years. It also indicates what the robbery rate was in Providence during the same year:

Year	1	2	3	4	5	6	7	8	9	10
Number of Patients	36	33	40	41	40	55	60	54	58	61
Robbery Rate per 1,000 Population	58.3	61.1	73.4	75.7	81.1	89.0	101.1	94.8	103.3	116.2

Using trend analysis, predict the number of patients Dr. Sweeney will see in years 11 and 12. How well does the model fit the data? **Px**

• •   40   Using the data in Problem 39, apply linear regression to study the relationship between the robbery rate and Dr. Sweeney's patient load. If the robbery rate increases to 131.2 in year 11, how many phobic patients will Dr. Sweeney treat? If the robbery rate drops to 90.6, what is the patient projection? **Px**

• • •   41   Bus and subway ridership for the summer months in London, England, is believed to be tied heavily to the number of tourists visiting the city. During the past 12 years, the following data have been obtained:

Year (summer months)	Number of Tourists (in millions)	Ridership (in millions)
1	7	1.5
2	2	1.0
3	6	1.3
4	4	1.5
5	14	2.5
6	15	2.7
7	16	2.4
8	12	2.0
9	14	2.7
10	20	4.4
11	15	3.4
12	7	1.7

a) Plot these data and decide if a linear model is reasonable.
b) Develop a regression relationship.
c) What is expected ridership if 10 million tourists visit London in a year?
d) Explain the predicted ridership if there are no tourists at all.
e) What is the standard error of the estimate?
f) What is the model's correlation coefficient and coefficient of determination? **Px**

Alan Copson, **Photolibrary.com**.

• • •   42   Des Moines Power and Light has been collecting data on demand for electric power in its western subregion for only the past 2 years. Those data are shown in the following table:

Demand in Megawatts		
Month	Last Year	This Year
January	5	17
February	6	14
March	10	20
April	13	23
May	18	30
June	15	38
July	23	44
August	26	41
September	21	33
October	15	23
November	12	26
December	14	17

To plan for expansion and to arrange to borrow power from neighboring utilities during peak periods, the utility needs to be able to forecast demand for each month next year. However, the standard forecasting models discussed in this chapter will not fit the data observed for the 2 years.
a) What are the weaknesses of the standard forecasting techniques as applied to this set of data?
b) Because known models are not appropriate here, propose your own approach to forecasting. Although there is no perfect solution to tackling data such as these (in other words, there are no 100% right or wrong answers), justify your model.
c) Forecast demand for each month next year using the model you propose.

• • •   43   Emergency calls to the 911 system of Gainesville, Florida, for the past 24 weeks are shown in the following table:

Week	1	2	3	4	5	6	7	8	9	10	11	12
Calls	50	35	25	40	45	35	20	30	35	20	15	40
Week	13	14	15	16	17	18	19	20	21	22	23	24
Calls	55	35	25	55	55	40	35	60	75	50	40	65

a) Compute the exponentially smoothed forecast of calls for each week. Assume an initial forecast of 50 calls in the first week, and use $\alpha = .2$. What is the forecast for week 25?
b) Reforecast each period using $\alpha = .6$.
c) Actual calls during week 25 were 85. Which smoothing constant provides a superior forecast? Explain and justify the measure of error you used. **Px**

• • •   44   Using the 911 call data in Problem 43, forecast calls for weeks 2 through 25 with a trend-adjusted exponential smoothing model. Assume an initial forecast for 50 calls for week 1 and an initial trend of zero. Use smoothing constants of $\alpha = .3$ and $\beta = .2$. Is this model better than that of Problem 43? What adjustment might be useful for further improvement? (Again, assume that actual calls in week 25 were 85.) **Px**

• • •   45   The following are monthly actual and forecast demand levels for May through December for units of a product manufactured by the N. Tamimi Pharmaceutical Company:

Month	Actual Demand	Forecast Demand
May	100	100
June	80	104
July	110	99
August	115	101
September	105	104
October	110	104
November	125	105
December	120	109

What is the value of the tracking signal as of the end of December?

•• 46 Thirteen students entered the business program at Hillcrest College 2 years ago. The following table indicates what each student scored on the high school SAT math exam and their grade-point averages (GPAs) after students were in the Hillcrest program for 2 years.

a) Is there a meaningful relationship between SAT math scores and grades?
b) If a student scores a 350, what do you think his or her GPA will be?
c) What about a student who scores 800?

Student	A	B	C	D	E	F	G
SAT Score	421	377	585	690	608	390	415
GPA	2.90	2.93	3.00	3.45	3.66	2.88	2.15
Student	H	I	J	K	L	M	
SAT Score	481	729	501	613	709	366	
GPA	2.53	3.22	1.99	2.75	3.90	1.60	PX

••• 47 City Cycles has just started selling the new Z-10 mountain bike, with monthly sales as shown in the table. First, co-owner Amit wants to forecast by exponential smoothing by initially setting February's forecast equal to January's sales with $\alpha = .1$. Co-owner, Barbara wants to use a three-period moving average.

	Sales	Amit	Barbara	Amit's Error	Barbara's Error
January	400	—			
February	380	400			
March	410				
April	375				
May					

a) Is there a strong linear trend in sales over time?
b) Fill in the table with what Amit and Barbara each forecast for May and the earlier months, as relevant.
c) Assume that May's actual sales figure turns out to be 405. Complete the table's columns and then calculate the mean absolute deviation for both Amit's and Barbara's methods.
d) Based on these calculations, which method seems more accurate? PX

•• 48 Sundar Balakrishnan, the general manager of Precision Engineering Corporation (PEC), thinks that his firm's engineering services contracted to highway construction firms are directly related to the volume of highway construction business contracted with companies in his geographic area. He wonders if this is really so, and if it is, can this information help him plan his operations better by forecasting the quantity of his engineering services required by construction firms in each quarter of the year? The following table presents the sales of his services and total amounts of contracts for highway construction over the last 8 quarters:

Quarter	1	2	3	4	5	6	7	8
Sales of PEC Services (in $ thousands)	8	10	15	9	12	13	12	16
Contracts Released (in $ thousands)	153	172	197	178	185	199	205	226

a) Using this data, develop a regression equation for predicting the level of demand of Precision's services.
b) Determine the coefficient of correlation and the standard error of the estimate. PX

••••49 Salinas Savings and Loan is proud of its long tradition in Topeka, Kansas. Begun by Teresita Salinas 18 years after World War II, the S&L has bucked the trend of financial and liquidity problems that has plagued the industry since 1985. Deposits have increased slowly but surely over the years, despite recessions in 1983, 1988, 1991, and 2001. Ms. Salinas believes it is necessary to have a long-range strategic plan for her firm, including a 1-year forecast and preferably even a 5-year forecast of deposits. She examines the past deposit data and also peruses Kansas's gross state product (GSP), over the same 44 years. (GSP is analogous to gross national product [GNP] but on the state level.) The resulting data are in the following table:

Year	Deposits[a]	GSP[b]	Year	Deposits[a]	GSP[b]
1964	.25	.4	1986	6.2	2.5
1965	.24	.4	1987	4.1	2.8
1966	.24	.5	1988	4.5	2.9
1967	.26	.7	1989	6.1	3.4
1968	.25	.9	1990	7.7	3.8
1969	.30	1.0	1991	10.1	4.1
1970	.31	1.4	1992	15.2	4.0
1971	.32	1.7	1993	18.1	4.0
1972	.24	1.3	1994	24.1	3.9
1973	.26	1.2	1995	25.6	3.8
1974	.25	1.1	1996	30.3	3.8
1975	.33	.9	1997	36.0	3.7
1976	.50	1.2	1998	31.1	4.1
1977	.95	1.2	1999	31.7	4.1
1978	1.70	1.2	2000	38.5	4.0
1979	2.3	1.6	2001	47.9	4.5
1980	2.8	1.5	2002	49.1	4.6
1981	2.8	1.6	2003	55.8	4.5
1982	2.7	1.7	2004	70.1	4.6
1983	3.9	1.9	2005	70.9	4.6
1984	4.9	1.9	2006	79.1	4.7
1985	5.3	2.3	2007	94.0	5.0

[a]In $ millions.
[b]In $ billions.

a) Using exponential smoothing, with $\alpha = .6$, then trend analysis, and finally linear regression, discuss which forecasting model fits best for Salinas's strategic plan. Justify the selection of one model over another.
b) Carefully examine the data. Can you make a case for excluding a portion of the information? Why? Would that change your choice of model? PX

Case Studies

Southwestern University: (B)*

Southwestern University (SWU), a large state college in Stephenville, Texas, enrolls close to 20,000 students. The school is a dominant force in the small city, with more students during fall and spring than permanent residents.

Always a football powerhouse, SWU is usually in the top 20 in college football rankings. Since the legendary Bo Pitterno was hired as its head coach in 2001 (in hopes of reaching the elusive number 1 ranking), attendance at the five Saturday home games each year increased. Prior to Pitterno's arrival, attendance generally averaged 25,000 to 29,000 per game. Season ticket sales bumped up by 10,000 just with the announcement of the new coach's arrival. Stephenville and SWU were ready to move to the big time!

The immediate issue facing SWU, however, was not NCAA ranking. It was capacity. The existing SWU stadium, built in 1953, has seating for 54,000 fans. The following table indicates attendance at each game for the past 6 years.

One of Pitterno's demands upon joining SWU had been a stadium expansion, or possibly even a new stadium. With attendance increasing, SWU administrators began to face the issue head-on. Pitterno had wanted dormitories solely for his athletes in the stadium as an additional feature of any expansion.

SWU's president, Dr. Joel Wisner, decided it was time for his vice president of development to forecast when the existing stadium would "max out." The expansion was, in his mind, a given. But Wisner needed to know how long he could wait. He also sought a revenue projection, assuming an average ticket price of $20 in 2008 and a 5% increase each year in future prices.

Discussion Questions

1. Develop a forecasting model, justifying its selection over other techniques, and project attendance through 2009.
2. What revenues are to be expected in 2008 and 2009?
3. Discuss the school's options.

*This integrated case study runs throughout the text. Other issues facing Southwestern's football stadium include (A) managing the stadium project; (C) quality of facilities; (D) break-even analysis of food services (Supplement 7 web site); (E) locating the new stadium; (F) inventory planning of football programs; and (G) scheduling of campus security officers/staff for game days.

Southwestern University Football Game Attendance, 2002–2007

Game	*2002* Attendees	Opponent	*2003* Attendees	Opponent	*2004* Attendees	Opponent
1	34,200	Baylor	36,100	Oklahoma	35,900	TCU
2[a]	39,800	Texas	40,200	Nebraska	46,500	Texas Tech
3	38,200	LSU	39,100	UCLA	43,100	Alaska
4[b]	26,900	Arkansas	25,300	Nevada	27,900	Arizona
5	35,100	USC	36,200	Ohio State	39,200	Rice

Game	*2005* Attendees	Opponent	*2006* Attendees	Opponent	*2007* Attendees	Opponent
1	41,900	Arkansas	42,500	Indiana	46,900	LSU
2[a]	46,100	Missouri	48,200	North Texas	50,100	Texas
3	43,900	Florida	44,200	Texas A&M	45,900	Prairie View A&M
4[b]	30,100	Miami	33,900	Southern	36,300	Montana
5	40,500	Duke	47,800	Oklahoma	49,900	Arizona State

[a]Homecoming games.

[b]During the 4th week of each season, Stephenville hosted a hugely popular southwestern crafts festival. This event brought tens of thousands of tourists to the town, especially on weekends, and had an obvious negative impact on game attendance.

Digital Cell Phone, Inc.

Paul Jordan has just been hired as a management analyst at Digital Cell Phone, Inc. Digital Cell manufactures a broad line of phones for the consumer market. Paul's boss, John Smithers, chief operations officer, has asked Paul to stop by his office this morning. After a brief exchange of pleasantries over a cup of coffee, he says he has a special assignment for Paul: "We've always just made an educated guess about how many phones we need to make each month. Usually we just look at how many we sold last month and plan to produce about the same number. This sometimes works fine. But most months we either have too many phones in inventory or we are out of stock. Neither situation is good."

Handing Paul the table shown here, Smithers continues, "Here are our actual orders entered for the past 36 months. There are 144 phones per case. I was hoping that since you graduated recently from the University of Alaska, you might have studied some techniques that would help us plan better. It's been awhile since I was in college—I think I forgot most of the details I learned then. I'd like you to analyze these data and give me an idea of what our business will look like over the next 6 to 12 months. Do you think you can handle this?"

"Of course," Paul replies, sounding more confident than he really is. "How much time do I have?"

"I need your report on the Monday before Thanksgiving—that would be November 20th. I plan to take it home with me and read it during the holiday. Since I'm sure you will not be around during the holiday, be sure that you explain things carefully so that I can understand your recommendation without having to ask you any more questions. Since you are new to the company, you should know that I like to see all the details and complete justification for recommendations from my staff."

With that, Paul was dismissed. Arriving back at his office, he began his analysis.

Orders Received by Month

Month	Cases 2005	Cases 2006	Cases 2007
January	480	575	608
February	436	527	597
March	482	540	612
April	448	502	603
May	458	508	628
June	489	573	605
July	498	508	627
August	430	498	578
September	444	485	585
October	496	526	581
November	487	552	632
December	525	587	656

Discussion Question

1. Prepare Paul Jordan's report to John Smithers using regression analysis. Provide a summary of the cell phone industry outlook as part of Paul's response.
2. Adding seasonality into your model, how does the analysis change?

Source: Professor Victor E. Sower, Sam Houston State University.

Forecasting at Hard Rock Cafe

Video Case

With the growth of Hard Rock Cafe—from one pub in London in 1971 to more than 110 restaurants in more than 40 countries today—came a corporatewide demand for better forecasting. Hard Rock uses long-range forecasting in setting a capacity plan and intermediate-term forecasting for locking in contracts for leather goods (used in jackets) and for such food items as beef, chicken, and pork. Its short-term sales forecasts are conducted each month, by cafe, and then aggregated for a headquarters view.

The heart of the sales forecasting system is the point-of-sale system (POS), which, in effect, captures transaction data on nearly every person who walks through a cafe's door. The sale of each entrée represents one customer; the entrée sales data are transmitted daily to the Orlando corporate headquarters' database. There, the financial team, headed by Todd Lindsey, begins the forecast process. Lindsey forecasts monthly guest counts, retail sales, banquet sales, and concert sales (if applicable) at each cafe. The general managers of individual cafes tap into the same database to prepare a daily forecast for their sites. A cafe manager pulls up prior years' sales for that day, adding information from the local Chamber of Commerce or Tourist Board on upcoming events such as a major convention, sporting event, or concert in the city where the cafe is located. The daily forecast is further broken into hourly sales, which drives employee scheduling. An hourly forecast of $5,500 in sales translates into 19 workstations, which are further broken down into a specific number of wait staff, hosts, bartenders, and kitchen staff. Computerized scheduling software plugs in people based on their availability. Variances between forecast and actual sales are then examined to see why errors occurred.

Hard Rock doesn't limit its use of forecasting tools to sales. To evaluate managers and set bonuses, a 3-year weighted moving average is applied to cafe sales. If cafe general managers exceed their targets, a bonus is computed. Todd Lindsey, at corporate headquarters, applies weights of 40% to the most recent year's sales, 40% to the year before, and 20% to sales 2 years ago in reaching his moving average.

An even more sophisticated application of statistics is found in Hard Rock's menu planning. Using multiple regression, managers can compute the impact on demand of other menu items if the price of one item is changed. For example, if the price of a cheeseburger increases from $7.99 to $8.99, Hard Rock can predict the effect this will have on sales of chicken sandwiches, pork sandwiches, and salads. Managers do the same analysis on menu placement, with the center section driving higher sales volumes. When an item such as a hamburger is moved off the center to one of the side flaps, the corresponding effect on related items, say french fries, is determined.

Hard Rock's Moscow Cafe[a]

Month	1	2	3	4	5	6	7	8	9	10
Guest count (in thousands)	21	24	27	32	29	37	43	43	54	66
Advertising (in $ thousand)	14	17	25	25	35	35	45	50	60	60

[a]These figures are used for purposes of this case study.

Discussion Questions*

1. Describe three different forecasting applications at Hard Rock. Name three other areas in which you think Hard Rock could use forecasting models.
2. What is the role of the POS system in forecasting at Hard Rock?

3. Justify the use of the weighting system used for evaluating managers for annual bonuses.
4. Name several variables besides those mentioned in the case that could be used as good predictors of daily sales in each cafe.
5. At Hard Rock's Moscow restaurant, the manager is trying to evaluate how a new advertising campaign affects guest counts.

Using data for the past 10 months (see the table) develop a least squares regression relationship and then forecast the expected guest count when advertising is $65,000.

*You may wish to review this video case on your DVD before answering these questions.

Additional Case Studies

Internet Case Study: Visit our Companion Web site at www.prenhall.com/heizer *for this free case study:*

- **North–South Airline:** Reflects the merger of two airlines and addresses their maintenance costs.

Harvard has selected these Harvard Business School case studies to accompany this chapter:

harvardbusinessonline.hbsp.harvard.edu

- **Merchandising at Nine West Retail Stores** (# 698-098): This large retail shoe store chain faces a merchandising decision.
- **New Technologies, New Markets: The Launch of Hong Kong Telecom's Video-on-Demand** (# HKU-011): Asks students to examine the forecasting behind a new technology.
- **Sport Obermeyer Ltd.** (# 695-022): This skiwear company has short-life-cycle products with uncertain demand and a globally dispersed supply chain.
- **L.L. Bean, Inc.** (# 893-003): L.L. Bean must forecast and manage thousands of inventory items sold through its catalogs.

Bibliography

Balakrishnan, R., B. Render, and R. M. Stair. *Managerial Decision Modeling with Spreadsheets*, 2nd ed. Upper Saddle River, NJ: Prentice Hall, 2007.

Berenson, Mark, Tim Krehbiel, and David Levine. *Basic Business Statistics*, 10th ed. Upper Saddle River, NJ: Prentice Hall, 2006.

Diebold, F. X. *Elements of Forecasting*, 4th ed. Cincinnati: Southwestern College Publishing, 2007.

Georgoff, D. M., and R. G. Murdick. "Manager's Guide to Forecasting." *Harvard Business Review* 64 (January–February 1986): 110–120.

Gilliland, M. "Is Forecasting a Waste of Time?" *Supply Chain Management Review* 1 (July 2002).

Gilliland, M., and M. Leonard. "Forecasting Software—The Past and the Future." *The Journal of Business Forecasting* 25, no. 1 (Spring 2006): 33–36.

Hanke, J. E., A. G. Reitsch, and D. W. Wichern. *Business Forecasting*, 9th ed. Upper Saddle River, NJ: Prentice Hall, 2007.

Heizer, Jay. "Forecasting with Stagger Charts." *IIE Solutions* 34 (June 2002): 46–49.

Jain, C. L. "Benchmarking Forecasting Models." *The Journal of Business Forecasting* 24, no. 4 (Winter 2005/2006): 9–11.

Lapide, Larry. "Evolution of the Forecasting Function." *The Journal of Business Forecasting* 25, no. 1 (Spring 2006): 22–24.

Meade, Nigel. "Evidence for the Selection of Forecasting Models." *Journal of Forecasting* 19, no. 6 (November 2000): 515–535.

Portougal, V. "Demand Forecast for a Catalog Retailing Company." *Production and Inventory Management Journal* (first–second quarter 2002): 29–34.

Render, B., R. M. Stair, and M. Hanna. *Quantitative Analysis for Management*, 9th ed. Upper Saddle River, NJ: Prentice Hall, 2006.

Sanders, N. R., and K. B. Manrodt. "Forecasting Software in Practice." *Interfaces* 33 (September–October 2003): 90–93.

Snyder, Ralph D., and Roland G. Shami. "Exponential Smoothing of Seasonal Data." *Journal of Forecasting* 20, no. 3 (April 2001): 197–202.

Wilson, J. H., B. Keating, and J. Galt. *Business Forecasting with Forecast X Software.* New York: McGraw-Hill, 2007.

Internet Resources

American Statistical Association: **www.amstat.org**
Institute of Business Forecasting: **www.ibf.org**
International Institute of Forecasters: **www.forecasters.org**

Journal of Time Series Analysis: **www.blackwellpublishers.co.uk**
Royal Statistical Society: **www.rss.org.uk**

Solutions to Even Numbered Problems

2 **(a)** None obvious.
　　(b) 7, 7.67, 9, 10, 11, 11, 11.33, 11, 9
　　(c) 6.4, 7.8, 11, 9.6, 10.9, 12.2, 10.5, 10.6, 8.4
　　(d) The 3-yr. moving average.
4 **(a)** 41.6
　　(b) 42.3
　　(c) Banking industry's seasonality.
6 **(b)** Naive = 23; 3-mo. moving = 21.33; 6-mo. weighted = 20.6; trend = 20.67
　　(c) Trend projection.
8 **(a)** 91.3
　　(b) 89
　　(c) MAD = 2.7
　　(d) MSE = 13.35
　　(e) MAPE = 2.99%
10 **(a)** 4.67, 5.00, 6.33, 7.67, 8.33, 8.00, 9.33, 11.67, 13.7
　　(b) 4.50, 5.00, 7.25, 7.75, 8.00, 8.25, 10.00, 12.25, 14.0
　　(c) Forecasts are about the same.
12 72
14 Method 1: MAD = .5; MSE = .085
　　Method 2: MAD = .51; MSE = .0721
16 $y = 421 + 33.6x$. When $x = 6$, $y = 622.8$.
18 49
20 $\alpha = .1$, $\beta = .8$, August forecast = \$71,303; MSE = 12.7 for $\beta = .8$ vs. MSE = 18.87 for $\beta = .2$ in Problem 4.19.
22 Confirm that you match the numbers in Table 1.
24 **(a)** Observations do not form a straight line but do cluster about one.
　　(b) $y = .676 + 1.03x$
　　(c) 10 drums
　　(d) $r^2 = .68$; $r = .825$
26 270, 390, 189, 351 for fall, winter, spring, and summer, respectively.

28 Index is 0.709, winter; 1.037, spring; 1.553, summer; 0.700, fall.
30 **(a)** 337
　　(b) 380
　　(c) 423
32 **(a)** $y = 50 + 18x$
　　(b) \$410
34 **(a)** 28
　　(b) 43
　　(c) 58
36 **(a)** \$452.50
　　(b) Request is higher than predicted, so seek additional documentation.
　　(c) Include other variables (such as a destination cost index) to try to increase r and r^2.
38 **(a)** $y = -.158 + .1308x$
　　(b) 2.719
　　(c) $r = .966$; $r^2 = .934$
40 131.2 → 72.7 patients; 90.6 → 50.6 patients
42 **(a)** They need more data and must be able to address seasonal *and* trend factors.
　　(b) Try to create your own naive model because seasonality is strong.
　　(c) Compute and graph your forecast.
44 Trend adjustment does not appear to give any significant improvement.
46 **(a)** $y = 1.03 + .0034x$, $r^2 = .479$
　　(b) For $x = 350$; $Y = 2.22$
　　(c) For $x = 800$; $Y = 3.75$
　　（Some rounding may occur, depending on software.)
48 **(a)** Sales (y) = $-9.349 + .1121$ (contracts)
　　(b) $r = .8963$; $S_{xy} = 1.3408$

Solutions to Self Test

1. d; **2.** d; **3.** b; **4.** d; **5.** a; **6.** a; **7.** simple regression has only one independent variable; **8.** exponential smoothing is a weighted moving average model in which all prior values are weighted with a set of exponentially declining weight; **9.** spot relationships between two variables.

Managing Quality

Outline

Ten OM Strategy Decisions

Design of Goods and Services

Managing Quality

Process Strategy

Location Strategies

Layout Strategies

Human Resources

Supply Chain Management

Inventory Management

Scheduling

Maintenance

Learning Objectives

When you complete this selection you should be able to

1. Define quality and TQM
2. Describe the ISO international quality standards
3. Explain Six Sigma
4. Explain how benchmarking is used

5. Explain quality robust products and Taguchi concepts
6. Use the seven tools of TQM

Global Company Profile: Arnold Palmer Hospital

Managing Quality Provides a Competitive Advantage at Arnold Palmer Hospital

Since 1989, the Arnold Palmer Hospital, named after its famous golfing benefactor, has touched the lives of over 7 million children and women and their families. Its patients come not only from its Orlando location but from all 50 states and around the world. More than 13,000 babies are delivered every year at Arnold Palmer, and its huge neonatal intensive care unit boasts one of the highest survival rates in the U.S.

Every hospital professes quality health care, but at Arnold Palmer quality is the mantra—practiced in a fashion like the Ritz-Carlton practices it in the hotel industry. The hospital typically scores in the top 10% of national benchmark studies in terms of patient satisfaction. And its managers follow patient questionnaire results daily. If anything is amiss, corrective action takes place immediately.

Virtually every quality management technique we present in this chapter is employed at Arnold Palmer Hospital:

- *Continuous improvement:* The hospital constantly seeks new ways to lower infection rates, readmission rates, deaths, costs, and hospital stay times.
- *Employee empowerment:* When employees see a problem, they are trained to take care of it. Just like at the Ritz, staff are empowered to give gifts to patients displeased with some aspect of service.
- *Benchmarking:* The hospital belongs to a 2,000-member organization that monitors standards in many areas and provides monthly feedback to the hospital.
- *Just-in-time:* Supplies are delivered to Arnold Palmer on a JIT basis. This keeps inventory costs low and keeps quality problems from hiding.

▼ *The lobby of Arnold Palmer Hospital, with its 20-foot-high Genie, is clearly intended as a warm and friendly place for children.*

▼ *The Storkboard is a visible chart of the status of each baby about to be delivered, so all nurses and doctors are kept up-to-date at a glance.*

Jonathan Bailey Associates

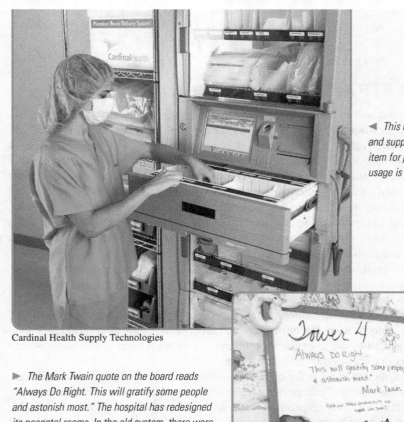

Cardinal Health Supply Technologies

◀ This PYXIS inventory station gives nurses quick access to medicines and supplies needed in their departments. When the nurse removes an item for patient use, the item is automatically billed to that account, and usage is noted at the main supply area.

▶ The Mark Twain quote on the board reads "Always Do Right. This will gratify some people and astonish most." The hospital has redesigned its neonatal rooms. In the old system, there were 16 neonatal beds in an often noisy and large room. The new rooms are semiprivate, with a quiet simulated-night atmosphere. These rooms have proven to help babies develop and improve more quickly.

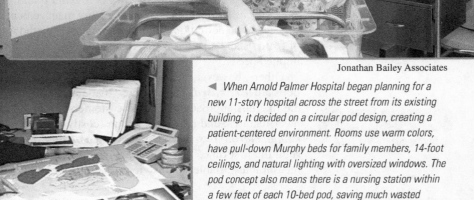

Jonathan Bailey Associates

Jonathan Bailey Associates

◀ When Arnold Palmer Hospital began planning for a new 11-story hospital across the street from its existing building, it decided on a circular pod design, creating a patient-centered environment. Rooms use warm colors, have pull-down Murphy beds for family members, 14-foot ceilings, and natural lighting with oversized windows. The pod concept also means there is a nursing station within a few feet of each 10-bed pod, saving much wasted walking time by nurses to reach the patient. The Video Case Study in next Chapter examines this layout in detail.

- *Tools such as Pareto charts and flowcharts:* These tools monitor processes and help the staff graphically spot problem areas and suggest ways they can be improved.

From their first day of orientation, employees from janitors to nurses learn that the patient comes first. Staff standing in hallways will never be heard discussing their personal lives or commenting on confidential issues of health care. This culture of quality at Arnold Palmer Hospital makes a hospital visit, often traumatic to children and their parents, a warmer and more comforting experience.

111

QUALITY AND STRATEGY

As Arnold Palmer Hospital and many other organizations have found, quality is a wonderful tonic for improving operations. Managing quality helps build successful strategies of *differentiation*, *low cost*, and *response*. For instance, defining customer quality expectations has helped Bose Corp. successfully *differentiate* its stereo speakers as among the best in the world. Nucor has learned to produce quality steel at *low cost* by developing efficient processes that produce consistent quality. And Dell Computers rapidly *responds* to customer orders because quality systems, with little rework, have allowed it to achieve rapid throughput in its plants. Indeed, quality may be the critical success factor for these firms just as it is at Arnold Palmer Hospital.

As Figure 1 suggests, improvements in quality help firms increase sales and reduce costs, both of which can increase profitability. Increases in sales often occur as firms speed response, lower selling prices as a result of economies of scale, and improve their reputation for quality products. Similarly, improved quality allows costs to drop as firms increase productivity and lower rework, scrap, and warranty costs. One study found that companies with the highest quality were five times as productive (as measured by units produced per labor-hour) as companies with the poorest quality. Indeed, when the implications of an organization's long-term costs and the potential for increased sales are considered, total costs may well be at a minimum when 100% of the goods or services are perfect and defect free.

Quality, or the lack of quality, affects the entire organization from supplier to customer and from product design to maintenance. Perhaps more importantly, *building* an organization that can achieve quality also affects the entire organization—and it is a demanding task. Figure 2 lays out the flow of activities for an organization to use to achieve total quality management (TQM). A successful quality strategy begins with an organizational environment that fosters quality, followed by an understanding of the principles of quality, and then an effort to engage employees in the necessary activities to implement quality. When these things are done well, the organization typically satisfies its customers and obtains a competitive advantage. The ultimate goal is to win customers. Because quality causes so many other good things to happen, it is a great place to start.

DEFINING QUALITY

The operations manager's objective is to build a total quality management system that identifies and satisfies customer needs. Total quality management takes care of the customer. Consequently, we accept the definition of **quality** as adopted by the American Society for Quality: "The totality of features and characteristics of a product or service that bears on its ability to satisfy stated or implied needs."[1]

Others, however, believe that definitions of quality fall into several categories. Some definitions are *user based*. They propose that quality "lies in the eyes of the beholder." Marketing people like this approach and so do customers. To them, higher quality means better performance, nicer features, and other (sometimes costly) improvements. To production managers, quality is *manufacturing based*. They believe that quality means conforming to standards and "making it right the first time." Yet a third approach is *product based*, which views quality as a precise and measurable variable. In this view, for example, really good ice cream has high butterfat levels.

Quality
The ability of a product or service to meet customer needs.

▶ **Figure 1**

Ways Quality Improves Profitability

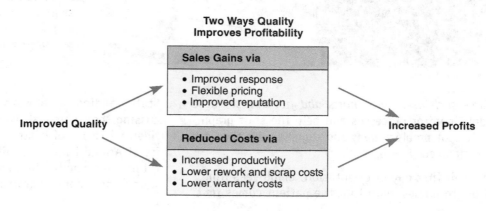

Two Ways Quality Improves Profitability

Improved Quality →

Sales Gains via
- Improved response
- Flexible pricing
- Improved reputation

Reduced Costs via
- Increased productivity
- Lower rework and scrap costs
- Lower warranty costs

→ Increased Profits

[1]See the American Society for Quality Web site, at **www.asq.org**.

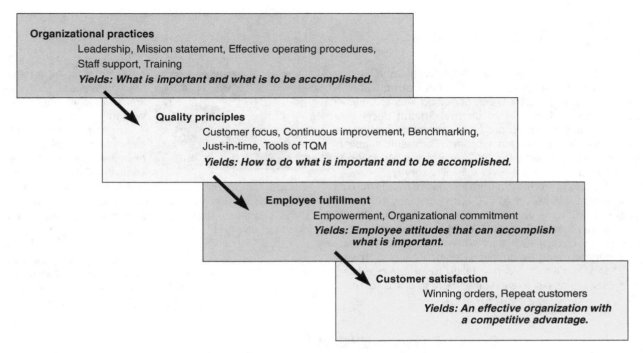

▲ Figure 2 The Flow of Activities that Are Necessary to Achieve Total Quality Management

This text develops approaches and techniques to address all three categories of quality. The characteristics that connote quality must first be identified through research (a user-based approach to quality). These characteristics are then translated into specific product attributes (a product-based approach to quality). Then, the manufacturing process is organized to ensure that products are made precisely to specifications (a manufacturing-based approach to quality). A process that ignores any one of these steps will not result in a quality product.

Quality may be in the eyes of the beholder, but to create a good or a service, operations managers must define what the beholder (the consumer) expects.

Implications of Quality

In addition to being a critical element in operations, quality has other implications. Here are three other reasons why quality is important:

1. *Company reputation:* An organization can expect its reputation for quality—be it good or bad—to follow it. Quality will show up in perceptions about the firm's new products, employment practices, and supplier relations. Self-promotion is not a substitute for quality products.
2. *Product liability:* The courts increasingly hold organizations that design, produce, or distribute faulty products or services liable for damages or injuries resulting from their use. Legislation such as the Consumer Product Safety Act sets and enforces product standards by banning products that do not reach those standards. Impure foods that cause illness, nightgowns that burn, tires that fall apart, or auto fuel tanks that explode on impact can all lead to huge legal expenses, large settlements or losses, and terrible publicity.
3. *Global implications:* In this technological age, quality is an international, as well as OM, concern. For both a company and a country to compete effectively in the global economy, products must meet global quality, design, and price expectations. Inferior products harm a firm's profitability and a nation's balance of payments.

Malcolm Baldrige National Quality Award

The global implications of quality are so important that the U.S. has established the *Malcolm Baldrige National Quality Award* for quality achievement. The award is named for former Secretary of Commerce Malcolm Baldrige. Winners include such firms as Motorola, Milliken, Xerox, FedEx, Ritz-Carlton Hotels, AT&T, Cadillac, and Texas Instruments.

The Japanese have a similar award, the Deming Prize, named after an American, Dr. W. Edwards Deming.

For further information regarding the Baldrige Award and its 1,000-point scoring system, visit www.quality.nist.gov.

The Very High Cost of Quality at Mercedes

Perhaps it was Mercedes's merger with Chrysler that first diverted management's attention from quality. Or perhaps it was the $4.7 billion operating loss at Chrysler in 2001. But Mercedes made the difficult decision—squeeze costs to pump out better corporate profits and demand lower prices from suppliers. The result: suppliers cut corners on quality. By 2003, Mercedes had fallen to the bottom of the J.D. Power reliability survey.

Mercedes is still reeling from a series of recalls from its $50,000 E-Class sedan. In 2004, the company suffered a spate of problems with brake control systems; 680,000 cars were recalled. Then in 2005, Mercedes announced the biggest recall in its history—1.3 million cars with faulty fuel pumps made by supplier Robert Bosch. Software problems and interfaces that failed to let complex electronics systems talk to each other were to blame for many

Koichi Kamoshida/Liaison, Getty Images

Mercedes E-Class on fire in Tokyo.

other defects. All totaled, Mercedes spent $600 million in one year to cover warranty costs.

The cost of the quality fiasco takes a toll in sales, of course, as well. Market shares in the U.S. and Europe are down. And rival BMW has just overtaken Mercedes as the world's number-one luxury carmaker. BMW's strategy: build only premium quality cars . . . and don't get diverted.

Sources: Business Week (August 15, 2005): 31–38; *Motor Trend* (November 2005): 4; *The Wall Street Journal* (January 30, 2006): B4; and *Automotive News* (May 2, 2005): 3.

Cost of Quality (COQ)

Cost of quality (COQ)
The cost of doing things wrong—that is, the price of nonconformance.

Four major categories of costs are associated with quality. Called the **cost of quality (COQ)**, they are:

- *Prevention costs:* costs associated with reducing the potential for defective parts or services (e.g., training, quality improvement programs).
- *Appraisal costs:* costs related to evaluating products, processes, parts, and services (e.g., testing, labs, inspectors).
- *Internal failure:* costs that result from production of defective parts or services before delivery to customers (e.g., rework, scrap, downtime).
- *External costs:* costs that occur after delivery of defective parts or services (e.g., rework, returned goods, liabilities, lost goodwill, costs to society).

The first three costs can be reasonably estimated, but external costs are very hard to quantify. When GE had to recall 3.1 million dishwashers recently (because of a defective switch alleged to have started seven fires), the cost of repairs exceeded the value of all the machines. This leads to the belief by many experts that the cost of poor quality is consistently underestimated. The *OM in Action* box "The Very High Cost of Quality at Mercedes" certainly reinforces that point.

Observers of quality management believe that, on balance, the cost of quality products is only a fraction of the benefits. They think the real losers are organizations that fail to work aggressively at quality. For instance, Philip Crosby stated that quality is free. "What costs money are the unquality things—all the actions that involve not doing it right the first time."[2]

TAKUMI

Takumi is a Japanese character that symbolizes a broader dimension than quality, a deeper process than education, and a more perfect method than persistence.

Leaders in Quality Besides Crosby there are several other giants in the field of quality management, including Deming, Feigenbaum, and Juran. Table 1 summarizes their philosophies and contributions.

Ethics and Quality Management

For operations managers, one of the most important jobs is to deliver healthy, safe, and quality products and services to customers. The development of poor-quality products, because of inadequate design and production processes, results not only in higher production costs but also leads to injuries, lawsuits, and increased government regulation.

[2]Philip B. Crosby, *Quality Is Free* (New York: McGraw-Hill, 1979). Further, J. M. Juran states, in his book *Juran on Quality by Design* (The Free Press 1992, p. 119), that costs of poor quality "are huge, but the amounts are not known with precision. In most companies the accounting system provides only a minority of the information needed to quantify this cost of poor quality. It takes a great deal of time and effort to extend the accounting system so as to provide full coverage."

▼ **Table 1** Leaders in the Field of Quality Management

Leader	Philosophy/Contribution
W. Edwards Deming	Deming insisted management accept responsibility for building good systems. The employee cannot produce products that on average exceed the quality of what the process is capable of producing. His 14 points for implementing quality improvement are presented in this chapter.
Joseph M. Juran	A pioneer in teaching the Japanese how to improve quality, Juran believes strongly in top-management commitment, support, and involvement in the quality effort. He is also a believer in teams that continually seek to raise quality standards. Juran varies from Deming somewhat in focusing on the customer and defining quality as fitness for use, not necessarily the written specifications.
Armand Feigenbaum	His 1961 book, *Total Quality Control*, laid out 40 steps to quality improvement processes. He viewed quality not as a set of tools but as a total field that integrated the processes of a company. His work in how people learn from each other's successes led to the field of cross-functional teamwork.
Philip B. Crosby	*Quality is Free* was Crosby's attention-getting book published in 1979. Crosby believed that in the traditional trade-off between the cost of improving quality and the cost of poor quality, the cost of poor quality is understated. The cost of poor quality should include all of the things that are involved in not doing the job right the first time. Crosby coined the term *zero defects* and stated, "There is absolutely no reason for having errors or defects in any product or service."

If a firm believes that it has introduced a questionable product, ethical conduct must dictate the responsible action. This may be a worldwide recall, as conducted by both Johnson & Johnson (for Tylenol) and Perrier (for sparkling water), when each of these products was found to be contaminated. A manufacturer must accept responsibility for any poor-quality product released to the public. Neither Ford (the Explorer SUV maker) nor Firestone (the radial tire maker) did this. In recent years, both firms have been accused of failing to issue product recalls, of withholding damaging information, and of handling complaints on an individual basis.[3]

High-quality products and services are the most profitable.

There are many stakeholders involved in the production and marketing of poor-quality products, including stockholders, employees, customers, suppliers, distributors, and creditors. As a matter of ethics, management must ask if any of these stakeholders are being wronged. Every company needs to develop core values that become day-to-day guidelines for everyone from the CEO to production-line employees.

◄ *The ISO 9000 Certified sign is up, but this Bridgestone/Firestone plant in Decatur, Illinois, produced millions of defective tires that resulted in thousands of accidents and 271 deaths. After lying before Congress, the firm was forced to admit that the Firestone 500 radial had 17.5% return rates (vs. 2.9% for competitor Goodyear). Before the investigation became public knowledge, Firestone held a half-price clearance sale of defective tires in the Southeast U.S. Congress later discovered that Firestone continued to manufacture the 500 radial tire after claiming it had stopped production. This case of unethical conduct eventually resulted in the recall of 14.4 million tires and cost Bridgestone/Firestone hundreds of millions of dollars.*

Tim Boyle, Getty Images, Inc.—Liasion

[3]For further reading, see M. R. Nayebpour and D. Koehn, "The Ethics of Quality: Problems and Preconditions" *Journal of Business Ethics* 44 (April, 2003): 37–48.

INTERNATIONAL QUALITY STANDARDS

ISO 9000

ISO 9000

A set of quality standards developed by the International Organization for Standardization (ISO).

Quality is so important globally that the world is uniting around a single quality standard, **ISO 9000**. ISO 9000 is the only quality standard with international recognition. In 1987, 91 member nations (including the U.S.) published a series of quality assurance standards, known collectively as ISO 9000. The U.S., through the American National Standards Institute, has adopted the ISO 9000 series as the ANSI/ASQ Q9000 series.[4] The focus of the standards is to establish quality management procedures, through leadership, detailed documentation, work instructions, and recordkeeping. These procedures, we should note, say nothing about the actual quality of the product—they deal entirely with standards to be followed.

"ISO" is Greek for equal or uniform, as in uniform throughout the world.

To become ISO 9000 certified, organizations go through a 9- to 18-month process that involves documenting quality procedures, an on-site assessment, and an ongoing series of audits of their products or services. To do business globally—and especially in Europe—being listed in the ISO directory is critical. As of 2007, there were well over 600,000 certifications awarded to firms in 158 countries. About 50,000 U.S. firms are ISO 9000 certified.

Visit the Web sites www.iso.ch and www.asq.org to learn more about ISO standards.

ISO revised its standards in 2000 into more of a quality management system, which is detailed in its ISO 9001: 2000 component. Leadership by top management and customer requirements and satisfaction play a much larger role, while documented procedures receive less emphasis under ISO 9001: 2000.

Learning Objective

2. Describe the ISO international quality standards

ISO 14000

The continuing internationalization of quality is evident with the development of **ISO 14000**. ISO 14000 is an environmental management standard that contains five core elements: (1) environmental management, (2) auditing, (3) performance evaluation, (4) labeling, and (5) life cycle assessment. The new standard could have several advantages:

ISO 14000

An environmental management standard established by the International Organization for Standardization (ISO).

- Positive public image and reduced exposure to liability.
- Good systematic approach to pollution prevention through the minimization of ecological impact of products and activities.
- Compliance with regulatory requirements and opportunities for competitive advantage.
- Reduction in need for multiple audits.

This standard is being accepted worldwide.

TOTAL QUALITY MANAGEMENT

Total quality management (TQM)

Management of an entire organization so that it excels in all aspects of products and services that are important to the customer.

Total quality management (TQM) refers to a quality emphasis that encompasses the entire organization, from supplier to customer. TQM stresses a commitment by management to have a continuing companywide drive toward excellence in all aspects of products and services that are important to the customer.

TQM is important because quality decisions influence each of the 10 decisions made by operations managers. Each of those 10 decisions deals with some aspect of identifying and meeting customer expectations. Meeting those expectations requires an emphasis on TQM if a firm is to compete as a leader in world markets.

Quality expert W. Edwards Deming used 14 points (see Table 2) to indicate how he implemented TQM. We develop these into seven concepts for an effective TQM program: (1) continuous improvement, (2) Six Sigma, (3) employee empowerment, (4) benchmarking, (5) just-in-time (JIT), (6) Taguchi concepts, and (7) knowledge of TQM tools.

Continuous Improvement

Respect for people is a cornerstone of continuous improvement.

Total quality management requires a never-ending process of continuous improvement that covers people, equipment, suppliers, materials, and procedures. The basis of the philosophy is that every aspect of an operation can be improved. The end goal is perfection, which is never achieved but always sought.

---

[4]ASQ is the American Society for Quality.

1. Create consistency of purpose.
2. Lead to promote change.
3. Build quality into the product; stop depending on inspections to catch problems.
4. Build long-term relationships based on performance instead of awarding business on the basis of price.
5. Continuously improve product, quality, and service.
6. Start training.
7. Emphasize leadership.
8. Drive out fear.
9. Break down barriers between departments.
10. Stop haranguing workers.
11. Support, help, and improve.
12. Remove barriers to pride in work.
13. Institute a vigorous program of education and self-improvement.
14. Put everybody in the company to work on the transformation.

Source: Deming revised his 14 points a number of times over the years. See J. Spigener and P. J. Angelo, "What Would Deming Say?" *Quality Progress* (March 2001): 61–65.

◄ **Table 2**

Deming's 14 Points for Implementing Quality Improvement

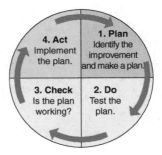

▲ **Figure 3**   **PDCA Cycle**

PDCA
A continuous improvement model of plan, do, check. act.

Plan-Do-Check-Act   Walter Shewhart, another pioneer in quality management, developed a circular model known as **PDCA** (plan, do, check, act) as his version of continuous improvement. Deming later took this concept to Japan during his work there after World War II. The PDCA cycle is shown in Figure 3 as a circle to stress the continuous nature of the improvement process.

The Japanese use the word *kaizen* to describe this ongoing process of unending improvement—the setting and achieving of ever-higher goals. In the U.S., *TQM* and *zero defects* are also used to describe continuous improvement efforts. But whether it's PDCA, *kaizen*, TQM, or zero defects, the operations manager is a key player in building a work culture that endorses continuous improvement.

Six Sigma

The term **Six Sigma**, popularized by Motorola, Honeywell, and General Electric, has two meanings in TQM. In a *statistical* sense, it describes a process, product, or service with an extremely high capability (99.9997% accuracy). For example, if 1 million passengers pass through the St. Louis Airport with checked baggage each month, a Six Sigma program for baggage handling will result in only 3.4 passengers with misplaced luggage. The more common three-sigma program (which we address in the supplement to this chapter) would result in 2,700 passengers with misplaced bags every month. See Figure 4.

The second TQM definition of Six Sigma is a program designed to reduce defects to help lower costs, save time, and improve customer satisfaction. Six Sigma is a comprehensive system—a strategy, a discipline, and a set of tools—for achieving and sustaining business success:

- It is a *strategy* because it focuses on total customer satisfaction.
- It is a *discipline* because it follows the formal Six Sigma Improvement Model known as **DMAIC**. This five-step process improvement model (1) **Defines** the project's purpose, scope, and outputs and then identifies the required process information, keeping in mind the customer's definition of quality; (2) **Measures** the process and collects data; (3) **Analyzes** the data, ensuring repeatability (the results can be duplicated), and reproducibility (others get the

Six Sigma
A program to save time, improve quality, and lower costs.

Learning Objective
3. Explain what Six Sigma is

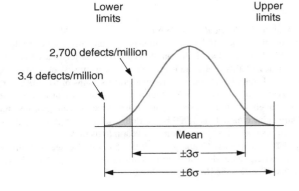

◄ **Figure 4**

Defects per Million for ±3σ vs. ± 6σ

same result); (4) *Improves*, by modifying or redesigning, existing processes and procedures; and (5) *Controls* the new process to make sure performance levels are maintained.

- It is a *set of seven tools* that we introduce shortly in this chapter: check sheets, scatter diagrams, cause-and-effect diagrams, Pareto charts, flowcharts, histograms, and statistical process control.

Motorola developed Six Sigma in the 1980s in response to customer complaints about its products, and to stiff competition. The company first set a goal of reducing defects by 90%. Within 1 year it had achieved such impressive results—through benchmarking competitors, soliciting new ideas from employees, changing reward plans, adding training, revamping critical processes—that it documented the procedures into what it called Six Sigma. Although the concept was rooted in manufacturing, GE later expanded Six Sigma into services, including human resources, sales, customer services, and financial/credit services. The concept of wiping out defects turns out to be the same in both manufacturing and services.

Implementing Six Sigma   Implementing Six Sigma "is a big commitment," says the head of that program at Praxair, a major industrial gas company. "We're asking our executives to spend upward of 15% of their time on Six Sigma. If you don't spend the time you don't get the results."[5] Indeed, successful Six Sigma programs in every firm, from GE to Motorola to DuPont to Texas Instruments require a major time commitment, especially from top management. These leaders have to formulate the plan, communicate their buy-in and the firm's objectives, and take a visible role in setting the example for others.

Successful Six Sigma projects are clearly related to the strategic direction of a company. It is a management-directed, team-based, and expert-led approach.[6]

Employee Empowerment

Employee empowerment means involving employees in every step of the production process. Consistently, business literature suggests that some 85% of quality problems have to do with materials and processes, not with employee performance. Therefore, the task is to design equipment and processes that produce the desired quality. This is best done with a high degree of involvement by those who understand the shortcomings of the system. Those dealing with the system on a daily basis understand it better than anyone else. One study indicated that TQM programs that delegate responsibility for quality to shop-floor employees tend to be twice as likely to succeed as those implemented with "top-down" directives.[7]

When nonconformance occurs, the worker is seldom wrong. Either the product was designed wrong, the system that makes the product was designed wrong, or the employee was improperly trained. Although the employee may be able to help solve the problem, the employee rarely causes it.

Techniques for building employee empowerment include (1) building communication networks that include employees; (2) developing open, supportive supervisors; (3) moving responsibility from both managers and staff to production employees; (4) building high-morale organizations; (5) and creating such formal organization structures as teams and quality circles.

Teams can be built to address a variety of issues. One popular focus of teams is quality. Such teams are often known as quality circles. A **quality circle** is a group of employees who meet regularly to solve work-related problems. The members receive training in group planning, problem solving, and statistical quality control. They generally meet once a week (usually after work but sometimes on company time). Although the members are not rewarded financially, they do

Employee empowerment
Enlarging employee jobs so that the added responsibility and authority is moved to the lowest level possible in the organization.

Quality circle
A group of employees meeting regularly with a facilitator to solve work-related problems in their work area.

[5]B. Schmitt, "Expanding Six Sigma," *Chemical Week* (February 21, 2001): 21–24.
[6]To train employees in how to improve quality and its relationship to customers, there are three other key players in the Six Sigma program: Master Black Belts, Black Belts, and Green Belts. Master Black Belts are full-time teachers who have extensive training in statistics, quality tools, and leadership. They mentor Black Belts, who in turn are project team leaders, directing perhaps a half-dozen projects per year (with average savings of $175,000 per project, according to the Six Sigma Academy). They receive about 4 weeks of Six Sigma training but must also have solid "people skills," so as to be able to see their changes through. Green Belts spend part of their time on team projects and the rest on their normal jobs. Dow Chemical and DuPont have more than 1,000 Black Belts each in their global operations. DuPont also has 160 Master Black Belts and introduces over 2,000 Green Belts per year into its ranks.
[7]"The Straining of Quality," *The Economist* (January 14, 1995): 55. We also see that this is one of the strengths of Southwest Airlines, which offers bare-bones domestic service but whose friendly and humorous employees help it obtain number one ranking for quality. (See *Fortune* [March 6, 2006]: 65–69.)

◀ *Workers at this TRW airbag manufacturing plant in Marshall, Illinois, are their own inspectors. Empowerment is an essential part of TQM. This man is checking the quality of a crash sensor he built.*

TRW Automobile, General Manley Ford

receive recognition from the firm. A specially trained team member, called the *facilitator*, usually helps train the members and keeps the meetings running smoothly. Teams with a quality focus have proven to be a cost-effective way to increase productivity as well as quality.

Benchmarking

Benchmarking is another ingredient in an organization's TQM program. **Benchmarking** involves selecting a demonstrated standard of products, services, costs, or practices that represent the very best performance for processes or activities very similar to your own. The idea is to develop a target at which to shoot and then to develop a standard or benchmark against which to compare your performance. The steps for developing benchmarks are:

1. Determine what to benchmark.
2. Form a benchmark team.
3. Identify benchmarking partners.
4. Collect and analyze benchmarking information.
5. Take action to match or exceed the benchmark.

Typical performance measures used in benchmarking include percentage of defects, cost per unit or per order, processing time per unit, service response time, return on investment, customer satisfaction rates, and customer retention rates. When considering company Web sites, this benchmark list is quite different, as we see in Table 3.

In the ideal situation, you find one or more similar organizations that are leaders in the particular areas you want to study. Then you compare yourself (benchmark yourself) against them. The company need not be in your industry. Indeed, to establish world-class standards, it may be best

Benchmarking
Selecting a demonstrated standard of performance that represents the very best performance for a process or an activity.

> **Learning Objective**
>
> 4. Explain how benchmarking is used in TQM

1. Use of meta tags (keywords)	Yes: 70%, No: 30%
2. A meaningful homepage title	Yes: 97%, No: 3%
3. Unique domain name	Yes: 91%, No: 9%
4. Search engine site registration	Above 96%
5. Average speed of homepage loading (in seconds)	28K: 19.31; 56K: 10.88; T1: 2.59
6. Average number of spelling errors	0.16
7. Visibility of contact information	Yes: 74%, No: 26%
8. Presence of a search engine	Yes: 59%, No: 41%
9. Translation to multiple languages	Yes: 11%; No: 89%

◀ **Table 3**

Benchmarking Factors Deemed Critical to Quality at *Fortune* 500 Company Web Sites (and survey results)

Sources: Adopted from M. Jenamani, P. K. J. Mohapatra, and S. Ghose, *Internet Research* 16, no. 3 (2006): 248; and N. Tamini, M. Rajan, and R. Sebastianelli, *Quality Progress* 33, no. 7 (July 2000): 47–51.

► Table 4

Best Practices for
Resolving Customer
Complaints

- *Make it easy for clients to complain:* It is free market research.
- *Respond quickly to complaints:* It adds customers and loyalty.
- *Resolve complaints on the first contact:* It reduces cost.
- *Use computers to manage complaints:* Discover trends, share them, and align your services.
- *Recruit the best for customer service jobs:* It should be part of formal training and career advancement.

Source: Canadian Government Guide on Complaint Mechanism.

to look outside your industry. If one industry has learned how to compete via rapid product development while yours has not, it does no good to study your industry.

This is exactly what Xerox and Mercedes Benz did when they went to L.L. Bean for order-filling and warehousing benchmarks. Xerox noticed that L.L. Bean was able to "pick" orders three times as fast as it could. After benchmarking, it was immediately able to pare warehouse costs by 10%. Mercedes Benz observed that L.L. Bean warehouse employees used flowcharts to spot wasted motions. The auto giant followed suit and now relies more on problem solving at the worker level.

Benchmarks often take the form of "best practices" found in other firms or in other divisions. Table 4 illustrates best practices for resolving customer complaints.

Likewise, British computer manufacturer ICL benchmarked Marks and Spencer (the food and clothing retailer) to improve its distribution system.

Internal Benchmarking   When an organization is large enough to have many divisions or business units, a natural approach is the internal benchmark. Data are usually much more accessible than from outside firms. Typically, one internal unit has superior performance worth learning from.

Xerox's almost religious belief in benchmarking has paid off not only by looking outward to L.L. Bean but by examining the operations of its various country divisions. For example, Xerox Europe, a $6 billion subsidiary of Xerox Corp., formed teams to see how better sales could result through internal benchmarking. Somehow, France sold five times as many color copiers as did other divisions in Europe. By copying France's approach, namely, better sales training and use of dealer channels to supplement direct sales, Norway increased sales by 152%, Holland by 300%, and Switzerland by 328%!

Benchmarks can and should be established in a variety of areas. Total quality management requires no less.[8]

Video 6.2

Xerox's Benchmarking Strategy

Just-in-Time (JIT)

The philosophy behind just-in-time (JIT) is one of continuing improvement and enforced problem solving. JIT systems are designed to produce or deliver goods just as they are needed. JIT is related to quality in three ways:

- *JIT cuts the cost of quality:* This occurs because scrap, rework, inventory investment, and damage costs are directly related to inventory on hand. Because there is less inventory on hand with JIT, costs are lower. Additionally, inventory hides bad quality, whereas JIT immediately *exposes* bad quality.
- *JIT improves quality:* As JIT shrinks lead time it keeps evidence of errors fresh and limits the number of potential sources of error. JIT creates, in effect, an early warning system for quality problems, both within the firm and with vendors.
- *Better quality means less inventory and a better, easier-to-employ JIT system:* Often the purpose of keeping inventory is to protect against poor production performance resulting from unreliable quality. If consistent quality exists, JIT allows firms to reduce all the costs associated with inventory.

[8]Note that benchmarking is good for evaluating how well you are doing the thing you are doing compared with the industry, but the more imaginative approach to process improvement is to ask, Should we be doing this at all? Comparing your warehousing operations to the marvelous job that L.L. Bean does is fine, but maybe you should be outsourcing the warehousing function (see Supplement 11).

Taguchi Concepts

Most quality problems are the result of poor product and process design. Genichi Taguchi has provided us with three concepts aimed at improving both product and process quality: *quality robustness*, *quality loss function*, and *target-oriented quality*.[9]

Quality robust products are products that can be produced uniformly and consistently in adverse manufacturing and environmental conditions. Taguchi's idea is to remove the *effects* of adverse conditions instead of removing the causes. Taguchi suggests that removing the effects is often cheaper than removing the causes and more effective in producing a robust product. In this way, small variations in materials and process do not destroy product quality.

A **quality loss function (QLF)** identifies all costs connected with poor quality and shows how these costs increase as the product moves away from being exactly what the customer wants. These costs include not only customer dissatisfaction but also warranty and service costs; internal inspection, repair, and scrap costs; and costs that can best be described as costs to society. Notice that Figure 5(a) shows the quality loss function as a curve that increases at an increasing rate. It takes the general form of a simple quadratic formula:

$$L = D^2 C$$

where L = loss to society
D^2 = square of the distance from the target value
C = cost of the deviation at the specification limit

All the losses to society due to poor performance are included in the loss function. The smaller the loss, the more desirable the product. The farther the product is from the target value, the more severe the loss.

Taguchi observed that traditional conformance-oriented specifications (i.e., the product is good as long as it falls within the tolerance limits) are too simplistic. As shown in Figure 5(b), conformance-oriented quality accepts all products that fall within the tolerance limits, producing more units farther from the target. Therefore, the loss (cost) is higher in terms of customer satisfaction and benefits to society. Target-oriented quality, on the other hand, strives to keep the product at the desired specification, producing more (and better) units near the target. **Target-oriented quality** is a philosophy of continuous improvement to bring the product exactly on target.

Quality robust
Products that are consistently built to meet customer needs in spite of adverse conditions in the production process.

Quality loss function (QLF)
A mathematical function that identifies all costs connected with poor quality and shows how these costs increase as product quality moves from what the customer wants.

Learning Objective

5. Explain quality robust products and Taguchi concepts

Target-oriented quality
A philosophy of continuous improvement to bring the product exactly on target.

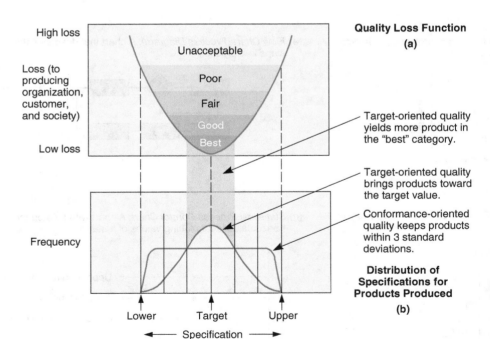

Quality Loss Function (a)

Target-oriented quality yields more product in the "best" category.

Target-oriented quality brings products toward the target value.

Conformance-oriented quality keeps products within 3 standard deviations.

Distribution of Specifications for Products Produced (b)

◄ **Figure 5**

(a) Quality Loss Function and (b) Distribution of Products Produced

Taguchi aims for the target because products produced near the upper and lower acceptable specifications result in higher quality loss function.

[9]G. Taguchi, S. Chowdhury, and Y. Wu, *Taguchi's Quality Engineering Handbook* (New York: Wiley, 2004).

Knowledge of TQM Tools

To empower employees and implement TQM as a continuing effort, everyone in the organization must be trained in the techniques of TQM. In the following section, we focus on some of the diverse and expanding tools that are used in the TQM crusade.

TOOLS OF TQM

Seven tools that are particularly helpful in the TQM effort are shown in Figure 6. We will now introduce these tools.

Learning Objective

6. Use the seven tools of TQM

Check Sheets

A check sheet is any kind of a form that is designed for recording data. In many cases, the recording is done so the patterns are easily seen while the data are being taken (see Figure 6[a]). Check sheets help analysts find the facts or patterns that may aid subsequent analysis. An example might be a drawing that shows a tally of the areas where defects are occurring or a check sheet showing the type of customer complaints.

Tools for Generating Ideas

(a) *Check Sheet:* An organized method of recording data

Defect	Hour							
	1	2	3	4	5	6	7	8
A	///	/		/	/	/	///	/
B	//	/	/	/			//	///
C	/	//					//	////

(b) *Scatter Diagram:* A graph of the value of one variable vs. another variable

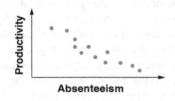

(c) *Cause-and-Effect Diagram:* A tool that identifies process elements (causes) that may effect an outcome

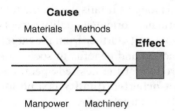

Tools for Organizing the Data

(d) *Pareto Chart:* A graph to identify and plot problems or defects in descending order of frequency

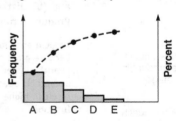

(e) *Flow Chart (Process Diagram):* A chart that describes the steps in a process

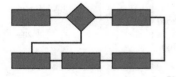

Tools for Identifying Problems

(f) *Histogram:* A distribution showing the frequency of occurrences of a variable

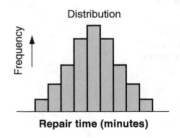

(g) *Statistical Process Control Chart:* A chart with time on the horizontal axis for plotting values of a statistic

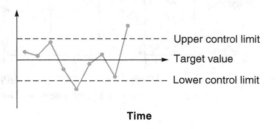

▲ **Figure 6**   Seven Tools of TQM

OM in Action   TQM Improves Copier Service

In the copier industry, technology in copier design has blurred the distinction between most companies' products. Savin, a copier manufacturer owned by Japan's Ricoh Corp., believes that competitive advantage is to be found in service and is stressing customer service rather than product specifications. Says Savin VP Robert Williams: "A company's fortunes ride on the quality of its service."

Here are two ways in which Savin reduced expenses while improving service quality:

- Using the tools of TQM, Savin found that significant time on service calls was being wasted when engineers had to go back to their trucks for spare parts. The firm assembled a "call kit," which allows engineers to carry onto customer premises all parts with

highest probability for use. Now service calls are faster and cost less, and more can be made per day.
- The Pareto principle, that 20% of your staff causes 80% of your errors, was used to tackle the "callback" problem. Callbacks meant the job was not done right the first time and that a second visit, at Savin's expense, was needed. Retraining only the 11% of customer engineers with the most callbacks resulted in a 19% drop in return visits.

"Total quality management," according to Williams, "is an approach to doing business that should permeate every job in the service industry."

Sources: Fortune (July 24, 2006): S16–S17; and *The Wall Street Journal* (May 19, 1998): B8.

Scatter Diagrams

Scatter diagrams show the relationship between two measurements. An example is the positive relationship between length of a service call and the number of trips the repairperson makes back to the truck for parts (as discussed in the *OM in Action* box "TQM Improves Copier Service"). Another example might be a plot of productivity and absenteeism, as shown in Figure 6(b). If the two items are closely related, the data points will form a tight band. If a random pattern results, the items are unrelated.

Cause-and-Effect Diagrams

Another tool for identifying quality issues and inspection points is the **cause-and-effect diagram**, also known as an **Ishikawa diagram** or a **fish-bone chart**. Figure 7 illustrates a chart (note the shape resembling the bones of a fish) for a basketball quality control problem—missed free throws. Each "bone" represents a possible source of error.

Cause-and-effect diagram
A schematic technique used to discover possible locations of quality problems.

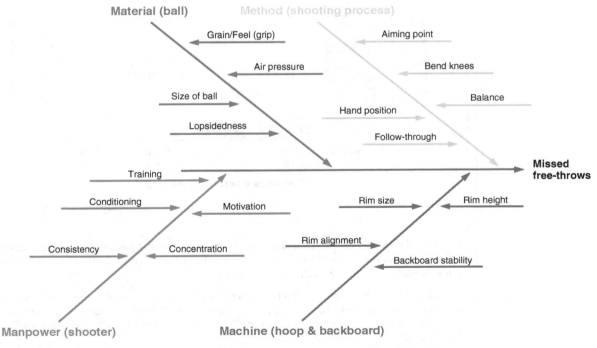

▲ **Figure 7**   Fish-Bone Chart (or Cause-and-Effect Diagram) for Problems with Missed Free Throws

Source: Adapted from MoreSteam.com, 2007.

123

The operations manager starts with four categories: material, machinery/equipment, manpower, and methods. These four *M*s are the "causes." They provide a good checklist for initial analysis. Individual causes associated with each category are tied in as separate bones along that branch, often through a brainstorming process. For example, the method branch in Figure 7 has problems caused by hand position, follow-through, aiming point, bent knees, and balance. When a fish-bone chart is systematically developed, possible quality problems and inspection points are highlighted.

Pareto Charts

Pareto charts are a method of organizing errors, problems, or defects to help focus on problem-solving efforts. They are based on the work of Vilfredo Pareto, a nineteenth-century economist. Joseph M. Juran popularized Pareto's work when he suggested that 80% of a firm's problems are a result of only 20% of the causes.

Example 1 indicates that of the five types of complaints identified, the vast majority were of one type, poor room service.

EXAMPLE 1

A Pareto chart at the Hard Rock Hotel

Active Model 6.1

Example 1 is further illustrated in Active Model 6.1 in the CD-ROM.

The Hard Rock Hotel in Bali has just collected the data from 75 complaint calls to the general manager during the month of October. The manager wants to prepare an analysis of the complaints. The data provided are room service, 54; check-in delays, 12; hours the pool is open, 4; minibar prices, 3; and miscellaneous, 2.

Approach: A Pareto chart is an excellent choice for this analysis.

Solution: The Pareto chart shown below indicates that 72% of the calls were the result of one cause: room service. The majority of complaints will be eliminated when this one cause is corrected.

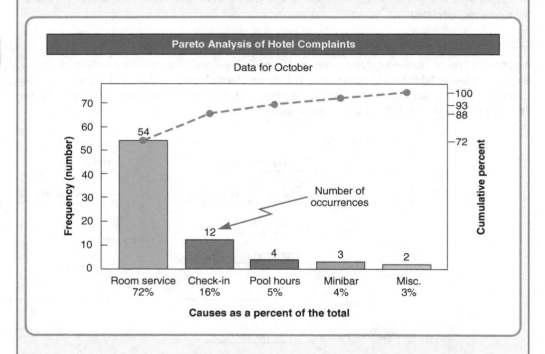

Insight: This visual means of summarizing data is very helpful—particularly with large amounts of data, as in the Southwestern University case study at the end of this chapter. We can immediately spot the top problems and prepare a plan to address them.

Learning exercise: Hard Rock's bar manager decides to do a similar analysis on complaints she has collected over the past year: too expensive, 22; weak drinks, 15; slow service, 65; short hours, 8; unfriendly bartender, 12. Prepare a Pareto chart. [Answer: slow service, 53%; expensive, 18%; drinks, 12%; bartender, 10%; hours, 7%.]

Related problems: 1, 3, 7b, 12, 13, 16c

Pareto analysis indicates which problems may yield the greatest payoff. Pacific Bell discovered this when it tried to find a way to reduce damage to buried phone cable, the number-one cause of phone outages. Pareto analysis showed that 41% of cable damage was caused by construction work. Armed with this information, Pacific Bell was able to devise a plan to reduce cable cuts by 24% in one year, saving $6 million.

Flowcharts

Flowcharts graphically present a process or system using annotated boxes and interconnected lines (see Figure 6[e]). They are a simple, but great tool for trying to make sense of a process or explain a process. Example 2 uses a flowchart to show the process of completing an MRI at a hospital.

Flowcharts
Block diagrams that graphically describe a process or system.

EXAMPLE 2

A flowchart for hospital MRI service

Arnold Palmer Hospital has undertaken a series of process improvement initiatives. One of these is to make the MRI service efficient for patient, doctor, and hospital. The first step, the administrator believes, is to develop a flowchart for this process.

Approach: A process improvement staffer observed a number of patients and followed them (and information flow) from start to end. Here are the 11 steps:

1. Physician schedules MRI after examining patient (START).
2. Patient taken to the MRI lab with test order and copy of medical records.
3. Patient signs in, completes required paperwork.
4. Patient is prepped by technician for scan.
5. Technician carries out the MRI scan.
6. Technician inspects film for clarity.
7. If MRI not satisfactory (20% of time), steps 5 and 6 are repeated.
8. Patient taken back to hospital room.
9. MRI is read by radiologist and report is prepared.
10. MRI and report are transferred electronically to physician.
11. Patient and physician discuss report (END).

Solution: Here is the flowchart:

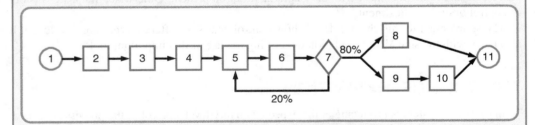

Insight: With the flowchart in hand, the hospital can analyze each step and identify value-added activities and activities that can be improved or eliminated.

Learning exercise: If the patient's blood pressure is over 200/120 when being prepped for the MRI, she is taken back to her room for 2 hours and the process returns to step 2. How does the flowchart change? Answer:

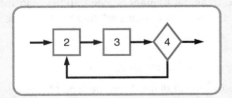

Related problems: 6, 15

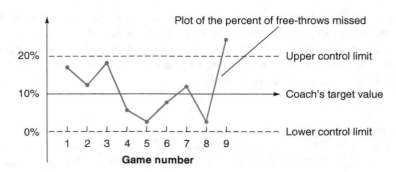

▶ **Figure 8**

Control Chart for Percentage of Free Throws Missed by the Chicago Bulls in Their First Nine Games of the New Season

Histograms

Histograms show the range of values of a measurement and the frequency with which each value occurs (see Figure 6[f]). They show the most frequently occurring readings as well as the variations in the measurements. Descriptive statistics, such as the average and standard deviation, may be calculated to describe the distribution. However, the data should always be plotted so the shape of the distribution can be "seen." A visual presentation of the distribution may also provide insight into the cause of the variation.

Statistical Process Control (SPC)

Statistical process control (SPC)

A process used to monitor standards, make measurements and take corrective action as a product or service is being produced.

Statistical process control monitors standards, makes measurements, and takes corrective action as a product or service is being produced. Samples of process outputs are examined; if they are within acceptable limits, the process is permitted to continue. If they fall outside certain specific ranges, the process is stopped and, typically, the assignable cause located and removed.

Control charts

Graphic presentations of process data over time, with predetermined control limits.

Control charts are graphic presentations of data over time that show upper and lower limits for the process we want to control (see Figure 6[g]). Control charts are constructed in such a way that new data can be quickly compared with past performance data. We take samples of the process output and plot the average of these samples on a chart that has the limits on it. The upper and lower limits in a control chart can be in units of temperature, pressure, weight, length, and so on.

Figure 8 shows the plot of percentages of a sample in a control chart. When the average of the samples falls within the upper and lower control limits and no discernible pattern is present, the process is said to be in control with only natural variation present. Otherwise, the process is out of control or out of adjustment.

The supplement to this chapter details how control charts of different types are developed. It also deals with the statistical foundation underlying the use of this important tool.

THE ROLE OF INSPECTION

To make sure a system is producing at the expected quality level, control of the process is needed. The best processes have little variation from the standard expected. The operations manager's task is to build such systems and to verify, often by inspection, that they are performing to standard. This **inspection** can involve measurement, tasting, touching, weighing, or testing of the product (sometimes even destroying it when doing so). Its goal is to detect a bad process immediately. Inspection does not correct deficiencies in the system or defects in the products; nor does it change a product or increase its value. Inspection only finds deficiencies and defects, and it is expensive.

Inspection

A means of ensuring that an operation is producing at the quality level expected.

Inspection should be thought of as an audit. Audits do not add value to the product. However, operations managers, like financial managers, need audits, and they need to know when and where to audit. Thus there are two basic issues relating to inspection: (1) *when to inspect* and (2) *where to inspect*.

When and Where to Inspect

Deciding when and where to inspect depends on the type of process and the value added at each stage. Inspections (audits) can take place at any of the following points:

1. At your supplier's plant while the supplier is producing.
2. At your facility upon receipt of goods from your supplier.

3. Before costly or irreversible processes.
4. During the step-by-step production process.
5. When production or service is complete.
6. Before delivery to your customer.
7. At the point of customer contact.

The seven tools of TQM discussed in the previous section aid in this "when and where to inspect" decision. However, inspection is not a substitute for a robust product produced by well-trained employees in a good process. In one well-known experiment conducted by an independent research firm, 100 defective pieces were added to a "perfect" lot of items and then subjected to 100% inspection.[10] The inspectors found only 68 of the defective pieces in their first inspection. It took another three passes by the inspectors to find the next 30 defects. The last two defects were never found. So the bottom line is that there is variability in the inspection process. Additionally, inspectors are only human: They become bored, they become tired, and the inspection equipment itself has variability. Even with 100% inspection, inspectors cannot guarantee perfection. Therefore, good processes, employee empowerment, and source control are a better solution than trying to find defects by inspection.

For example, at Velcro Industries, as in many organizations, quality was viewed by machine operators as the job of "those quality people." Inspections were based on random sampling, and if a part showed up bad, it was thrown out. The company decided to pay more attention to operators, machine repair and design, measurement methods, communications, and responsibilities, and to invest more money in training. Over time as defects declined, Velcro was able to pull half its quality control people out of the process.

One of the themes of our treatment of quality is that "quality cannot be inspected into a product."

Source Inspection

The best inspection can be thought of as no inspection at all; this "inspection" is always done at the source—it is just doing the job properly with the operator ensuring that this is so. This may be called **source inspection** (or source control) and is consistent with the concept of employee empowerment, where individual employees self-check their own work. The idea is that each supplier, process, and employee *treats the next step in the process as the customer*, ensuring perfect product to the next "customer." This inspection may be assisted by the use of checklists and controls such as a fail-safe device called a *poka-yoke*, a name borrowed from the Japanese.

A **poka-yoke** is a foolproof device or technique that ensures production of good units every time.[11] These special devices avoid errors and provide quick feedback of problems. A simple example of a poka-yoke device is the diesel or leaded gas pump nozzle that will not fit into the "unleaded" gas tank opening on your car. In McDonald's, the french fry scoop and standard-size

Source inspection
Controlling or monitoring at the point of production or purchase—at the source.

Poka-yoke
Literally translated, "foolproof"; it has come to mean a device or technique that ensures the production of a good unit every time.

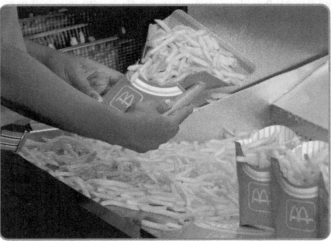

◄ *Good methods analysis and the proper tools can result in poka-yokes that improve both quality and speed. Here, two poka-yokes are demonstrated. First, the aluminum scoop automatically positions the French fries vertically, and second, the properly sized container ensures that the portion served is correct. This combination also speeds delivery, ensuring that french fries are delivered just as the customer requests them.*

Ralf-Finn Hestoft, Corbis/SABA Press Photos, Inc.

[10] *Statistical Quality Control* (Springfield, MA: Monsanto Chemical Company, n.d.): 19.
[11] For further discussion, see D. M. Stewart and S. A. Melnyk, "Effective Process Improvement Developing Poka-Yoke Procedures," *Production & Inventory Management Journal* 41, no. 4 (4th quarter, 2000): 11–17.

► **Table 5**

Examples of Inspection in Services

Organization	What Is Inspected	Standard
Jones Law Offices	Receptionist performance Billing Attorney	Phone answered by the second ring Accurate, timely, and correct format Promptness in returning calls
Hard Rock Hotel	Reception desk Doorman Room Minibar	Use customer's name Greet guest in less than 30 seconds All lights working, spotless bathroom Restocked and charges accurately posted to bill
Arnold Palmer Hospital	Billing Pharmacy Lab Nurses Admissions	Accurate, timely, and correct format Prescription accuracy, inventory accuracy Audit for lab-test accuracy Charts immediately updated Data entered correctly and completely
Olive Garden Restaurant	Busboy Busboy Waiter	Serves water and bread within 1 minute Clears all entrée items and crumbs prior to dessert Knows and suggests specials, desserts
Nordstrom Department Store	Display areas Stockrooms Salesclerks	Attractive, well organized, stocked, good lighting Rotation of goods, organized, clean Neat, courteous, very knowledgeable

bag used to measure the correct quantity are poka-yokes. Similarly, in a hospital, the prepackaged surgical coverings that contain exactly the items needed for a medical procedure are poka-yokes. Checklists are another type of poka-yoke. The idea of source inspection and poka-yokes is to ensure that 100% good product or service is provided at each step in the process.

Service Industry Inspection

In *service*-oriented organizations, inspection points can be assigned at a wide range of locations, as illustrated in Table 5. Again, the operations manager must decide where inspections are justified and may find the seven tools of TQM useful when making these judgments.

Inspection of Attributes versus Variables

When inspections take place, quality characteristics may be measured as either *attributes* or *variables*. **Attribute inspection** classifies items as being either good or defective. It does not address the *degree* of failure. For example, the lightbulb burns or it does not. **Variable inspection** measures such dimensions as weight, speed, height, or strength to see if an item falls within an acceptable range. If a piece of electrical wire is supposed to be 0.01 inch in diameter, a micrometer can be used to see if the product is close enough to pass inspection.

Knowing whether attributes or variables are being inspected helps us decide which statistical quality control approach to take, as we will see in the supplement to this chapter.

TQM IN SERVICES

The personal component of services is more difficult to measure than the quality of the tangible component. Generally, the user of a service, like the user of a good, has features in mind that form a basis for comparison among alternatives. Lack of any one feature may eliminate the service from further consideration. Quality also may be perceived as a bundle of attributes in which many lesser characteristics are superior to those of competitors. This approach to product comparison differs little between goods and services. However, what is very different about the selection of services is the poor definition of the (1) *intangible differences between products* and (2) *the intangible expectations customers have of those products*.[12] Indeed, the intangible attributes may not

Attribute inspection
An inspection that classifies items as being either good or defective.

Variable inspection
Classifications of inspected items as falling on a continuum scale, such as dimension, size, or strength.

[12] V. Zeithaml, L. Berry, and A. Parasuraman, "The Behavioral Consequence of Service Quality," *Journal of Marketing* (April 1996): 31–47.

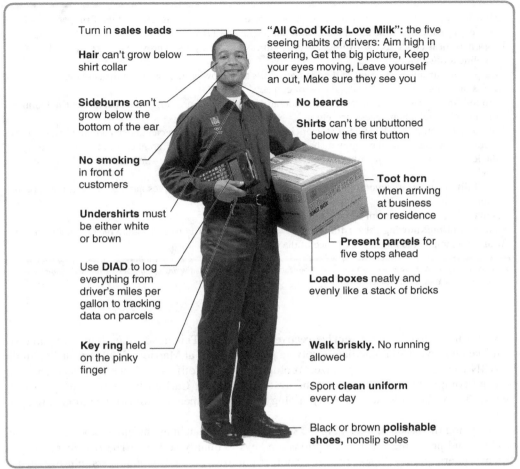

Turn in **sales leads**

Hair can't grow below shirt collar

Sideburns can't grow below the bottom of the ear

No smoking in front of customers

Undershirts must be either white or brown

Use **DIAD** to log everything from driver's miles per gallon to tracking data on parcels

Key ring held on the pinky finger

"All Good Kids Love Milk": the five seeing habits of drivers: Aim high in steering, Get the big picture, Keep your eyes moving, Leave yourself an out, Make sure they see you

No beards

Shirts can't be unbuttoned below the first button

Toot horn when arriving at business or residence

Present parcels for five stops ahead

Load boxes neatly and evenly like a stack of bricks

Walk briskly. No running allowed

Sport **clean uniform** every day

Black or brown **polishable shoes,** nonslip soles

Ann States Photography

◄ *UPS drivers are taught 340 precise methods of how to correctly deliver a package. Regimented? Absolutely. But UPS credits its uniformity and efficiency with laying the foundation for its high-quality service.*

Source: Forbes (January 10, 2000): 80.

be defined at all. They are often unspoken images in the purchaser's mind. This is why all of those marketing issues such as advertising, image, and promotion can make a difference (see the photo of the UPS driver).

The operations manager plays a significant role in addressing several major aspects of service quality. First, the *tangible component of many services is important.* How well the service is designed and produced does make a difference. This might be how accurate, clear, and complete your checkout bill at the hotel is, how warm the food is at Taco Bell, or how well your car runs after you pick it up at the repair shop.

Second, another aspect of service and service quality is the process. Notice in Table 6 that 9 out of 10 of the determinants of service quality are related to *the service process.* Such things as reliability and courtesy are part of the process. An operations manager can *design processes (service products) that have these attributes* and can ensure their quality through the TQM techniques discussed in this chapter.

Third, the operations manager should realize that the customer's expectations are the standard against which the service is judged. Customers' perceptions of service quality result from a comparison of their before-service expectations with their actual-service experience. In other words, service quality is judged on the basis of whether it meets expectations. The *manager may be able to influence both the quality of the service and the expectation.* Don't promise more than you can deliver.

Fourth, the manager must expect exceptions. There is a standard quality level at which the regular service is delivered, such as the bank teller's handling of a transaction. However, there are "exceptions" or "problems" initiated by the customer or by less-than-optimal operating conditions (e.g., the computer "crashed"). This implies that the quality control system must recognize and *have a set of alternative plans for less-than-optimal operating conditions.*

 Video 6.3

TQM at Ritz-Carlton Hotels

► **Table 6**

Determinants of Service Quality

Reliability involves consistency of performance and dependability. It means that the firm performs the service right the first time and that the firm honors its promises.

Responsiveness concerns the willingness or readiness of employees to provide service. It involves timeliness of service.

Competence means possession of the required skills and knowledge to perform the service.

Access involves approachability and ease of contact.

Courtesy involves politeness, respect, consideration, and friendliness of contact personnel (including receptionists, telephone operators, etc.).

Communication means keeping customers informed in language they can understand and listening to them. It may mean that the company has to adjust its language for different consumers—increasing the level of sophistication with a well-educated customer and speaking simply and plainly with a novice.

Credibility involves trustworthiness, believability, and honesty. It involves having the customer's best interests at heart.

Security is the freedom from danger, risk, or doubt.

Understanding/knowing the customer involves making the effort to understand the customer's needs.

Tangibles include the physical evidence of the service.

Source: Adapted from A. Parasuranam, Valarie A. Zeithaml, and Leonard L. Berry, *Delivering Quality Service and Balancing Customer Expectations* (New York: The Free Press, 1990).

Service recovery

Training and empowering frontline workers to solve a problem immediately.

Well-run companies have **service recovery** strategies. This means they train and empower frontline employees to immediately solve a problem. Staff at Marriott Hotels are drilled in the LEARN routine—*L*isten, *E*mpathize, *A*pologize, *R*eact, *N*otify—with the final step ensuring that the complaint is fed back into the system. The Ritz-Carlton trains its staff not to say merely "sorry" but "please accept my apology" and gives them a budget for reimbursing upset guests.

Designing the product, managing the service process, matching customer expectations to the product, and preparing for the exceptions are keys to quality services. The *OM in Action* box "Richey International's Spies" provides another glimpse of how OM managers improve quality in services.

OM in Action   Richey International's Spies

How do luxury hotels maintain quality? They inspect. But when the product is one-on-one service, largely dependent on personal behavior, how do you inspect? You hire spies!

Richey International is the spy. Preferred Hotels and Resorts Worldwide and Intercontinental Hotels have both hired Richey to do quality evaluations via spying. Richey employees posing as customers perform the inspections. However, even then management must have established what the customer expects and specific services that yield customer satisfaction. Only then do managers know where and how to inspect. Aggressive training and objective inspections reinforce behavior that will meet those customer expectations.

The hotels use Richey's undercover inspectors to ensure performance to exacting standards. The hotels do not know when the evaluators will arrive or what aliases they will use. More than 50 different standards are evaluated before the inspectors even check in at a luxury hotel. Over the next 24 hours, using checklists, tape recordings,

and photos, written reports are prepared and include evaluation of standards such as the following:

- Does the doorman greet each guest in less than 30 seconds?
- Does the front-desk clerk use the guest's name during check-in?
- Is the bathroom tub and shower spotlessly clean?
- How many minutes does it take to get coffee after the guest sits down for breakfast?
- Did the waiter make eye contact?
- Were minibar charges posted correctly on the bill?

Established standards, aggressive training, and inspections are part of the TQM effort at these hotels. Quality does not happen by accident.

Sources: Hotel and Motel Management (August 2002): 128; *The Wall Street Journal* (May 12, 1999): B1, B12; and *Forbes* (October 5, 1998): 88–89.

Summary

Quality is a term that means different things to different people. It is defined in this chapter as "the totality of features and characteristics of a product or service that bears on its ability to satisfy stated or implied needs." Defining quality expectations is critical to effective and efficient operations.

Quality requires building a total quality management (TQM) environment because quality cannot be inspected into a product. The selection also addresses seven TQM *concepts* : continuous improvement, Six Sigma, employee empowerment, benchmarking, just-in-time, Taguchi concepts, and knowledge of TQM tools. The seven TQM *tools* introduced in this chapter are check sheets, scatter diagrams, cause-and-effect diagrams, Pareto charts, flowcharts, histograms, and statistical process control (SPC).

Key Terms

Quality
Cost of quality (COQ)
ISO 9000
ISO 14000
Total quality management (TQM)
PDCA
Six Sigma
Employee empowerment
Quality circle

Benchmarking
Quality robust
Quality loss function (QLF)
Target-oriented quality
Cause-and-effect diagram, Ishikawa
 diagram, or fish-bone chart
Pareto charts
Flowcharts
Statistical process control (SPC)

Control charts
Inspection
Source inspection
Poka-yoke
Attribute inspection
Variable inspection
Service recovery

Active Model Exercise

This Active Model appears on your CD-ROM. It allows you to evaluate important elements in the Pareto chart.

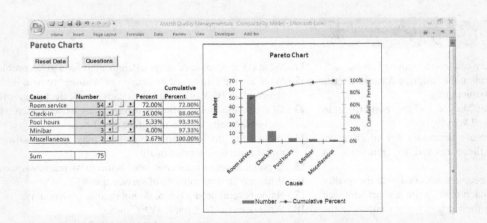

◀ **Active Model 6.1**

Pareto Analysis of Hotel Data from Example 1

Questions

1. What percentage of overall defects do the room service complaints account for?

2. If we could reduce the room service complaints in half how would this affect the chart?

Self-Test

- **Before taking the self-test,** *refer to the learning objectives listed at the beginning of the chapter and the key terms listed at the end of the selection.*
- *Use the key at the back of the text to* **correct** *your answers.*
- **Restudy** *pages that correspond to any questions you answered incorrectly or material you feel uncertain about.*

1. In this selection, *quality* is defined as:
   a) the degree of excellence at an acceptable price and the control of variability at an acceptable cost
   b) how well a product fits patterns of consumer preferences
   c) the totality or features and characteristics of a product or service that bears on its ability to satisfy stated or implied needs
   d) even though it cannot be defined, you know what it is

2. 100% inspection:
   a) will always catch all of the defective parts
   b) means that only good parts will be shipped to a customer
   c) is practical and generally a good idea
   d) means that every part is checked to see whether or not it is defective

3. The seven basic concepts of TQM are _____, _____, _____, _____, _____, _____, and _____.

4. ISO 14000 is an EC standard to address _____.

5. The seven tools of total quality management are _____, _____, _____, _____, _____, _____, and _____.

6. Cause-and-effect diagrams are also known as:
   a) quality loss charts
   b) target specification graphs
   c) fish-bone charts
   d) Ishikawa diagrams
   e) a and b
   f) c and d

7. The Taguchi method includes all except which of the following major concepts:
   a) employee involvement
   b) remove the effects of adverse conditions
   c) quality loss function
   d) target specifications

8. Quality cannot be _____ into a product.

Internet and Student CD-ROM/DVD Exercises

Visit our Companion Web site or your student CD-ROM/DVD to help with material in this chapter.

 On Our Companion Web Site,
www.prenhall.com/heizer
- Self-Study Quizzes
- Practice Problems
- Virtual Company Tour
- Internet Case
- PowerPoint Lecture

 On Your Student CD-ROM
- Practice Problems
- Active Model Exercise

 On Your Student DVD
- Video Clips and Video Cases

Discussion Questions

1. Explain how improving quality can lead to reduced costs.
2. As an Internet exercise, determine the Baldrige Award Criteria. See the Web site **www.quality.nist.gov**.
3. Which 3 of Deming's 14 points do you feel are most critical to the success of a TQM program? Why?
4. List the seven concepts that are necessary for an effective TQM program. How are these related to Deming's 14 points?
5. Name three of the important people associated with the quality concepts of this chapter. In each case, write a short sentence about each one summarizing their primary contribution to the field of quality management.
6. What are seven tools of TQM?
7. How does fear in the workplace (and in the classroom) inhibit learning?
8. How can a university control the quality of its output (that is, its graduates)?
9. Philip Crosby said that quality is free. Why?
10. List the three concepts central to Taguchi's approach.

11. What is the purpose of using a Pareto chart for a given problem?
12. What are the four broad categories of "causes" to help initially structure an Ishikawa diagram or cause-and-effect diagram?
13. Of the several points where inspection may be necessary, which apply especially well to manufacturing?
14. What roles do operations managers play in addressing the major aspects of service quality?
15. Explain, in your own words, what is meant by *source inspection*.
16. What are 10 determinants of service quality?
17. Name several products that do not require high quality.
18. What does the formula $L = D^2C$ mean?
19. In this chapter, we have suggested that building quality into a process and its people is difficult. Inspections are also difficult. To indicate just how difficult inspections are, count the number of *E*s (both capital *E* and lowercase *e*) in the *OM in Action* box "Richey International's Spies" (include the title but not the footnote). How many did you find? If each student does this individually, you are very likely to find a distribution rather than a single number!

Ethical Dilemma

A lawsuit a few years ago made headlines worldwide when a McDonald's drive-through customer spilled a cup of scalding hot coffee on herself. Claiming the coffee was too hot to be safely consumed in a car, the badly burned 80-year-old woman won $2.9 million in court. (The judge later reduced the award to $640,000.) McDonald's claimed the product was served to the correct specifications and was of proper quality. Further, the cup read "Caution—Contents May Be Hot." McDonald's coffee, at 180°, is substantially hotter (by corporate rule) than typical restaurant coffee,

despite hundreds of coffee-scalding complaints in the past 10 years. Similar court cases, incidentally, resulted in smaller verdicts, but again in favor of the plaintiffs. For example, Motor City Bagel Shop was sued for a spilled cup of coffee by a drive-through patron, and Starbucks by a customer who spilled coffee on her own ankle.

Are McDonald's, Motor City, and Starbucks at fault in situations such as these? How do quality and ethics enter into these cases?

Problems

• **1** An avant-garde clothing manufacturer runs a series of high-profile, risqué ads on a billboard on Highway 101 and regularly collects protest calls from people who are offended by them. The company has no idea how many people in total see the ad, but it has been collecting statistics on the number of phone calls from irate viewers:

Type	Description	Number of Complaints
R	Offensive racially/ethnically	10
M	Demeaning to men	4
W	Demeaning to women	14
I	Ad is Incomprehensible	6
O	Other	2

a) Depict this data with a Pareto chart. Also depict the cumulative complaint line.
b) What percent of the total complaints can be attributed to the most prevalent complaint?

• **2** Develop a scatter diagram for two variables of interest (say pages in the newspaper by day of the week; see example in Figure 6b).

• **3** Develop a Pareto chart of the following causes of poor grades on an exam:

Reason for Poor Grade	Frequency
Insufficient time to complete	15
Late arrival to exam	7
Difficulty understanding material	25
Insufficient preparation time	2
Studied wrong material	2
Distractions in exam room	9
Calculator batteries died during exam	1
Forgot exam was scheduled	3
Felt ill during exam	4

• **4** Develop a histogram of the time it took for you or your friends to receive six recent orders at a fast-food restaurant.

•• **5** Theresa Shotwell's restaurant in Tallahassee, Florida, has recorded the following data for eight recent customers:

Customer Number, i	Minutes from Time Food Ordered Until Food Arrived (y_i)	No. of Trips to Kitchen by Waitress (x_i)
1	10.50	4
2	12.75	5
3	9.25	3
4	8.00	2
5	9.75	3
6	11.00	4
7	14.00	6
8	10.75	5

a) Theresa wants you to graph the eight points (x_i, y_i), i = 1, 2, . . . 8. She has been concerned because customers have been waiting too long for their food, and this graph is intended to help her find possible causes of the problem.
b) This is an example of what type of graph?

•• **6** Develop a flowchart (as in Figure 6[e] and Example 2) showing all the steps involved in planning a party.

•• **7** Consider the types of poor driving habits that might occur at a traffic light. Make a list of the 10 you consider most likely to happen. Add the category of "other" to that list.
a) Compose a check sheet (like that in Figure 6[a]) to collect the frequency of occurrence of these habits. Using your check sheet, visit a busy traffic light intersection at four different times of the day, with two of these times being during high-traffic periods (rush hour, lunch hour). For 15 to 20 minutes each visit, observe the frequency with which the habits you listed occurred.
b) Construct a Pareto chart showing the relative frequency of occurrence of each habit.

•• **8** Draw a fish-bone chart detailing reasons why an airline customer might be dissatisfied.

•• **9** Consider the everyday task of getting to work on time or arriving at your first class on time in the morning. Draw a fish-bone chart showing reasons why you might arrive late in the morning.

•• **10** Construct a cause-and-effect diagram to reflect "student dissatisfied with university registration process." Use the "four Ms" or create your own organizing scheme. Include at least 12 causes.

•• **11** Draw a fish-bone chart depicting the reasons that might give rise to an incorrect fee statement at the time you go to pay for your registration at school.

••• 12   Mary Beth Marrs, the manager of an apartment complex, feels overwhelmed by the number of complaints she is receiving. Below is the check sheet she has kept for the last 12 weeks. Develop a Pareto chart using this information. What recommendations would you make?

Week	Grounds	Parking/ Drives	Pool	Tenant Issues	Electrical/ Plumbing
1	✓✓✓	✓✓	✓	✓✓✓	
2	✓	✓✓✓	✓✓	✓✓	✓
3	✓✓✓	✓✓✓	✓✓	✓	
4	✓	✓✓✓✓	✓	✓	✓✓
5	✓✓	✓✓✓	✓✓✓✓	✓✓	
6	✓	✓✓✓✓	✓✓		
7		✓✓✓	✓✓	✓✓	
8	✓	✓✓✓✓	✓✓	✓✓✓	✓
9	✓	✓✓	✓		
10	✓	✓✓✓✓	✓✓	✓✓	
11		✓✓✓	✓✓	✓	
12	✓✓	✓✓✓	✓✓✓	✓	

•   13   Use Pareto analysis to investigate the following data collected on a printed-circuit-board assembly line:

Defect	Number of Defect Occurrences
Components not adhering	143
Excess adhesive	71
Misplaced transistors	601
Defective board dimension	146
Mounting holes improperly positioned	12
Circuitry problems on final test	90
Wrong component	212

a) Prepare a graph of the data.
b) What conclusions do you reach?

•• 14   A list of 16 issues that led to incorrect formulations in Richard Dulski's jam manufacturing unit is provided below:

List of Issues

1. Incorrect measurement	9. Variability
2. Antiquated scales	10. Equipment in disrepair
3. Lack of clear instructions	11. Technician calculation off
4. Damaged raw material	12. Jars mislabeled
5. Operator misreads display	13. Temperature controls off
6. Inadequate cleanup	14. Incorrect weights
7. Incorrect maintenance	15. Priority miscommunication
8. Inadequate flow controls	16. Inadequate instructions

Create a fish-bone diagram and categorize each of these issues correctly, using the "four *M*s" method.

•• 15   Develop a flowchart for one of the following:
a) Filling up with gasoline at a self-serve station.
b) Determining your account balance and making a withdrawal at an ATM.
c) Getting a cone of yogurt or ice cream from an ice cream store.

••••16   Boston Electric Generators has been getting many complaints from its major customer, Home Station, about the quality of its shipments of home generators. Daniel Shimshak, the plant manager, is alarmed that a customer is providing him with the only information the company has on shipment quality. He decides to collect information on defective shipments through a form he has asked his drivers to complete on arrival at customers' stores. The forms for the first 279 shipments have been turned in. They show the following over the last 8 weeks:

			Reason for Defective Shipment			
Week	No. of Ship-ments	No. of Ship-ments with Defects	Incorrect Bill of Lading	Incorrect Truck-load	Damaged Product	Trucks Late
1	23	5	2	2	1	
2	31	8	1	4	1	2
3	28	6	2	3	1	
4	37	11	4	4	1	2
5	35	10	3	4	2	1
6	40	14	5	6	3	
7	41	12	3	5	3	1
8	44	15	4	7	2	2

Even though Daniel increased his capacity by adding more workers to his normal contingent of 30, he knew that for many weeks he exceeded his regular output of 30 shipments per week. A review of his turnover over the last 8 weeks shows the following:

Week	No. of New Hires	No. of Terminations	Total No. of Workers
1	1	0	30
2	2	1	31
3	3	2	32
4	2	0	34
5	2	2	34
6	2	4	32
7	4	1	35
8	3	2	36

a) Develop a scatter diagram using total number of shipments and number of defective shipments. Does there appear to be any relationship?
b) Develop a scatter diagram using the variable "turnover" (number of new hires plus number of terminations) and the number of defective shipments. Does the diagram depict a relationship between the two variables?
c) Develop a Pareto chart for the type of defects that have occurred.
d) Draw a fish-bone chart showing the possible causes of the defective shipments.

Case Study

Southwestern University: (C)*

The popularity of Southwestern University's football program under its new coach, Bo Pitterno, surged in each of the 5 years since his arrival at the Stephenville, Texas, college. With a football stadium close to maxing out at 54,000 seats and a vocal coach pushing for a new stadium, SWU president Joel Wisner faced some difficult decisions. After a phenomenal upset victory over its archrival, the University of Texas, at the homecoming game in the fall, Dr. Wisner was not as happy as one would think. Instead of ecstatic alumni, students, and faculty, all Wisner heard were complaints. "The lines at the concession stands were too long"; "Parking was harder to find and farther away than in the old days" (that is, before the team won regularly); "Seats weren't comfortable"; "Traffic was backed up halfway to Dallas"; and on

and on. "A college president just can't win," muttered Wisner to himself.

At his staff meeting the following Monday, Wisner turned to his VP of administration, Leslie Gardner. "I wish you would take care of these football complaints, Leslie," he said. "See what the *real* problems are and let me know how you've resolved them." Gardner wasn't surprised at the request. "I've already got a handle on it, Joel," she replied. "We've been randomly surveying 50 fans per game for the past year to see what's on their minds. It's all part of my campuswide TQM effort. Let me tally things up and I'll get back to you in a week."

When she returned to her office, Gardner pulled out the file her assistant had compiled (see Table 7). "There's a lot of information here," she thought.

		Overall Grade				
		A	**B**	**C**	**D**	**E**
Game Day	A. Parking	90	105	45	5	5
	B. Traffic	50	85	48	52	15
	C. Seating	45	30	115	35	25
	D. Entertainment	160	35	26	10	19
	E. Printed Program	66	34	98	22	30
Tickets	A. Pricing	105	104	16	15	10
	B. Season Ticket Plans	75	80	54	41	0
Concessions	A. Prices	16	116	58	58	2
	B. Selection of Foods	155	60	24	11	0
	C. Speed of Service	35	45	46	48	76

Respondents

Alumnus	113
Student	83
Faculty/Staff	16
None of the above	38

Open-Ended Comments on Survey Cards:

Parking a mess	More hot dog stands	Put in bigger seats	My company will buy a skybox—build it!
Add a skybox	Seats are all metal	Friendly ushers	Programs overpriced
Get better cheerleaders	Need skyboxes	Need better seats	Want softer seats
Double the parking attendants	Seats stink	Expand parking lots	Beat those Longhorns!
Everything is okay	Go SWU!	Hate the bleacher seats	I'll pay for a skybox
Too crowded	Lines are awful	Hot dogs cold	Seats too small
Seats too narrow	Seats are uncomfortable	$3 for a coffee? No way!	Band was terrific
Great food	I will pay more for better view	Get some skyboxes	Love Pitterno
Joe P. for President!	Get a new stadium	Love the new uniforms	Everything is great
I smelled drugs being smoked	Student dress code needed	Took an hour to park	Build new stadium
Stadium is ancient	I want cushioned seats	Coach is terrific	Move games to Dallas
Seats are like rocks	Not enough police	More water fountains	No complaints
Not enough cops for traffic	Students too rowdy	Better seats	Dirty bathroom
Game starts too late	Parking terrible	Seats not comfy	
Hire more traffic cops	Toilets weren't clean	Bigger parking lot	
Need new band	Not enough handicap spots in lot	I'm too old for bench seats	
Great!	Well done, SWU	Cold coffee served at game	

▲ **Table 7** Fan Satisfaction Survey Results (*N* = 250)

Discussion Questions

1. Using at least two different quality tools, analyze the data and present your conclusions.
2. How could the survey have been more useful?
3. What is the next step?

*This integrated case study runs throughout the text. Other issues facing Southwestern's football stadium include: (A) Managing the renovation project; (B) Forecasting game attendance; (C) Quality of facilities; (D) Break-even analysis of food services; (E) Locating the new stadium; (F) Inventory planning of football programs; and (G) Scheduling of campus security officers/staff for game days.

The Culture of Quality at Arnold Palmer Hospital

Video Case

Founded in 1989, Arnold Palmer Hospital is one of the largest hospitals for women and children in the U.S., with 431 beds in two facilities totaling 676,000 square feet. Located in downtown Orlando, Florida, and named after its famed golf benefactor, the hospital, with more than 2,000 employees serves an 18-county area in central Florida and is the only Level 1 trauma center for children in that region. Arnold Palmer Hospital provides a broad range of medical services including neonatal and pediatric intensive care, pediatric oncology and cardiology, care for high-risk pregnancies, and maternal intensive care.

The Issue of Assessing Quality Health Care

Quality health care is a goal all hospitals profess, but Arnold Palmer Hospital has actually developed comprehensive and scientific means of asking customers to judge the quality of care they receive. Participating in a national benchmark comparison against other hospitals, Arnold Palmer Hospital consistently scores in the top 10% in overall patient satisfaction. Executive Director Kathy Swanson states, "Hospitals in this area will be distinguished largely on the basis of their customer satisfaction. We must have accurate information about how our patients and their families judge the quality of our care, so I follow the questionnaire results daily. The in-depth survey helps me and others on my team to gain quick knowledge from patient feedback." Arnold Palmer Hospital employees are empowered to provide gifts in value up to $200 to patients who find reason to complain about any hospital service such as food, courtesy, responsiveness, or cleanliness.

Swanson doesn't focus just on the customer surveys, which are mailed to patients one week after discharge, but also on a variety of internal measures. These measures usually start at the grassroots level, where the staff sees a problem and develops ways to track performance. The hospital's longstanding philosophy supports the concept that each patient is important and respected as a person. That patient has the right to comprehensive, compassionate family-centered health care provided by a knowledgeable physician-directed team.

Some of the measures Swanson carefully monitors for continuous improvement are morbidity, infection rates, readmission rates, costs per case, and length of stays. The tools she uses daily include Pareto charts, flowcharts and process charts, in addition to benchmarking against hospitals both nationally and in the southeast region.

The result of all of these efforts has been a quality culture as manifested in Arnold Palmer's high ranking in patient satisfaction and one of the highest survival rates of critically ill babies.

Discussion Questions*

1. Why is it important for Arnold Palmer Hospital to get a patient's assessment of health care quality? Does the patient have the expertise to judge the health care she receives?
2. How would you build a culture of quality in an organization, such as Arnold Palmer Hospital?
3. What techniques does Arnold Palmer Hospital practice in its drive for quality and continuous improvement?
4. Develop a fish-bone diagram illustrating the quality variables for a patient who just gave birth at Arnold Palmer Hospital (or any other hospital).

*You may wish to review this video case on your DVD before answering these questions.

Quality at the Ritz-Carlton Hotel Company

Video Case

Ritz-Carlton. The name alone evokes images of luxury and quality. As the first hotel company to win the Malcolm Baldrige National Quality Award, the Ritz treats quality as if it is the heartbeat of the company. This means a daily commitment to meeting customer expectations and making sure that each hotel is free of any deficiency.

In the hotel industry, quality can be hard to quantify. Guests do not purchase a product when they stay at the Ritz: They buy an experience. Thus, creating the right combination of elements to make the experience stand out is the challenge and goal of every employee, from maintenance to management.

Before applying for the Baldrige Award, company management undertook a rigorous self-examination of its operations in an attempt to measure and quantify quality. Nineteen processes were studied, including room service delivery, guest reservation and registration, message delivery, and breakfast service. This period of self-study included statistical measurement of process work flows and cycle times for areas ranging from room service delivery times and reservations to valet parking and housekeeping efficiency. The results were used to develop performance benchmarks against which future activity could be measured.

With specific, quantifiable targets in place, Ritz-Carlton managers and employees now focus on continuous improvement. The goal is 100% customer satisfaction: If a guest's experience does not meet expectations, the Ritz-Carlton risks losing that guest to competition.

One way the company has put more meaning behind its quality efforts is to organize its employees into "self-directed" work teams. Employee teams determine work scheduling, what work needs to be done, and what to do about quality problems in their own areas. In order that they can see the relationship of their specific area to the overall goals, employees are also given the opportunity to take additional training in hotel operations. Ritz-Carlton believes that a more educated and informed employee is in a better position to make decisions in the best interest of the organization.

Discussion Questions*

1. In what ways could the Ritz-Carlton monitor its success in achieving quality?
2. Many companies say that their goal is to provide quality products or services. What actions might you expect from a company that intends quality to be more than a slogan or buzzword?
3. Why might it cost the Ritz-Carlton less to "do things right" the first time?
4. How could control charts, Pareto diagrams, and cause-and-effect diagrams be used to identify quality problems at a hotel?
5. What are some nonfinancial measures of customer satisfaction that might be used by the Ritz-Carlton?

*You may wish to view this video case on your DVD before addressing these questions.

Source: Adapted from C. T. Horngren, S. M. Datar, and G. Foster, *Cost Accounting*, 12th ed. (Upper Saddle River, NJ: Prentice Hall, 2006).

Additional Case Studies

Internet Case Study: Visit our Companion Web site at www.prenhall.com/heizer for this free case study:

• **Westover Electrical, Inc.:** This electric motor manufacturer has a large log of defects in its wiring process.

Harvard has selected these Harvard Business School cases to accompany this chapter:

harvardbusinessonline.hbsp.harvard.edu

• **GE: We Bring Good Things to Life (A)** (#899-162): Illustrates the complexity of managing change and the momentum that initiatives can provide.
• **Wainwright Industries (A): Beyond the Baldrige** (#396-219): Traces the growth of an auto supply company and its culture of quality.
• **Romeo Engine Plant** (#197-100): The employees at this auto engine plant must solve problems and ensure quality, not watch parts being made.
• **Motorola-Penang** (#494-135): The female manager of this Malaysia factory is skeptical of empowerment efforts at other Motorola sites.
• **Measure of Delight: The Pursuit of Quality at AT&T Universal Card Service (A)** (#694-047): Links performance measurement and compensation policies to precepts of quality management.

Bibliography

Aikens, C. *Quality*. Upper Saddle River, NJ: Prentice Hall, 2006.

Beer, M. "Why Total Quality Management Programs Do Not Persist." *Decision Sciences* 34, no. 4 (Fall 2003): 623–642.

Brown, Mark G. *Baldrige Award Winning Quality*, 13th ed. University Park, IL: Productivity Press, 2004.

Crosby, P. B. *Quality Is Still Free*. New York: McGraw-Hill, 1996.

Evans, J. R., and W. M. Lindsay. *An Introduction to Six Sigma and Process Improvement*. Mason, OH: Thompson-Southwestern, 2005.

Foster, S. Thomas. *Managing Quality*, 3rd ed. Upper Saddle River, NJ: Prentice Hall, 2007.

Gitlow, H. S., et al. *Quality Management*, 3rd ed. New York: McGraw-Hill, 2005.

Goetsch, David L., and Stanley B. Davis. *Quality Management*, 5th ed. Upper Saddle River, NJ: Prentice Hall, 2006.

Gryna, F. M., R. C. H. Chua, and J. A. DeFeo. *Juran's Quality Planning and Analysis for Enterprise Quality*, 5th ed. New York: McGraw-Hill, 2007.

Henderson, G. R. *Six Sigma Quality Improvement with Minitab*. New York: Wiley, 2006.

King, J., and R. Cichy. *Managing for Quality in the Hospitality Industry*. Upper Saddle River, NJ: Prentice Hall, 2006.

Pande, P. S., R. P. Neuman, R. R. Cavanagh. *What Is Design for Six Sigma?* New York: McGraw-Hill, 2005.

Pil, F. K., and S. Rothenberg. "Environmental Performance as a Driver of Superior Quality." *Production and Operations Management* 12, no. 3 (Fall 2003): 404–415.

Prahalad, C. K., and M. S. Krishnan. "The New Meaning of Quality in the Information Age." *Harvard Business Review* (September–October, 1999): 109–118.

Stewart, D. M. "Piecing Together Service Quality: A Framework for Robust Service." *Production and Operations Management* (Summer 2003): 246–265.

Summers, Donna. *Quality*. 4th ed. Upper Saddle River, NJ: Prentice Hall, 2006.

Tonkin, L. P. "Supercharging Business Improvements: Motorola's Six Sigma Leadership Tools." *Target: Innovation at Work* 20, no. 1 (first issue 2004): 50–53.

Vastag, Gyula. "Revisiting ISO 14000 Diffusion: A New 'Look' at the Drivers of Certification." *Production and Operations Management* 13, no. 3 (Fall 2004): 260–267.

Internet Resources

American Society for Quality: **www.asq.org/**
ISO Central Secretariat: **www.iso.ch/**
Juran Institute: **www.juran.com/**
Links to benchmarking sites: **www.ebenchmarking.com**

National Institute of Standards and Technology: **www.quality.nist.gov/**
Quality Assurance Institute: **www.qai.worldwide.org**
Quality Digest: **www. qualitydigest.com**
Quality Progress: **www.qualityprogress.asq.org**

Solutions to Even Numbered Problems

2 Individual answer, in the style of Figure 6(b).

4 Individual answer, in the style of Figure 6(f).

6 Partial flowchart for planning a party:

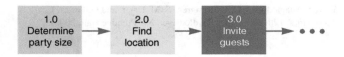

8 See figure on next page.

10 Individual answer, in the style of Figure 7 in the chapter.

12 Pareto chart, in the style of Example 1 with parking/drives most frequent, pool second, etc

14 See figure on next page.
Materials: 4, 12, 14; Methods: 3, 7, 15, 16; Manpower: 1, 5, 6, 11; Machines: 2, 8, 9, 10, 13.

16 **(a)** A scatter diagram in the style of Figure 6(b) that shows a strong positive relationship between shipments and defects
(b) A scatter diagram in the style of Figure 6(b) that shows a mild relationship between shipments and turnover

▼ *Figure for problem 8.*

Fish-Bone Chart for Dissatisfied Airline Customer

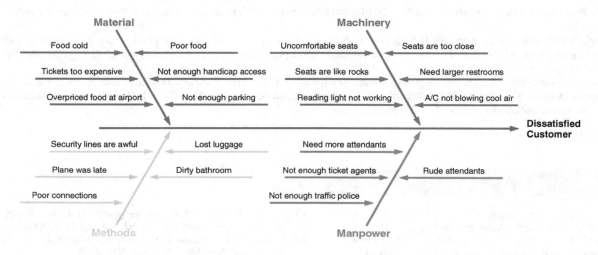

▼ *Figure for problem 14.*

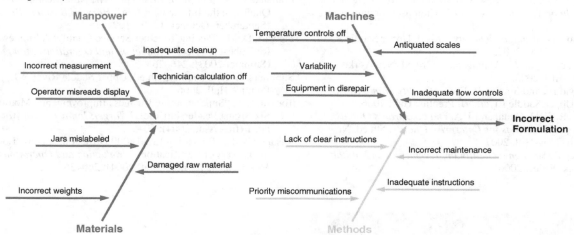

(c) A Pareto chart in the style of Figure 6(d) that shows frequency
of each type of defect

(d) A fishbone chart in the style of Figure 6(c) with the 4 *M*s
showing possible causes of increasing defects in shipments

Solutions to Self Test

1. c; **2.** d; **3.** continuous improvement; Six Sigma; Taguchi concepts;
empowerment; benchmarking; JIT; TQM tools; **4.** environmental
procedures; **5.** check sheets, scatter diagrams, cause-and-effect diagrams,
Pareto charts, flowcharts, histograms, SPC charts; **6.** f; **7.** a; **8.** inspected.

Statistical Process Control

Outline

Statistical Process Control (SPC)
Control Charts for Variables
The Central Limit Theorem
Setting Mean Chart Limits ($\bar{x}$-Charts)
Setting Range Chart Limits (R-Charts)
Using Mean and Range Charts
Control Charts for Attributes
Managerial Issues and Control Charts

Process Capability
Process Capability Ratio (C_p)
Process Capability Index (C_{pk})

Acceptance Sampling
Operating Characteristic Curve
Average Outgoing Quality
Summary
Key Terms

Using Software for SPC
Solved Problems
Active Model Exercise
Self-Test
Internet and Student CD-ROM/DVD
    Exercises
Discussion Questions
Problems
Case Studies: Bayfield Mud Company;
    Alabama Airlines's On-Time Schedule
Video Case: Farm to Fork: Quality at
    Darden Restaurants
Additional Case Studies
Bibliography
Internet Resources

Learning Objectives

When you complete this selection you should be able to

1. Explain the purpose of a control chart
2. Explain the role of the central limit theorem in SPC
3. Build $\bar{x}$-charts and R-charts
4. List the five steps involved in building control charts
5. Build p-charts and c-charts
6. Explain process capability and compute C_p and C_{pk}
7. Explain acceptance sampling
8. Compute the AOQ

▶ *BetzDearborn, A Division of Hercules Incorporated, is headquartered in Trevose, Pennsylvania. It is a global supplier of specialty chemicals for the treatment of industrial water, wastewater, and process systems. The company uses statistical process control to monitor the performance of treatment programs in a wide variety of industries throughout the world. BetzDearborn's quality assurance laboratory (shown here) also uses statistical sampling techniques to monitor manufacturing processes at all of the company's production plants.*

P.L. Vidor, BetzDearborn, Inc.

Statistical process control (SPC)

A process used to monitor standards by taking measurements and corrective action as a product or service is being produced.

In this supplement, we address statistical process control—the same techniques used at BetzDearborn, at IBM, at GE, and at Motorola to achieve quality standards. We also introduce acceptance sampling. **Statistical process control** is the application of statistical techniques to the control of processes. *Acceptance sampling* is used to determine acceptance or rejection of material evaluated by a sample.

STATISTICAL PROCESS CONTROL (SPC)

Statistical process control (SPC) is a statistical technique that is widely used to ensure that processes meet standards. All processes are subject to a certain degree of variability. While studying process data in the 1920s, Walter Shewhart of Bell Laboratories made the distinction between the common and special causes of variation. Many people now refer to these variations as *natural* and *assignable* causes. He developed a simple but powerful tool to separate the two—the **control chart**.

Control chart

A graphical presentation of process data over time.

We use statistical process control to measure performance of a process. A process is said to be operating *in statistical control* when the only source of variation is common (natural) causes. The process must first be brought into statistical control by detecting and eliminating special (assignable) causes of variation.[1] Then its performance is predictable, and its ability to meet customer expectations can be assessed. The *objective* of a process control system is to *provide a statistical signal when assignable causes of variation are present*. Such a signal can quicken appropriate action to eliminate assignable causes.

Natural variations

Variability that affects every production process to some degree and is to be expected; also known as common cause.

Natural Variations   Natural variations affect almost every production process and are to be expected. **Natural variations** are the many sources of variation that occur within a process that is in statistical control. Natural variations behave like a constant system of chance causes. Although individual values are all different, as a group they form a pattern that can be described as a *distribution*. When these distributions are *normal*, they are characterized by two parameters:

- Mean, μ (the measure of central tendency—in this case, the average value)
- Standard deviation, σ (the measure of dispersion)

As long as the distribution (output measurements) remains within specified limits, the process is said to be "in control," and natural variations are tolerated.

---

[1]Removing assignable causes is work. Quality expert W. Edwards Deming observed that a state of statistical control is not a natural state for a manufacturing process. Deming instead viewed it as an achievement, arrived at by elimination, one by one, by determined effort, of special causes of excessive variation. See J. R. Thompson and J. Koronacki, *Statistical Process Control, The Deming Paradigm and Beyond*. Boca Raton, FL: Chapman and Hall, 2002.

Assignable Variations   **Assignable variation** in a process can be traced to a specific reason. Factors such as machine wear, misadjusted equipment, fatigued or untrained workers, or new batches of raw material are all potential sources of assignable variations.

Natural and assignable variations distinguish two tasks for the operations manager. The first is to *ensure that the process is capable* of operating under control with only natural variation. The second is, of course, to *identify and eliminate assignable variations* so that the processes will remain under control.

Samples   Because of natural and assignable variation, statistical process control uses averages of small samples (often of four to eight items) as opposed to data on individual parts. Individual pieces tend to be too erratic to make trends quickly visible.

Figure 1 provides a detailed look at the important steps in determining process variation. The horizontal scale can be weight (as in the number of ounces in boxes of cereal) or length (as in fence posts) or any physical measure. The vertical scale is frequency. The samples of five boxes of cereal in Figure 1 (**a**) are weighed; (**b**) form a distribution, and (**c**) can vary. The distributions formed in (**b**) and (**c**) will fall in a predictable pattern (**d**) if only natural variation is present. If assignable causes of variation are present, then we can expect either the mean to vary or the dispersion to vary, as is the case in (**e**).

Control Charts   The process of building control charts is based on the concepts presented in Figure 2. This figure shows three distributions that are the result of outputs from three types of processes. We plot small samples and then examine characteristics of the resulting data to see if the process is within "control limits." The purpose of control charts is to help distinguish between natural variations and variations due to assignable causes. As seen in Figure 2, a process is (**a**) in control *and the process is capable of producing within established control limits*, (**b**) in control *but the process is not capable of producing within established limits*, or (**c**) out of control. We now look at ways to build control charts that help the operations manager keep a process under control.

Assignable variation
Variation in a production process that can be traced to specific causes.

Video S6.1

SPC at Harley-Davidson

Learning Objective

1. Explain the purpose of a control chart

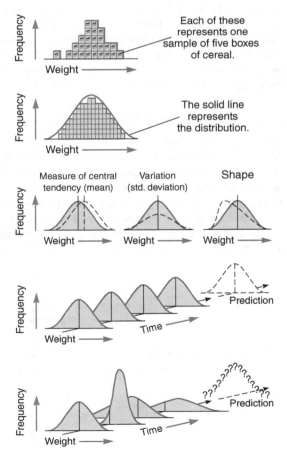

(a) Samples of the product, say five boxes of cereal taken off the filling machine line, vary from one another in weight.

Each of these represents one sample of five boxes of cereal.

(b) After enough samples are taken from a stable process, they form a pattern called a *distribution*.

The solid line represents the distribution.

(c) There are many types of distributions, including the normal (bell-shaped) distribution, but distributions do differ in terms of central tendency (mean), standard deviation or variance, and shape.

Measure of central tendency (mean)   Variation (std. deviation)   Shape

(d) If only natural causes of variation are present, the output of a process forms a distribution that is stable over time and is predictable.

Prediction

(e) If assignable causes of variation are present, the process output is not stable over time and is not predictable. That is, when causes that are not an expected part of the process occur, the samples will yield unexpected distributions that vary by central tendency, standard deviation, and shape.

Prediction

◄ **Figure 1**

Natural and Assignable Variation

▶ Figure 2

Process Control: Three Types of Process Outputs

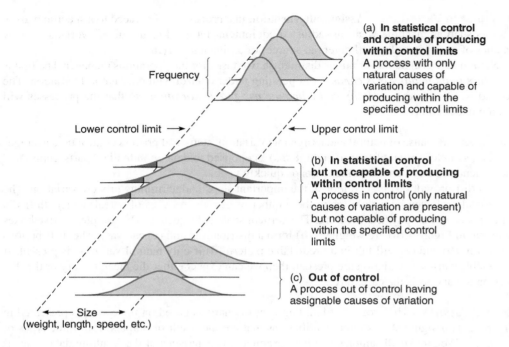

Frequency

Lower control limit →

← Upper control limit

(a) In statistical control and capable of producing within control limits
A process with only natural causes of variation and capable of producing within the specified control limits

(b) In statistical control but not capable of producing within control limits
A process in control (only natural causes of variation are present) but not capable of producing within the specified control limits

(c) Out of control
A process out of control having assignable causes of variation

← Size →
(weight, length, speed, etc.)

$\bar{x}$-chart

A quality control chart for variables that indicates when changes occur in the central tendency of a production process.

R-chart

A control chart that tracks the "range" within a sample; it indicates that a gain or loss in uniformity has occurred in dispersion of a production process.

Central limit theorem

The theoretical foundation for $\bar{x}$-charts, which states that regardless of the distribution of the population of all parts or services, the distribution of $\bar{x}$s will tend to follow a normal curve as the number of samples increases.

Control Charts for Variables

The variables of interest here are those that have continuous dimensions. They have an infinite number of possibilities. Examples are weight, speed, length, or strength. Control charts for the mean, $\bar{x}$ or x-bar, and the range, R, are used to monitor processes that have continuous dimensions. The $\bar{x}$-chart tells us whether changes have occurred in the central tendency (the mean, in this case) of a process. These changes might be due to such factors as tool wear, a gradual increase in temperature, a different method used on the second shift, or new and stronger materials. The **R-chart** values indicate that a gain or loss in dispersion has occurred. Such a change may be due to worn bearings, a loose tool, an erratic flow of lubricants to a machine, or to sloppiness on the part of a machine operator. The two types of charts go hand in hand when monitoring variables because they measure the two critical parameters: central tendency and dispersion.

The Central Limit Theorem

The theoretical foundation for $\bar{x}$-charts is the **central limit theorem**. This theorem states that regardless of the distribution of the population, the distribution of $\bar{x}$s (each of which is a mean of a sample drawn from the population) will tend to follow a normal curve as the number of samples increases. Fortunately, even if the sample (n) is fairly small (say, 4 or 5), the distributions of the averages will still roughly follow a normal curve. The theorem also states that: (1) the mean of the distribution of the $\bar{x}$s (called $\bar{\bar{x}}$) will equal the mean of the overall population (called μ); and (2) the standard deviation of the *sampling distribution*, $\sigma_{\bar{x}}$, will be the *population standard deviation*, σ, divided by the square root of the sample size, n. In other words:[2]

$$\bar{\bar{x}} = \mu \tag{1}$$

and:

$$\sigma_{\bar{x}} = \frac{\sigma}{\sqrt{n}} \tag{2}$$

Figure 3 shows three possible population distributions, each with its own mean, μ, and standard deviation, σ. If a series of random samples ($\bar{x}_1, \bar{x}_2, \bar{x}_3, \bar{x}_4$, and so on), each of size n, is drawn

[2]*Note:* The standard deviation is easily calculated as $\sigma = \sqrt{\dfrac{\sum_{i=1}^{n}(x_i - \bar{x})^2}{n-1}}$.

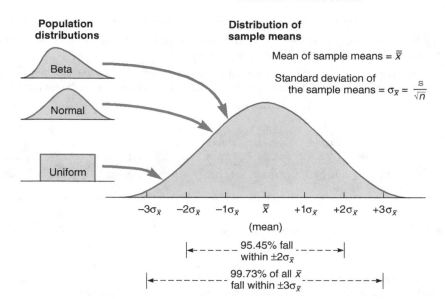

The Relationship between Population and Sampling Distributions

Regardless of the population distribution (e.g., normal, beta, uniform), each with its own mean (μ) and standard deviation (σ), the distribution of sample means is normal.

from any population distribution (which could be normal, beta, uniform, and so on), the resulting distribution of $\bar{x}_i$s will appear as they do in Figure 3.

Moreover, the sampling distribution, as is shown in Figure 4, will have less variability than the process distribution. Because the sampling distribution is normal, we can state that:

- 95.45% of the time, the sample averages will fall within $\pm 2\sigma_{\bar{x}}$ if the process has only natural variations.
- 99.73% of the time, the sample averages will fall within $\pm 3\sigma_{\bar{x}}$ if the process has only natural variations.

If a point on the control chart falls outside of the $\pm 3\sigma_{\bar{x}}$ control limits, then we are 99.73% sure the process has changed. This is the theory behind control charts.

Learning Objective

2. Explain the role of the central limit theorem in SPC

Setting Mean Chart Limits ($\bar{x}$-Charts)

If we know, through past data, the standard deviation of the process population, σ, we can set upper and lower control limits by using these formulas:

$$\text{Upper control limit (UCL)} = \bar{\bar{x}} + z\sigma_{\bar{x}} \tag{3}$$

$$\text{Lower control limit (LCL)} = \bar{\bar{x}} - z\sigma_{\bar{x}} \tag{4}$$

where
$\bar{\bar{x}}$ = mean of the sample means or a target value set for the process
z = number of normal standard deviations (2 for 95.45% confidence, 3 for 99.73%)
$\sigma_{\bar{x}}$ = standard deviation of the sample means = $\sigma / \sqrt{n}$
σ = population (process) standard deviation
n = sample size

Example 1 shows how to set control limits for sample means using standard deviations.

Learning Objective

3. Build $\bar{x}$-charts and R-charts

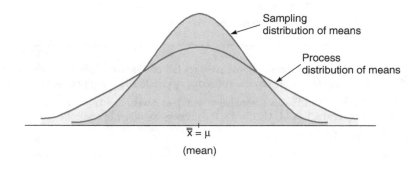

◄ **Figure 4**

The Sampling Distribution of Means Is Normal and Has Less Variability Than the Process Distribution

In this figure, the process distribution from which the sample was drawn was also normal, but it could have been any distribution.

The weights of boxes of Oat Flakes within a large production lot are sampled each hour. Managers want to set control limits that include 99.73% of the sample means.

Approach: Randomly select and weigh nine ($n = 9$) boxes each hour. Then find the overall mean and use Equations (3) and (4) to compute the control limits. Here are the nine boxes chosen for Hour 1:

Solution: The average weight in the first sample $= \dfrac{17+13+16+18+17+16+15+17+16}{9}$

$$= 16.1 \text{ oz.}$$

Also, the *population* standard deviation (σ) is known to be 1 ounce. We do not show each of the boxes randomly selected in hours 2 through 12, but here are all twelve hourly samples:

Hour	Weight of Sample (Avg. of 9 Boxes)	Hour	Weight of Sample (Avg. of 9 Boxes)	Hour	Weight of Sample (Avg. of 9 Boxes)
1	16.1	5	16.5	9	16.3
2	16.8	6	16.4	10	14.8
3	15.5	7	15.2	11	14.2
4	16.5	8	16.4	12	17.3

The average mean of the 12 samples is calculated to be exactly 16 ounces. We therefore have $\bar{\bar{x}} = 16$ ounces, $\sigma = 1$ ounce, $n = 9$, and $z = 3$. The control limits are:

$$\text{UCL}_{\bar{x}} = \bar{\bar{x}} + z\sigma_{\bar{x}} = 16 + 3\left(\frac{1}{\sqrt{9}}\right) = 16 + 3\left(\frac{1}{3}\right) = 17 \text{ ounces}$$

$$\text{LCL}_{\bar{x}} = \bar{\bar{x}} - z\sigma_{\bar{x}} = 16 - 3\left(\frac{1}{\sqrt{9}}\right) = 16 - 3\left(\frac{1}{3}\right) = 15 \text{ ounces}$$

The 12 samples are then plotted on the following control chart:

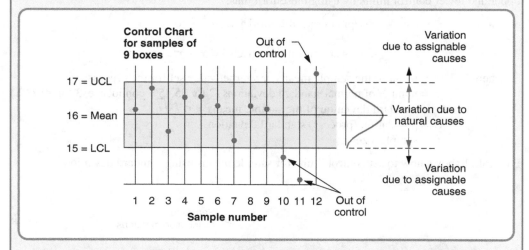

Insight: Because the means of recent sample averages fall outside the upper and lower control limits of 17 and 15, we can conclude that the process is becoming erratic and is *not* in control.

Learning exercise: If Oat Flakes's population standard deviation (σ) is 2 (instead of 1), what is your conclusion? [Answer: LCL = 14, UCL = 18; the process would be in control.]

Related problems: 1, 2, 4, 8, 10a,b

Sample Size, n	Mean Factor, A_2	Upper Range, D_4	Lower Range, D_3
2	1.880	3.268	0
3	1.023	2.574	0
4	.729	2.282	0
5	.577	2.115	0
6	.483	2.004	0
7	.419	1.924	0.076
8	.373	1.864	0.136
9	.337	1.816	0.184
10	.308	1.777	0.223
12	.266	1.716	0.284

◄ **Table 1**

Factors for Computing Control Chart Limits (3 sigma)

Source: Reprinted by permission of American Society for Testing Materials. Copyright 1951. Taken from Special Technical Publication 15-C, "Quality Control of Materials," pp. 63 and 72.

Because process standard deviations are either not available or difficult to compute, we usually calculate control limits based on the average *range* values rather than on standard deviations. Table 1 provides the necessary conversion for us to do so. The *range* is defined as the difference between the largest and smallest items in one sample. For example, the heaviest box of Oat Flakes in Hour 1 of Example S1 was 18 ounces and the lightest was 13 ounces, so the range for that hour is 5 ounces. We use Table 1 and the equations:

$$UCL_{\bar{x}} = \bar{\bar{x}} + A_2\bar{R} \qquad (5)$$

and:

$$LCL_{\bar{x}} = \bar{\bar{x}} - A_2\bar{R} \qquad (6)$$

where $\bar{R}$ = average range of the samples

A_2 = value found in Table 1

$\bar{\bar{x}}$ = mean of the sample means

Example 2 shows how to set control limits for sample means by using Table 1 and the average range.

> The range is the difference between the largest and the smallest items in a sample.

EXAMPLE 2

Setting mean limits using table values

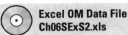
Excel OM Data File Ch06SExS2.xls

Super Cola bottles soft drinks labeled "net weight 12 ounces." Indeed, an overall process average of 12 ounces has been found by taking many samples, in which each sample contained 5 bottles. The average range of the process is .25 ounce. The OM team wants to determine the upper and lower control limits for averages in this process.

Approach: Super Cola applies Equations (5) and (6) and uses the A_2 column of Table 1.

Solution: Looking in Table 1 for a sample size of 5 in the mean factor A_2 column, we find the value .577. Thus, the upper and lower control chart limits are:

$$UCL_{\bar{x}} = \bar{\bar{x}} + A_2\bar{R}$$

$$= 12 + (.577)(.25)$$

$$= 12 + .144$$

$$= 12.144 \text{ ounces}$$

$$LCL_{\bar{x}} = \bar{\bar{x}} - A_2\bar{R}$$

$$= 12 - .144$$

$$= 11.856 \text{ ounces}$$

Insight: The advantage of using this range approach, instead of the standard deviation, is that it is easy to apply and may be less confusing.

Learning exercise: If the sample size was $n = 4$ and the average range = .20 ounces, what are the revised $UCL_{\bar{x}}$ and $LCL_{\bar{x}}$? [Answer: 12.146, 11.854.]

Related problems: 3a, 5, 6, 7, 9, 10b,c,d 11, 34

▶ *Salmon filets are monitored by Darden Restaurant's SPC software, which includes C_p, C_{pk}, $\bar{x}$-, and R-charts and a process capability histogram. The video case study "Farm to Fork," at the end of this supplement, asks you to interpret these figures.*

Video S6.2

Farm to Fork: Quality of Darden Restaurants

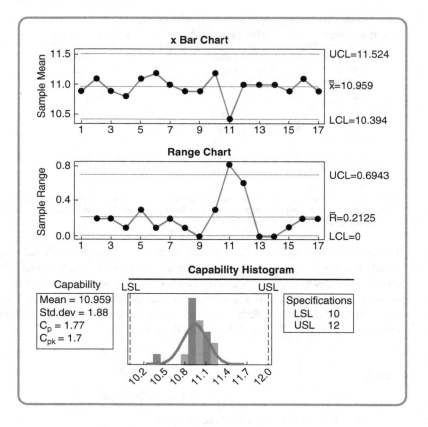

Setting Range Chart Limits (*R*-Charts)

In Examples 1 and 2, we determined the upper and lower control limits for the process *average*. In addition to being concerned with the process average, operations managers are interested in the process *dispersion*, or *range*. Even though the process average is under control, the dispersion of the process may not be. For example, something may have worked itself loose in a piece of equipment that fills boxes of Oat Flakes. As a result, the average of the samples may remain the same, but the variation within the samples could be entirely too large. For this reason, operations managers use control charts for ranges to monitor the process variability, as well as control charts for averages, which monitor the process central tendency. The theory behind the control charts for ranges is the same as that for process average control charts. Limits are established that contain ±3 standard deviations of the distribution for the average range $\bar{R}$. We can use the following equations to set the upper and lower control limits for ranges:

> *When determining the UCL_R and LCL_R, use the average range, $\bar{R}$. But when plotting points once the R-chart is developed, use the individual range values for each sample.*

$$UCL_R = D_4\bar{R} \tag{7}$$

$$LCL_R = D_3\bar{R} \tag{8}$$

where UCL_R = upper control chart limit for the range
           LCL_R = lower control chart limit for the range
     D_4 and D_3 = values from Table 1

Example 3 shows how to set control limits for sample ranges using Table 1 and the average range.

EXAMPLE 3

Setting range limits using table values

The average *range* of a product at Clinton Manufacturing is 5.3 pounds. With a sample size of 5, owner Roy Clinton wants to determine the upper and lower control chart limits.

Approach: Looking in Table 1 for a sample size of 5, he finds that $D_4 = 2.115$ and $D_3 = 0$.

Solution: The range control limits are:

$$UCL_R = D_4\bar{R} = (2.115)(5.3 \text{ pounds}) = 11.2 \text{ pounds}$$

$$LCL_R = D_3\bar{R} = (0)(5.3 \text{ pounds}) = 0$$

Insight: Computing ranges with Table 1 is straightforward and an easy way to evaluate dispersion.

Learning exercise: Clinton decides to increase the sample size to $n = 7$. What are the new UCL_R and LCL_R values? [Answer: 10.197, 0.40.]

Related problems: 3b, 5, 6, 7, 9, 10c, 11, 12, 34

Using Mean and Range Charts

The normal distribution is defined by two parameters, the *mean* and *standard deviation*. The $\bar{x}$ (mean)-chart and the R-chart mimic these two parameters. The $\bar{x}$-chart is sensitive to shifts in the process mean, whereas the R-chart is sensitive to shifts in the process standard deviation. Consequently, by using both charts we can track changes in the process distribution.

For instance, the samples and the resulting $\bar{x}$-chart in Figure 5(a) show the shift in the process mean, but because the dispersion is constant, no change is detected by the R-chart. Conversely, the samples and the $\bar{x}$-chart in Figure 5(b) detect no shift (because none is present), but the R-chart does detect the shift in the dispersion. Both charts are required to track the process accurately.

Steps to Follow When Using Control Charts   There are five steps that are generally followed in using $\bar{x}$- and R-charts:

1. Collect 20 to 25 samples, often of $n = 4$ or $n = 5$ observations each, from a stable process and compute the mean and range of each.
2. Compute the overall means ($\bar{\bar{x}}$ and $\bar{R}$), set appropriate control limits, usually at the 99.73% level, and calculate the preliminary upper and lower control limits. Refer to Table 2 for other control limits. *If the process is not currently stable*, use the desired mean, μ, instead of $\bar{\bar{x}}$ to calculate limits.

Desired Control Limit (%)	z-Value (standard deviation required for desired level of confidence)
90.0	1.65
95.0	1.96
95.45	2.00
99.0	2.58
99.73	3.00

> **Learning Objective**
>
> 4. List the five steps involved in building control charts

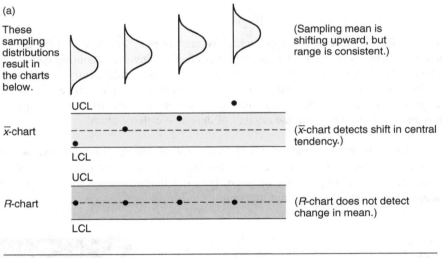

(a)

These sampling distributions result in the charts below.

(Sampling mean is shifting upward, but range is consistent.)

$\bar{x}$-chart — ($\bar{x}$-chart detects shift in central tendency.)

R-chart — (R-chart does not detect change in mean.)

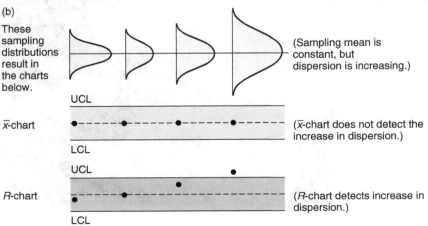

(b)

These sampling distributions result in the charts below.

(Sampling mean is constant, but dispersion is increasing.)

$\bar{x}$-chart — ($\bar{x}$-chart does not detect the increase in dispersion.)

R-chart — (R-chart detects increase in dispersion.)

> *The two parameters are:*
> *Mean → measure of central tendency.*
> *Range → measure of dispersion.*

◀ **Figure 5**

Mean and Range Charts Complement Each Other by Showing the Mean and Dispersion of the Normal Distribution

OM in Action   Frito-Lay Uses SPC to Keep Its Ruffles Tasty

No one wants to bite into a potato chip that is too salty—nor one that has no taste at all. Frito-Lay's Ruffles brand potato chips have to have just the right salt content, crispiness, and thickness.

Frito-Lay uses $\bar{x}$ charts and SPC to control its production at critical points in the process—instead of its old system of inspecting chips at the end of the process. Every 15 minutes, three batches of chips are taken from the conveyor, ground up, weighed, dissolved in distilled water, and filtered into a beaker. The salt content of the batches is analyzed electronically and averaged to get a mean for that sample. The sample mean is then plotted on an $\bar{x}$ chart whose target value is 1.6%. The lower and upper control limits are 1.12% and 2.08%, respectively;

Donna McWilliam, AP Wide World Photos

so if a batch is out of control, the process can be corrected before a huge number of defective Ruffles are produced. With SPC, variability among bags of chips has decreased by 50%.

Sources: Knight Ridder Tribune Business News (October 24, 2004): 1; COMAP, Annenberg/ CPB Project (Needham Heights, MA: Allyn & Bacon); and *Strategic Direction* (February 2002): 8–11.

3. Graph the sample means and ranges on their respective control charts and determine whether they fall outside the acceptable limits.
4. Investigate points or patterns that indicate the process is out of control. Try to assign causes for the variation, address the causes, and then resume the process.
5. Collect additional samples and, if necessary, revalidate the control limits using the new data.

Applications of control charts appear in examples in this supplement, as well as in the *OM in Action* box "Frito-Lay Uses SPC to Keep Its Ruffles Tasty."

Control Charts for Attributes

Control charts for $\bar{x}$ and R do not apply when we are sampling *attributes*, which are typically classified as *defective* or *nondefective*. Measuring defectives involves counting them (for example, number of bad lightbulbs in a given lot, or number of letters or data entry records typed with errors), whereas *variables* are usually measured for length or weight. There are two kinds of attribute control charts: (1) those that measure the *percent* defective in a sample—called *p*-charts—and (2) those that count the *number* of defects—called *c*-charts.

p-chart

A quality control chart that is used to control attributes.

p-**Charts**   Using **p-charts** is the chief way to control attributes. Although attributes that are either good or bad follow the binomial distribution, the normal distribution can be used to calculate *p*-chart limits when sample sizes are large. The procedure resembles the $\bar{x}$-chart approach, which is also based on the central limit theorem.

▶ *Although SPC charts can be generated by computer, this one is being prepared by hand. This chart is updated each hour and reflects a week of workshifts.*

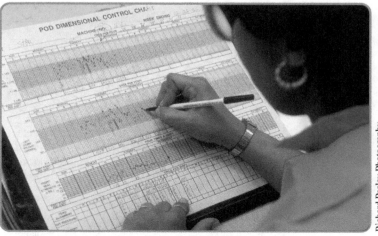
Richard Pasley Photography

The formulas for *p*-chart upper and lower control limits follow:

$$UCL_p = \bar{p} + z\sigma_{\hat{p}} \tag{9}$$

$$LCL_p = \bar{p} - z\sigma_{\hat{p}} \tag{10}$$

where $\bar{p}$ = mean fraction defective in the sample
             z = number of standard deviations ($z = 2$ for 95.45% limits; $z = 3$ for 99.73% limits)
             $\sigma_{\hat{p}}$ = standard deviation of the sampling distribution

$\sigma_{\hat{p}}$ is estimated by the formula

$$\sigma_{\hat{p}} = \sqrt{\frac{\bar{p}(1-\bar{p})}{n}} \tag{11}$$

where n = number of observations in *each* sample

Example S4 shows how to set control limits for *p*-charts for these standard deviations.

Clerks at Mosier Data Systems key in thousands of insurance records each day for a variety of client firms. CEO Donna Mosier wants to set control limits to include 99.73% of the random variation in the data entry process when it is in control.

Approach: Samples of the work of 20 clerks are gathered (and shown in the table). Mosier carefully examines 100 records entered by each clerk and counts the number of errors. She also computes the fraction defective in each sample. Equations (9), (10), and (11) are then used to set the control limits.

Sample Number	Number of Errors	Fraction Defective	Sample Number	Number of Errors	Fraction Defective
1	6	.06	11	6	.06
2	5	.05	12	1	.01
3	0	.00	13	8	.08
4	1	.01	14	7	.07
5	4	.04	15	5	.05
6	2	.02	16	4	.04
7	5	.05	17	11	.11
8	3	.03	18	3	.03
9	3	.03	19	0	.00
10	2	.02	20	4	.04
				80	

Solution: $\bar{p} = \dfrac{\text{Total number of errors}}{\text{Total number of records examined}} = \dfrac{80}{(100)(20)} = .04$

$\sigma_{\hat{p}} = \sqrt{\dfrac{(.04)(1-.04)}{100}} = .02$ (rounded up from .0196)

(*Note:* 100 is the size of *each* sample = *n*.)

$$UCL_p = \bar{p} + z\sigma_{\hat{p}} = .04 + 3(.02) = .10$$

$$LCL_p = \bar{p} - z\sigma_{\hat{p}} = .04 - 3(.02) = 0$$

(because we cannot have a negative percent defective)

Insight: When we plot the control limits and the sample fraction defectives, we find that only one data-entry clerk (number 17) is out of control. The firm may wish to examine that individual's work a bit more closely to see if a serious problem exists (see Figure 6).

EXAMPLE 4

Setting control limits for percent defective

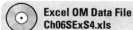
Excel OM Data File
Ch06SExS4.xls

Active Model S6.1

Example 4 is further illustrated in Active Model S6.1 on the CD-ROM.

► **Figure 6**

p-Chart for Data Entry
for Example 4

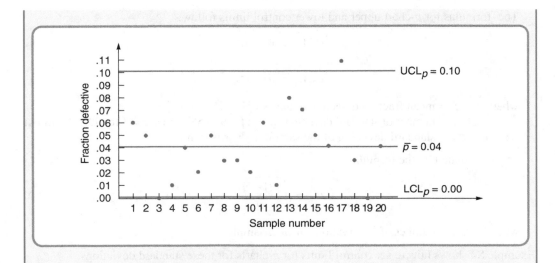

Learning exercise: Mosier decides to set control limits at 95.45% instead. What are the new UCL$_p$ and LCL$_p$? [Answer: 0.08, 0.]

Related problems: 13, 14, 15, 16, 17, 18, 19, 20, 25

The *OM in Action* box "Unisys Corp.'s Costly Experiment in Health Care Services" provides a real-world follow-up to Example 4.

c-Charts   In Example 4, we counted the number of defective records entered. A defective record was one that was not exactly correct because it contained at least one defect. However, a bad record may contain more than one defect. We use **c-charts** to control the *number* of defects per unit of output (or per insurance record, in the preceding case).

c-chart

A quality control chart used to control the number of defects per unit of output.

Control charts for defects are helpful for monitoring processes in which a large number of potential errors can occur, but the actual number that do occur is relatively small. Defects may be errors in newspaper words, bad circuits in a microchip, blemishes on a table, or missing pickles on a fast-food hamburger.

OM in Action   Unisys Corp.'s Costly Experiment in Health Care Services

When Unisys Corp. expanded into the computerized health care service business things looked rosy. It had just beat out Blue Cross/Blue Shield of Florida for an $86 million contract to serve Florida's state employee health-insurance services. Its job was to handle the 215,000 Florida employees' claims processing—a seemingly simple and lucrative growth area for an old-line computer company like Unisys.

But 1 year later the contract was not only torn up, Unisys was fined more than $500,000 for not meeting quality standards. Here are two of the measures of quality, both attributes (that is, either "defective" or "not defective") on which the firm was out of control:

1. *Percent of claims processed with errors:* An audit over a 3-month period, by Coopers & Lybrand, found that Unisys made errors in 8.5% of claims processed. The industry standard is 3.5% "defectives."

2. *Percent of claims processed within 30 days:* For this attribute measure, a "defect" is a processing time longer than the contract's time allowance. In one month's sample, 13% of the claims exceeded the 30-day limit, far above the 5% allowed by the State of Florida.

The Florida contract was a migraine for Unisys, which underestimated the labor-intensiveness of health claims. CEO James Unruh pulled the plug on future ambitions in health care. Meanwhile, the State of Florida's Ron Poppel says, "We really need somebody that's in the insurance business."

Sources: Knight Ridder Tribune Business News (October 20, 2004): 1 and (February 7, 2002): 1; and *Business Week* (June 16, 1997): 6.

Charles O'Rear, CORBIS—NY

◄ *Sampling wine from these wooden barrels, to make sure it is aging properly, uses both SPC (for alcohol content and acidity) and subjective measures (for taste).*

The Poisson probability distribution,[3] which has a variance equal to its mean, is the basis for c-charts. Because $\bar{c}$ is the mean number of defects per unit, the standard deviation is equal to $\sqrt{\bar{c}}$. To compute 99.73% control limits for $\bar{c}$, we use the formula:

$$\text{Control limits} = \bar{c} \pm 3\sqrt{\bar{c}} \qquad (12)$$

Example 5 shows how to set control limits for a $\bar{c}$-chart.

Red Top Cab Company receives several complaints per day about the behavior of its drivers. Over a 9-day period (where days are the units of measure), the owner, Gordon Hoft, received the following numbers of calls from irate passengers: 3, 0, 8, 9, 6, 7, 4, 9, 8, for a total of 54 complaints. Hoft wants to compute 99.73% control limits.

Approach: He applies Equation (12).

Solution: $\bar{c} = \dfrac{54}{9} = 6$ complaints per day

Thus:

$$\text{UCL}_c = \bar{c} + 3\sqrt{\bar{c}} = 6 + 3\sqrt{6} = 6 + 3(2.45) = 13.35, \text{ or } 13$$

$$\text{LCL}_c = \bar{c} - 3\sqrt{\bar{c}} = 6 - 3\sqrt{6} = 6 - 3(2.45) = 0 \leftarrow \text{(since it cannot be negative)}$$

Insight: After Hoft plotted a control chart summarizing these data and posted it prominently in the drivers' locker room, the number of calls received dropped to an average of three per day. Can you explain why this occurred?

Learning exercise: Hoft collects 3 more days' worth of complaints (10, 12, and 8 complaints) and wants to combine them with the original 9 days to compute updated control limits. What are the revised UCL_c and LCL_c? [Answer: 14.94, 0.]

Related problems: 21, 22, 23, 24

EXAMPLE 5

Setting control limits for number defective

Excel OM Data File Ch06SExS5.xls

Managerial Issues and Control Charts

In an ideal world, there is no need for control charts. Quality is uniform and so high that employees need not waste time and money sampling and monitoring variables and attributes. But because most processes have not reached perfection, managers must make three major decisions regarding control charts.

---

[3]A Poisson probability distribution is a discrete distribution commonly used when the items of interest (in this case, defects) are infrequent and/or occur in time and space.

► **Table 3**

Helping You Decide Which
Control Chart to Use

Variable Data

Using an $\bar{x}$-Chart and an R-Chart

1. Observations are *variables*, which are usually products measured for size or weight. Examples are the width or length of a wire being cut and the weight of a can of Campbell's soup.
2. Collect 20 to 25 samples, usually of $n = 4$, $n = 5$, or more, each from a stable process, and compute the mean for an $\bar{x}$-chart and the range for an R-chart.
3. We track samples of n observations each, as in Example 1.

Attribute Data

Using a p-Chart

1. Observations are *attributes* that can be categorized as good or bad (or pass–fail, or functional–broken), that is, in two states.
2. We deal with fraction, proportion, or percent defectives.
3. There are several samples, with many observations in each. For example, 20 samples of $n = 100$ observations in each, as in Example 4.

Using a c-Chart

1. Observations are *attributes* whose defects per unit of output can be counted.
2. We deal with the number counted, which is a small part of the possible occurrences.
3. Defects may be: number of blemishes on a desk; complaints in a day; crimes in a year; broken seats in a stadium; typos in a chapter of this text; or flaws in a bolt of cloth, as is shown in Example 5.

First, managers must select the points in their process that need SPC. They may ask "Which parts of the job are critical to success?" or "Which parts of the job have a tendency to become out of control?"

Second, managers need to decide if variable charts (i.e., $\bar{x}$ and R) or attribute charts (i.e., p and c) are appropriate. Variable charts monitor weights or dimensions. Attribute charts are more of a "yes–no" or "go–no go" gauge and tend to be less costly to implement. Table 3 can help you understand when to use each of these types of control charts.

Third, the company must set clear and specific SPC policies for employees to follow. For example, should the data-entry process be halted if a trend is appearing in percent defective records being keyed? Should an assembly line be stopped if the average length of five successive samples is above the centerline? Figure 7 illustrates some of the patterns to look for over time in a process.

A tool called a **run test** is available to help identify the kind of abnormalities in a process that we see in Figure 7. In general, a run of 5 points above or below the target or centerline may suggest that an assignable, or nonrandom, variation is present. When this occurs, even though all the points may

Run test

A test used to examine the points in a control chart to see if nonrandom variation is present.

► **Figure 7**

Patterns to Look for on Control Charts

Source: Adapted from Bertrand L. Hansen, *Quality Control: Theory and Applications* (1991): 65. Reprinted by permission of Prentice Hall, Upper Saddle River, New Jersey.

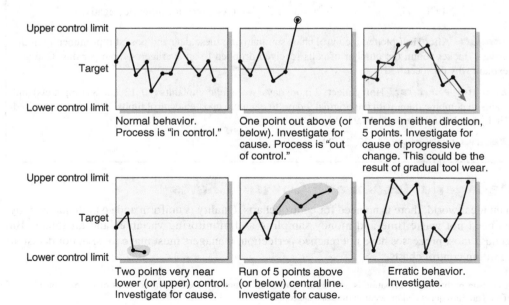

fall inside the control limits, a flag has been raised. This means the process may not be statistically in control. A variety of run tests are described in books on the subject of quality methods.[4]

PROCESS CAPABILITY

Statistical process control means keeping a process in control. This means that the natural variation of the process must be stable. But a process that is in statistical control may not yield goods or services that meet their *design specifications* (tolerances). The ability of a process to meet design specifications, which are set by engineering design or customer requirements, is called **process capability**. Even though that process may be statistically in control (stable), the output of that process may not conform to specifications.

For example, let's say the time a customer expects to wait for the completion of a lube job at Quik Lube is 12 minutes, with an acceptable tolerance of ±2 minutes. This tolerance gives an upper specification of 14 minutes and a lower specification of 10 minutes. The lube process has to be capable of operating within these design specifications—if not, some customers will not have their requirements met. As a manufacturing example, the tolerances for Harley-Davidson cam gears are extremely low, only 0.0005 inch—and a process must be designed that is capable of achieving this tolerance.

There are two popular measures for quantitatively determining if a process is capable: process capability ratio (C_p) and process capability index (C_{pk}).

Process Capability Ratio (C_p)

For a process to be capable, its values must fall within upper and lower specifications. This typically means the process capability is within ±3 standard deviations from the process mean. Since this range of values is 6 standard deviations, a capable process tolerance, which is the difference between the upper and lower specifications, must be greater than or equal to 6.

The process capability ratio, C_p, is computed as:

$$C_p = \frac{\text{Upper specification} - \text{Lower specification}}{6\sigma}$$

(13)

Example 6 shows the computation of C_p.

> **Process capability**
> The ability to meet design specifications.

> **Learning Objective**
> 6. Explain process capability and compute C_p and C_{pk}

> **C_p**
> A ratio for determining whether a process meets design specifications; a ratio of the specification to the process variation.

EXAMPLE 6

Process capability ratio (C_p)

In a GE insurance claims process, $\bar{x}$ = 210.0 minutes, and σ = .516 minutes.

The design specification to meet customer expectations is 210 ± 3 minutes. So the Upper Specification is 213 minutes and the lower specification is 207 minutes. The OM manager wants to compute the process capability ratio.

Approach: GE applies Equation (13).

Solution: $C_p = \dfrac{\text{Upper specification} - \text{Lower specification}}{6\sigma} = \dfrac{213 - 207}{6(.516)} = 1.938$

Insight: Since a ratio of 1.00 means that 99.73% of a process's outputs are within specifications, this ratio suggests a very capable process, with nonconformance of less than 4 claims per million.

Learning exercise: If σ = .60 (instead of .516), what is the new C_p? [Answer: 1.667, a very capable process still.]

Related problems: 26, 27

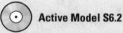

Active Model S6.2

Example 6 is further illustrated in Active Model S6.2 on the CD-ROM.

A capable process has a C_p of at least 1.0. If the C_p is less than 1.0, the process yields products or services that are outside their allowable tolerance. With a C_p of 1.0, 2.7 parts in 1,000 can be expected to be "out of spec."[5] The higher the process capability ratio, the greater the likelihood

---

[4]See Gerald Smith, *Statistical Process Control and Process Improvement*, 6th ed. (Upper Saddle River, NJ: Prentice Hall, 2007).

[5]This is because a C_p of 1.0 has 99.73% of outputs within specifications. So 1.00 − .9973 = .0027; with 1,000 parts, there are .0027 × 1,000 = 2.7 defects.

For a C_p of 2.0, 99.99966% of outputs are "within spec." So 1.00 − .9999966 = .0000034; with 1 million parts, there are 3.4 defects.

the process will be within design specifications. Many firms have chosen a C_p of 1.33 (a 4-sigma standard) as a target for reducing process variability. This means that only 64 parts per million can be expected to be out of specification.

The concept of *Six Sigma* quality is championed by GE and Motorola. This standard equates to a C_p of 2.0, with only 3.4 defective parts per million (very close to zero defects) instead of the 2.7 parts per 1,000 with 3-sigma limits.

Although C_p relates to the spread (dispersion) of the process output relative to its tolerance, it does not look at how well the process average is centered on the target value.

Process Capability Index (C_{pk})

C_{pk}
A proportion of variation (3σ) between the center of the process and the nearest specification limit.

The process capability index, **C_{pk}**, measures the difference between the desired and actual dimensions of goods or services produced.

The formula for C_{pk} is:

$$C_{pk} = \text{Minimum of} \left[\frac{\text{Upper specification limit} - \bar{X}}{3\sigma}, \frac{\bar{X} - \text{Lower specification limit}}{3\sigma} \right] \quad (14)$$

where $\bar{X}$ = process mean
σ = standard deviation of the process population

When the C_{pk} index for both the upper and lower specification limits equals 1.0, the process variation is centered and the process is capable of producing within ±3 standard deviations (fewer than 2,700 defects per million). A C_{pk} of 2.0 means the process is capable of producing fewer than 3.4 defects per million. For C_{pk} to exceed 1, σ must be less than $\frac{1}{3}$ of the difference between the specification and the process mean ($\bar{X}$). Figure 8 shows the meaning of various measures of C_{pk}, and Example 7 shows an application of C_{pk}.

EXAMPLE 7

Process capability index (C_{pk})

You are the process improvement manager and have developed a new machine to cut insoles for the company's top-of-the-line running shoes. You are excited because the company's goal is no more than 3.4 defects per million and this machine may be the innovation you need. The insoles cannot be more than ±.001 of an inch from the required thickness of .250". You want to know if you should replace the existing machine, which has a C_{pk} of 1.0.

Approach: You decide to determine the C_{pk}, using Equation (14), for the new machine and make a decision on that basis.

Solution:
Upper specification limit = .251 inch
Lower specification limit = .249 inch

Mean of the new process $\bar{X}$ = .250 inch.
Estimated standard deviation of the new process = σ = .0005 inch.

$$C_{pk} = \text{Minimum of} \left[\frac{\text{Upper specification limit} - \bar{X}}{3\sigma}, \frac{\bar{X} - \text{Lower specification limit}}{3\sigma} \right]$$

$$C_{pk} = \text{Minimum of} \left[\frac{(.251) - .250}{(3).0005}, \frac{.250 - (.249)}{(3).0005} \right]$$

Both calculations result in: $\frac{.001}{.0015} = .67$.

Insight: Because the new machine has a C_{pk} of only 0.67, the new machine should *not* replace the existing machine.

Learning exercise: If the insoles can be ±.002" (instead of .001") from the required .250", what is the new C_{pk}? [Answer: 1.33 and the new machine *should* replace the existing one.]

Related problems: 27, 28, 29, 30, 31

Note that C_p and C_{pk} will be the same when the process is centered. However, if the mean of the process is not centered on the desired (specified) mean, then the smaller numerator in Equation (14) is used (the minimum of the difference between the upper specification limit and the mean or the lower specification limit and the mean). This application of C_{pk} is shown in Solved Problem 4. C_{pk} is the standard criterion used to express process performance.

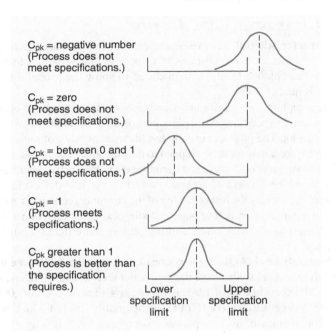

Meanings of C_{pk} Measures

A C_{pk} index of 1.0 for both the upper and lower control limits indicates that the process variation is within the upper and lower control limits. As the C_{pk} index goes above 1.0, the process becomes increasingly target-oriented with fewer defects. If the C_{pk} is less than 1.0, the process will not produce within the specified tolerance. Because a process may not be centered, or may "drift," a C_{pk} above 1 is desired.

ACCEPTANCE SAMPLING[6]

Acceptance sampling is a form of testing that involves taking random samples of "lots," or batches, of finished products and measuring them against predetermined standards. Sampling is more economical than 100% inspection. The quality of the sample is used to judge the quality of all items in the lot. Although both attributes and variables can be inspected by acceptance sampling, attribute inspection is more commonly used, as illustrated in this section.

Acceptance sampling can be applied either when materials arrive at a plant or at final inspection, but it is usually used to control incoming lots of purchased products. A lot of items rejected, based on an unacceptable level of defects found in the sample, can (1) be returned to the supplier or (2) be 100% inspected to cull out all defects, with the cost of this screening usually billed to the supplier. However, acceptance sampling is not a substitute for adequate process controls. In fact, the current approach is to build statistical quality controls at suppliers so that acceptance sampling can be eliminated.

Acceptance sampling
A method of measuring random samples of lots or batches of products against predetermined standards.

7. Explain acceptance sampling

Georgia Institute of Technology

◀ *Flowers Bakery in Villa Rica, Georgia, uses a digital camera to inspect just-baked sandwich buns as they move along the production line. Items that don't measure up in terms of color, shape, seed distribution, or size are identified and removed automatically from the conveyor.*

[6]Refer to Tutorial 2 on your CD-ROM for an extended discussion of Acceptance Sampling.

Operating Characteristic Curve

The **operating characteristic (OC) curve** describes how well an acceptance plan discriminates between good and bad lots. A curve pertains to a specific plan—that is, to a combination of n (sample size) and c (acceptance level). It is intended to show the probability that the plan will accept lots of various quality levels.

With acceptance sampling, two parties are usually involved: the producer of the product and the consumer of the product. In specifying a sampling plan, each party wants to avoid costly mistakes in accepting or rejecting a lot. The producer usually has the responsibility of replacing all defects in the rejected lot or of paying for a new lot to be shipped to the customer. The producer, therefore, wants to avoid the mistake of having a good lot rejected (**producer's risk**). On the other hand, the customer or consumer wants to avoid the mistake of accepting a bad lot because defects found in a lot that has already been accepted are usually the responsibility of the customer (**consumer's risk**). The OC curve shows the features of a particular sampling plan, including the risks of making a wrong decision.[7]

Figure 9 can be used to illustrate one sampling plan in more detail. Four concepts are illustrated in this figure.

The **acceptable quality level (AQL)** is the poorest level of quality that we are willing to accept. In other words, we wish to accept lots that have this or a better level of quality, but no lower. If an acceptable quality level is 20 defects in a lot of 1,000 items or parts, then AQL is $20/1,000 = 2\%$ defectives.

The **lot tolerance percent defective (LTPD)** is the quality level of a lot that we consider bad. We wish to reject lots that have this or a poorer level of quality. If it is agreed that an unacceptable quality level is 70 defects in a lot of 1,000, then the LTPD is $70/1,000 = 7\%$ defective.

To derive a sampling plan, producer and consumer must define not only "good lots" and "bad lots" through the AQL and LTPD, but they must also specify risk levels.

Producer's risk (α) is the probability that a "good" lot will be rejected. This is the risk that a random sample might result in a much higher proportion of defects than the population of all items. A lot with an acceptable quality level of AQL still has an α chance of being rejected. Sampling plans are often designed to have the producer's risk set at $\alpha = .05$, or 5%.

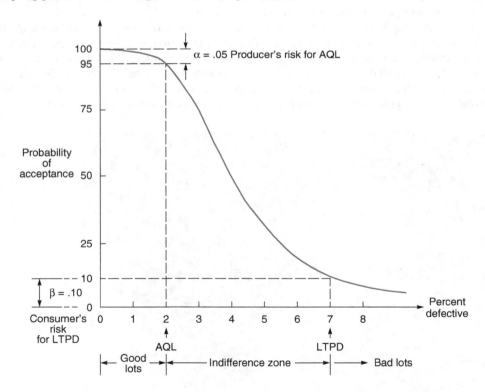

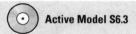
[7]Note that sampling always runs the danger of leading to an erroneous conclusion. Let us say in one company that the total population under scrutiny is a load of 1,000 computer chips, of which in reality only 30 (or 3%) are defective. This means that we would want to accept the shipment of chips, because for this particular firm 4% is the allowable defect rate. However, if a random sample of $n = 50$ chips was drawn, we could conceivably end up with 0 defects and accept that shipment (that is, it is okay), or we could find all 30 defects in the sample. If the latter happened, we could wrongly conclude that the whole population was 60% defective and reject them all.

 This laser tracking device, by Faro Technologies, enables quality control personnel to measure and inspect parts and tools during production. The tracker can measure objects from 100 feet away and takes up to 1,000 readings per second.

Consumer's risk (β) is the probability that a "bad" lot will be accepted. This is the risk that a random sample may result in a lower proportion of defects than the overall population of items. A common value for consumer's risk in sampling plans is β = .10, or 10%.

The probability of rejecting a good lot is called a **type I error**. The probability of accepting a bad lot is a **type II error**.

Sampling plans and OC curves may be developed by computer (as seen in the software available with this text), by published tables, or by calculation, using binomial or Poisson distributions.

Type I error
Statistically, the probability of rejecting a good lot.

Type II error
Statistically, the probability of accepting a bad lot.

Average Outgoing Quality

In most sampling plans, when a lot is rejected, the entire lot is inspected and all defective items replaced. Use of this replacement technique improves the average outgoing quality in terms of percent defective. In fact, given (1) any sampling plan that replaces all defective items encountered and (2) the true incoming percent defective for the lot, it is possible to determine the **average outgoing quality (AOQ)** in percent defective. The equation for AOQ is:

$$AOQ = \frac{(P_d)(P_a)(N - n)}{N} \tag{15}$$

where P_d = true percent defective of the lot
   P_a = probability of accepting the lot for a given sample size and quantity defective
   N = number of items in the lot
   n = number of items in the sample

Average outgoing quality (AOQ)
The percent defective in an average lot of goods inspected through acceptance sampling.

The maximum value of AOQ corresponds to the highest average percent defective or the lowest average quality for the sampling plan. It is called the *average outgoing quality limit (AOQL)*.

Acceptance sampling is useful for screening incoming lots. When the defective parts are replaced with good parts, acceptance sampling helps to increase the quality of the lots by reducing the outgoing percent defective.

Figure 10 compares acceptance sampling, SPC, and C_{pk}. As Figure 10 shows, (a) acceptance sampling by definition accepts some bad units, (b) control charts try to keep the process in control, but (c) the C_{pk} index places the focus on improving the process. As operations managers, that is what we want to do—improve the process.

Learning Objective

8. Compute the AOQ

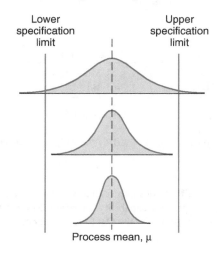

Lower specification limit

Upper specification limit

(a) Acceptance sampling
(Some bad units accepted; the "lot" is good or bad.)

(b) Statistical process control
(Keep the process "in control.")

(c) C_{pk} > 1
(Design a process that is in control.)

Process mean, μ

◄ **Figure 10**

The Application of Statistical Process Techniques Contributes to the Identification and Systematic Reduction of Process Variability

Summary

Statistical process control is a major statistical tool of quality control. Control charts for SPC help operations managers distinguish between natural and assignable variations. The $\bar{x}$-chart and the R-chart are used for variable sampling, and the p-chart and the c-chart for attribute sampling. The C_{pk} index is a way to express process capability. Operating characteristic (OC) curves facilitate acceptance sampling and provide the manager with tools to evaluate the quality of a production run or shipment.

Key Terms

Statistical process control (SPC)
Control chart
Natural variations
Assignable variation
$\bar{x}$-chart
R-chart
Central limit theorem
p-chart

c-chart
Run test
Process capability
C_p
C_p
Acceptance sampling
Operating characteristic (OC) curve
Producer's risk

Consumer's risk
Acceptable quality level (AQL)
Lot tolerance percent defective (LTPD)
Type I error
Type II error
Average outgoing quality (AOQ)

Using Software for

Excel, Excel OM, and POM for Windows may be used to develop control charts for most of the problems in this chapter.

✗ Creating Excel Spreadsheets to Determine Control Limits for a *c*-Chart

Excel and other spreadsheets are extensively used in industry to maintain control charts. Program 1 is an example of how to use Excel to determine the control limits for a c-chart. C-charts are used when the number of defects per unit of output is known. The data from Example 5 are used. In this example, 54 complaints occurred over 9 days. Excel also contains a built-in graphing ability with Chart Wizard.

► **Program 1**

An Excel Spreadsheet for Creating a c-Chart for Example 5

	A	B	C	D	E	F	G	H
1	**Red Top Cab Company**							
2								
3	Number of samples	9						
4								
5		Complaints		Results				
6	Day 1	3		Total Defects	54			
7	Day 2	0		Defect rate, λ	6			
8	Day 3	8		Standard deviation	2.45			
9	Day 4	9		z value	3			99.73%
10	Day 5	6						
11	Day 6	7		Upper Control Limit	13.348469			
12	Day 7	4		Center Line	6			
13	Day 8	9		Lower Control Limit	0			
14	Day 9	8						

Value	Cell	Excel Formula
Total Defects	E6	=SUM(B6:B14)
Defect rate, λ	E7	=E6/B3
Standard deviation	E8	=SQRT(E7)
Upper Control Limit	E11	=E7+E9*E8
Center Line	E12	=E7
Lower Control Limit	E13	=IF(E7-E9*E8>0,E7-E9*E8,0)

✗ Using Excel OM

Excel OM's Quality Control module has the ability to develop $\bar{x}$-charts, p-charts, and c-charts. It also handles OC curves, acceptance sampling, and process capability. Program 2 illustrates Excel OM's spreadsheet approach to computing the $\bar{x}$ control limits for the Oat Flakes company in Example 1.

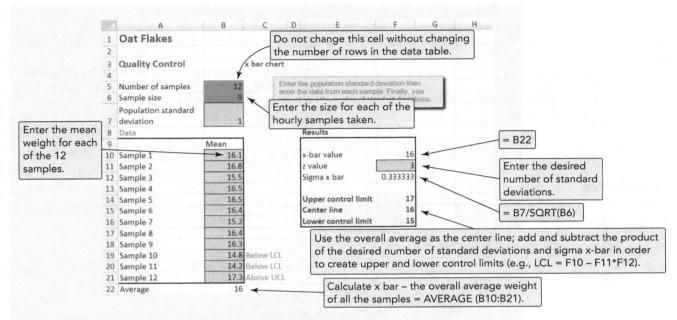

▲ **Program 2**   **Excel OM Input and Selected Formulas for the Oat Flakes Example 1**

Using POM for Windows

The POM for Windows Quality Control module has the ability to compute all the SPC control charts we introduced in this supplement, as well as OC curves, acceptance sampling, and process capability. See Appendix: Using Excel OM and POM for Windows for further details.

Solved Problems

 Virtual Office Hours help is available on Student DVD.

Solved Problem 1

A manufacturer of precision machine parts produces round shafts for use in the construction of drill presses. The average diameter of a shaft is .56 inch. Inspection samples contain 6 shafts each. The average range of these samples is .006 inch. Determine the upper and lower $\bar{x}$ control chart limits.

Solution

The mean factor A_2 from Table 1 where the sample size is 6, is seen to be .483. With this factor, you can obtain the upper and lower control limits:

$$\text{UCL}_{\bar{x}} = .56 + (.483)(.006)$$
$$= .56 + .0029$$
$$= .5629 \text{ inch}$$
$$\text{LCL}_{\bar{x}} = .56 - .0029$$
$$= .5571 \text{ inch}$$

Solved Problem 2

Nocaf Drinks, Inc., a producer of decaffeinated coffee, bottles Nocaf. Each bottle should have a net weight of 4 ounces. The machine that fills the bottles with coffee is new, and the operations manager wants to make sure that it is properly adjusted. Bonnie Crutcher, the operations manager, randomly selects and weighs $n = 8$ bottles and records the average and range in ounces for each sample. The data for several samples is given in the following table. Note that every sample consists of 8 bottles.

Sample	Sample Range	Sample Average	Sample	Sample Range	Sample Average
A	.41	4.00	E	.56	4.17
B	.55	4.16	F	.62	3.93
C	.44	3.99	G	.54	3.98
D	.48	4.00	H	.44	4.01

Is the machine properly adjusted and in control?

Solution

We first find that $\bar{\bar{x}} = 4.03$ and $\bar{R} = .505$. Then, using Table 1, we find:

$$\text{UCL}_{\bar{x}} = \bar{\bar{x}} + A_2\bar{R} = 4.03 + (.373)(.505) = 4.22$$

$$\text{LCL}_{\bar{x}} = \bar{\bar{x}} - A_2\bar{R} = 4.03 - (.373)(.505) = 3.84$$

$$\text{UCL}_R = D_4\bar{R} = (1.864)(.505) = .94$$

$$\text{LCL}_R = D_3\bar{R} = (.136)(.505) = .07$$

It appears that the process average and range are both in statistical control.

The operations manager needs to determine if a process with a mean (4.03) slightly above the desired mean of 4.00 is satisfactory; if it is not, the process will need to be changed.

Solved Problem 3

Altman Distributors, Inc., fills catalog orders. Samples of size $n = 100$ orders have been taken each day over the past six weeks. The average defect rate was .05. Determine the upper and lower limits for this process for 99.73% confidence.

Solution

$z = 3$, $\bar{p} = .05$. Using Equations 9, 10, and 11,

$$\text{UCL}_p = \bar{p} + 3\sqrt{\frac{\bar{p}(1-\bar{p})}{n}} = .05 + 3\sqrt{\frac{(.05)(1-.05)}{100}}$$

$$= .05 + 3(0.0218) = .1154$$

$$\text{LCL}_p = \bar{p} - 3\sqrt{\frac{\bar{p}(1-\bar{p})}{n}} = .05 - 3(.0218)$$

$$= .05 - .0654 = 0 \text{ (because percent defective cannot be negative)}$$

Solved Problem 4

Ettlie Engineering has a new catalyst injection system for your countertop production line. Your process engineering department has conducted experiments and determined that the mean is 8.01 grams with a standard deviation of .03. Your specifications are:

$\mu = 8.0$ and $\sigma = .04$, which means an upper specification limit of 8.12 [= 8.0 + 3(.04)] and a lower specification limit of 7.88 [= 8.0 − 3(.04)].

What is the C_{pk} performance of the injection system?

Solution

Using Equation (14):

$$C_{pk} = \text{Minimum of} \left[\frac{\text{Upper specification limit} - \bar{X}}{3\sigma}, \frac{\bar{X} - \text{Lower specification limit}}{3\sigma} \right]$$

where $\bar{X}$ = process mean
        σ = standard deviation of the process population

$$C_{pk} = \text{minimum of} \left[\frac{8.12 - 8.01}{(3)(.03)}, \frac{8.01 - 7.88}{(3)(.03)} \right]$$

$$\left[\frac{.11}{.09} = 1.22, \frac{.13}{.09} = 1.44 \right]$$

The minimum is 1.22, so the C_{pk} of 1.22 is within specifications and has an implied error rate of less than 2,700 defects per million.

Active Model Exercise

This Active Model, as well as Active Models S6.2 and S6.3, appears on your CD. Active Model S6.1 allows you to evaluate important elements in the p-charts.

Questions

1. Has the process been in control?

2. Suppose we use a 95 percent p-chart. What are the upper and lower control limits? Has the process gotten more out of control?

p-Chart

Reset Data   Questions

	# Defects	Fraction Defective
Number of samples	20	
Sample size	100	
z value	3.0000	
Confidence	99.73%	

Total Sample Size	2000	Upper Control Limit	0.10
Total Defects	80	Center Line	0.04
Percentage defects	0.04	Lower Control Limit	0.00
Std dev of p-bar	0.019596		

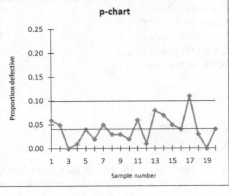

	# Defects	Fraction Defective
Sample 1	6	0.06
Sample 2	5	0.05
Sample 3	0	0.00
Sample 4	1	0.01
Sample 5	4	0.04
Sample 6	2	0.02
Sample 7	5	0.05
Sample 8	3	0.03
Sample 9	3	0.03
Sample 10	2	0.02
Sample 11	6	0.06
Sample 12	1	0.01
Sample 13	8	0.08
Sample 14	7	0.07
Sample 15	5	0.05
Sample 16	4	0.04
Sample 17	11	0.11 Above UCL
Sample 18	3	0.03
Sample 19	0	0.00
Sample 20	4	0.04

◄ **Active Model S6.1**

p-Chart for the Mosier Data Systems in Example 4.

3. Suppose that the sample size used was actually 120 instead of the 100 that it was supposed to be. How would this affect the chart?

4. What happens to the chart as we reduce the *z*-value?

5. What happens to the chart as we reduce the percentage defects?

Self-Test

- *Before taking the self-test, refer to the learning objectives listed at the beginning of the selection and the key terms listed at the end of the supplement.*
- *Use the key at the back of the text to **correct** your answers.*
- *Restudy pages that correspond to any questions you answered incorrectly or material you feel uncertain about.*

1. The type of chart used to control the central tendency of variables with continuous dimensions is:
   a) $\bar{x}$-bar chart
   b) *R*-chart
   c) *p*-chart
   d) *c*-chart
   e) none of the above

2. Control charts for attributes are:
   a) *p*-charts
   b) *c*-charts
   c) *R*-charts
   d) $\bar{x}$-charts
   e) all of the above

3. If parts in a sample are measured and the mean of the sample measurement is outside the tolerance limits:
   a) the process is out of control, and the cause should be established
   b) the process is in control, but not capable of producing within the established control limits
   c) the process is within the established control limits with only natural causes of variation
   d) all of the above are true

4. If *parts* in a sample are measured and the mean of the sample measurement is in the middle of the tolerance limits but some parts measure outside the control limits:
   a) the process is in control, with only assignable causes of variation
   b) the process is not producing within the established control limits
   c) the process is within the established control limits with only natural causes of variation
   d) the process has both natural and assignable causes of variation

5. If a 95.45% level of confidence is desired, the $\bar{x}$-chart limits will be set plus or minus _____.

6. The two techniques discussed to find and resolve assignable variations in process control are the _____ and the _____.

7. The _____ risk is the probability that a lot will be rejected despite the quality level exceeding or meeting the _____.

8. The ability of a process to meet design specifications is called:
   a) Taguchi
   b) process capability
   c) capability index
   d) acceptance sampling
   e) average outgoing quality

Internet and Student CD-ROM/DVD Exercises

Visit our Companion Web site or use your student CD-ROM/DVD to help with material in this supplement.

 On Our Companion Web Site,
www.prenhall.com/heizer
- Self-Study Quizzes
- Practice Problems
- Virtual Company Tour
- Internet Case Study
- PowerPoint Lecture

 On Your Student CD-ROM
- Practice Problems
- Active Model Exercises
- Excel OM Software
- Excel OM Data Files
- POM for Windows

 On Your Student DVD
- Video Clips and Video Case Study
- Virtual Office Hours for Solved Problems

Discussion Questions

1. List Shewhart's two types of variation. What are they also called?
2. Define "in statistical control."
3. Explain briefly what an $\bar{x}$-chart and an R-chart do.
4. What might cause a process to be out of control?
5. List five steps in developing and using $\bar{x}$-charts and R-charts.
6. List some possible causes of assignable variation.
7. Explain how a person using 2-sigma control charts will more easily find samples "out of bounds" than 3-sigma control charts. What are some possible consequences of this fact?
8. When is the desired mean, μ, used in establishing the centerline of a control chart instead of $\bar{\bar{x}}$?
9. Can a production process be labeled as "out of control" because it is too good? Explain.

10. In a control chart, what would be the effect on the control limits if the sample size varied from one sample to the next?
11. Define C_{pk} and explain what a C_{pk} of 1.0 means. What is C_p?
12. What does a run of 5 points above or below the centerline in a control chart imply?
13. What are the acceptable quality level (AQL) and the lot tolerance percent defective (LTPD)? How are they used?
14. What is a run test and when is it used?
15. Discuss the managerial issues regarding the use of control charts.
16. What is an OC curve?
17. What is the purpose of acceptance sampling?
18. What two risks are present when acceptance sampling is used?
19. Is a *capable* process a *perfect* process? That is, does a capable process generate only output that meets specifications? Explain.

Problems*

• **1** Boxes of Organic Flakes are produced to contain 14 ounces, with a standard deviation of .1 ounce. Set up the 3-sigma $\bar{x}$-chart for a sample size of 36 boxes. **Px**

• **2** The overall average on a process you are attempting to monitor is 50 units. The process standard deviation is 1.72. Determine the upper and lower control limits for a mean chart, if you choose to use a sample size of 5. Set $z = 3$. **Px**

• **3** Thirty-five samples of size 7 each were taken from a fertilizer-bag-filling machine. The results were: Overall mean = 57.75 lb; Average range = 1.78 lb.
a) Determine the upper and lower control limits of the $\bar{x}$-chart, where $\sigma = 3$.
b) Determine the upper and lower control limits of the R-chart, where $\sigma = 3$. **Px**

• **4** Pioneer Chicken advertises "lite" chicken with 30% fewer calories than standard chicken. When the process for "lite" chicken breast production is in control, the average chicken breast contains 420 calories, and the standard deviation in caloric content of the chicken breast population is 25 calories.
Pioneer wants to design an $\bar{x}$-chart to monitor the caloric content of chicken breasts, where 25 chicken breasts would be chosen at random to form each sample. What are the lower and upper con-

trol limits for this chart if these limits are chosen to be *four* standard deviations from the target? **Px**

• **5** Cordelia Barrera is attempting to monitor a filling process that has an overall average of 705 cc. The average range is 6 cc. If you use a sample size of 10, what are the upper and lower control limits for the mean and range? **Px**

•• **6** Sampling 4 pieces of precision-cut wire (to be used in computer assembly) every hour for the past 24 hours has produced the following results:

Hour	$\bar{x}$	R	Hour	$\bar{x}$	R
1	3.25″	.71″	13	3.11″	.85″
2	3.10	1.18	14	2.83	1.31
3	3.22	1.43	15	3.12	1.06
4	3.39	1.26	16	2.84	.50
5	3.07	1.17	17	2.86	1.43
6	2.86	.32	18	2.74	1.29
7	3.05	.53	19	3.41	1.61
8	2.65	1.13	20	2.89	1.09
9	3.02	.71	21	2.65	1.08
10	2.85	1.33	22	3.28	.46
11	2.83	1.17	23	2.94	1.58
12	2.97	.40	24	2.64	.97

Develop appropriate control charts and determine whether there is any cause for concern in the cutting process. Plot the information and look for patterns. **Px**

Note: **Px** means the problem may be solved with POM for Windows and/or Excel OM/Excel.

·· 7 Auto pistons at Yongpin Zhou's plant in Shanghai are produced in a forging process, and the diameter is a critical factor that must be controlled. From sample sizes of 10 pistons produced each day, the mean and the range of this diameter have been as follows:

Day	Mean (mm)	Range (mm)
1	156.9	4.2
2	153.2	4.6
3	153.6	4.1
4	155.5	5.0
5	156.6	4.5

Construct the 3-sigma $\bar{x}$-chart and the 3-sigma R-chart for this dimension, using the data observed in the table above. **PX**

·· 8 Bill Kime's bowling ball factory makes bowling balls of adult size and weight only. The standard deviation in the weight of a bowling ball produced at the factory is known to be 0.12 pounds. Each day for 24 days, the average weight, in pounds, of nine of the bowling balls produced that day has been assessed as follows:

Day	Average (lb)	Day	Average (lb)
1	16.3	13	16.3
2	15.9	14	15.9
3	15.8	15	16.3
4	15.5	16	16.2
5	16.3	17	16.1
6	16.2	18	15.9
7	16.0	19	16.2
8	16.1	20	15.9
9	15.9	21	15.9
10	16.2	22	16.0
11	15.9	23	15.5
12	15.9	24	15.8

Establish a control chart for monitoring the average weights of the bowling balls in which the upper and lower control limits are each two standard deviations from the mean. What are the values of the control limits? **PX**

·· 9 Whole Grains LLC uses statistical process control to ensure that its health-conscious, low-fat, multigrain sandwich loaves have the proper weight. Based on a previously stable and in-control process, the control limits of the $\bar{x}$- and R-charts are: $UCL_{\bar{x}} = 6.56$, $LCL_{\bar{x}} = 5.84$, $UCL_R = 1.141$, $LCL_R = 0$. Over the past few days, they have taken five random samples of four loaves each and have found the following:

	Net Weight			
Sample	Loaf #1	Loaf #2	Loaf #3	Loaf #4
1	6.3	6.0	5.9	5.9
2	6.0	6.0	6.3	5.9
3	6.3	4.8	5.6	5.2
4	6.2	6.0	6.2	5.9
5	6.5	6.6	6.5	6.9

Is the process still in control? **PX**

··· 10 A process that is considered to be in control measures an ingredient in ounces. Below are the last 10 samples (each of size $n = 5$) taken. The population standard deviation is 1.36.

	Samples									
1	**2**	**3**	**4**	**5**	**6**	**7**	**8**	**9**	**10**
10	9	13	10	12	10	10	13	8	10
9	9	9	10	10	10	11	10	8	12
10	11	10	11	9	8	10	8	12	9
9	11	10	10	11	12	8	10	12	8
12	10	9	10	10	9	9	8	9	12

a) What is the process standard deviation σ? What is $\sigma_{\bar{x}}$?
b) If $z = 3$, what are the control limits for the mean chart?
c) What are the control limits for the range chart?
d) Is the process in control? **PX**

··· 11 Twelve samples, each containing five parts, were taken from a process that produces steel rods. The length of each rod in the samples was determined. The results were tabulated and sample means and ranges were computed. The results were:

Sample	Sample Mean (in.)	Range (in.)
1	10.002	0.011
2	10.002	0.014
3	9.991	0.007
4	10.006	0.022
5	9.997	0.013
6	9.999	0.012
7	10.001	0.008
8	10.005	0.013
9	9.995	0.004
10	10.001	0.011
11	10.001	0.014
12	10.006	0.009

Determine the upper and lower control limits and the overall means for $\bar{x}$-charts and R-charts. Draw the chart and plot the values of the sample means and ranges. Do the data indicate a process that is in control? Why or why not? **PX**

·· 12 Eagletrons are all-electric automobiles produced by Mogul Motors, Inc. One of the concerns of Mogul Motors is that the Eagletrons be capable of achieving appropriate maximum speeds. To monitor this, Mogul executives take samples of eight Eagletrons at a time. For each sample, they determine the average maximum speed and the range of the maximum speeds within the sample. They repeat this with 35 samples to obtain 35 sample means and 35 ranges. They find that the average sample mean is 88.50 miles per hour, and the average range is 3.25 miles per hour. Using these results, the executives decide to establish an R chart. They would like this chart to be established so that when it shows that the range of a sample is not within the control limits, there is only approximately a 0.0027 probability that this is due to natural variation. What will be the upper control limit (UCL) and the lower control limit (LCL) in this chart? **PX**

· 13 The defect rate for data entry of insurance claims has historically been about 1.5%. What are the upper and lower control chart limits if you wish to use a sample size of 100 and 3-sigma limits? **PX**

·· 14 You are attempting to develop a quality monitoring system for some parts purchased from Charles Sox Manufacturing Co. These parts are either good or defective. You have decided to take a sample of 100 units. Develop a table of the appropriate upper and lower control chart limits for various values of the average fraction defective in the samples taken. The values for $\bar{p}$ in this table should range from 0.02 to 0.10 in increments of 0.02. Develop the upper and lower control limits for a 99.73% confidence level.

n = 100		
p̄	UCL	LCL
0.02		
0.04		
0.06		
0.08		
0.10		

PX

•• **15** The results of inspection of DNA samples taken over the past 10 days are given below. Sample size is 100.

Day	1	2	3	4	5	6	7	8	9	10
Defectives	7	6	6	9	5	6	0	8	9	1

a) Construct a 3-sigma *p*-chart using this information.
b) If the number of defectives on the next three days are 12, 5, and 13, is the process in control? PX

• **16** In the past, the defect rate for your product has been 1.5%. What are the upper and lower control chart limits if you wish to use a sample size of 500 and $z = 3$? PX

• **17** Refer to Problem 16. If the defect rate was 3.5% instead of 1.5%, what would be the control limits ($z = 3$)? PX

•• **18** Five data entry operators work at the data processing department of the Georgia Bank. Each day for 30 days, the number of defective records in a sample of 250 records typed by these operators has been noted, as follows:

Sample No.	No. Defective	Sample No.	No. Defective	Sample No.	No. Defective
1	7	11	18	21	17
2	5	12	5	22	12
3	19	13	16	23	6
4	10	14	4	24	7
5	11	15	11	25	13
6	8	16	8	26	10
7	12	17	12	27	14
8	9	18	4	28	6
9	6	19	6	29	12
10	13	20	16	30	3

Establish 3σ upper and lower control limits. PX

•• **19** Detroit Central Hospital is trying to improve its image by providing a positive experience for its patients and their relatives. Part of the "image" program involves providing tasty, inviting patient meals that are also healthful. A questionnaire accompanies each meal served, asking the patient, among other things, whether he or she is satisfied or unsatisfied with the meal. A 100-patient sample of the survey results over the past 7 days yielded the following data:

Day	No. of Unsatisfied Patients	Sample Size
1	24	100
2	22	100
3	8	100
4	15	100
5	10	100
6	26	100
7	17	100

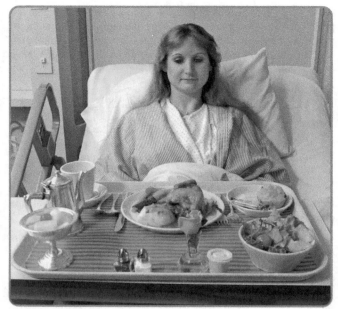

Corbis Digital Stock

Construct a *p*-chart that plots the percentage of patients unsatisfied with their meals. Set the control limits to include 99.73% of the random variation in meal satisfaction. Comment on your results. PX

•• **20** Chicago Supply Company manufactures paper clips and other office products. Although inexpensive, paper clips have provided the firm with a high margin of profitability. Samples of 200 are taken. Results are given for the last 10 samples. Establish upper and lower control limits for the control chart and graph the data. Is the process in control?

Sample	1	2	3	4	5	6	7	8	9	10
Defectives	5	7	4	4	6	3	5	6	2	8

PX

• **21** Peter Ittig's department store, Ittig Brothers, is Amherst's largest independent clothier. The store receives an average of six returns per day. Using $z = 3$, would nine returns in a day warrant action? PX

•• **22** An ad agency tracks the complaints, by week received, about the billboards in its city:

Week	No. of Complaints
1	4
2	5
3	4
4	11
5	3
6	9

a) What type of control chart would you use to monitor this process and why?
b) What are the 3-sigma control limits for this process? Assume that the historical complaint rate is unknown.
c) Is the process mean in control, according to the control limits? Why or why not?
d) Assume now that the historical complaint rate has been 4 calls a week. What would the 3-sigma control limits for this process be now? Is the process in control according to the control limits? PX

•• 23   The school board is trying to evaluate a new math program introduced to second-graders in five elementary schools across the county this year. A sample of the student scores on standardized math tests in each elementary school yielded the following data:

School	No. of Test Errors
A	52
B	27
C	35
D	44
E	55

Construct a c-chart for test errors, and set the control limits to contain 99.73% of the random variation in test scores. What does the chart tell you? Has the new math program been effective? **Px**

•• 24   Telephone inquiries of 100 IRS "customers" are monitored daily at random. Incidents of incorrect information or other nonconformities (such as impoliteness to customers) are recorded. The data for last week follow:

Day	No. of Nonconformities
1	5
2	10
3	23
4	20
5	15

Construct a 3-standard deviation c-chart of nonconformities. What does the control chart tell you about the IRS telephone operators? **Px**

••• 25   The accounts receivable department at Rick Wing Manufacturing has been having difficulty getting customers to pay the full amount of their bills. Many customers complain that the bills are not correct and do not reflect the materials that arrived at their receiving docks. The department has decided to implement SPC in its billing process. To set up control charts, 10 samples of 50 bills each were taken over a month's time and the items on the bills checked against the bill of lading sent by the company's shipping department to determine the number of bills that were not correct. The results were:

Sample No.	No. of Incorrect Bills	Sample No.	No. of Incorrect Bills
1	6	6	5
2	5	7	3
3	11	8	4
4	4	9	7
5	0	10	2

a) Determine the value of p-bar, the mean fraction defective. Then determine the control limits for the p-chart using a 99.73% confidence level (3 standard deviations). Is this process in control? If not, which sample(s) were out of control?

b) How might you use the quality tools discussed in Chapter 6 to determine the source of the billing defects and where you might start your improvement efforts to eliminate the causes? **Px**

• 26   The difference between the upper specification and the lower specification for a process is 0.6″. The standard deviation is 0.1″. What is the process capability ratio, C_p? Interpret this number. **Px**

•• 27   Meena Chavan Corp.'s computer chip production process yields DRAM chips with an average life of 1,800 hours and $\sigma = 100$ hours. The tolerance upper and lower specification limits are 2,400 hours and 1,600 hours, respectively. Is this process capable of producing DRAM chips to specification? **Px**

•• 28   Blackburn, Inc., an equipment manufacturer in Nashville, has submitted a sample cutoff valve to improve your manufacturing process. Your process engineering department has conducted experiments and found that the valve has a mean (μ) of 8.00 and a standard deviation (σ) of .04. Your desired performance is $\mu = 8.0$ and $\sigma = .045$. What is the C_{pk} of the Blackburn valve? **Px**

•• 29   The specifications for a plastic liner for concrete highway projects calls for a thickness of 3.0 mm ±.1 mm. The standard deviation of the process is estimated to be .02 mm. What are the upper and lower specification limits for this product? The process is known to operate at a mean thickness of 3.0 mm. What is the C_{pk} for this process? About what percentage of all units of this liner will meet specifications? **Px**

•• 30   The manager of a food processing plant desires a quality specification with a mean of 16 ounces, an upper specification limit of 16.5, and a lower specification limit of 15.5. The process has a mean of 16 ounces and a standard deviation of 1 ounce. Determine the C_{pk} of the process. **Px**

•• 31   A process filling small bottles with baby formula has a target of 3 ounces ±0.150 ounce. Two hundred bottles from the process were sampled. The results showed the average amount of formula placed in the bottles to be 3.042 ounces. The standard deviation of the amounts was 0.034 ounce. Determine the value of C_{pk}. Roughly what proportion of bottles meet the specifications? **Px**

••• 32   As the supervisor in charge of shipping and receiving, you need to determine *the average outgoing quality* in a plant where the known incoming lots from your assembly line have an average defective rate of 3%. Your plan is to sample 80 units of every 1,000 in a lot. The number of defects in the sample is not to exceed 3. Such a plan provides you with a probability of acceptance of each lot of .79 (79%). What is your average outgoing quality? **Px**

••• 33   An acceptance sampling plan has lots of 500 pieces and a sample size of 60. The number of defects in the sample may not exceed 2. This plan, based on an OC curve, has a probability of .57 of accepting lots when the incoming lots have a defective rate of 4%, which is the historical average for this process. What do you tell your customer the average outgoing quality is? **Px**

••••34   West Battery Corp. has recently been receiving complaints from retailers that its 9-volt batteries are not lasting as long as other name brands. James West, head of the TQM program at West's Austin plant, believes there is no problem because his batteries have had an average life of 50 hours, about 10% longer than competitors' models. To raise the lifetime above this level would require a new level of technology not available to West. Nevertheless, he is concerned enough to set up hourly assembly line checks. Previously, after ensuring that the process was running properly, West took size-5 samples of 9-volt batteries for each of 25 hours to establish the standards for control chart limits. Those 25 samples are shown in the following table:

West Battery Data—Battery Lifetimes (in hours)

Hour	Sample 1	2	3	4	5	$\bar{x}$	R
1	51	50	49	50	50	50.0	2
2	45	47	70	46	36	48.8	34
3	50	35	48	39	47	43.8	15
4	55	70	50	30	51	51.2	40
5	49	38	64	36	47	46.8	28
6	59	62	40	54	64	55.8	24
7	36	33	49	48	56	44.4	23
8	50	67	53	43	40	50.6	27
9	44	52	46	47	44	46.6	8
10	70	45	50	47	41	50.6	29
11	57	54	62	45	36	50.8	26
12	56	54	47	42	62	52.2	20
13	40	70	58	45	44	51.4	30
14	52	58	40	52	46	49.6	18
15	57	42	52	58	59	53.6	17
16	62	49	42	33	55	48.2	29
17	40	39	49	59	48	47.0	20
18	64	50	42	57	50	52.6	22
19	58	53	52	48	50	52.2	10

Hour	Sample 1	2	3	4	5	$\bar{x}$	R
20	60	50	41	41	50	48.4	19
21	52	47	48	58	40	49.0	18
22	55	40	56	49	45	49.0	16
23	47	48	50	50	48	48.6	3
24	50	50	49	51	51	50.2	2
25	51	50	51	51	62	53.0	12

With these limits established, West now takes 5 more hours of data, which are shown in the following table:

Hour	Sample 1	2	3	4	5
26	48	52	39	57	61
27	45	53	48	46	66
28	63	49	50	45	53
29	57	70	45	52	61
30	45	38	46	54	52

a) Determine means and the upper and lower control limits for $\bar{x}$ and R (using the first 25 hours only).
b) Is the manufacturing process in control?
c) Comment on the lifetimes observed. **Px**

Case Studies

Bayfield Mud Company

In November 2007, John Wells, a customer service representative of Bayfield Mud Company, was summoned to the Houston warehouse of Wet-Land Drilling, Inc., to inspect three boxcars of mud-treating agents that Bayfield had shipped to the Houston firm. (Bayfield's corporate offices and its largest plant are located in Orange, Texas, which is just west of the Louisiana–Texas border.) Wet-Land had filed a complaint that the 50-pound bags of treating agents just received from Bayfield were short-weight by approximately 5%.

The short-weight bags were initially detected by one of Wet-Land's receiving clerks, who noticed that the railroad scale tickets indicated that net weights were significantly less on all three boxcars than those of identical shipments received on October 25, 2007. Bayfield's traffic department was called to determine if lighter-weight pallets were used on the shipments. (This might explain the lighter net weights.) Bayfield indicated, however, that no changes had been made in loading or palletizing procedures. Thus, Wet-Land engineers randomly checked 50 bags and discovered that the average net weight was 47.51 pounds. They noted from past shipments that the process yielded bag net weights averaging exactly 50.0 pounds, with an acceptable standard deviation σ of 1.2 pounds. Consequently, they concluded that the sample indicated a significant short-weight. (The reader may wish to verify this conclusion.) Bayfield was then contacted, and Wells was sent to investigate the complaint. Upon arrival, Wells verified the complaint and issued a 5% credit to Wet-Land.

Wet-Land management, however, was not completely satisfied with the issuance of credit. The charts followed by their mud engineers on the drilling platforms were based on 50-pound bags of

treating agents. Lighter-weight bags might result in poor chemical control during the drilling operation and thus adversely affect drilling efficiency. (Mud-treating agents are used to control the pH and other chemical properties of the core during drilling operation.) This defect could cause severe economic consequences because of the extremely high cost of oil and natural gas well-drilling operations. Consequently, special-use instructions had to accompany the delivery of these shipments to the drilling platforms. Moreover, the short-weight shipments had to be isolated in Wet-Land's warehouse, causing extra handling and poor space utilization. Thus, Wells was informed that Wet-Land might seek a new supplier of mud-treating agents if, in the future, it received bags that deviated significantly from 50 pounds.

The quality control department at Bayfield suspected that the lightweight bags might have resulted from "growing pains" at the Orange plant. Because of the earlier energy crisis, oil and natural gas exploration activity had greatly increased. In turn, this increased activity created increased demand for products produced by related industries, including drilling muds. Consequently, Bayfield had to expand from a one-shift (6:00 A.M. to 2:00 P.M.) to a two-shift (2:00 P.M. to 10:00 P.M.) operation in mid-2005, and finally to a three-shift operation (24 hours per day) in the fall of 2007.

The additional night-shift bagging crew was staffed entirely by new employees. The most experienced foremen were temporarily assigned to supervise the night-shift employees. Most emphasis was placed on increasing the output of bags to meet ever-increasing demand. It was suspected that only occasional reminders were made to double-check the bag weight-feeder. (A double-check is per-

Time	Average Weight (pounds)	Range		Time	Average Weight (pounds)	Range	
		Smallest	Largest			Smallest	Largest
6:00 A.M.	49.6	48.7	50.7	6:00	46.8	41.0	51.2
7:00	50.2	49.1	51.2	7:00	50.0	46.2	51.7
8:00	50.6	49.6	51.4	8:00	47.4	44.0	48.7
9:00	50.8	50.2	51.8	9:00	47.0	44.2	48.9
10:00	49.9	49.2	52.3	10:00	47.2	46.6	50.2
11:00	50.3	48.6	51.7	11:00	48.6	47.0	50.0
12 Noon	48.6	46.2	50.4	12 Midnight	49.8	48.2	50.4
1:00 P.M.	49.0	46.4	50.0	1:00 A.M.	49.6	48.4	51.7
2:00	49.0	46.0	50.6	2:00	50.0	49.0	52.2
3:00	49.8	48.2	50.8	3:00	50.0	49.2	50.0
4:00	50.3	49.2	52.7	4:00	47.2	46.3	50.5
5:00	51.4	50.0	55.3	5:00	47.0	44.1	49.7
6:00	51.6	49.2	54.7	6:00	48.4	45.0	49.0
7:00	51.8	50.0	55.6	7:00	48.8	44.8	49.7
8:00	51.0	48.6	53.2	8:00	49.6	48.0	51.8
9:00	50.5	49.4	52.4	9:00	50.0	48.1	52.7
10:00	49.2	46.1	50.7	10:00	51.0	48.1	55.2
11:00	49.0	46.3	50.8	11:00	50.4	49.5	54.1
12 Midnight	48.4	45.4	50.2	12 Noon	50.0	48.7	50.9
1:00 A.M.	47.6	44.3	49.7	1:00 P.M.	48.9	47.6	51.2
2:00	47.4	44.1	49.6	2:00	49.8	48.4	51.0
3:00	48.2	45.2	49.0	3:00	49.8	48.8	50.8
4:00	48.0	45.5	49.1	4:00	50.0	49.1	50.6
5:00	48.4	47.1	49.6	5:00	47.8	45.2	51.2
6:00	48.6	47.4	52.0	6:00	46.4	44.0	49.7
7:00	50.0	49.2	52.2	7:00	46.4	44.4	50.0
8:00	49.8	49.0	52.4	8:00	47.2	46.6	48.9
9:00	50.3	49.4	51.7	9:00	48.4	47.2	49.5
10:00	50.2	49.6	51.8	10:00	49.2	48.1	50.7
11:00	50.0	49.0	52.3	11:00	48.4	47.0	50.8
12 Noon	50.0	48.8	52.4	12 Midnight	47.2	46.4	49.2
1:00 P.M.	50.1	49.4	53.6	1:00 A.M.	47.4	46.8	49.0
2:00	49.7	48.6	51.0	2:00	48.8	47.2	51.4
3:00	48.4	47.2	51.7	3:00	49.6	49.0	50.6
4:00	47.2	45.3	50.9	4:00	51.0	50.5	51.5
5:00	46.8	44.1	49.0	5:00	50.5	50.0	51.9

formed by systematically weighing a bag on a scale to determine if the proper weight is being loaded by the weight-feeder. If there is significant deviation from 50 pounds, corrective adjustments are made to the weight-release mechanism.)

To verify this expectation, the quality control staff randomly sampled the bag output and prepared the chart above. Six bags were sampled and weighed each hour.

Discussion Questions

1. What is your analysis of the bag-weight problem?
2. What procedures would you recommend to maintain proper quality control?

Source: Professor Jerry Kinard, Western Carolina University.

Alabama Airlines's On-Time Schedule

Alabama Airlines opened its doors in December 2001 as a commuter service with its headquarters and only hub located in Birmingham. A product of airline deregulation, Alabama Air joined the growing number of short-haul, point-to-point airlines, including Lone Star, Comair, Atlantic Southeast, and Skywest.

Alabama Air was started and managed by two former pilots, David Douglas (who had been with now-defunct Midway Airlines) and Michael Hanna (formerly with Continental). It acquired a fleet of

12 used prop-jet planes and the airport gates vacated by Delta Airlines in 2001 when it curtailed flights due to the terrorist attacks of 9/11.

One of Alabama Air's top competitive priorities is on-time arrivals. The airline defines "on-time" to mean any arrival that is within 20 minutes of the scheduled time.

Mike Hanna decided to personally monitor Alabama Air's performance. Each week for the past 30 weeks, Hanna checked a random sample of 100 flight arrivals for on-time performance. The table that follows contains the number of flights that did not meet Alabama Air's definition of on time:

Sample (week)	Late Flights	Sample (week)	Late Flights
1	2	16	2
2	4	17	3
3	10	18	7
4	4	19	3
5	1	20	2
6	1	21	3
7	13	22	7
8	9	23	4
9	11	24	3
10	0	25	2
11	3	26	2
12	4	27	0
13	2	28	1
14	2	29	3
15	8	30	4

Discussion Questions

1. Using a 95% confidence level, plot the overall percentage of late flights (p) and the upper and lower control limits on a control chart.
2. Assume that the airline industry's upper and lower control limits for flights that are not on time are .1000 and .0400, respectively. Draw them on your control chart.
3. Plot the percentage of late flights in each sample. Do all samples fall within Alabama Airlines's control limits? When one falls outside the control limits, what should be done?
4. What can Mike Hanna report about the quality of service?

Farm to Fork: Quality at Darden Restaurants

Darden Restaurants, the $5.2 billion owner of such popular brands as Olive Garden, Red Lobster, Seasons 52, and Bahama Breeze, serves more than 300 million meals annually in its 1,450 restaurants across the U.S. and Canada. Before any one of these meals is placed before a guest, the ingredients for each recipe must pass quality control inspections from the source, ranging from measurement and weighing, to tasting, touching, or lab testing. Darden has differentiated itself from its restaurant peers by developing the gold standard in continuous improvement.

To assure both customers and the company that quality expectations are met, Darden uses a rigorous inspection process, employing statistical process control (SPC) as part of its "Farm to Fork" program. More than 50 food scientists, microbiologists, and public health professionals report to Ana Hooper, director of quality assurance.

As part of Darden's Point Source program, Hooper's team, based in Southeast Asia (in China, Thailand, and Singapore) and Latin America (in Equador, Honduras, and Chile), approves and inspects—and works with Darden buyers to purchase—more than 50 million pounds of seafood each year for restaurant use. Darden used to build quality in at the end by inspecting shipments as they reached U.S. distribution centers. Now, thanks to coaching and partnering with vendors abroad, Darden needs but a few domestic inspection labs to verify compliance to its exacting standards. Food vendors in source countries know that when supplying Darden, they are subject to regular audits that are stricter than U.S. Food & Drug Administration (FDA) standards.

Two Quality Success Stories

Quality specialists' jobs include raising the bar and improving quality and safety at all plants in their geographic area. The Thai quality representative, for example, worked closely with several of Darden's largest shrimp vendors to convert them to a production-line-integrated quality assurance program. The vendors were able to improve the quality of shrimp supplied and reduce the percentage of defects by 19%.

Likewise, when the Darden quality teams visited fields of growers/shippers in Mexico recently, it identified challenges such as low employee hygiene standards, field food safety problems, lack of portable toilets, child labor, and poor working conditions. Darden addressed these concerns and hired third party independent food safety verification firms to ensure continued compliance to standards.

SPC Charts

SPC charts, such as the one shown in this supplement, are particularly important. These charts document precooked food weights; meat, seafood and poultry temperatures; blemishes on produce; and bacteria counts on shrimp—just to name a few. Quality assurance is part of a much bigger process that is key to Darden's success—its supply chain. That's because quality comes from the source and flows through distribution to the restaurant and guests.

Discussion Questions*

1. How does Darden build quality into the supply chain?
2. Select two potential problems—one in the Darden supply chain and one in a restaurant—that can be analyzed with a fish-bone chart. Draw a complete chart to deal with each problem.
3. Darden applies SPC in many product attributes. Identify where these are probably used.
4. The SPC chart illustrates Darden's use of control charts to monitor the weight of salmon filets. Given these data, what conclusion do you, as a Darden quality control inspector, draw? What report do you issue to your supervisor? How do you respond to the salmon vendor?

*You might want to watch this video case on your DVD before answering these questions.

Additional Case Studies

Internet Case Study: Visit our Companion Web site at www.prenhall.com/heizer for this free case study:

- **Green River Chemical Company:** Involves a company that needs to set up a control chart to monitor sulfate content because of customer complaints.

Harvard has selected these Harvard Business School cases to accompany this supplement:

harvardbusinessonline.hbsp.harvard.edu

- **Deutsche Allgemeinversicherung** (#696-084): A German insurance company tries to adopt *p*-charts to a variety of services it performs.
- **Process Control at Polaroid (A)** (#696-047): This film-production plant moves from traditional QC inspection to worker-based SPC charts.

Bibliography

Bakir, S. T. "A Quality Control Chart for Work Performance Appraisal." *Quality Engineering* 17, no. 3 (2005): 429.

Burr, J. T. *Elementary Statistical Quality Control.* Boca Raton, FL: CRC Press, 2005.

Goetsch, David L., and Stanley B. Davis. *Quality Management,* 5th ed. Upper Saddle River, NJ: Prentice Hall, 2006.

Gryna, F. M., R. C. H. Chua, and J. A. DeFeo. *Juran's Quality Planning and Analysis,* 5th ed. New York: McGraw-Hill, 2007.

Johnson, K. "Six Sigma Delivers On-Time Service." *Quality Progress* 38, no. 12 (December 2005): 57–60.

Lin, H., and G. Sheen. "Practical Implementation of the Capability Index C_{pk} Based on Control Chart Data." *Quality Engineering* 17, no. 3 (2005): 371.

Montgomery, D. C. *Introduction to Statistical Quality Control,* 5th ed. New York: Wiley, 2004.

Roth, H. P. "How SPC Can Help Cut Costs." *Journal of Corporate Accounting and Finance* 16, no. 3 (March–April 2005): 21–30.

Smith, Gerald. *Statistical Process Control and Process Improvement.* 6th ed. Upper Saddle River, NJ: Prentice Hall, 2007.

Summers, Donna. *Quality,* 4th ed. Upper Saddle River, NJ: Prentice Hall, 2006.

Spigener, J. B., and P. J. Angelo. "What Would Deming Say?" *Quality Progress* 34, no. 3 (March 2001): 61–65.

Sumukadas, N., J. W. Fairfield-Sonn, and S. Morgan. "Ready-to-Use Simulation: Demystifying Statistical Process Control." *Simulation & Gaming* 36, no. 1 (March 2005): 134.

Internet Resources

American Society for Quality: **www.asq.org**
American Statistical Association: **www.amstat.org**
Associated Quality Consultants: **www.quality.org**
Business Process Improvement: **spcforexcel.com**
Institute of Statistics and Decision Science at Duke University: **www.isds.duke.edu**

Statistical Engineering Division of the Department of Commerce: **www.itl.nist.gov/div898/**
Total Quality Engineering: **www.tqe.com**

Solutions to Even Numbered Problems

2 $\text{UCL}_{\bar{x}} = 52.31$
$\text{LCL}_{\bar{x}} = 47.69$

4 $\text{UCL}_{\bar{x}} = 440$ calories
$\text{LCL}_{\bar{x}} = 400$ calories

6 $\text{UCL}_{\bar{x}} = 3.728$
$\text{LCL}_{\bar{x}} = 2.236$
$\text{UCL}_R = 2.336$
$\text{LCL}_R = 0.0$
The process is in control.

8 (a) $\text{UCL}_{\bar{x}} = 16.08$
$\text{LCL}_{\bar{x}} = 15.92$

10 (a) 1.36, 0.61
(b) Using $\sigma_{\bar{x}}$, $\text{UCL}_{\bar{x}} = 11.83$, and $\text{LCL}_{\bar{x}} = 8.17$.
Using A_2, $\text{UCL}_{\bar{x}} = 11.90$, and $\text{LCL}_{\bar{x}} = 8.10$.
(c) $\text{UCL}_R = 6.98$; $\text{LCL}_R = 0$
(d) Yes

12 $\text{UCL}_R = 6.058$; $\text{LCL}_R = 0.442$
Averages are increasing.

14

UCL	LCL
.062	0
.099	0
.132	0
.161	0
.190	.01

16 $\text{UCL}_p = .0313$; $\text{LCL}_p = 0$

18 $\text{UCL}_p = 0.077$; $\text{LCL}_p = 0.003$

20 (a) $\text{UCL}_p = .0581$
$\text{LCL}_p = 0$

22 (a) c-chart
(b) $\text{UCL}_c = 13.3$
$\text{LCL}_c = 0$

(c) in control
(d) not in control

24 $UCL_c = 26.063$
   $LCL_c = 3.137$

26 $C_p = 1.0$. The process is barely capable.

28 $C_{pk} = 1.125$. Process *is* centered and will produce within tolerance.

30 $C_{pk} = .166$

32 $AOQ = 2.2\%$

34 (a) $UCL_{\bar{x}} = 61.131$, $LCL_{\bar{x}} = 38.421$, $UCL_R = 41.62$, $LCL_R = 0$
   (b) Yes, the process is in control for both $\bar{x}$- and R-charts.
   (c) They support West's claim. But variance from the mean needs to be reduced and controlled.

Solutions to Self Test

1. a; 2. a; 3. a; 4. b; 5. 2 std. dev.; 6. $\bar{x}$-chart and R-chart; 7. producer's risk, AQL; 8. b.

Process Strategy

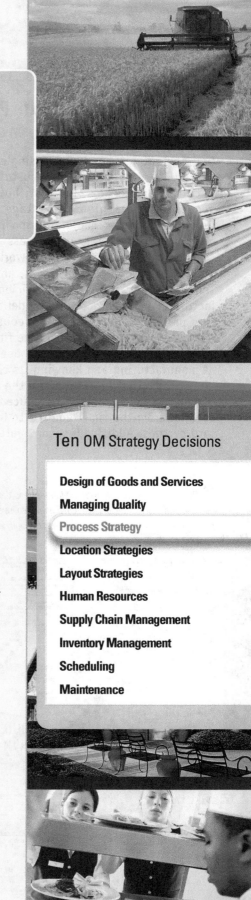

Outline

Ten OM Strategy Decisions

Design of Goods and Services

Managing Quality

Process Strategy

Location Strategies

Layout Strategies

Human Resources

Supply Chain Management

Inventory Management

Scheduling

Maintenance

Learning Objectives

When you complete this selection you should be able to

1. Describe four production processes
2. Compute crossover points for
   different processes
3. Use the tools of process analysis

4. Describe customer interaction in
   process design
5. Identify recent advances in
   production technology

Global Company Profile: Dell Computer Corp.

Mass Customization Provides Dell Computer's Competitive Advantage

Dell Computer started with a single premise: selling a custom PC directly to end customers, thus eliminating markups in the distribution chain that accounted for a high percentage of a PC's price. Dell's concept and manufacturing process made the company an innovative business model, allowing Dell to grab first place in sales worldwide.

Dell's plants in Austin, Texas, and Nashville, Tennessee, are showcases of efficient custom manufacturing. Dell's direct-sales model and lean production practices provide instantaneous customer feedback. Because of this, Dell is the first to know of changes in the market. Dell has been so successful at manufacturing and knowing its customers that huge productivity increases are the norm, with manufacturing space constantly reduced. Robots shave seconds from the time required to load computers into cartons. Additional seconds are saved by com-

Dell Inc.

▲ Michael Dell founded Dell Computer, at age 19, from his college dorm at the University of Texas. He dreamed of competing with IBM and in 1999 bypassed IBM in PC sales. Dell is now number one in the world.

▼ Dell computers are sold over the Internet and then efficiently produced and shipped directly to individual customers. No inventories are kept. Mass customization allows models to change continually as new technologies become available.

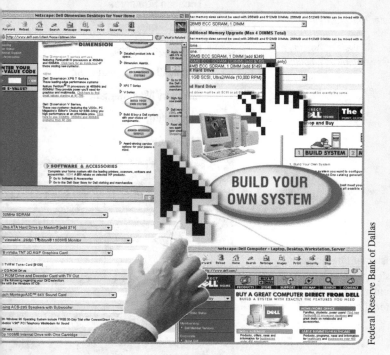

Federal Reserve Bank of Dallas

bining the downloading of software and computer testing into one step. Dell keeps product design under constant review, simplifying components, speeding assembly, and saving even more seconds. Time saved improves throughput, adds capacity, and contributes to flexibility. The added throughput, capacity, and flexibility allow Dell to respond to the sudden and frequent shifts in demand that characterize the PC market.

Both Dell's suppliers and in-house purchasing personnel evaluate inventories on an hour-by-hour basis to hold work-in-process (WIP) to a minimum. Despite a long and diverse global supply chain, Dell operates with just 4 days of inventory, a fraction of its competitors'. Six-person teams assemble 18 computers each hour, with parts that arrive via an overhead conveyor system. When a work cell has a prob-

Although more than 90% of Dell's personal computer business is build to order, the throughput time for each machine is less than 8 hours, and manufacturing cycle time is about 3 hours.

Dell, Inc.

Greg Smith, Corbis/Bettmann

◄ Kits of components are prepared for each customer. Parts are then delivered as needed to work cells, and the final product is assembled by highly trained generalists who put together the entire computer.

lem, parts are instantly shifted to another cell, avoiding delays that are common in traditional assembly lines.

Dell's direct sales model embraces the Internet. Few companies have been as successful in turning the Internet into an everyday tool to enhance productivity. Dell has integrated the Web into every aspect of its business—design, production, sales, and service. Dell has set the standard for quick delivery and mass customization. This process has prevented the major problem of outdated inventory and obsolete PCs. Dell trims inventory by taking

delivery of components just *minutes* before they are needed.

One reason mass customization works at Dell is because instead of investing resources in developing computer components (as many competitors do), it focuses much of its research and development on software designed to make the installation and configuration of its PCs fast and simple. Dell's performance impresses many large organizations that now use Dell as their de facto supplier. The firm's reputation is such that CEO Michael Dell now counsels other firms on mass customization.

A major decision for an operations manager is finding the best way to produce. Let's look at ways to help managers design a process for achieving this goal.

A **process** (or transformation) **strategy** is an organization's approach to transforming resources into goods and services. *The objective of a process strategy is to build a production process that meets customer requirements and product specifications within cost and other managerial constraints.* The process selected will have a long-term effect on efficiency and flexibility of production, as well as on cost and quality of the goods produced. Therefore, much of a firm's operations strategy is determined at the time of this process decision.

FOUR PROCESS STRATEGIES

Virtually every good or service is made by using some variation of one of four process strategies: (1) process focus, (2) repetitive focus, (3) product focus, and (4) mass customization. The relationship of these four strategies to volume and variety is shown in Figure 1. Although the figure shows only four strategies, an innovative operations manager can build processes anywhere in the matrix to meet the necessary volume and variety requirements.

Let's look at each of these strategies with an example and a flow diagram. We examine *Standard Register* as a process-focused firm, *Harley-Davidson* as a repetitive producer, *Nucor Steel* as a product-focused operation, and *Dell* as a mass customizer.

Process Focus

The vast majority of global production is devoted to making *low-volume, high-variety* products in places called "job shops." Such facilities are organized around specific activities or processes. In a factory, these processes might be departments devoted to welding, grinding, and painting. In an office, the processes might be accounts payable, sales, and payroll. In a restaurant, they might be bar, grill, and bakery. Such facilities are **process focused** in terms of equipment, layout, and supervision. They provide a high degree of product flexibility as products move intermittently between processes. Each process is designed to perform a wide variety of activities and handle frequent changes. Consequently, they are also called *intermittent processes*.

These facilities have high variable costs with extremely low utilization of facilities, as low as 5%. This is the case for many restaurants, hospitals, and machine shops. However, some facilities now do somewhat better through the use of innovative equipment, often with electronic controls. With the development of machines controlled by computer software, it is possible to program machine tools, piece movement, and tool changing, and even to automate placement of the parts on the machine and the movement of materials between machines.

Process strategy
An organization's approach to transforming resources into goods and services.

Learning Objective

1. Describe four production processes

Process focus
A production facility organized around processes to facilitate low-volume, high-variety production.

► **Figure 1**

Process Selected Must Fit with Volume and Variety

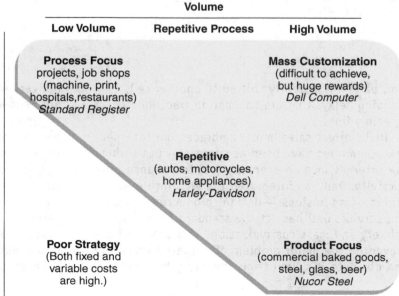

Example 1 shows how Standard Register, a billion-dollar printer and document processor headquartered in Dayton, Ohio, produces paper business forms.

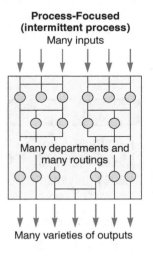

EXAMPLE 1

Job Shop Process Focus at Standard Register

If you've had a pizza delivered to your home recently, there is a good chance that Standard Register printed the order and delivery tag on the box. You probably came in contact with one of Standard's forms this week without knowing it. Thousands of different products are made by the firm, a typical one being a multisheet (three- or four-layer) business form. Forms used for college student applications, hospital patient admissions, bank drafts, store orders, and job applications are examples. The company has 11 U.S. plants in its Forms Division.

Figure 2 is a flow diagram of the entire production process, from order submission to shipment, at Standard's Kirksville, Missouri, plant. This job shop groups people and machines that perform specific activities, such as printing, cutting, or binding, into departments. Entire orders are processed in batches, moving from department to department.

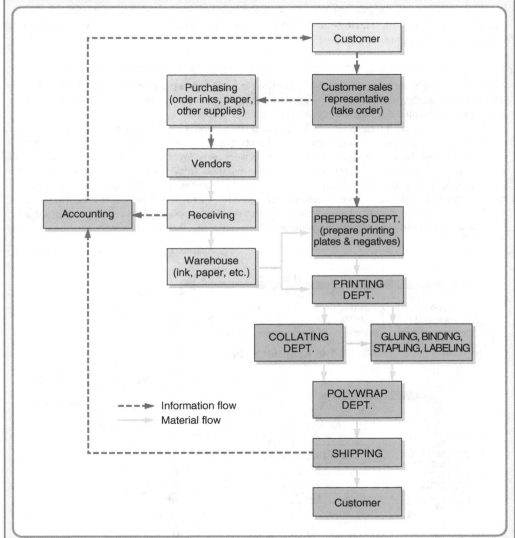

◄ Figure 2

Flow Diagram of the Production Process at Standard Register's Plant in Kirksville, Missouri

Source: Adapted with permission from J. S. Martinich, *Production and Operations Management* (New York: Wiley, 1997): 79–87.

The process begins with a sales representative helping the customer design the business form. Once the form is established, the order is transmitted electronically to the Sales Support Department at the manufacturing plant. An order coordinator determines what materials will be needed in production (ink, paper, labels, etc.), computes the production *time* needed, and schedules the job on a particular machine.

The Prepress Department uses computer-aided design (CAD) to convert the product design into printing plates for the presses and then "burns" the image of the form onto an aluminum printing plate. Machine operators in the Printing Department install the plates and inks on their presses and print the forms. After leaving the presses, most products are collated on a machine that places up to 14 copies together. Some products undergo additional processing (for example, gluing, binding, stapling, or labeling). When the forms are completed, most are wrapped in polyethylene before being placed in cartons for shipping. The order is shipped, a "job ticket" is sent to Accounting, and an invoice goes to the customer.

Repetitive Focus

A repetitive process falls between the product and process focuses seen in Figure 1. Repetitive processes use modules. Modules are parts or components previously prepared, often in a continuous process.

Repetitive process
A product-oriented production process that uses modules.

The **repetitive process** line is the classic assembly line. Widely used in the assembly of virtually all automobiles and household appliances, it has more structure and consequently less flexibility than a process-focused facility.

Modules
Parts or components of a product previously prepared, often in a continuous process.

Fast-food firms are an example of a repetitive process using **modules**. This type of production allows more customizing than a continuous process; modules (for example, meat, cheese, sauce, tomatoes, onions) are assembled to get a quasi-custom product, a cheeseburger. In this manner, the firm obtains both the economic advantages of the continuous model (where many of the modules are prepared) and the custom advantage of the low-volume, high-variety model.

Example 2 shows the Harley-Davidson assembly line. Harley is a repetitive manufacturer located toward the center of Figure 1.

EXAMPLE 2

Repetitive Manufacturing at Harley-Davidson

Repetitive Focus
Raw material and module inputs

Few modules

Modules combined for many output options

 Video 7.1

Saturn Auto's Mass Production

▶ **Figure 3**

Flow Diagram Showing the Production Process at Harley-Davidson's York, Pennsylvania, Assembly Plant

Harley-Davidson assembles modules. Most repetitive manufacturers produce on a form of assembly line where the end product can take a variety of shapes depending on the mix of modules. This is the case at Harley, where the modules are motorcycle components and options.

Harley engines are produced in Milwaukee and shipped on a just-in-time basis to the company's York, Pennsylvania, plant. At York, Harley groups parts that require similar processes together into families (see the flow diagram in Figure 3). The result is *work cells*. Work cells perform in one location all the operations necessary for the production of specific modules. These work cells feed the assembly line.

Harley-Davidson assembles 2 engine types in 3 displacement sizes for 20 street bike models, which are available in 13 colors and 2 wheel options, adding up to 95 total combinations. Harley also produces 4 police and 2 Shriner motorcycles, and offers many custom paint options. This strategy requires that no fewer than 20,000 different pieces be assembled into modules and then into motorcycles.

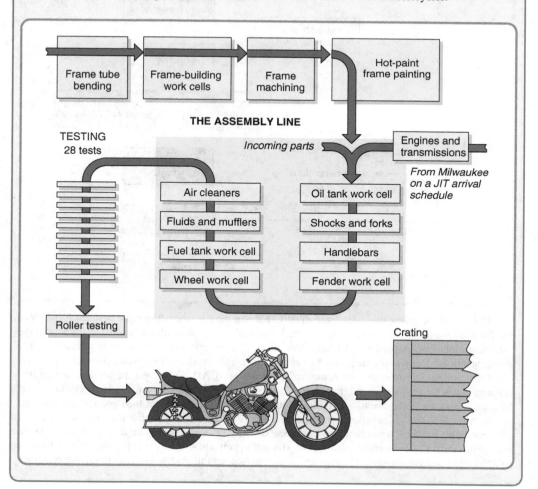

Product Focus

High-volume, low-variety processes are **product focused**. The facilities are organized around *products*. They are also called *continuous processes*, because they have very long, continuous production runs. Products such as glass, paper, tin sheets, lightbulbs, beer, and bolts are made via a continuous process. Some products, such as lightbulbs, are discrete; others, such as rolls of paper, are nondiscrete. Still others, such as repaired hernias at Shouldice Hospital, are services. It is only with standardization and effective quality control that firms have established product-focused facilities. An organization producing the same lightbulb or hot dog bun day after day can organize around a product. Such an organization has an inherent ability to set standards and maintain a given quality, as opposed to an organization that is producing unique products every day, such as a print shop or general-purpose hospital.

A product-focused facility produces high volume and low variety. The specialized nature of the facility requires high fixed cost, but low variable costs reward high facility utilization. The Nucor example follows.

Product focus

A facility organized around products; a product-oriented, high-volume, low-variety process.

Video 7.2

Wassau Paper's Continuous Work Flow

EXAMPLE 3

Product-Focused Production at Nucor Steel

Steel is manufactured in a product-oriented facility. Figure 4 illustrates Nucor's product-focused flow.

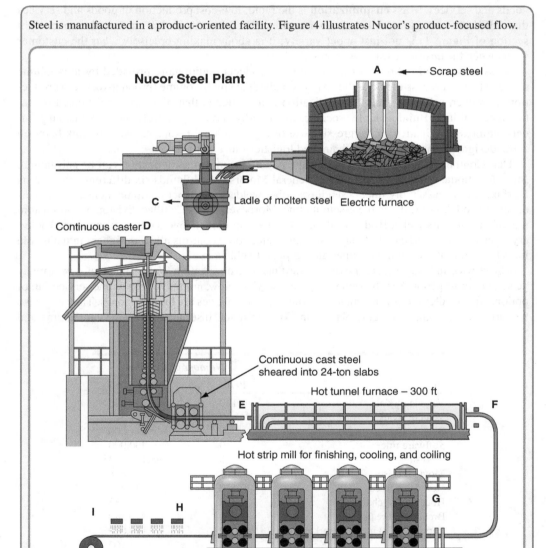

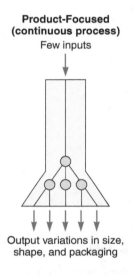

Product-Focused (continuous process)
Few inputs

Output variations in size, shape, and packaging

◄ **Figure 4**

A Flow Diagram Showing the Steelmaking Process at Nucor's Crawfordsville, Indiana, Plant

In this process flow diagram, cold scrap steel is first lowered into a furnace that uses an electric arc to melt the steel in 20 seconds (A). Then molten steel pours from the furnace into a preheated ladle (B). The ladle moves on an overhead-track crane to the continuous caster (C). The ladle then opens and steel exits into the caster (D). Shaped steel exits the caster mold as a 2″ × 52″ slab (E). The slab exits the tunnel furnace (F) at a specific temperature needed for rolling. A higher-quality sheet can be produced if the slab temperature is uniform. The steel then enters the rolling mill (G). Water cools the hot-rolled steel before it is coiled (H). The rolled sheet of steel is coiled into rolls of about 25 tons each (I). Finally, a variety of finishing operations can modify the characteristics of the sheet steel to meet customer needs.

Nucor operates 24 hours a day, 6 days a week, with the seventh day reserved for scheduled maintenance.

Mass Customization Focus

Mass customization

Rapid, low-cost production that caters to constantly changing unique customer desires.

Our increasingly wealthy and sophisticated world demands individualized goods and services. A peek at the rich variety of goods and services that operations managers are called on to supply is shown in Table 1. The explosion of variety has taken place in automobiles, movies, breakfast cereals, and thousands of other areas. In spite of this proliferation of products, operations managers have improved product quality while reducing costs. Consequently, the variety of products continues to grow. Operations managers use *mass customization* to produce this vast array of goods and services. **Mass customization** is the rapid, low-cost production of goods and services that fulfill increasingly unique customer desires. But mass customization (see the upper-right section of Figure 1) is not just about variety; it is about making precisely *what* the customer wants *when* the customer wants it economically.

Mass customization brings us the variety of products traditionally provided by low-volume manufacture (a process focus) at the cost of standardized high-volume (product-focused) production. However, achieving mass customization is a challenge that requires sophisticated operational capabilities. Building agile processes that rapidly and inexpensively produce custom products requires imaginative and aggressive use of organizational resources. And the link between sales, design, production, supply chain, and logistics must be tight.[1]

Dell Computer has demonstrated that the payoff for mass customization can be substantial. More traditional manufacturers include General Motors, which builds six different styles on its Fairfax, Kansas, assembly line. GM adjusts robot welders and other equipment electronically as different models come down the assembly line. Moreover, GM's Cadillac division is now custom manufacturing cars with a 10-day lead time. Not to be outdone, Toyota recently announced delivery of custom-ordered cars in 5 days. Similarly, electronic controls allow designers in the textile industry to rapidly revamp their lines and respond to changes.

The service industry is also moving toward mass customization. For instance, not very many years ago, most people had the same telephone service. Now, not only is the phone service full of options, from caller ID to voice mail, but contemporary phones are hardly phones. They may also be part camera, computer, game player, and Web browser. Insurance companies are adding and

▶ **Table 1**

Mass Customization Provides More Choices Than Ever[a]

Source: Various; however, many of the data are from the Federal Reserve Bank of Dallas.

Item	Number of Choices	
	1970s	**21st Century**
Vehicle models	140	286
Vehicle styles	18	1,212
Bicycle types	8	211,000[c]
Software titles	0	400,000
Web sites	0	98,116,993[d]
Movie releases	267	458
New book titles	40,530	77,446
Houston TV channels	5	185
Breakfast cereals	160	340
Items (SKUs) in supermarkets	14,000[b]	150,000[e]
LCD TVs	0	102

[a]Variety available in America; worldwide the variety increases even more.
[b]1989.
[c]Possible combinations for one manufacturer.
[d]2007, **www.ipwalk.com** (July 2, 2007).
[e]SKUs managed by H. E. Butts grocery chain.

[1]Paul Zipkin, "The Limits of Mass Customization," *MIT Sloan Management Review* (spring 2001): p. 81.

Mass Customization at Borders Books and at Smooth FM Radio

So you want a hard-to-get, high-quality paperback book in 15 minutes? Borders can take care of you—even if you want a book that the store does not carry or have in stock. First, a Borders employee checks the digital database of titles that have been licensed from publishers. If the title is available, a digital file of the book is downloaded to two printers from a central server in Atlanta. One printer makes the book cover and the other the pages. Then the employee puts the two pieces together in a bookbinding machine. A separate machine cuts the book to size. And your book is ready. You get the book you want now, and Borders gets a sale. Books sold this way also avoid both inventory and incoming shipping cost, as well as the cost of returning books that do not sell.

Smooth FM provides a "customized" radio broadcast for Houston, Boston, Milwaukee, Albany, and Jacksonville from its midtown Manhattan station. Here is how it works. During Smooth FM's 40-minute music blocks, an announcer in Manhattan busily records 30-second blocks of local weather and traffic, commercials, promotions, and 5-second station IDs. Then the recorded material is transmitted to the affiliate stations. When the music block is over, the Manhattan announcer hits a button that signals computers at all the affiliates to simultaneously air the prerecorded "local" segments. Any "national" news or "national" ads can also be added from Manhattan. The result is the economy of mass production *and* a customized product for the local market. Radio people call it "local customization."

Sources: Hoover's Company Records (January 15, 2006): 51511; *The New York Times* (February 16, 2004): C3; *The Wall Street Journal* (June 1, 1999): B1, B4.

tailoring new products with shortened development times to meet the unique needs of their customers. And emusic of California maintains a music sound bite inventory on the Internet that allows customers to select a dozen songs of their choosing and have them made into a custom CD.[2] Similarly, the number of new books and movies increases each year. Mass customization places new demands on operations managers who must build the processes that provide this expanding variety of goods and services.

One of the essential ingredients in mass customization is a reliance on modular design. In all the examples cited, as well as those in the *OM in Action* box "Mass Customization at Borders Books and at Smooth FM Radio," modular design is the key. However, as Figure 5 shows, very effective scheduling, personnel and facility flexibility, supportive supply chains, and rapid throughput are also required. These items influence all 10 of the OM decisions and therefore require excellent operations management.

Making Mass Customization Work Mass customization suggests a system in which products are built-to-order.[3] **Build-to-order** means producing to customer orders, not forecasts.

Build-to-order (BTO)
Produce to customer order rather than to a forecast.

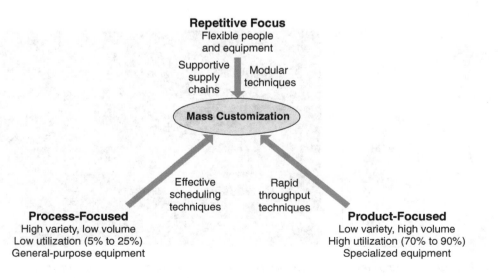

◄ **Figure 5**

Requirements to Achieve Mass Customization

[2]www.emusic.com.
[3]Build-to-order (BTO) may be referred to and refined as engineer-to-order (ETO) and design-to-order (DTO), depending on the extent of the customization.

As Dell Computers has shown, build-to-order can be a successful order-winning strategy when executed successfully. But build-to-order is difficult. Some major challenges are:

- *Product design* must be imaginative and fast. Successful build-to-order designs often use modules. Ping Inc. uses different combinations of club heads, grips, shafts, and angles to make 20,000 variations of its golf clubs. Another design technique is to do the customization as late in the production process as possible. For instance, to accommodate different orders, Dell installs both requested hardware and software modules at final assembly. At organizations such as Ping and Dell, the individual modules are made to a forecast but assembled on a "mix and match" basis to meet mass customization demands.

- *Process design* must be rapid, flexible, and able to accommodate changes in design and technology. Flexibility allows a BMW customer to change an order up to 6 days before the car's final assembly. In addition to process flexibility that facilitates change, a process technique that has proven effective is to postpone customization until late in the production process. The auto industry installs or outsources unique interior modules until very late in the production, as they do with customized vans.

- *Inventory management* requires tight control. To be successful, a firm must avoid being stuck with unpopular or obsolete components. With virtually no raw material, work in process, or finished goods, Dell puts custom computers together in less than a day.

- *Tight schedules* that track orders and material from design through delivery can be effectively implemented only with dedicated personnel. National Bicycle (see the photo) accomplishes this with virtually no inventory and a 3-hour build schedule. Product and process design that allow customization to be scheduled late in the production process also contribute to efficient mass customization. This type of scheduling is often referred to as **postponement**.

- *Responsive partners* in the supply chain yield effective collaboration. Cooperation with fast, open information exchange is critical as operations moves to an era in which competition is not between individual companies but between supply chains. Vans Inc. can custom tailor a pair of shoes, have them manufactured thousands of miles away in a Chinese factory, and have them delivered in a matter of weeks. Forecasting, inventory management, and ordering for JCPenney men's dress shirts are all handled by a supplier in Hong Kong.

Mass customization/build-to-order is difficult, but is the new imperative for operations. There are advantages to mass customization and building to order: first, by meeting the demands of the market place, firms win orders and stay in business; in addition, they reduce the enormous expenses present in organizations (from personnel to inventory to facilities) that exist because of inaccurate sales forecasting. Mass customization and build-to-order can be done—and operations managers in leading organizations are accepting the challenge.

Postponement

The delay of any modifications or customization to a product as long as possible in the production process.

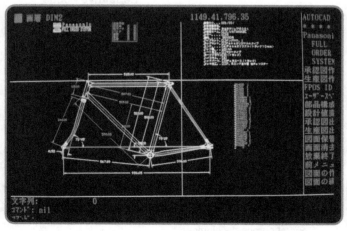

Louis Psihoyos, Science Faction

▲ *Mass customization improves customer service and provides competitive advantage. National Bicycle's customized bicycle production process begins by defining individual customer needs. The customer mounts the special frame in a bicycle store from which measurements are taken. These custom measurements are then sent to the factory, where CAD software produces a blueprint in about 3 minutes. At the same time, a bar-code label is prepared that will identify bicycle components as they move through production. Time—from beginning to end—is only 3 hours.*

Comparison of Process Choices

The characteristics of the four processes are shown in Table 2 and Figure 5. Advantages exist across the continuum of processes, and firms may find strategic advantage in any process. Each of the processes, when properly matched to volume and variety, can produce a low-cost advantage. For instance, unit costs will be less in the continuous-process case if high volume (and high utilization) exists. However, we do not always use the continuous-process (that is, specialized equipment and facilities) because it is too expensive when volumes are low or flexibility is required. A low-volume, unique, highly differentiated good or service is more economical when produced under process focus; this is the way fine-dining restaurants and general-purpose hospitals are organized. Just as all four processes, when appropriately selected and well managed, can yield low cost, so too can all four be responsive and produce differentiated products.

Figure 5 indicated that equipment utilization in a process-focused facility is often in the range of 5% to 25%. When utilization goes above 15%, moving toward a repetitive or product focus, or

> *Manufactured housing is now used for 32% of all new homes sold in the U.S. This industry has increased sales, reduced costs, and moved production from a process focus to a repetitive focus.*

▼ **Table 2** Comparison of the Characteristics of Four Types of Processes

Process Focus (low volume, high variety) (e.g., Standard Register)	Repetitive Focus (modular) (e.g., Harley-Davidson)	Product Focus (high volume, low variety) (e.g., Nucor Steel)	Mass Customization (high volume, high variety) (e.g., Dell Computer)
1. Small quantity and large variety of products are produced.	1. Long runs, usually a standardized product with options, are produced from modules.	1. Large quantity and small variety of products are produced.	1. Large quantity and large variety of products are produced.
2. Equipment used is general purpose.	2. Special equipment aids in use of an assembly line.	2. Equipment used is special purpose.	2. Rapid changeover on flexible equipment.
3. Operators are broadly skilled.	3. Employees are modestly trained.	3. Operators are less broadly skilled.	3. Flexible operators are trained for the necessary customization.
4. There are many job instructions because each job changes.	4. Repetitive operations reduce training and changes in job instructions.	4. Work orders and job instructions are few because they are standardized.	4. Custom orders require many job instructions.
5. Raw-material inventories are high relative to the value of the product.	5. Just-in-time procurement techniques are used.	5. Raw material inventories are low relative to the value of the product.	5. Raw material inventories are low relative to the value of the product.
6. Work-in-process is high compared to output.	6. Just-in-time inventory techniques are used.	6. Work-in-process inventory is low compared to output.	6. Work-in-process inventory is driven down by JIT, kanban, lean production.
7. Units move slowly through the plant.	7. Movement is measured in hours and days.	7. Swift movement of units through the facility is typical.	7. Goods move swiftly through the facility.
8. Finished goods are usually made to order and not stored.	8. Finished goods are made to frequent forecasts.	8. Finished goods are usually made to a forecast and stored.	8. Finished goods are often build-to-order (BTO).
9. Scheduling orders is complex and concerned with the trade-off between inventory availability, capacity, and customer service.	9. Scheduling is based on building various models from a variety of modules to forecasts.	9. Scheduling is relatively simple and concerned with establishing a rate of output sufficient to meet sales forecasts.	9. Sophisticated scheduling is required to accommodate custom orders.
10. Fixed costs tend to be low and variable costs high.	10. Fixed costs are dependent on flexibility of the facility.	10. Fixed costs tend to be high and variable costs low.	10. Fixed costs tend to be high, but variable costs must be low.
11. Costing, often done by the job, is estimated prior to doing the job, but known only after the job.	11. Costs are usually known because of extensive prior experience.	11. Because fixed costs are high, costs are highly dependent on utilization of capacity.	11. High fixed costs and dynamic variable costs make costing a challenge.

► **Figure 6**

Crossover Charts

Three different processes can be expected to have three different costs. However, at any given volume, only one will have the lowest cost.

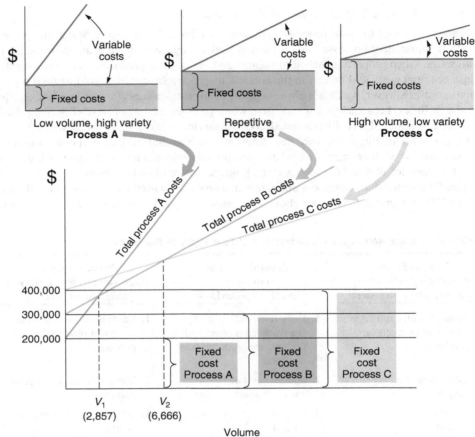

Low volume, high variety
Process A

Repetitive
Process B

High volume, low variety
Process C

2. Compute crossover points for different processes

Crossover chart

A chart of costs at the possible volumes for more than one process.

even mass customization, may be advantageous. A cost advantage usually exists by improving utilization, provided the necessary flexibility is maintained. McDonald's started an entirely new industry by moving its limited menu from process focus to repetitive focus. McDonald's is now trying to add more variety by moving toward mass customization.

Much of what is produced in the world is still produced in very small lots—often as small as one. This is true for legal services, medical services, dental services, and restaurants. An X-ray machine in a dentist's office and much of the equipment in a fine-dining restaurant have low utilization. Hospitals, too, have low utilization, which suggests why their costs are considered high. Why such low utilization? In part because excess capacity for peak loads is desirable. Hospital administrators, as well as managers of other service facilities and their patients and customers, expect equipment to be available as needed. Another reason is poor scheduling (although substantial efforts have been made to forecast demand in the service industry) and the resulting imbalance in the use of facilities.

Crossover Charts The comparison of processes can be further enhanced by looking at the point where the total cost of the processes changes. For instance, Figure 6 shows three alternative processes compared on a single chart. Such a chart is sometimes called a **crossover chart**. Process A has the lowest cost for volumes below V_1, process B has the lowest cost between V_1 and V_2, and process C has the lowest cost at volumes above V_2.

Example 4 illustrates how to determine the exact volume where one process becomes more expensive than another.

EXAMPLE 4

Crossover chart

Kleber Enterprises would like to evaluate three accounting software products (A, B, and C) to support changes in its internal accounting processes. The resulting processes will have cost structures similar to those shown in Figure 6. The costs of the software for these processes are:

	Total Fixed Cost	Dollars Required per Accounting Report
Software A	$200,000	$60
Software B	$300,000	$25
Software C	$400,000	$10

Approach: Solve for the crossover point for software A and B and then the crossover point for software B and C.

Solution: Software A yields a process that is most economical up to V_1, but to exactly what number of reports (volume)? To determine the volume at V_1, we set the cost of software A equal to the cost of software B. V_1 is the unknown volume:

$$200,000 + (60)V_1 = 300,000 + (25)V_1$$

$$35V_1 = 100,000$$

$$V_1 = 2,857$$

This means that software A is most economical from 0 reports to 2,857 reports (V_1)

Similarly, to determine the crossover point for V_2, we set the cost of software B equal to the cost of software C:

$$300,000 + (25)V_2 = 400,000 + (10)V_2$$

$$15V_2 = 100,000$$

$$V_2 = 6,666$$

This means that software B is most economical if the number of reports is between 2,857 (V_1) and 6,666 (V_2) and that software C is most economical if reports exceed 6,666 (V_2).

Insight: As you can see, the software and related process chosen is highly dependent on the forecasted volume.

Learning exercise: If the vendor of software A reduces the fixed cost to $150,000, what is the new crossover point between A and B? [Answer: 4,286.]

Related problems: 5, 6, 7, 8, 9, 10, 11, 12, 14

 Active Model 7.1

Example 4 is further illustrated in Active Model 7.1 on the CD-ROM.

Focused Processes   In an ongoing quest for efficiency, industrialized societies continue to move toward specialization. The focus that comes with specialization contributes to efficiency. Managers who focus on a limited number of activities, products, and technologies do better. As the variety of products in a facility increase, overhead costs increase even faster. Similarly, as the variety of products, customers, and technology increases, so does complexity. The resources necessary to cope with the complexity expand disproportionately. A focus on depth of product line as opposed to breadth is typical of outstanding firms, of which Intel, Motorola, L.M. Ericsson, Nokia, and Bosch are world-class examples. Specialization, simplification, concentration, and *focus* yield efficiency. They also contribute to building a core competence that yields market and financial success. The focus can be:

 Video 7.3

Process Strategy at Wheeled Coach Ambulance

- *Customers* (such as Winterhalter Gastronom, a German company that focuses on dishwashers for hotels and restaurants, for whom spotless glasses and dishes are critical)
- *Products* with similar attributes (such as Nucor Steel's Crawford, Ohio, plant, which processes only high-quality sheet steels, and Gallagher, a New Zealand company, which has 45% of the world market in electric fences)
- *Service* (such as Orlando's Arnold Palmer Hospital, with a focus on children and women; or Shouldice Hospital, in Canada, with a focus on hernia repair).
- *Technology* (such as Texas Instruments, with a focus on only certain specialized kinds of semiconductors; and SAP, which in spite of a world of opportunities, remains focused on software).

The key for the operations manager is to move continuously toward specialization, focusing on the products, technology, customers, processes, and talents necessary to excel in that specialty.

Changing Processes   Changing the production system from one process model to another is difficult and expensive. In some cases, the change may mean starting over. Consider what would be required of a rather simple change—McDonald's adding the flexibility necessary to serve you a charbroiled hamburger. What appears to be rather straightforward would require changes in

Agile organizations are quick and flexible in their response to changing customer requirements.

many of our 10 OM decisions. For instance, changes may be necessary in (1) purchasing (a different quality of meat, perhaps with more fat content, and supplies such as charcoal); (2) quality standards (how long and at what temperature the patty will cook); (3) equipment (the charbroiler); (4) layout (space for the new process and for new exhaust vents); and (5) training. So choosing where to operate on the process strategy continuum may determine the transformation strategy for an extended period. This critical decision must be done right the first time.

PROCESS ANALYSIS AND DESIGN

When analyzing and designing processes to transform resources into goods and services, we ask questions such as the following:

Learning Objective

3. Use the tools of process analysis

- Is the process designed to achieve competitive advantage in terms of differentiation, response, or low cost?
- Does the process eliminate steps that do not add value?
- Does the process maximize customer value as perceived by the customer?
- Will the process win orders?

A number of tools help us understand the complexities of process design and redesign. They are simply ways of making sense of what happens or must happen in a process. Let's look at five of them: flow diagrams, time-function mapping, value-stream mapping, process charts, and service blueprinting.

Flow Diagrams

Flow diagram

A drawing used to analyze movement of people or material.

The first tool is the **flow diagram**, which is a schematic or drawing of the movement of material, product, or people. For instance, Figures 2, 3, and 4 showed the processes for Standard Register, Harley-Davidson, and Nucor Steel, respectively. Such diagrams can help understanding, analysis, and communication of a process.

Time-Function Mapping

Time-function mapping (or process mapping)

A flow diagram with time added on the horizontal axis.

A second tool for process analysis and design is a flow diagram, but with time added on the horizontal axis. Such charts are sometimes called **time-function mapping**, or **process mapping**. With time-function mapping, nodes indicate the activities and the arrows indicate the flow direction, with time on the horizontal axis. This type of analysis allows users to identify and eliminate waste such as extra steps, duplication, and delay. Figure 7 shows the use of process mapping before and after

▼ **Figure 7** Time-Function Mapping (Process Mapping) for a Product Requiring Printing and Extruding Operations at American National Can Company

This technique clearly shows that waiting and order processing contributed substantially to the 46 days that can be eliminated in this operation.

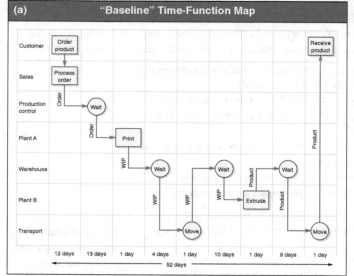

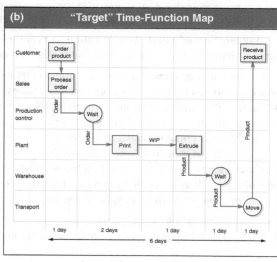

Source: Excerpted from Elaine J. Labach, "Faster, Better, and Cheaper," *Target* no. 5: 43 with permission of the Association for Manufacturing Excellence, 380 West Palatine Road, Wheeling, IL 60090-5863, 847/520-3282. **www.ame.org**.

process improvement at American National Can Company. In this example, substantial reduction in waiting time and process improvement in order processing contributed to a savings of 46 days.

Value-Stream Mapping

A variation of time-function mapping is **value-stream mapping** (VSM); however, value-stream mapping takes an expanded look at where value is added (and not added) in the entire production process, including the supply chain. As with time-function mapping, the idea is to start with the customer and understand the production process, but value-stream mapping extends the analysis back to suppliers.[4]

Value-stream mapping (VSM)

A process that helps managers understand how to add value in the flow of material and information through the entire production process.

EXAMPLE 5

Value-stream mapping

Motorola has received an order for 11,000 cell phones per month and wants to understand how the order will be processed through manufacturing.

Approach: To fully understand the process from customer to supplier, Motorola wants to prepare a value-stream map.

Solution: Although value-stream maps appear complex, their construction is easy. Here are the steps needed to complete the value-stream map shown in Figure 8

◄ **Figure 8**

Value-Stream Mapping (VSM)

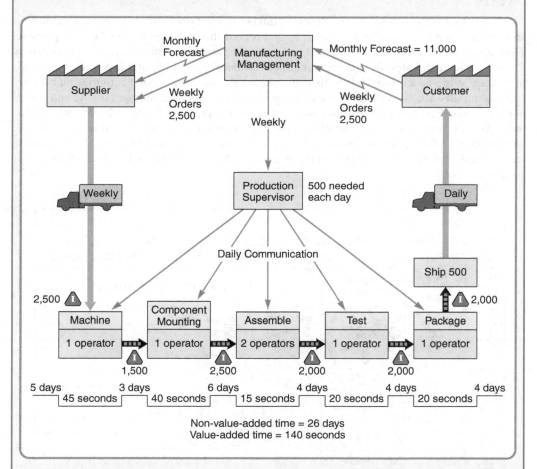

1. Begin with symbols for customer, supplier, and production to ensure the big picture.
2. Enter customer order requirements.
3. Calculate the daily production requirements.
4. Enter the outbound shipping requirements and delivery frequency.
5. Determine inbound shipping method and delivery frequency.
6. Add the process steps (i.e., machine, assemble) in sequence, left to right.

[4]See Mike Rother and John Shook, *Learning to See*. Brookline, MA: Lean Enterprise Institute, Inc., 1999.

7. Add communication methods, add their frequency, and show the direction with arrows.
8. Add inventory quantities (shown with ▲I) between every step of the entire flow.
9. Determine total working time (value-added time) and delay (non-value-added time).

Insight: From Figure 8 we note that large inventories exist in incoming raw material and between processing steps, and that the value-added time is low as a proportion of the entire process.

Learning exercise: How might raw material inventory be reduced? [Answer: Have deliveries twice per week rather than once per week.]

Related problem: 13

Value-stream mapping takes into account not only the process but, as shown in Example 5, also the management decisions and information systems that support the process.

Process Charts

Process charts

Charts that use symbols to analyze the movement of people or material.

The fourth tool is the *process chart*. **Process charts** use symbols, time, and distance to provide an objective and structured way to analyze and record the activities that make up a process. They allow us to focus on value-added activities. For instance, the process chart shown in Figure 9, which includes the present method of hamburger assembly at a fast-food restaurant, includes a value-added line to help us distinguish between value-added activities and waste. Identifying all value-added operations (as opposed to inspection, storage, delay, and transportation, which add no value) allows us to determine the percent of value added to total activities.[5] We can see from the computation at the bottom of Figure 9 that the value added in this case is 85.7%. The operations manager's job is to reduce waste and increase the percent of value added. The non-value-added items are a waste; they are resources lost to the firm and to society forever.

▶ **Figure 9**

Process Chart Showing a Hamburger Assembly Process at a Fast-Food Restaurant

Present Method ☒		PROCESS CHART		Proposed Method ☐
SUBJECT CHARTED *Hamburger Assembly Process*			DATE *8/1/07*	
DEPARTMENT _____		CHART BY *KH*	SHEET NO. *1* OF *1*	

DIST. IN FEET	TIME IN MINS.	CHART SYMBOLS	PROCESS DESCRIPTION
	—	○ ⇨ ☐ D ▽	*Meat Patty in Storage*
1.5	.05	○ ⇨ ☐ D ▽	*Transfer to Broiler*
	2.50	⊗ ⇨ ☐ D ▽	*Broiler*
	.05	○ ⇨ ☐ D ▽	*Visual Inspection*
1.0	.05	○ ⇨ ☐ D ▽	*Transfer to Rack*
	.15	○ ⇨ ☐ D ▽	*Temporary Storage*
.5	.10	○ ⇨ ☐ D ▽	*Obtain Buns, Lettuce, etc.*
	.20	⊗ ⇨ ☐ D ▽	*Assemble Order*
.5	.05	○ ⇨ ☐ D ▽	*Place in Finish Rack*
		○ ⇨ ☐ D ▽	
3.5	3.15	2 4 1 – 2	TOTALS

Value-added time = Operation time/Total time = (2.50+.20)/3.15 = 85.7%

○ = operation; ⇨ = transportation; ☐ = inspection; D = delay; ▽ = storage.

[5]Waste includes *inspection* (if the task is done properly, then inspection is unnecessary); *transportation* (movement of material within a process may be a necessary evil, but it adds no value); *delay* (an asset sitting idle and taking up space is waste); *storage* (unless part of a "curing" process, storage is waste).

Service Blueprinting

Products with a high service content may warrant use of yet a fifth process technique. **Service blueprinting** is a process analysis technique that focuses on the customer and the provider's interaction with the customer.[6] For instance, the activities at level one of Figure 10 are under the control of the customer. In the second level are activities of the service provider interacting with the customer. The third level includes those activities that are performed away from, and not immediately visible to, the customer. Each level suggests different management issues. For instance, the top level may suggest educating the customer or modifying expectations, whereas the second level may require a focus on personnel selection and training. Finally, the third level lends itself to more typical process innovations. The service blueprint shown in Figure 10 also notes potential failure points and shows how poka-yoke techniques can be added to improve quality. The consequences of these failure points can be greatly reduced if identified at the design stage when modifications or appropriate poka-yokes can be included. A time dimension is included in Figure 10 to aid understanding, extend insight, and provide a focus on customer service.[7]

Service blueprinting
A process analysis technique that lends itself to a focus on the customer and the provider's interaction with the customer.

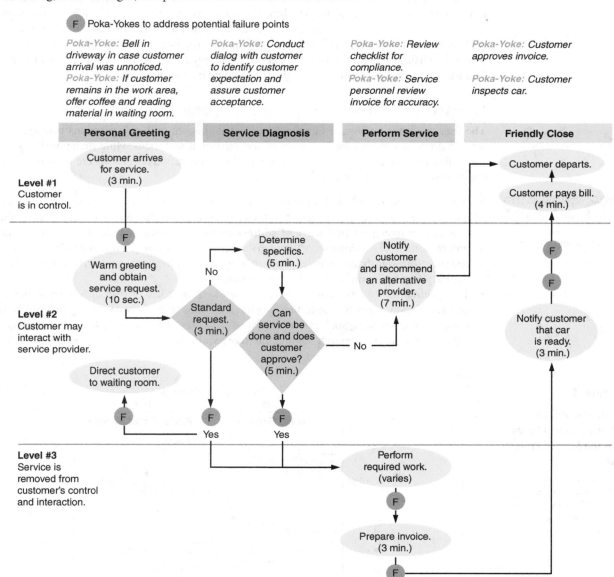

▲ **Figure 10** Service Blueprint for Service at Speedy Lube, Inc.

[6]G. L. Shostack is given credit for the term *service blueprint.* See G. L. Shostack, "Designing Services That Deliver," *Harvard Business Review* 62, no. 1 (January–February, 1984): 133–139.

[7]See related work by James P. Womack and Daniel T. Jones, "Lean Consumption," *Harvard Business Review* 84, no. 4 (March 2005): 58–68.

Each of these five process analysis tools has its strengths and variations. Flowcharts are a quick way to view the big picture and try to make sense of the entire system. Time-function mapping adds some rigor and a time element to the macro analysis. Value-stream mapping extends beyond the immediate organization to customers and suppliers. Process charts are designed to provide a much more detailed view of the process, adding items such as value-added time, delay, distance, storage, and so forth. Service blueprinting, on the other hand, is designed to help us focus on the customer interaction part of the process. Because customer interaction is often an important variable in process design, we now examine some additional aspects of service process design.

SERVICE PROCESS DESIGN

Interaction with the customer often affects process performance adversely. But a service, by its very nature, implies that some interaction and customization is needed. Recognizing that the customer's unique desires tend to play havoc with a process, the more the manager designs the process to accommodate these special requirements, the more effective and efficient the process will be. Notice how well Dell Computer has managed the interface between the customer and the process by using the Internet (see the *Global Company Profile* at the beginning of this chapter). The trick is to find the right combination of cost and customer interaction.

Customer Interaction and Process Design

The four quadrants of Figure 11 provide additional insight on how operations managers design service processes to find the best level of specialization and focus while maintaining the necessary customer interaction and customization. The 10 operations decisions are used with a different emphasis in each quadrant. For instance:

Learning Objective

4. Describe customer interaction in process design

- In the upper sections (quadrants) of *mass service* and *professional service*, where *labor content is high*, we expect the manager to focus extensively on human resources. These quadrants require that managers find ways of addressing unique issues that satisfy customers and win orders. This is often done with very personalized services, requiring high labor involvement and therefore significant selection and training issues in the human resources area. This is particularly true in the professional service quadrant.
- The quadrants with *low customization* tend to (1) standardize or restrict some offerings, as do fast-food restaurants, (2) automate, as have airlines with ticket-vending machines, or (3) remove some services, such as seat assignments, as has Southwest Airlines. Off-loading some aspect of the service through automation may require innovations in process design as well as

▶ **Figure 11**

Services Moving toward Specialization and Focus within the Service Process Matrix

Source: Adapted from work by Roger Schmenner, "Service Business and Productivity," *Decision Sciences* 35, no. 3 (summer 2004): 333–347.

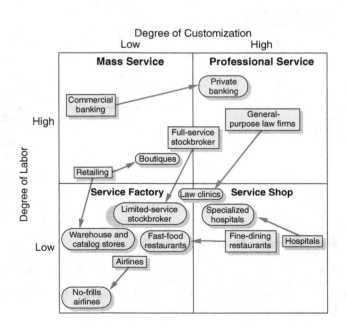

Strategy	Technique	Example
Separation	*Structuring service* so customers must go where the service is offered	Bank customers go to a manager to open a new account, to loan officers for loans, and to tellers for deposits
Self-service	*Self-service* so customers examine, compare, and evaluate at their own pace	Supermarkets and department stores Internet ordering
Postponement	*Customizing at delivery*	Customizing vans at delivery rather than at production
Focus	*Restricting* the offerings	Limited-menu restaurant
Modules	*Modular* selection of service *Modular* production	Investment and insurance selection Prepackaged food modules in restaurants
Automation	*Separating services* that may lend themselves to some type of automation	Automatic teller machines
Scheduling	Precise personnel *scheduling*	Scheduling ticket counter personnel at 15-minute intervals at airlines
Training	*Clarifying the service* options *Explaining how to avoid problems*	Investment counselor, funeral directors After-sale maintenance personnel

◄ **Table 3**

Techniques for Improving Service Productivity

capital investment. Such is the case with airline ticket vending and bank ATMs. This move to standardization and automation may require added capital expenditure, as well as putting operations managers under pressure to develop new skills for the purchase and maintenance of such equipment. A reduction in a customization capability will require added strength in other areas.

- Because customer feedback is lower in the quadrants with *low customization*, tight control may be required to maintain quality standards.
- Operations with *low labor intensity* may lend themselves particularly well to innovations in process technology and scheduling.

Table 3 shows some additional techniques for innovative process design in services. Managers focus on designing innovative processes that enhance the service. For instance, supermarket *self-service* reduces cost while it allows customers to check for the specific features they want, such as freshness or color. Dell Computer provides another version of self-service by allowing customers to design their own product on the Web. Customers seem to like this, and it is cheaper and faster for Dell.

More Opportunities to Improve Service Processes

Layout Layout design is an integral part of many service processes, particularly in retailing, dining, and banking. In retailing, layout can provide not only product exposure but also customer education and product enhancement. In restaurants, layout can enhance the dining experience as well as provide an effective flow between bar, kitchen, and dining area. In banks, layout provides security as well as work flow and personal comfort. Because layout is such an integral part of many services, it provides continuing opportunity for winning orders.

 Video 7.4

Process Analysis at Arnold Palmer Hospital

Human Resources Because so many services involve direct interaction with the customer (as the upper quadrants of Figure 11 suggest), the human resource issues of recruiting and training can be particularly important ingredients in service processes. Additionally, a committed workforce that exhibits flexibility when schedules are made and is cross-trained to fill in when the process requires less than a full-time person, can have a tremendous impact on overall process performance.

SELECTION OF EQUIPMENT AND TECHNOLOGY

Ultimately, the decisions about a particular process require decisions about equipment and technology. Those decisions can be complex because alternative methods of production are present in virtually all operations functions, be they hospitals, restaurants, or manufacturing facilities.

Picking the best equipment means understanding the specific industry and available processes and technology. That choice of equipment, be it an X-ray machine for a hospital, a computer-controlled lathe for a factory, or a new computer for an office, requires considering cost, quality, capacity, and flexibility. To make this decision, operations personnel develop documentation that indicates the capacity, size, and tolerances of each option, as well as its maintenance requirements. Any one of these attributes may be the deciding factor regarding selection.

The selection of equipment for a particular type of process can also provide competitive advantage. Many firms, for instance, develop unique machines or techniques within established processes that provide an advantage. This advantage may result in added flexibility in meeting customer requirements, lower cost, or higher quality. Innovations and equipment modification might also allow for a more stable production process that takes less adjustment, maintenance, and operator training. In any case, specialized equipment often provides a way to win orders.

Modern technology also allows operations managers to enlarge the scope of their processes. As a result, an important attribute to look for in new equipment and process selection is flexible equipment. **Flexibility** is the ability to respond with little penalty in time, cost, or customer value. This may mean modular, movable, even cheap equipment. Flexibility may also mean the development of sophisticated electronic equipment, which increasingly provides the rapid changes that mass customization demands. The technological advances that influence OM process strategy are substantial and are discussed next.

Flexibility
The ability to respond with little penalty in time, cost, or customer value.

5. Identify recent advances in production technology

PRODUCTION TECHNOLOGY

Advances in technology that enhance production and productivity have a wide range of applications in both manufacturing and services. In this section, we introduce nine areas of technology: (1) machine technology, (2) automatic identification systems (AIS), (3) process control, (4) vision systems, (5) robots, (6) automated storage and retrieval systems (ASRSs), (7) automated guided vehicles (AGVs), (8) flexible manufacturing systems (FMSs), and (9) computer-integrated manufacturing (CIM).

Machine Technology

Most of the world's machinery that performs operations such as cutting, drilling, boring, and milling is undergoing tremendous progress in both precision and control. New machinery turns out metal components that vary less than a micron—1/76 the width of a human hair. They can accelerate water to three times the speed of sound to cut titanium for surgical tools. Machinery of the 21st century is often five times more productive than that of previous generations while being smaller and using less power. The space and power savings are both significant. And continuing advances in lubricants now allow the use of water-based lubricants rather than oil based. Using water-based lubricants eliminates hazardous waste and allows shavings to be easily recovered and recycled.

▶ Three critical success factors in the trucking industry are (1) getting shipments to customers promptly (rapid response); (2) keeping trucks busy (capacity utilization); and (3) buying inexpensive fuel (driving down costs). Many firms have now developed devices like the one shown here (on the right) to track location of trucks and facilitate communication between drivers and dispatchers. Some systems use global positioning satellites (shown on the left), to speed shipment response, maximize utilization of the truck, and ensure purchase of fuel at the most economical location. Sensors are also being added inside trailers. These sensors communicate whether the trailer is empty or full and detect if the trailer is connected to a truck or riding on a railroad car.

NYT Graphics, New York Times Agency

Tony Freeman, PhotoEdit Inc.

The intelligence now available for the control of new machinery via computer chips allows more complex and precise items to be made faster. Electronic controls increase speed by reducing changeover time, reducing waste (because of fewer mistakes), and enhancing flexibility. Machinery with its own computer and memory is called **computer numerical control (CNC)** machinery.

Advanced versions of such technology are used on Pratt and Whitney's turbine blade plant in Connecticut. The machinery has improved the loading and alignment task so much that Pratt has cut the total time for the grinding process of a turbine blade from 10 days to 2 hours. The new machinery has also contributed to process improvements that mean the blades now travel just 1,800 feet in the plant, down from 8,100 feet. The total throughput time for a turbine blade has been cut from 22 days to 7 days.

Computer numerical control (CNC)
Machinery with its own computer and memory.

Automatic Identification Systems (AISs) and RFID

New equipment, from numerically controlled manufacturing machinery to ATM machines, is controlled by digital electronic signals. Electrons are a great vehicle for transmitting information, but they have a major limitation—most OM data does not start out in bits and bytes. Therefore, operations managers must get the data into an electronic form. Making data digital is done via computer keyboards, bar codes, radio frequencies, optical characters on bank checks, and so forth. These **automatic identification systems (AISs)** help us move data into electronic form, where it is easily manipulated.

Because of its decreasing cost and increasing pervasiveness, **radio frequency identification (RFID)** warrants special note. RFID is integrated circuitry with its own tiny antennas that use radio waves to send signals a limited range—usually a matter of yards. These RFID tags (sometimes called RFID circuits) provide unique identification that enables the tracking and monitoring of parts, pallets, people, and pets—virtually everything that moves. RFID requires no line of sight between tag and reader.

Innovative OM examples of AISs and RFID include:[8]

Automatic identification system (AIS)
A system for transforming data into electronic form, for example, bar codes.

Radio frequency identification (RFID)
A wireless system in which integrated circuits with antennas send radio waves.

- Nurses reduce errors in hospitals by matching bar codes on medication to ID bracelets on patients.
- RFID tags in agriculture monitor the temperature at which fruit is kept. They can also track what chemicals and fertilizers have been used on the fruit.
- Transponders attached to cars allow McDonald's to identify and bill customers who can now zip through the drive-through line without having to stop and pay. The transponders use the same technology that permits motorists to skip stops on some toll roads. McDonald's estimates that the change speeds up throughput time by 15 seconds.
- Stanford University School of Medicine doctors are using sponges embedded with RFID tags. Waving a detector over an incision can tell if a surgeon accidentally left a sponge in the patient.
- FedEx tags major airplane parts, which allows them to be scanned so maintenance data (e.g., part number, installation date, country of origin) can be tracked.

With RFID, a cashier could scan the entire contents of a shopping cart in seconds.

Process Control

Process control is the use of information technology to monitor and control a physical process. For instance, process control is used to measure the moisture content and thickness of paper as it travels over a paper machine at thousands of feet per minute. Process control is also used to determine and control temperatures, pressures, and quantities in petroleum refineries, petrochemical processes, cement plants, steel mills, nuclear reactors, and other product-focused facilities.

Process control systems operate in a number of ways, but the following is typical:

Process control
The use of information technology to control a physical process.

- Sensors collect data.
- Devices read data on some periodic basis, perhaps once a minute or once every second.
- Measurements are translated into digital signals, which are transmitted to a digital computer.
- Computer programs read the file (the digital data) and analyze the data.
- The resulting output may take numerous forms. These include messages on computer consoles or printers, signals to motors to change valve settings, warning lights or horns, statistical process control charts, or schematics.

[8]See *Industrial Engineer* 38, no. 8 (August 2006): 10; and *The Wall Street Journal* (July 18, 2006): D3.

▶ *Process control software, such as Factory Link IV, shown here, controls the flow of sugars and fruits into a juice mixer. The production report in the lower left corner provides a current status report.*

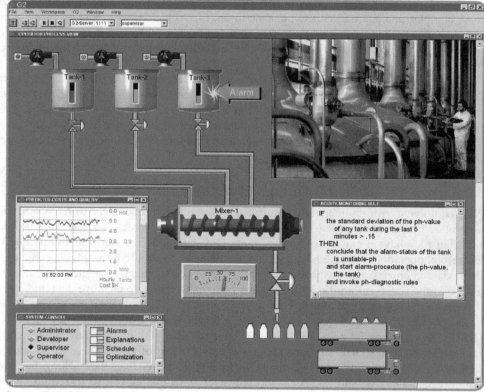

Gensym Corporation

Vision Systems

Vision systems
Systems that use video cameras and computer technology in inspection roles.

Vision systems combine video cameras and computer technology and are often used in inspection roles. Visual inspection is an important task in most food-processing and manufacturing organizations. Moreover, in many applications, visual inspection performed by humans is tedious, mind-numbing, and error prone. Thus vision systems are widely used when the items being inspected are very similar. For instance, vision systems are used to inspect french fries so that imperfections can be identified as the fries proceed down the production line. Vision systems are used to ensure that sealant is present and in the proper amount on Whirlpool's washing-machine transmissions, and to inspect switch assemblies at the Foster Plant in Des Plaines, Illinois. Vision systems are consistently accurate, do not become bored, and are of modest cost. These systems are vastly superior to individuals trying to perform these tasks.

Robots

Robot
A flexible machine with the ability to hold, move, or grab items. It functions through electronic impulses that activate motors and switches.

When a machine is flexible and has the ability to hold, move, and perhaps "grab" items, we tend to use the word *robot*. **Robots** are mechanical devices that may have a few electronic impulses stored on semiconductor chips that will activate motors and switches. Robots may be used effectively to perform tasks that are especially monotonous or dangerous or those that can be improved by the substitution of mechanical for human effort. Such is the case when consistency, accuracy, speed, strength, or power can be enhanced by the substitution of machines for people. Ford, for example, uses robots to do 98% of the welding on some automobiles.

Automated Storage and Retrieval Systems (ASRSs)

Automated storage and retrieval system (ASRS)
Computer-controlled warehouses that provide for the automatic placement of parts into and from designated places within a warehouse.

Because of the tremendous labor involved in error-prone warehousing, computer-controlled warehouses have been developed. These systems, known as **automated storage and retrieval systems (ASRSs)**, provide for the automatic placement and withdrawal of parts and products into and from designated places in a warehouse. Such systems are commonly used in distribution facilities of retailers such as Wal-Mart, Tupperware, and Benetton. These systems are also found in inventory and test areas of manufacturing firms.

Automated Guided Vehicles (AGVs)

Automated material handling can take the form of monorails, conveyors, robots, or automated guided vehicles. **Automated guided vehicles (AGVs)** are electronically guided and controlled carts used in manufacturing to move parts and equipment. They are also used in offices to move mail and in hospitals and in jails to deliver meals.

Automated guided vehicle (AGV)
Electronically guided and controlled cart used to move materials.

Flexible Manufacturing Systems (FMSs)

When a central computer provides instructions to each workstation *and* to the material-handling equipment (which moves material to that station), the system is known as an automated work cell or, more commonly, a **flexible manufacturing system (FMS)**. An FMS is flexible because both the material-handling devices and the machines themselves are controlled by easily changed electronic signals (computer programs). Operators simply load new programs, as necessary, to produce different products. The result is a system that can economically produce low volume but high variety. For example, the Lockheed Martin facility, near Dallas, efficiently builds one-of-a-kind spare parts for military aircraft. The costs associated with changeover and low utilization have been reduced substantially. FMSs bridge the gap between product-focused and process-focused facilities.

Flexible manufacturing system (FMS)
A system that uses an automated work cell controlled by electronic signals from a common centralized computer facility.

FMSs are not a panacea, however, because the individual components (machines and material-handling devices) have their own physical constraints. The Lockheed Martin plant, for example, handles only light machining. Other FMSs are capable of handling electronic assembly of products of only limited size. Moreover, an FMS also has stringent communications requirements between the unique components within it. And, of course, sophisticated equipment means substantial capital investment. However, reduced changeover time and more accurate scheduling result in faster throughput and improved utilization. Because there are fewer mistakes, reduced waste also contributes to lowering costs. These features are what operations managers are looking for: flexibility to provide customized products, improved utilization to reduce costs, and improved throughput to improve response.

Computer-Integrated Manufacturing (CIM)

Flexible manufacturing systems can be extended backward electronically into the engineering and inventory control departments and forward to the warehousing and shipping departments. In this way, computer-aided design (CAD) generates the necessary electronic instructions to run a numerically controlled machine. In a computer-integrated manufacturing environment, a design change initiated at a CAD terminal can result in that change being made in the part produced on the shop floor in a matter of minutes. When this capability is integrated with inventory control, warehousing, and shipping as a part of a flexible manufacturing system, the entire system is called **computer-integrated manufacturing (CIM)** (Figure 12).

 Video 7.5

Computer-Integrated Manufacturing at Harley-Davidson

Flexible manufacturing systems and computer-integrated manufacturing are reducing the distinction between low-volume/high-variety and high-volume/low-variety production. Information technology is allowing FMS and CIM to handle increasing variety while expanding to include a growing range of volumes.

Computer-integrated manufacturing (CIM)
A manufacturing system in which CAD, FMS, inventory control, warehousing, and shipping are integrated.

TECHNOLOGY IN SERVICES

Just as we have seen rapid advances in technology in the manufacturing sector, so we also find dramatic changes in the service sector. These range from electronic diagnostic equipment at auto repair shops, to blood- and urine-testing equipment in hospitals, to retinal security scanners at airports and high-security facilities. The hospitality industry provides other examples, as discussed

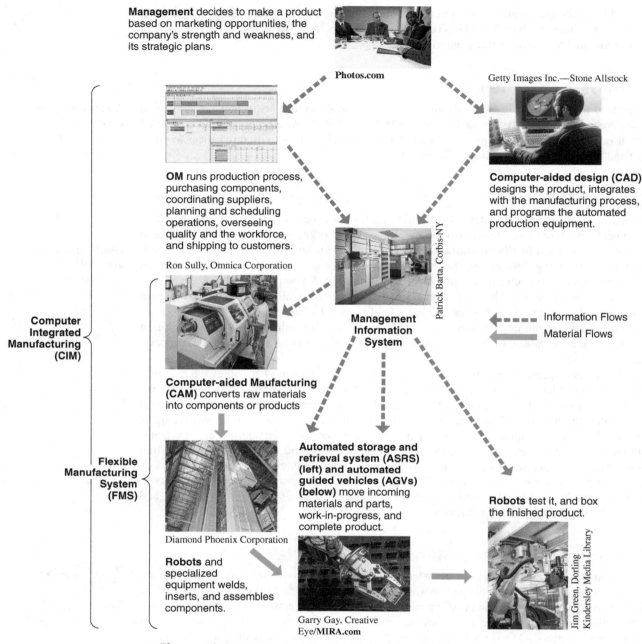

▲ **Figure 12** Computer-Integrated Manufacturing (CIM)

CIM includes computer-aided design (CAD), computer-aided manufacturing (CAM), flexible manufacturing systems (FMSs), automated storage and retrieval systems (ASRSs), automated guided vehicles (AGVs), and robots to provide an integrated and flexible manufacturing process.

in the *OM in Action* box "Technology Changes the Hotel Industry." The McDonald's approach is to use self-serve kiosks. The labor savings when ordering and speedier checkout service provide valuable productivity increases for both the restaurant and the customer.

Similarly, Andersen Windows, of Minnesota, has developed user-friendly computer software that enables customers to design their own window specifications. The customer calls up a product information guide, promotion material, a gallery of designs, and a sketch pad to create the designs desired. The software also allows the customer to determine likely energy savings and see a graphic view of their home fitted with the new window.

In retail stores, POS terminals now download prices quickly to reflect changing costs or market conditions, and sales are tracked in 15-minute segments to aid production and scheduling.

Technology Changes the Hotel Industry

Technology is introducing "intelligent rooms" to the hotel industry. Hotel management can now precisely track a maid's time through the use of a security system. When a maid enters a room, a card is inserted that notifies the front-desk computer of the maid's location. "We can show her a printout of how long she takes to do a room," says one manager.

Security systems also enable guests to use their own credit cards as keys to unlock their doors. There are also other uses for the system. The computer can bar a guest's access to the room after checkout time and automatically control the air conditioning or heat, turning it on at check-in and off at checkout.

Minibars are now equipped with sensors that alert the central computer system at the hotel when an item is removed. Such items are immediately billed to the room. And now, with a handheld infrared unit, housekeeping staff can check, from the hallway, to see if a room is physically occupied. This both eliminates the embarrassment of having a hotel staffer walk in on a guest *and* improves security for housekeepers.

At Loew's Portofino Bay Hotel at Universal Studios, Orlando, guest smart cards act as credit cards in both the theme park and the hotel, and staff smart cards (programmed for different levels of security access) create an audit trail of employee movement. Starwood Hotels, which runs such properties as Sheraton and Westins, use Casio Pocket PCs to communicate with a hotel wireless network. Now guests can check in and out from any place on the property, such as at their restaurant table after breakfast or lunch.

Sources: Hotel and Motel Management (August 2004): 128–133; *Hotels* (April, 2004): 51–54; and *Newsweek* (international ed.) (September 27, 2004): 73.

Drug companies, such as Purdue Pharma LP, have begun tracking critical medications with radio frequency identification (RFID) tags to reduce counterfeiting and theft.

Table 4 provides a glimpse of the impact of technology on services. Operations managers in services, as in manufacturing, must be able to evaluate the impact of technology on their firm. This ability requires particular skill when evaluating reliability, investment analysis, human resource requirements, and maintenance/service.

PROCESS REDESIGN

Often a firm finds that the initial assumptions of its process are no longer valid. The world is a dynamic place, and customer desires, product technology, and product mix change. Consequently, processes are redesigned. **Process redesign** is the fundamental rethinking of business processes to

Process redesign
The fundamental rethinking of business processes to bring about dramatic improvements in performance.

▲ At Orlando's Wet 'n Wild water park, instead of using credit cards or cash, visitors use RFID technology. The technology is embedded in wristbands that can transmit a serial number to scanners alongside the park's cash registers. At the end of the day, visitors get a receipt that lists all their charges. The bands are disabled once they are cut off.

Orlando Sentinel Communication, The Orlando Sentinel

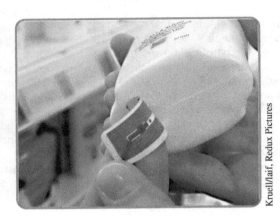

Kruell/laif, Redux Pictures

▲ Pharmaceutical companies are counting on RFID to aid the tracking and tracing of drugs in the distribution system to reduce losses that total over $30 billion a year.

	Service Industry	Example
▶ **Table 4** **Examples of Technology's Impact on Services**	Financial Services	Debit cards, electronic funds transfer, automatic teller machines, Internet stock trading
	Education	Online newspapers, online journals, interactive assignments via Web CT and Blackboard
	Utilities and government	Automated one-man garbage trucks, optical mail and bomb scanners, flood-warning systems.
	Restaurants and foods	Wireless orders from waiters to the kitchen, robot butchering, transponders on cars that track sales at drive-throughs.
	Communications	Electronic publishing, interactive TV
	Hotels	Electronic check-in/checkout, electronic key/lock systems
	Wholesale/retail trade	Use of ATM-like kiosks, point-of-sale (POS) terminals, e-commerce, electronic communication between store and supplier, bar-coded data
	Transportation	Automatic toll booths, satellite-directed navigation systems
	Health care	Online patient-monitoring systems, online medical information systems, robotic surgery
	Airlines	Ticketless travel, scheduling, Internet purchases

bring about dramatic improvements in performance.[9] Effective process redesign relies on reevaluating the purpose of the process and questioning both purpose and underlying assumptions. It works only if the basic process and its objectives are reexamined (see the *OM in Action* box "Operations Management at the Barber Shop?").

Process redesign also focuses on those activities that cross functional lines. Because managers are often in charge of specific "functions" or specialized areas of responsibility, those activities (processes) that cross from one function or specialty to another may be neglected.

OM in Action   Operations Management at the Barber Shop?

While Kuniyoshi Konishi was getting his hair cut one day, he found himself growing irritated with the drawn-out ritual of hot towels and shoulder rubs that is standard practice in Japanese barber shops. For the haircut and other amenities, Tokyo barbers charge 3,000 to 6,000 yen ($25 to $50).

Mr. Konishi recognized the need for a new system of delivering fast, inexpensive haircuts, so he formed QB House, a fast, no-frills men's barber shop: no reservations, no phones, and no shampoo (just an "air wash" system, to vacuum heads clean).

To free barbers from any task that took them away from snipping, each QB House is equipped with a ticket vending machine. Customers buy a ticket from the machine and then give the ticket to the barber before getting their cut.

High-tech touches were added along the way. Sensors under each seat in the waiting area convey signals to a signpost in front of each shop. A green light on the sign-post means there is no waiting, a yellow light indicates a wait of about 5 minutes, and a red light indicates the waiting time may be as long as 15 minutes. The barber chair sensor and the ticket vending machine sensor transmit data over the Internet to the head office in Tokyo, where traffic volume and sales can be monitored in real time. When sales volume for a particular store is much higher than average, QB House looks into opening another outlet nearby.

Seven years after opening his first barber shop, Konishi has 200 outlets nationwide providing the formerly impossible: 10-minute haircuts for 1,000 yen. With OM techniques, the company has creatively improved productivity in a very traditional service and is now going global. Next stop Singapore.

Sources: The Wall Street Journal (September 22, 2003): R4, R7; and *American Way* (December 15, 2003): 54–60.

[9]Michael Hammer and Steven Stanton call process redesign *process reengineering* in *The Reengineering Revolution* (New York: HarperCollins, 1995): 3.

Redesign casts aside all notions of how the process is currently being done and focuses on dramatic improvements in cost, time, and customer value. Any process is a candidate for radical redesign. The process can be a factory layout, a purchasing procedure, a new way of processing credit applications, or a new order-fulfillment process.

Shell Lubricants, for example, reinvented its order-fulfillment process by replacing a group of people who handled different parts of an order with one individual who does it all. As a result, Shell has cut the cycle time of turning an order into cash by 75%, reduced operating expenses by 45%, and boosted customer satisfaction 105%—all by introducing a new way of handling orders. Time, cost, and customer satisfaction—the dimension of performance shaped by operations—get major boosts from operational innovation.[10]

ETHICS AND ENVIRONMENTALLY FRIENDLY PROCESSES

We introduce some process approaches that address ethics, social responsibility, and environmental concerns. Many firms have found opportunities in their production processes to reduce the negative impact on the environment. The opportunities range from activities that society perceives as ethical and socially responsible to actions that are legally required, such as pollution prevention. These activities include a focus on such issues as efficient use of resources, reduction of waste by-products, emission controls, and recycling.

Operations managers can be environmentally sensitive and still achieve a differentiation strategy—and even a low-cost strategy. Here are four examples:

- British cosmetic firm The Body Shop has successfully differentiated its products by stressing environmental sensitivity. It pursues a product design, development, and testing strategy that it believes to be ethical and socially responsible. This includes environment-friendly ingredients and elimination of animal testing.
- Ben & Jerry's pursues its socially responsible image (and saves $250,000 annually) just by using energy-efficient lighting.
- Standard Register, described in Example 1, produces considerable paper scrap—almost 20 tons of punch holes alone per month—which creates a significant waste issue. But the company developed ways to recycle the paper scrap, as well as aluminum and silver from the plate-making process shown in the flow diagram in Figure 2.
- Anheuser-Busch saves $30 million per year in energy and waste-treatment costs by using treated plant wastewater to generate the gas that powers its St. Louis brewery.

Processes can be ethical, environmentally friendly, and socially responsible while still contributing to profitable strategies.

Summary

Effective operations managers understand how to use process strategy as a competitive weapon. They select a production process with the necessary quality, flexibility, and cost structure to meet product and volume requirements. They also seek creative ways to combine the low unit cost of high-volume, low-variety manufacturing with the customization available through low-volume, high-variety facilities. Managers use the techniques of lean production and employee participation to encourage the development of efficient equipment and processes. They design their equipment and processes to have capabilities beyond the tolerance required by their customers, while ensuring the flexibility needed for adjustments in technology, features, and volumes.

[10]Michael Hammer, "Deep Change: How Operational Innovation Can Transform Your Company," *Harvard Business Review* 82, no. 4 (April 2004): 85–93.

Key Terms

Process strategy
Process focus
Repetitive process
Modules
Product focus
Mass customization
Build-to-order (BTO)
Postponement
Crossover chart
Flow diagram

Time-function mapping (or process mapping)
Value-stream mapping (VSM)
Process charts
Service blueprinting
Flexibility
Computer numerical control (CNC)
Automatic identification system (AIS)
Radio frequency identification (RFID)
Process control

Vision systems
Robot
Automated storage and retrieval system (ASRS)
Automated guided vehicle (AGV)
Flexible manufacturing system (FMS)
Computer-integrated manufacturing (CIM)
Process redesign

Solved Problem

 Virtual Office Hours help is available on Student DVD.

Solved Problem 1

Bagot Copy Shop has a volume of 125,000 black-and-white copies per month. Two salesmen have made presentations to Gordon Bagot for machines of equal quality and reliability. The Print Shop 5 has a cost of $2,000 per month and a variable cost of $.03. The other machine (a Speed Copy 100) will cost only $1,500 per month but the toner is more expensive, driving the cost per copy up to $.035. If cost and volume are the only considerations, which machine should Bagot purchase?

Solution

$$2,000 + .03\,X = 1,500 + .035\,X$$
$$2,000 - 1,500 = .035\,X - .03\,X$$
$$500 = .005\,X$$
$$100,000 = X$$

Because Bagot expects his volume to exceed 100,000 units, he should choose the Print Shop 5.

Active Model Exercise

This active model appears on your CD-ROM. It allows you to evaluate important elements in the crossover chart in Example 4.

▶ **Active Model 7.1**

Crossover Chart Illustration of Example 4's Three Software Products

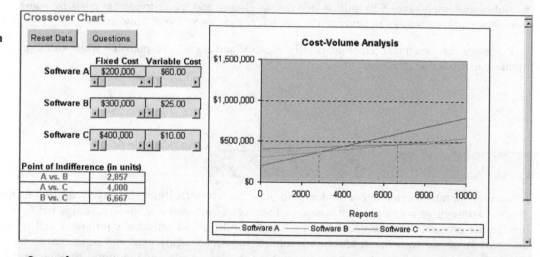

Questions

1. Suppose that Kleber Enterprises wants to lower the point of indifference between software A and software B to 2,000 units. What would the fixed costs need to be for software B?

2. Examine the graph. If the expected volume is 1,500 reports, which process should be used?

3. Examine the graph. If the expected volume is 15,000 reports, which process should be used?

4. As the fixed costs for developing software B drop, what happens to the graph?

Self-Test

- *Before taking the self-test*, refer to the learning objectives listed at the beginning of the selection and the key terms listed at the end of the selection.
- Use the key at the back of the text to **correct** your answers.
- *Restudy* pages that correspond to any questions you answered incorrectly or material you feel uncertain about.

1. Low-volume, high-variety processes are also known as:
   a) continuous processes
   b) intermittent processes
   c) repetitive processes
   d) product focused

2. Advantages of a flexible manufacturing system (FMS) include:
   a) lower direct labor cost
   b) consistent and perhaps better quality
   c) reduced inventory
   d) all of the above

3. Repetitive process lines:
   a) use modules
   b) are the classic assembly lines
   c) have more structure and less flexibility than a job shop layout
   d) include the assembly of basically all automobiles
   e) all of the above

4. Computer-integrated manufacturing (CIM) includes manufacturing systems that have:
   a) computer-aided design, direct numerical control machines, material handling equipment controlled by automation
   b) transaction processing, management information system, and decision support systems

   c) automated guided vehicles, robots, and process control
   d) robots, automated guided vehicles, and transfer equipment

5. As the quantity produced increases and you move toward product-focused production:
   a) the variable cost per unit increases
   b) the total fixed cost for the production operation increases
   c) the equipment utilization rate decreases
   d) more general-purpose equipment is used
   e) all of the above

6. Characteristics of a modular production process (repetitive focus) include:
   a) the use of just-in-time procurement techniques
   b) the use of just-in-time inventory control techniques
   c) costs are usually known
   d) standardized product options
   e) all of the above

7. Advantages of flexible manufacturing systems include all of the following except:
   a) lower setup costs
   b) ability to adapt to wide range of sizes and configuration
   c) high utilization of facilities
   d) lower direct labor costs
   e) all of the above are advantages

8. Process control is used to control physical processes in:
   a) discrete manufacturing facilities
   b) repetitive manufacturing facilities
   c) intermittent facilities
   d) job shops
   e) product-oriented facilities

Internet and Student CD-ROM/DVD Exercises

Visit our Companion Web Site or use your student CD-ROM/DVD to help with material in this chapter.

 On Our Companion Web Site,
www.prenhall.com/heizer
- Self-Study Quizzes
- Practice Problems
- Virtual Company Tour
- Internet Case
- PowerPoint Lecture

On Your Student CD-ROM
- Practice Problems
- Active Model Exercise
- POM for Windows

On Your Student DVD
- Video Clips and Video Cases
- Virtual Office Hours for Solved Problem

Discussion Questions

1. What is process strategy?
2. What type of process is used for making each of the following products?
   (a) beer
   (b) wedding invitations
   (c) automobiles
   (d) paper
   (e) Big Macs
   (f) custom homes
   (g) motorcycles

3. What is service blueprinting?
4. What is process redesign?
5. What are the techniques for improving service productivity?
6. Name the four quadrants of the service process matrix. Discuss how the matrix is used to classify services into categories.
7. What is CIM?
8. What do we mean by a process-control system and what are the typical elements in such systems?
9. Identify *manufacturing* firms that compete on each of the four processes shown in Figure 1.

10. Identify the competitive advantage of each of the four firms identified in discussion question 9.
11. Identify *service* firms that compete on each of the four processes shown in Figure 1.
12. Identify the competitive advantage of each of the four firms identified in discussion question 11.
13. What are numerically controlled machines?

14. Describe briefly what an automatic identification system (AIS) is and how service organizations could use AIS to increase productivity and at the same time increase the variety of services offered.
15. Name some of the advances being made in technology that enhance production and productivity.
16. Explain what a flexible manufacturing system (FMS) is.
17. In what ways do CAD and FMS connect?

Ethical Dilemma

For the sake of efficiency and lower costs, Premium Standard Farms of Princeton, Missouri, has turned pig production into a standardized product-focused process. Slaughterhouses have done this for a hundred years—but after the animal was dead. Doing it while the animal is alive is a relatively recent innovation. Here is how it works.

Impregnated female sows wait for 40 days in metal stalls so small that they cannot turn around. After an ultrasound test, they wait 67 days in a similar stall until they give birth. Two weeks after delivering 10 or 11 piglets, the sows are moved back to breeding rooms for another cycle. After 3 years, the sow is slaughtered. Animal-welfare advocates say such confinement drives pigs crazy. Premium Standard replies that its hogs are in fact comfortable, arguing that only 1% die before Premium Standard wants them to.

Discuss the productivity and ethical implications of this industry and these two divergent opinions.

Problems*

•   **1**   Prepare a flow diagram for one of the following:
a) The registration process at a school.
b) The process at the local car wash.
c) A shoe shine.
d) Some other process with the approval of the instructor.

•   **2**   Prepare a process chart for one of the activities in Problem 1.

••   **3**   Prepare a time-function map for one of the activities in Problem 1.

••   **4**   Prepare a service blueprint for one of the activities in Problem 1.

•   **5**   Meile Machine Shop, Inc., has a 1-year contract for the production of 200,000 gear housings for a new off-road vehicle. Owner Larry Meile hopes the contract will be extended and the volume increased next year. Meile has developed costs for three alternatives. They are general-purpose equipment (GPE), flexible manufacturing system (FMS), and expensive, but efficient, dedicated machine (DM). The cost data follow:

	General-Purpose Equipment (GPE)	Flexible Manufacturing System (FMS)	Dedicated Machine (DM)
Annual contracted units	200,000	200,000	200,000
Annual fixed cost	$100,000	$200,000	$500,000
Per unit variable cost	$ 15.00	$ 14.00	$ 13.00

Which process is best for this contract? **Px**

•   **6**   Using the data in Problem 5, determine the economical volume for each process. **Px**

•   **7**   Using the data in Problem 5, determine the best process for each of the following volumes: (1) 75,000, (2) 275,000, and (3) 375,000.

•   **8**   Refer to Problem 5. If a contract for the second and third years is pending, what are the implications for process selection?

••   **9**   Stan Fawcett's company is considering producing a gear assembly that it now purchases from Salt Lake Supply, Inc. Salt Lake Supply charges $4 per unit with a minimum order of 3,000 units. Stan estimates that it will cost $15,000 to set up the process and then $1.82 per unit for labor and materials.
a) Draw a graph illustrating the crossover (or indifference) point.
b) Determine the number of units where either choice has the same cost. **Px**

••   **10**   Ski Boards, Inc., wants to enter the market quickly with a new finish on its ski boards. It has three choices: (a) refurbish the old equipment at a cost of $800, (b) make major modifications at the

Robert Michael, CORBIS-NY

Note: **Px** means the problem may be solved with POM for Windows and/or Excel OM.

cost of $1,100, or (c) purchase new equipment at a net cost of $1,800. If the firm chooses to refurbish the equipment, materials and labor will be $1.10 per board. If it chooses to make modifications, materials and labor will be $0.70 per board. If it buys new equipment, variable costs are estimated to be $.40 per board.

a) Graph the three total cost lines on the same chart.
b) Which alternative should Ski Boards, Inc., choose if it thinks it can sell more than 3,000 boards?
c) Which alternative should the firm use if it thinks the market for boards will be between 1,000 and 2,000? **Px**

•• 11 Susan Meyer, owner/manager of Meyer's Motor Court in Key West, is considering outsourcing the daily room cleanup for her motel to Duffy's Maid Service. Susan rents an average of 50 rooms for each of 365 nights (365 × 50 equals the total rooms rented for the year). Susan's cost to clean a room is $12.50. The Duffy's Maid Service quote is $18.50 per room plus a fixed cost of $25,000 for sundry items such as uniforms with the motel's name. Susan's annual fixed cost for space, equipment, and supplies is $61,000. Which is the preferred process for Susan, and why? **Px**

•• 12 Keith Whittingham, as manager of Designs by Whittingham, is upgrading his CAD software. The high-performance (HP) software rents for $3,000 per month per workstation. The standard-performance (SP) software rents for $2,000 per month per workstation. The productivity figures that he has available suggest that the HP software is faster for his kind of design. Therefore, with the HP software he will need five engineers and with the SP soft-

ware he will need six. This translates into a variable cost of $200 per drawing for the HP system and $240 per drawing for the SP system. At his projected volume of 80 drawings per month, which system should he rent? **Px**

•• 13 Using Figure 8 in the discussion of value-stream mapping as a starting point, analyze an opportunity for improvement in a process with which you are familiar and develop an improved process.

••• 14 Creative Cabinets, Inc., needs to choose a production method for its new office shelf, the Maxistand. To help accomplish this, the firm has gathered the following production cost data:

	Annualized Fixed Cost of	Variable Costs (per unit) ($)		
Process Type	Plant & Equip.	Labor	Material	Energy
Mass Customization	$1,260,000	30	18	12
Intermittent	$1,000,000	24	26	20
Repetitive	$1,625,000	28	15	12
Continuous	$1,960,000	25	15	10

Creative Cabinets projects an annual demand of 24,000 units for the Maxistand. The Maxistand will sell for $120 per unit.

a) Which process type will maximize the annual profit from producing the Maxistand?
b) What is the value of this annual profit? **Px**

Case Studies

Rochester Manufacturing Corporation

Rochester Manufacturing Corporation (RMC) is considering moving some of its production from traditional numerically controlled machines to a flexible manufacturing system (FMS). Its computer numerical control machines have been operating in a high-variety, low-volume, intermittent manner. Machine utilization, as near as it can determine, is hovering around 10%. The machine tool salespeople and a consulting firm want to put the machines together in an FMS. They believe that a $3 million expenditure on machinery and the transfer machines will handle about 30% of RMC's work. There will, of course, be transition and startup costs in addition to this.

The firm has not yet entered all its parts into a comprehensive group technology system, but believes that the 30% is a good estimate of products suitable for the FMS. This 30% should fit very nicely into a "family." A reduction, because of higher utilization, should take place in the number of pieces of machinery. The firm should be able to go from 15 to about 4 machines and personnel should go from 15 to perhaps as low as 3. Similarly, floor space reduction will go from 20,000 square feet to about 6,000. Throughput of orders should also

improve with processing of this family of parts in 1 to 2 days rather than 7 to 10. Inventory reduction is estimated to yield a one-time $750,000 savings, and annual labor savings should be in the neighborhood of $300,000.

Although the projections all look very positive, an analysis of the project's return on investment showed it to be between 10% and 15% per year. The company has traditionally had an expectation that projects should yield well over 15% and have payback periods of substantially less than 5 years.

Discussion Questions

1. As a production manager for RMC, what do you recommend? Why?
2. Prepare a case by a conservative plant manager for maintaining the status quo until the returns are more obvious.
3. Prepare the case for an optimistic sales manager that you should move ahead with the FMS now.

Process Analysis at Arnold Palmer Hospital

Video Case

The Arnold Palmer Hospital (APH) in Orlando, Florida, is one of the busiest and most respected hospitals for the medical treatment of children and women in the U.S. Since its opening on golfing legend

Arnold Palmer's birthday September 10, 1989, more than 1.6 million children and women have passed through its doors. It is the fourth busiest labor and delivery hospital in the U.S. and one of the largest neonatal intensive care units in the Southeast. APH ranks in the top 10% of hospitals nationwide in patient satisfaction.

"Part of the reason for APH's success," says Executive Director Kathy Swanson, "is our continuous improvement process. Our goal is 100% patient satisfaction. But getting there means constantly examining and reexamining everything we do, from patient flow, to cleanliness, to layout space, to a work-friendly environment, to speed of medication delivery from the pharmacy to a patient. Continuous improvement is a huge and never-ending task."

One of the tools the hospital uses consistently is the process flowchart (like those in Figures 1 to 3 in this chapter). Staffer Diane Bowles, who carries the title "clinical practice improvement consultant," charts scores of processes. Bowles's flowcharts help study ways to improve the turnaround of a vacated room (especially important in a hospital that has pushed capacity for years), speed up the admission process, and deliver warm meals warm.

Lately, APH has been examining the flow of maternity patients (and their paperwork) from the moment they enter the hospital until they are discharged, hopefully with their healthy baby a day or two later. The flow of maternity patients follows these steps:

1. Enter APH's Labor & Delivery check-in desk entrance.
2. If the baby is born en route or if birth is imminent, the mother and baby are taken directly to Labor & Delivery on the second floor and registered and admitted directly at the bedside. If there are no complications, the mother and baby go to step 6.
3. If the baby is *not* yet born, the front desk asks if the mother is pre-registered. (Most do pre-register at the 28- to 30-week pregnancy mark). If she is not, she goes to the registration office on the first floor.
4. The pregnant woman is then taken to Labor & Delivery Triage on the 8th floor for assessment. If she is in active labor, she is taken to a Labor & Delivery (L&D) room on the 2nd floor until the baby is born. If she is not ready, she goes to step 5.
5. Pregnant women not ready to deliver (i.e., no contractions or false alarm) are either sent home to return on a later date

and reenter the system at that time, or if contractions are not yet close enough, they are sent to walk around the hospital grounds (to encourage progress) and then return to Labor & Delivery Triage at a prescribed time.

6. When the baby is born, if there are no complications, after 2 hours the mother and baby are transferred to a "mother–baby care unit" room on floors 3, 4, or 5 for an average of 40–44 hours.
7. If there *are* complications with the mother, she goes to an operating room and/or intensive care unit. From there, she goes back to a mother–baby care room upon stabilization—or is discharged at another time if not stabilized. Complications for the baby may result in a stay in the neonatal intensive care unit (NICU) before transfer to the baby nursery near the mother's room. If the baby is not stable enough for discharge with the mother, the baby is discharged later.
8. Mother and/or baby, when ready, are discharged and taken by wheelchair to the discharge exit for pickup to travel home.

Discussion Questions*

1. As Diane's new assistant, you need to flowchart this process. Explain how the process might be improved once you have completed the chart.
2. If a mother is scheduled for a Caesarean-section birth (i.e., the baby is removed from the womb surgically), how would this flowchart change?
3. If *all* mothers were electronically (or manually) preregistered, how would the flowchart change? Redraw the chart to show your changes.
4. Describe in detail a process that the hospital could analyze, besides the ones mentioned in this case.

*You may wish to view this video case on your DVD before addressing these questions.

Process Strategy at Wheeled Coach

Video Case

Wheeled Coach, based in Winter Park, Florida, is the world's largest manufacturer of ambulances. Working four 10-hour days each week, 350 employees make only custom-made ambulances: Virtually every vehicle is unique. Wheeled Coach accommodates the marketplace by providing a wide variety of options and an engineering staff accustomed to innovation and custom design. Continuing growth, which now requires that more than 20 ambulances roll off the assembly line each week, makes process design a continuing challenge. Wheeled Coach's response has been to build a focused factory: Wheeled Coach builds nothing but ambulances. Within the focused factory, Wheeled Coach established work cells for every major module feeding an assembly line, including aluminum bodies, electrical wiring harnesses, interior cabinets, windows, painting, and upholstery.

Labor standards drive the schedule so that every work cell feeds the assembly line on schedule, just-in-time for installations. The chassis, usually that of a Ford truck, moves to a station at which the aluminum body is mounted. Then the vehicle is moved to painting. Following a custom paint job, it moves to the assembly line, where it will spend 7 days. During each of these 7 workdays, each work cell delivers its respective module to the appropriate position

on the assembly line. During the first day, electrical wiring is installed; on the second day, the unit moves forward to the station at which cabinetry is delivered and installed, then to a window and lighting station, on to upholstery, to fit and finish, to further customizing, and finally to inspection and road testing. The *Global Company Profile* featuring Wheeled Coach provides further details about this process.

Discussion Questions*

1. Why do you think major auto manufacturers do not build ambulances?
2. What is an alternative process strategy to the assembly line that Wheeled Coach currently uses?
3. Why is it more efficient for the work cells to prepare "modules" and deliver them to the assembly line than it would be to produce the component (e.g., interior upholstery) on the line?
4. How does Wheeled Coach manage the tasks to be performed at each work station?

*You may wish to view this video case on your DVD before addressing these questions.

Additional Case Studies

Internet case study: Visit our Companion Web site at **www.prenhall.com/heizer** *for this free case study:*

• **Matthew Yachts, Inc.:** Examines a possible process change as the market for yachts changes.

Harvard has selected these Harvard Business School cases to accompany this chapter:

harvardbusinessonline.hbsp.harvard.edu

• **Massachusetts General Hospital** (#696-015): Describes efforts at Massachusetts General Hospital to reengineer the service delivery process for heart bypass surgery.
• **John Crane UK Ltd.: The CAD/CAM Link** (#691-021): Describes the improvement of manufacturing performance in a job shop.
• **Product Development at Dell** (#699-010): Discusses the new product and process and the management of development risk.

Bibliography

Carrillo, Janice E., and Cheryl Gaimon. "Improving Manufacturing Performance through Process Change and Knowledge Creation." *Management Science* 46, no. 2 (February 2000): 265–288.

Davenport, T. H. "The Coming Commoditization of Processes." *Harvard Business Review* 83, no. 6 (June 2005): 101–108.

Debo, L. G., L. B. Toktay, and L. N. Van Wassenhove. "Market Segmentation and Product Technology Selection for Remanufacturable Products." *Management Science* 51, no. 8 (August 2005): 1193–1205.

Duray, R., P. T. Ward, G. W. Milligan, and W. L. Berry. "Approaches to Mass Customization: Configurations and Empirical Validation." *Journal of Operations Management* 18, no. 6 (November 2000): 605–625.

Gilmore, James H., and Joseph Pine II (eds.). *Markets of One: Creating Customer-Unique Value through Mass Customization.* Harvard Business Review Book, 2000.

Hegde, V. G. et al. "Customization: Impact on Product and Process Performance." *Production and Operations Management* 14, no. 4 (Winter 2005): 388–399.

Hounshell, D. A. *From the American System to Mass Production, 1800–1932.* Baltimore: Johns Hopkins University Press, 1984.

Inderfurth, Karl, I. M. Langella. "An Approach for Solving Disassembly-to-order Problems under Stochastic Yields." In *Logistik Management.* Heidelberg: Physica, 2004: 309–331.

Moeeni, F. "From Light Frequency Identification to Radio Frequency Identification in the Supply Chain," *Decision Line* 37, no. 3 (May 2006): 8–13.

Su, J. C. P., Y. Chang, and M. Ferguson. "Evaluation of Postponement Structures to Accommodate Mass Customization." *Journal of Operations Management* 23, nos. 3–4 (April 2005): 305–318.

Swamidass, Paul M. *Innovations in Competitive Manufacturing.* Dordrecht, NL: Kluwer, 2000.

Tu, Qiang, et al. "Measuring Modularity-Based Manufacturing Practices and Their Impact on Mass Customization Capability: A Customer-Driven Perspective." *Decision Sciences* 35, no. 2 (Spring 2004): 147–168.

Zipkin, Paul. "The Limits of Mass Customization." *MIT Sloan Management Review* 40, no. 1 (spring 2001): 81–88.

Internet Resources

American Council of Engineering Companies: **www.acec.org**
Association of Automatic Identification and Mobility:
    www.aimglobal.org
Association for Manufacturing Excellence: **www.ame.org**
Business Process Reengineering online learning center tutorial:
    www.prosci.com/index.html
DARPA: U.S. Defense Dept., Innovative Prototype Systems:
    www.ARPA.mil
Dassault Systems: **www.dsweb.com**

Graham Process Improvement Methodology: **www.worksimp.com**
iGraphic's approach to Value Stream Mapping: **www.iGrafx.com**
Strategos Inc.'s approach to value-stream mapping:
    www.strategosinc.com
Traleon GMBH's approach to value-stream mapping:
    www.valuestreamdesigner.com
WARIA, the Workflow and Reengineering International Association:
    www.waria.com

Solutions to Even Numbered Problems

2

Present Method [X]		PROCESS CHART	Proposed Method [ ]
SUBJECT CHARTED	Shoe Shine		DATE 1/15/08
			CHART BY J.C.
DEPARTMENT			SHEET NO. 1 OF 1

DIST. IN FEET	TIME IN MINS.	CHART SYMBOLS	PROCESS DESCRIPTION
	.5	○⇨□D▽	Clean/Brush Shoes
1.	.05	○⇨□D▽	Obtain Polish
	.5	○⇨□D▽	Open and Apply Polish
	.75	○⇨□D▽	Buff
	.05	○⇨□D▽	Inspect
	.25	○⇨□D▽	Collect Payment
1.	2.10	4 1 1	Totals

4

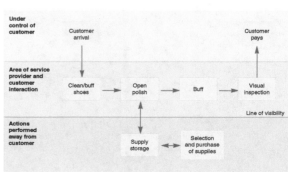

6 GPE is best below 100,000.
 FMS is best between 100,000 and 300,000.
 DM is best over 300,000.

8 Optimal process will change at 100,000 and 300,000.

10 **(a)**

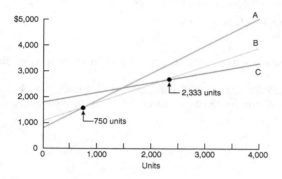

(b) Plan c

(c) Plan b

12 Rent HP software since projected volume of 80 is above the crossover point of 75.

14 **(a)** Intermittent

 (b) $200,000

Solutions to Self Test

1. d; **2.** d; **3.** e; **4.** a; **5.** b; **6.** e; **7.** e; **8.** e.

Capacity Planning

Outline

Learning Objectives

When you complete this selection you should be able to

1. Define capacity
2. Determine design capacity, effective capacity, and utilization
3. Compute break-even
4. Apply decision trees to capacity decisions
5. Compute net present value

John Garrett, Getty Images, Inc.—Stone Allstock

► When designing a concert hall, management hopes that the forecasted capacity (the product mix—opera, symphony, and special events—and the technology needed for these events) is accurate and adequate for operation above the break-even point. However, in many concert halls, even when operating at full capacity, break-even is not achieved, and supplemental funding must be obtained.

CAPACITY

How many concertgoers should a facility seat? How many customers per day should an Olive Garden or a Hard Rock Cafe be able to service? How many computers should Dell's Nashville plant be able to produce in an 8-hour shift? And how should we build facilities to meet these uncertain demands?

After selection of a production process, we need to determine capacity. **Capacity** is the "throughput," or the number of units a facility can hold, receive, store, or produce in a period of time. The capacity often determines capital requirements and therefore a large portion of fixed cost. Capacity also determines if demand will be satisfied or if facilities will be idle. If the facility is too large, portions of it will sit idle and add cost to existing production. If the facility is too small, customers and perhaps entire markets are lost. So determining facility size, with an objective of achieving high levels of utilization and a high return on investment, is critical.

Capacity planning can be viewed in three time horizons. In Figure 1 we note that long-range capacity (greater than 1 year) is a function of adding facilities and equipment that have a long lead time. In the intermediate range (3 to 18 months), we can add equipment, personnel, and shifts; we can subcontract; and we can build or use inventory. This is the aggregate planning task. In the short run (usually up to 3 months), we are primarily concerned with scheduling jobs and people, and allocating machinery. It is difficult to modify capacity in the short run; we are using capacity that already exists.

Capacity
The "throughput" or number of units a facility can hold, receive, store, or produce in a period of time.

1. Define capacity

► **Figure 1**

Types of Planning over a Time Horizon

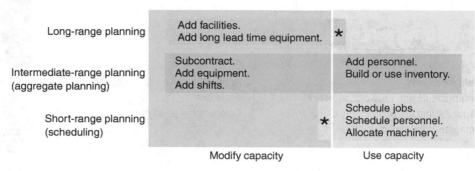

	Modify capacity	Use capacity
Long-range planning	Add facilities. Add long lead time equipment.	*
Intermediate-range planning (aggregate planning)	Subcontract. Add equipment. Add shifts.	Add personnel. Build or use inventory.
Short-range planning (scheduling)	*	Schedule jobs. Schedule personnel. Allocate machinery.

* Limited options exist

Design and Effective Capacity

Design capacity is the maximum theoretical output of a system in a given period under ideal conditions. It is normally expressed as a rate, such as the number of tons of steel that can be produced per week, per month, or per year. For many companies, measuring capacity can be straightforward: It is the maximum number of units produced in a specific time. However, for some organizations, determining capacity can be more difficult. Capacity can be measured in terms of beds (a hospital), active members (a church), or classroom size (a school). Other organizations use total work time available as a measure of overall capacity.

Most organizations operate their facilities at a rate less than the design capacity. They do so because they have found that they can operate more efficiently when their resources are not stretched to the limit. Instead, they expect to operate at perhaps 82% of design capacity. This concept is called effective capacity.

Effective capacity is the capacity a firm *expects* to achieve given the current operating constraints. Effective capacity is often lower than design capacity because the facility may have been designed for an earlier version of the product or a different product mix than is currently being produced.

Two measures of system performance are particularly useful: utilization and efficiency. **Utilization** is simply the percent of *design capacity* actually achieved. **Efficiency** is the percent of *effective capacity* actually achieved. Depending on how facilities are used and managed, it may be difficult or impossible to reach 100% efficiency. Operations managers tend to be evaluated on efficiency. The key to improving efficiency is often found in correcting quality problems and in effective scheduling, training, and maintenance. Utilization and efficiency are computed below:

$$\text{Utilization} = \text{Actual output/Design capacity} \qquad (1)$$

$$\text{Efficiency} = \text{Actual output/Effective capacity} \qquad (2)$$

In Example 1 we determine these values.

Design capacity
The theoretical maximum output of a system in a given period under ideal conditions.

Effective capacity
The capacity a firm can expect to achieve, given its product mix, methods of scheduling, maintenance, and standards of quality.

Utilization
Actual output as a percent of design capacity.

Efficiency
Actual output as a percent of effective capacity.

EXAMPLE 1

Determining capacity utilization and efficiency

 Active Model S7.1

Example 1 is further illustrated in Active Model S7.1 on your CD-ROM.

Sara James Bakery has a plant for processing *Deluxe* breakfast rolls and wants to better understand its capability. Determine the design capacity, utilization, and efficiency for this plant when producing this *Deluxe* roll.

Approach: Last week the facility produced 148,000 rolls. The effective capacity is 175,000 rolls. The production line operates 7 days per week, with three 8-hour shifts per day. The line was designed to process the nut-filled, cinnamon-flavored *Deluxe* roll at a rate of 1,200 per hour. The firm first computes the design capacity and then uses Equation (1) to determine utilization and Equation (2) to determine efficiency.

Solution: Design capacity = (7 days × 3 shifts × 8 hours) × (1,200 rolls per hour) = 201,600 rolls

Utilization = Actual output/Design capacity = 148,000/201,600 = 73.4%

Efficiency = Actual output/Effective capacity = 148,000/175,000 = 84.6%

Insight: The bakery now has the information necessary to evaluate efficiency.

Learning exercise: If the actual output is 150,000, what is the efficiency? [Answer: 85.7%.]

Related problems: 1, 2, 4, 5, 11

Design capacity, utilization, and efficiency are all important measures for an operations manager. But managers often need to know the expected output of a facility or process. To do this, we solve for actual (or in this case, future or expected) output as shown in Equation (3):

$$\text{Actual (or Expected) output} = (\text{Effective capacity})(\text{Efficiency}) \qquad (3)$$

Expected output is sometimes referred to as *rated capacity*. With a knowledge of effective capacity and efficiency, a manager can find the expected output of a facility. We do so in Example 2.

Learning Objective

2. Determine design capacity, effective capacity, and utilization

EXAMPLE 2

Determining expected output

The manager of Sara James Bakery (see Example 1) now needs to increase production of the increasingly popular *Deluxe* roll. To meet this demand, she will be adding a second production line.

Approach: The manager must determine the expected output of this second line for the sales department. Effective capacity on the second line is the same as on the first line, which is 175,000 *Deluxe* rolls. The first line is operating at an efficiency of 84.6%, as computed in Example 1. But output on the second line will be less than the first line because the crew will be primarily new hires; so the efficiency can be expected to be no more than 75%. What is the expected output?

Solution: Use Equation (3) to determine the expected output:

Expected output = (Effective capacity)(Efficiency) = (175,000)(.75) = 131,250 rolls

Insight: The sales department can now be told the expected output is 131,250 *Deluxe* rolls.

Learning exercise: After 1 month of training, the crew on the second production line is expected to perform at 80% efficiency. What is the revised expected output of *Deluxe* rolls? [Answer: 140,000.]

Related problems: 3, 6, 7, 8, 10

If the expected output is inadequate, additional capacity may be needed. Much of the remainder of this supplement addresses how to effectively and efficiently add that capacity.

Capacity and Strategy

Sustained profits come from building competitive advantage, not just from a good financial return on a specific process. Capacity decisions must be integrated into the organization's mission and strategy. Investments are not to be made as isolated expenditures, but as part of a coordinated plan that will place the firm in an advantageous position.[1] The questions to be asked are, Will these investments eventually win customers? and What competitive advantage (such as process flexibility, speed of delivery, improved quality, and so on) do we obtain?

All 10 decisions of operations management we discuss in this text, as well as other organizational elements such as marketing and finance, are affected by changes in capacity. Change in capacity will have sales and cash flow implications, just as capacity changes have quality, supply chain, human resource, and maintenance implications. All must be considered.

Capacity Considerations

In addition to tight integration of strategy and investments, there are four special considerations for a good capacity decision:

1. *Forecast demand accurately:* An accurate forecast is paramount to the capacity decision. The new product may be Olive Garden's veal scampi, a dish that places added demands on the restaurant's food service, or the product may be a new maternity capability at Arnold Palmer Hospital, or the new hybrid Lexus. Whatever the new product, its prospects and the life cycle of existing products, must be determined. Management must know which products are being added and which are being dropped, as well as their expected volumes.

2. *Understand the technology and capacity increments:* The number of initial alternatives may be large, but once the volume is determined, technology decisions may be aided by analysis of cost, human resources required, quality, and reliability. Such a review often reduces the number of alternatives to a few. The technology may dictate the capacity increment. Meeting added demand with a few extra tables in an Olive Garden may not be difficult, but meeting increased demand for a new automobile by adding a new assembly line at BMW may be very difficult—and expensive. The operations manager is held responsible for the technology and the correct capacity increment.

3. *Find the optimum operating level (volume):* Technology and capacity increments often dictate an optimal size for a facility. A roadside motel may require 50 rooms to be viable. If

[1]For an excellent discussion on investments that support competitive advantage, see Terry Hill, *Operations Management*, 2nd ed. (New York: Palgrave Macmillan, 2005).

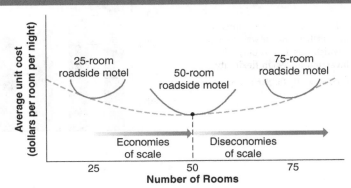

◄ Figure 2

Economies and Diseconomies of Scale

Chitose Suzuki, AP Wide World Photos

smaller, the fixed cost is too burdensome; if larger, the facility becomes more than one manager can supervise. A hypothetical optimum for the motel is shown in Figure 2. This issue is known as *economies and diseconomies of scale*. GM at one time believed that the optimum auto plant was one with 600 employees. As the Krispy Kreme photo suggests, most businesses have an optimal size—at least until someone comes along with a new business model. For decades, very large integrated steel mills were considered optimal. Then along came Nucor, CMC, and other minimills with a new process and a new business model that changed the optimum size of a steel mill.

4. *Build for change:* In our fast-paced world, change is inevitable. So operations managers build flexibility into the facility and equipment (see Figure 3. They evaluate the sensitivity of the decision by testing several revenue projections on both the upside and downside for potential risks. Buildings can often be built in phases; and buildings and equipment can be designed with modifications in mind to accommodate future changes in product, product mix, and processes.

Rather than strategically manage capacity, managers may tactically manage demand.

Managing Demand

Even with good forecasting and facilities built to that forecast, there may be a poor match between the actual demand that occurs and available capacity. A poor match may mean demand exceeds capacity or capacity exceeds demand. However, in both cases, firms have options.

◄ *Krispy Kreme originally had 8,000-square-foot stores but found them too large and too expensive for many markets. Then they tried tiny 1,300-square-foot stores, which required less investment, but such stores were too small to provide the mystique of seeing and smelling Krispy Kreme donuts being made. Krispy Kreme finally got it right with a 2,600-foot-store. This one includes a huge glass window to view doughnut production.*

Chitose Suzuki, AP Wide World Photos

▶ **Figure 3** **Percent of North American Vehicles Made on Flexible Assembly Lines***

A large and growing percent of cars are made on flexible assembly lines. Chrysler, for example, discovered several years ago that its underutilized Belvidere, Illinois, plant was not flexible enough to paint a PT Cruiser (which was 1″ too tall). The company learned its lesson and is now a leader in investing in design flexibility.

*2007 estimate, *The Wall Street Journal* (April 11, 2006): A1 and (January 14–15, 2006): B14.

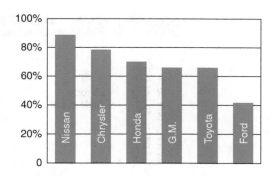

Demand Exceeds Capacity   When *demand exceeds capacity*, the firm may be able to curtail demand simply by raising prices, scheduling long lead times (which may be inevitable), and discouraging marginally profitable business. However, because inadequate facilities reduce revenue below what is possible, the long-term solution is usually to increase capacity (as we see in the *OM in Action* box "Too Little Capacity at Dalrymple Bay").

Capacity Exceeds Demand   When *capacity exceeds demand*, the firm may want to stimulate demand through price reductions or aggressive marketing, or it may accommodate the market through product changes. When decreasing customer demand is combined with old and inflexible processes, layoffs and plant closings may be necessary to bring capacity in line with demand. The *OM in Action* box "Too Much Capacity at G.M. and Ford" indicates how difficult adjusting capacity to declining demand can be.

Adjusting to Seasonal Demands   A seasonal or cyclical pattern of demand is another capacity challenge. In such cases, management may find it helpful to offer products with complementary demand patterns—that is, products for which the demand is high for one when low for the other. For example, in Figure 4 the firm is adding a line of snowmobile motors to its line of jet skis to smooth demand. With appropriate complementing of products, perhaps the utilization of facility, equipment, and personnel can be smoothed.

OM in Action   Too Little Capacity at Dalrymple Bay

Nearly 20 ships were anchored in the Coral Sea on a recent morning. They were waiting to be loaded with coal to fuel Asia's voracious steel mills. Australia has some of the most prolific coal mines in the world, but its key port of Dalrymple Bay, just outside Queensland, isn't big enough to meet demand. So the ships sit idle for days. Capacity at the port is far below what is needed for the current worldwide demand. This makes Dalrymple Bay one of the key choke points.

The process is rather simple but expensive. Trains are loaded with coal at the mines, travel several hours to the port, and dump their coal into piles that are sprayed with water to prevent black coal dust from blowing onto homes and beaches. Eventually, the coal is loaded onto a conveyor belt that moves 2.5 miles out into the Coral Sea, to be loaded onto ships.

The current plan is to invest $610 million to expand port capacity to 85 million metric tons of coal in the next 3 years. But this is still less than the estimated demand requirement of 107 million metric tons needed. As a result, coal companies, even after the expansion is completed, may still find access to shipping rationed.

The demand must exist, the port must expand, and the mines must enlarge. Without that assurance, the risk remains high and the necessary ROI (return on investment) is not there. Managers are not going to put significant money into expanding port capacity until they are comfortable that both the demand and coal supply support a larger port. To justify investment in capacity, each phase of the chain must support that investment.

Source: Australasian Business Intelligence (June 22, 2006); and *The Wall Street Journal* (July 7, 2005): C1, C4.

Too Much Capacity at G.M. and Ford

For decades G.M. and Ford added capacity. The auto and truck market expanded, and they expanded along with it. They were the world's greatest automobile companies. They built specialized product-focused plants with little flexibility. And they grew capacity to millions of cars per year. G.M. alone produced over half of the cars sold in the U.S. But the world changed. Cars now arrive in the U.S. from every corner of the world. Germany, Italy, Japan, Korea, and now even Mexico and Brazil are making inroads into the U.S. market—with China on the horizon. And G.M. now makes fewer than one-fourth of the cars sold in the U.S.

Toyota, VW, Honda, BMW, Mercedes, and others are stealing sales. They are stealing sales with imports, and they are stealing sales with domestic production. Recently Toyota's U.S. plants were operating at 111% of expected output compared with 87% for G.M. and 79% for Ford.

G.M. and Ford are not sitting still. In an effort to drive down costs, both companies are increasing productivity and flexibility. For instance, in the past 6 years, the total labor-hours per vehicle necessary for stamping, assembly, and engine production have dropped by 26%, from 46.5 hours to 34.3 hours. The number of stamping machines necessary to make the fenders, hoods, doors, and so on have dropped from 330 to 241. This potent combination of lower sales and increased productivity means G.M. and Ford must cut capacity. By 2010, employment at the two automakers will drop by 50,000 people. Capacity adjustments, particularly on the down side, can be painful.

Source: The Wall Street Journal (January 21–22, 2006): A2; *The Economist* (January 7, 2006): 61; and *Knight Ridder Tribune Business News* (January 4, 2006): 1.

Tactics for Matching Capacity to Demand   Various tactics for matching capacity to demand exist. Options for adjusting capacity include:

1. Making staffing changes (increasing or decreasing the number of employees or shifts)
2. Adjusting equipment (purchasing additional machinery or selling or leasing out existing equipment)
3. Improving processes to increase throughput
4. Redesigning products to facilitate more throughput
5. Adding process flexibility to better meet changing product preferences
6. Closing facilities

The foregoing tactics can be used to adjust demand to existing facilities. The strategic issue is, of course, how to have a facility of the correct size.

Demand and Capacity Management in the Service Sector

In the service sector, scheduling customers is *demand management*, and scheduling the workforce is *capacity management*.

Demand Management   When demand and capacity are fairly well matched, demand management can often be handled with appointments, reservations, or a first-come, first-served rule. In some businesses, such as doctors' and lawyers' offices, an *appointment system* is the schedule and is adequate. *Reservations systems* work well in rental car agencies, hotels, and some restaurants as

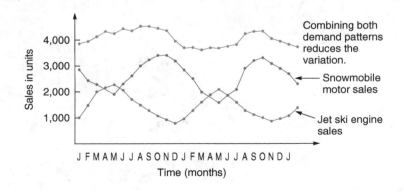

◄ **Figure 4**

By Combining Products That Have Complementary Seasonal Patterns, Capacity Can Be Better Utilized

A smoother sales demand contributes to improved scheduling and better human resource strategies.

▶ *Many U.S. hospitals use services abroad to manage capacity for radiologists during night shifts. Night Hawk, an Idaho-based service with 50 radiologists in Zurich and Sydney, contracts with 900 facilities (20% of all U.S. hospitals). These trained experts, wide awake and alert in their daylight hours, usually return a diagnosis in 10 to 20 minutes, with a guarantee of 30 minutes.*

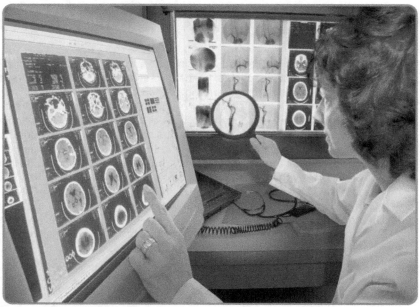

Lester Lefkowitz, Corbis—NY

a means of minimizing customer waiting time and avoiding disappointment over unfilled service. In retail shops, a post office, or a fast-food restaurant, a *first-come, first-served* rule for serving customers may suffice. Each industry develops its own approaches to matching demand and capacity. Other more aggressive approaches to demand management include many variations of discounts: "early bird" specials in restaurants, discounts for matinee performances or for seats at odd hours on an airline, and cheap weekend phone calls.

Capacity Management   When managing demand is not feasible, then managing capacity through changes in full-time, temporary, or part-time staff may be an option. This is the approach in many services. For instance, hospitals may find capacity limited by a shortage of board-certified radiologists willing to cover the graveyard shifts. Getting fast and reliable radiology readings can be the difference between life and death for an emergency room patient. As the photo above illustrates, when an overnight reading is required (and 40% of CT scans are done between 8 P.M. and 8 A.M.), the image can be sent by e-mail to a doctor in Europe or Australia for immediate analysis.

▶ *FedEx's huge aircraft fleet is used to near capacity for nighttime delivery of packages but is 100% idle during the daytime. In an attempt to better utilize capacity (and leverage assets), FedEx considered two services with opposite or countercyclical demand patterns to its nighttime service—commuter passenger service and passenger charter service. However, after a thorough analysis, the 12% to 13% return on investment was judged insufficient for the risks involved. Facing the same issues, though, UPS decided to begin a charter airline that operates on weekends.*

Charles Thatcher, C. Thatcher, Inc.

CAPACITY PLANNING

 **Video S7.1**

Capacity Planning at
Arnold Palmer Hospital

Setting future capacity requirements can be a complicated procedure, one based in large part on future demand. When demand for goods and services can be forecast with a reasonable degree of precision, determining capacity requirements can be straightforward. Determining capacity normally requires two phases. During the first phase, future demand is forecast with traditional models. During the second phase, this forecast is used to determine capacity requirements and the incremental size of each addition to capacity.[2] Interestingly, demand growth is typically gradual in small units, while capacity additions are typically instantaneous in large units. This contradiction often makes capacity expansion difficult.

Figure 5 reveals four approaches to new capacity. As we see in Figure 5(a), new capacity is acquired at the beginning of year 1. This capacity will handle increased demand until the beginning of year 2. At the beginning of year 2, new capacity is again acquired, which will allow the organization to stay ahead of demand until the beginning of year 3. This process can be continued indefinitely into the future.

The capacity plan shown in Figure 5(a) is only one of an almost limitless number of plans to satisfy future demand. In this figure, new capacity was acquired *incrementally*—at the beginning of year 1 *and* at the beginning of year 2. In Figure 5(b), a large increase in capacity is acquired at the beginning of year 1 to satisfy expected demand until the beginning of year 3.

The excess capacity provided by plans Figure 5(a) and Figure 5(b) gives operations managers flexibility. For instance, in the hotel industry, added capacity in the form of rooms can allow a

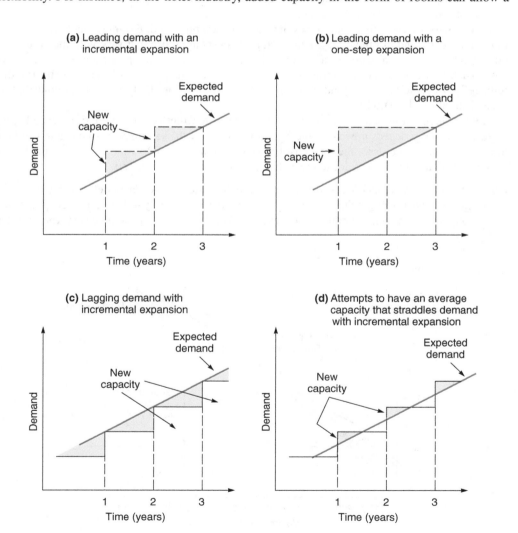

◄ **Figure 5**

Approaches to Capacity Expansion

(a) Leading demand with an incremental expansion

(b) Leading demand with a one-step expansion

(c) Lagging demand with incremental expansion

(d) Attempts to have an average capacity that straddles demand with incremental expansion

[2]At this point, we make the assumption that management knows the technology and the *type* of facilities to be employed to satisfy future demand requirements—not a minor issue, but beyond the scope of this text.

wider variety of room options and perhaps flexibility in room cleanup schedules. In manufacturing, the excess capacity can be used to do more setups to shorten production runs, driving down inventory. The added capacity may also allow management to build excess inventory and thus delay the capital expenditure and disruption that come with adding additional new capacity.[3]

Alternatives Figure 5(a) and Figure 5(b) *lead* capacity—that is, acquire capacity to stay ahead of demand—but Figure 5(c) shows an option that *lags* capacity, perhaps using overtime or subcontracting to accommodate excess demand. Figure 5(d) straddles demand by building capacity that is "average," sometimes lagging demand and sometimes leading it.

In some cases, deciding between alternatives can be relatively easy. The total cost of each alternative can be computed, and the alternative with the least total cost can be selected. In other cases, determining the capacity and how to achieve it can be much more complicated. In most cases, numerous subjective factors are difficult to quantify and measure. These factors include technological options; competitor strategies; building restrictions; cost of capital; human resource options; and local, state, and federal laws and regulations.

BREAK-EVEN ANALYSIS

Break-even analysis

A means of finding the point, in dollars and units, at which costs equal revenues.

Fixed costs

Costs that continue even if no units are produced.

Variable costs

Costs that vary with the volume of units produced.

Contribution

The difference between selling price and variable costs.

Revenue function

The function that increases by the selling price of each unit.

Break-even analysis is a critical tool for determining the capacity a facility must have to achieve profitability. The objective of **break-even analysis** is to find the point, in dollars and units, at which costs equal revenue. This point is the break-even point. Firms must operate above this level to achieve profitability. As shown in Figure 6, break-even analysis requires an estimation of fixed costs, variable costs, and revenue.

Fixed costs are costs that continue even if no units are produced. Examples include depreciation, taxes, debt, and mortgage payments. **Variable costs** are those that vary with the volume of units produced. The major components of variable costs are labor and materials. However, other costs, such as the portion of the utilities that varies with volume, are also variable costs. The difference between selling price and variable cost is **contribution**. Only when total contribution exceeds total fixed cost will there be profit.

Another element in break-even analysis is the **revenue function**. In Figure 6, revenue begins at the origin and proceeds upward to the right, increasing by the selling price of each unit. Where the revenue function crosses the total cost line (the sum of fixed and variable costs), is the break-even point, with a profit corridor to the right and a loss corridor to the left.

Assumptions   A number of assumptions underlie the basic break-even model. Notably, costs and revenue are shown as straight lines. They are shown to increase linearly—that is, in direct proportion to the volume of units being produced. However, neither fixed costs nor variable costs (nor, for that

▶ **Figure 6**

Basic Break-Even Point

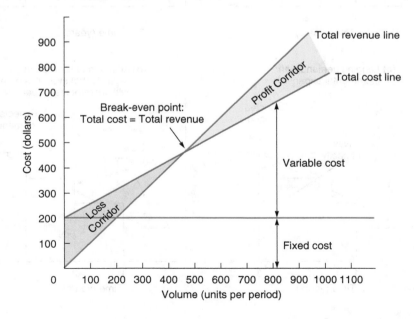

[3]See related discussion in S. Rajagopalan and J. M. Swaminathan, "Coordinated Production Planning Model with Capacity Expansion and Inventory Management," *Management Science* 47, no. 11, (November 2001): 1562–1580.

matter, the revenue function) need be a straight line. For example, fixed costs change as more capital equipment or warehouse space is used; labor costs change with overtime or as marginally skilled workers are employed; the revenue function may change with such factors as volume discounts.

Graphic Approach   The first step in the graphic approach to break-even analysis is to define those costs that are fixed and sum them. The fixed costs are drawn as a horizontal line beginning at that dollar amount on the vertical axis. The variable costs are then estimated by an analysis of labor, materials, and other costs connected with the production of each unit. The variable costs are shown as an incrementally increasing cost, originating at the intersection of the fixed cost on the vertical axis and increasing with each change in volume as we move to the right on the volume (or horizontal) axis. Both fixed- and variable-cost information is usually available from a firm's cost accounting department, although an industrial engineering department may also maintain cost information.

Fixed costs do not remain constant over all volume; new warehouses and new overhead charges result in step functions in fixed cost.

Algebraic Approach   The respective formulas for the break-even point in units and dollars are shown below. Let:

BEP_x = break-even point in units TR = total revenue = Px
$BEP_\$$ = break-even point in dollars F = fixed costs
P = price per unit (after all discounts) V = variable costs per unit
x = number of units produced TC = total costs = $F + Vx$

The break-even point occurs where total revenue equals total costs. Therefore:

$$TR = TC \quad \text{or} \quad Px = F + Vx$$

Solving for x, we get

$$BEP_x = \frac{F}{P - V}$$

and:

$$BEP_\$ = BEP_x P = \frac{F}{P - V} P = \frac{F}{(P - V)/P}$$
$$= \frac{F}{1 - V/P}$$

$$\text{Profit} = TR - TC$$
$$= Px - (F + Vx) = Px - F - Vx$$
$$= (P - V)x - F$$

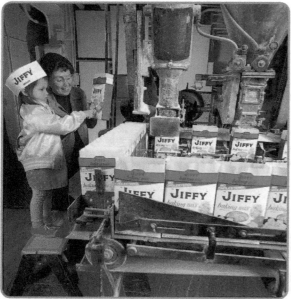

◄ Some companies adjust for a capacity change by modifying machinery or using older equipment—even though it may not be the most efficient. For instance, managers at the family-owned maker of Jiffy brand mixes decided that their OM strategy did not support additional capital investment in new equipment. Consequently, when making repairs, modifying equipment, or adjusting for peak loads, they draw on spare, often old, equipment.

James Schnepf Photography, Inc.

Using these equations, we can solve directly for break-even point and profitability. The two break-even formulas of particular interest are:

$$\text{Break-even in units} = \frac{\text{Total fixed cost}}{\text{Price} - \text{Variable cost}} \quad (4)$$

$$\text{Break-even in dollars} = \frac{\text{Total fixed cost}}{1 - \dfrac{\text{Variable cost}}{\text{Selling price}}} \quad (5)$$

Single-Product Case

In Example 3, we determine the break-even point in dollars and units for one product.

<table>
<tr><td>

EXAMPLE 3

Single product break-even analysis

Excel OM Data File
Ch07SExS3.xls

Active Model S7.2

Example 3 is further illustrated in Active Model S7.2 on the CD-ROM.

</td><td>

Stephens, Inc., wants to determine the minimum dollar volume and unit volume needed at its new facility to break even.

Approach: The firm first determines that it has fixed costs of $10,000 this period. Direct labor is $1.50 per unit, and material is $.75 per unit. The selling price is $4.00 per unit.

Solution: The break-even point in dollars is computed as follows:

$$BEP_\$ = \frac{F}{1-(V/P)} = \frac{\$10,000}{1-[(1.50+.75)/(4.00)]} = \frac{\$10,000}{.4375} = \$22,857.14$$

The break-even point in units is:

$$BEP_x = \frac{F}{P-V} = \frac{\$10,000}{4.00-(1.50+.75)} = 5,714$$

Note that we use total variable costs (that is, both labor and material).

Insight: The management of Stevens, Inc., now has an estimate in both units and dollars of the volume necessary for the new facility.

Learning exercise: If Stevens finds that fixed cost will increase to $12,000, what happens to the break-even in units and dollars? [Answer: The break-even in units increases to 6,857, and break-even in dollars increases to $27,428.57.]

Related problems: 9, 12, 13, 14, 15, 16, 17, 18, 19, 20, 21, 22, 23

</td></tr>
</table>

Multiproduct Case

Most firms, from manufacturers to restaurants (even fast-food restaurants), have a variety of offerings. Each offering may have a different selling price and variable cost. Utilizing break-even analysis, we modify Equation (5) to reflect the proportion of sales for each product. We do this by "weighting" each product's contribution by its proportion of sales. The formula is then:

$$BEP_\$ = \frac{F}{\sum \left[\left(1 - \dfrac{V_i}{P_i}\right) \times (W_i) \right]} \quad (6)$$

where
V = variable cost per unit
P = price per unit
F = fixed cost
W = percent each product is of total dollar sales
i = each product

Example 4 shows how to determine the break-even point for the multiproduct case at the Le Bistro restaurant.

◄ *Paper machines such as the one shown here, at International Paper, require a high capital investment. This investment results in a high fixed cost but allows production of paper at a very low variable cost. The production manager's job is to maintain utilization above the break-even point to achieve profitability.*

Jack Kenner, International Paper Company

EXAMPLE 4

Multiproduct break-even analysis

Le Bistro makes more than one product and would like to know its break-even point in dollars.

Approach: Information for Le Bistro follows. Fixed costs are $3,500 per month.

Item	Price	Cost	Annual Forecasted Sales Units
Sandwich	$2.95	$1.25	7,000
Soft drink	.80	.30	7,000
Baked potato	1.55	.47	5,000
Tea	.75	.25	5,000
Salad bar	2.85	1.00	3,000

With a variety of offerings, we proceed with break-even analysis just as in a single-product case, except that we weight each of the products by its proportion of total sales using Equation (6).

Solution: Multiproduct Break-Even: Determining Contribution

1	2	3	4	5	6	7	8
Item (i)	Selling Price (P)	Variable Cost (V)	(V/P)	$1 - (V/P)$	Annual Forecasted Sales $	% of Sales	Weighted Contribution (col. 5 × col. 7)
Sandwich	$2.95	$1.25	.42	.58	$20,650	.446	.259
Soft drink	.80	.30	.38	.62	5,600	.121	.075
Baked potato	1.55	.47	.30	.70	7,750	.167	.117
Tea	.75	.25	.33	.67	3,750	.081	.054
Salad bar	2.85	1.00	.35	.65	8,550	.185	.120
					$46,300	1.000	.625

Note: Revenue for sandwiches is $20,650 (2.95 × 7,000), which is 44.6% of the total revenue of $46,300. Therefore, the contribution for sandwiches is "weighted" by .446. The weighted contribution is .446 × .58 = .259. In this manner, its *relative* contribution is properly reflected.

Using this approach for each product, we find that the total weighted contribution is .625 for each dollar of sales, and the break-even point in dollars is $67,200:

$$BEP_\$ = \frac{F}{\sum\left[\left(1 - \frac{V_i}{P_i}\right) \times (W_i)\right]} = \frac{\$3,500 \times 12}{.625} = \frac{\$42,000}{.625} = \$67,200$$

The information given in this example implies total daily sales (52 weeks at 6 days each) of:

$$\frac{\$67,200}{312 \text{ days}} = \$215.38$$

Insight: The management of Le Bistro now knows that it must generate average sales of $215.38 each day to break even. Management also knows that if the forecasted sales of $46,300 are correct, Le Bistro will lose money, as break-even is $67,200.

Learning exercise: If the manager of Le Bistro wants to make an additional $2,000 per month and considers this a fixed cost, what is the new break-even point in average sales per day? [Answer: $338.46.]

Related problems: 24a, 25, 26a

Break-even figures by product provide the manager with added insight as to the realism of his or her sales forecast. They indicate exactly what must be sold each day, as we illustrate in Example 5.

EXAMPLE 5

Unit sales at break-even

Le Bistro also wants to know the break-even for the number of sandwiches that must be sold every day.

Approach: Using the data in Example 4, we take the forecast sandwich sales of 44.6% times the daily break-even of $215.38 divided by the selling price of each sandwich ($2.95).

Solution: At break-even, sandwich sales must then be:

$$\frac{.446 \times \$215.38}{\$2.95} = \text{Number of sandwiches} = 32.6 \approx 33 \text{ sandwiches each day}$$

Insight: With knowledge of individual product sales, the manager has a basis for determining material and labor requirements.

Learning exercise: At a dollar break-even of $338.46 per day, how many sandwiches must Le Bistro sell each day? [Answer: 51.]

Related problems: 24b, 26b, 35

Once break-even analysis has been prepared, analyzed, and judged to be reasonable, decisions can be made about the type and capacity of equipment needed. Indeed, a better judgment of the likelihood of success of the enterprise can now be made.

When capacity requirements are subject to significant unknowns, "probabilistic" models may be appropriate. One technique for making successful capacity planning decisions with an uncertain demand is decision theory, including the use of decision trees.

Learning Objective

4. Apply decision trees to capacity decisions

APPLYING DECISION TREES TO CAPACITY DECISIONS

Decision trees require specifying alternatives and various states of nature. For capacity planning situations, the state of nature usually is future demand or market favorability. By assigning probability values to the various states of nature, we can make decisions that maximize the expected value of the alternatives. Example 6 shows how to apply decision trees to a capacity decision.

EXAMPLE 6

Decision tree applied to capacity decision

Southern Hospital Supplies, a company that makes hospital gowns, is considering capacity expansion.

Approach: Southern's major alternatives are to do nothing, build a small plant, build a medium plant, or build a large plant. The new facility would produce a new type of gown, and currently the potential or marketability for this product is unknown. If a large plant is built and a favorable market exists, a profit of $100,000 could be realized. An unfavorable market would yield a $90,000 loss.

However, a medium plant would earn a $60,000 profit with a favorable market. A $10,000 loss would result from an unfavorable market. A small plant, on the other hand, would return $40,000 with favorable market conditions and lose only $5,000 in an unfavorable market. Of course, there is always the option of doing nothing.

Recent market research indicates that there is a .4 probability of a favorable market, which means that there is also a .6 probability of an unfavorable market. With this information, the alternative that will result in the highest expected monetary value (EMV) can be selected.

Solution: Prepare a decision tree and compute the EMV for each branch:

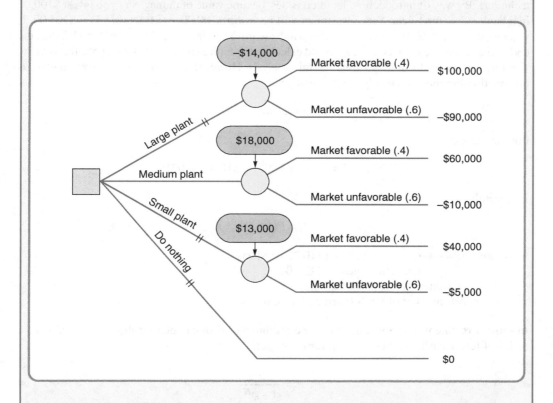

$$\text{EMV (large plant)} = (.4)(\$100,000) + (.6)(-\$90,000) = -\$14,000$$
$$\text{EMV (medium plant)} = (.4)(\$60,000) + (.6)(-\$10,000) = +\$18,000$$
$$\text{EMV (small plant)} = (.4)(\$40,000) + (.6)(-\$5,000) = +\$13,000$$
$$\text{EMV (do nothing)} = \$0$$

Based on EMV criteria, Southern should build a medium plant.

Insight: If Southern makes many decisions like this, then determining the EMV for each branch and selecting the highest EMV is a good decision criterion.

Learning exercise: If a new estimate of the loss from a medium plant in an unfavorable market increases to −$20,000 what is the new EMV for this branch? [Answer: $12,000, which changes the decision because the small plant EMV is now higher.]

Related problems: 27, 28.

APPLYING INVESTMENT ANALYSIS TO STRATEGY-DRIVEN INVESTMENTS

Once the strategy implications of potential investments have been considered, traditional investment analysis is appropriate. We introduce the investment aspects of capacity next.

An operations manager may be the one held responsible for return on investment (ROI).

Investment, Variable Cost, and Cash Flow

Because capacity and process alternatives exist, so do options regarding capital investment and variable cost. Managers must choose from among different financial options as well as capacity and process alternatives. Analysis should show the capital investment, variable cost, and cash flows as well as net present value for each alternative.

Net Present Value

Net present value
A means of determining the discounted value of a series of future cash receipts.

Determining the discount value of a series of future cash receipts is known as the **net present value** technique. By way of introduction, let us consider the time value of money. Say you invest $100.00 in a bank at 5% for 1 year. Your investment will be worth $100.00 + ($100.00)(.05) = $105.00. If you invest the $105.00 for a second year, it will be worth $105.00 + ($105.00)(.05) = $110.25 at the end of the second year. Of course, we could calculate the future value of $100.00 at 5% for as many years as we wanted by simply extending this analysis. However, there is an easier way to express this relationship mathematically. For the first year:

$$\$105 = \$100(1 + .05)$$

For the second year:

$$\$110.25 = \$105(1 + .05) = \$100(1 + .05)^2$$

In general:

$$F = P(1 + i)^N \tag{7}$$

where
F = future value (such as $110.25 or $105)
P = present value (such as $100.00)
i = interest rate (such as .05)
N = number of years (such as 1 year or 2 years)

Learning Objective

5. Compute net present value

In most investment decisions, however, we are interested in calculating the present value of a series of future cash receipts. Solving for P, we get:

$$P = \frac{F}{(1+i)^N} \tag{8}$$

When the number of years is not too large, the preceding equation is effective. However, when the number of years, N, is large, the formula is cumbersome. For 20 years, you would have to compute $(1 + i)^{20}$. Without a sophisticated calculator, this computation would be difficult.

▲ *Matching capacity and demand can be a challenge. When market share is declining and facilities are old and inflexible, as is the case at this General Motors plant, the mismatch between demand and capacity means empty plants and laying off employees (left photo). On the other hand, when demand exceeds capacity, as at this opening of the Apple store on the outskirts of Rome, Italy, the mismatch may mean frustrated customers and lost revenue (right photo).*

Year	5%	6%	7%	8%	9%	10%	12%	14%
1	.952	.943	.935	.926	.917	.909	.893	.877
2	.907	.890	.873	.857	.842	.826	.797	.769
3	.864	.840	.816	.794	.772	.751	.712	.675
4	.823	.792	.763	.735	.708	.683	.636	.592
5	.784	.747	.713	.681	.650	.621	.567	.519
6	.746	.705	.666	.630	.596	.564	.507	.456
7	.711	.665	.623	.583	.547	.513	.452	.400
8	.677	.627	.582	.540	.502	.467	.404	.351
9	.645	.592	.544	.500	.460	.424	.361	.308
10	.614	.558	.508	.463	.422	.386	.322	.270
15	.481	.417	.362	.315	.275	.239	.183	.140
20	.377	.312	.258	.215	.178	.149	.104	.073

◄ **Table 1**

Present Value of $1

Interest-rate tables, such as Table 1, alleviate this situation. First, let us restate the present value equation:

$$P = \frac{F}{(1+i)^N} = FX \qquad (9)$$

where X = a factor from Table 1 defined as = $1/(1+i)^N$ and F = future value

Thus, all we have to do is find the factor X and multiply it by F to calculate the present value, P. The factors, of course, are a function of the interest rate, i, and the number of years, N. Table 1 lists some of these factors.

Equations (8) and (9) are used to determine the present value of one future cash amount, but there are situations in which an investment generates a series of uniform and equal cash amounts. This type of investment is called an *annuity*. For example, an investment might yield $300 per year for 3 years. Of course, you could use Equation (8) three times, for 1, 2, and 3 years, but there is a shorter method. Although there is a formula that can be used to solve for the present value of an annual series of uniform and equal cash flows (an annuity), an easy-to-use table has been developed for this purpose. Like the customary present value computations, this calculation involves a factor. The factors for annuities are in Table 2. The basic relationship is

$$S = RX$$

where X = factor from Table 2
S = present value of a series of uniform annual receipts
R = receipts that are received every year for the life of the investment (the annuity)

The present value of a uniform annual series of amounts is an extension of the present value of a single amount, and thus Table 2 can be directly developed from Table 1. The factors for any given interest rate in Table 2 are nothing more than the cumulative sum of the values in Table 1.

Year	5%	6%	7%	8%	9%	10%	12%	14%
1	.952	.943	.935	.926	.917	.909	.893	.877
2	1.859	1.833	1.808	1.783	1.759	1.736	1.690	1.647
3	2.723	2.673	2.624	2.577	2.531	2.487	2.402	2.322
4	3.546	3.465	3.387	3.312	3.240	3.170	3.037	2.914
5	4.329	4.212	4.100	3.993	3.890	3.791	3.605	3.433
6	5.076	4.917	4.766	4.623	4.486	4.355	4.111	3.889
7	5.786	5.582	5.389	5.206	5.033	4.868	4.564	4.288
8	6.463	6.210	5.971	5.747	5.535	5.335	4.968	4.639
9	7.108	6.802	6.515	6.247	5.985	5.759	5.328	4.946
10	7.722	7.360	7.024	6.710	6.418	6.145	5.650	5.216
15	10.380	9.712	9.108	8.559	8.060	7.606	6.811	6.142
20	12.462	11.470	10.594	9.818	9.128	8.514	7.469	6.623

◄ **Table 2**

Present Value of an Annuity of $1

In Table 1, for example, .952, .907, and .864 are the factors for years 1, 2, and 3 when the interest rate is 5%. The cumulative sum of these factors is 2.723 = .952 + .907 + .864. Now look at the point in Table 2 where the interest rate is 5% and the number of years is 3. The factor for the present value of an annuity is 2.723, as you would expect. Table 2 can be very helpful in reducing the computations necessary to make financial decisions. (Note, however, that there may be minor rounding differences between the tables.)

Example 7 shows how to determine the present value of an annuity.

EXAMPLE 7

Determining net present value of future receipts of equal value

River Road Medical Clinic is thinking of investing in a sophisticated new piece of medical equipment. It will generate $7,000 per year in receipts for 5 years.

Approach: Determine the present value of this cash flow; assume an interest rate of 6%.

Solution: The factor from Table 2 (4.212) is obtained by finding that value when the interest rate is 6% and the number of years is 5:

$$S = RX = \$7,000(4.212) = \$29,484$$

Insight: There is another way of looking at this example. If you went to a bank and took a loan for $29,484 today, your payments would be $7,000 per year for 5 years if the bank used an interest rate of 6% compounded yearly. Thus, $29,484 is the present value.

Learning exercise: If the interest rate is 8%, what is the present value? [Answer: $27,951.]

Related problems: 29, 30, 31

The net present value method is one of the best methods of ranking investment alternatives. The procedure is straightforward: You simply compute the present value of all cash flows for each investment alternative. When deciding among investment alternatives, you pick the investment with the highest net present value. Similarly, when making several investments, those with higher net present values are preferable to investments with lower net present values.

Example 8 shows how to use the net present value to choose between investment alternatives.

EXAMPLE 8

Determining net present value of future receipts of different value

Quality Plastics, Inc., is considering two different investment alternatives.

Approach: To find the net present value of each investment, Quality first needs to determine the initial investment, cash flows, and interest rate. Investment A has an initial cost of $25,000, and investment B has an initial cost of $26,000. Both investments have a useful life of 4 years. The cash flows for these investments follow. The cost of capital or the interest rate (i) is 8%. (Factors come from Table 1).

Investment A's Cash Flow	Investment B's Cash Flow	Year	Present Value Factor at 8%
$10,000	$9,000	1	.926
9,000	9,000	2	.857
8,000	9,000	3	.794
7,000	9,000	4	.735

Solution: To find the present value of the cash flows for each investment, we multiply the present value factor by the cash flow for each investment for each year. The sum of these present value calculations minus the initial investment is the net present value of each investment. The computations appear in the following table:

Year	Investment A's Present Values	Investment B's Present Values
1	$ 9,260 = (.926)($10,000)	$ 8,334 = (.926)($9,000)
2	7,713 = (.857)($9,000)	7,713 = (.857)($9,000)
3	6,352 = (.794)($8,000)	7,146 = (.794)($9,000)
4	5,145 = (.735)($7,000)	6,615 = (.735)($9,000)
Totals	$28,470	$29,808
Minus initial investment	−25,000	−26,000
Net present value	$ 3,470	$ 3,808

Insight: The net present value criterion shows investment B to be more attractive than investment A because it has a higher present value.

Learning exercise: If the interest rate is 10%, does this change the decision? [Answer: no, but the difference between the two investments does narrow. NPV of investment A = $2,243; B = $2,500.]

Related problems: 32, 33, 34, 36

In Example 8, it was not necessary to make all those present value computations for investment B. Because the cash flows are uniform, Table 2, the annuity table, gives the present value factor. Of course, we would expect to get the same answer. As you recall, Table 2 gives factors for the present value of an annuity. In this example, for payments of $9,000, cost of capital is 8% and the number of years is 4. Looking at Table 2 under 8% and 4 years, we find a factor of 3.312. Thus, the present value of this annuity is (3.312)($9,000) = $29,808, the same value as in Example 8.

Although net present value is one of the best approaches to evaluating investment alternatives, it does have its faults. Limitations of the net present value approach include the following:

1. Investments with the same net present value may have significantly different projected lives and different salvage values.
2. Investments with the same net present value may have different cash flows. Different cash flows may make substantial differences in the company's ability to pay its bills.
3. The assumption is that we know future interest rates, which we do not.
4. Payments are always made at the end of the period (week, month, or year), which is not always the case.

Summary

Managers tie equipment selection and capacity decisions to the organization's missions and strategy. They design their equipment and processes to have capabilities beyond the tolerance required by their customers while ensuring the flexibility needed for adjustments in technology, features, and volumes.

Good forecasting, break-even analysis, decision trees, cash flow, and net present value (NPV) techniques are par-

ticularly useful to operations managers when making capacity decisions.

Capacity investments are made effective by ensuring that the investments support a long-term strategy. The criteria for investment decisions are contributions to the overall strategic plan and winning profitable orders, not just return on investment. Efficient firms select the correct process and the correct capacity that contributes to their long-term strategy.

Key Terms

Capacity	Efficiency	Contribution
Design capacity	Break-even analysis	Revenue function
Effective capacity	Fixed costs	Net present value
Utilization	Variable costs	

Using Software for Break-Even Analysis

Excel, Excel OM, and POM for Windows all handle break-even and cost–volume analysis problems.

Using Excel
It is a straightforward task to develop the formulas to do a break-even analysis in Excel. Although we do not demonstrate the basics here, you can see most of the spreadsheet analysis in the Excel OM preprogrammed software that accompanies this text.

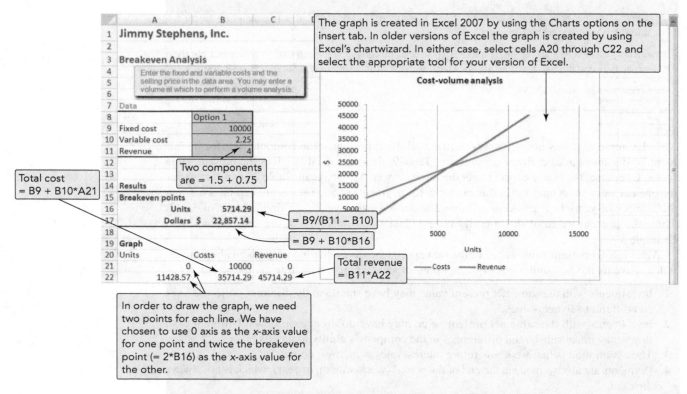

The graph is created in Excel 2007 by using the Charts options on the insert tab. In older versions of Excel the graph is created by using Excel's chartwizard. In either case, select cells A20 through C22 and select the appropriate tool for your version of Excel.

Total cost = B9 + B10*A21

Two components are = 1.5 + 0.75

= B9/(B11 − B10)

= B9 + B10*B16

Total revenue = B11*A22

In order to draw the graph, we need two points for each line. We have chosen to use 0 axis as the x-axis value for one point and twice the breakeven point (= 2*B16) as the x-axis value for the other.

▲ **Program 1**   Excel OM's Break-Even Analysis, Using Example 3 Data

Using Excel OM

Excel OM's Break-Even Analysis module is illustrated in Program 1. Using the Stephens, Inc., information in Example 3, Program 1 shows input data, the Excel formulas used to compute the break-even points, and the solution and graphical output.

Using POM for Windows

Similar to Excel OM, POM for Windows also contains a break-even/cost–volume analysis module.

Solved Problems

 Virtual Office Hours help is available on Student DVD.

Solved Problem 1

Sara James Bakery, described earlier in Examples 1 and 2, has decided to increase its facilities by adding one additional process line. The firm will have two process lines, each working 7 days a week, 3 shifts per day, 8 hours per shift. Effective capacity is now 300,000 rolls. This addition, however, will reduce overall system efficiency to 85%. Compute the expected production with this new effective capacity.

Solution

$$\text{Expected production} = (\text{Effective capacity})(\text{Efficiency})$$
$$= 300,000(.85)$$
$$= 255,000 \text{ rolls per week}$$

Solved Problem 2

Marty McDonald has a business packaging software in Wisconsin. His annual fixed cost is $10,000, direct labor is $3.50 per package, and material is $4.50 per package. The selling price will be $12.50 per package. What is the break-even point in dollars? What is break-even in units?

Solution

$$BEP_\$ = \frac{F}{1 - (V/P)} = \frac{\$10,000}{1 - (\$8.00 / \$12.50)} = \frac{\$10,000}{.36} = \$27,777$$

$$BEP_x = \frac{F}{P - V} = \frac{\$10,000}{\$12.50 - \$8.00} = \frac{\$10,000}{\$4.50} = 2,222 \text{ units}$$

Solved Problem 3

John has been asked to determine whether the $22.50 cost of tickets for the community dinner theater will allow the group to achieve break-even and whether the 175 seating capacity is adequate. The cost for each performance of a 10-performance run is $2,500. The facility rental cost for the entire 10 performances is $10,000. Drinks and parking are extra charges and have their own price and variable costs, as shown below:

	1	2	3	4	5	6	7	8	9
				Percent		Estimated Quantity of	Dollar		Contribution Weighted by
	Selling Price (P)	Variable Cost (V)	Variable Cost (V/P)	Contribution 1 – (V/P)	Sales Units (sales)	Sales (Sales × P)	Percent of Sales	Percent Sales (col. 5 × col. 8)
Tickets with Dinner	$22.50	$10.50	0.467	0.533	175	$3,938	0.741	0.395
Drinks	$ 5.00	$ 1.75	0.350	0.650	175	$ 875	0.165	0.107
Parking	$ 5.00	$ 2.00	0.400	0.600	100	$ 500	0.094	0.056
					450	$5,313	1.000	0.558

Solution

$$BEP_\$ = \frac{F}{\sum\left[\left(1-\frac{V_i}{P_i}\right)\times(W_i)\right]} = \frac{\$(10\times 2,500)+\$10,000}{0.558} = \frac{\$35,000}{0.558} = \$62,724$$

Revenue for each day (from column 7) = $5,313
Total forecasted revenue for the 10 performances = (10 × $5,313) = $53,130
Forecasted revenue with this mix of sales shows a breakeven of $62,724

Thus, given this mix of costs, sales, and capacity John determines that the theatre will not break even.

Solved Problem 4

Your boss has told you to evaluate the cost of two machines. After some questioning, you are assured that they have the costs shown at the right. Assume:
a) The life of each machine is 3 years, and
b) The company thinks it knows how to make 14% on investments no riskier than this one.
Determine via the present value method which machine to purchase.

	Machine A	Machine B
Original cost	$13,000	$20,000
Labor cost per year	2,000	3,000
Floor space per year	500	600
Energy (electricity) per year	1,000	900
Maintenance per year	2,500	500
Total annual cost	$ 6,000	$ 5,000
Salvage value	$ 2,000	$ 7,000

Solution

		Machine A			Machine B		
		Column 1	Column 2	Column 3	Column 4	Column 5	Column 6
Now	Expense	1.000	$13,000	$13,000	1.000	$20,000	$20,000
1 yr.	Expense	.877	6,000	5,262	.877	5,000	4,385
2 yr.	Expense	.769	6,000	4,614	.769	5,000	3,845
3 yr.	Expense	.675	6,000	4,050	.675	5,000	3,375
				$26,926			$31,605
3 yr.	Salvage Revenue	.675	$ 2,000	−1,350	.675	$ 7,000	−4,725
				$25,576			$26,880

We use 1.0 for payments with no discount applied against them (that is, when payments are made now, there is no need for a discount). The other values in columns 1 and 4 are from the 14% column and the respective year in Table 1 (for example, the intersection of 14% and 1 year is .877, etc.). Columns 3 and 6 are the products of the present value figures times the combined costs. This computation is made for each year and for the salvage value.

The calculation for machine A for the first year is:

$$.877 \times (\$2,000 + \$500 + \$1,000 + \$2,500) = \$5,262$$

The salvage value of the product is *subtracted* from the summed costs, because it is a receipt of cash. Since the sum of the net costs for machine B is larger than the sum of the net costs for machine A, machine A is the low-cost purchase, and your boss should be so informed.

Self-Test

- *Before taking the self-test*, refer to the learning objectives listed at the beginning of the supplement and the key terms listed at the end of the supplement.
- Use the key at the end of the chapter to **correct** your answers.
- *Restudy* pages that correspond to any questions you answered incorrectly or material you feel uncertain about.

1. Capacity decisions should be made on the basis of:
   a) building sustained competitive advantage
   b) good financial returns
   c) a coordinated plan
   d) integration into the company's strategy
   e) all of the above

2. Assumptions of the standard break-even model are:
   a) fixed and variable costs are linear and revenue is exponential
   b) fixed cost is linear and variable and revenue are exponential
   c) fixed cost, variable cost and revenue are linear
   d) break-even is computed in dollars only
   e) break-even is computed in units only

3. Effective capacity is:
   a) the capacity a firm expects to achieve given the current operating constraints
   b) percent of design capacity actually achieved
   c) the percent of capacity actually achieved
   d) actual output
   e) efficiency

4. Utilization is:
   a) the capacity a firm expects to achieve given the current operating constraints
   b) percent of design capacity actually achieved
   c) the percent of capacity actually achieved
   d) actual output
   e) efficiency

5. Efficiency is:
   a) the capacity a firm expects to achieve given the current operating constraints
   b) percent of design capacity actually achieved
   c) the percent of effective capacity actually achieved
   d) actual output
   e) design capacity

6. Capacity adjustments are accomplished through:
   a) making staffing changes
   b) adjusting equipment
   c) improving processes
   d) product redesign
   e) all of the above

7. The break-even point is:
   a) adding processes to meet the point of changing product demands
   b) improving processes to increase throughput point
   c) the point in dollars or units at which cost equals revenue
   d) adding or removing capacity to meet demand
   e) the total cost of a process alternative

8. Contribution is:
   a) cost that continues even if no units are produced
   b) the difference between selling price and the variable costs
   c) the revenue that is directly in proportion to the units sold
   d) those cost that vary with the units sold
   e) all of the above

Internet and Student CD-ROM/DVD Exercises

Visit our Companion Web site or use your student CD-ROM/DVD to help with material in this supplement.

 On Our Companion Web Site,
www.prenhall.com/heizer
- Self-Study Quizzes
- Practice Problems
- Virtual Company Tour
- Internet Cases
- PowerPoint Lecture

 On Your Student CD-ROM
- Practice Problems
- Active Model Exercises
- Excel OM
- Excel OM Data Files
- POM for Windows

 On Your Student DVD
- Video Clips and Video Case
- Virtual Office Hours for Solved Problems

Discussion Questions

1. Distinguish between design capacity and effective capacity.
2. What are the assumptions of break-even analysis?
3. Where does the manager obtain data for break-even analysis?
4. What keeps plotted revenue data from falling on a straight line in a break-even analysis?
5. Under what conditions would a firm want its capacity to lag demand? to lead demand?
6. Explain how net present value is an appropriate tool for comparing investments.
7. What is effective capacity?
8. What is efficiency?
9. How is actual, or expected, output computed?

Problems*

• 1 If a plant was designed to produce 7,000 hammers per day but is limited to making 6,000 hammers per day because of the time needed to change equipment between styles of hammers, what is the utilization?

• 2 For the past month, the plant in Problem 1, which has an effective capacity of 6,500, has made only 4,500 hammers per day because of material delay, employee absences, and other problems. What is its efficiency?

• 3 If a plant has an effective capacity of 6,500 and an efficiency of 88%, what is the actual (planned) output?

• 4 A plant has an effective capacity of 900 units per day and produces 800 units per day with its product mix; what is its efficiency?

• 5 Material delays have routinely limited production of household sinks to 400 units per day. If the plant efficiency is 80%, what is the effective capacity?

•• 6 What is the expected output for a plant with a design capacity of 108 chairs per day, if its effective capacity is 90 chairs and its efficiency is 90%?

• 7 A work center containing 4 machines of equal capability operates 2 shifts per day 5 days per week (8 hours per shift). This is the effective capacity. If the work center has a system efficiency of 95%, what is the expected output in hours per week?

• 8 The effective capacity and efficiency for the next quarter at MMU Mfg. in Waco, Texas, for each of three departments are shown:

Department	Effective Capacity	Recent Efficiency
Design	93,600	.95
Fabrication	156,000	1.03
Finishing	62,400	1.05

Compute the expected production for next quarter for each department.

• 9 Smithson Cutting is opening a new line of scissors for supermarket distribution. It estimates its fixed cost to be $500.00 and its variable cost to be $0.50 per unit. Selling price is expected to average $0.75 per unit.
a) What is Smithson's break-even point in units?
b) What is the break-even point in dollars? **Px**

•• 10 Under ideal conditions, a service bay at a Fast Lube can serve 6 cars per hour. The effective capacity and efficiency of a Fast Lube service bay are known to be 5.5 and 0.880, respectively. What is the minimum number of service bays Fast Lube needs to achieve an anticipated production of 200 cars per 8-hour day?

•• 11 Southeastern Oklahoma State University's business program has the facilities and faculty to handle an enrollment of 2,000 new students per semester. However, in an effort to limit class sizes to a "reasonable" level (under 200, generally), Southeastern's dean, Tom Choi, placed a ceiling on enrollment of 1,500 new students. Although there was ample demand for business courses last semester, conflicting schedules allowed only 1,450 new students to take business courses. What are the utilization and efficiency of this system?

*Note: **Px** means the problem may be solved with POM for Windows and/or Excel OM.

• 12 Markland Manufacturing intends to increase capacity by overcoming a bottleneck operation by adding new equipment. Two vendors have presented proposals. The fixed costs for proposal A are $50,000, and for proposal B, $70,000. The variable cost for A is $12.00, and for B, $10.00. The revenue generated by each unit is $20.00.
a) What is the break-even point in units for proposal A?
b) What is the break-even point in units for proposal B? **Px**

• 13 Using the data in Problem 12:
a) What is the break-even point in dollars for proposal A if you add $10,000 installation to the fixed cost?
b) What is the break-even point in dollars for proposal B if you add $10,000 installation to the fixed cost? **Px**

• 14 Given the data in Problem 12, at what volume (units) of output would the two alternatives yield the same profit? **Px**

•• 15 Janelle Heinke, the owner of Ha'Peppas!, is considering a new oven in which to bake the firm's signature dish, vegetarian pizza. Oven type A can handle 20 pizzas an hour. The fixed costs associated with oven A are $20,000 and the variable costs are $2.00 per pizza. Oven B is larger and can handle 40 pizzas an hour. The fixed costs associated with oven B are $30,000 and the variable costs are $1.25 per pizza. The pizzas sell for $14 each.
a) What is the break-even point for each oven?
b) If the owner expects to sell 9,000 pizzas, which oven should she purchase?
c) If the owner expects to sell 12,000 pizzas, which oven should she purchase?
d) At what volume should Janelle switch ovens? **Px**

Corbis Digital Stock

• 16 Given the following data, calculate: a) $BEP(x)$; b) $BEP(\$)$; and c) the profit at 100,000 units:

$$P = \$8/unit \quad V = \$4/unit \quad F = \$50,000 \text{ Px}$$

•• 17 You are considering opening a copy service in the student union. You estimate your fixed cost at $15,000 and the variable cost of each copy sold at $.01. You expect the selling price to average $.05.
a) What is the break-even point in dollars?
b) What is the break-even point in units? **Px**

•• 18   Dr. Aleda Roth, a prolific author, is considering starting her own publishing company. She will call it DSI Publishing, Inc. DSI's estimated costs are:

Fixed	$250,000.00
Variable cost per book	$20.00
Selling price per book	$30.00

How many books must DSI sell to break even? What is its break-even point in dollars? **Px**

•• 19   In addition to the costs in Problem 18, Dr. Roth wants to pay herself a salary of $75,000 per year.
a) Now what is her break-even point in units?
b) What is her break-even point in dollars? **Px**

•• 20   An electronics firm is currently manufacturing an item that has a variable cost of $.50 per unit and a selling price of $1.00 per unit. Fixed costs are $14,000. Current volume is 30,000 units. The firm can substantially improve the product quality by adding a new piece of equipment at an additional fixed cost of $6,000. Variable cost would increase to $.60, but volume should jump to 50,000 units due to a higher-quality product. Should the company buy the new equipment? **Px**

•• 21   The electronics firm in Problem 20 is now considering the new equipment and increasing the selling price to $1.10 per unit. With the higher-quality product, the new volume is expected to be 45,000 units. Under these circumstances, should the company purchase the new equipment and increase the selling price? **Px**

•••• 22   Zan Azlett and Angela Zesiger have joined forces to start A&Z Lettuce Products, a processor of packaged shredded lettuce for institutional use. Zan has years of food processing experience, and Angela has extensive commercial food preparation experience. The process will consist of opening crates of lettuce and then sorting, washing, slicing, preserving, and finally packaging the prepared lettuce. Together, with help from vendors, they feel they can adequately estimate demand, fixed costs, revenues, and variable cost per 5-pound bag of lettuce. They think a largely manual process will have monthly fixed costs of $37,500 and variable costs of $1.75 per bag. A more mechanized process will have fixed costs of $75,000 per month with variable costs of $1.25 per 5-pound bag. They expect to sell the shredded lettuce for $2.50 per 5-pound bag.
a) What is the break-even quantity for the manual process?
b) What is the revenue at the break-even quantity for the manual process?
c) What is the break-even quantity for the mechanized process?
d) What is the revenue at the break-even quantity for the mechanized process?
e) What is the monthly profit or loss of the *manual* process if they expect to sell 60,000 bags of lettuce per month?
f) What is the monthly profit or loss of the *mechanized* process if they expect to sell 60,000 bags of lettuce per month?
g) At what quantity would Zan and Angela be indifferent to the process selected?
h) Over what range of demand would the *manual* process be preferred over the mechanized process? Over what range of demand would the *mechanized* process be preferred over the manual process? **Px**

•• 23   Carter Manufacturing is currently producing a tape holder that has a variable cost of $0.75 per unit and a selling price of $2.00 per unit. Fixed costs are $20,000. Current volume is 40,000 units. The firm can produce a better product by adding a new piece of equipment to the process line. This equipment represents an increase of $5,000 in fixed cost. The variable cost would decrease $0.25 per unit. Volume for the new and improved product should rise to 50,000 units.
a) Should the company invest in the new equipment?
b) At what volume does the equipment choice change?
c) At a volume of 15,000 units, which process should be used?

••• 24   As a prospective owner of a club known as the Red Rose, you are interested in determining the volume of sales dollars necessary for the coming year to reach the break-even point. You have decided to break down the sales for the club into four categories, the first category being beer. Your estimate of the beer sales is that 30,000 drinks will be served. The selling price for each unit will average $1.50; the cost is $.75. The second major category is meals, which you expect to be 10,000 units with an average price of $10.00 and a cost of $5.00. The third major category is desserts and wine, of which you also expect to sell 10,000 units, but with an average price of $2.50 per unit sold and a cost of $1.00 per unit. The final category is lunches and inexpensive sandwiches, which you expect to total 20,000 units at an average price of $6.25 with a food cost of $3.25. Your fixed cost (that is, rent, utilities, and so on) is $1,800 per month plus $2,000 per month for entertainment.
a) What is your break-even point in dollars per month?
b) What is the expected number of meals each day if you are open 30 days a month?

••• 25   Using the data in Problem 24, make the problem more realistic by adding labor cost (as a variable cost) at one-third the total cost of meals and sandwiches. Also add variable expenses (kitchen supplies, tablecloths, napkins, etc.) at 10% of the food cost for each category.
a) What is your break-even point?
b) If you expect to make an annual profit of $35,000 (before taxes) for your 12-hour days, what must your total sales be?

••• 26   As manager of the St. Cloud Theatre Company, you have decided that concession sales will support themselves. The following table provides the information you have been able to put together thus far:

Item	Selling Price	Variable Cost	% of Revenue
Soft drink	$1.00	$ .65	25
Wine	1.75	.95	25
Coffee	1.00	.30	30
Candy	1.00	.30	20

Last year's manager, Jim Freeland, has advised you to be sure to add 10% of variable cost as a waste allowance for all categories.

You estimate labor cost to be $250.00 (5 booths with 3 people each). Even if nothing is sold, your labor cost will be $250.00, so you decide to consider this a fixed cost. Booth rental, which is a contractual cost at $50.00 for *each* booth per night, is also a fixed cost.
a) What is break-even volume per evening performance?
b) How much wine would you expect to sell at the break-even point?

•• 27   James Lawson's Bed and Breakfast, in a small historic Mississippi town, must decide how to subdivide (remodel) the large old home that will become its inn. There are three alternatives: Option A would modernize all baths and combine rooms, leaving the inn with four suites, each suitable for two to four adults.

Option B would modernize only the second floor; the results would be six suites, four for two to four adults, two for two adults only. Option C (the status quo option) leaves all walls intact. In this case, there are eight rooms available, but only two are suitable for four adults, and four rooms will not have private baths. Below are the details of profit and demand patterns that will accompany each option:

Alternatives	Annual Profit under Various Demand Patterns			
	High	p	Average	p
A (modernize all)	$90,000	.5	$25,000	.5
B (modernize 2nd)	$80,000	.4	$70,000	.6
C (status quo)	$60,000	.3	$55,000	.7

a) Draw the decision tree for Lawson.
b) Which option has the highest expected value? **Px**

••• **28** As operations manager of Holz Furniture, you must make a decision about adding a line of rustic furniture. In discussing the possibilities with your sales manager, Steve Gilbert, you decide that there will definitely be a market and that your firm should enter that market. However, because rustic furniture has a different finish than your standard offering, you decide you need another process line. There is no doubt in your mind about the decision, and you are sure that you should have a second process. But you do question how large to make it. A large process line is going to cost $400,000; a small process line will cost $300,000. The question, therefore, is the demand for rustic furniture. After extensive discussion with Mr. Gilbert and Tim Ireland of Ireland Market Research, Inc., you determine that the best estimate you can make is that there is a two-out-of-three chance of profit from sales as large as $600,000 and a one-out-of-three chance as low as $300,000.

With a large process line, you could handle the high figure of $600,000. However, with a small process line you could not and would be forced to expand (at a cost of $150,000), after which time your profit from sales would be $500,000 rather than the $600,000 because of the lost time in expanding the process. If you do not expand the small process, your profit from sales would be held to $400,000. If you build a small process and the demand is low, you can handle all of the demand.

Should you open a large or small process line?

•• **29** What is the net present value of an investment that costs $75,000 and has a salvage value of $45,000? The annual profit from the investment is $15,000 each year for 5 years. The cost of capital at this risk level is 12%. **Px**

• **30** The initial cost of an investment is $65,000 and the cost of capital is 10%. The return is $16,000 per year for 8 years. What is the net present value? **Px**

• **31** An investment will produce $2,000 three years from now. What is the amount worth today? That is, what is the present value if the interest rate is 9%? **Px**

• **32** What is the present value of $5,600 when the interest rate is 8% and the return of $5,600 will not be received for 15 years? **Px**

•• **33** Tim Smunt has been asked to evaluate two machines. After some investigation, he determines that they have the costs shown in the following table. He is told to assume that:
a) the life of each machine is 3 years, and
b) the company thinks it knows how to make 12% on investments no more risky than this one.

	Machine A	Machine B
Original cost	$10,000	$20,000
Labor per year	2,000	4,000
Maintenance per year	4,000	1,000
Salvage value	2,000	7,000

Determine, via the present value method, which machine Tim should recommend.

•• **34** Your boss has told you to evaluate two ovens for Tink-the-Tinkers, a gourmet sandwich shop. After some questioning of vendors and receipt of specifications, you are assured that the ovens have the attributes and costs shown in the following table. The following two assumptions are appropriate:
1) The life of each machine is 5 years.
2) The company thinks it knows how to make 14% on investments no more risky than this one.

	Three Small Ovens at $1,250 Each	Two Large Ovens at $2,500 Each
Original cost	$3,750	$5,000
Labor per year in excess of larger models	$ 750 (total)	
Cleaning/ maintenance	$ 750 ($250 each)	$ 400 ($200 each)
Salvage value	$ 750 ($250 each)	$1,000 ($500 each)

a) Determine via the present value method which machine to tell your boss to purchase.
b) What assumption are you making about the ovens?
c) What assumptions are you making in your methodology?

••••**35** Andre is investigating setting up a crepe stand on campus. He could rent space in the student union (which costs $300/month in rent and overhead). His materials and labor costs are $1 per crepe, and the sale price is $4 per crepe.
a) What is the break-even quantity for this option (i.e., how many crepes per month will Andre have to sell before making a profit)?
b) Andre could use a portable crepe maker from a friend and set up a booth outside the student union. He'd have no rent or other general overhead costs (i.e., no fixed costs), but his friend would demand $1.50 per crepe sold. What is the break-even quantity for this option?
c) Assume that an informal survey shows that Andre could expect 350 crepes to be sold per month. Which capacity option should he elect: student union stand or portable crepe maker?
d) What would his total monthly profit be on the better option?
e) By how much (and in what direction) would the demand have to be different before he would consider switching to the other capacity option?

••••**36** Bold's Gym, a health club chain, is considering expanding into a new location: the initial investment would be $1 million in equipment, renovation, and a 6-year lease, and its annual upkeep and expenses would be $75,000. Its planning horizon is 6 years out, and at the end, it can sell the equipment for $50,000. Club capacity is 500 members who would pay an annual fee of $600. Bold's expects to have no problems filling membership slots. Assume that the interest rate is 10%. (See Table 1)
a) What is the present value profit/loss of the deal?
b) The club is considering offering a special deal to the members in the first year. For $3,000 upfront they get a full 6-year membership (i.e., 1 year free). Would it make financial sense to offer this deal?

Case Study

Capacity Planning at Arnold Palmer Hospital

Since opening day in 1989, the Arnold Palmer Hospital has experienced an explosive growth in demand for its services. One of only six hospitals in the U.S. to specialize in health care for women and children, Arnold Palmer Hospital has cared for over 1,500,000 patients who came to the Orlando facility from all 50 states and more than 100 countries. With patient satisfaction scores in the top 10% of U.S. hospitals surveyed (over 95% of patients would recommend the hospital to others), one of Arnold Palmer Hospital's main focuses is delivery of babies. Originally built with 281 beds and a capacity for 6,500 births per year, the hospital steadily approached and then passed 10,000 births. Looking at Table 3, Executive Director Kathy Swanson knew an expansion was necessary.

▼ **Table 3** **Births at Arnold Palmer Hospital**

Year	Births
1995	6,144
1996	6,230
1997	6,432
1998	6,950
1999	7,377
2000	8,655
2001	9,536
2002	9,825
2003	10,253
2004	10,555
2005	12,316
2006	13,070
2007 (est.)	13,600

With continuing population growth in its market area serving 18 central Florida counties, Arnold Palmer Hospital was delivering the equivalent of a kindergarten class of babies every day and still not meeting demand. Supported with substantial additional demographic analysis, the hospital was ready to move ahead with a capacity expansion plan and a new 11-story hospital building across the street from the existing facility.

Thirty-five planning teams were established to study such issues as (1) their specific forecasts, (2) services that would transfer to the new facility, (3) services that would remain in the existing facility, (4) staffing needs, (5) capital equipment, (6) pro forma accounting data, and (7) regulatory requirements. Ultimately, Arnold Palmer Hospital was ready to move ahead with a budget of $100 million and a commitment to an additional 150 beds. But given the growth of the central Florida region, Swanson decided to expand the hospital in stages: the top two floors would be empty interiors ("shell") to be completed at a later date, and the fourth-floor operating room could be doubled in size when needed. "With the new facility in place, we are now able to handle up to 16,000 births per year," says Swanson.

Discussion Questions*

1. Given the capacity planning discussion in the text (see Figure 5) what approach is being taken by Arnold Palmer Hospital toward matching capacity to demand?
2. What kind of major changes could take place in Arnold Palmer Hospital's demand forecast that would leave the hospital with an underutilized facility (namely, what are the risks connected with this capacity decision)?
3. Use regression analysis to forecast the point at which Swanson needs to "build out" the top two floors of the new building, namely, when demand will exceed 16,000 births.

*You may wish to view this video case on your DVD before addressing these questions.

Additional Case Studies

Internet case study: Visit our Companion Web site at www.prenhall.com/heizer for this free case study:

- **Southwestern University D:** Requires the development of a multiproduct break-even solution.

Harvard has selected these Harvard Business School cases to accompany this supplement:

harvardbusinessonline.hbsp.harvard.edu

- **National Cranberry Cooperative** (#688-122): Requires the student to analyze process, bottlenecks, and capacity.
- **Lenzing AG: Expanding in Indonesia** (#796-099): Considers how expansion affects the company's competitive position.
- **Chaparral Steel** (#687-045): Examines a major capacity expansion proposal of Chaparral Steel, a steel minimill.
- **Align Technology, Inc., Matching Manufacturing Capacity to Sales Demand** (#603-058): Analyzing and planning production capacity.
- **Samsung Heavy Industries: The Koje Shipyard** (#695-032): Explores manufacturing improvement but falling performance after major capital expansion.

Bibliography

Atamturk, A., and D. S. Hochbaum. "Capacity Acquisition, Subcontracting, and Lot-Sizing." *Management Science* 47, no. 8 (August 2001): 1081–1100.

Bowers, John, et al. "Modelling Outpatient Capacity for a Diagnosis and Treatment Center." *Health Care Management Science* 8, no. 3 (August 2005): 205.

Cheng, H. K., K. Dogan, R. A. Einicki. "Pricing and Capacity Decisions for Non-Profit Internet Service Providers." *Information Technology and Management* 7, no. 2 (April, 2006): 91.

Goodale, John C., Rohit Verma, and Madeleine E. Pullman. "A Market Utility-Based Model for Capacity Scheduling in Mass Services." *Production and Operations Management* 12, no. 2 (summer 2003): 165–185.

Hanfield, Robert B., and Kevin McCormack. "What You Need to Know About Sourcing from China." *Supply Chain Management Review* 9, no. 6 (September 2005): 28–37.

Jack, Eric P., and Amitabh S. Raturi. "Measuring and Comparing Volume Flexibility in the Capital Goods Industry." *Production and Operations Management* 12, no. 4 (winter 2003): 480–501.

Jonsson, Patrik, and Stig-Arne Mattsson. "Use and Applicability of Capacity Planning Methods." *Production and Inventory Management Journal* (3rd/4th quarter 2002): 89–95.

Kekre, Sunder, et al. "Reconfiguring a Remanufacturing Line at Visteon, Mexico." *Interfaces* 33, no. 6 (November–December 2003): 30–43.

Koste, L. L., M. K. Malhotra, and S. Sharma. "Measuring Dimensions of Manufacturing Flexibility." *Journal of Operations Management* 22, no. 2 (April 2004): 171–196.

Lovejoy, William S., and Ying Li. "Hospital Operating Room Expansion." *Management Science* 48, no. 11 (November 2002): 1369–1387.

Wacker, J. G., and C. Sheu. "Effectiveness of Manufacturing Planning and Central Systems on Manufacturing Competitiveness." *International Journal of Production Research* 44, no. 5 (March 2006): 1015.

Internet Resources

American Council of Engineering Companies: **www.acec.org**
Association for Manufacturing Excellence: **www.ame.org**

DARPA: U.S. Defense Dept., Innovative Prototype Systems: **www.DARPA.mil**

Solutions to Even Numbered Problems

2 69.2%
4 88.9%
6 81 chairs
8 Design = 88,920
Fabrication = 160,680
Finishing = 65,520
10 5.17 (or 6) bays
12 (a) 6,250 units
(b) 7,000 units
14 $x = 10,000$
16 (a) 12,500 units
(b) $100,000
(c) $350,000
18 $BEP_x = 25,000$
20 Present equipment = $1,000 profit
New equipment = 0 profit
22 (a) 50,000 bags
(b) $125,000
(c) 60,000 bags
(d) $150,000

(e) $7,500
(f) 0.0
(g) Indifferent at 75,000.
(h) Manual process below 75,000.
Mechanized process above 75,000.
24 $BEP_\$ = \$7,584.83$ per mo.
Daily meals = 9
26 (a) $986.19
(b) 140.9 servings
28 Large line payoff = $100,000
Small line payoff = $66,666
30 NPV = $20,360
32 NPV = $1,764
34 (a) Purchase two large ovens.
(b) Equal quality, equal capacity.
(c) Payments are made at end of each time period. And future interest rates are known.
36 (a) $77,750
(b) Yes, NPV = $2,274

Solutions to Self Test

1. e; **2.** c; **3.** a; **4.** b; **5.** c; **6.** e; **7.** c; **8.** b.

Layout Strategies

Outline

Ten OM Strategy Decisions

Design of Goods and Services

Managing Quality

Process Strategy

Location Strategies

Layout Strategies

Human Resources

Supply Chain Management

Inventory Management

Scheduling

Maintenance

Learning Objectives

When you complete this chapter you should be able to

1. Discuss important issues in office layout
2. Define the objectives of retail layout
3. Discuss modern warehouse management and terms such as ASRS, cross-docking, and random stocking
4. Identify when fixed-position layouts are appropriate
5. Explain how to achieve a good process-oriented facility layout
6. Define work cell and the requirements of a work cell
7. Define product-oriented layout
8. Explain how to balance production flow in a repetitive or product-oriented facility

McDonald's Looks for Competitive Advantage through Layout

In its half century of existence, McDonald's revolutionized the restaurant industry by inventing the limited-menu fast-food restaurant. It has also made seven major innovations. The first, the introduction of *indoor seating* (1950s), was a layout issue, as was the second, *drive-through windows* (1970s). The third, adding *breakfasts* to the menu (1980s), was a product strategy. The fourth, *adding play areas* (late 1980s), was again a layout decision.

In the 1990s, McDonald's completed its fifth innovation, a radically new *redesign of the kitchens* in its 13,500 North America outlets to facilitate a mass customization process. Dubbed the "Made by You" kitchen system, sandwiches were assembled to order with the revamped layout.

In 2004, the chain began the rollout of its sixth innovation, a new food ordering layout: the *self-service kiosk*. Self-service kiosks have been infiltrating the service sector since the introduction of ATMs in 1985 (there are over ½ million ATMs in banking). Alaska Airlines was the first airline to provide self-service airport check-in, in 1996. Most passengers of the major airlines now check themselves in for flights. Kiosks take up less space than an employee and reduce waiting line time.

Now, McDonald's is working on its seventh innovation, and not surprisingly, it also deals with restaurant layout. The company, on an unprecedented scale, is redesigning all 30,000 eateries around the globe to take on a *21st century look*. The dining area will be separated into three sections with distinct personalities: (1) the "linger" zone focuses on young adults and offers comfortable furniture and Wi-Fi connections; (2) the "grab and go" zone features tall counters, bar stools, and plasma TVs; and (3) the "flexible" zone has colorful family booths, flexible seating, and kid-oriented music. The cost per outlet: a whopping $300,000–$400,000 renovation fee.

As McDonald's has discovered, facility layout is indeed a source of competitive advantage.

▼ *McDonald's finds that kiosks reduce both space requirements and waiting; order taking is faster. An added benefit is that customers like them. Also, kiosks are reliable—they don't call in sick. And, most importantly, sales are up 10%–15% (an average of $1) when a customer orders from a kiosk, which consistently recommends the larger size and other extras.*

Rick Wiliking, Corbis/Reuters America LLC

► *The redesigned kitchen of a McDonald's in Manhattan. The more efficient layout requires less labor, reduces waste, and provides faster service. A graphic of this "assembly line" is shown in Figure 12.*

▼ Linger Zone

Cozy armchairs and sofas, plus Wi-Fi connections, make these areas attractive to those who want to hang out and socialize.

▼ Grab & Go Zone

This section has tall counters with bar stools for customers who eat alone. Plasma TVs keep them company.

▲ Flexible Zone

Booths with colorful fabric cushions make up the area geared to family and larger groups. Tables and chairs are movable.

THE STRATEGIC IMPORTANCE OF LAYOUT DECISIONS

Layout is one of the key decisions that determines the long-run efficiency of operations. Layout has numerous strategic implications because it establishes an organization's competitive priorities in regard to capacity, processes, flexibility, and cost, as well as quality of work life, customer contact, and image. An effective layout can help an organization achieve a strategy that supports differentiation, low cost, or response. Benetton, for example, supports a *differentiation* strategy by heavy investment in warehouse layouts that contribute to fast, accurate sorting and shipping to its 5,000 outlets. Wal-Mart store layouts support a strategy of *low cost*, as do its warehouse and store layouts. Hallmark's office layouts, where many professionals operate with open communication in work cells, support *rapid development* of greeting cards. *The objective of layout strategy is to develop an effective and efficient layout that will meet the firm's competitive requirements.* These firms have done so.

In all cases, layout design must consider how to achieve the following:

1. Higher utilization of space, equipment, and people
2. Improved flow of information, materials, or people
3. Improved employee morale and safer working conditions
4. Improved customer/client interaction
5. Flexibility (whatever the layout is now, it will need to change).

In our increasingly short-life-cycle, mass-customized world, layout designs need to be viewed as dynamic. This means considering small, movable, and flexible equipment. Store displays need to be movable, office desks and partitions modular, and warehouse racks prefabricated. To make quick and easy changes in product models and in production rates, operations managers must design flexibility into layouts. To obtain flexibility in layout, managers cross train their workers, maintain equipment, keep investments low, place workstations close together, and use small, movable equipment. In some cases, equipment on wheels is appropriate, in anticipation of the next change in product, process, or volume.

> *The objective of layout strategy is to develop a cost-effective layout that meets a firm's competitive needs.*

Video 9.1

Layout at Service Organizations

TYPES OF LAYOUT

Layout decisions include the best placement of machines (in production settings), offices and desks (in office settings), or service centers (in settings such as hospitals or department stores). An effective layout facilitates the flow of materials, people, and information within and between areas. To achieve these objectives, a variety of approaches has been developed. We will discuss seven of them in this chapter:

1. *Office layout:* Positions workers, their equipment, and spaces/offices to provide for movement of information.
2. *Retail layout:* Allocates shelf space and responds to customer behavior.
3. *Warehouse layout:* Addresses trade-offs between space and material handling.
4. *Fixed-position layout:* Addresses the layout requirements of large, bulky projects such as ships and buildings.
5. *Process-oriented layout:* Deals with low-volume, high-variety production (also called "job shop," or intermittent production).
6. *Work-cell layout:* Arranges machinery and equipment to focus on production of a single product or group of related products.
7. *Product-oriented layout:* Seeks the best personnel and machine utilization in repetitive or continuous production.

Examples for each of these classes of layout problems are noted in Table 1.

Because only a few of these seven classes can be modeled mathematically, layout and design of physical facilities are still something of an art. However, we do know that a good layout requires determining the following:

1. *Material handling equipment:* Managers must decide about equipment to be used, including conveyors, cranes, automated storage and retrieval systems, and automatic carts to deliver and store material.
2. *Capacity and space requirements:* Only when personnel, machines, and equipment requirements are known can managers proceed with layout and provide space for each component.

▼ **Table 1** **Layout Strategies**

Office	Retail	Warehouse (storage)	Project (fixed position)	Job Shop (process oriented)	Work Cell (product families)	Repetitive/ Continuous (product oriented)
			Examples			
Allstate Insurance	Kroger's Supermarket	Federal-Mogul's warehouse	Ingall Ship Building Corp.	Arnold Palmer Hospital	Hallmark Cards	Sony's TV assembly line
Microsoft Corp.	Walgreen's	The Gap's distribution center	Trump Plaza	Hard Rock Cafe	Wheeled Coach	Toyota Scion
	Bloomingdale's		Pittsburgh Airport	Olive Garden	Standard Aero	
			Problems/Issues			
Locate workers requiring frequent contact close to one another	Expose customer to high-margin items	Balance low-cost storage with low-cost material handling	Move material to the limited storage areas around the site	Manage varied material flow for each product	Identify a product family, build teams, cross train team members	Equalize the task time at each workstation

In the case of office work, operations managers must make judgments about the space requirements for each employee. It may be a 6×6-foot cubicle plus allowance for hallways, aisles, rest rooms, cafeterias, stairwells, elevators, and so forth, or it may be spacious executive offices and conference rooms. Management must also consider allowances for requirements that address safety, noise, dust, fumes, temperature, and space around equipment and machines.

3. *Environment and aesthetics:* Layout concerns often require decisions about windows, planters, and height of partitions to facilitate air flow, reduce noise, provide privacy, and so forth.

4. *Flows of information:* Communication is important to any organization and must be facilitated by the layout. This issue may require decisions about proximity as well as decisions about open spaces versus half-height dividers versus private offices.

5. *Cost of moving between various work areas:* There may be unique considerations related to moving materials or to the importance of having certain areas next to each other. For example, moving molten steel is more difficult than moving cold steel.

Chuck Keeler, Getty Images, Inc.—Stone Allstock

◄ *This open office offers a large shared space that encourages employees to interact. Before Steelcase, the office furniture maker, went to an open office system, 80% of its office space was private; now it is just 20% private. The CEO even went from a private 700-square-foot office to a 48-square-foot enclosure in an open area. This dramatically increases unplanned and spontaneous communication between employees.*

OFFICE LAYOUT

Concepts of office space are not universal. In the Tokyo office of Toyota about 110 people work in one large room. When important visitors arrive for meetings, they are ushered into special rooms and do not see these cramped offices.

Office layouts require the grouping of workers, their equipment, and spaces to provide for comfort, safety, and movement of information. The main distinction of office layouts is the importance placed on the flow of information. Office layouts are in constant flux as the technological change sweeping society alters the way offices function.

Even though the movement of information is increasingly electronic, analysis of office layouts still requires a task-based approach. Paper correspondence, contracts, legal documents, confidential patient records, and hard-copy scripts, artwork, and designs still play a major role in many offices. Managers therefore examine both electronic and conventional communication patterns, separation needs, and other conditions affecting employee effectiveness. A useful tool for such an analysis is the *relationship chart* shown in Figure 1. This chart, prepared for an office of product designers, indicates that the chief marketing officer must be (1) near the designers' area, (2) less near the secretary and central files, and (3) not at all near the copy center or accounting department.

General office-area guidelines allot an average of about 100 square feet per person (including corridors). A major executive is allotted about 400 square feet, and a conference room area is based on 25 square feet per person.

On the other hand, some layout considerations are universal (many of which apply to factories as well as to offices). They have to do with working conditions, teamwork, authority, and status. Should offices be private or open cubicles, have low file cabinets to foster informal communication or high cabinets to reduce noise and contribute to privacy? (See the Steelcase photo on the previous page). Should all employees use the same entrance, rest rooms, lockers, and cafeteria? As mentioned earlier, layout decisions are part art and part science.

As a final comment on office layout, we note two major trends. First, technology, such as cell phones, iPods, faxes, the Internet, laptop computers, and PDAs, allows increasing layout flexibility by moving information electronically and allowing employees to work offsite. Second, modern firms create dynamic needs for space and services.

Here are two examples[1]:

1. When Deloitte & Touche found that 30% to 40% of desks were empty at any given time, the firm developed its "hoteling programs." Consultants lost their permanent offices; anyone who plans to be in the building (rather than out with clients) books an office through a "concierge," who hangs that consultant's name on the door for the day and stocks the space with requested supplies.
2. Cisco Systems cut rent and workplace service costs by 37% and saw productivity benefits of $2.4 billion per year by reducing square footage, reconfiguring space, creating movable, everything-on-wheels offices, and designing "get away from it all" innovation areas.

► **Figure 1**

Office Relationship Chart

Source: Adapted from Richard Muther, *Simplified Systematic Layout Planning*, 3rd ed. (Kansas City, Mgt. & Ind'l Research Publications). Used by permission of the publisher.

Value	CLOSENESS
A	Absolutely necessary
E	Especially important
I	Important
O	Ordinary OK
U	Unimportant
X	Not desirable

[1]"Square Feet. Oh, How Square!" *Business Week* (July 3, 2006): 100–101.

RETAIL LAYOUT

Retail layouts are based on the idea that sales and profitability vary directly with customer exposure to products. Thus, most retail operations managers try to expose customers to as many products as possible. Studies do show that the greater the rate of exposure, the greater the sales and the higher the return on investment. The operations manager can alter *both* with the overall arrangement of the store and the allocation of space to various products within that arrangement.

Five ideas are helpful for determining the overall arrangement of many stores:

1. Locate the high-draw items around the periphery of the store. Thus, we tend to find dairy products on one side of a supermarket and bread and bakery products on another. An example of this tactic is shown in Figure 2.
2. Use prominent locations for high-impulse and high-margin items. Best Buy puts fast-growing, high-margin digital goods—such as cameras and DVDs—in the front and center of its stores.
3. Distribute what are known in the trade as "power items"—items that may dominate a purchasing trip—to both sides of an aisle, and disperse them to increase the viewing of other items.
4. Use end-aisle locations because they have a very high exposure rate.
5. Convey the mission of the store by carefully selecting the position of the lead-off department. For instance, if prepared foods are part of a supermarket's mission, position the bakery and deli up front to appeal to convenience-oriented customers. Wal-Mart's push to increase sales of clothes means those departments are in broad view upon entering a store.

Once the overall layout of a retail store has been decided, products need to be arranged for sale. Many considerations go into this arrangement. However, the main *objective of retail layout is to maximize profitability per square foot of floor space* (or, in some stores, on linear foot of shelf space). Big-ticket, or expensive, items may yield greater dollar sales, but the profit per square foot may be lower. Computerized programs are available to assist managers in evaluating the profitability of various merchandising plans for hundreds of categories: this technique is know as category management.

An additional, and somewhat controversial, issue in retail layout is called slotting. **Slotting fees** are fees manufacturers pay to get their goods on the shelf in a retail store or supermarket chain. The result of massive new-product introductions, retailers can now demand up to $25,000 to place an item in their chain. During the last decade, marketplace economics, consolidations, and technology have provided retailers with this leverage. The competition for shelf space is advanced by POS systems and scanner technology, which improve supply chain management and inventory control. Many small firms question the legality and ethics of slotting fees, claiming the fees stifle new products, limit their ability to expand, and cost consumers money.[2] (See the Ethical Dilemma at the end of this chapter).

Retail layout
An approach that addresses flow, allocates space, and responds to customer behavior.

2. Define the objectives of retail layout

Slotting fees
Fees manufacturers pay to get shelf space for their products.

Wal-Mart is one of the few major retailers that does not demand slotting fees. This removes the barrier to entry that small companies usually face.

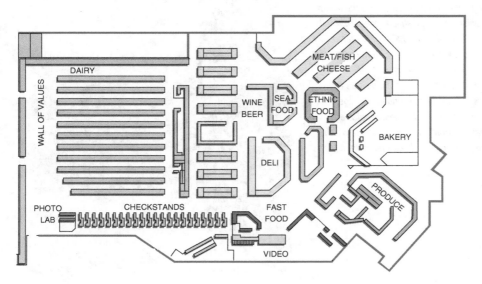

► **Figure 2**

Store Layout with Dairy and Bakery, High-Draw Items, in Different Areas of the Store

---

[2]For an interesting discussion of slotting fees, see J. G. Kaikati and A. M. Kaikati, "Slotting and Promotional Allowances," *Supply Chain Management* 11, no. 2 (2006): 140–147; or J. L. Stanton and K. C. Herbst, "Slotting Allowances," *International Journal of Retail & Distribution Management* 34, no. 2/3 (2006): 187–197.

► *Trying to penetrate urban areas that have lofty land prices and strong antidevelopment movements, Wal-Mart is changing its layout to up, not out. A new generation of multi-level stores take only one-third the space of the traditional 25-acre swaths. Here, in the El Cajon, California, store, Wal-Mart trained workers to help shoppers confused by the device next to the escalator that carries shopping carts from one floor to another.*

Wal Mart

Servicescapes

Servicescape

The physical surroundings in which a service takes place, and how they affect customers and employees.

Although the main objective of retail layout is to maximize profit through product exposure, there are other aspects of the service that managers consider. The term **servicescape** describes the physical surroundings in which the service is delivered and how the surroundings have a humanistic effect on customers and employees.[3] To provide a good service layout, a firm considers three elements:

1. *Ambient conditions*, which are background characteristics such as lighting, sound, smell, and temperature. All these affect workers *and* customers and can affect how much is spent and how long a person stays in the building.
2. *Spatial layout and functionality*, which involve customer circulation path planning, aisle characteristics (such as width, direction, angle, and shelf spacing), and product grouping.
3. *Signs, symbols, and artifacts*, which are characteristics of building design that carry social significance (such as carpeted areas of a department store that encourage shoppers to slow down and browse).

► *A critical element contributing to the bottom line at Hard Rock Cafe is the layout of each cafe's retail shop space. The retail space, from 600 to 1,300 square feet in size, is laid out in conjunction with the restaurant area to create the maximum traffic flow before and after eating. The payoffs for cafes like this one in London are huge. Almost half of a cafe's annual sales are generated from these small shops, which have very high retail sales per square foot.*

Hard Rock Café

[3]See either A. Tombs and J. R. McColl-Kennedy, "Social Servicescapes Conceptual Model," *Marketing Theory* (December 2003): 447; or Mary Jo Bitner, "Servicescapes: The Impact of Physical Surroundings on Customers and Employees," *Journal of Marketing* 56 (April 1992): 57–71.

Examples of each of these three elements of servicescape are:

- *Ambient conditions:* Fine-dining restaurant with linen tablecloths and candlelit atmosphere; Mrs. Field's Cookie bakery smells permeating the shopping mall; leather chairs at Starbucks
- *Layout/functionality:* Kroger's long aisles and high shelves; Best Buys' wide center aisle
- *Signs, symbols, and artifacts:* Wal-Mart's greeter at the door; Hard Rock Cafe's wall of guitars

WAREHOUSING AND STORAGE LAYOUTS

The objective of **warehouse layout** is to find the optimum trade-off between handling cost and costs associated with warehouse space. Consequently, management's task is to maximize the utilization of the total "cube" of the warehouse—that is, utilize its full volume while maintaining low material handling costs. We define *material handling costs* as all the costs related to the transaction. This consists of incoming transport, storage, and outgoing transport of the materials to be warehoused. These costs include equipment, people, material, supervision, insurance, and depreciation. Effective warehouse layouts do, of course, also minimize the damage and spoilage of material within the warehouse.

Management minimizes the sum of the resources spent on finding and moving material plus the deterioration and damage to the material itself. The variety of items stored and the number of items "picked" has direct bearing on the optimum layout. A warehouse storing a few unique items lends itself to higher density than a warehouse storing a variety of items. Modern warehouse management is, in many instances, an automated procedure using *automated storage and retrieval systems* (ASRSs).

The Stop & Shop grocery chain, with 350 supermarkets in New England, has recently completed the largest ASRS in the world. The 1.3 million-square-foot distribution center in Freetown, Massachusetts, employs 77 rotating-fork automated storage and retrieval machines. These 77 cranes each access 11,500 pick slots on 90 aisles—a total of 64,000 pallets of food. The Wolfsburg, Germany parking garage photo (below) indicates that an ASRS can take many forms.

An important component of warehouse layout is the relationship between the receiving/unloading area and the shipping/loading area. Facility design depends on the type of supplies unloaded, what they are unloaded from (trucks, rail cars, barges, and so on), and where they are unloaded. In some companies, the receiving and shipping facilities, or *docks*, as they are called, are even the same area; sometimes they are receiving docks in the morning and shipping docks in the afternoon.

Warehouse layout
A design that attempts to minimize total cost by addressing trade-offs between space and material handling.

Learning Objective

3. Discuss modern warehouse management and terms such as ASRS, cross-docking, and random stocking

◄ *Automated storage and retrieval systems are not found only in traditional warehouses. This parking garage in Wolfsburg, Germany, occupies only 20% of the space of a traditionally designed garage. The ASRS "retrieves" autos in less time, without the potential of the cars being damaged by an attendant.*

Fabian Bimmer, AP Wide World Photos

Automated storage and retrieval systems are reported to improve productivity by an estimated 500% over manual methods.

Cross-docking
Avoiding the placement of materials or supplies in storage by processing them as they are received for shipment.

Cross-Docking

Cross-docking means to avoid placing materials or supplies in storage by processing them as they are received. In a manufacturing facility, product is received directly to the assembly line. In a distribution center, labeled and presorted loads arrive at the shipping dock for immediate rerouting, thereby avoiding formal receiving, stocking/storing, and order-selection activities. Because these activities add no value to the product, their elimination is 100% cost savings. Wal-Mart, an early advocate of cross-docking, uses the technique as a major component of its continuing low-cost strategy. With cross-docking, Wal-Mart reduces distribution costs and speeds restocking of stores, thereby improving customer service. Although cross-docking reduces product handling, inventory, and facility costs, it requires both (1) tight scheduling and (2) accurate inbound product identification.

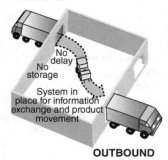

INBOUND

No delay
No storage
System in place for information exchange and product movement

OUTBOUND

Random Stocking

Automatic identification systems (AISs), usually in the form of bar codes, allow accurate and rapid item identification. When automatic identification systems are combined with effective management information systems, operations managers know the quantity and location of every unit. This information can be used with human operators or with automatic storage and retrieval systems to load units anywhere in the warehouse—randomly. Accurate inventory quantities and locations mean the potential utilization of the whole facility because space does not need to be reserved for certain stock-keeping units (SKUs) or part families. Computerized **random stocking** systems often include the following tasks:

Random stocking
Used in warehousing to locate stock wherever there is an open location.

1. Maintaining a list of "open" locations
2. Maintaining accurate records of existing inventory and its locations
3. Sequencing items to minimize the travel time required to "pick" orders
4. Combining orders to reduce picking time
5. Assigning certain items or classes of items, such as high-usage items, to particular warehouse areas so that the total distance traveled within the warehouse is minimized

Random stocking systems can increase facility utilization and decrease labor cost, but they require accurate records.

Customizing

Customizing
Using warehousing to add value to a product through component modification, repair, labeling, and packaging.

Although we expect warehouses to store as little product as possible and hold it for as short a time as possible, we are now asking warehouses to customize products. Warehouses can be places where value is added through **customizing**. Warehouse customization is a particularly useful way to generate competitive advantage in markets with rapidly changing products. For instance, a warehouse can be a place where computer components are put together, software

▶ The Gap strives for both high quality and low costs. It does so by (1) designing its own clothes, (2) ensuring quality control among its vendors, and (3) maintaining downward pressure on distribution costs. A new automatic distribution center near Baltimore allows The Gap to stock East Coast stores daily rather than only three times a week.

Chris Usher, Chris Usher Photography & Associates, Inc.

loaded, and repairs made. Warehouses may also provide customized labeling and packaging for retailers so items arrive ready for display.

Increasingly, this type of work goes on adjacent to major airports, in facilities such as the FedEx terminal in Memphis. Adding value at warehouses adjacent to major airports also facilitates overnight delivery. For example, if your computer terminal has failed, the replacement may be sent to you from such a warehouse for delivery the next morning. When your old terminal arrives back at the warehouse, it is repaired and sent to someone else. These value-added activities at "quasi-warehouses" contribute to strategies of differentiation, low cost, and rapid response.

FIXED-POSITION LAYOUT

In a **fixed-position layout**, the project remains in one place and workers and equipment come to that one work area. Examples of this type of project are a ship, a highway, a bridge, a house, and an operating table in a hospital operating room.

The techniques for addressing the fixed-position layout are not well developed and are complicated by three factors. First, there is limited space at virtually all sites. Second, at different stages of a project, different materials are needed; therefore, different items become critical as the project develops. Third, the volume of materials needed is dynamic. For example, the rate of use of steel panels for the hull of a ship changes as the project progresses.

Fixed-position layout
A system that addresses the layout requirements of stationary projects.

Here are three versions of the fixed-position layout.

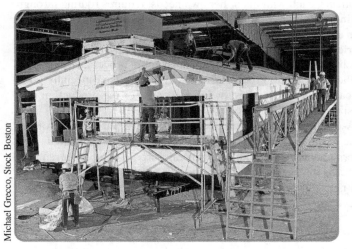

◄ *A house built via traditional fixed-position layout would be constructed onsite, with equipment, materials, and workers brought to the site for a "meeting of the trades" to assign space for various time periods. However, the home pictured here can be built at a much lower cost. The house is built in two movable modules in a factory. Scaffolding and hoists make the job easier, quicker, and cheaper, and the indoor work environment aids labor productivity.*

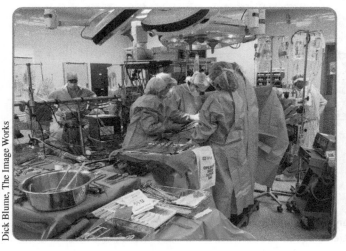

▲ *A service example of a fixed-position layout is an operating room; the patient remains stationary on the table, and medical personnel and equipment are brought to the site.*

▲ *In shipbuilding, there is limited space next to the fixed-position layout. Shipyards call these loading areas platens, and they are assigned for various time periods to each contractor.*

Because problems with fixed-position layouts are so difficult to solve well onsite, an alternative strategy is to complete as much of the project as possible offsite. This approach is used in the shipbuilding industry when standard units—say, pipe-holding brackets—are assembled on a nearby assembly line (a product-oriented facility). In an attempt to add efficiency to shipbuilding, Ingall Ship Building Corporation has moved toward product-oriented production when sections of a ship (modules) are similar or when it has a contract to build the same section of several similar ships. Also, as the top photo on the previous page shows, many home builders are moving from a fixed-position layout strategy to one that is more product oriented. About one-third of all new homes in the U.S. are built this way. In addition, many houses that are built onsite (fixed position) have the majority of components such as doors, windows, fixtures, trusses, stairs, and wallboard built as modules with more efficient offsite processes.

PROCESS-ORIENTED LAYOUT

Process-oriented layout
A layout that deals with low-volume, high-variety production in which like machines and equipment are grouped together.

A **process-oriented layout** can simultaneously handle a wide variety of products or services. This is the traditional way to support a product differentiation strategy. It is most efficient when making products with different requirements or when handling customers, patients, or clients with different needs. A process-oriented layout is typically the low-volume, high-variety strategy. In this job-shop environment, each product or each small group of products undergoes a different sequence of operations. A product or small order is produced by moving it from one department to another in the sequence required for that product. A good example of the process-oriented layout is a hospital or clinic. Figure 3 illustrates the process for two patients, A and B, at an emergency clinic in Chicago. An inflow of patients, each with his or her own needs, requires routing through admissions, laboratories, operating rooms, radiology, pharmacies, nursing beds, and so on. Equipment, skills, and supervision are organized around these processes.

A big advantage of process-oriented layout is its flexibility in equipment and labor assignments. The breakdown of one machine, for example, need not halt an entire process; work can be transferred to other machines in the department. Process-oriented layout is also especially good for handling the manufacture of parts in small batches, or **job lots**, and for the production of a wide variety of parts in different sizes or forms.

Job lots
Groups or batches of parts processed together.

The disadvantages of process-oriented layout come from the general-purpose use of the equipment. Orders take more time to move through the system because of difficult scheduling, changing setups, and unique material handling. In addition, general-purpose equipment requires high labor skills, and work-in-process inventories are higher because of imbalances in the production process. High labor-skill needs also increase the required level of training and experience, and high work-in-process levels increase capital investment.

Video 9.2

Layout at Arnold Palmer Hospital

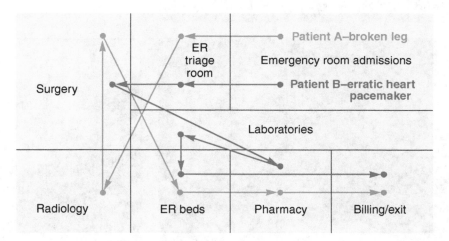

▲ **Figure 3** **An Emergency Room Process Layout Showing the Routing of Two Patients**

Patient A (broken leg) proceeds (blue arrow) to ER triage, to radiology, to surgery, to a bed, to pharmacy, to billing. Patient B (pacemaker problem) moves (purple arrow) to ER triage, to surgery, to pharmacy, to lab, to a bed, to billing.

When designing a process layout, the most common tactic is to arrange departments or work centers so as to minimize the costs of material handling. In other words, departments with large flows of parts or people between them should be placed next to one another. Material handling costs in this approach depend on (1) the number of loads (or people) to be moved between two departments during some period of time and (2) the distance-related costs of moving loads (or people) between departments. Cost is assumed to be a function of distance between departments. The objective can be expressed as follows:

Learning Objective

5. Explain how to achieve a good process-oriented facility layout

$$\text{Minimize cost} = \sum_{i=1}^{n} \sum_{j=1}^{n} X_{ij} C_{ij} \qquad \text{(1)}$$

where n = total number of work centers or departments
i, j = individual departments
X_{ij} = number of loads moved from department i to department j
C_{ij} = cost to move a load between department i and department j

Process-oriented facilities (and fixed-position layouts as well) try to minimize loads or trips, times distance-related costs. The term C_{ij} combines distance and other costs into one factor. We thereby assume not only that the difficulty of movement is equal but also that the pickup and set-down costs are constant. Although they are not always constant, for simplicity's sake we summarize these data (that is, distance, difficulty, and pickup and setdown costs) in this one variable, cost. The best way to understand the steps involved in designing a process layout is to look at an example.

Walters Company management wants to arrange the six departments of its factory in a way that will minimize interdepartmental material handling costs. They make an initial assumption (to simplify the problem) that each department is 20 × 20 feet and that the building is 60 feet long and 40 feet wide.

Approach and Solution: The process layout procedure that they follow involves six steps:

Step 1:   *Construct a "from–to matrix"* showing the flow of parts or materials from department to department (see Figure 4).

EXAMPLE 1

Designing a process layout

Number of loads per week

Department	Assembly (1)	Painting (2)	Machine Shop (3)	Receiving (4)	Shipping (5)	Testing (6)
Assembly (1)		50	100	0	0	20
Painting (2)			30	50	10	0
Machine Shop (3)				20	0	100
Receiving (4)					50	0
Shipping (5)						0
Testing (6)						

◄ **Figure 4**

Interdepartmental Flow of Parts

The high flows between 1 and 3 and between 3 and 6 are immediately apparent. Departments 1, 3, and 6, therefore, should be close together.

Step 2:   *Determine the space requirements* for each department. (Figure 5 shows available plant space.)

Excel OM Data File Ch09Ex1.xls

▶ **Figure 5**

Building Dimensions and One Possible Department Layout

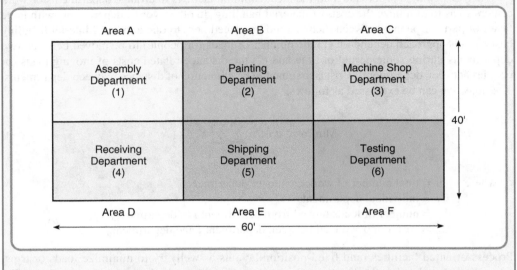

Step 3: *Develop an initial schematic diagram* showing the sequence of departments through which parts must move. Try to place departments with a heavy flow of materials or parts next to one another. (See Figure 6.)

▶ **Figure 6**

Interdepartmental Flow Graph Showing Number of Weekly Loads

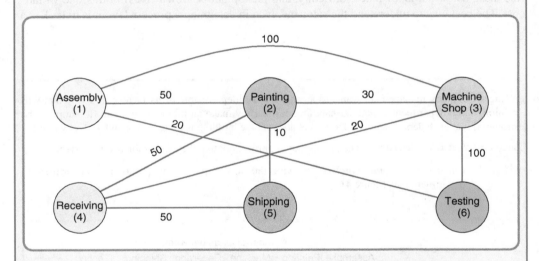

Step 4: *Determine the cost of this layout* by using the material-handling cost equation:

$$\text{Cost} = \sum_{i=1}^{n}\sum_{j=1}^{n} X_{ij}C_{ij}$$

For this problem, Walters Company assumes that a forklift carries all interdepartmental loads. The cost of moving one load between adjacent departments is estimated to be $1. Moving a load between nonadjacent departments costs $2. Looking at Figures 4 and 5, we thus see that the handling cost between departments 1 and 2 is $50 ($1 × 50 loads), $200 between departments 1 and 3 ($2 × 100 loads), $40 between departments 1 and 6 ($2 × 20 loads), and so on. Work areas that are diagonal to one another, such as 2 and 4, are treated as adjacent. The total cost for the layout shown in Figure 6 is:

$$
\begin{aligned}
\text{Cost} = \quad & \$50 \; + \; \$200 \; + \; \$40 \; + \; \$30 \; + \; \$50 \\
& \text{(1 and 2)} \;\; \text{(1 and 3)} \;\; \text{(1 and 6)} \;\; \text{(2 and 3)} \;\; \text{(2 and 4)} \\[4pt]
& + \;\; \$10 \;\; + \;\; \$40 \;\; + \;\; \$100 \;\; + \;\; \$50 \\
& \quad \text{(2 and 5)} \;\; \text{(3 and 4)} \;\; \text{(3 and 6)} \;\; \text{(4 and 5)} \\[4pt]
& = \$570
\end{aligned}
$$

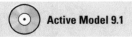

Example 1 is further illustrated in Active Model 9.1 on the CD-ROM.

Step 5: By trial and error (or by a more sophisticated computer program approach that we discuss shortly), *try to improve the layout* pictured in Figure 5 to establish a better arrangement of departments.

By looking at both the flow graph (Figure 6) and the cost calculations, we see that placing departments 1 and 3 closer together appears desirable. They currently are nonadjacent, and the high volume of flow between them causes a large handling expense. Looking the situation over, we need to check the effect of shifting departments and possibly raising, instead of lowering, overall costs.

One possibility is to switch departments 1 and 2. This exchange produces a second departmental flow graph (Figure 7), which shows a reduction in cost to $480, a savings in material handling of $90:

$$\text{Cost} = \underset{\text{(1 and 2)}}{\$50} + \underset{\text{(1 and 3)}}{\$100} + \underset{\text{(1 and 6)}}{\$20} + \underset{\text{(2 and 3)}}{\$60} + \underset{\text{(2 and 4)}}{\$50}$$
$$+ \underset{\text{(2 and 5)}}{\$10} + \underset{\text{(3 and 4)}}{\$40} + \underset{\text{(3 and 6)}}{\$100} + \underset{\text{(4 and 5)}}{\$50}$$
$$= \$480$$

Process layouts are common not only in manufacturing but in colleges, banks, auto-repair shops, airlines, and libraries.

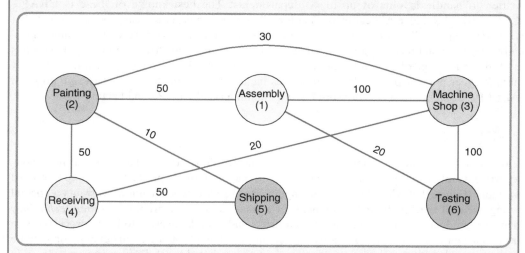

◀ **Figure 7**

Second Interdepartmental Flow Graph

Suppose Walters Company is satisfied with the cost figure of $480 and the flow graph of Figure 7. The problem may not be solved yet. Often, a sixth step is necessary:

Step 6: *Prepare a detailed plan* arranging the departments to fit the shape of the building and its nonmovable areas (such as the loading dock, washrooms, and stairways). Often this step involves ensuring that the final plan can be accommodated by the electrical system, floor loads, aesthetics, and other factors.

In the case of Walters Company, space requirements are a simple matter (see Figure 8).

◀ **Figure 8**

A Feasible Layout for Walters Company

Area A	Area B	Area C
Painting Department (2)	Assembly Department (1)	Machine Shop Department (3)
Receiving Department (4)	Shipping Department (5)	Testing Department (6)
Area D	Area E	Area F

Insight: This switch of departments is only one of a large number of possible changes. For a six-department problem, there are actually 720 (or 6! = $6 \times 5 \times 4 \times 3 \times 2 \times 1$) potential arrangements! In layout problems, we may not find the optimal solution and may have to be satisfied with a "reasonable" one.

Learning exercise: Can you improve on the layout in Figures 7 and 8? [Answer: Yes, it can be lowered to $430 by placing Shipping in area A, Painting in area B, Assembly in area C, Receiving in area D (no change), Machine Shop in area E, and Testing in area F (no change).]

Related problems: 1, 2, 3, 4, 5, 6, 7, 8, 9

Computer Software for Process-Oriented Layouts

CRAFT

A computer program that systematically examines alternative departmental rearrangements to reduce total material handling cost.

The graphic approach in Example 1 is fine for small problems. It does not, however, suffice for larger problems. When 20 departments are involved in a layout problem, more than 600 *trillion* different department configurations are possible. Fortunately, computer programs have been written to handle layouts of up to 40 departments. The best-known of these is **CRAFT** (Computerized Relative Allocation of Facilities Technique), a program that produces "good" but not always "optimal" solutions. CRAFT is a search technique that systematically examines alternative departmental rearrangements to reduce total "handling" cost (see Figure 9). CRAFT has the added advantage of examining not only load and distance but also a third factor, a difficulty rating.[4] Other popular process layout packages include the Automated Layout Design program (ALDEP), Computerized Relationship Layout Planning (CORELAP), and Factory Flow.

WORK CELLS

Work cell

An arrangement of machines and personnel that focuses on making a single product or family of related products.

A **work cell** reorganizes people and machines that would ordinarily be dispersed in various departments into a group so that they can focus on making a single product or a group of related products (Figure 10). Cellular work arrangements are used when volume warrants a special arrangement of machinery and equipment. In a manufacturing environment, *group technology* identifies products that have similar characteristics and lend themselves to being processed in a particular work cell. These work cells are reconfigured as product designs change or volume fluctuates. Although the idea of work cells was first presented by R. E. Flanders in 1925, only with the increasing use of group technology has the technique reasserted itself. The advantages of work cells are:

1. *Reduced work-in-process inventory* because the work cell is set up to provide one-piece flow from machine to machine.
2. *Less floor space* required because less space is needed between machines to accommodate work-in-process inventory.

▶ **Figure 9**

In This Six-Department Outpatient Hospital Example, (a) CRAFT Has Rearranged the Initial Layout, with a Cost of $20,100, into (b) the New Layout with a Lower Cost of $14,390.

CRAFT does this by systematically testing pairs of departments to see if moving them closer to each other lowers total cost.

Legend:

☐ A = X-ray/MRI rooms
☐ B = laboratories
☐ C = admissions
☐ D = exam rooms
☐ E = operating rooms
☐ F = recovery rooms

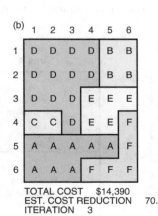

[4]Y. A. Bozer, R. R. Meller, and S. J. Erlebacher, "An Improvement-Type Layout Algorithm for Single and Multiple Floor Facilities," *Management Science* 40, no. 7 (1994): 918–933.

◄ *Contemporary software such as this from e-factory (UGS Corp.) allows operations managers to quickly place and connect symbols for factory equipment for a full three-dimensional view of the layout. Such presentations provide added insight into the issues of facility layout in terms of process, material handling, efficiency, and safety.*

UGS

3. *Reduced raw material and finished goods inventories* because less work-in-process allows more rapid movement of materials through the work cell.
4. *Reduced direct labor cost* because of improved communication among employees, better material flow, and improved scheduling.
5. *Heightened sense of employee participation* in the organization and the product: employees accept the added responsibility of product quality because it is directly associated with them and their work cell.
6. *Increased equipment and machinery utilization* because of better scheduling and faster material flow.
7. *Reduced investment in machinery and equipment* because good utilization reduces the number of machines and the amount of equipment and tooling.

Learning Objective

6. Define work cell and the requirements of a work cell

Requirements of Work Cells

The requirements of cellular production include:

1. Identification of families of products, often through the use of group technology codes or equivalents
2. A high level of training, flexibility, and empowerment of employees
3. Being self-contained, with its own equipment and resources.
4. Test (poka-yoke) at each station in the cell

Work cells have at least five advantages over assembly lines and process facilities: (1) because tasks are grouped, inspection is often immediate; (2) fewer workers are needed; (3) workers can reach more of the work area; (4) the work area can be more efficiently balanced; and (5) communication is enhanced. Work cells are sometimes organized in a U shape, as shown on the right side of Figure 10.

About half of U.S. plants with fewer than 100 employees use some sort of cellular system, whereas 75% of larger plants have adopted cellular production methods. Bayside Controls in Queens, New York, for example, has in the past decade increased sales from $300,000 per year to $11 million. Much of the gain was attributed to its move to cellular manufacturing. As noted in the *OM in Action* box, Rowe Furniture has had similar success with work cells.

 Video 9.3

Work Cells at Kurt Manufacturing

Staffing and Balancing Work Cells

Once the work cell has the appropriate equipment located in the proper sequence, the next task is to staff and balance the cell. Efficient production in a work cell requires appropriate staffing.

► **Figure 10**

Improving Layouts by Moving to the Work Cell Concept

Note in both (a) and (b) that U-shaped work cells can reduce material and employee movement. The U shape may also reduce space requirements, enhance communication, cut the number of workers, and make inspection easier.

(a)

Current layout–workers in small closed areas. Cannot increase output without a third worker.

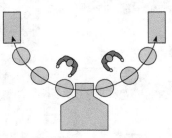

Improved layout–cross-trained workers can assist each other. May be able to add a third worker as added output is needed.

(b)

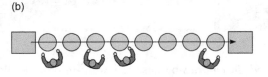

Current layout–straight lines make it hard to balance tasks because work may not be divided evenly.

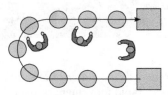

Improved layout–in U shape, workers have better access. Four cross-trained workers were reduced to three.

Takt time

Pace of production to meet customer demands.

This involves two steps. First, determine the **takt time**,[5] which is the pace (frequency) of production units necessary to meet customer orders:

$$\text{Takt time} = \text{Total work time available / Units required} \qquad (2)$$

Second, determine the number of operators required. This requires dividing the total operation time in the work cell by the takt time:

$$\text{Workers required} = \text{Total operation time required / Takt time} \qquad (3)$$

Example 2 considers these two steps when staffing work cells.

OM in Action   Work Cells at Rowe Furniture

Furniture customers usually want a much wider selection of options than showrooms display. What they really want is customization—unique styles, fabrics, and colors. And they are unhappy waiting months to get them. With imports claiming over 50% of the U.S. dining room/bedroom market, custom furniture is an opportunity for American manufacturers. Rowe Furniture Corp. of Salem, Virginia, took advantage of this opportunity by creating a computer network on which customers could order customized combinations of styles, fabrics, and colors. This strategy provided the orders for customization, but the real trick was how operations people could build ordered furniture quickly (in 10 days from order to delivery), with no increase in cost.

First, Rowe got rid of its old assembly line. Then it formed unique work cells, called "focused factories," each containing teams of workers with the necessary skills—gluers, sewers, staplers, and stuffers. Instead of being scattered along an assembly line, about three dozen team members found themselves in work cells. The work cells enhanced communication among team members and with management. Cross-training followed; gluers began to understand what staplers needed, and stuffers began to understand sewing requirements. Soon, team members realized that they could successfully deal with daily problems and began to develop improved methods. Moreover, both team members and management began to work together to solve problems.

The work cells yielded record productivity. The plant now produces 5% more with 10% fewer workers, and absenteeism has been cut in half. In addition, immediate feedback in the work cell has driven the error rate down to 1/10 of 1%.

Sources: Upholstery Design and Management (February 2001): 16–22; *Fast Company* (July 2004): 80–82; *The Wall Street Journal* (September 13, 1996): B1; and **www.rowefurniture.com**.

[5]*Takt* is German for "time," "measure," "beat" and is used in this context as the rate at which completed units must be produced to satisfy customer demand.

EXAMPLE 2

Staffing work cells

Stephen Hall's company in Dayton makes auto mirrors. The major customer is the Honda plant nearby. Honda expects 600 mirrors delivered daily, and the work cell producing the mirrors is scheduled for 8 hours. Hall wants to determine the takt time and the number of workers required.

Approach: Hall uses Equations (2) and (3) and develops a work balance chart to help determine the time for each operation in the work cell, as well as total time.

Solution: Takt time = (8 hours × 60 minutes) / 600 units = 480/600 =.8 minute = 48 seconds

Therefore, the customer requirement is one mirror every 48 seconds.

The *work balance chart* in Figure 11 shows that 5 operations are necessary, for a total operation time of 140 seconds:

$$\text{Workers required} = \text{Total operation time required} / \text{Takt time}$$
$$= (50 + 45 + 10 + 20 + 15) / 48$$
$$= 140 / 48 = 2.91$$

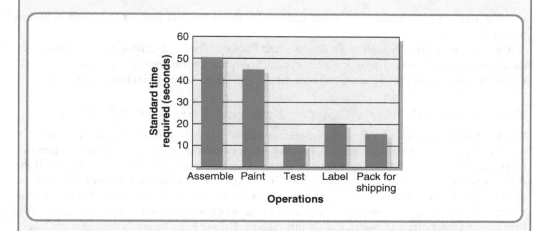

◄ **Figure 11**

Work Balance Chart for Mirror Production

Insight: To produce one unit every 48 seconds will require 2.91 people. With three operators this work cell will be producing one unit each 46.67 seconds (140 seconds / 3 employees = 46.67) and 617 units per day (480 minutes available × 60 seconds) / 46.67 seconds for each unit = 617).

Learning exercise: If testing time is expanded to 20 seconds, what is the staffing requirement? [Answer: 3.125 employees.]

Related problem: 10

A *work balance chart* (like the one in Example 2) is also valuable for evaluating the operation times in work cells. Some consideration must be given to determining the bottleneck operation. Bottleneck operations can constrain the flow through the cell. Imbalance in a work cell is seldom an issue if the operation is manual, as cell members by definition are part of a cross-trained team. Consequently, the many advantages of work cells typically overcome modest imbalance issues within a cell. However, if the imbalance is a machine constraint, then an adjustment in machinery, process, or operations may be necessary. In such situations the use of traditional assembly-line-balancing analysis, the topic of our next section, may be helpful.

In many arrangements, without cells and without cross training, if one operation is halted for whatever reason (reading a drawing, getting a tool, machine maintenance, etc.), the entire flow stops. Multiple-operator cells are therefore preferred.

The success of work cells is not limited to manufacturing. Kansas City's Hallmark, which has over half the U.S. greeting card market and produces some 40,000 different cards, has modified the offices into a cellular design. In the past, its 700 creative professionals would take up to 2 years to develop a new card. Hallmark's decision to create work cells consisting of artists, writers, lithographers, merchandisers, and accountants, all located in the same area, has resulted in card preparation in a fraction of the time that the old layout required. Work cells have also

▶ **Table 2**

Work Cells, Focused Work Centers, and the Focused Factory

Work Cell	Focused Work Center	Focused Factory
A work cell is a temporary product-oriented arrangement of machines and personnel in what is ordinarily a process-oriented facility	A focused work center is a permanent product-oriented arrangement of machines and personnel in what is ordinarily a process-oriented facility	A focused factory is a permanent facility to produce a product or component in a product-oriented facility. Many of the focused factories currently being built were originally part of a process-oriented facility
Example: A job shop with machinery and personnel rearranged to produce 300 unique control panels	*Example:* Pipe bracket manufacturing at a shipyard	*Example:* A plant to produce window mechanisms for automobiles

yielded higher performance and better service for the American Red Cross blood donation process.[6]

Commercial software, such as ProPlanner and Factory Flow, is available to aid managers in their move to work cells. These programs typically require information that includes AutoCAD layout drawings; part routing data; and cost, times, and speeds of material handling systems.

The Focused Work Center and the Focused Factory

When a firm has *identified a family of similar products that have a large and stable demand*, it may organize a focused work center. A **focused work center** moves production from a general-purpose, process-oriented facility to a large work cell that remains part of the present plant. If the focused work center is in a separate facility, it is often called a **focused factory**. A fast-food restaurant is a focused factory—most are easily reconfigured for adjustments to product mix and volume. Burger King, for example, changes the number of personnel and task assignments rather than moving machines and equipment. In this manner, Burger King balances the assembly line to meet changing production demands. In effect, the "layout" changes numerous times each day.

The term *focused factories* may also refer to facilities that are focused in ways other than by product line or layout. For instance, facilities may be focused in regard to meeting quality, new product introduction, or flexibility requirements.

Focused facilities in manufacturing and in services appear to be better able to stay in tune with their customers, to produce quality products, and to operate at higher margins. This is true whether they are steel mills like CMC, Nucor, or Chaparral; restaurants like McDonald's and Burger King; or a hospital like Arnold Palmer.

Table 2 summarizes our discussion of work cells, focused work centers, and focused factories.

REPETITIVE AND PRODUCT-ORIENTED LAYOUT

Product-oriented layouts are organized around products or families of similar high-volume, low-variety products. Repetitive production and continuous production, use product layouts. The assumptions are that:

1. Volume is adequate for high equipment utilization
2. Product demand is stable enough to justify high investment in specialized equipment
3. Product is standardized or approaching a phase of its life cycle that justifies investment in specialized equipment
4. Supplies of raw materials and components are adequate and of uniform quality (adequately standardized) to ensure that they will work with the specialized equipment

Two types of a product-oriented layout are fabrication and assembly lines. The **fabrication line** builds components, such as automobile tires or metal parts for a refrigerator, on a series of

Focused work center
A permanent or semi-permanent product-oriented arrangement of machines and personnel.

Focused factory
A facility designed to produce similar products or components.

Learning Objective

7. Define product-oriented layout

Fabrication line
A machine-paced, product-oriented facility for building components.

[6]Mark Pagell and Steven A. Melnyk, "Assessing the Impact of Alternative Manufacturing Layouts in a Service Setting," *Journal of Operations Management* 22 (2004): 413–429.

machines. An **assembly line** puts the fabricated parts together at a series of workstations. Both are repetitive processes, and in both cases, the line must be "balanced": That is, the time spent to perform work on one machine must equal or "balance" the time spent to perform work on the next machine in the fabrication line, just as the time spent at one workstation by one assembly-line employee must "balance" the time spent at the next workstation by the next employee. The same issues arise when designing the "disassembly lines" of slaughterhouses and automobile makers (see the *OM in Action* box "From Assembly Lines to Disassembly Lines").

Fabrication lines tend to be machine-paced and require mechanical and engineering changes to facilitate balancing. Assembly lines, on the other hand, tend to be paced by work tasks assigned to individuals or to workstations. Assembly lines, therefore, can be balanced by moving tasks from one individual to another. The central problem, then, in product-oriented layout planning is to balance the tasks at each workstation on the production line so that it is nearly the same while obtaining the desired amount of output.

Management's goal is to create a smooth, continuous flow along the assembly line with a minimum of idle time at each workstation. A well-balanced assembly line has the advantage of high personnel and facility utilization and equity among employees' work loads. Some union contracts require that work loads be nearly equal among those on the same assembly line. The term most often used to describe this process is **assembly-line balancing**. Indeed, the *objective of the product-oriented layout is to minimize imbalance in the fabrication or assembly line.*

The main advantages of product-oriented layout are:

1. The low variable cost per unit usually associated with high-volume, standardized products
2. Low material handling costs
3. Reduced work-in-process inventories
4. Easier training and supervision
5. Rapid throughput

The disadvantages of product layout are:

1. The high volume required because of the large investment needed to establish the process
2. That work stoppage at any one point ties up the whole operation
3. A lack of flexibility when handling a variety of products or production rates

Assembly line
An approach that puts fabricated parts together at a series of workstations; used in repetitive processes.

Assembly-line balancing
Obtaining output at each workstation on a production line so delay is minimized.

Product layout can handle only a few products and process designs.

OM in Action   From Assembly Lines to Disassembly Lines

Almost 100 years have passed since assembly lines were developed to *make* automobiles—and now we're developing disassembly lines to take them apart. Sprawling graveyards of rusting cars and trucks bear testimony to the need for automotive disassembly lines. But those graveyards are slowly beginning to shrink as we learn the art of automobile disassembly. New *disassembly* lines now take apart so many automobiles that recycling is the 16th-largest industry in the U.S. The motivation for this disassembly comes from many sources, including mandated industry recycling standards and a growing consumer interest in purchasing cars based on how "green" they are.

New car designs have traditionally been unfriendly to recyclers, with little thought given to disassembly. However, manufacturers now design in such a way that materials can be easily reused in the next generation of cars. The 2007 Mercedes S-class is 95% recyclable and already meets the 2015 EU standard. BMW has disassembly plants in Europe and Japan as well as U.S. salvage centers in New York, Los Angeles, and Orlando. A giant 200,000-square-foot facility in Baltimore (called CARS) can disassemble up to 30,000 vehicles per year. At CARS's ini-

tial "greening station," special tools puncture tanks and drain fluids, and the battery and gas tank are removed. Then on a semi-automated track, which includes a giant steel vise that can flip a 7,500-pound car upside-down, wheels, doors, hood, and trunk are removed; next comes the interior items; then plastic parts are removed and sorted for recycling; then glass and interior and trunk materials. Eventually the chassis is in a bale and sold as a commodity to minimills that use scrap steel.

Disassembly lines are not easy. Some components, like air bags, are hard to handle and dangerous. Reusable parts are bar coded and entered into a database. Various color-coded plastics must be recycled differently to support being remelted and turned into new parts, such as intake manifolds. After the engines, transmissions, radios, and exhausts have been removed, the remaining metal parts of the disassembly line are easier: with shredders and magnets, baseball-sized chunks of metal are sorted. Assembly lines put cars together, and disassembly lines take them apart.

Sources: The New York Times (September 19, 2005): D5; *Forbes* (April 16, 2001): 314–315; and *Automotive Industry Trends* (March 2004).

▶ The Boeing 737, the world's most popular commercial airplane, is produced on a moving production line, traveling at 2 inches a minute through the final assembly process. The moving line, one of several lean manufacturing innovations at the Renton, Washington, facility, has enhanced quality, reduced flow time, slashed inventory levels, and cut space requirements. Final assembly is only 11 days—a time savings of 50%—and inventory is down more than 55%. Boeing has expanded the moving line concept to its 747 jumbo jet.

Boeing Commercial Airplane Group

Video 9.4

Facility Layout at Wheeled Coach Ambulances

Because the problems of fabrication lines and assembly lines are similar, we focus our discussion on assembly lines. On an assembly line, the product typically moves via automated means, such as a conveyor, through a series of workstations until completed. This is the way automobiles and some planes (see the photo of the Boeing 737) are assembled, television sets and ovens are produced, and fast-food hamburgers are made (see Figure 12). Product-oriented layouts use more automated and specially designed equipment than do process layouts.

Assembly-Line Balancing

Learning Objective

8. Explain how to balance production flow in a repetitive or product-oriented facility

Line balancing is usually undertaken to minimize imbalance between machines or personnel while meeting a required output from the line. To produce at a specified rate, management must know the tools, equipment, and work methods used. Then the time requirements for each assembly task (e.g., drilling a hole, tightening a nut, or spray-painting a part) must be determined. Management also needs to know the *precedence relationship* among the activities—that is, the sequence in which various tasks must be performed. Example 3 shows how to turn these task data into a precedence diagram.

▶ **Figure 12**

McDonald's Hamburger Assembly Line

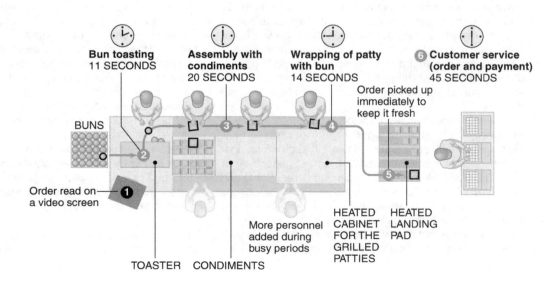

Bun toasting 11 SECONDS

Assembly with condiments 20 SECONDS

Wrapping of patty with bun 14 SECONDS

❻ Customer service (order and payment) 45 SECONDS

Order picked up immediately to keep it fresh

BUNS

Order read on a video screen ❶

More personnel added during busy periods

HEATED CABINET FOR THE GRILLED PATTIES

HEATED LANDING PAD

TOASTER   CONDIMENTS

EXAMPLE 3

Developing a
precedence diagram
for an assembly line

Boeing wants to develop a precedence diagram for an electrostatic wing component that requires a total assembly time of 66 minutes.

Approach: Staff gather tasks, assembly times, and sequence requirements for the component in Table 3.

Task	Performance Time (minutes)	Task Must Follow Task Listed Below	
A	10	—	This means that tasks B and E cannot be done until task A has been completed.
B	11	A	
C	5	B	
D	4	B	
E	12	A	
F	3	C, D	
G	7	F	
H	11	E	
I	3	G, H	
	Total time 66		

Solution: Figure 13 shows the precedence diagram.

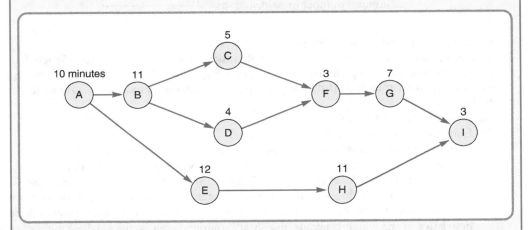

Insight: The diagram helps structure an assembly line and workstations, and it makes it easier to visualize the sequence of tasks.

Learning exercise: If task D had a second preceding task (C), how would Figure 13 change? [Answer: There would also be an arrow pointing from C to D.]

Related problems: 12a, 14a, 15a, 16a, 19a

Once we have constructed a precedence chart summarizing the sequences and performance times, we turn to the job of grouping tasks into job stations so that we can meet the specified production rate. This process involves three steps:

1. Take the units required (demand or production rate) per day and divide it into the productive time available per day (in minutes or seconds). This operation gives us what is called the **cycle time**[7]—namely, the maximum time allowed at each workstation if the production rate is to be achieved:

$$\text{Cycle time} = \frac{\text{Production time available per day}}{\text{Units required per day}} \quad (4)$$

Cycle time

The maximum time that a product is allowed at each workstation.

[7]*Cycle time* is the actual time to accomplish a task or process step. Several process steps may be necessary to complete the product. *Takt time*, discussed earlier, is determined by the customer and is the speed at which completed units must be produced to satisfy customer demand.

► **Table 4**

Layout Heuristics That May Be Used to Assign Tasks to Work Stations in Assembly-Line Balancing

1. *Longest task (operation) time*	From the available tasks, choose the task with the largest (longest) time.
2. *Most following tasks*	From the available tasks, choose the task with the largest number of following tasks.
3. *Ranked positional weight*	From the available tasks, choose the task for which the sum of the times for each following task is longest. (In Example 4 we will see that the ranked positional weight of task C = 5(C) + 3(F) + 7(G) + 3(I) = 18, whereas the ranked positional weight of task D = 4(D) + 3(F) + 7(G) + 3(I) = 17; therefore, C would be chosen first.)
4. *Shortest task (operations) time*	From the available tasks, choose the task with the shortest task time.
5. *Least number of following tasks*	From the available tasks, choose the task with the least number of subsequent tasks.

2. Calculate the theoretical minimum number of workstations. This is the total task-duration time (the time it takes to make the product) divided by the cycle time. Fractions are rounded to the next higher whole number:

$$\text{Minimum number of workstations} = \frac{\sum\limits_{i=1}^{n} \text{Time for task } i}{\text{Cycle time}} \qquad (5)$$

where n is the number of assembly tasks.

3. Balance the line by assigning specific assembly tasks to each workstation. An efficient balance is one that will complete the required assembly, follow the specified sequence, and keep the idle time at each workstation to a minimum. A formal procedure for doing this is the following:

   a. Identify a master list of tasks.

   b. Eliminate those tasks that have been assigned.

   c. Eliminate those tasks whose precedence relationship has not been satisfied.

   d. Eliminate those tasks for which inadequate time is available at the workstation.

   e. Use one of the line-balancing "heuristics" described in Table 4. The five choices are (1) longest task time, (2) most following tasks, (3) ranked positional weight, (4) shortest task time, and (5) least number of following tasks. You may wish to test several of these **heuristics** to see which generates the "best" solution—that is, the smallest number of workstations and highest efficiency. Remember, however, that although heuristics provide solutions, they do not guarantee an optimal solution.

Heuristic

Problem solving using procedures and rules rather than mathematical optimization.

Example 4 illustrates a simple line-balancing procedure.

EXAMPLE 4

Balancing the assembly line

On the basis of the precedence diagram and activity times given in Example 3, Boeing determines that there are 480 productive minutes of work available per day. Furthermore, the production schedule requires that 40 units of the wing component be completed as output from the assembly line each day. It now wants to group the tasks into workstations.

Approach: Following the three steps above, we compute the cycle time using Equation (4) and minimum number of workstations using Equation (5), and we assign tasks to workstations—in this case using the *most following tasks* heuristic.

Solution:

$$\text{Cycle time (in minutes)} = \frac{480 \text{ minutes}}{40 \text{ units}}$$

$$= 12 \text{ minutes/unit}$$

$$\text{Minimum number of workstations} = \frac{\text{Total task time}}{\text{Cycle time}} = \frac{66}{12}$$

$$= 5.5 \text{ or } 6 \text{ stations}$$

Figure 14 shows one solution that does not violate the sequence requirements and that groups tasks into six stations. To obtain this solution, activities with the most following tasks were moved into workstations to use as much of the available cycle time of 12 minutes as possible. The first workstation consumes 10 minutes and has an idle time of 2 minutes.

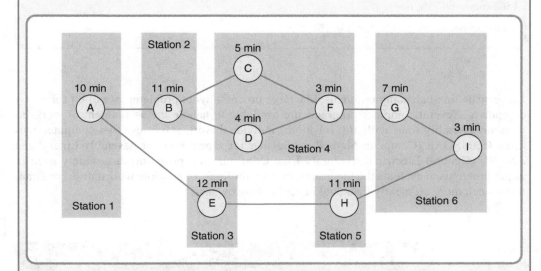

◄ **Figure 14**

A Six-Station Solution to the Line-Balancing Problem

Insight: This is a reasonably well-balanced assembly line. The second workstation uses 11 minutes, and the third consumes the full 12 minutes. The fourth workstation groups three small tasks and balances perfectly at 12 minutes. The fifth has 1 minute of idle time, and the sixth (consisting of tasks G and I) has 2 minutes of idle time per cycle. Total idle time for this solution is 6 minutes per cycle.

Learning exercise: If task I required 6 minutes (instead of 3 minutes), how would this change the solution? [Answer: The cycle time would not change, and the *theoretical* minimum number of workstations would still be 6 (rounded up from 5.75), but it would take 7 stations to balance the line.]

Related problems: 11, 12, 13, 14, 15, 16, 17, 18, 19, 20, 21, 22, 23

We can compute the efficiency of a line balance by dividing the total task time by the product of the number of workstations required times the assigned (actual) cycle time of the longest workstation:

$$\text{Efficiency} = \frac{\Sigma \text{ Task times}}{(\text{Actual number of workstations}) \times (\text{Largest assigned cycle time})} \qquad (6)$$

Operations managers compare different levels of efficiency for various numbers of workstations. In this way, a firm can determine the sensitivity of the line to changes in the production rate and workstation assignments.

Two issues in line balancing are the production rate and the efficiency.

EXAMPLE 5

Determining line efficiency

Boeing needs to calculate the balance efficiency for Example 4.

Approach: Equation (6) is applied.

Solution:
$$\text{Efficiency} = \frac{66 \text{ minutes}}{(6 \text{ stations}) \times (12 \text{ minutes})} = \frac{66}{72} = 91.7\%$$

Note that opening a seventh workstation, for whatever reason, would decrease the efficiency of the balance to 78.6% (assuming that at least one of the workstations still required 12 minutes):

$$\text{Efficiency} = \frac{66 \text{ minutes}}{(7 \text{ stations}) \times (12 \text{ minutes})} = 78.6\%$$

Insight: Increasing efficiency may require that some tasks be divided into smaller elements and reassigned to other tasks. This facilitates a better balance between workstations and means higher efficiency.

Learning exercise: What is the efficiency if an eighth workstation is opened? [Answer: Efficiency = 68.75%.]

Related problems: 12f, 13c, 14f, 16c, 17b, 18b, 19e,g

Large-scale line-balancing problems, like large process-layout problems, are often solved by computers. Several computer programs are available to handle the assignment of workstations on assembly lines with 100 (or more) individual work activities. Two computer routines, COMSOAL (Computer Method for Sequencing Operations for Assembly Lines)[8] and ASYBL (General Electric's Assembly Line Configuration program), are widely used in larger problems to evaluate the thousands, or even millions, of possible workstation combinations much more efficiently than could ever be done by hand.

▶ *In the case of slaughtering operations, the assembly line is actually a disassembly line. The line-balancing procedures described in this chapter are the same as for an assembly line. The chicken-processing plant shown here must balance the work of several hundred employees. The total labor content in each of the chickens processed is a few minutes.*

Cary Wolinsky, Jupiter Images—Foodpix-Cretas-Brand
X-Banana Stock-Picture Quest

Summary

Layouts make a substantial difference in operating efficiency. The seven layout situations discussed in this chapter are (1) office, (2) retail, (3) warehouse, (4) fixed position, (5) process oriented, (6) work cells, and (7) product oriented. A variety of techniques have been developed to solve these layout problems. Office layouts often seek to maximize information flows, retail firms focus on product exposure, and warehouses attempt to optimize the trade-off between storage space and material handling cost.

The fixed-position layout problem attempts to minimize material handling costs within the constraint of limited space at the site. Process layouts minimize travel distances times the number of trips. Product layouts focus on reducing waste and the imbalance in an assembly line. Work cells are the result of identifying a family of products that justify a special configuration of machinery and equipment that reduces material travel and adjusts imbalances with cross-trained personnel.

Often, the issues in a layout problem are so wide-ranging that finding an optimal solution is not possible. For this reason, layout decisions, although the subject of substantial research effort, remain something of an art.

[8]G. W. De Puy, "Applying the COMSOAL Computer Heuristic," *Computers & Industrial Engineering* 38, no. 3 (October 2000): 413–422.

Key Terms

Office layout	Customizing	Focused work center *(p. 364)*
Retail layout	Fixed-position layout	Focused factory *(p. 364)*
Slotting fees	Process-oriented layout	Fabrication line *(p. 364)*
Servicescape	Job lots	Assembly line *(p. 365)*
Warehouse layout	CRAFT	Assembly-line balancing *(p. 365)*
Cross-docking	Work cell	Cycle time *(p. 367)*
Random stocking	Takt time	Heuristic *(p. 368)*

Using Software to Solve Layout Problems

In addition to the many commercial software packages available for addressing layout problems, Excel OM and POM for Windows, both of which accompany this text, contain modules for the process problem and the assembly-line-balancing problem.

✗ Using Excel OM

Excel OM can assist in evaluating a series of department to work area assignments like the one we saw for the Walters Company in Example 1. The layout module can generate an optimal solution by enumeration or by computing the "total movement" cost for each layout you wish to examine. As such, it provides a speedy calculator for each flow–distance pairing.

Program 1 illustrates our inputs in the top two tables. We first enter department flows, then provide distances between work areas. Entering area assignments on a trial-and-error basis in the upper left of the top table generates movement computations at the bottom of the screen. Total movement is recalculated each time we try a new area assignment. It turns out that the assignment shown is optimal at 430 feet of movement.

P Using POM for Windows

The POM for Windows facility layout module can be used to place up to 10 departments in 10 rooms to minimize the total distance traveled as a function of the distances between the rooms and the flow between departments. The program exchanges departments until no exchange will reduce the total amount of movement, meaning an optimal solution has been reached.

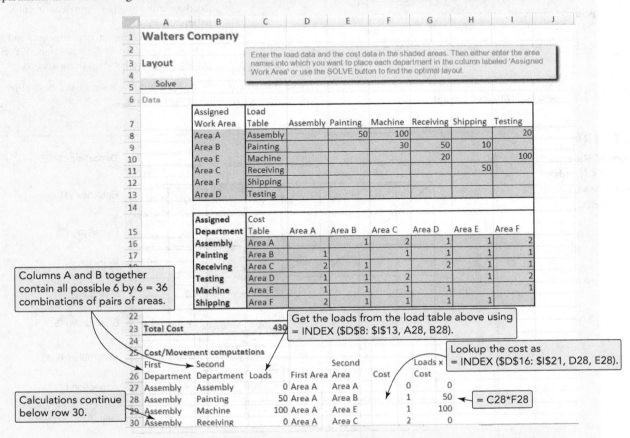

▲ **Program 1** Using Excel OM's Process Layout Module to Solve the Walters Company Problem in Example 1

The POM for Windows and Excel OM modules for line balancing can handle a line with up to 99 tasks, each with up to 6 immediate predecessors. In this program, cycle time can be entered either (1) *given*, if known, or (2) the *demand* rate can be entered with time available as shown. All five "heuristic rules" are used: (1) longest operation (task) time, (2) most following tasks, (3) ranked positional weight, (4) shortest operation (task) time, and (5) least number of following tasks. No one rule can guarantee an optimal solution, but POM for Windows displays the number of stations needed for each rule.

Solved Problems

⊙ **Virtual Office Hours help is available on Student DVD.**

Solved Problem 1

Aero Maintenance is a small aircraft engine maintenance facility located in Wichita, Kansas. Its new administrator, Ann Daniel, decides to improve material flow in the facility, using the process-layout method she studied at Wichita State University. The current layout of Aero Maintenance's eight departments is shown in Figure 15.

Current Aero Maintenance Layout

Area A	Area B	Area C	Area D	
Entrance (1)	Receiving (2)	Parts (3)	Metallurgy (4)	10'
Breakdown (5)	Assembly (6)	Inspection (7)	Test (8)	10'
Area E	Area F	Area G	Area H	

← 40' →

▲ **Figure 15** Aero Maintenance Layout

The only physical restriction perceived by Daniel is the need to keep the entrance in its current location. All other departments can be moved to a different work area (each 10 feet square) if layout analysis indicates a move would be beneficial.

First, Daniel analyzes records to determine the number of material movements among departments in an average month. These data are shown in Figure 16. Her objective, Daniel decides, is to lay out the departments so as to minimize the total movement (distance traveled) of material in the facility. She writes her objective as:

$$\text{Minimize material movement} = \sum_{i=1}^{8} \sum_{j=1}^{8} X_{ij} C_{ij}$$

where X_{ij} = number of material movements per month (loads or trips) moving from department i to department j

        C_{ij} = distance in feet between departments i and j (which, in this case, is the equivalent of cost per load to move between departments)

Note that this is only a slight modification of the cost-objective equation shown earlier in the selection.

► **Figure 16**

Number of Material Movements (Loads) between Departments in One Month

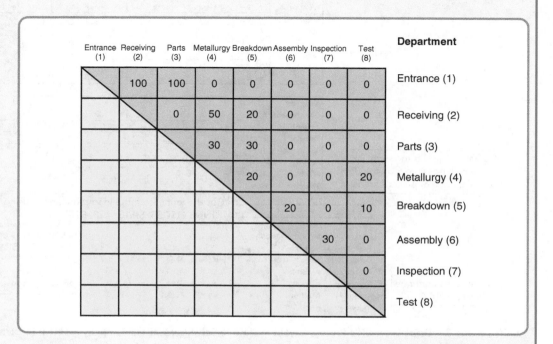

	Entrance (1)	Receiving (2)	Parts (3)	Metallurgy (4)	Breakdown (5)	Assembly (6)	Inspection (7)	Test (8)	Department
		100	100	0	0	0	0	0	Entrance (1)
			0	50	20	0	0	0	Receiving (2)
				30	30	0	0	0	Parts (3)
					20	0	0	20	Metallurgy (4)
						20	0	10	Breakdown (5)
							30	0	Assembly (6)
								0	Inspection (7)
									Test (8)

Daniel assumes that adjacent departments, such as entrance (now in work area A) and receiving (now in work area B), have a walking distance of 10 feet. Diagonal departments are also considered adjacent and assigned a distance of 10 feet. Nonadjacent departments, such as the entrance and parts (now in area C) or the entrance and inspection (area G) are 20 feet apart, and nonadjacent rooms, such as entrance and metallurgy (area D), are 30 feet apart. (Hence, 10 feet is considered 10 units of cost, 20 feet is 20 units of cost, and 30 feet is 30 units of cost.)

Given the above information, redesign Aero Maintenance's layout to improve its material flow efficiency.

solution

First, establish Aero Maintenance's current layout, as shown in Figure 17. Then, by analyzing the current layout, compute material movement:

$$
\begin{aligned}
\text{Total movement} = \quad & (100 \times 10') \quad + \quad (100 \times 20') \quad + \quad (50 \times 20') \quad + \quad (20 \times 10') \\
& \quad\; \text{1 to 2} \qquad\qquad\quad \text{1 to 3} \qquad\qquad\; \text{2 to 4} \qquad\qquad\; \text{2 to 5} \\
+ \quad & (30 \times 10') \quad + \quad (30 \times 20') \quad + \quad (20 \times 30') \quad + \quad (20 \times 10') \\
& \quad\; \text{3 to 4} \qquad\qquad\quad \text{3 to 5} \qquad\qquad\; \text{4 to 5} \qquad\qquad\; \text{4 to 8} \\
+ \quad & (20 \times 10') \quad + \quad (10 \times 30') \quad + \quad (30 \times 10') \\
& \quad\; \text{5 to 6} \qquad\qquad\quad \text{5 to 8} \qquad\qquad\; \text{6 to 7} \\
= \quad & 1{,}000 + 2{,}000 + 1{,}000 + 200 + 300 + 600 + 600 \\
& + 200 + 200 + 300 + 300 \\
= \quad & 6{,}700 \text{ feet}
\end{aligned}
$$

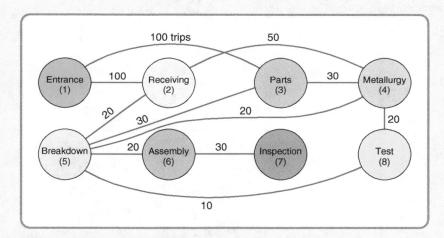

▲ **Figure 17** Current Material Flow

Propose a new layout that will reduce the current figure of 6,700 feet. Two useful changes, for example, are to switch departments 3 and 5 and to interchange departments 4 and 6. This change would result in the schematic shown in Figure 18:

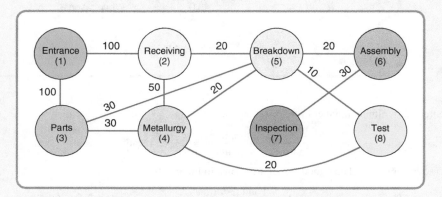

▲ **Figure 18** Improved Layout

$$\text{Total movement} = \begin{matrix} (100 \times 10') & + & (100 \times 10') & + & (50 \times 10') & + & (20 \times 10') \\ \text{1 to 2} & & \text{1 to 3} & & \text{2 to 4} & & \text{2 to 5} \end{matrix}$$

$$\begin{matrix} + & (30 \times 10') & + & (30 \times 20') & + & (20 \times 10') & + & (20 \times 20') \\ & \text{3 to 4} & & \text{3 to 5} & & \text{4 to 5} & & \text{4 to 8} \end{matrix}$$

$$\begin{matrix} + & (20 \times 10') & + & (10 \times 10') & + & (30 \times 10') \\ & \text{5 to 6} & & \text{5 to 8} & & \text{6 to 7} \end{matrix}$$

$$= 1{,}000 + 1{,}000 + 500 + 200 + 300 + 600 + 200$$
$$+ 400 + 200 + 100 + 300$$

$$= 4{,}800 \text{ feet}$$

Do you see any room for further improvement?

Solved Problem 2

The assembly line whose activities are shown in Figure 19 has an 8-minute cycle time. Draw the precedence graph and find the minimum possible number of workstations. Then arrange the work activities into workstations so as to balance the line. What is the efficiency of your line balance?

Task	Performance Time (minutes)	Task Must Follow This Task
A	5	—
B	3	A
C	4	B
D	3	B
E	6	C
F	1	C
G	4	D, E, F
H	2	G
	28	

▶ **Figure 19**

Four-Station Solution to the Line-Balancing Problem

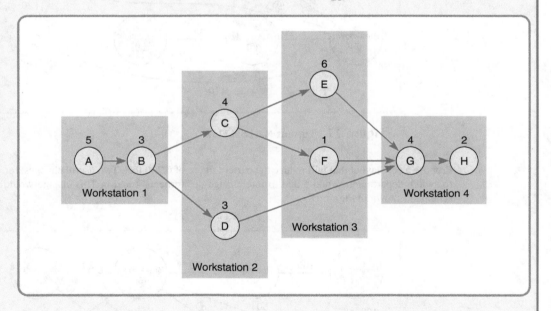

Solution

The theoretical minimum number of workstations is:

$$\frac{\Sigma t_i}{\text{Cycle time}} = \frac{28 \text{ minutes}}{8 \text{ minutes}} = 3.5, \text{ or 4 stations}$$

The precedence graph and one good layout are shown in Figure 19.

$$\text{Efficiency} = \frac{\text{Total task time}}{(\text{Number of workstations}) \times (\text{Largest cycle time})} = \frac{28}{(4)(8)} = 87.5\%$$

Self-Test

- **Before taking the self-test**, *refer to the learning objectives listed at the beginning of the chapter and the key terms listed at the end of the selection.*
- *Use the key at the back of the text to **correct** your answers.*
- **Restudy** *pages that correspond to any questions you answered incorrectly or material you feel uncertain about.*

1. In process-oriented and fixed-position layouts, it is important to minimize the costs of:
   a) raw materials
   b) material handling
   c) special purpose machinery
   d) skilled labor

2. A major assumption of stability of demand is important for justifying which of the following layout types?
   a) product layout
   b) process layout
   c) fixed-position layout
   d) all of the above

3. A fixed-position layout:
   a) groups workers to provide for movement of information
   b) addresses the layout requirements of large, bulky projects such as ships and buildings
   c) seeks the best machine utilization in continuous production
   d) allocates shelf space based on customer behavior
   e) deals with low-volume, high-variety production

4. A process-oriented layout:
   a) groups workers to provide for movement of information
   b) addresses the layout requirements of large, bulky projects such as ships and buildings
   c) seeks the best machine utilization in continuous production
   d) allocates shelf space based on customer behavior
   e) deals with low-volume, high-variety production

5. A big advantage of a process-oriented layout is:
   a) its low cost
   b) its flexibility in equipment and labor assignment
   c) the simplified scheduling problem presented by this layout strategy
   d) the ability to employ low-skilled labor

6. The fundamental layout strategies include:
   a) _____
   b) _____
   c) _____
   d) _____
   e) _____
   f) _____

7. For a focused work center or focused factory to be appropriate requires:
   a) _____
   b) _____
   c) _____

8. Before considering a product-oriented layout, we would wish to be certain that:
   a) _____
   b) _____
   c) _____
   d) _____

Active Model Exercise

This active model appears on your CD-ROM. It allows you to evaluate parameters in a process layout analysis. Active Model 9.1 contains a device for pairwise exchange of processes in work areas. There is a drop-down box that tells the software which two processes to swap. There is a Swap button that will make the switch. If the switch does not help, pressing the Swap button a second time will return the two processes to the work areas they were in before the swap.

Questions

1. What is the current total cost?

2. Assembly and Machine Shop have the highest degree of interaction. Would it be better to swap Assembly and Painting or Machine Shop and Painting to get Assembly and Machine Shop next to each other?

3. Use the Swap button one swap at a time. If the swap helps, move to the next pair. If not, press Swap to put the departments back. What is the minimum total cost after all swaps have been tried?

4. Look at the two data tables and use the yellow-shaded column to put processes in areas. What assignments lead to the minimum cost? What is this cost?

▼ **Active Model 1** Process Layout Model Using Walters Co. Data in Example 1

Process - Oriented Layout

	Area A	Area B	Area C
	Assembly	Painting	Machine Shop
	Receiving	Shipping	Testing
	Area D	Area E	Area F

Reset Data   Questions

Assigned Work Area	Load Table	Assembly	Painting	Machine Shop	Receiving	Shipping	Testing
Area A	Assembly		50	100	0	0	20
Area B	Painting			30	50	10	0
Area C	Machine Shop				20	0	100
Area D	Receiving					50	0
Area E	Shipping						0
Area F	Testing						

Assembly & Painting   Swap

Total cost $ 570

Assigned Department	Cost table	Area A	Area B	Area C	Area D	Area E	Area F
Assembly	Area A		1	2	1	2	2
Painting	Area B			1	1	1	2
Machine Shop	Area C				2	2	1
Receiving	Area D					1	2
Shipping	Area E						1
Testing	Area F						

Cost/Movement computations

First Department	Second Department	Loads	First Area	Second Area	Cost	Loads x Cost
Assembly	Assembly	0	Area A	Area A	0	0
Assembly	Painting	50	Area A	Area B	1	50
Assembly	Machine Shop	100	Area A	Area C	2	200
Assembly	Receiving	0	Area A	Area D	1	0
Assembly	Shipping	0	Area A	Area E	2	0
Assembly	Testing	20	Area A	Area F	2	40
Painting	Assembly	0	Area B	Area A	1	0
Painting	Painting	0	Area B	Area B	0	0

Internet and Student CD-ROM/DVD Exercises

Visit our Companion Web site or use your student CD-ROM/DVD to help with material in this chapter.

 On Our Companion Web Site,
www.prenhall.com/heizer
- Self-Study Quizzes
- Internet Case
- Practice Problems
- Virtual Company Tour
- PowerPoint Lecture

 On Your Student CD-ROM
- Practice Problems
- Active Model Exercise
- Excel OM
- Excel OM Data Files
- POM for Windows

 On Your Student DVD
- Video Clips and Video Cases
- Virtual Office Hours for Solved Problems

Discussion Questions

1. What are the seven layout strategies presented in this chapter?
2. What are the three factors that complicate a fixed-position layout?
3. What are the advantages and disadvantages of process layout?
4. How would an analyst obtain data and determine the number of trips in:
   (a) a hospital?
   (b) a machine shop?
   (c) an auto-repair shop?
5. What are the advantages and disadvantages of product layout?
6. What are the four assumptions (or preconditions) of establishing layout for high-volume, low-variety products?
7. What are the three forms of work cells discussed in the textbook?
8. What are the advantages and disadvantages of work cells?
9. What are the requirements for a focused work center or focused factory to be appropriate?
10. What are the two major trends influencing office layout?
11. What layout variables would you consider particularly important in an office layout where computer programs are written?
12. What layout innovations have you noticed recently in retail establishments?
13. What are the variables that a manager can manipulate in a retail layout?
14. Visit a local supermarket and sketch its layout. What are your observations regarding departments and their locations?
15. What is random stocking?
16. What information is necessary for random stocking to work?
17. Explain the concept of cross-docking.
18. What is a heuristic? Name several that can be used in assembly-line balancing.

Ethical Dilemma

Although buried by mass customization and a proliferation of new products of numerous sizes and variations, grocery chains continue to seek to maximize payoff from their layout. Their layout includes a marketable commodity—shelf space—and they charge for it. This charge is known as a *slotting fee*. Recent estimates are that food manufacturers now spend some 13% of sales on trade promotions, which is paid to grocers to get them to promote and discount the manufacturer's products. A portion of these fees is for slotting; but slotting fees drive up the manufacturer's cost. They also put the small company with a new product at a disadvantage, because small companies with limited resources are squeezed out of the market place. Slotting fees may also mean that customers may no longer be able to find the special local brand. How ethical are slotting fees?

Problems*

• • **1** Michael Plumb's job shop has four work areas, A, B, C, and D. Distances in feet between centers of the work areas are:

	A	B	C	D
A	—	4	9	7
B	—	—	6	8
C	—	—	—	10
D	—	—	—	—

Workpieces moved, in 100s of workpieces per week, between pairs of work areas, are:

	A	B	C	D
A	—	8	7	4
B	—	—	3	2
C	—	—	—	6
D	—	—	—	—

It costs Michael $1 to move 1 work piece 1 foot. What is the weekly total material handling cost of the layout? **Px**

• • **2** A Missouri job shop has four departments—machining (M), dipping in a chemical bath (D), finishing (F), and plating (P)—assigned to four work areas. The operations manager, Mary Marrs, has gathered the following data for this job shop as it is currently laid out (Plan A).

100s of Workpieces Moved Between Work Areas Each Year Plan A

	M	D	F	P
M	—	6	18	2
D	—	—	4	2
F	—	—	—	18
P	—	—	—	—

Distances Between Work Areas (Departments) in Feet

	M	D	F	P
M	—	20	12	8
D	—	—	6	10
F	—	—	—	4
P	—	—	—	—

It costs $0.50 to move 1 workpiece 1 foot in the job shop. Marrs' goal is to find a layout that has the lowest material handling cost.
a) Determine cost of the current layout, Plan A, from the data above.

Note: **Px** means the problem may be solved with POM for Windows and/or Excel OM.

b) One alternative is to switch those departments with the high loads, namely, finishing (F) and plating (P), which alters the distance between them and machining (M) and dipping (D), as follows:

Distances Between Work Areas (Departments) in Feet Plan B

	M	D	F	P
M	—	20	8	12
D	—	—	10	6
F	—	—	—	4
P	—	—	—	—

What is the cost of *this* layout?
c) Marrs now wants you to evaluate Plan C, which also switches milling (M) and drilling (D), below.

Distance Between Work Areas (Departments) in Feet Plan C

	M	D	F	P
M	—	20	10	6
D	—	—	8	12
F	—	—	—	4
P	—	—	—	—

What is the cost of *this* layout?
d) Which layout is best from a cost perspective? **Px**

• **3** Three departments—milling (M), drilling (D), and sawing (S)—are assigned to three work areas in Samuel Smith's machine shop in Baltimore. The number of work pieces moved per day and the distances between the centers of the work areas, in feet, are shown below.

Pieces Moved Between Work Areas Each Day

	M	D	S
M	—	23	32
D	—	—	20
S	—	—	—

Distances Between Centers of Work Areas (Departments) in Feet

	M	D	S
M	—	10	5
D	—	—	8
S	—	—	—

It costs $2 to move 1 workpiece 1 foot.
What is the cost? **Px**

• • 4 Roy Creasey Enterprises, a machine shop, is planning to move to a new, larger location. The new building will be 60 feet long by 40 feet wide. Creasey envisions the building as having six distinct production areas, roughly equal in size. He feels strongly about safety and intends to have marked pathways throughout the building to facilitate the movement of people and materials. See the following building schematic.

Building Schematic (with work areas 1–6)

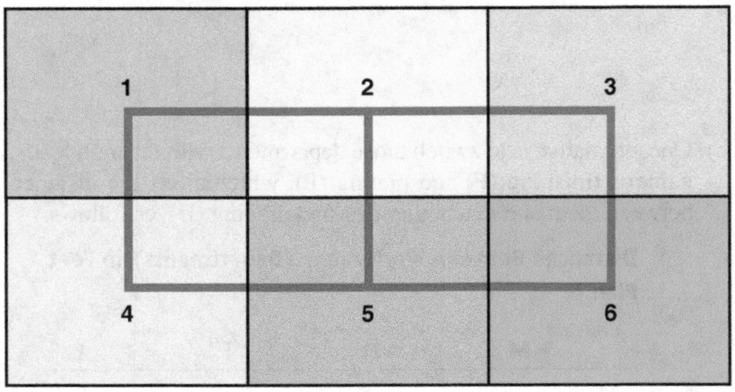

His foreman has completed a month-long study of the number of loads of material that have moved from one process to another in the current building. This information is contained in the following flow matrix.

Flow Matrix between Production Processes

To From	Materials	Welding	Drills	Lathes	Grinders	Benders
Materials	0	100	50	0	0	50
Welding	25	0	0	50	0	0
Drills	25	0	0	0	50	0
Lathes	0	25	0	0	20	0
Grinders	50	0	100	0	0	0
Benders	10	0	20	0	0	0

Finally, Creasey has developed the following matrix to indicate distances between the work areas shown in the building schematic.

Distance between Work Areas

	1	2	3	4	5	6
1		20	40	20	40	60
2			20	40	20	40
3				60	40	20
4					20	40
5						20
6						

What is the appropriate layout of the new building?

• • 5 Registration at Southern University has always been a time of emotion, commotion, and lines. Students must move among four stations to complete the trying semiannual process. Last semes-

Interstation Activity Mix

	Pick up paperwork and forms (A)	Advising station (B)	Pick up class cards (C)	Verification of status and payment (D)
Paperwork/forms (A)	---	450	550	50
Advising (B)	350	---	200	0
Class cards (C)	0	0	---	750
Verification/payment (D)	0	0	0	---

Existing Layout

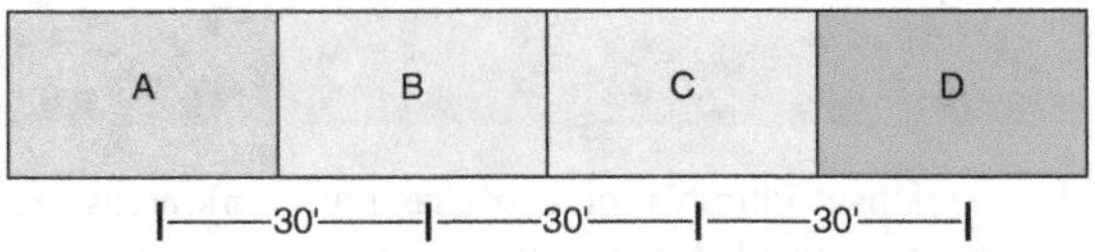

▲ **Figure 20** Registration Flow of Students

ter's registration, held in the fieldhouse, is described in Figure 20. You can see, for example, that 450 students moved from the paperwork station (A) to advising (B), and 550 went directly from A to picking up their class cards (C). Graduate students, who for the most part had preregistered, proceeded directly from A to the station where registration is verified and payment collected (D). The layout used last semester is also shown in Figure 20. The registrar is preparing to set up this semester's stations and is anticipating similar numbers.

a) What is the "load × distance," or "movement cost," of the layout shown?

b) Provide an improved layout and compute its movement cost. **Px**

• • • 6 You have just been hired as the director of operations for Reid Chocolates, a purveyor of exceptionally fine candies. Reid Chocolates has two kitchen layouts under consideration for its recipe making and testing department. The strategy is to provide the best kitchen layout possible so that food scientists can devote their time and energy to product improvement, not wasted effort in the kitchen. You have been asked to evaluate these two kitchen layouts and to prepare a recommendation for your boss, Mr. Reid, so that he can proceed to place the contract for building the kitchens. (See Figure 21(a), and Figure 21(b) on the next page.) **Px**

▼ **Figure 21(a)** Layout Options

Number of trips between work centers:

To: From:	Refrigerator 1	Counter 2	Sink 3	Storage 4	Stove 5
Refrig. 1	0	8	13	0	0
Counter 2	5	0	3	3	8
Sink 3	3	12	0	4	0
Storage 4	3	0	0	0	5
Stove 5	0	8	4	10	0

(*continued*)

Kitchen layout #1

Walking distance in feet

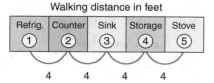

Kitchen layout #2

Walking distance in feet

▲ **Figure 21(b)** (*continued*)

• • **7** Reid Chocolates (see Problem 6) is considering a third layout, as shown below. Evaluate its effectiveness in trip-distance feet. **Px**

Kitchen layout #3

Walking distance in feet

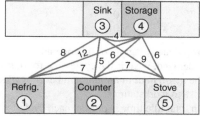

• • **8** Reid Chocolates (see Problems 6 and 7) has yet two more layouts to consider.

a) Layout 4 is shown below. What is the total trip distance?

b) Layout 5, which also follows, has what total trip distance? **Px**

Kitchen layout #4

Walking distance in feet

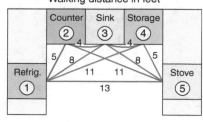

Kitchen layout #5

Walking distance in feet

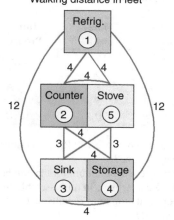

• • **9** Six processes are to be laid out in six areas along a long corridor at Linda Babat Accounting Services. The distance between adjacent work centers is 40 feet. The number of trips between work centers is given in the following table:

	Trips between Processes					
		To				
From	**A**	**B**	**C**	**D**	**E**	**F**
A		18	25	73	12	54
B			96	23	31	45
C				41	22	20
D					19	57
E						48
F						

a) Assign the processes to the work areas in a way that minimizes the total flow, using a method that places processes with highest flow adjacent to each other.

b) What assignment minimizes the total traffic flow? **Px**

• • **10** After an extensive product analysis using group technology, Bob Buerlein has identified a product he believes should be pulled out of his process facility and handled in a work cell. Bob has identified the following operations as necessary for the work cell. The customer expects delivery of 250 units per day, and the work day is 420 minutes.

a) What is the takt time?

b) How many employees should be cross-trained for the cell?

c) Which operations may warrant special consideration?

Operation	**Standard Time (min)**
Shear	1.1
Bend	1.1
Weld	1.7
Clean	3.1
Paint	1.0

• • **11** Stanford Rosenberg Electronics wants to establish an assembly line for producing a new product, the Personal Little

Assistant (PLA). The tasks, task times, and immediate predecessors for the tasks are as follows:

Task	Time (sec)	Immediate Predecessors
A	12	—
B	15	A
C	8	A
D	5	B, C
E	20	D

Rosenberg's goal is to produce 180 PLAs per hour.
a) What is the cycle time?
b) What is the theoretical minimum for the number of workstations that Rosenberg can achieve in this assembly line?
c) Can the theoretical minimum actually be reached when workstations are assigned? **Px**

•• **12**   South Carolina Furniture, Inc., produces all types of office furniture. The "Executive Secretary" is a chair that has been designed using ergonomics to provide comfort during long work hours. The chair sells for $130. There are 480 minutes available during the day, and the average daily demand has been 50 chairs. There are eight tasks:

Task	Performance Time (min)	Task Must Follow Task Listed Below
A	4	—
B	7	—
C	6	A, B
D	5	C
E	6	D
F	7	E
G	8	E
H	6	F, G

a) Draw a precedence diagram of this operation.
b) What is the cycle time for this operation?
c) What is the *theoretical* minimum number of workstations?
d) Assign tasks to workstations.
e) How much total idle time is present each day?
f) What is the overall efficiency of the assembly line? **Px**

•• **13**   Rita Gibson Appliances wants to establish an assembly line to manufacture its new product, the Mini-Me Microwave Oven. The goal is to produce five Mini-Me Microwave Ovens per hour. The tasks, task times, and immediate predecessors for producing one Mini-Me Microwave Oven are as follows:

Task	Time (min)	Immediate Predecessors
A	10	—
B	12	A
C	8	A, B
D	6	B, C
E	6	C
F	6	D, E

a) What is the *theoretical* minimum for the smallest number of workstations that Gibson can achieve in this assembly line?
b) Graph the assembly line and assign workers to workstations. Can you assign them with the theoretical minimum?
c) What is the efficiency of *your* assignment? **Px**

•• **14**   The Temple Toy Company has decided to manufacture a new toy tractor, the production of which is broken into six steps. The demand for the tractor is 4,800 units per 40-hour workweek:

Task	Performance Time (sec)	Predecessors
A	20	None
B	30	A
C	15	A
D	15	A
E	10	B, C
F	30	D, E

a) Draw a precedence diagram of this operation.
b) Given the demand, what is the cycle time for this operation?
c) What is the *theoretical* minimum number of workstations?
d) Assign tasks to workstations.
e) How much total idle time is present each cycle?
f) What is the overall efficiency of the assembly line with five stations; and with six stations? **Px**

•• **15**   The following table details the tasks required for Dallas-based T. Liscio Industries to manufacture a fully portable industrial vacuum cleaner. The times in the table are in minutes. Demand forecasts indicate a need to operate with a cycle time of 10 minutes.

Activity	Activity Description	Immediate Predecessors	Time
A	Attach wheels to tub	—	5
B	Attach motor to lid	—	1.5
C	Attach battery pack	B	3
D	Attach safety cutoff	C	4
E	Attach filters	B	3
F	Attach lid to tub	A, E	2
G	Assemble attachments	—	3
H	Function test	D, F, G	3.5
I	Final inspection	H	2
J	Packing	I	2

a) Draw the appropriate precedence diagram for this production line.
b) Assign tasks to workstations and determine how much idle time is present each cycle?
c) Discuss how this balance could be improved to 100%
d) What is the *theoretical* minimum number of workstations? **Px**

•• **16**   Tailwind, Inc., produces high-quality but expensive training shoes for runners. The Tailwind shoe, which sells for $210, contains both gas- and liquid-filled compartments to provide more stability and better protection against knee, foot, and back injuries. Manufacturing the shoes requires 10 separate tasks. There are 400 minutes available for manufacturing the shoes in the plant each day. Daily demand is 60. The information for the tasks is as follows:

Task	Performance Time (min)	Task Must Follow Task Listed Below
A	1	—
B	3	A
C	2	B
D	4	B
E	1	C, D
F	3	A
G	2	F
H	5	G
I	1	E, H
J	3	I

a) Draw the precedence diagram.
b) Assign tasks to the minimum feasible number of workstations according to the "ranked positioned weight" decision rule.
c) What is the efficiency of the process?
d) What is the idle time per cycle? **Px**

•• **17** Mach 10 is a one-person sailboat designed to be used in the ocean. Manufactured by Creative Leisure, Mach 10 can handle 40-mph winds and seas over 10 feet. The final assembly plant is in Cupertino, California. At this time, 200 minutes are available each day to manufacture Mach 10. The daily demand is 60 boats. Given the following information,
a) Draw the precedence diagram and assign tasks to the fewest workstations possible.
b) What is the efficiency of the assembly line?
c) What is the *theoretical* minimum number of workstations?
d) What is the idle time?

Task	Performance Time (min)	Task Must Follow Task Listed Below
A	1	—
B	1	A
C	2	A
D	1	C
E	3	C
F	1	C
G	1	D, E, F
H	2	B
I	1	G, H **Px**

•• **18** Because of the expected high demand for Mach 10, Creative Leisure has decided to increase manufacturing time available to produce the Mach 10 (see Problem 17).
a) If demand remained the same and 300 minutes were available each day, how many workstations would be needed?
b) What would be the efficiency of the new system?
c) What would be the impact on the system if 400 minutes were available? **Px**

••• **19** Dr. Lori Baker, operations manager at Nesa Electronics, prides herself on excellent assembly-line balancing. She has been told that the firm needs to complete 96 instruments per 24-hour day. The assembly-line activities are:

Task	Time (min)	Predecessors
A	3	—
B	6	—
C	7	A
D	5	A, B
E	2	B
F	4	C
G	5	F
H	7	D, E
I	1	H
J	6	E
K	4	G, I, J
	50	

a) Draw the precedence diagram.
b) If the daily (24-hour) production rate is 96 units, what is the highest allowable cycle time?
c) If the cycle time after allowances is given as 10 minutes, what is the daily (24-hour) production rate?

d) With a 10-minute cycle time, what is the theoretical minimum number of stations with which the line can be balanced?
e) With a 10-minute cycle time and six workstations, what is the efficiency?
f) What is the total idle time per cycle with a 10-minute cycle time and six workstations?
g) What is the best work station assignment you can make without exceeding a 10-minute cycle time and what is its efficiency? **Px**

•• **20** Suppose production requirements in Solved Problem 2 increase and require a reduction in cycle time from 8 minutes to 7 minutes. Balance the line once again, using the new cycle time. Note that it is not possible to combine task times so as to group tasks into the minimum number of workstations. This condition occurs in actual balancing problems fairly often. **Px**

•• **21** The preinduction physical examination given by the U.S. Army involves the following seven activities:

Activity	Average Time (min)
Medical history	10
Blood tests	8
Eye examination	5
Measurements (i.e., weight, height, blood pressure)	7
Medical examination	16
Psychological interview	12
Exit medical evaluation	10

These activities can be performed in any order, with two exceptions: Medical history must be taken first, and exit medical evaluation is last. At present, there are three paramedics and two physicians on duty during each shift. Only physicians can perform exit evaluations and conduct psychological interviews. Other activities can be carried out by either physicians or paramedics.
a) Develop a layout and balance the line.
b) How many people can be processed per hour?
c) Which activity accounts for the current bottleneck?
d) What is the total idle time per cycle?
e) If one more physician and one more paramedic can be placed on duty, how would you redraw the layout? What is the new throughput?

••• **22** Frank Pianki's company wants to establish an assembly line to manufacture its new product, the iScan phone. Frank's goal

271

is to produce 60 iScans per hour. Tasks, task times, and immediate predecessors are as follows:

Task	Time (sec)	Immediate Predecessors	Task	Time (sec)	Immediate Predecessors
A	40	—	F	25	C
B	30	A	G	15	C
C	50	A	H	20	D, E
D	40	B	I	18	F, G
E	6	B	J	30	H, I

a) What is the theoretical minimum for the number of workstations that Frank can achieve in this assembly line?

b) Use the *most following tasks* heuristic to balance an assembly line for the iScan phone.

c) How many workstations are in your answer to (b)?

d) What is the efficiency of your answer to (b)? **Px**

•••• **23** As the Cottrell Bicycle Co. of St. Louis completes plans for its new assembly line, it identifies 25 different tasks in the production process. VP of Operations Jonathan Cottrell now faces the job of balancing the line. He lists precedences and provides time estimates for each step based on work-sampling tech-

niques. His goal is to produce 1,000 bicycles per standard 40-hour workweek.

Task	Time (sec)	Precedence Tasks	Task	Time (sec)	Precedence Tasks
K3	60	—	E3	109	F3
K4	24	K3	D6	53	F4
K9	27	K3	D7	72	F9, E2, E3
J1	66	K3	D8	78	E3, D6
J2	22	K3	D9	37	D6
J3	3	—	C1	78	F7
G4	79	K4, K9	B3	72	D7, D8, D9, C1
G5	29	K9, J1	B5	108	C1
F3	32	J2	B7	18	B3
F4	92	J2	A1	52	B5
F7	21	J3	A2	72	B5
F9	126	G4	A3	114	B7, A1, A2
E2	18	G5, F3			

a) Balance this operation, using various heuristics. Which is best and why?

b) What happens if the firm can change to a 41-hour workweek? **Px**

Case Studies

State Automobile License Renewals

Henry Coupe, the manager of a metropolitan branch office of the state department of motor vehicles, attempted to analyze the driver's license–renewal operations. He had to perform several steps. After examining the license-renewal process, he identified those steps and associated times required to perform each step, as shown in the following table:

State Automobile License-Renewal Process Times

Step	Average Time to Perform (sec)
1. Review renewal application for correctness	15
2. Process and record payment	30
3. Check file for violations and restrictions	60
4. Conduct eye test	40
5. Photograph applicant	20
6. Issue temporary license	30

Coupe found that each step was assigned to a different person. Each application was a separate process in the sequence shown. He determined that his office should be prepared to accommodate a maximum demand of processing 120 renewal applicants per hour.

He observed that work was unevenly divided among clerks and that the clerk responsible for checking violations tended to shortcut her task to keep up with the others. Long lines built up during the maximum-demand periods.

Coupe also found that steps 1 to 4 were handled by general clerks who were each paid $12 per hour. Step 5 was performed by a photographer paid $16 per hour. (Branch offices were charged $10 per hour for each camera to perform photography.) Step 6, issuing temporary licenses, was required by state policy to be handled by uniformed motor vehicle officers. Officers were paid $18 per hour but could be assigned to any job except photography.

A review of the jobs indicated that step 1, reviewing applications for correctness, had to be performed before any other step could be taken. Similarly, step 6, issuing temporary licenses, could not be performed until all the other steps were completed.

Henry Coupe was under severe pressure to increase productivity and reduce costs, but he was also told by the regional director that he must accommodate the demand for renewals. Otherwise, "heads would roll."

Discussion Questions

1. What is the maximum number of applications per hour that can be handled by the present configuration of the process?

2. How many applications can be processed per hour if a second clerk is added to check for violations?

3. Assuming the addition of a second clerk, what is the maximum number of applications the process can handle?

4. How would you suggest modifying the process to accommodate 120 applications per hour?

Source: Updated from a case by W. Earl Sasser, Paul R. Olson, and D. Daryl Wyckoff, *Management of Services Operations: Text, Cases, and Readings* (Boston: Allyn & Bacon).

Laying Out Arnold Palmer Hospital's New Facility

When Orlando's Arnold Palmer Hospital began plans to create a new 273-bed, 11-story hospital across the street from its existing facility, which was bursting at the seams in terms of capacity, a massive planning process began. The $100 million building, opened in 2006, was long overdue, according to Executive Director Kathy Swanson. "We started Arnold Palmer Hospital in 1989, with a mission to provide quality services for children and women in a comforting, family-friendly environment. Since then we have served well over 1.5 million women and children and now deliver more than 12,000 babies a year. By 2001, we simply ran out of room, and it was time for us to grow."

The new hospital's unique, circular pod design provides a maximally efficient layout in all areas of the hospital, creating a patient-centered environment. *Servicescape* design features include a serene environment created through the use of warm colors, private rooms with pull-down Murphy beds for family members, 14-foot ceilings, and natural lighting with oversized windows in patient rooms. But these radical new features did not come easily. "This pod concept with a central nursing area and pie-shaped rooms resulted from over 1,000 planning meetings of 35 user groups, extensive motion and time studies, and computer simulations of the daily movements of nurses," says Swanson.

In a traditional linear hospital layout, called the *racetrack* design, patient rooms line long hallways, and a nurse might walk 2.7 miles per day serving patient needs at Arnold Palmer. "Some nurses spent 30% of their time simply walking. With the nursing shortage and the high cost of health care professionals, efficiency is a major concern," added Swanson. With the nursing station in the center of 10- or 12-bed circular pods, no patient room is more than 14 feet from a station. The time savings are in the 20% range. Swanson pointed to Figures 22 and 23 as examples of the old and new walking and trip distances.*

Layout and walking distances, including some of the numbers in Figures 22 and 23, have been simplified for purposes of this case.

▶ Figure 22

Traditional Hospital Layout

Patient rooms are on two linear hallways with exterior windows. Supply rooms are on interior corridors. This layout is called a "racetrack" design.

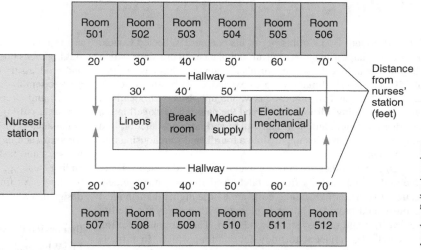

▶ Figure 23

New Pod Design for Hospital Layout

Note that each room is 14 feet from the pod's *local* nursing station. The *break rooms* and the *central medical station* are each about 60 feet from the local nursing pod. Pod *linen supply* rooms are also 14 feet from the local nursing station.

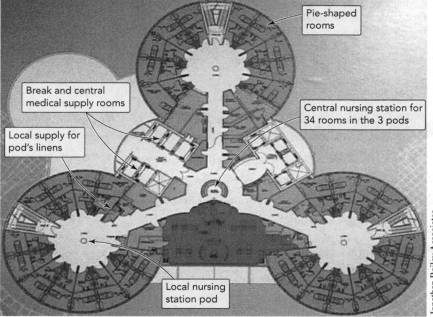

273

"We have also totally redesigned our neonatal rooms," says Swanson. "In the old system, there were 16 neonatal beds in a large and often noisy rectangular room. The new building features semiprivate rooms for these tiny babies. The rooms are much improved, with added privacy and a quiet, simulated night atmosphere, in addition to pull-down beds for parents to use. Our research shows that babies improve and develop much more quickly with this layout design. Layout and environment indeed impact patient care!"

Discussion Questions**

1. Identify the many variables that a hospital needs to consider in layout design.
2. What are the advantages of the circular pod design over the traditional linear hallway layout found in most hospitals?
3. Figure 22 illustrates a sample linear hallway layout. During a period of random observation, nurse Thomas Smith's day includes 6 trips from the nursing station to each of the 12 patient rooms (back and forth), 20 trips to the medical supply room, 5 trips to the break room, and 12 trips to the linen supply room. What is his total distance traveled in miles?
4. Figure 23 illustrates an architect's drawing of Arnold Palmer Hospital's new circular pod system. If nurse Susan Jones's day includes 7 trips from the nursing pod to each of the 12 rooms (back and forth), 20 trips to central medical supply, 6 trips to the break room, and 12 trips to the pod linen supply, how many miles does she walk during her shift? What are the differences in the travel times between the two nurses for this random day?
5. The concept of *servicescapes* is discussed in this chapter. Describe why this is so important at Arnold Palmer Hospital and give examples of its use in layout design.

**You may wish to view this video case on your DVD before addressing these questions.

Facility Layout at Wheeled Coach

Video Case

When President Bob Collins began his career at Wheeled Coach, the world's largest manufacturer of ambulances, there were only a handful of employees. Now the firm's Florida plant has a workforce of 350. The physical plant has also expanded, with offices, R&D, final assembly, and wiring, cabinetry, and upholstery work cells in one large building. Growth has forced the painting work cell into a separate building, aluminum fabrication and body installation into another, inspection and shipping into a fourth, and warehousing into yet another.

Like many other growing companies, Wheeled Coach was not able to design its facility from scratch. And although management realizes that material handling costs are a little higher than an ideal layout would provide, Collins is pleased with the way the facility has evolved and employees have adapted. The aluminum cutting work cell lies adjacent to body fabrication, which, in turn, is located next to the body-installation work cell. And while the vehicle must be driven across a street to one building for painting and then to another for final assembly, at least the ambulance is on wheels. Collins is also satisfied with the flexibility shown in design of the work cells. Cell construction is flexible and can accommodate changes in product mix and volume. Additionally, work cells are typically small and movable, with many work benches and staging racks borne on wheels so that they can be easily rearranged and products transported to the assembly line.

Assembly-line balancing is one key problem facing Wheeled Coach and every other repetitive manufacturer. Produced on a schedule calling for four 10-hour work days per week, once an ambulance is on one of the six final assembly lines, it *must* move forward each day to the next workstation. Balancing just enough workers and tasks at each of the seven workstations is a never-ending challenge. Too many workers end up running into each other; too few can't finish an ambulance in 7 days. Constant shifting of design and mix and improved analysis has led to frequent changes.

Discussion Questions*

1. What analytical techniques are available to help a company like Wheeled Coach deal with layout problems?
2. What suggestions would you make to Bob Collins about his layout?
3. How would you measure the "efficiency" of this layout?

*You may wish to view this video case on your DVD before addressing these questions.

Additional Case Studies

Internet case study: Visit our Companion Web site at www.prenhall.com/heizer for this free case study:

- **Microfix, Inc.:** This company needs to balance its PC manufacturing assembly line and deal with sensitivity analysis of time estimates.

Harvard has selected these Harvard Business School cases to accompany this chapter:

harvardbusinessonline.hbsp.harvard.edu

- **Toshiba; Ome Works** (#696-059): Deals with the design of an efficient notebook computer assembly line in the Ome, Japan, factory.
- **Mouawad Bangkok Rare Jewels Manufacturers Co. Ltd.** (A) (#696-056): This small Thai factory faces a challenging production control process.
- **Copeland Corp. (B)** (#686-089): A plant layout must be selected from two alternatives available to this Sydney, Australia, manufacturer.

Bibliography

Dekker, R., et al. "Improving Order-Picking Response Time at Ankor's Warehouse." *Interfaces* 34, no. 4 (July–August 2004): 303–313.

Francis, R. L., L. F. McGinnis, and J. A. White. *Facility Layout and Location*, 3rd ed. Upper Saddle River, NJ: Prentice Hall, 1998.

Heyer, N., and U. Wemmerlöv. *Reorganizing the Factory: Competing through Cellular Manufacturing.* Portland, OR: Productivity Press, 2002.

Kee, Micah R. "The Well-Ordered Warehouse." *APICS: The Performance Advantage* (March 2003): 20–24.

Kulwiec, Ray. "Crossdocking as a Supply Chain Strategy." *Target* 20, no. 3 (third issue 2004): 28–35.

Larson, S. "Extreme Makover—OR Edition." *Nursing Management* (November 2005): 26.

Owen, Robin. "Modeling Future Factories." *IIE Solutions* (August 2001): 24–35.

Panchalavarapu, P. R., and V. Chankong. "Design of Cellular Manufacturing System with Assembly Considerations."

Computers & Industrial Engineering 48, no. 3 (May 2005): 448.

Roodbergen, K. J., and I. F. A. Vis. "A Model for Warehouse Layout." *IIE Transactions* 38, no. 10 (October 2006): 799–811.

Seppala, P. "How to Carry Out Sustainable Change? An Analysis of Introducing Manufacturing Cells in a Finnish Engineering Company." *Human Factors and Ergonomics in Manufacturing* 16, no. 1 (Winter 2006): 17.

Stanowy, A. "Evolutionary Strategy for Manufacturing Cell Design." *Omega* 34, no. 1 (January 2006): 1.

Upton, David. "What Really Makes Factories Flexible?" *Harvard Business Review* 73, no. 4 (July–August 1995): 74–84.

Zeng, A. Z., M. Mahan, and N. Fleut. "Designing an Efficient Warehouse Layout to Facilitate the Order-Filling Process." *Production and Inventory Management Journal* 43, no. 3–4 (3rd/4th quarter 2002): 83–88.

Internet Resources

Commercial layout software from Cimtechnologies: **www.cimtech.com**

Factory flow for layout analysis: **www.ugs.com**

Layout iQ: **www.rapidmodeling.com**

Proplanner's Flow Planner calculator: **www.proplanner.com/product/details/flowpath.aspx**

Various facility designs plans: **www.manufacturing.net**

Solutions to Even Numbered Problems

2 **(a)** $23,400
   (b) $20,600
   (c) $22,000
   (d) Plan B

4 Benders to area 1; Materials to 2; Welders to 3; Drills to 4; Grinder to 5; and Lathes to 6; Trips × Distance = 13,000 ft.

6 Layout #1, distance = 600 with areas fixed
   Layout #2, distance = 602 with areas fixed

8 Layout #4, distance = 609
   Layout #5, distance = 478

10 **(a)** 1.68 minutes
   (b) 4.76 ≈ 5
   (c) cleaning

12 **(b)** Cycle time = 9.6 min.; **(e)** There are 15 idle hours per day; **(f)** 8 workstations with 76.6% efficiency is possible.

14 **(a)**
   (b) cycle time = 30 sec./unit
   (c) 4 stations = *theoertical* minimum, but 5 are needed
   (d) Station 1–Task A; 2–B; 3–C, D; 4–E; 5–F
   (e) Total idle = 30 sec.
   (f) E = 80% with 5 stations; E = 66.6% with 6 stations

16 **(a, b)** Cycle time = 6.67 min./unit. Multiple solutions with 5 stations. Here is a sample: A, F, G to station 1; B, C to station 2; D, E to station 3; H to station 4; and I, J to station 5. **(d)** Idle time = 5 min./cycle.

18 **(a)** Minimum no. of workstations = 2.6 (or 3).
   (b) Efficiency = 86.7%.
   (c) Cycle time = 6.67 min./unit with 400 min./day; minimum no. of workstations = 1.95 (or 2).

20 Minimum (theoretical) = 4 stations. Efficiency = 93.3% with 5 stations and 6 min. cycle time. Several assignments with 5 are possible.

22 **(a)** Theoretical min. no. workstations = 5
   (b) There are several possibilities. For example; Station 1–Task A; 2–C; 3–B and F; 4–D and G; 5–E, H, and I; 6–J. Or 1–A; 2–C; 3–B and F; 4–D and G; 5–E, H and I; 6–J.
   (c) $n = 6$
   (d) E = .7611

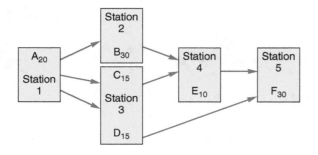

Solutions to Self Test

1. b; **2.** a; **3.** b; **4.** e; **5.** b; **6.** fixed, process, product, retail, warehouse, office; **7.** family of products, stable forecast (demand), volume; **8.** adequate volume, stable demand, standardized product; adequate/quality supplies.

276

Supply Chain Management

Outline

Ten OM Strategy Decisions

Design of Goods and Services

Managing Quality

Process Strategy

Location Strategies

Layout Strategies

Human Resources

Supply Chain Management

Inventory Management

Scheduling

Maintenance

Learning Objectives

When you complete this selection you should be able to

1. Explain the strategic importance of the supply chain
2. Identify five supply chain strategies
3. Explain issues and opportunities in the supply chain
4. Describe approaches to supply chain negotiations
5. Evaluate supply chain performance
6. Compute percent of assets committed to inventory
7. Compute inventory turnover

Darden's Supply Chain Yields a Competitive Edge

Darden Restaurants, Inc., is the largest publicly traded casual dining restaurant company in the world. It serves over 300 million meals annually from more than 1,400 restaurants in the U.S. and Canada. Each of its well-known flagship brands—Olive Garden and Red Lobster—generates sales of $2.4 billion annually. Darden's other brands include Bahama Breeze and Seasons 52; with the $1.4 billion addition in late 2007 of the Capital Grille and Long Horn Steakhouse chains. The firm employs more than 150,000 people.

"Operations is typically thought of as an execution of strategy. For us it is the strategy," Darden's former chairman, Joe R. Lee, recently stated.

In the restaurant business, a winning strategy requires a winning supply chain. Nothing is more important than sourcing and delivering healthy, high-quality food; and there are very few other industries where supplier performance is so closely tied to the customer.

Darden sources its food from five continents and thousands of suppliers. To meet Darden's needs for fresh ingredients, the company has developed four distinct supply chains: one for seafood; one for dairy/produce/other refrigerated foods; a third for other food items, like baked goods; and a fourth for restaurant supplies (everything from dishes to ovens to uniforms). Over $1.5 billion is spent in these supply chains annually. (See the *Video Case Study* at the end of this chapter for details.)

Jay Heizer

▲ **Product tracking:** *Darden's seafood inspection team developed an integral system that uses a lot ID to track seafood from its origin through shipping and receipt. Darden uses a modified atmosphere packaging (MAP) process to extend the shelf life and preserve the quality of its fresh fish. The tracking includes time temperature monitoring.*

 Video 11.1

Darden's Global Supply Chain

▶ **Qualifying the supplier:** *Long before a supplier is qualified to sell to Darden, a total quality team is appointed. The team, consisting of personnel from the quality assurance, culinary, purchasing, and distribution departments spends time at the supplier's facility to understand the processes and to evaluate the effectiveness of its food safety/quality management. The team provides guidance, assistance, support, and training to the supplier to ensure that overall objectives and desired results are accomplished.*

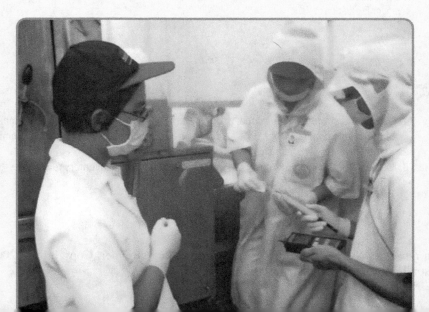

► **Worldwide sources:** Parts of the supply chain begin in the frigid waters off the coast of Alaska, where crabs are harvested. For many products, temperature monitoring begins immediately and is tracked through the entire supply chain, to the kitchen, and ultimately to the guest.

◄ **Independent audits of suppliers:** To provide fair and accurate assessment, Darden's Total Quality Supplier Program includes an independent verification program. Each supplier is evaluated regularly by independent auditors on a risk-based schedule to determine the supplier's effectiveness.

► **JIT delivery:** JIT delivery and quality service at each of Darden's 1,450 restaurants is the final step in the supply chain.

Jay Heizer

Darden's four supply channels have some common characteristics. They all require *supplier qualification*, have *product tracking*, are subject to *independent audits*, and employ *just-in-time delivery*. With best-in-class techniques and processes, Darden creates world-wide supply chain partnerships and alliances that are rapid, transparent, and efficient. Darden achieves competitive advantage through its superior supply chain.

Most firms, like Darden, spend a huge portion of their sales dollars on purchases. Because such a high percentage of an organization's costs are determined by purchasing, relationships with suppliers are increasingly integrated and long term. Joint efforts that improve innovation, speed design, and reduce costs are common. Such efforts, when part of a corporate-wide strategy, can dramatically improve both partners' competitiveness. This integrated focus places added emphasis on procurement and supplier relationships which must be managed. The discipline that manages these relationships is known as *supply chain management.*

THE SUPPLY CHAIN'S STRATEGIC IMPORTANCE

Supply chain management

Management of activities that procure materials and services, transforming them into intermediate goods and final products, and delivering the products through a distribution system.

Supply chain management is the integration of the activities that procure materials and services, transform them into intermediate goods and final products, and deliver them to customers. These activities include purchasing and outsourcing activities, plus many other functions that are important to the relationship with suppliers and distributors. As Figure 1 suggests, supply-chain management includes determining (1) transportation vendors, (2) credit and cash transfers, (3) suppliers, (4) distributors, (5) accounts payable and receivable, (6) warehousing and inventory, (7) order fulfillment, and (8) sharing customer, forecasting, and production information. The *objective is to build a chain of suppliers that focuses on maximizing value to the ultimate customer.* Competition is no longer between companies; it is between supply chains. And those supply chains are often global.

As firms strive to increase their competitiveness via product customization, high quality, cost reductions, and speed to market, added emphasis is placed on the supply chain. Effective supply chain management makes suppliers "partners" in the firm's strategy to satisfy an ever-changing marketplace. A competitive advantage may depend on a close long-term strategic relationship with a few suppliers.

▼ **Figure 1** A Supply Chain for Beer

The supply chain includes all the interactions among suppliers, manufacturers, distributors, and customers. The chain includes transportation, scheduling information, cash and credit transfers, as well as ideas, designs, and material transfers. Even can and bottle manufacturers have their own tiers of suppliers providing components such as glass, lids, labels, packing containers, etc. (Costs are approximate and include substantial taxes.)

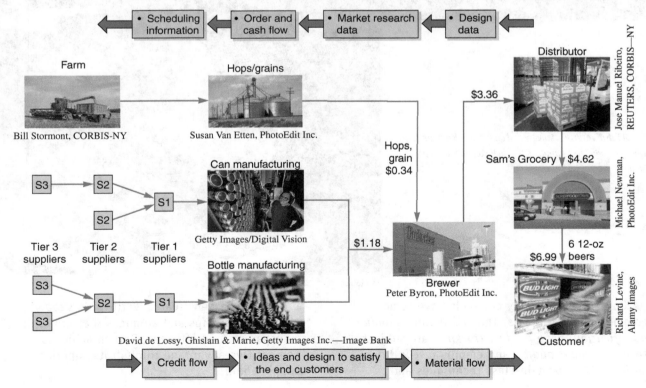

▼ **Table 1** How Supply Chain Decisions Affect Strategy*

	Low-Cost Strategy	**Response Strategy**	**Differentiation Strategy**
Supplier's goal	Supply demand at lowest possible cost (e.g., Emerson Electric, Taco Bell)	Respond quickly to changing requirements and demand to minimize stockouts (e.g., Dell Computers)	Share market research; jointly develop products and options (e.g., Benetton)
Primary selection criteria	Select primarily for cost	Select primarily for capacity, speed, and flexibility	Select primarily for product development skills
Process characteristics	Maintain high average utilization	Invest in excess capacity and flexible processes	Use modular processes that lend themselves to mass customization
Inventory characteristics	Minimize inventory throughout the chain to hold down costs	Develop responsive system, with buffer stocks positioned to ensure supply	Minimize inventory in the chain to avoid obsolescence
Lead-time characteristics	Shorten lead time as long as it does not increase costs	Invest aggressively to reduce production lead time	Invest aggressively to reduce development lead time
Product-design characteristics	Maximize performance and minimize cost	Use product designs that lead to low setup time and rapid production ramp-up	Use modular design to postpone product differentiation for as long as possible

*See related table and discussion in Marshall L. Fisher, "What Is the Right Supply Chain for Your Product?" *Harvard Business Review* (March–April 1997): 105.

To ensure that the supply chain supports the firm's strategy, managers need to consider the supply chain issues shown in Table 1. Activities of supply chain managers cut across accounting, finance, marketing, and the operations discipline. Just as the OM function supports the firm's overall strategy, the supply chain must support the OM strategy. Strategies of low cost or rapid response demand different things from a supply chain than a strategy of differentiation. For instance, a low-cost strategy, as Table 1 indicates, requires suppliers be selected based primarily on cost. Such suppliers should have the ability to design low-cost products that meet the functional requirements, minimize inventory, and drive down lead times. The firm must achieve integration of its selected strategy up and down the supply chain, and must expect that strategy to be different for different products and change as products move through their life cycle.

Learning Objective

1. Explain the strategic importance of the supply chain

Global Supply Chain Issues

When companies enter growing global markets such as eastern Europe, China, South America, or even Mexico, expanding their supply chains becomes a strategic challenge. Quality production in those areas may be a challenge, just as distribution systems may be less reliable, suggesting higher inventory levels than would be needed in one's home country. Also, tariffs and quotas may block nonlocal companies from doing business. Moreover, both political and currency risk remain high in much of the world.[1]

Thus, the development of a successful strategic plan for supply chain management requires innovative planning and careful research. Supply chains in a global environment must be able to:

1. React to sudden changes in parts availability, distribution or shipping channels, import duties, and currency rates
2. Use the latest computer and transmission technologies to schedule and manage the shipment of parts in and finished products out
3. Staff with local specialists who handle duties, freight, customs, and political issues

McDonald's planned for a global supply chain challenge 6 years in advance of its opening in Russia. Creating a $60 million "food town," it developed independently owned supply plants in

[1]Note the devaluation of the Mexican peso in 1992, the Thai bhat and the Malaysian ringgit in 1997, and the Argentine peso in 2002, as well as armed conflicts in about two dozen countries at any given time. Even the stable U.S. dollar reached record lows compared with the euro in 2007.

Moscow to keep its transportation costs and handling times low and its quality and customer-service levels high. Every component in this food chain—meat plant, chicken plant, bakery, fish plant, and lettuce plant—is closely monitored to make sure that all the system's links are strong.

Firms like Ford and Boeing also face global procurement decisions. Ford's Mercury has only 227 suppliers worldwide, a small number compared with the 700 involved in previous models. Ford has set a trend to develop a global network of *fewer* suppliers who provide the lowest cost and highest quality regardless of home country. So global is the production of the Boeing 787 that 75% to 80% of the plane is built by non-Boeing companies, with most of that figure outside the U.S. The *OM in Action* box "A Rose Is a Rose, But Only if It Is Fresh" details a global supply chain that ends with your local florist.

▼ **Table 2**

Supply Chain Costs as a Percent of Sales

Industry	% Purchased
All industry	52
Automobile	67
Food	60
Lumber	61
Paper	55
Petroleum	79
Transportation	62

SUPPLY CHAIN ECONOMICS

The supply chain receives such attention because it is an integral part of a firm's strategy and the most costly activity in most firms. For both goods and services, supply chain costs as a percent of sales are often substantial (see Table 2). Because such a huge portion of revenue is devoted to the supply chain, an effective strategy is vital. The supply chain provides a major opportunity to reduce costs and increase contribution margins.

Table 3 and Example 1 illustrate the amount of leverage available to the operations manager through the supply chain.

EXAMPLE 1

Profit potential in the supply chain

Hau Lee Furniture Inc. spends 50% of its sales dollar in the supply chain and has a net profit of 4%. Hau wants to know how many dollars of sales is equivalent to supply chain savings of $1.

Approach: Table 3 (given Hau's assumptions) can be used to make the analysis.

Solution: Table 3 indicates that every $1 Hau can save in the supply chain results in the same profit that would be generated by $3.70 in sales.

Percent Net Profit of Firm	Percent of Sales Spent in the Supply Chain						
	30%	40%	50%	60%	70%	80%	90%
2	$2.78	$3.23	$3.85	$4.76	$6.25	$9.09	$16.67
4	$2.70	$3.13	$3.70	$4.55	$5.88	$8.33	$14.29
6	$2.63	$3.03	$3.57	$4.35	$5.56	$7.69	$12.50
8	$2.56	$2.94	$3.45	$4.17	$5.26	$7.14	$11.11
10	$2.50	$2.86	$3.33	$4.00	$5.00	$6.67	$10.00

[a]The required increase in sales assumes that 50% of the costs other than purchases are variable and that half the remaining costs (less profit) are fixed. Therefore, at sales of $100 (50% purchases and 2% margin), $50 are purchases, $24 are other variable costs, $24 are fixed costs, and $2 profit. Increasing sales by $3.85 yields the following:

Purchases at 50%	$ 51.93
Other Variable Costs	24.92
Fixed Cost	24.00
Profit	3.00
	$103.85

Through $3.85 of additional sales, we have increased profit by $1, from $2 to $3. The same increase in margin could have been obtained by reducing supply chain costs by $1.

Insight: Effective management of the supply chain can generate substantial benefits.

Learning exercise: If Hau increases his profit to 6%, how much of an increase in sales is necessary to equal $1 savings? [Answer: $3.57.]

Related problems: 6, 7

These numbers indicate the strong role that procurement can play in profitability.

Make-or-Buy Decisions

A wholesaler or retailer buys everything that it sells; a manufacturing operation hardly ever does. Manufacturers, restaurants, and assemblers of products buy components and subassemblies that go into final products. Choosing products and services can be advantageously obtained *externally* as opposed to produced *internally* is known as the **make-or-buy decision**. Supply chain personnel evaluate alternative suppliers and provide current, accurate, complete data relevant to the buy alternative. Table 4 lists a variety of considerations in the make-or-buy decision. Regardless of the decision, supply chain performance should be reviewed periodically. Vendor competence and costs change, as do a firm's own strategy, production capabilities, and costs.

Make-or-buy decision
A choice between producing a component or service in-house or purchasing it from an outside source.

◄ **Table 4**

Considerations for the Make-or-Buy Decision

Reasons for Making	Reasons for Buying
1. Maintain core competence	1. Frees management to deal with its core competence
2. Lower production cost	
3. Unsuitable suppliers	2. Lower acquisition cost
4. Assure adequate supply (quantity or delivery)	3. Preserve supplier commitment
5. Utilize surplus labor or facilities and make a marginal contribution	4. Obtain technical or management ability
	5. Inadequate capacity
6. Obtain desired quality	6. Reduce inventory costs
7. Remove supplier collusion	7. Ensure alternative sources
8. Obtain unique item that would entail a prohibitive commitment for a supplier	8. Inadequate managerial or technical resources
	9. Reciprocity
9. Protect personnel from a layoff	10. Item is protected by a patent or trade secret
10. Protect proprietary design or quality	
11. Increase or maintain size of the company (management preference)	

Outsourcing

Outsourcing
Transferring a firm's activities that have traditionally been internal to external suppliers.

Outsourcing transfers some of what are traditional internal activities and resources of a firm to outside vendors, making it slightly different from the traditional make-or-buy decision. Outsourcing is part of the continuing trend toward utilizing the efficiency that comes with specialization. The vendor performing the outsourced service is an expert in that particular specialty. This leaves the outsourcing firm to focus on its critical success factors, that is, its core competencies that yield a competitive advantage. Outsourcing is the focus of the supplement to this chapter.

ETHICS IN THE SUPPLY CHAIN

As we have stressed throughout this text, ethical decisions are critical to the long-term success of any organization. However, the supply chain is particularly susceptible to ethical lapses, as the opportunities for unethical behavior are enormous. With sales personnel anxious to sell, and purchasing agents spending huge sums, the temptation for unethical behavior is substantial. Many salespeople become friends with customers, do favors for them, take them to lunch, or present small (or large) gifts. Determining when tokens of friendship become a bribe can be a challenge. Many companies have strict rules and codes of conduct that limit what is acceptable. Recognizing these issues, the Institute for Supply Management has developed principles and standards to be used as guidelines for ethical behavior. An abbreviated version is shown in Table 5.

As the supply chain becomes international, operations managers need to expect an additional set of ethical issues to manifest themselves as they deal with labor laws, culture, and whole new sets of values. For instance, Gap Inc. recently reported that of its 3,000 plus factories worldwide, about 90% failed their initial evaluation.[2] The report indicated that between 10% and 25% of its Chinese factories engaged in psychological or verbal abuse, and more than 50% of the factories visited in sub-Saharan Africa operate without proper safety devices. The challenge of ethics in the supply chain is significant, but responsible firms such as Gap are finding ways to deal with a difficult issue.

SUPPLY CHAIN STRATEGIES

For goods and services to be obtained from outside sources, the firm must decide on a supply chain strategy. One such strategy is the approach of *negotiating with many suppliers* and playing one supplier against another. A second strategy is to develop *long-term "partnering"* relation-

▶ **Table 5**

Principles and Standards of Ethical Supply Management Conduct

LOYALTY TO YOUR ORGANIZATION; JUSTICE TO THOSE WITH WHOM YOU DEAL; FAITH IN YOUR PROFESSION
1. Avoid the intent and appearance of unethical or compromising practice.
2. Demonstrate loyalty to the employer by diligently following the lawful instructions of the employer.
3. Avoid any activity that would create a conflict between personal and employer interest.
4. Avoid any activity that might influence, or appear to influence, supply management decisions.
5. Handle confidential or proprietary information with due care and proper consideration.
6. Promote positive supplier relationships.
7. Avoid improper reciprocal agreements.
8. Know and obey the letter and spirit of laws.
9. Encourage support for small, disadvantaged, and minority-owned businesses.
10. Acquire and maintain professional competence.
11. Conduct activities in accordance with national and international laws, customs, practices, and ethics.
12. Enhance the stature of the supply management profession.

Source: Adapted from the Institute for Supply Management™, **www.ism.ws/about/content/cfm**.

[2]Amy Merrick, "Gap Offers Unusual Look at Factory Conditions," *The Wall Street Journal* (May 12, 2004): A1, A12.

ships with a few suppliers to satisfy the end customer. A third strategy is *vertical integration*, in which a firm decides to use vertical backward integration by actually buying the supplier. A fourth variation is a combination of few suppliers and vertical integration, known as a *keiretsu*. In a *keiretsu, suppliers become part of a company coalition.* Finally, a fifth strategy is to develop *virtual companies that use suppliers on an as-needed basis.* We will now discuss each of these strategies.

Video 11.2

Supply Chain Management at Regal Marine

Many Suppliers

With the many-suppliers strategy, a supplier responds to the demands and specifications of a "request for quotation," with the order usually going to the low bidder. This is a common strategy when products are commodities. This strategy plays one supplier against another and places the burden of meeting the buyer's demands on the supplier. Suppliers aggressively compete with one another. Although many approaches to negotiations can be used with this strategy, long-term "partnering" relationships are not the goal. This approach holds the supplier responsible for maintaining the necessary technology, expertise, and forecasting abilities, as well as cost, quality, and delivery competencies.

Few Suppliers

A strategy of few suppliers implies that rather than looking for short-term attributes, such as low cost, a buyer is better off forming a long-term relationship with a few dedicated suppliers. Long-term suppliers are more likely to understand the broad objectives of the procuring firm and the end customer. Using few suppliers can create value by allowing suppliers to have economies of scale and a learning curve that yields both lower transaction costs and lower production costs.

Few suppliers, each with a large commitment to the buyer, may also be more willing to participate in JIT systems as well as provide design innovations and technological expertise. Many firms have moved aggressively to incorporate suppliers into their supply systems. Chrysler, for one, now seeks to choose suppliers even before parts are designed. Motorola also evaluates suppliers on rigorous criteria, but in many instances has eliminated traditional supplier bidding, placing added emphasis on quality and reliability. On occasion these relationships yield contracts that extend through the product's life cycle. The expectation is that both the purchaser and supplier collaborate, becoming more efficient and reducing prices over time. The natural outcome of such relationships is fewer suppliers, but those that remain have long-term relationships.

Service companies like Marks & Spencer, a British retailer, have also demonstrated that cooperation with suppliers can yield cost savings for customers and suppliers alike. This strategy has resulted in suppliers that develop new products, winning customers for Marks & Spencer and the supplier. The move toward tight integration of the suppliers and purchasers is occurring in both manufacturing and services.

Like all strategies, a downside exists. With few suppliers, the cost of changing partners is huge, so both buyer and supplier run the risk of becoming captives of the other. Poor supplier performance is only one risk the purchaser faces. The purchaser must also be concerned about trade secrets and suppliers that make other alliances or venture out on their own. This happened when the U.S. Schwinn Bicycle Co., needing additional capacity, taught Taiwan's Giant Manufacturing Company to make and sell bicycles. Giant Manufacturing is now the largest bicycle manufacturer in the world, and Schwinn was acquired out of bankruptcy by Pacific Cycle LLC.

About 100 years ago, Henry Ford surrounded himself with reliable suppliers, many on his own property, making his assembly operation close to self-sufficient.

Vertical Integration

Purchasing can be extended to take the form of vertical integration. By **vertical integration**, we mean developing the ability to produce goods or services previously purchased or actually buying a supplier or a distributor. As shown in Figure 2, vertical integration can take the form of *forward* or *backward integration*.

Backward integration suggests a firm purchase its suppliers, as in the case of Ford Motor Company deciding to manufacture its own car radios. Forward integration, on the other hand, suggests that a manufacturer of components make the finished product. An example is Texas Instruments, a manufacturer of integrated circuits that also makes calculators and flat-screens containing integrated circuits for TVs.

Vertical integration
Developing the ability to produce goods or services previously purchased or actually buying a supplier or a distributor.

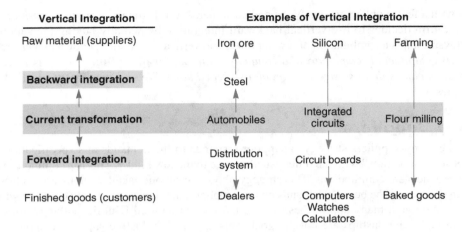

► Figure 2

Vertical Integration Can Be Forward or Backward

Vertical integration can offer a strategic opportunity for the operations manager. For firms with the capital, managerial talent, and required demand, vertical integration may provide substantial opportunities for cost reduction, quality adherence, and timely delivery. Other advantages, such as inventory reduction and scheduling can accrue to the company that effectively manages vertical integration or close, mutually beneficial relationships with suppliers.

Because purchased items represent such a large part of the costs of sales, it is obvious why so many organizations find interest in vertical integration. Vertical integration appears to work best when the organization has large market share and the management talent to operate an acquired vendor successfully.

The relentless march of specialization continues, meaning that a model of "doing everything" or "vertical integration" is increasingly difficult. Backward integration may be particularly dangerous for firms in industries undergoing technological change if management cannot keep abreast of those changes or invest the financial resources necessary for the next wave of technology. The alternative, particularly in high-tech industries, is to establish close-relationship suppliers. This allows partners to focus on their specific contribution. Research and development costs are too high and technology changes too rapid for one company to sustain leadership in every component. Most organizations are better served concentrating on their specialty and leveraging the partners' contributions. Exceptions do exist. Where capital, management talent, and technology are available and the components are also highly integrated, vertical integration may make sense. On the other hand, it made no sense for Jaguar to make commodity components for its autos as it did until it was purchased by Ford.

Keiretsu Networks

Keiretsu

A Japanese term that describes suppliers who become part of a company coalition.

Many large Japanese manufacturers have found a middle ground between purchasing from few suppliers and vertical integration. These manufacturers are often financial supporters of suppliers through ownership or loans. The supplier becomes part of a company coalition known as a *keiretsu*. Members of the *keiretsu* are assured long-term relationships and are therefore expected to function as partners, providing technical expertise and stable quality production to the manufacturer. Members of the *keiretsu* can also have suppliers farther down the chain, making second- and even third-tier suppliers part of the coalition.

Virtual Companies

Virtual companies

Companies that rely on a variety of supplier relationships to provide services on demand. Also known as hollow corporations or network companies.

The limitations to vertical integration are severe. Our technological society continually demands more specialization, which complicates vertical integration. Moreover, a firm that has a department or division of its own for everything may be too bureaucratic to be world class. So rather than letting vertical integration lock an organization into businesses that it may not understand or be able to manage, another approach is to find good flexible suppliers. **Virtual companies** rely on a variety of supplier relationships to provide services on demand. Virtual companies have fluid, moving organizational boundaries that allow them to create a unique enterprise to meet changing market demands. Suppliers may provide a variety of services that include doing the payroll, hiring personnel, designing products, providing consulting services, manufacturing components, conducting tests, or distributing products. The relationships may be short- or long-term and may include true partners, collaborators, or simply able suppliers and subcontractors. Whatever the formal relationship, the result can be exceptionally lean performance. The advantages of virtual companies include specialized management expertise, low capital investment, flexibility, and speed. The result is efficiency.

The apparel business provides a *traditional* example of virtual organizations. The designers of clothes seldom manufacture their designs; rather, they license the manufacture. The manufacturer may then rent space, lease sewing machines, and contract for labor. The result is an organization that has low overhead, remains flexible, and can respond rapidly to the market.

A *contemporary* example is the semiconductor industry, exemplified by Visioneer in Palo Alto. This California firm subcontracts almost everything: Software is written by several partners, hardware is manufactured by a subcontractor in Silicon Valley, printed circuit boards are made in Singapore, and plastic cases are made in Boston, where units are also tested and packed for shipment. In the virtual company, managing the supply chain is demanding and dynamic.

MANAGING THE SUPPLY CHAIN

As managers move toward integration of the supply chain, substantial efficiencies are possible. The cycle of materials—as they flow from suppliers, to production, to warehousing, to distribution, to the customer—takes place among separate and often very independent organizations. Therefore, there are significant management issues that may result in serious inefficiencies. Success begins with mutual agreement on goals, followed by mutual trust, and continues with compatible organizational cultures.

Video 11.3

Arnold Palmer Hospital's
Supply Chain

Mutual Agreement on Goals An integrated supply chain requires more than just agreement on the contractual terms of a buy/sell relationship. Partners in the chain must appreciate that the only entity that puts money into a supply chain is the end customer. Therefore, establishing a mutual understanding of the mission, strategy, and goals of participating organizations is essential. The integrated supply chain is about adding economic value and maximizing the total content of the product.

Trust Trust is critical to an effective and efficient supply chain. Members of the chain must enter into a relationship that shares information. Visibility throughout the supply chain—what Darden Restaurants calls a transparent supply chain—is a requirement. Supplier relationships are more likely to be successful if risk and cost savings are shared—and activities such as end-customer research, sales analysis, forecasting, and production planning are joint activities. Such relationships are built on mutual trust.

The supplier must be treated as an extension of the company.

Compatible Organizational Cultures A positive relationship between the purchasing and supplying organizations that comes with compatible organizational cultures can be a real advantage when making a supply chain hum. A champion within one of the two firms promotes both formal and informal contacts, and those contacts contribute to the alignment of the organizational cultures, further strengthening the relationship.

The operations manager is dealing with a supply chain that is made up of independent specialists, each trying to satisfy its own customers at a profit. This leads to actions that may not optimize the entire chain. On the other hand, the supply chain is replete with opportunities to reduce waste and enhance value. We now look at some of the significant issues and opportunities.

Issues in an Integrated Supply Chain

Three issues complicate development of an efficient, integrated supply chain: local optimization, incentives, and large lots.

Learning Objective

3. Explain issues and opportunities in the supply chain

Local Optimization Members of the chain are inclined to focus on maximizing local profit or minimizing immediate cost based on their limited knowledge. Slight upturns in demand are overcompensated for because no one wants to be caught short. Similarly, slight downturns are overcompensated for because no one wants to be caught holding excess inventory. So fluctuations are magnified. For instance, a pasta distributor does not want to run out of pasta for its retail customers;

the natural response to an extra large order from the retailer is to compensate with an even larger order to the manufacturer on the assumption that retail sales are picking up. Neither the distributor nor the manufacturer knows that the retailer had a major one-time promotion that moved a lot of pasta. This is exactly the issue that complicated the implementation of efficient distribution at the Italian pasta maker Barilla.

Incentives (Sales Incentives, Quantity Discounts, Quotas, and Promotions)

Incentives push merchandise into the chain for sales that have not occurred. This generates fluctuations that are ultimately expensive to all members of the chain.

Large Lots

There is often a bias toward large lots because large lots tend to reduce unit costs. A logistics manager wants to ship large lots, preferably in full trucks, and a production manager wants long production runs. Both actions drive down unit shipping and production costs, but fail to reflect actual sales and increased holding costs.

These three common occurrences—local optimization, incentives, and large lots—contribute to distortions of information about what is really occurring in the supply chain. A well-running supply system needs to be based on accurate information about how many products are truly being pulled through the chain. The inaccurate information is unintentional, but it results in distortions and fluctuations in the supply chain and causes what is known as the bullwhip effect.

Bullwhip effect

The increasing fluctuation in orders that often occurs as orders move through the supply chain.

The **bullwhip effect** occurs as orders are relayed from retailers, to wholesalers, to manufacturers, with fluctuations increasing at each step in the sequence. The "bullwhip" fluctuations in the supply chain increase the costs associated with inventory, transportation, shipping, and receiving while decreasing customer service and profitability. Procter & Gamble found that although the use of Pampers diapers was steady and the retail-store orders had little fluctuation, as orders moved through the supply chain, fluctuations increased. By the time orders were initiated for raw material, the variability was substantial. Similar behavior has been observed and documented at many companies, including Campbell Soup, Hewlett-Packard, and Applied Materials.[3] A number of opportunities exist for reducing the bullwhip effect and improving opportunities in the supply chain. These are discussed in the following section.

Opportunities in an Integrated Supply Chain

Opportunities for effective management in the supply chain include the following 10 items.

Pull data

Accurate sales data that initiate transactions to "pull" product through the supply chain.

Accurate "Pull" Data

Accurate **pull data** are generated by sharing (1) point-of-sales (POS) information so that each member of the chain can schedule effectively and (2) computer-assisted ordering (CAO). This implies using POS systems that collect sales data and then adjusting that data for market factors, inventory on hand, and outstanding orders. Then a net order is sent directly to the supplier who is responsible for maintaining the finished-goods inventory.

Lot Size Reduction

Lot sizes are reduced through aggressive management. This may include (1) developing economical shipments of less than truckload lots; (2) providing discounts based on total annual volume rather than size of individual shipments; and (3) reducing the cost of ordering through techniques such as standing orders and various forms of electronic purchasing.

Single stage control of replenishment

Fixing responsibility for monitoring and managing inventory for the retailer.

Single Stage Control of Replenishment

Single stage control of replenishment means designating a member in the chain as responsible for monitoring and managing inventory in the supply chain based on the "pull" from the end user. This approach removes distorted information and multiple forecasts that create the bullwhip effect. Control may be in the hands of:

- A sophisticated retailer who understands demand patterns. How Wal-Mart does this for some of its inventory with radio frequency (RFID) tags is shown in the *OM in Action* box "Radio Frequency Tags: Keeping the Shelves Stocked."
- A distributor who manages the inventory for a particular distribution area. Distributors who handle grocery items, beer, and soft drinks may do this. Anheuser-Busch manages beer inventory and delivery for many of its customers.

---

[3]See R. Croson and K. Donahue, "Behavioral Causes of the Bullwhip Effect," *Management Science* 52, no. 3 (March 2006): 323–336; R. D. H. Warburton, "An Analytical Investigation of the Bullwhip Effect," *Production and Operations Management* 13, no. 2 (summer 2004): 150–160; and Robert Ristelhueber, "Supply Chain Strategies—Applied Materials Seek to Snap Bullwhip Effect," *EBN* (January 22, 2001): 61.

OM in Action — Radio Frequency Tags: Keeping the Shelves Stocked

Supply chains work smoothly when sales are steady, but often break down when confronted by a sudden surge in demand. Radio frequency ID (or RFID) tags can change that by providing real-time information about what's happening on store shelves. Here's how the system works for Procter & Gamble's (P&G's) Pampers.

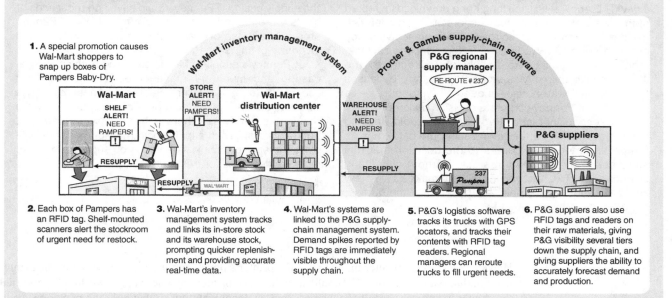

1. A special promotion causes Wal-Mart shoppers to snap up boxes of Pampers Baby-Dry.

2. Each box of Pampers has an RFID tag. Shelf-mounted scanners alert the stockroom of urgent need for restock.

3. Wal-Mart's inventory management system tracks and links its in-store stock and its warehouse stock, prompting quicker replenishment and providing accurate real-time data.

4. Wal-Mart's systems are linked to the P&G supply-chain management system. Demand spikes reported by RFID tags are immediately visible throughout the supply chain.

5. P&G's logistics software tracks its trucks with GPS locators, and tracks their contents with RFID tag readers. Regional managers can reroute trucks to fill urgent needs.

6. P&G suppliers also use RFID tags and readers on their raw materials, giving P&G visibility several tiers down the supply chain, and giving suppliers the ability to accurately forecast demand and production.

Sources: Information Week (January 23, 2006): 20; *Business 2.0* (May 2002): 86; and *Knight Ridder Tribune Business News* (August 6, 2006): 1.

- A manufacturer who has a well-managed forecasting, manufacturing, and distribution system. TAL Apparel Ltd., discussed in the *OM in Action* box, "The JCPenney Supply Chain for Dress Shirts," does this for JCPenney.

Vendor-Managed Inventory Vendor-managed inventory (VMI) means the use of a local supplier (usually a distributor) to maintain inventory for the manufacturer or retailer. The supplier delivers directly to the purchaser's using department rather than to a receiving dock or stockroom. If the supplier can maintain the stock of inventory for a variety of customers who use the same product or whose differences are very minor (say, at the packaging stage), then there should be a net savings. These systems work without the immediate direction of the purchaser.

> **Vendor-managed inventory (VMI)**
> A system in which a supplier maintains material for the buyer, often delivering directly to the buyer's using department.

Blanket Orders Blanket orders are unfilled orders with a vendor.[4] A **blanket order** is a contract to purchase certain items from a vendor. It is not an authorization to ship anything. Shipment is made only on receipt of an agreed-on document, perhaps a shipping requisition or shipment release.

> **Blanket order**
> A long-term purchase commitment to a supplier for items that are to be delivered against short-term releases to ship.

Standardization The purchasing department should make special efforts to increase levels of standardization. That is, rather than obtaining a variety of similar components with labeling, coloring, packaging, or perhaps even slightly different engineering specifications, the purchasing agent should try to have those components standardized. Consider GM's automobile seat frame. GM makes 26 different versions; Toyota makes 2. The cost advantage to Toyota is about $500 million.[5]

Postponement **Postponement** withholds any modification or customization to the product (keeping it generic) as long as possible. The concept is to minimize internal variety while maximizing external variety. For instance, after analyzing the supply chain for its printers,

> **Postponement**
> Delaying any modifications or customization to a product as long as possible in the production process.

---

[4]Unfilled orders are also referred to as "open" orders, or "incomplete" orders.
[5]David Welch, "Renault—Nissan: Say Hello to Bo," *Business Week* (July 31, 2006): 56–58.

The JCPenney Supply Chain for Dress Shirts

Purchase a white Stafford wrinkle-free dress shirt, size 17 neck, 34/35 sleeve at JCPenney at Atlanta's Northlake Mall on a Tuesday, and the supply chain responds. Within a day, TAL Apparel Ltd. in Hong Kong downloads a record of the sale. After a run through its forecasting model, TAL decides how many shirts to make and in what styles, colors, and sizes. By Wednesday afternoon, the replacement shirt is packed to be shipped directly to the JCPenney Northlake Mall store. The system bypasses the JCPenney warehouse—indeed all warehouses—as well as the JCPenney corporate decision makers.

In a second instance, two shirts are sold, leaving none in stock. TAL, after downloading the data, runs its forecasting model but comes to the decision that this store needs to have two in stock. Without consulting JCPenney, a TAL factory in Taiwan makes two new shirts. It sends one by ship, but because of the outage, the other goes by air.

As retailers deal with mass customization, fads, and seasonal swings they also strive to cut costs—making a responsive supply chain critical. Before globalization of the supply chain, JCPenney would have had thousands of shirts warehoused across the country. Now JCPenney stores, like those of many retailers, hold a very limited inventory of shirts.

JCPenney's supplier, TAL, is providing both sales forecasting and inventory management, a situation not acceptable to many retailers. But what is most startling is that TAL also places its own orders! A supply chain like this works only when there is trust between partners. The rapid changes in supply chain management not only place increasing technical demands on suppliers but also increase demands for trust between the parties.

Sources: Apparel (April 2006): 14–18; *The Wall Street Journal* (September 11, 2003): A1, A9; and *International Trade Forum* (Issue 3, 2005): 12–13.

Hewlett-Packard (HP) determined that if the printer's power supply was moved out of the printer itself and into a power cord, HP could ship the basic printer anywhere in the world. HP modified the printer, its power cord, its packaging, and its documentation so that only the power cord and documentation needed to be added at the final distribution point. This modification allowed the firm to manufacture and hold centralized inventories of the generic printer for shipment as demand changed. Only the unique power system and documentation had to be held in each country. This understanding of the entire supply chain reduced both risk and investment in inventory.

Drop shipping

Shipping directly from the supplier to the end consumer rather than from the seller, saving both time and reshipping costs.

Drop Shipping and Special Packaging **Drop shipping** means the supplier will ship directly to the end consumer, rather than to the seller, saving both time and reshipping costs. Other cost-saving measures include the use of special packaging, labels, and optimal placement of labels and bar codes on containers. The final location down to the department and number of units in each shipping container can also be indicated. Substantial savings can be obtained through management techniques such as these. Some of these techniques can be of particular benefit to wholesalers and retailers by reducing shrinkage (lost, damaged, or stolen merchandise) and handling cost.

For instance, Dell Computer has decided that its core competence is not in stocking peripherals, but in assembling PCs. So if you order a PC from Dell, with a printer and perhaps other components, the computer comes from Dell, but the printer and many of the other components will be drop shipped from the manufacturer.

Pass-through facility

Expedites shipment by holding merchandise and delivering from shipping hubs.

Pass-through Facility A **pass-through facility** is a distribution center where merchandise is held, but it functions less as a holding area and more as a shipping hub. These facilities, often run by logistics vendors, use the latest technology and automated systems to expedite orders. For instance, UPS works with Nike at such a facility in Louisville, Kentucky, to immediately handle orders. Similarly, FedEx's warehouse next to the airport in Memphis can receive an order after a store closes for the evening and can locate, package, and ship the merchandise that night. Delivery is guaranteed by 10 A.M. the next day.

Channel assembly

Postpones final assembly of a product so the distribution channel can assemble it.

Channel Assembly Channel assembly is an extension of the pass-through facility. **Channel assembly** sends individual components and modules, rather than finished products, to the distributor. The distributor then assembles, tests, and ships. Channel assembly treats distributors more as manufacturing partners than as distributors. This technique has proven successful in industries where products are undergoing rapid change, such as personal computers. With this strategy, finished-goods inventory is reduced because units are built to a shorter, more accurate forecast. Consequently, market response is better, with lower investment—a nice combination.

E-PROCUREMENT

E-procurement uses the Internet to facilitate purchasing. E-procurement speeds purchasing, reduces costs, and integrates the supply chain, enhancing an organization's competitive advantage. The traditional supply chain is full of paper transactions, such as requisitions, requests for bids, bid evaluations, purchase orders, order releases, receiving documents, invoices, and the issuance of checks. E-procurement reduces this barrage of paperwork.

In this section, we discuss traditional techniques of electronic ordering and funds transfer and then move on to online catalogs, auctions, RFQs, and real-time inventory tracking.

Electronic Ordering and Funds Transfer   Electronic ordering and bank transfers are traditional approaches to speeding transactions and reducing paperwork. Transactions between firms often use **electronic data interchange (EDI)**, which is a standardized data-transmittal format for computerized communications between organizations. EDI provides data transfer for virtually any business application, including purchasing. Under EDI, data for a purchase order, such as order date, due date, quantity, part number, purchase order number, address, and so forth, are fitted into the standard EDI format. EDI also provides for the use of **advanced shipping notice (ASN)**, which notifies the purchaser that the vendor is ready to ship. Although some firms are still moving to EDI and ASN, the Internet's ease of use and lower cost is proving more popular.

Online Catalogs

Purchase of standard items is often accomplished via online catalogs. Such catalogs provide current information about products in electronic form. Online catalogs support cost comparisons and are efficient for both buyers and sellers. These electronic catalogs can enrich traditional catalogs by incorporating voice and video clips, much as do the CD-ROM and DVD that accompany this text. Online catalogs are available in three versions:

1. Typical of *catalogs provided by vendors* are those of W. W. Grainger and Office Depot. W. W. Grainger is probably the world's largest seller of MRO items (items for maintenance, repair, and operations), while Office Depot provides the same service for office supplies. Systems such as Grainger's and Office Depot's take care of frequent, relatively low-dollar purchases. Customized catalogs can take orders 24 hours a day and reflect discounts applicable to each customer. Online catalogs are often available on every employee's desktop computer. Once approved and established, each employee can do his or her own purchasing. Many of these purchases are individually small dollar value and as such have historically failed to receive the attention of other "normal" purchases. The result has been a huge inefficiency. E-procurement provides an opportunity for substantial savings; and the paper trails related to ordering become less-expensive electronic trails.

2. *Catalogs provided by intermediaries* are Internet sites where business buyers and sellers can meet. These intermediaries typically create industry specific catalogs with content from many suppliers. Qualified buyers can place orders with selling companies. The cost is significantly less than with traditional faxes, telephone calls, and purchase orders.

3. One of the first online *exchanges provided by buyers* was Covisint, created by auto giants GM, Ford, and Chrysler. Although focusing on the auto industry, Covisint buys virtually everything, from paper clips to stamping presses to contract manufacturing. As Figure 3 suggests, virtually every other industry quickly followed. For instance, Global Health Care Exchange, the first exchange listed in Figure 3, provides similar service for the hospital

E-procurement
Purchasing facilitated through the Internet.

Electronic data interchange (EDI)
A standardized data-transmittal format for computerized communications between organizations.

Advanced shipping notice (ASN)
A shipping notice delivered directly from vendor to purchaser.

"... e-procurement ... integrates supply chains between different buyers and sellers, and makes a company's supply chain a key competitive advantage."

Robert Derocher
Deloitte Consulting

Health care products—set up by Johnson & Johnson, GE Medical Systems, Baxter International, Abbott Laboratories, and Medtronic Inc; called the Global Health Care Exchange (**ghx.com**).

Retail Goods—set up by Sears and France's Carrefour; called GlobalNetXchange for retailers (**gnx.com**).

Defense and aerospace products— created by Boeing, Raytheon, Lockheed-Martin, Rolls-Royce, and Britain's BAE Systems; called the Aerospace and Defense Industry Trading Exchange (**exostar.com**).

Food, beverage, consumer products—set up by 49 leading food and beverage firms; called Transora (**transora.com**).

Steel and metal products—such as Metal-Site (**metalsite.com**).

Hotels—created by Marriott and Hyatt, and later joined by Fairmont, Six Continents, and Club Corp; called Avendra (**avendra.com**) buys for 2,800 hotels.

◄ **Figure 3**

Internet Trading Exchanges

sector. These exchanges, by moving from a multitude of individual phone calls, faxes, and e-mails to a centralized online exchange, are driving billions of dollars of waste out of the supply chain. Online exchanges can be expected to continue to put downward pressure on price while improving transaction efficiency.

Auctions

Online auction sites can be maintained by sellers, buyers, or intermediaries. GM's approach to selling excess steel is to post it on the Web and expect that its own suppliers who need steel will buy it. Operations managers find online auctions a fertile area for disposing of excess raw material and discontinued or excess inventory. Online auctions lower entry barriers, which encourages sellers to join and simultaneously increase the potential number of buyers.

The key for auction firms, such as Ariba of Sunnyvale, California, is to find and build a huge base of potential bidders (see photo). Indeed, most of Ariba's employees spend their time not running electronic auctions but improving client buying procedures and qualifying new suppliers.

Sun Microsystems claims savings of over $1 billion a year using its in-house reverse auction system (called Dynamic Bidding). The firm now spends 1 hour pricing out items that used to take weeks or months to negotiate. For an operations manager, online auctions are a significant opportunity to improve supply chain performance.

RFQs

When purchasing requirements are nonstandard, time spent preparing requests for quotes (RFQs) and the related bid package can be substantial. Consequently, e-procurement has now moved these often expensive parts of the purchasing process online. At General Electric, for example, e-procurement now provides purchasing personnel with an extensive database of vendor, delivery, and quality data. With this extensive history, supplier selection has improved. Electronic files containing engineering drawings are also available. These resources allow purchasing agents to attach electronic copies of the necessary drawings to RFQs and inexpensively send the entire electronic-encrypted package to vendors in a matter of hours.

Real-Time Inventory Tracking

FedEx's pioneering efforts at tracking packages from pickup to delivery has shown the way for operations managers to do the same for their shipments and inventory. Because tracking cars and trucks has been a chronic and embarrassingly inexact science, Ford has recently hired UPS to track more than 4 million vehicles as they move from factory to dealers. Using bar codes and the Internet, Ford dealers are now able to log onto a Web site and find out exactly where the ordered vehicles are in the distribution system. As operations managers move to an era of mass customization, with customers ordering exactly the cars they want, customers will expect to know

▶ *Here an Ariba team monitors an online market from the firm's Global Market Operations Center. Ariba provides support for the entire global sourcing process, including software, supplier development, competitive negotiations, and savings implementation. Online bidding leads to greater cost savings than more traditional procurement.*

Ariba

where their cars are and exactly when they can be picked up. E-procurement, supported by bar codes and RFID, can provide economical inventory tracking on the shop floor, in warehouses, and in logistics.

VENDOR SELECTION

For those goods and services a firm buys, vendors must be selected. Vendor selection considers numerous factors, such as strategic fit, vendor competence, delivery, and quality performance. Because a firm may have some competence in all areas and may have exceptional competence in only a few, selection can be challenging. Procurement policies also need to be established. Those might address issues such as percent of business done with any one supplier or with minority businesses. We now examine vendor selection as a three-stage process: (1) vendor evaluation, (2) vendor development, and (3) negotiations.

Vendor Evaluation

The first stage of vendor selection, *vendor evaluation*, involves finding potential vendors and determining the likelihood of their becoming good suppliers. This phase requires the development of evaluation criteria such as criteria shown in Example 2.[6] However, both the criteria and the weights selected vary depending on the supply chain strategy being implemented. (Refer to Table 1 shown earlier in the chapter.)

EXAMPLE 2

Weighted approach to vendor evaluation

Erin Davis, president of Creative Toys in Palo Alto, is interested in evaluating suppliers who will work with him to make nontoxic, environmentally friendly paints and dyes for his line of children's toys. This is a critical strategic element of his supply chain, and he desires a firm that will contribute to his product.

Approach: Erin begins his analysis of one potential supplier, Faber Paint and Dye, by using the weighted approach to vendor evaluation.

Solution: Erin first reviews the supplier differentiation attributes in Table 1 and develops the following list of selection criteria. He then assigns the weights shown to help him perform an objective review of potential vendors. His staff assigns the scores shown and computes the total weighted score.

Criteria	Weights	Scores (1–5) (5 highest)	Weight × Score
Engineering/research/innovation skills	.20	5	1.0
Production process capability (flexibility/technical assistance)	.15	4	.6
Distribution/delivery capability	.05	4	.2
Quality systems and performance	.10	2	.2
Facilities/location	.05	2	.1
Financial and managerial strength (stability and cost structure)	.15	4	.6
Information systems capability (e-procurement, ERP)	.10	2	.2
Integrity (environmental compliance/ethics)	.20	5	1.0
	1.00		3.9 Total

Faber Paint and Dye receives an overall score of 3.9.

Insight: Erin now has a basis for comparison with other potential vendors, selecting the one with the highest overall rating.

Learning exercise: If Erin believes that the weight for "engineering/research/innovation skills" should be increased to .25 and the weight for "financial and managerial strength" reduced to .10, what is the new score? [Answer: Faber Paint and Dye now goes to 3.95.]

Related problems: 2, 3, 4

---

[6]A discussion of vendor selection criteria can be found in Chapter 8 of Robert Monczka, Robert Trent, and Robert Handfield, *Purchasing and Supply Chain Management*, 3rd ed. (Mason, Ohio: South-Western, 2005); and Chapters 2 and 3 of Joel D. Wisner, G. Keong Leong, and K. C. Tan, *Principles of Supply Chain Management* (Mason, Ohio: South-Western, 2005).

The selection of competent suppliers is critical. If good suppliers are not selected, then all other supply-chain efforts are wasted. As firms move toward using fewer longer-term suppliers, the issues of financial strength, quality, management, research, technical ability, and potential for a close long-term relationship play an increasingly important role. These attributes should be noted in the evaluation process.

Vendor Development

The second stage of vendor selection is *vendor development*. Assuming that a firm wants to proceed with a particular vendor, how does it integrate this supplier into its system? The buyer makes sure the vendor has an appreciation of quality requirements, product specifications, schedules and delivery, the purchaser's payment system, and procurement policies. *Vendor development* may include everything from training, to engineering and production help, to procedures for information transfer.

Negotiations

Negotiation strategies
Approaches taken by supply chain personnel to develop contractual relationships with suppliers.

Regardless of the supply chain strategy adopted, negotiations regarding the critical elements of the contractual relationship must take place. These negotiations often focus on quality, delivery, payment, and cost. We will look at three classic types of **negotiation strategies**: the cost-based model, the market-based price model, and competitive bidding.

Cost-Based Price Model   The *cost-based price model* requires that the supplier open its books to the purchaser. The contract price is then based on time and materials or on a fixed cost with an escalation clause to accommodate changes in the vendor's labor and materials cost.

Learning Objective

4. Describe approaches to supply chain negotiations

Market-Based Price Model   In the market-based price model, price is based on a published, auction, or index price. Many commodities (agriculture products, paper, metal, etc.) are priced this way. Paperboard prices, for instance, are available via the *Official Board Markets* weekly publication (**www.advanstar.com**). Nonferrous metal prices are quoted in *Platt's Metals Week* (**www.platts.com/plattsmetals/**), and prices of other metals are quoted at **www.metalworld.com**.

Competitive Bidding   When suppliers are not willing to discuss costs or where near-perfect markets do not exist, competitive bidding is often appropriate. Infrequent work (such as construction, tooling, and dies) is usually purchased based on a bid. Bidding may take place via mail, fax, or an Internet auction. Competitive bidding is the typical policy in many firms for the majority of their purchases. Bidding policies usually require that the purchasing agent have several potential suppliers of the product (or its equivalent) and quotations from each. The major disadvantage of this method, as mentioned earlier, is that the development of long-term relations between buyer and seller is hindered. Competitive bidding may effectively determine initial cost. However, it may also make difficult the communication and performance that are vital for engineering changes, quality, and delivery.

Negotiations should not be viewed as a win-lose game; they can be a win-win game.

Yet a fourth approach is *to combine one or more* of the preceding negotiation techniques. The supplier and purchaser may agree on review of certain cost data, accept some form of market data for raw material costs, or agree that the supplier will "remain competitive." In any case, a good supplier relationship is one in which both partners have established a degree of mutual trust and a belief in each other's competence, honesty, and fair dealing.

LOGISTICS MANAGEMENT

Logistics management
An approach that seeks efficiency of operations through the integration of all material acquisition, movement, and storage activities.

Procurement activities may be combined with various shipping, warehousing, and inventory activities to form a logistics system. The purpose of **logistics management** is to obtain efficiency of operations through the integration of all material acquisition, movement, and storage activities. When transportation and inventory costs are substantial on both the input and output sides of the production process, an emphasis on logistics may be appropriate. When logistics issues are significant or expensive, many firms opt for outsourcing the logistics function. Logistics specialists can often bring expertise not available in-house. For instance, logistics companies often have tracking technology that reduces transportation losses and supports delivery schedules that adhere to precise delivery windows. The potential for competitive advantage is found via both reduced costs and improved customer service.

Firms recognize that the distribution of goods to and from their facilities can represent as much as 25% of the cost of products. In addition, the total distribution cost in the U.S. is over 10% of the gross national product (GNP). Because of this high cost, firms constantly evaluate their means of distribution. Five major means of distribution are trucking, railroads, airfreight, waterways, and pipelines.

Distribution Systems

Trucking   The vast majority of manufactured goods moves by truck. The flexibility of shipping by truck is only one of its many advantages. Companies that have adopted JIT programs in recent years have put increased pressure on truckers to pick up and deliver on time, with no damage, with paperwork in order, and at low cost. Trucking firms are using computers to monitor weather, find the most effective route, reduce fuel cost, and analyze the most efficient way to unload. In spite of these advances, the motor carrier industry averages a capacity utilization of only 50%. That under-utilized space costs the U.S. economy over $31 billion per year. To improve logistics efficiency, the industry is establishing Web sites such as Schneider National's connection (**www.schneider.com**), which lets shippers and truckers find each other to use some of this idle capacity. Shippers may pick from thousands of approved North American carriers that have registered with Schneider logistics.

Railroads   Railroads in the U.S. employ 200,000 people and ship 90% of all coal, 67% of autos, 68% of paper products, and about half of all food, lumber, and chemicals. Containerization has made intermodal shipping of truck trailers on railroad flat cars, often piggybacked as double-deckers, a popular means of distribution. More than 13 million trailer loads are moved in the U.S. each year by rail. With the growth of JIT, however, rail transport has been the biggest loser because small-batch manufacture requires frequent, smaller shipments that are likely to move via truck or air.

Airfreight   Airfreight represents only about 1% of tonnage shipped in the U.S. However, the recent proliferation of airfreight carriers such as FedEx, UPS, and DHL makes it the fastest-growing mode of shipping. Clearly, for national and international movement of lightweight items, such as medical and emergency supplies, flowers, fruits, and electronic components, airfreight offers speed and reliability.

Waterways   Waterways are one of the nation's oldest means of freight transportation, dating back to construction of the Erie Canal in 1817. Included in U.S. waterways are the nation's rivers, canals, the Great Lakes, coastlines, and oceans connecting to other countries. The usual cargo on waterways is bulky, low-value cargo such as iron ore, grains, cement, coal, chemicals, limestone, and petroleum products. Internationally, millions of containers are shipped at very

◄ As this photo of the port of Charleston suggests, with 16 million containers entering the U.S. annually, tracking location, content, and condition of trucks and containers is a challenge. But new technology may improve both security and JIT shipments.

South Carolina State Ports Authority

► *Seven farms within a 2-hour drive of Kenya's Nairobi Airport supply 300 tons of fresh beans, bok choy, okra, and other produce that is packaged at the airport and shipped overnight to Europe. The time between harvest and arrival in Europe is 2 days. When a good supply chain and good logistics work together, the results can be startling—and fresh food.*

Francesco Broli

low cost via huge oceangoing ships each year. Water transportation is important when shipping cost is more important than speed.

Pipelines   Pipelines are an important form of transporting crude oil, natural gas, and other petroleum and chemical products. An amazing 90% of the state of Alaska's budget is derived from the 1.5 million barrels of oil pumped daily through the pipeline at Prudhoe Bay.

Third-Party Logistics

Supply chain managers may find that outsourcing logistics is advantageous in driving down inventory investment and costs while improving delivery reliability and speed. Specialized logistics firms support this goal by coordinating the supplier's inventory system with the service capabilities of the delivery firm. FedEx, for example, has a successful history of using the Internet for online tracking. At **FedEx.com**, a customer can compute shipping costs, print labels, adjust invoices, and track package status all on the same Web site. FedEx, UPS, and DHL play a core role in other firms' logistics processes. In some cases, they even run the server for retailer Web sites. In other cases, such as for Dell Computer, FedEx operates warehouses that pick, pack, test, and assemble products, then it handles delivery and customs clearance when necessary. The *OM in Action* box "DHL's Role in the Supply Chain" provides another example of how outsourcing logistics can reduce costs while shrinking inventory and delivery times.

OM in Action   DHL's Role in the Supply Chain

It's the dead of night at DHL International's air express hub in Brussels, yet the massive building is alive with busy forklifts and sorting workers. The boxes going on and off the DHL plane range from Dell computers and Cisco routers to Caterpillar mufflers and Komatsu hydraulic pumps. Sun Microsystems computers from California are earmarked for Finland; CD-ROMs from Teac's plant in Malaysia are destined for Bulgaria.

The door-to-door movement of time-sensitive packages is key to the global supply chain. JIT, short product life cycles, mass customization, and reduced inventories depend on logistics firms such as DHL, FedEx, and UPS. These powerhouses are in continuous motion.

With a decentralized network covering 227 countries and territories (more than are in the UN), DHL is a true multinational. The Brussels headquarters has only 450 of the company's 60,000 employees but includes 26 nationalities.

DHL has assembled an extensive global network of express logistics centers for strategic goods. In its Brussels logistics center, for instance, DHL upgrades, repairs, and configures Fijitsu computers, InFocus projectors, and Johnson & Johnson medical equipment. It stores and provides parts for EMC and Hewlett-Packard and replaces Nokia and Philips phones. "If something breaks down on a Thursday at 4 o'clock, the relevant warehouse knows at 4:05, and the part is on a DHL plane at 7 or 8 that evening," says Robert Kuijpers, DHL International's CEO.

Sources: Journal of Commerce (August 15, 2005): 1; *EBN* (February 25, 2002): 27; and *Forbes* (October 18, 1999): 120–124.

Cost of Shipping Alternatives

The longer a product is in transit, the longer the firm has its money invested. But faster shipping is usually more expensive than slow shipping. A simple way to obtain some insight into this trade-off is to evaluate carrying cost against shipping options. We do this in Example 3.

A shipment of new connectors for semiconductors needs to go from San Jose to Singapore for assembly. The value of the connectors is $1,750 and holding cost is 40% per year. One airfreight carrier can ship the connectors 1 day faster than its competitor, at an extra cost of $20.00. Which carrier should be selected?

Approach: First we determine the daily holding cost and then compare the daily holding cost with the cost of faster shipment.

Solution: Daily cost of holding the product = (Annual holding cost × Product value)/365

$$= (.40 \times \$1,750)/365$$

$$= \$1.92$$

Since the cost of saving one day is $20.00, which is much more than the daily holding cost of $1.92, we decide on the less costly of the carriers and take the extra day to make the shipment. This saves $18.08 ($20.00 − $1.92).

Insight: The solution becomes radically different if the 1-day delay in getting the connectors to Singapore delays delivery (making a customer angry) or delays payment of a $150,000 final product. (Even 1 day's interest on $150,000 or an angry customer makes a savings of $18.08 insignificant.)

Learning exercise: If the holding cost is 100% per year, what is the decision? [Answer: Even with a holding cost of $4.79 per day, the less costly carrier is selected.]

Related problems: 8, 9, 10

Example 3 looks only at holding costs versus shipping cost. For the operations or logistics manager there are many other considerations, including coordinating shipments to maintain a schedule, getting a new product to market, and keeping a customer happy.[7] Estimates of these other costs can be added to the estimate of daily holding cost. Determining the impact and cost of these many other considerations makes the evaluation of shipping alternatives interesting.

Federal Express Corporation

▲ *Speed and accuracy in the supply chain are supported by bar-code tracking of shipments. At each step of a journey, from initial pickup to final destination, bar codes (left) are read and stored. Within seconds, this tracking information is available online to customers worldwide (right).*

---

[7]The cost of an unhappy customer can be equated to the stockout cost discussed in further Chapter.

▶ *The global supply chain puts new demands on logistics: In Boeing's case, sections of the 787 Dreamliner need to be moved around the world in a timely fashion. Boeing's in-house solution was to build three of these new Large Cargo Freight liners. "Some people say this plane is ugly, but I call it an elegant logistics solution," says a Boeing supply chain executive. (The Wall Street Journal, January 8, 2007: A1, A14).*

Boeing Commercial Airplane Group

Logistics, Security, and JIT

There is probably no society more open than the U.S. This includes its borders and ports. With removal of the last constraints on the North American Free Trade Agreement (NAFTA), expanding globalization, and increased use of JIT deliveries, U.S. borders and ports are swamped. About 16 million containers enter U.S. ports each year, along with thousands of planes, cars, and trucks each day. Even under the best of conditions, some 5% of the container movements are misrouted, stolen, damaged, or excessively delayed.

Since the September 11, 2001, terrorist attacks, supply chains have become more complex, and they can be expected to become even more so. However, technological innovations in the supply chain are improving logistics, security, and JIT. Technology is now capable of knowing truck and container location, content, and condition. New devices can detect whether someone has broken into a sealed container and can communicate that information to the shipper or receiver via satellite or radio. Motion detectors can also be installed inside containers. Other sensors can record interior data including temperature, shock, radioactivity, and whether a container is moving. Tracking lost containers, identifying delays, or just reminding individuals in the supply chain that a shipment is on its way will help expedite shipments. Improvements in security may aid JIT, and improvements in JIT may aid security—both of which can improve supply chain logistics.

MEASURING SUPPLY CHAIN PERFORMANCE

Learning Objective

5. Evaluate supply chain performance

Like all other managers, supply chain managers require standards (or *metrics*, as they are often called) to evaluate performance. Evaluation of the supply chain is particularly critical for these managers because they spend most of the organization's money. In addition, they make scheduling and quantity decisions that determine the assets committed to inventory. Only with effective metrics can managers determine how well the *supply chain is performing* and *how well assets are utilized*. We will now discuss these two metrics.

Supply Chain Performance   The benchmark metrics shown in Table 6 focus on procurement and vendor performance issues. World-class benchmarks are the result of well-managed supply chains that drive down costs, lead times, late deliveries, and shortages while improving quality.

▶ **Table 6**

Supply Chain Performance

	Typical Firms	**Benchmark Firms**
Lead time (weeks)	15	8
Time spent placing an order	42 minutes	15 minutes
Percent of late deliveries	33%	2%
Percent of rejected material	1.5%	.0001%
Number of shortages per year	400	4

Source: Adapted from a McKinsey & Company report.

Assets Committed to Inventory   Three specific measures can be helpful here. The first is the amount of money invested in inventory, usually expressed as a percent of assets, as shown in Equation (1):

$$\text{Percent invested in inventory} = (\text{Total inventory investment/Total assets}) \times 100 \qquad (1)$$

Learning Objective
6. Compute percent of assets committed to inventory

EXAMPLE 4

Tracking Home Depot's inventory investment

Home Depot's management wishes to track its investment in inventory as one of its performance measures. Home Depot had $11.4 billion invested in inventory and total assets of $44.4 billion in 2006.

Approach: Determine the investment in inventory and total assets and then use Equation (1).

Solution: Percent invested in inventory = (11.4/44.4) × 100 = 25.7%

Insight: Over one-fourth of Home Depot assets are committed to inventory.

Learning exercise: If Home Depot can drive its investment down to 20% of assets, how much money will it free up for other uses? [Answer: 11.4 − (44.5 × .2) = $2.5 billion.]

Related problems: 11b, 12b

Specific comparisons with competitors may assist evaluation. Total assets committed to inventory in manufacturing approach 20%, in wholesale 34%, and retail 27%—with wide variations, depending on the specific business model and management (see Table 7).

The second common measure of supply chain performance is *inventory turnover* (see Table 8) and its reciprocal, *weeks of supply*. **Inventory turnover** is computed on an annual basis, using Equation (2):

$$\text{Inventory turnover} = \text{Cost of goods sold/Inventory investment} \qquad (2)$$

Inventory turnover
Cost of goods sold divided by average inventory.

Cost of goods sold is the cost to produce the goods or services sold for a given period. Average inventory investment is the average inventory value for the same period. This may be the average of several periods of inventory or beginning and ending inventory added together and divided by 2. Often, average inventory investment is based on nothing more than the inventory investment at the end of the period—typically at year-end.[8]

In Example 5, we look at inventory turnover applied to PepsiCo.

Learning Objective
7. Compute inventory turnover

▼ **Table 7**   **Inventory as Percent of Total Assets (with examples of exceptional performance)**

Manufacturer (Toyota 5%)	20%
Wholesale (Coca-Cola 2.9%)	34%
Restaurants (McDonald's .05%)	2.9%
Retail (Home Depot 25.7%)	27%

▼ **Table 8**   **Examples of Annual Inventory Turnover**

Food, Beverage, Retail	
Anheuser Busch	15
Coca-Cola	14
Home Depot	5
McDonald's	112
Manufacturing	
Dell Computer	90
Johnson Controls	22
Toyota (overall)	13
Nissan (assembly)	150

[8]Inventory quantities often fluctuate wildly, and various types of inventory exist (e.g., raw material, work-in-process, finished goods, and maintenance, repair, and operating supplies [MRO]). Therefore, care must be taken when using inventory values; they may reflect more than just supply chain performance.

EXAMPLE 5

Inventory turnover at PepsiCo, Inc.

PepsiCo, Inc., manufacturer and distributor of drinks, snacks, and Quaker Foods, provides the following in its 2005 annual report (shown here in $ billions). Determine PepsiCo's turnover and weeks of inventory.

Net revenue		$32.5
Cost of goods sold		$14.2
Inventory:		
Raw material inventory	$.74	
Work-in-process inventory	$.11	
Finished goods inventory	$.84	
Total inventory investment		$1.69

Approach: Use the inventory turnover computation in Equation (2) to measure inventory performance. Cost of goods sold is $14.2 billion. Total inventory is the sum of raw material at $.74 billion, work-in-process at $.11 billion, and finished goods at $.84 billion, for total inventory investment of $1.69 billion.

Solution: Inventory Turnover = Cost of goods sold / Inventory investment

$$= 14.2/1.69$$

$$= 8.4$$

Insight: We now have a standard, popular measure by which to evaluate performance.

Learning exercise: If Coca-Cola's cost of goods sold is $10.8 billion and inventory investment is $.76 billion, what is its inventory turnover? [Answer: 14.2.]

Related problems: 11a, 12c, 13

Weeks of supply may have more meaning in the wholesale and retail portions of the service sector than in manufacturing. It is computed below as the reciprocal of inventory turnover:

Weeks of supply = Inventory investment/(Annual cost of goods sold/52 weeks) (3)

EXAMPLE 6

Determining weeks of supply at PepsiCo

Using the PepsiCo data in Example 5, management wants to know the weeks of supply.

Approach: We know that inventory investment is $1.69 billion and that weekly sales equal annual cost of goods sold ($14.2 billion) divided by 52 = $14.2/52 = $.273 billion.

Solution: Using Equation (3), we compute weeks of supply as:

Weeks of supply = (Inventory investment/Average weekly cost of goods sold)

$$1.69/.273 = 6.19 \text{ weeks}$$

Insight: We now have a standard measurement by which to evaluate a company's continuing performance or by which to compare companies.

Learning exercise: If Coca-Cola's average inventory investment is $.76 billion and its average weekly cost of goods sold is $.207 billion, what is the firm's weeks of supply? [Answer: 3.67 weeks.]

Related problems: 12a, 14

Supply chain management is critical in driving down inventory investment. The rapid movement of goods is key. Wal-Mart, for example, has set the pace in the retailing sector with its world-renowned supply chain management. By doing so, it has established a competitive advantage. With its own truck fleet, distribution centers, and a state-of-the-art communication system, Wal-Mart (with the help of its suppliers) replenishes store shelves an average of twice per week. Competitors resupply every other week. Economical and speedy resupply means both rapid response to product changes and customer preferences, as well as lower inventory investment. Similarly, while many manufacturers struggle to move inventory turnover up to 10 times per year, Dell Computer has inventory turns exceeding 90 and supply measured in *days*—not weeks. Supply chain management provides a competitive advantage when firms effectively respond to the demands of global markets and global sources.

For most companies, the percent of revenue spent on labor is going down but the percent spent in the supply chain is going up.

Summary

Competition is not just between companies but between supply chains. For many firms, the supply chain determines a substantial portion of product cost and quality, as well as opportunities for responsiveness and differentiation. Five supply chain strategies have been identified: (1) many suppliers, (2) few suppliers, (3) vertical integration, (4) *keiretsu* networks, and (5) virtual companies. Skillful supply chain management provides a great strategic opportunity for competitive advantage.

Key Terms

Supply chain management
Make-or-buy decision
Outsourcing
Vertical integration
Keiretsu
Virtual companies
Bullwhip effect
Pull data

Single stage control of replenishment
Vendor-managed inventory (VMI)
Blanket order
Postponement
Drop shipping
Pass-through facility
Channel assembly
E-procurement

Electronic data interchange (EDI)
Advanced shipping notice (ASN)
Negotiation strategies
Logistics management
Inventory turnover

Solved Problem

 Virtual Office Hours help is available on Student DVD.

Solved Problem 1

Jack's Pottery Outlet has total end-of-year assets of $5 million. The first-of-the-year inventory was $375,000, with a year-end inventory of $325,000. The annual cost of goods sold was $7 million. The owner, Eric Jack, wants to evaluate his supply chain performance by measuring his percent of assets in inventory, his inventory turnover, and his weeks of supply. We use Equations (1), (2), and (3) to provide these measures.

solution

First, determine *average inventory*:

$$(\$375,000 + \$325,000)/2 = \$350,000$$

Then, use Equation (1) to determine percent invested in inventory:

$$\text{Percent invested in inventory} = (\text{Total inventory investment}/\text{Total assets}) \times 100$$
$$= (350,000/5,000,000) \times 100$$
$$= 7\%$$

Third, determine inventory turnover, using Equation (2):

$$\text{Inventory turnover} = \text{Cost of goods sold}/\text{Inventory investment}$$
$$= 7,000,000/350,000$$
$$= 20$$

Finally, to determine weeks of inventory, use Equation (3), adjusted to weeks:

$$\text{Weeks of inventory} = \text{Inventory investment}/\text{Weekly cost of goods sold}$$
$$= 350,000/(7,000,000/52)$$
$$= 350,000/134,615$$
$$= 2.6$$

We conclude that Jack's Pottery Outlet has 7% of its assets invested in inventory, that the inventory turnover is 20, and that weeks of supply is 2.6.

Self-Test

- ***Before taking the self-test***, *refer to the learning objectives listed at the beginning of the selection and the key terms listed at the end of the selection.*
- *Use the key at the back of the text to **correct** your answers.*
- ***Restudy*** *pages that correspond to any questions you answered incorrectly or material you feel uncertain about.*

1. A *keiretsu* is:
   a) a purchasing agent
   b) an expediter
   c) a virtual company
   d) part of a company coalition
   e) a variation of the bullwhip effect

2. A pull system is aimed toward _____.

3. Two measures of supply chain performance are:
   a) inventory turnover and amount of vertical integration
   b) assets committed to inventory and amount of vertical integration
   c) weeks of supply and number of blanket orders
   d) inventory turnover and assets committed to inventory
   e) level of bullwhip and inventory turnover

4. The term *vertical integration* means to:
   a) develop the ability to produce products that complement or supplement the original product
   b) produce goods or services previously purchased
   c) develop the ability to produce the specified good more efficiently
   d) all of the above

5. Postponement:
   a) is shipping directly from the supplier to the end customer
   b) requires the use of EDI or the Internet
   c) uses e-procurement to facilitate purchasing
   d) delays modifications as long as possible in the production process
   e) uses single stage replenishment

6. Vendor-managed inventories and blanket orders:
   a) mean the same thing
   b) both lead to vastly reduced overall purchasing costs for a particular item
   c) both tend to reduce the amount of paperwork involved in the transaction
   d) both require multiplicity of suppliers

7. Single-stage replenishment means:
   a) vendor-managed inventory
   b) a single member of the supply chain is responsible for managing resupply
   c) sharing POS information
   d) drop shipping directly to the end customer
   e) delaying modifications to the product as long as possible

8. The objective of supply chain management is: _____.

9. A market-based model for negotiations is based on:
   a) the supplier opening its books to the purchaser
   b) supplier and vendor agreeing on price
   c) competitive bidding
   d) a published, auction, or index price

10. The bullwhip effect can be aggravated by:
    a) local optimization
    b) sales incentives
    c) quantity discounts
    d) promotions
    e) all of the above

Internet and Student CD-ROM/DVD Exercises

Visit our Companion Web site or use your student CD-ROM/DVD to help with material in this chapter.

 On Our Companion Web Site, www.prenhall.com/heizer
- Self-Study Quizzes
- Practice Problems
- Virtual Company Tour
- Internet Case
- PowerPoint Lecture

On Your Student CD-ROM
- Practice Problems

 On Your Student DVD
- Video Clips and Video Cases
- Virtual Office Hours for Solved Problem

Discussion Questions

1. Define supply chain management.
2. What are the objectives of supply chain management?
3. What is the objective of logistics management?
4. How do we distinguish between supply chain management, purchasing, and logistics management?
5. What is vertical integration? Give examples of backward and forward integration.
6. What are three basic approaches to negotiations?
7. How does a traditional adversarial relationship with suppliers change when a firm makes a decision to move to a few suppliers?
8. What is the difference between postponement and channel assembly?
9. Explain each of the three versions of online catalogs.
10. What is the value of online auctions in e-commerce?
11. Explain how FedEx uses the Internet to meet requirements for quick and accurate delivery.

12. How does Wal-Mart use drop shipping?
13. What are blanket orders? How do they differ from invoiceless purchasing?
14. What can purchasing do to implement just-in-time deliveries?
15. What is e-procurement?

16. How does Darden Restaurants, described in the *Global Company Profile*, find competitive advantage in its supply chain?
17. What are the cultural impediments to establishing *keiretsu* networks in countries other than Japan?

Ethical Dilemma

For generations, the policy of Sears Roebuck and Company, the granddaddy of retailers, was not to purchase more than 50% of any of its suppliers' output. The rationale of this policy was that it allowed Sears to move to other suppliers, as the market dictated, without destroying the supplier's ability to stay in business. In contrast, Wal-Mart purchases more and more of a supplier's output. Eventually, Wal-Mart can be expected to sit down with that supplier and explain why the supplier no longer needs a sales force and that the supplier should eliminate the sales force, passing the cost savings on to Wal-Mart.

Sears is losing market share, has been acquired by K-Mart, and is eliminating jobs; Wal-Mart is gaining market share and hiring. What are the ethical issues involved, and which firm has a more ethical position?

Problems

•• 1 Choose a local establishment that is a member of a relatively large chain. From interviews with workers and information from the Internet, identify the elements of the supply chain. Determine whether the supply chain represents a low-cost, rapid response, or differentiation strategy. Are the supply chain characteristics significantly different from one product to another?

•• 2 As purchasing agent for Woolsey Enterprises in Golden, Colorado, you ask your buyer to provide you with a ranking of "excellent," "good," "fair," or "poor" for a variety of characteristics for two potential vendors. You suggest that "Products" total be weighted 40% and the other three categories' totals be weighted 20% each. The buyer has returned the following ranking:

VENDOR RATING

Company	Excellent (4)	Good (3)	Fair (2)	Poor (1)
Financial Strength			K	D
Manufacturing Range			KD	
Research Facilities	K		D	
Geographical Locations		K	D	
Management		K	D	
Labor Relations			K	D
Trade Relations			KD	

Service	Excellent (4)	Good (3)	Fair (2)	Poor (1)
Deliveries on Time		KD		
Handling of Problems		KD		
Technical Assistance		K	D	

Products	Excellent (4)	Good (3)	Fair (2)	Poor (1)
Quality	KD			
Price			KD	
Packaging			KD	

Sales	Excellent (4)	Good (3)	Fair (2)	Poor (1)
Product Knowledge			D	K
Sales Calls			K	D
Sales Service			K	D

DONNA INC. = D
KAY CORP. = K

Which of the two vendors would you select?

•• 3 Using the data in Problem 2, assume that both Donna, Inc., and Kay Corp. are able to move all their "poor" ratings to "fair." How would you then rank the two firms?

•• 4 Develop a vendor-rating form that represents your comparison of the education offered by universities in which you considered (or are considering) enrolling. Fill in the necessary data, and identify the "best" choice. Are you attending that "best" choice? If not, why not?

•• 5 Using sources from the Internet, identify some of the problems faced by a company of your choosing as it moves toward, or operates as, a virtual organization. Does its operating as a virtual organization simply exacerbate old problems, or does it create new ones?

• 6 Using Table 3, determine the sales necessary to equal a dollar of savings on purchases for a company that has:
a) A net profit of 4% and spends 40% of its revenue on purchases.
b) A net profit of 6% and spends 80% of its revenue on purchases.

• **7** Using Table 3, determine the sales necessary to equal a dollar of savings on purchases for a company that has:
a) A net profit of 6% and spends 60% of its revenue on purchases.
b) A net profit of 8% and spends 80% of its revenue on purchases.

•• **8** Your options for shipping $100,000 of machine parts from Baltimore to Kuala Lumpur, Malaysia, are (1) use a ship that will take 30 days at a cost of $3,800, or (2) truck the parts to Los Angeles and then ship at a total cost of $4,800. The second option will take only 20 days. You are paid via a letter of credit the day the parts arrive. Your holding cost is estimated at 30% of the value per year.
a) Which option is more economical?
b) What customer issues are not included in the data presented?

Thomas Raupach, Peter Arnold Inc.

•• **9** If you have a third option for the data in Problem 8, and it costs only $4,000 and also takes 20 days, what is your most economical plan?

•• **10** Monczka-Trent Shipping is the logistics vendor for Handfield Manufacturing Co. in Ohio. Handfield has daily shipments of a power-steering pump from its Ohio plant to an auto assembly line in Alabama. The value of the standard shipment is $250,000. Monczka-Trent has two options: (1) its standard 2-day shipment or (2) a subcontractor who will team drive overnight with an effective delivery of 1 day. The extra driver costs $175. Handfield's holding cost is 35% annually for this kind of inventory.
a) Which option is more economical?
b) What production issues are not included in the data presented?

▼ **Table 9** **For Problems 11 and 12**

Arrow Distributing Corp.

Net revenue	$16,500
Cost of sales	$13,500
Inventory	$ 1,000
Total assets	$ 8,600

Baker Mfg. Inc.

Net revenue	$27,500
Cost of sales	$21,500
Inventory	$ 1,250
Total assets	$16,600

•• **11** Baker Mfg Inc. (see Table 9) wishes to compare its inventory turnover to those of industry leaders, who have turnover of about 13 times per year and 8% of their assets invested in inventory.
a) What is Baker's inventory turnover?
b) What is Baker's percent of assets committed to inventory?
c) How does Baker's performance compare to the industry leaders?

•• **12** Arrow Distributing Corp. (see Table 9) likes to track inventory by using weeks of supply as well as by inventory turnover.
a) What is its weeks of supply?
b) What percent of Arrow's assets are committed to inventory?
c) What is Arrow's inventory turnover?
d) Is Arrow's supply chain performance, as measured by these inventory metrics, better than that of Baker, in Problem 11?

• **13** The grocery industry has an annual inventory turnover of about 14 times. Organic Grocers, Inc., had a cost of goods sold last year of $10.5 million; its average inventory was $1.0 million. What was Organic Grocers's inventory turnover, and how does that performance compare with that of the industry?

•• **14** Mattress Wholesalers, Inc. is constantly trying to reduce inventory in its supply chain. Last year, cost of goods sold was $7.5 million and inventory was $1.5 million. This year, costs of goods sold is $8.6 million and inventory investment is $1.6 million.
a) What were the weeks of supply last year?
b) What are the weeks of supply this year?
c) Is Mattress Wholesalers making progress in its inventory-reduction effort?

Case Studies

Dell's Value Chain

Dell, the computer manufacturer highlighted in *Global Company Profile*, develops close relationships with suppliers. It encourages suppliers to focus on their individual technological capabilities to sustain leadership in their components. Research and development costs are too high and technological changes are too rapid for any one company to sustain leadership in every component. Suppliers are also pressed to drive down lead times, lot sizes, and inventories. Dell, in turn, keeps its research customer focused and leverages that research to help itself and suppliers. Dell also constructs special Web pages for suppliers, allowing them to view orders for components they produce as well as current levels of inventory at Dell. This allows suppliers to plan based on actual end customer demand; as a result, it reduces the bullwhip effect. The intent is to work with suppliers to keep the supply chain moving rapidly, products current, and the customer order queue short. Then, with supplier collaboration, Dell can offer the latest options, can build to order, and can achieve rapid throughput. The payoff is a competitive advantage, growing market share, and low capital investment.

On the distribution side, Dell uses direct sales, primarily via the Internet, to increase revenues by offering a virtually unlimited variety of desktops, notebooks, and enterprise products. Options displayed over the Internet allow Dell to attract customers that value choice. Customers select recommended product configurations or customize them. Dell's customers place orders at any time of the day from anywhere in the world. And Dell's price is cheaper; retail stores have additional costs because of their brick-and-mortar model. Dell has also customized Web pages that enable large business customers to track past purchases and place orders consistent with their purchase history and current needs. Assembly begins immediately after receipt of a customer order. Competing firms have previously assembled products filling the distribution channels (including shelves at retailers) before a product reaches the customer. Dell, in contrast, introduces a new product to customers over the Internet as soon as the first of that model is ready. In an industry where products have life cycles measured in months, Dell enjoys a huge early-to-market advantage.

Dell's model also has cash flow advantages. Direct sales allow Dell to eliminate distributor and retailer margins and increase its own margin. Dell collects payment in a matter of days after products are sold. But Dell pays its suppliers according to the more traditional billing schedules. Given its low levels of inventory, Dell is able to operate its business with negative working capital because it manages to receive payment before it pays its suppliers for components. These more traditional supply chains often require 60 or more days for the cash to flow from customer to supplier—a huge demand on working capital.

Dell has designed its order processing, products, and assembly lines so that customized products can be assembled in a matter of hours. This allows Dell to postpone assembly until after a customer order has been placed. In addition, any inventory is often in the form of components that are common across a wide variety of finished products. Postponement, component modularity, and tight scheduling allow low inventory and support mass customization. Dell maximizes the benefit of postponement by focusing on new products for which demand is difficult to forecast. Manufacturers who sell via distributors and retailers find postponement virtually impossible. Therefore, traditional manufacturers are often stuck with product configurations that are not selling while simultaneously being out of the configurations that *are* selling. Dell is better able to match supply and demand.

One of the few negatives for Dell's model is that it results in higher outbound shipping costs than selling through distributors and retailers. Dell sends individual products directly to customers from its factories. But many of these shipments are small (often one or a few products), while manufacturers selling through distributors and retailers ship with some economy of scale, using large shipments via truck to warehouses and retailers, with the end user providing the final portion of delivery. As a result, Dell's outbound transportation costs are higher, but the relative cost is low (typically 2% to 3%), and thus the impact on the overall cost is low.

What Dell has done is build a collaborative supply chain and an innovative ordering and production system. The result is what Dell likes to refer to as its *value chain*—a chain that brings value from supplier to the customer and provides Dell with a competitive advantage.

Discussion Questions

1. How has Dell used its direct sales and build-to-order model to develop an exceptional supply chain?
2. How has Dell exploited the direct sales model to improve operations performance?
3. What are the main disadvantages of Dell's direct sales model?
4. How does Dell compete with a retailer who already has a stock?
5. How does Dell's supply chain deal with the bullwhip effect?

Sources: Adapted from S. Chopra and P. Meindl, *Supply Chain Management*, 3rd ed. (Upper Saddle River, NJ: Prentice Hall, 2007); R. Kapuscinski, et al., "Inventory Decisions in Dell's Supply Chain," *Interfaces* 34, no. 3 (May–June 2004): 191–205; and A. A. Thompson, A. J. Strickland, and J. E. Gamble, "Dell, Inc. in 2006: Can Rivals Beat Its Strategy?" *Crafting and Executing Strategy*, 15th ed. (New York: McGraw-Hill, 2007).

Darden's Global Supply Chains

Video Case

Darden Restaurants (subject of the *Global Company Profile* at the beginning of this chapter), owner of popular brands such as Olive Garden and Red Lobster, requires unique supply chains to serve more than 300 million meals annually. Darden's strategy is operations excellence, and Senior VP Jim Lawrence's task is to ensure competitive advantage via Darden's supply chains. For a firm with purchases exceeding $1.5 billion, managing the supply chains is a complex and challenging task.

Darden, like other casual dining restaurants, has unique supply chains that reflect its menu options. Darden's supply chains are rather shallow, often having just one tier of suppliers. But it has four distinct supply chains.

First, "smallware" is a restaurant industry term for items such as linens, dishes, tableware and kitchenware, and silverware. These are purchased, with Darden taking title as they are received at the Darden Direct Distribution (DDD) warehouse in Orlando, Florida. From this single warehouse, smallware items are shipped via common carrier (trucking companies) to Olive Garden, Red Lobster, Bahama Breeze, and Seasons 52 restaurants.

Second, frozen, dry, and canned food products are handled economically by Darden's 11 distribution centers in North America, which are managed by major U.S. food distributors, such as MBM, Maines, and Sygma. This is Darden's second supply line.

Third, the fresh food supply chain (not frozen and not canned), where life is measured in days, includes dairy products, produce, and meat. This supply chain is B2B, where restaurant managers directly place orders with a preselected group of independent suppliers.

Fourth, Darden's worldwide seafood supply chain is the final link. Here Darden has developed independent suppliers of salmon, shrimp, tilapia, scallops, and other fresh fish that are source inspected by Darden's overseas representatives to ensure quality. These fresh products are flown to the U.S. and shipped to 16 distributors, with 22 locations, for quick delivery to the restaurants. With suppliers in 35 countries, Darden must be on the cutting edge when it comes to collaboration, partnering, communication, and food safety. It does this with heavy travel schedules for purchasing and quality control personnel, native-speaking employees onsite, and aggressive communication.

Communication is a critical element; Darden tries to develop as much forecasting transparency as possible. "Point of sale (POS) terminals," says Lawrence, "feed actual sales every night to suppliers."

Discussion Questions*

1. What are the advantages of each of Darden's four supply chains?
2. What are the complications of having four supply chains?
3. Where would you expect ownership/title to change in each of Darden's four supply chains?

4. How do Darden's four supply chains compare with those of other firms, such as Dell or an automobile manufacturer? Why do the differences exist, and how are they addressed?

*You may wish to view this video on your DVD before answering these questions.

Source: Written by Professors Barry Render (Rollins College), Jay Heizer (Texas Lutheran University), and Beverly Amer (Northern Arizona University).

Arnold Palmer Hospital's Supply Chain

Video Case

Arnold Palmer Hospital, one of the nation's top hospitals dedicated to serving women and children, is a large business with over 2,000 employees working in a 431-bed facility totaling 676,000 square feet in Orlando, Florida. Like many other hospitals, and other companies, Arnold Palmer Hospital had been a long-time member of a large buying group, one servicing 900 members. But the group did have a few limitations. For example, it might change suppliers for a particular product every year (based on a new lower-cost bidder) or stock only a product that was not familiar to the physicians at Arnold Palmer Hospital. The buying group was also not able to negotiate contracts with local manufacturers to secure the best pricing.

So in 2003, Arnold Palmer Hospital, together with seven other partner hospitals in central Florida, formed its own much smaller, but still powerful (with $200 million in annual purchases) Healthcare Purchasing Alliance (HPA) corporation. The new alliance saved the HPA members $7 million in its first year from two main changes. First, it was structured and staffed to assure that the bulk of the savings associated with its contracting efforts went to its eight members. Second, it struck even better deals with vendors by guaranteeing a *committed* volume and signing not 1-year deals but 3–5 year contracts. "Even with a new internal cost of $400,000 to run HPA, the savings and ability to contract for what our member hospitals really want makes the deal a winner," says George DeLong, head of HPA.

Effective supply chain management in manufacturing often focuses on development of new product innovations and efficiency through buyer–vendor collaboration. However, the approach in a service industry has a slightly different emphasis. At Arnold Palmer Hospital, supply chain opportunities often manifest themselves through the Medical Economic Outcomes Committee. This committee (and its subcommittees) consists of users (including the medical and nursing staff) who evaluate purchase options with a goal of

better medicine while achieving economic targets. For instance, the heart pacemaker negotiation by the cardiology subcommittee allowed for the standardization to two manufacturers, with annual savings of $2 million for just this one product.

Arnold Palmer Hospital is also able to develop custom products that require collaboration down to the third tier of the supply chain. This is the case with custom packs that are used in the operating room. The custom packs are delivered by a distributor, McKesson General Medical, but assembled by a pack company that uses materials the hospital wanted purchased from specific manufacturers. The HPA allows Arnold Palmer Hospital to be creative in this way. With major cost savings, standardization, blanket purchase orders, long-term contracts, and more control of product development, the benefits to the hospital are substantial.

Discussion Questions*

1. How does this supply chain differ from that in a manufacturing firm?
2. What are the constraints on making decisions based on economics alone at Arnold Palmer Hospital?
3. What role do doctors and nurses play in supply chain decisions in a hospital? How is this participation handled at Arnold Palmer Hospital?
4. Doctor Smith just returned from the Annual Physician's Orthopedic Conference, where she saw a new hip joint replacement demonstrated. She decides she wants to start using the replacement joint at Arnold Palmer Hospital. What process will Dr. Smith have to go through at the hospital to introduce this new product into the supply chain for future surgical use?

*You may wish to view this video on your DVD before answering the questions.

Supply Chain Management at Regal Marine

Video Case

Like most other manufacturers, Regal Marine finds that it must spend a huge portion of its revenue on purchases. Regal has also found that the better its suppliers understand its end users, the better are both the supplier's product and Regal's final product. As one of the 10 largest U.S. power boat manufacturers, Regal is trying to differentiate its products from the vast number of boats supplied by 300 other companies. Thus, the firm works closely with suppliers to ensure innovation, quality, and timely delivery.

Regal has done a number of things to drive down costs while driving up quality, responsiveness, and innovation. First, working on partnering relationships with suppliers ranging from providers of wind-

shields to providers of instrument panel controls, Regal has brought timely innovation at reasonable cost to its product. Key vendors are so tightly linked with the company that they meet with designers to discuss material changes to be incorporated into new product designs.

Second, the company has joined about 15 other boat manufacturers in a purchasing group, known as American Boat Builders Association, to work with suppliers on reducing the costs of large purchases. Third, Regal is working with a number of local vendors to supply hardware and fasteners directly to the assembly line on a just-in-time basis. In some of these cases, Regal has worked out an arrangement with the vendor so that title does not transfer until parts are used by Regal. In other cases, title transfers when items are delivered to the property. This practice drives down total inventory and the costs associated with large-lot delivery.

Finally, Regal works with a personnel agency to outsource part of the recruiting and screening process for employees. In all these cases, Regal is demonstrating innovative approaches to supply chain management that help the firm and, ultimately, the end user. The *Global Company Profile* featuring Regal Marine provides further background on Regal's operations.

Discussion Questions*

1. What other techniques might Regal use to improve supply chain management?
2. What kind of response might members of the supply chain expect from Regal in response to their "partnering" in the supply chain?
3. Why is supply chain management important to Regal?

*You may wish to view this case on your DVD before answering the questions.

Additional Case Studies

Internet case study: Visit our Companion Web site at www.prenhall.com/heizer for this free case study:

- **Amazon.com:** Discusses opportunities and issues in an innovative business model for the Internet.

Harvard has selected these Harvard Business School cases to accompany this chapter:

harvardbusinessonline.hbsp.harvard.edu

- **Supply Chain Management at World Co. Ltd.** (#601-072): Illustrates the value of response times and how response times can be reduced.
- **Ford Motor Co.: Supply Chain Strategy** (#699-198): Evaluation of whether Ford should "virtually integrate" on the Dell Computer model.
- **Sport Obermeyer Ltd.** (#695-022): Examines how to match supply with demand for products with high demand uncertainty.
- **Barilla SpA (A)** (#694-046): Allows students to analyze how a company can implement a continuous replenishment system.
- **Tale of Two Electronic Components Distributors** (#697-064): Examines distributor consolidation and growth of the Internet.

Bibliography

Ballou, Ronald H. *Business Logistics Management*, 5th ed. Upper Saddle River, NJ: Prentice Hall (2004).

Benton, W. C., and Michael Maloni. "The Influence of Power Driven Buyer/Seller Relationships on Supply Chain Satisfaction." *Journal of Operations Management* 23, vol. 1 (January 2005): 1–22.

Boswell, Tim, et al. "How Supplier Development Helps Harley-Davidson Go Lean." *Target: Innovation at Work* 20, no. 1 (first issue 2004): 18–30.

Boyer, Kenneth K., and G. Tomas M. Hult. "Extending the Supply Chain: Integrating Operations and Marketing in the Online Grocery Industry." *Journal of Operations Management* 23, no. 6 (September 2005): 642–661.

Chen, I. J., and A. Paulraj. "Towards a Theory of Supply Chain Management: The Constructs and Measurements." *Journal of Operations Management* 22, no. 2 (April 2004): 119–150.

Chopra, Sunil, and Peter Meindl. *Supply Chain Management*, 3rd ed. Upper Saddle River, NJ: Prentice Hall (2007).

Davenport, Thomas H. "The Coming Commoditization of Processes." *Harvard Business Review* (June 2005): 100–108.

Gardner, Dan. "The Impact of Globalization on Supply Chain Management." *APICS—The Performance Advantage* (April 2004): 30–35.

Gaur, Vishal, Marshall L. Fisher, and Ananth Raman. "An Econometric Analysis of Inventory Turnover Performance in Retail Services." *Management Science* 51, no. 2 (February 2005): 181–194.

Kapuscinski, Roman, et al. "Inventory Decisions in Dell's Supply Chain." *Interfaces* 34, no. 3 (May–June 2004): 191–205.

Kleindorfer, Paul R., and Germaine H. Saad. "Managing Disruption Risks in Supply Chains." *Production and Operations Management* 14, no. 1 (spring 2005): 53–68.

Kreipl, Stephan, and Michael Pinedo. "Planning and Scheduling in Supply Chains: An Overview of Issues in Practice." *Production and Operations Management* 13, no. 1 (spring 2004): 77–92.

Mentzer, John T., Soonhong Min, and L. Michelle Bobbitt. "Toward a Unified Theory of Logistics." *International Journal of Physical Distribution and Logistics Management* 34, no. 8 (2004): 606–627.

Shirodkar, S., and K. Kempf. "Supply Chain Collaboration Through Shared Capacity Models." *Interfaces* 36, no. 5 (September–October 2006): 420–432.

Stanley, L. L., and V. R. Singhal. "Service Quality Along the Supply Chain: Implications for Purchasing." *Journal of Operations Management* 19, no. 3 (May 2001): 287–306.

de Treville, Suzanne, Roy D. Shapiro, and Ari-Pekka Hameri. "From Supply Chain to Demand Chain: The Role of Lead-Time Reduction in Improving Demand Chain Performance." *Journal of Operations Management* 21, no. 6 (January 2004): 613–627.

Wisner, Joel and Linda Stanley. *Process Management: Creating Value Along the Supply Chain.* Mason OH: Thomson (2008).

Internet Resources

American Supplier Institute (ASI): **www.amsup.com**
Commerce One: **www.commerceone.com**
Council of Supply Chain Management: **www.escmp.org**
Erasmus Center for Maritime Economics and Logistics: **www.maritimeeconomics.com**
Institute for Logistics Management: **www.logistics-edu.com/**

Institute for Supply Management: **www.ism.ws**
Distribution Solutions International: **www2.dsii.com**
Purchasing Magazine's Business Intelligence Center: **www.purchasingdata.com**
Purchasing Magazine Web Site: **www.purchasing.com**

Solutions to Even Numbered Problems

2 Donna Inc, 8.2; Kay Corp., 9.8
4 Individual responses. Issues might include: academics, location, financial support, size, facilities, etc.
6 (a) $3.13
   (b) $7.69
8 (a) Option a is most economical.
   (b) The customer requirements may demand a faster schedule.
10 (a) Go with faster subcontractor.
   (b) Internal production or testing may require a faster schedule.

12 (a) Weeks of supply = 3.85
   (b) % of assets in inventory = 11.63%
   (c) Turnover = 13.5
   (d) No, but note they are in different industries
14 (a) Last year = 10.4
   (b) This year = 9.67
   (c) Yes

Solutions to Self Test

1. d; **2.** requesting/pulling rather than pushing orders through the supply chain; **3.** d; **4.** b; **5.** d; **6.** c; **7.** b; **8.** to build a chain of suppliers that focuses on maximizing value to the ultimate customer; **9.** d; **10.** e.

Outsourcing as a Supply Chain Strategy

Outline

What Is Outsourcing?
Types of Outsourcing

Strategic Planning and Core
Competencies
The Theory of Comparative Advantage

Outsourcing Trends and Political
Repercussions

Risks in Outsourcing

Methodologies for Outsourcing
Evaluating Multiple Criteria with
Factor Rating
Break-even Analysis

Advantages and Disadvantages
of Outsourcing
Advantages of Outsourcing
Disadvantages of Outsourcing

Audits and Metrics to Evaluate
Outsourcing Performance

Ethical Issues in Outsourcing
Summary
Key Terms
Using Software to Solve Outsourcing
Problems
Solved Problem
Self-Test
Internet and Student CD-ROM/DVD
Exercises
Discussion Questions
Problems
Case Study: Outsourcing to Tata
Video Case: Outsourcing Offshore at Darden
Bibliography
Internet Resources

Learning Objectives

When you complete this selection you should be able to

1. Explain how core competencies relate
to outsourcing

2. Describe the risks of outsourcing

3. Use factor rating to evaluate both
country and provider outsourcers

4. Use break-even analysis to determine
if outsourcing is cost-effective

5. List the advantages and
disadvantages of outsourcing

▶ *Sara Lee contracts with external bakeries to prepare many of its food products. By outsourcing most of its supply chain, Sara Lee can focus on managing its most important competitive advantage—its brand name. But there are risks involved in outsourcing. Outsourcing decisions, as part of the supply chain strategy, are explored in this supplement.*

Michael Abramson, Woodfin Camp & Associates

Outsourcing is a creative management strategy. Indeed, some organizations use outsourcing to replace entire purchasing, information systems, marketing, finance, and operations departments. Outsourcing is applicable to firms throughout the world. And because outsourcing decisions are risky and many are not successful, making the right decision may mean the difference between a firm's success and failure.[1]

Because outsourcing grows by double digits every year, students and managers need to understand the issues, concepts, models, philosophies, procedures, and practices of outsourcing. The purpose of this supplement is to provide current concepts and methodologies that can help you understand and use outsourcing strategies.

WHAT IS OUTSOURCING?

Outsourcing
Procuring from external sources services or products that are normally part of an organization.

Offshoring
Moving a business process to a foreign country but retaining control of it.

Client firm
An organization that outsources.

Outsource provider
A firm that provides outsourcing activity.

Outsourcing means procuring from external suppliers services or products that are normally a part of an organization. In other words, a firm takes functions it was performing in-house (such as accounting, janitorial, or call center functions) and has another company do the same job. If a company owns two plants and reallocates production from the first to the second, this is not considered outsourcing. In addition, if a company moves some of its business processes to a foreign country but retains control, we define this move as **offshoring**, not outsourcing. For example, China's Haier Group recently offshored a $40 million refrigerator factory to South Carolina (with huge savings in transportation costs).

A firm that outsources its internal business activities is called the **client firm**. A company that provides outsourcing is called the **outsource provider**.

Early in their life cycle, many businesses handle their activities internally. As businesses mature and grow, however, they often find competitive advantage in the specialization provided by outside firms. They may also find limitations on locally available labor, services, materials, or other resources. So organizations balance the potential benefits of outsourcing with its potential risks. Outsourcing the wrong activities can cause major problems.

Outsourcing is not a new concept; it is simply an extension of the long-standing practice of *subcontracting* production activities. Indeed, the classic make-or-buy decisions concerning products are examples of outsourcing.

[1]The authors wish to thank Professor Marc J. Schneiderjans, of the University of Nebraska–Lincoln, for help with the development of this supplement. His book *Outsourcing and Insourcing in an International Context*, with Ashlyn Schniederjans and Dara Schniederjans (Armonk, NY: M.E. Sharpe, 2005), provided insight, content, and references that shaped our approach to the topic.

So why has outsourcing expanded to become a major strategy in business the world over? From an economic perspective, it is due to the continuing move toward specialization in an increasingly technological society. More specifically, outsourcing's continuing growth is due to (1) increasing expertise, (2) reduced costs of more reliable transportation, and (3) the rapid development and deployment of advancements in telecommunications and computers. Low-cost communication, including the Internet, permits firms anywhere in the world to provide information services that were previously limited geographically. This communication ability also supplies the connectivity needed to support the global outsourcing growth engine.

Examples of outsourcing include:

- Call centers for the French in Angola (a former French colony in Africa) and for the U.S. and England in India
- DuPont's legal services and Procter & Gamble's (P&G's) finance services routed to the Philippines
- Electronic Data Systems (EDS) providing information technology for Delphi Automotive and Nextel
- IBM handling travel services and payroll, and Hewlett-Packard providing IT services to P&G
- ADP providing payroll services for thousands of firms
- Solectron (a specialist in electronic assembly) producing many of IBM's computers
- Production of the Chrysler Crossfire, Audi A4 convertible, and Mercedes CLK convertible by Wilheim Karmann in Osnabruck, Germany

Outsourced manufacturing, also known as contract manufacturing, is becoming standard practice in many industries, from computers (as shown in the photo) to automobiles.

Paralleling the growth of outsourcing is the growth of international trade. With the passage of landmark trade agreements like the North American Free Trade Agreement (NAFTA), the work of the World Trade Organization and the European Union, and other international trade zones established throughout the world, we are witnessing the greatest expansion of international commerce in history.

Types of Outsourcing

Nearly any business activity can be outsourced. A general contractor in the building industry, who subcontracts various construction activities needed to build a home, is a perfect example of an outsourcer. Every component of the building process, including the architect's design, a consultant's site location analysis, a lawyer's work to obtain the building permits, plumbing, electrical work, dry walling, painting, furnace installation, landscaping, and sales, is usually outsourced. Outsourcing implies an agreement (typically a legally binding contract) with an external organization.

> *"Offshoring is when a company takes one of its factories that it is operating in Canton, Ohio and moves the whole factory to Canton, China."*
>
> Thomas Friedman,
> The World Is Flat

> *When outsourcing does work, it can deliver tremendous value.*

Keith Dannemiller, Alamy Images

◄ *Contract manufacturers such as Solectron provide outsourcing service not only to IBM but also to Cisco Systems, HP, Microsoft, Motorola, Sony, Nortel, Ericsson, and Sun. Solectron is a high-quality producer that has won over 450 awards, including the Malcolm Baldrige Award. One of the side benefits of outsourcing is that client firms such as IBM can actually improve their performance by using the competencies of an outstanding firm like Solectron.*

Among the business processes outsourced are (1) purchasing, (2) logistics, (3) R&D, (4) operation of facilities, (5) management of services, (6) human resources, (7) finance/accounting, (8) customer relations, (9) sales/marketing, (10) training, and (11) legal processes. Note that the first six of these are OM functions that we discuss in this text.

STRATEGIC PLANNING AND CORE COMPETENCIES

Organizations develop missions, long-term goals, and strategies as general guides for operating their businesses. The strategic planning process begins with a basic mission statement and establishing goals. Given the mission and goals, strategic planners next undertake an internal analysis of the organization to identify how much or little each business activity contributes to the achievement of the mission.

During such an analysis, firms identify their strengths—what they do well or better than their competitors. These unique skills, talents, and capabilities are called **core competencies**. Core competencies may include specialized knowledge, proprietary technology or information, and unique production methods. The trick is to identify what the organization does better than anyone else. Common sense dictates that core competencies are the activities that a firm should perform. By contrast, *non-core activities*, which can be a sizable portion of an organization's total business, are good candidates for outsourcing.

Sony's core competency, for example, is electromechanical design of chips. This is its core, and Sony is one of the best in the world when it comes to rapid response and specialized production of these chips. But, as Figure 1 suggests, outsourcing could offer Sony continuous innovation and flexibility. Leading specialized outsource providers are likely to come up with major innovations in such areas as software, human resources, and distribution. That is their business, not Sony's.

Managers evaluate their strategies and core competencies and ask themselves how to use the assets entrusted to them. Do they want to be the offshore company that does low-margin work at 3%–4% or the innovative firm that makes a 30%–40% margin? PC or iPod assemblers in China and Taiwan earn 3%–4%, but Apple, which innovates, designs, and sells, has a margin 10 times as large.

Core competencies

An organization's unique skills, talents, and capabilities.

Learning Objective

1. Explain how core competencies relate to outsourcing

▶ **Figure 1**

Sony, an Outsourcing Company*

*Adapted from J. B. Quinn. "Outsourcing Innovation." *Sloan Management Review* (Summer 2000): 20.

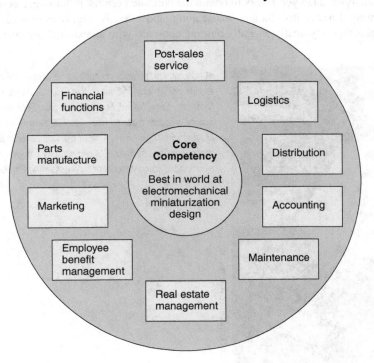

Outsourcers *could* provide Sony with:

The Theory of Comparative Advantage

The motivation for international outsourcing comes from the **theory of comparative advantage**. This theory focuses on the basic economics of outsourcing internationally. According to the theory, if an external outsourcing provider, regardless of its geographic location, can perform activities more productively than the client firm, the client firm should allow the external outsourcing provider firm to do the work. This allows the client firm to focus on what it does best (namely, on its core competencies).

Countries such as India, China, and Russia have made it a government priority and set up agencies to support the easy transition of foreign-based client firms into their outsourcing markets. Work and jobs go to countries that reduce risk through necessary legal structures, build an infrastructure, and have an educated workforce.

Ford's president calls the theory of comparative advantage "Economics 101, Adam Smith."[2] Ford has told its suppliers to match the world's "optimal" prices on auto parts, which usually means parts companies are forced to move work to Mexico or China. But Mexico is in a precarious position. Foster Electric, Ford's speaker supplier, recently shifted its entire production from Mexico to China to shave an additional 20% off its cost. With wages 1/20 of those in the U.S., the term "China price" has become the global benchmark—interchangeable with "lowest price possible." General Motors, which buys more than $80 billion of parts a year, expects its suppliers to meet the best price the firm can find worldwide—or else face termination.[3]

Theory of comparative advantage

A theory which states that countries benefit from specializing in (and exporting) products and services in which they have relative advantage, and importing goods in which they have a relative disadvantage.

"Although you may be good at something tactically, someone else may do it better and at lower cost."

James Champy

OUTSOURCING TRENDS AND POLITICAL REPERCUSSIONS

In a survey of 52 major corporations (83% of them U.S. based), executives were asked what they felt were the most important reasons for outsourcing. The top reasons included cost savings (77%), gaining outside expertise (70%), improving services (61%), focusing on core competencies (59%), and gaining access to technology (56%).[4] The study also revealed that in addition to outsourcing business activities (e.g., computer help desk services), whole business departmental functions (e.g., accounting, marketing, finance, operations management, information systems) were being outsourced. When asked about future plans, 35% said they would continue or expand outsourcing, 40% said they would continue outsourcing but revise their outsourcing arrangements, and a significant percent said they would reduce outsourcing or choose to bring their work inside. Apparently, those with experience in outsourcing are not always completely satisfied, suggesting that executives still have a lot to learn about using outsourcing to boost productivity.

One of the risks is the political backlash that results from outsourcing in foreign countries. The loss of U.S. jobs (as well as the loss of jobs in European countries) has fueled anti-outsourcing rhetoric and action from government officials. (See the *OM in Action* box "Outsourcing to Small-Town U.S.A.") In 2004, the governor of Tennessee signed an anti-outsourcing bill that made the state the first to give businesses an incentive for not outsourcing information systems work to cheaper offshore locations. The law requires state procurement officials to give preference in bids for information systems services to contractors employing workers only in the U.S. Almost 100 other bills aimed at keeping jobs in the U.S. have been introduced in 30 states. On the federal level, the *Thomas-Voinovich Amendment*, which also passed in 2004, prohibits some federal contracts from being outsourced overseas if U.S. government employees had previously done the work. One federal bill requires call centers to disclose their locations to consumers.

[2]N. Shirouzu, "Big Three's Outsourcing Plan: Make Part Suppliers Do It." *The Wall Street Journal* (June 10, 2004): A1, A6 and (September 26, 2005): A1.

[3]T. C. Fishman, "How China Will Change Your Business." *Inc. Magazine* (March 2005): 70–84.

[4]N. M. Goldsmith, *Outsourcing Trends* (New York: The Conference Board, 2003).

Outsourcing to Small-Town U.S.A.

U.S. companies continue their global search for efficiency by outsourcing call centers and back-office operations, but many find they need to look no farther than a place like Nacogdoches, Texas.

To U.S. firms facing quality problems with their outsourcing operations overseas and bad publicity at home, small-town America is emerging as a pleasant alternative. Nacogdoches (population 29,914) or Twin Falls, Idaho (population 34,469), may be the perfect call center location. Even though the pay is only $7 an hour, the jobs are some of the best available to small-town residents.

By moving out of big cities to the cheaper labor and real estate of small towns, companies can save millions and still increase productivity. A call center in a town that just lost its major manufacturing plant finds the jobs easy to fill. U.S. Bank recently picked Coeur d'Alene, Idaho, for its credit card call center. The city "has pretty serious unemployment," says VP Schott Hansen. "We can go in with 500 jobs and really make a difference in the community."

But taking advantage of cheap wages in countries like India will not stop soon. A few years ago, IBM bought Daksh eServices Ltd., a 9,000-employee Indian call center firm, for $170 million. So is India the unstoppable overseas call center capital? Not necessarily. Despite its population of 1.2 billion, only a small percent of its workers have the language skills and education to be employable in Western-style industries. Already, India has been warned that if call centers can't recruit at reasonable wages, its jobs will move to the Philippines, South Africa, and Ghana. And, indeed, in 2006, Apple Computer and Britain's Powergen pulled the plug on Indian call centers, claiming their costs had become too high.

Sources: Information Week (May 9, 2005): 47–53; *Business Week* (August 7, 2006): 40–41; *Business World* (October 11, 2005): 1; *Knight Ridder Tribune Business News* (October 2, 2005): 1.

Other developed countries have similar restrictions. A 2005 survey by the *Financial Times* found that 59% of French, 56% of Belgian, and 51% of German residents feared their jobs moving to other countries. (Ironically, developing countries are also concerned with developed nations exploiting labor and markets and dominating their countries' economic landscapes.)

Despite the negative impression created by government actions, the press, and current public opinion, the latest U.S. government data suggest that foreigners outsource far more services to the U.S. than American companies send abroad. And while U.S. jobs are outsourced, a minuscule few are outsourced offshore. One estimate is that 2/10 of 1% of jobs are outsourced each year, while the dynamic U.S. economy, in the natural course of capitalism, destroys millions of jobs but creates even more.[5] People flock to the U.S. for jobs, and unemployment remains low. The value of U.S. exports of services (e.g., legal work, computer programming, telecommunications, banking) was recently at $54 billion more than the value of U.S. imports of the same services. But outsourcing is a two-way street. India's cartoon producer Jadoo Works has even outsourced projects to U.S. animators!

In summary, the trend toward outsourcing continues to grow. This does not mean all existing outsourcing practices are perfect. The term **backsourcing** has been created to describe the return of business activity to the original firm. We will now discuss the risks associated with outsourcing.

Backsourcing
The return of business activity to the client firm.

RISKS IN OUTSOURCING

"The biggest challenge executives have is that they see outsourcing as a panacea, without investing sufficient time into making sure they do it right."

Dr. James Tompkins

Outsourcing can look very risky. And indeed it is. Perhaps half of all outsourcing agreements fail because of inappropriate planning and analysis.[6] For one thing, few promoters of international outsourcing mention the erratic power grids in some foreign countries or the difficulties with local government officials, inexperienced managers, and unmotivated employees. On the other hand, when managers set an outsourcing goal of 75% cost reduction and receive only a 30%–40% cost reduction, they view the outsourcing as a failure, when, in fact, it may be a success.

Table 1 lists some of the risks inherent in outsourcing.

[5]D. W. Drezner, "The Outsourcing Bogeyman," *Foreign Affairs* 83, no. 3 (May–June 2004): 22.
[6]See S. E. Fawcett, L. M. Ellram, and J. A. Ogden, *Supply Chain Management* [Upper Saddle River, N.J.: Prentice Hall, 2007): 282–300; P. Puranum and K. Srikanth "Seven Myths of Outsourcing" *The Wall Street Journal* (June 16–17, 2007): R6; and J. A. Tompkins, "Don't Outsource the Relationship," *Industrial Engineer* 87, no. 11 (2005): 28–33.

Outsourcing Process	Examples of Possible Risks
Identify non-core competencies	Can be incorrectly identified as a non-core competency.
Identify non-core activities that should be outsourced	Just because the activity is not a core competency for your firm does not mean an outsource provider is more competent and efficient.
Identify impact on existing facilities, capacity, and logistics	May fail to understand the change in resources and talents needed internally.
Establish goals and draft outsourcing agreement specifications	Goals can be set so high that failure is certain.
Identify and select outsource provider	Can select the wrong outsource provider.
Negotiate goals and measures of outsourcing performance	Can misinterpret measures and goals, how they are measured, and what they mean.
Monitor and control current outsourcing program	May be unable to control product development, schedules, and quality.
Evaluate and give feedback to outsource provider	May have a non-responsive provider (i.e., one that ignores feedback).
Evaluate international political and currency risks	Country's currency may be unstable, a country may be politically unstable, or cultural and language differences may inhibit successful operations.
Evaluate coordination needed for shipping and distribution	May not understand the timing necessary to manage flows to different facilities and markets.

◀ **Table 1**

The Outsourcing Process and Related Risks

The *OM in Action* box "Dell Brings Home Its Help Desks" is a case study in the *cultural* risks related to language. Understanding culture and all its implications is fundamental to any international business activity, and it is critically important in outsourcing.

In addition to the external risks, operations managers must deal with other issues that outsourcing brings. These include (1) changes in employment levels, (2) changes in facilities and processes needed to receive components in a different state of assembly, and (3) vastly expanded logistics issues, such as insurance, customs, and timing.

2. Describe the risks of outsourcing

OM in Action   Dell Brings Home Its Help Desks

Dell Computer is considered one of the best PC manufacturers in the world. Its business model, marketing strategies, and management have succeeded even in the most difficult economic times. When it saw other competitors (Gateway and Hewlett-Packard) moving some operations offshore, Dell quickly decided to adopt an international outsourcing strategy as well.

Dell believed it could cut labor costs by moving some of its technical support ("help desk" services) for corporate customers to Bangalore, India. Customers who had problems with their Dell computers could call a help desk service number, and a Dell service technician in India could provide basic technical information to help the customer to resolve the problems. Unfortunately, customer complaints quickly surfaced concerning the difficulty of understanding Indian service technicians.

Despite the best efforts of the provider firm in India, the accent of the Indian technicians was frequently too difficult

▲ *A call centre in Bangalore, India*

Sherwin Crasto, CORBIS/REUTERS America LLC

for customers to understand, a problem reported in the media. When Dell's customers started to complain, Dell management responded by backsourcing, shifting some help desk service phone calls previously routed to Bangalore to locations in Idaho, Tennessee, and Texas. Four of Dell's 30 call centers remain in India, partly to handle calls for help from its growing base of PC owners there.

Sources: CIO (June 1, 2006): 1; *Knight Ridder Tribune Business News* (May 29, 2005): 1 and (May 23, 2006): 1; and MSNBC *Nightly News* (February 19, 2004).

What can be done to mitigate the risks of outsourcing? Research indicates that of all the reasons given for outsourcing failure, the most common is that the decision was made without sufficient understanding of the options through quantitative analysis. The next section provides an analytical framework and some methodologies that help analyze the outsourcing decision process.

METHODOLOGIES FOR OUTSOURCING

In this section we introduce two analytical approaches that can be applied to an outsourcing decision: factor rating and break-even analysis.

Evaluating Multiple Criteria with Factor Rating

The factor-rating method is an excellent tool for dealing with both country risk assessment and source provider selection problems.

Rating International Risk Factors Suppose a company has identified for outsourcing a functional area of production that is a non-core competency. Example 1 shows how to subjectively rate several international risk factors using an *unweighted* factor rating approach.

<table>
<tr><td>

EXAMPLE 1

Establishing risk factors for four countries

▶ **Table 2**

Toronto Airbag's International Risk Factors, by Country (an unweighted approach)

</td><td>

Toronto Airbags produces auto and truck airbags for Nissan, Chrysler, Mercedes, and BMW. It wants to conduct a risk assessment of outsourcing manufacturing. Four countries—England, Mexico, Spain, and Canada (the current home nation)—are being considered. Only English- or Spanish-speaking countries are included because they "fit" with organizational capabilities.

Approach: Toronto's management identifies nine factors, listed in Table 2, and subjectively rates each country on a 0–3 scale, where 0 is no risk and 3 is high risk. Risk ratings are added to find the lowest-risk location.

Risk Factor	England	Mexico	Spain	Canada (home country)
Economic: Labor cost/laws	1	0	2	1
Economic: Capital availability	0	2	1	0
Economic: Infrastructure	0	2	2	0
Culture: Language	0	0	0	0
Culture: Social norms	2	0	1	2
Migration: Uncontrolled	0	2	0	0
Politics: Ideology	2	0	1	2
Politics: Instability	0	1	2	2
Politics: Legalities	3	0	2	3
Total risk rating scores	8	7	11	10

Risk rating scale: 0 = no risk, 1 = minor risk, 2 = average risk, 3 = high risk

Solution: Based on these ratings, Mexico is the least risky of the four locations being considered.

Insight: As with many other quantitative methods, assessing risk factors is not easy and may require considerable research, but the technique adds objectivity to a decision.

Learning exercise: Social norms in England have just been rescored by an economist, and the new rating is "no risk." How does this affect Toronto's decision? [Answer: England now has the lowest rating for risk.]

Related problems: 1, 3

</td></tr>
</table>

Learning Objective

3. Use factor rating to evaluate both country and provider outsourcers

In Example 1, Toronto Airbags considered only English- and Spanish-speaking countries. But it is worth mentioning that countries like China, India, and Russia have millions of English-speaking personnel. This may have an impact on the final decision.

Example 1 considered the home country of the client firm. This inclusion helps document the risks that a domestic outsourcing provider poses compared to the risks posed by international

▲ *Outsourcing office jobs and technical jobs is often feasible because the distance issue is overcome with electronic communication. However, on occasion, outsourcing can take unusual forms. Here, outsourcing the casting of more than 2,000 individual panels (left) to Pretecsa of Mexico and then shipping them 2,350 miles north for Salt Lake City's public library (right) is unusual, but indicates the growing magnitude of outsourcing.*

providers. Including the home country in the analysis also helps justify final strategy selection to stakeholders who might question it.

Indeed, **nearshoring** (i.e., choosing an outsource provider located in the home country or in a nearby country) can be a good strategy for businesses and governments seeking both control and cost advantages. U.S. firms are interested in nearshoring to Canada because of Canada's cultural similarity and geographic nearness to the U.S. This allows the company wanting to outsource to exert more control than would be possible when outsourcing to most other countries. Nearshoring represents a compromise in which some cost savings are sacrificed for greater control because Canada's smaller wage differential limits the labor cost reduction advantage.

Nearshoring
Choosing an outsource provider in the home country or in a nearby country.

Rating Outsource Providers The factor-rating method's computations are when each factor has its own importance weight. We now apply that concept in Example 2 to compare outsourcing providers being considered by a firm.

National Architects, Inc., a San Francisco–based designer of high-rise buildings, has decided to outsource its information technology (IT) function. Three outsourcing providers are being actively considered: one in the U.S., one in India, and one in Israel.

Approach: National's VP–Operations, Susan Cholette, has made a list of seven criteria she considers critical. After putting together a committee of four other VPs, she has rated each firm (on a 1–5 scale with 5 being highest) and has also placed an importance weight on each of the factors, as shown in Table 3.

EXAMPLE 2

Rating tactical provider selection criteria

◄ **Table 3**

Factor Ratings Applied to National Architects's Potential IT Outsourcing Providers

Factor (criterion)*	Importance Weight	Outsource Providers		
		BIM (U.S.)	S.P.C. (India)	Telco (Israel)
1. Can reduce operating costs	.2	3	3	5
2. Can reduce capital investment	.2	4	3	3
3. Skilled personnel	.2	5	4	3
4. Can improve quality	.1	4	5	2
5. Can gain access to technology not in company	.1	5	3	5
6. Can create additional capacity	.1	4	2	4
7. Aligns with policy/ philosophy/culture	.1	2	3	5
Totals	1.0	3.9	3.3	3.8

*These seven major criteria are based on a survey of 165 procurement executives, as reported in J. Schildhouse, "Outsourcing Ins and Outs," *Inside Supply Management* (December 2005): 22–29.

Solution: Susan multiplies each rating by the weight and sums the products in each column to generate a total score for each outsourcing provider. She selects BIM, which has the highest overall rating.

Insight: When the total scores are as close (3.9 vs. 3.8) as they are in this case, it is important to examine the sensitivity of the results to inputs. For example, if one of the importance weights or factor scores changes even marginally, the final selection may change. Management preference may also play a role here.

Learning exercise: Susan decides that "Skilled personnel" should instead get a weight of 0.1 and "Aligns with policy/philosophy/culture" should increase to 0.2. How do the total scores change? [Answer: BIM = 3.6, S.P.C. = 3.2, and Telco = 4.0, so Telco is selected.]

Related problems: 2, 4, 5, 6, 7

Break-even Analysis

In situations in which a firm's production is identified as a possible candidate for outsourcing, a break-even analysis may be applied. We first define total cost in-house as:

$$TC_{in} = F_{in} + (V_{in} \times X_{in}) \tag{1}$$

where TC_{in} is the total cost of an item produced in-house
F_{in} is the total in-house fixed cost
V_{in} is the variable cost/unit produced in-house
X_{in} is the total number of units produced in-house

Using the same approach, total cost under outsourcing is:

$$TC_{out} = F_{out} + (V_{out} \times X_{out}) \tag{2}$$

At an ideal break-even point, $X_{in} = X_{out}$ and $TC_{in} = TC_{out}$. If we let $X = X_{in} = X_{out}$, the two equations can be restated as:

$$F_{in} + (V_{in} \times X) = F_{out} + (V_{out} \times X) \tag{3}$$

By solving for X in Equation (S11-3), we compute how many units must be outsourced in order to reach a break-even point in total costs from both possible sources:

$$X = \frac{F_{in} - F_{out}}{V_{out} - V_{in}} \tag{4}$$

If X is less than the expected demand, we would select the source with the lower *variable* cost and higher *fixed* cost. If X is greater than the expected demand, the source with lower *fixed* cost and higher *variable* cost is chosen. Example 3 applies Equation (4) to a specific company.[7]

▶ *Most U.S. toy companies now outsource their production to Chinese manufacturers. Cost savings are significant, but there are several downsides, including loss of control over such issues as quality. In 2007 alone, Mattel had to recall 10.5 million Elmos, Big Birds, and SpongeBobs. Thomas & Friends recalled 1.5 million wooden trains, and Target recalled 20,000 kid's flashlights. All these made-in-China toys contained excessive levels of lead in their paint or other life-threatening ingredients.*

Ramey, PhotoEdit Inc.

[7]The simple unit break-even model in Equation (4) can also be mathematically adjusted to reflect risk factors inherent in financial parameters when using international outsourcing as a strategy. See M. J. Schniederjans and K. Zuckweiler, "A Quantitative Approach to the Outsourcing–Insourcing Decision in an International Context," *Management Decision* 42, no. 8 (2004): 974–986.

EXAMPLE 3

Outsource break-even analysis for Baker Toys

Toledo's Baker Toys produces a popular toy, the Astro Transformer, invented by its 30-year-old founder Ron Baker. The present annual fixed cost at the Ohio plant is $2 million, and the variable cost per toy is $3. A Chinese manufacturer, Jumbo Products, has approached Ron. Jumbo can produce an Astro Transformer of equal quality for a yearly fixed-cost payment of $1 million and a variable cost per unit of $4. Baker Toys now faces a yearly demand of 1.1 million Astro Transformers. Should Baker outsource to Jumbo?

Approach: Baker applies the outsource break-even model of Equation (4).

Solution: The unit break-even point is:

$$X = \frac{F_{in} - F_{out}}{V_{out} - V_{in}} = \frac{2,000,000 - 1,000,000}{4 - 3}$$
$$= 1,000,000 \text{ units}$$

Since the computed X of 1,000,000 is less than the expected demand of 1,100,000 units, the decision is to produce in-house since Baker has the lower variable cost.

Insight: For firms looking to outsource the manufacture of a single product or a group of products to an outsource provider, where cost is a major factor, this model may apply.

Learning exercise: Jumbo believes it can lower its variable cost per toy from $4 to $3.80 through better training and quality control. Should Baker now outsource to Jumbo? [Answer: Yes, $X = 1,250,000$ units now. So $X > 1,100,000$ units of expected demand.]

Related problems: 8, 9

If cost minimization is a driving force in an outsourcing decision, this break-even approach may be an excellent initial decision methodology. Note that this approach is similar to the crossover chart model.

ADVANTAGES AND DISADVANTAGES OF OUTSOURCING[8]

Advantages of Outsourcing

As mentioned earlier, companies outsource for five main reasons. They are, in order of importance: (1) cost savings, (2) gaining outside expertise, (3) improving operations and service, (4) focusing on core competencies, and (5) gaining outside technology.

Cost Savings The number-one reason driving outsourcing for many firms is the possibility of significant cost savings, particularly for labor. (See the *OM in Action* box "Wal-Mart's Competitive Advantage Is Its Supply Chain").

Gaining Outside Expertise In addition to gaining access to a broad base of skills that are unavailable in-house, an outsourcing provider may be a source of innovation for improving products, processes, and services.

Improving Operations and Service An outsourcing provider may have production flexibility. This may allow the client firm to win orders by more quickly introducing new products and services.

Focusing on Core Competencies An outsourcing provider brings *its* core competencies to the supply chain. This frees up the client firm's human, physical, and financial resources to reallocate to core competencies.

---

[8]See M. Weidenbaum, "Outsourcing: Pros and Cons," *Business Horizons* 48, no. 4 (July/August, 2005): 311; and P. Engardio, "The Future of Outsourcing," *Business Week* (January 30, 2006): 50–64.

OM in Action — Wal-Mart's Competitive Advantage Is Its Supply Chain

Competition is no longer between companies—it is now between supply chains, and Wal-Mart knows the way. No other company has a more efficient supply chain, and no other company has embraced outsourcing to China more vigorously than Wal-Mart. Perhaps as much as 85% of Wal-Mart's merchandise is made abroad, and Chinese factories are by far the most important and fastest growing of these sources.

A whopping 10%–13% of everything China sends to the U.S. ends up on Wal-Mart's shelves—well over $15 billion worth of goods a year. *The Washington Post* reported in 2004 that "more than 80% of the 6,000 factories in Wal-Mart's worldwide database of suppliers are in China." Wal-Mart has almost 600 people on the ground in China just to negotiate and make purchases.

As much as Wal-Mart has been demonized for its part in offshoring jobs and pushing the "China price" on all producers, it has expertly managed and accelerated that trend. Wal-Mart's critical mass allows Chinese firms to build assembly lines that are so huge that they drive prices down through economies of scale.

Wal-Mart's Chinese suppliers achieve startling, market-shaking price cuts. For example, the price of portable DVDs with 7″ LCD screens dropped in half when Wal-Mart found a Chinese factory to build in giant quantities. Likewise, Wal-Mart's Apex brand TVs from Changhong Electric undercut the competition by more than $100. Wal-Mart's success in going abroad and pressing suppliers for price breaks has forced both retailers and manufacturers to seriously reevaluate their supply chains and their operational processes.

Sources: The Booklist (February 1, 2006): 12; *Barron's* (November 20, 2006): 44; *Inc. Magazine* (March 2005): 80; and *Money Marketing* (April 8, 2004): 46.

Gaining Outside Technology The client firm can outsource to state-of-the-art providers instead of retaining "legacy" systems. The client firm does not have to invest in new technology, thereby cutting risks.

Other Advantages There are additional advantages in outsourcing. For example, the client firm may improve its performance and image by associating with an outstanding provider. Outsourcing can also be used as a strategy for downsizing, or "reengineering," a client firm.

Disadvantages of Outsourcing

There are a number of potential disadvantages in outsourcing. Here are just a few:

Increased Transportation Costs Delivery costs may rise substantially if distance increases from an outsourcing provider to a client firm.

Loss of Control This disadvantage can permeate and link to all other problems with outsourcing. When managers lose control of some operations, costs may increase because it's harder to assess and control them. For example, production of most of the world's laptops is now outsourced. This means that companies like Dell and HP find themselves using the same contractor (Quanta) to make their machines in China. This can leave them struggling to maintain control over the supplier.

Creating Future Competition Intel, for example, outsourced a core competency, chip production, to AMD when it could not keep up with early demands. Within a few years, AMD became a leading competitor, manufacturing its own chips.

Negative Impact on Employees Employee morale may drop when functions are outsourced, particularly when friends lose their jobs. Employees believe they may be next, and indeed they may be. Productivity, loyalty, and trust—all of which are needed for a healthy, growing business—may suffer.

Longer-Term Impact Some disadvantages of outsourcing tend to be longer term than the advantages of outsourcing. In other words, many of the risks firms run by outsourcing may not show up on the bottom line until some time in the future. This permits CEOs who prefer short-term planning and are interested only in bottom-line improvements to use the outsourcing strategy to make quick gains at the expense of longer-term objectives.

The advantages and disadvantages of outsourcing may or may not occur but should be thought of as possibilities to be managed effectively.

AUDITS AND METRICS TO EVALUATE OUTSOURCING PERFORMANCE

Regardless of the techniques and success in selection of outsourcing providers, agreements must specify results and outcomes. Whatever the outsourced component or service, management needs an evaluation process to ensure satisfactory continuing performance. At a minimum, the product or service must be defined in terms of quality, customer satisfaction, delivery, cost, and improvement. The mix and detail of the performance measures will depend on the nature of the product.

In situations where the outsourced product or service plays a major role in strategy and winning orders, the relationship needs to be more than after-the-fact audits and reports. It needs to be based on continuing communication, understanding, trust, and performance. The relationship should manifest itself in the mutual belief that "we are in this together" and go well beyond the written agreement.

However, when outsourcing is for less critical components, agreements that include the traditional mix of audits and metrics (such as cost, logistics, quality, and delivery) may be reported weekly or monthly. When a *service* has been outsourced, more imaginative metrics may be necessary. For instance, in an outsourced call center, these metrics may deal with personnel evaluation and training, call volume, call type, and response time, as well as tracking complaints. In this dynamic environment, reporting of such metrics may be required daily.[9]

As the client's needs change, the outsourcing agreements need to evolve also.

ETHICAL ISSUES IN OUTSOURCING

Laws, trade agreements, and business practices are contributing to a growing set of international, ethical practices for the outsourcing industry. Table 4 presents several tenets of conduct that have fairly universal acceptance.

In the electronics industry, HP, Dell, IBM, Intel and twelve other companies have created the Electronics Industry Code of Conduct (EICC). The EICC sets environmental standards, bans child labor and excessive overtime, and audits outsourcing producers to ensure compliance.[10]

Ethics Principle	Outsourcing Linkage
Seek to do no harm to indigenous cultures	Don't use outsourcing in a way that violates religious holidays (e.g., making employees work during religious holidays).
Seek to do no harm to the ecological systems of the world	Don't use outsourcing to move pollution from one country to another.
Seek to uphold universal labor standards	Don't use outsourcing to take advantage of cheap child labor that leads to child abuse.
Seek to uphold basic human rights	Don't accept outsourcing that violates basic human rights.
Seek to pursue long-term involvement in foreign countries	Don't use outsourcing as a short-term arrangement to reduce costs; view it as a long-term partnership.
Seek to share knowledge and technology with foreign countries	Don't think an outsourcing agreement will prevent sharing of technology, but use the inevitable sharing to build a good relationship with foreign outsourcing firms.

◄ **Table 4**

Ethical Principles and Related Outsourcing Linkages

[9]S. H. Huang and H. Keskar, "Comprehensive and Configurable Metrics for Supplier Selection," *International Journal of Production Economics* 105, no. 2 (February, 2007): 510–523.
[10]P. Burrows, "Stalking High-Tech Sweatshops," *Business Week* (June 19, 2006): 62–63.

Summary

Companies can give many different reasons why they outsource, but the reality is that outsourcing's most attractive feature is that it helps firms cut costs. Workers in low-cost countries simply work much more cheaply, with fewer fringe benefits, work rules, and legal restrictions, than their U.S. and European counterparts. For example, a comparable hourly wage of $20 in the U.S. and $30 in Europe is well above the $1 per hour in China. Yet China often achieves quality levels equivalent to (or even higher than) plants in the West.

There is a growing economic pressure to outsource. But there is also a need for planning outsourcing to make it acceptable to all participants. When outsourcing is done in the right way, it creates a win–win situation.

Key Terms

Outsourcing
Offshoring
Client firm

Outsource provider
Core competencies
Theory of comparative advantage

Backsourcing
Nearshoring

Using Software to Solve Outsourcing Problems

Excel, Excel OM, and POM for Windows may be used to solve most of the problems in this supplement. Excel OM and POM for Windows both contain Factor Rating modules that can address issues such as the ones we saw in Examples 1 and 2. They also both contain Cost-volume/Break-even Analysis modules that handle problems like we saw in Example 3.

Solved Problem

 Virtual Office Hours help is available on Student DVD.

Solved Problem 1

Mark Berenson is CEO of Montclair Electronics. He is currently producing 70,000 video telephones a year in his New Jersey plant, where fixed costs are $900,000 and the variable cost per unit is $6. By outsourcing to a Mexican firm, annual fixed cost (F) payments will rise to $1 million, but the variable cost (V) will drop to $5 per unit. Should Berenson outsource?

Solution

Use Equation (4) to compute how many units must be outsourced to reach a break-even point in total costs:

$$X = \frac{F_{in} - F_{out}}{V_{out} - V_{in}} = \frac{900,000 - 1,000,000}{5 - 6}$$

$$= \frac{-100,000}{-1} = 100,000 \text{ units}$$

Since a production level of 70,000 units is less than $X = 100,000$, Berenson should keep producing in New Jersey, where there are lower fixed costs and higher variable costs.

Self-Test

- ***Before taking the self-test***, *refer to the learning objectives listed at the beginning of the selection and the key terms listed at the end of the selection.*
- *Use the key at the back of the text to **correct** your answers.*
- ***Restudy*** *pages that correspond to any question you answered incorrectly or material you feel uncertain about.*

1. Outsourcing is procuring services or products from:
   a) other countries where the company owns facilities
   b) Canada or Mexico
   c) sources external to the organization
   d) offshore firms
   e) all of the above

2. Outsourcing has become a major force in business:
   a) because the Internet allows firms anywhere in the world to provide information services
   b) because of advancement in telecommunications
   c) because of rapid development of technology
   d) because there is more expertise in our knowledge society
   e) all of the above

3. Companies like IBM, HP, and Cisco outsource to Solectron because
   a) they can't build quality products themselves
   b) Solectron is an award-winning company with a good reputation
   c) it is not possible to manufacture computer parts in the U.S. anymore
   d) Solectron only manufactures in India, where costs are lower
   e) IBM, HP, and Cisco do not outsource

4. Core competencies are those strengths in a firm that include:
   a) specialized skills
   b) unique production methods
   c) proprietary information/knowledge
   d) things a company does better than others
   e) all of the above

5. The theory of comparative advantage means:
   a) Russia and China will almost always be selected for outsourcing
   b) a firm should typically outsource if a provider can do the work more productively than the outsourcing firm
   c) international outsourcing is better than outsourcing to other U.S. firms
   d) core competencies are never as strong as a good outsource provider
   e) the same as the theory of constraints

6. Outsourcing can be a risky proposition because:
   a) about half of all outsourcing agreements fail
   b) it only saves about 30% in labor costs
   c) labor costs are increasing throughout the world
   d) a non-core competency is outsourced
   e) shipping costs are increasing

7. Nearshoring is a good strategy for U.S. firms because:
   a) Mexico's culture is identical to that of the U.S.
   b) Canada is a low-cost producer
   c) geographic nearness allows more control than outsourcing to India or China
   d) Latin America is a lower-cost producer than Europe
   e) international trade is declining

8. Advantages of outsourcing include:
   a) focusing on core competencies and cost savings
   b) gaining outside technology and creating new markets in India for U.S. products
   c) improving operations by closing plants in Malaysia
   d) employees will want to leave the firm
   e) reduced problems with logistics

Internet and Student CD-ROM/DVD Exercises

Visit our Companion Web site or use your student CD-ROM/DVD to help with material in this supplement.

 On Our Companion Web Site,
www.prenhall.com/heizer
- Self-Study Quizzes
- Practice Problems
- PowerPoint Lecture

 On Your Student CD-ROM
- Practice Problems
- Excel OM Software
- Excel OM Data Files
- POM for Windows

 On Your Student DVD
- Video Clip and Video Case
- Virtual Office Hours for Solved Problem

Discussion Questions

1. How would you summarize outsourcing trends?
2. What potential cost saving advantages might firms experience by using outsourcing?
3. What internal issues must managers address when outsourcing?
4. How should a company select an outsourcing provider?
5. What are we trying to find the break-even point for in outsourcing break-even analysis?
6. What are international risk factors in the outsourcing decision?
7. How can ethics be beneficial in an outsourcing organization?
8. What are some of the possible consequences of poor outsourcing?

Problems*

• **1** Claudia Pragram Technologies, Inc., has narrowed its choice of outsourcing provider to two firms located in different countries. Pragram wants to decide which one of the two countries is the better choice, based on risk-avoidance criteria. She has polled her executives and established four criteria. The resulting ratings for the two countries are presented in the table below, where 1 is a lower risk and 3 is a higher risk. Using the unweighted factor-rating method, which country would you select?

Selection Criterion	England	Canada
Price of service from outsourcer	2	3
Nearness of facilities to client	3	1
Level of technology	1	3
History of successful outsourcing	1	2 PX

• **2** Using the same ratings given in Problem 1, assume that the executives have determined four criteria weightings: Price, with a weight of 0.1; Nearness, with 0.6; Technology, with 0.2; and History, with 0.1. Using the weighted factor-rating method, which country would you select? Why? PX

• **3** Ranga Ramasesh is the operations manager for a firm that is trying to decide which one of four countries it should research for possible outsourcing providers. The first step is to select a country based on cultural risk factors, which are critical to eventual business success with the provider. Ranga has reviewed outsourcing provider directories and found that the four countries in the table below have an ample number of providers from which they can choose. To aid in the country selection step, he has enlisted the aid of a cultural expert, John Wang, who has provided ratings of the various criteria in the table below. The resulting ratings are on a 1 to 10 scale, where 1 is a low risk and 10 is a high risk. Using the unweighted factor-rating method, which country should Ranga select based on risk avoidance?

Culture Selection Criterion	Mexico	Panama	Costa Rica	Peru
Trust	1	2	2	1
Society value of quality work	7	10	9	10
Religious attitudes	3	3	3	5
Individualism attitudes	5	2	4	8
Time orientation attitudes	4	6	7	3
Uncertainty avoidance attitudes	3	2	4	2 PX

•• **4** Using the same ratings given in Problem 3, assume that John Wang has determined six criteria weightings: Trust, with a weight of 0.4; Quality, with 0.2; Religious, with 0.1; Individualism, with 0.1; Time, with 0.1; and Uncertainty, with 0.1. Using the weighted factor-rating method, which country should Ranga select? PX

Note: PX means the problem may be solved with POM for Windows and/or Excel OM.

• **5** Charles Teplitz's firm wishes to use factor rating to help select an outsourcing provider of logistics services. With weights from 1–5 (5 highest) and ratings from 1–100 (100 highest), use the following table to help Teplitz make his decision:

		Rating of Logistics Providers		
Criterion	Weight	Atlanta Shipping	Seattle Delivery	Utah Freight
Quality	5	90	80	75
Delivery	3	70	85	70
Cost	2	70	80	95 PX

• **6** Walker Accounting Software is marketed to small accounting firms throughout the U.S. and Canada. Owner George Walker has decided to outsource the company's help desk and is considering three providers: Manila Call Center (Philippines), Delhi Services (India), and Moscow Bell (Russia). The following table summarizes the data Walker has assembled. Which outsourcing firm has the best rating? (Higher weights imply higher importance and higher ratings imply more desirable providers.)

		Provider Ratings		
Criterion	Importance Weight	Manila	Delhi	Moscow
Flexibility	0.5	5	1	9
Trustworthiness	0.1	5	5	2
Price	0.2	4	3	6
Delivery	0.2	5	6	6 PX

•••• **7** Price Technologies, a California-based high-tech manufacturer, is considering outsourcing some of its electronics production. Four firms have responded to its request for bids, and CEO Willard Price has started to perform an analysis on the scores his OM team has entered in the table below.

		Ratings of Outsource Providers			
Factor	Weight	A	B	C	D
Labor	w	5	4	3	5
Quality procedures	30	2	3	5	1
Logistics system	5	3	4	3	5
Price	25	5	3	4	4
Trustworthiness	5	3	2	3	5
Technology in place	15	2	5	4	4
Management team	15	5	4	2	1

Weights are on a scale from 1 through 30, and the outsourcing provider scores are on a scale of 1 through 5. The weight for the labor factor is shown as a w because Price's OM team cannot agree on a value for this weight. For what range of values of w, if any, is company C a recommended outsourcing provider, according to the factor-rating method?

•• **8** Kamal-Gursoy Electronics is currently insourcing all its single-product production, with a yearly fixed cost (F_{in}) of $5 million and a variable cost per unit (V_{in}) of $2. The firm is approached by a Vietnamese outsourcing provider that can manufacture the product with equal quality for a yearly fixed cost payment (F_{out}) of \$2 million and a variable cost per unit (V_{out}) of \$6. Kamal-Gursoy is now facing a yearly demand of 2 million units.

a) Using the unit break-even model, should the firm outsource or continue to insource the manufacture of this product?

b) What is the break-even point in units? **Px**

•• **9** Nye Products is currently insourcing all its telephone answering machines (its only product), with a yearly fixed cost of \$7 million and a variable cost per unit of \$3. CEO Harvey Nye has published a request for information and found an outsourcing provider that can manufacture the product with equal quality for a yearly fixed-cost payment of \$3 million and a variable cost per unit of \$8. Nye Products is now facing a yearly demand of 1.5 million telephones.

a) Using the unit break-even model, should Nye outsource or continue to insource the manufacture of this product?

b) What is the break-even point in units? **Px**

Case Studies

Outsourcing to Tata

While some states, such as Tennessee, have been quick to ban or limit international outsourcing of government activities, other state governments have sought to take advantage of low-cost opportunities that international outsourcing can offer.

The state of New Mexico's Labor Department hired Tata Consultancy Services, an Indian outsourcing firm, to redo New Mexico's unemployment compensation computer system. While Tata had completed work for other states, including Pennsylvania and New York, it had never worked on an unemployment compensation system. Also, New Mexico agreed to allow Tata to do all computer software work in India, apparently with insufficient monitoring of progress by New Mexico officials responsible for the outsourcing project.

The new system should have been completed in 6 months, which put the due date in December 2001. Unfortunately, things did not work out well. The initial system was delivered 1 year later. But in late 2004 it was still not working. Also, the outsourcing project went way over the budget of \$3.6 million, up to \$13 million. The warranty for the system ended in 2003, leaving New Mexico with a situation of either suing Tata to complete the project (it was estimated at 80% complete) or hiring someone to fix it. Tata's position was that it had complied with the outsourcing agreement and was willing to continue fixing the system if it could receive additional compensation to justify additional work.

Discussion Questions

1. Use the process in Table 1 to analyze what New Mexico could have done to achieve a more successful outcome.

2. Is this a case of cultural misunderstanding, or could the same result have occurred if a U.S. firm, such as IBM, had been selected?

3. Conduct your own research to assess the risks of outsourcing any information technology project. (*Computerworld* is one good source.)

Outsourcing Offshore at Darden

Video Case

Darden Restaurants, owner of popular brands such as Olive Garden and Red Lobster, serves more than 300 million meals annually in over 1,400 restaurants across the U.S. and Canada. To achieve competitive advantage via its supply chain, Darden must achieve excellence at each step. With purchases from 35 countries, and seafood products with a shelf life as short as 4 days, this is a complex and challenging task.

Those 300 million meals annually mean 40 million pounds of shrimp and huge quantities of tilapia, swordfish, and other fresh purchases. Fresh seafood is typically flown to the U.S. and monitored each step of the way to ensure that 34°F is maintained.

Darden's purchasing agents travel the world to find competitive advantage in the supply chain. Darden personnel from supply chain and development, quality assurance, and environmental relations contribute to developing, evaluating, and checking suppliers. Darden also has seven native-speaking representatives living on other continents to provide continuing support and evaluation of suppliers. All suppliers must abide by Darden's food standards, which typically exceed FDA and other industry standards. Darden expects continuous improvement in durable relationships that increase quality and reduce cost.

Darden's aggressiveness and development of a sophisticated supply chain provides an opportunity for outsourcing. Much food preparation is labor intensive and is often more efficient when handled in bulk. This is particularly true where large volumes may justify capital investment. For instance, Tyson and Iowa Beef prepare meats to Darden's specifications much more economically than can individual restaurants. Similarly, Darden has found that it can outsource both the cutting of salmon to the proper portion size and the cracking/peeling of shrimp more cost-effectively offshore than in U.S. distribution centers or individual restaurants.

Discussion Questions*

1. What are some outsourcing opportunities in a restaurant?

2. What supply chain issues are unique to a firm sourcing from 35 countries?

3. Examine how other firms or industries develop international supply chains as compared to Darden.

4. Why does Darden outsource harvesting and preparation of much of its seafood?

*You may wish to view this video case study on your DVD before answering the questions.

Source: Professors Barry Render (Rollins College), Jay Heizer (Texas Lutheran University), and Beverly Amer (Northern Arizona University).

Bibliography

Aron, R., and J. V. Singh. "Getting Offshoring Right." *Harvard Business Review* (December 2005): 135–143.

Bravard, J., and R. Morgan. *Smarter Outsourcing.* Upper Saddle River, NJ: Pearson (2006).

Champy, James. *Avoiding the Seven Deadly Sins of Outsourcing Relationships.* Plano, TX: Perot Systems (2005).

Friedman, Thomas. *The World Is Flat: A Brief History of the 21st Century.* New York: Farrar, Straus, and Giroux (2005).

Gray, J. V., A. Roth, and B. Tomlin. "An Empirical Study of Manufacturing Outsourcing." *Annual Decision Sciences Institute Proceedings.* San Francisco (2005).

Halvey, J. K., and B. M. Melby. *Business Process Outsourcing*, 2nd ed. New York: Wiley (2007).

Kotabe, M., and Murray, J. Y. "Global Sourcing Strategy and Sustainable Competitive Advantage." *Industrial Marketing Management* 33, no. 1 (2004): 7–15.

Lee, Hau L., and Chung-Yee Lee. *Building Supply Chain Excellence in Emerging Economies.* Secaucus, NJ: Springer (2007).

Rasheed, A. A., and K. M. Gilley. "Outsourcing: National- and Firm-Level Implications." *Thunderbird International Business Review* 47, no. 5 (September/October 2005): 513.

Schildhouse, Jill. "Outsourcing Ins and Outs." *Inside Supply Management* (December 2005): 22–29.

Schniederjans, Marc J., A. M. Schniederjans, and D. G. Schniederjans. *Outsourcing and Insourcing in an International Context.* Armonk, NY: M.E. Sharpe (2005).

Steak, M., and R. Downing. "Another Look at Offshoring." *Business Horizons* 48, no. 6 (November–December 2005): 513.

Thomas, A. R., and T. J. Wilkinson. "The Outsourcing Compulsion." *MIT Sloan Management Review* 48, no. 1 (Fall 2006): 10.

Tompkins, J. A., et al. *Logistics and Manufacturing Outsourcing: Harness Your Core Competencies.* Raleigh, NC: Tompkins Press (2005).

Webb, L., and J. Laborde. "Crafting a Successful Outsourcing Vendor/Client Relationship." *Business Process Management Journal* 11, no. 5 (2005): 437–443.

Whitten, Dwayne, and Dorothy Leidner. "Bringing IT Back: An Analysis of the Decision to Backsource or Switch Vendors." *Decision Sciences* 37, no. 4 (November 2006): 605–621.

Yourdon, Edward. *Outsource: Competing in the Global Productivity Race.* Upper Saddle River, NJ: Prentice Hall (2005).

Internet Resources

Center for Global Outsourcing **www.outsourceglobal.org**
Council on Foreign Affairs **www.foreignaffairs.org**
Global Aquaculture Alliance **www.gaalliance.org**
Institute for Supply Management **www.ism.ws**

Outsourcing directory **www.offshorexperts.com**
Outsourcing global services directory **www.outsourcing.org**
The Outsourcing Institute **www.outsourcing.com**
World Trade Organization **www.wto.org**

Solutions to Even Numbered Problems

2 Canada, 1.7
4 Mexico, 3.3

6 Moscow Bell, 7.1
8 Insource, $X = 750,000$ units, which is less than expected demand.

Solutions to Self Test

1. c; **2.** e; **3.** b; **4.** e; **5.** b; **6.** a; **7.** c; **8.** a.

Inventory Management

Outline

Ten OM Strategy Decisions

Design of Goods and Services

Managing Quality

Process Strategy

Location Strategies

Layout Strategies

Human Resources

Supply Chain Management

Inventory Management

   Independent Demand

   Dependent Demand

   JIT & Lean Operations

Scheduling

Maintenance

Learning Objectives

When you complete this selection you should be able to

1. Conduct an ABC analysis
2. Explain and use cycle counting
3. Explain and use the EOQ model for independent inventory demand
4. Compute a reorder point and explain safety stock
5. Apply the production order quantity model
6. Explain and use the quantity discount model
7. Understand service levels and probabilistic inventory models

Inventory Management Provides Competitive Advantage at Amazon.com

When Jeff Bezos opened his revolutionary business in 1995, Amazon.com was intended to be a "virtual" retailer—no inventory, no warehouses, no overhead—just a bunch of computers taking orders and authorizing others to fill them. Things clearly didn't work out that way. Now, Amazon stocks millions of items of inventory, amid hundreds of thousands of bins on metal shelves, in warehouses (seven around the U.S. and three in Europe) that have twice the floor space of the Empire State Building.

Precisely managing this massive inventory has forced Amazon into becoming a world-class leader in warehouse management and automation, with annual sales of over $8 billion. This profile shows what goes on behind the scenes.

When you place an order at Amazon.com, not only are you doing business with an Internet company, you are doing business with a company that obtains competitive advantage through inventory management.

▶ *1. You order three items, and a computer in Seattle takes charge.* A computer assigns your order—a book, a game, and a digital camera—to one of Amazon's massive U.S. distribution centers, such as the 750,000-square-foot facility in Coffeyville, Kansas.

2. The "flow meister" in Coffeyville receives your order. She determines which workers go where to fill your order.

Marilyn Newton

David Burnett, Contact Press Images, Inc.

◀ *3. Rows of red lights show which products are ordered.* Workers move from bulb to bulb, retrieving an item from the shelf above and pressing a button that resets the light. This is known as a "pick-to-light" system. This system doubles the picking speed of manual operators and drops the error rate to nearly zero.

▼ *4. Your items are put into crates on moving belts.* Each item goes into a large green crate that contains many customers' orders. When full, the crates ride a series of conveyor belts that wind more than 10 miles through the plant at a constant speed of 2.9 feet per second. The bar code on each item is scanned 15 times, by machines and by many of the 600 workers. The goal is to reduce errors to zero—returns are very expensive.

David Burnett, Contact Press Images, Inc.

▶ *5. All three items converge in a chute and then inside a box.* All the crates arrive at a central point where bar codes are matched with order numbers to determine who gets what. Your three items end up in a 3-foot-wide chute—one of several thousand—and are placed into a cardboard box with a new bar code that identifies your order. Picking is sequenced to reduce operator travel.

6. Any gifts you've chosen are wrapped by hand. Amazon trains an elite group of gift wrappers, each of whom processes 30 packages an hour.

David Burnett, Contact Press Images, Inc.

Contact Press Images, Inc.

◀ *7. The box is packed, taped, weighed, and labeled before leaving the warehouse in a truck.* The Coffeyville plant was designed to ship as many as 200,000 pieces a day. About 60% of orders are shipped via the U.S. Postal Service; nearly everything else goes through United Parcel Service.

8. Your order arrives at your doorstep. Within a week, your order is delivered.

As Amazon.com well knows, inventory is one of the most expensive assets of many companies, representing as much as 50% of total invested capital. Operations managers around the globe have long recognized that good inventory management is crucial. On the one hand, a firm can reduce costs by reducing inventory. On the other hand, production may stop and customers become dissatisfied when an item is out of stock. *The objective of inventory management is to strike a balance between inventory investment and customer service.* You can never achieve a low-cost strategy without good inventory management.

All organizations have some type of inventory planning and control system. A bank has methods to control its inventory of cash. A hospital has methods to control blood supplies and pharmaceuticals. Government agencies, schools, and, of course, virtually every manufacturing and production organization are concerned with inventory planning and control.

In cases of physical products, the organization must determine whether to produce goods or to purchase them. Once this decision has been made, the next step is to forecast demand. Then operations managers determine the inventory necessary to service that demand. In this chapter, we discuss the functions, types, and management of inventory. We then address two basic inventory issues: how much to order and when to order.

Inventory investment: your company's largest asset.

FUNCTIONS OF INVENTORY

Inventory can serve several functions that add flexibility to a firm's operations. The four functions of inventory are:

1. To *"decouple"* or separate various parts of the production process. For example, if a firm's supplies fluctuate, extra inventory may be necessary to decouple the production process from suppliers.
2. To *decouple the firm from fluctuations in demand* and *provide a stock of goods that will provide a selection for customers*. Such inventories are typical in retail establishments.
3. To *take advantage of quantity discounts*, because purchases in larger quantities may reduce the cost of goods or their delivery.
4. To *hedge against inflation* and upward price changes.

Types of Inventory

To accommodate the functions of inventory, firms maintain four types of inventories: (1) raw material inventory, (2) work-in-process inventory, (3) maintenance/repair/operating supply (MRO) inventory, and (4) finished-goods inventory.

Raw material inventory has been purchased but not processed. This inventory can be used to decouple (i.e., separate) suppliers from the production process. However, the preferred approach is to eliminate supplier variability in quality, quantity, or delivery time so that separation is not needed. **Work-in-process (WIP) inventory** is components or raw material that have undergone some change but are not completed. WIP exists because of the time it takes for a product to be made (called *cycle time*). Reducing cycle time reduces inventory. Often this task is not difficult: During most of the time a product is "being made," it is in fact sitting idle. As Figure 1

Raw material inventory
Materials that are usually purchased but have yet to enter the manufacturing process.

Work-in-process (WIP) inventory
Products or components that are no longer raw materials but have yet to become finished products.

▼ **Figure 1** **The Material Flow Cycle**

Most of the time that work is in-process (95% of the cycle time) is not productive time.

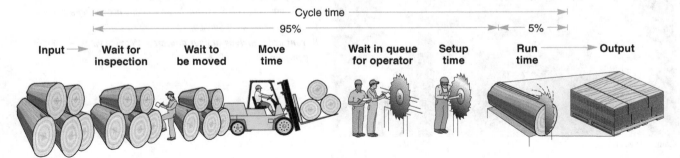

shows, actual work time, or "run" time, is a small portion of the material flow time, perhaps as low as 5%.

MROs are inventories devoted to **maintenance/repair/operating** supplies necessary to keep machinery and processes productive. They exist because the need and timing for maintenance and repair of some equipment are unknown. Although the demand for MRO inventory is often a function of maintenance schedules, other unscheduled MRO demands must be anticipated. **Finished-goods inventory** is completed product awaiting shipment. Finished goods may be inventoried because future customer demands are unknown.

MRO
Maintenance, repair, and operating materials.

Finished-goods inventory
An end item ready to be sold, but still an asset on the company's books.

INVENTORY MANAGEMENT

Operations managers establish systems for managing inventory. In this section, we briefly examine two ingredients of such systems: (1) how inventory items can be classified (called *ABC analysis*) and (2) how accurate inventory records can be maintained. We will then look at inventory control in the service sector.

ABC Analysis

ABC analysis divides on-hand inventory into three classifications on the basis of annual dollar volume. ABC analysis is an inventory application of what is known as the *Pareto principle*. The Pareto principle states that there are a "critical few and trivial many."[1] The idea is to establish inventory policies that focus resources on the *few critical* inventory parts and not the many trivial ones. It is not realistic to monitor inexpensive items with the same intensity as very expensive items.

To determine annual dollar volume for ABC analysis, we measure the *annual demand* of each inventory item times the *cost per unit. Class A* items are those on which the annual dollar volume is high. Although such items may represent only about 15% of the total inventory items, they represent 70% to 80% of the total dollar usage. *Class B* items are those inventory items of medium annual dollar volume. These items may represent about 30% of inventory items and 15% to 25% of the total value. Those with low annual dollar volume are *Class C*, which may represent only 5% of the annual dollar volume but about 55% of the total inventory items.

Graphically, the inventory of many organizations would appear as presented in Figure 2. An example of the use of ABC analysis is shown in Example 1.

ABC analysis
A method for dividing on-hand inventory into three classifications based on annual dollar volume.

Learning Objective

1. Conduct an ABC analysis

◄ **Figure 2**

Graphic Representation of ABC Analysis

EXAMPLE 1

ABC analysis for a chip manufacturer

Silicon Chips, Inc., maker of superfast DRAM chips, wants to categorize its 10 major inventory items using ABC analysis.

Approach: ABC analysis organizes the items on an annual dollar-volume basis. Shown on the following page (in columns 1–4) are the 10 items (identified by stock numbers), their annual demands, and unit costs.

Solution: Annual dollar volume is computed in column 5, along with the percent of the total represented by each item in column 6. Column 7 groups the 10 items into A, B, and C categories.

[1]After Vilfredo Pareto, 19th-century Italian economist.

ABC Calculation

(1) Item Stock Number	(2) Percent of Number of Items Stocked	(3) Annual Volume (units)	×	(4) Unit Cost	=	(5) Annual Dollar Volume	(6) Percent of Annual Dollar Volume		(7) Class
#10286	20%	1,000		$ 90.00		$ 90,000	38.8%	72%	A
#11526		500		154.00		77,000	33.2%		A
#12760	30%	1,550		17.00		26,350	11.3%	23%	B
#10867		350		42.86		15,001	6.4%		B
#10500		1,000		12.50		12,500	5.4%		B
#12572	50%	600		14.17		8,502	3.7%	5%	C
#14075		2,000		.60		1,200	.5%		C
#01036		100		8.50		850	.4%		C
#01307		1,200		.42		504	.2%		C
#10572		250		.60		150	.1%		C
		8,550				$232,057	100.0%		

Insight: The breakdown into A, B, and C categories is not hard and fast. The objective is to try to separate the "important" from the "unimportant."

Learning exercise: The unit cost for Item #10286 has increased from $90.00 to $120.00. How does this impact the ABC analysis? [Answer: The total annual dollar volume increases by $30,000, to $262,057, and the two A items now comprise 75% of that amount.]

Related problems: 1, 2, 3

Criteria other than annual dollar volume can determine item classification. For instance, anticipated engineering changes, delivery problems, quality problems, or high unit cost may dictate upgrading items to a higher classification. The advantage of dividing inventory items into classes allows policies and controls to be established for each class.

Policies that may be based on ABC analysis include the following:

1. Purchasing resources expended on supplier development should be much higher for individual A items than for C items.
2. A items, as opposed to B and C items, should have tighter physical inventory control; perhaps they belong in a more secure area, and perhaps the accuracy of inventory records for A items should be verified more frequently.
3. Forecasting A items may warrant more care than forecasting other items.

Better forecasting, physical control, supplier reliability, and an ultimate reduction in safety stock can all result from appropriate inventory management policies. ABC analysis guides the development of those policies.

Record Accuracy

Good inventory policies are meaningless if management does not know what inventory is on hand. Accuracy of records is a critical ingredient in production and inventory systems. Record accuracy allows organizations to focus on those items that are needed, rather than settling for being sure that "some of everything" is in inventory. Only when an organization can determine accurately what it has on hand can it make precise decisions about ordering, scheduling, and shipping.

To ensure accuracy, incoming and outgoing record keeping must be good, as must be stockroom security. A well-organized stockroom will have limited access, good housekeeping, and storage areas that hold fixed amounts of inventory. Bins, shelf space, and parts will be labeled accurately. The U.S. Marines' approach to improved inventory record accuracy is discussed in the *OM in Action* box "What the Marines Learned about Inventory from Wal-Mart."

OM in Action   What the Marines Learned about Inventory from Wal-Mart

The U.S. Marine Corps knew it had inventory problems. A few years ago, when a soldier at Camp Pendleton, near San Diego, put in an order for a spare part, it took him a week to get it—from the other side of the base. Worse, the Corps had 207 computer systems worldwide. Called the "Rats' Nest" by Marine techies, most systems didn't even talk to each other.

To execute a victory over uncontrolled supplies, the Corps studied Wal-Mart, Caterpillar, Inc., and UPS. "We're in the middle of a revolution," says General Gary McKissock. McKissock aims to reduce inventory for the Corps by half, saving $200 million, and to shift 2,000 Marines from inventory detail to the battlefield.

By replacing inventory with information, the Corps won't have to stockpile tons of supplies near the battle-field, like it did during the Gulf War, only to find it couldn't keep track of what was in containers. Then there was the Marine policy requiring a 60-day supply of everything. McKissock figured out there was no need to overstock commodity items, like office supplies, that can be obtained anywhere. And with advice from the private sector, the Marines have been upgrading warehouses, adding wireless scanners for real-time inventory placement and tracking. Now, if containers need to be sent into a war zone, they will have radio frequency transponders that, when scanned, will link to a database detailing what's inside.

Sources: Modern Materials Handling (August 2005): 24–25; and *Business Week* (December 24, 2001): 24.

Cycle Counting

Even though an organization may have made substantial efforts to record inventory accurately, these records must be verified through a continuing audit. Such audits are known as **cycle counting**. Historically, many firms performed annual physical inventories. This practice often meant shutting down the facility and having inexperienced people count parts and material. Inventory records should instead be verified via cycle counting. Cycle counting uses inventory classifications developed through ABC analysis. With cycle counting procedures, items are counted, records are verified, and inaccuracies are periodically documented. The cause of inaccuracies is then traced and appropriate remedial action taken to ensure integrity of the inventory system. A items will be counted frequently, perhaps once a month; B items will be counted less frequently, perhaps once a quarter; and C items will be counted perhaps once every 6 months. Example 2 illustrates how to compute the number of items of each classification to be counted each day.

Cycle counting
A continuing reconciliation of inventory with inventory records.

Learning Objective
2. Explain and use cycle counting

◄ At John Deere, two workers fill orders for 3,000 parts from a six-stand carousel system, using a sophisticated computer system. The computer saves time searching for parts and speeds orders in the miles of warehouse shelving. While a worker pulls a part from one carousel, the computer sends the next request to the adjacent carousel.

Deere & Company

Cole's Trucks, Inc., a builder of high-quality refuse trucks, has about 5,000 items in its inventory. It wants to determine how many items to cycle count each day.

Approach: After hiring Matt Clark, a bright young OM student, for the summer, the firm determined that it has 500 A items, 1,750 B items, and 2,750 C items. Company policy is to count all A items every month (every 20 working days), all B items every quarter (every 60 working days), and all C items every 6 months (every 120 working days). The firm then allocates some items to be counted each day.

EXAMPLE 2

Cycle counting at a truck manufacturer

Solution:

Item Class	Quantity	Cycle Counting Policy	Number of Items Counted per Day
A	500	Each month (20 working days)	500/20 = 25/day
B	1,750	Each quarter (60 working days)	$1,750/60 \cong 29$/day
C	2,750	Every 6 months (120 working days)	2,750/120 = 23/day
			77/day

Seventy-seven items are counted each day.

Insight: This daily audit of 77 items is much more efficient and accurate than conducting a massive inventory count once a year.

Learning exercise: Cole's reclassifies some B and C items so there are now 1,500 B items and 3,000 C items. How does this change the cycle count? [Answer: B and C both change to 25 items each per day, for a total of 75 items per day.]

Related problem: 4

In Example 2, the particular items to be cycle counted can be sequentially or randomly selected each day. Another option is to cycle count items when they are reordered.

Cycle counting also has the following advantages:

1. Eliminates the shutdown and interruption of production necessary for annual physical inventories.
2. Eliminates annual inventory adjustments.
3. Trained personnel audit the accuracy of inventory.
4. Allows the cause of the errors to be identified and remedial action to be taken.
5. Maintains accurate inventory records.

Control of Service Inventories

Shrinkage
Retail inventory that is unaccounted for between receipt and sale.

Pilferage
A small amount of theft.

Management of service inventories deserves special consideration. Although we may think of the service sector of our economy as not having inventory, that is not always the case. For instance, extensive inventory is held in wholesale and retail businesses, making inventory management crucial and often a factor in a manager's advancement. In the food-service business, for example, control of inventory can make the difference between success and failure. Moreover, inventory that is in transit or idle in a warehouse is lost value. Similarly, inventory damaged or stolen prior to sale is a loss. In retailing, inventory that is unaccounted for between receipt and time of sale is known as **shrinkage**. Shrinkage occurs from damage and theft as well as from sloppy paperwork. Inventory theft is also known as **pilferage**. Retail inventory loss of 1% of sales is consid-

▶ *Pharmaceutical distributor McKesson Corp., which is one of Arnold Palmer Hospital's main suppliers of surgical materials, makes heavy use of bar-code readers to automate inventory control. The device on the warehouse worker's arm combines a scanner, a computer, and a two-way radio to check orders. With rapid and accurate data, items are easily verified, improving inventory and shipment accuracy.*

McKesson Corporation

ered good, with losses in many stores exceeding 3%. Because the impact on profitability is substantial, inventory accuracy and control are critical. Applicable techniques include the following:

1. *Good personnel selection, training, and discipline:* These are never easy but very necessary in food-service, wholesale, and retail operations, where employees have access to directly consumable merchandise.
2. *Tight control of incoming shipments:* This task is being addressed by many firms through the use of bar-code and radio frequency ID (RFID) systems that read every incoming shipment and automatically check tallies against purchase orders. When properly designed, these systems are very hard to defeat. Each item has its own unique stock keeping unit (SKU; pronounced "skew").
3. *Effective control of all goods leaving the facility:* This job is accomplished with bar codes on items being shipped, magnetic strips on merchandise, or via direct observation. Direct observation can be personnel stationed at exits (as at Costco and Sam's Club wholesale stores) and in potentially high-loss areas or can take the form of one-way mirrors and video surveillance.

Successful retail operations require very good store-level control with accurate inventory in its proper location. One recent study found that consumers and clerks could not find 16% of the items at one of the U.S.'s largest retailers—not because the items were out of stock but because they were misplaced (in a backroom, a storage area, or on the wrong aisle). By the researcher's estimates, major retailers lose 10% to 25% of overall profits due to poor or inaccurate inventory records.[2]

Handheld reader can scan RFID tags, aiding control of both incoming and outgoing shipments.

INVENTORY MODELS

We now examine a variety of inventory models and the costs associated with them.

Independent vs. Dependent Demand

Inventory control models assume that demand for an item is either independent of or dependent on the demand for other items. For example, the demand for refrigerators is *independent* of the demand for toaster ovens. However, the demand for toaster oven components is *dependent* on the requirements of toaster ovens.

This selection focuses on managing inventory where demand is *independent*.

◄ *Even for a firm that manages its inventory better than most, Amazon was overwhelmed with the warehousing costs of the latest Harry Potter book. With popular products and seasonality causing surges in demand, retailers and suppliers often rely on large inventories. Full warehouses in November, in preparation for the holiday season, can mean huge holding costs.*

Jens Meyer, AP Wide World Photos

[2]See E. Malykhina, "Retailers Take Stock," *Information Week* (February 7, 2005): 20–22 and A. Raman, N. DeHoratius, and Z. Ton, "Execution: The Missing Link in Retail Operations," *California Management Review* 43, no. 3 (spring 2001): 136–141.

► Table 1

Determining Inventory Holding Costs

Category	Cost (and range) as a Percent of Inventory Value
Housing costs (building rent or depreciation, operating cost, taxes, insurance)	6% (3–10%)
Material handling costs (equipment lease or depreciation, power, operating cost)	3% (1–3.5%)
Labor cost (receiving, warehousing, security)	3% (3–5%)
Investment costs (borrowing costs, taxes, and insurance on inventory)	11% (6–24%)
Pilferage, scrap, and obsolescence (much higher in rapid-change industries like PCs and cell phones)	3% (2–5%)
Overall carrying cost	**26%**

Note: All numbers are approximate, as they vary substantially depending on the nature of the business, location, and current interest rates. Any inventory holding cost of less than 15% is suspect, but annual inventory holding costs often approach 40% of the value of inventory and even more in high tech and fashion industries.

Holding, Ordering, and Setup Costs

Holding cost
The cost to keep or carry inventory in stock.

Holding costs are the costs associated with holding or "carrying" inventory over time. Therefore, holding costs also include obsolescence and costs related to storage, such as insurance, extra staffing, and interest payments. Table 1 shows the kinds of costs that need to be evaluated to determine holding costs. Many firms fail to include all the inventory holding costs. Consequently, inventory holding costs are often understated.

Ordering cost
The cost of the ordering process.

Setup cost
The cost to prepare a machine or process for production.

Setup time
The time required to prepare a machine or process for production.

Ordering cost includes costs of supplies, forms, order processing, purchasing, clerical support, and so forth. When orders are being manufactured, ordering costs also exist, but they are a part of what is called setup costs. **Setup cost** is the cost to prepare a machine or process for manufacturing an order. This includes time and labor to clean and change tools or holders. Operations managers can lower ordering costs by reducing setup costs and by using such efficient procedures as electronic ordering and payment.

In many environments, setup cost is highly correlated with **setup time**. Setups usually require a substantial amount of work before a setup is actually performed at the work center. With proper planning much of the preparation required by a setup can be done prior to shutting down the machine or process. Setup times can thus be reduced substantially. Machines and processes that traditionally have taken hours to set up are now being set up in less than a minute by the more imaginative world-class manufacturers. As we shall see later in this chapter, reducing setup times is an excellent way to reduce inventory investment and to improve productivity.

INVENTORY MODELS FOR INDEPENDENT DEMAND

In this section, we introduce three inventory models that address two important questions: *when to order* and *how much to order*. These *independent* demand models are:

1. Basic economic order quantity (EOQ) model
2. Production order quantity model
3. Quantity discount model

The Basic Economic Order Quantity (EOQ) Model

Economic order quantity (EOQ) model
An inventory-control technique that minimizes the total of ordering and holding costs.

The **economic order quantity (EOQ) model** is one of the oldest and most commonly known inventory-control techniques.[3] This technique is relatively easy to use but is based on several assumptions:

1. Demand is known, constant, and independent.
2. Lead time—that is, the time between placement and receipt of the order—is known and constant.
3. Receipt of inventory is instantaneous and complete. In other words, the inventory from an order arrives in one batch at one time.
4. Quantity discounts are not possible.

[3]The research on EOQ dates to 1915; see Ford W. Harris, *Operations and Cost* (Chicago: A. W. Shaw, 1915).

Inventory Management

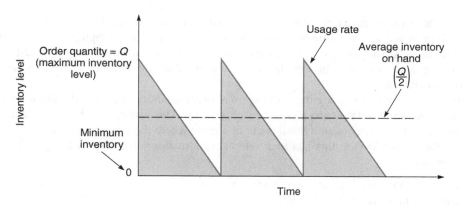

5. The only variable costs are the cost of setting up or placing an order (setup cost) and the cost of holding or storing inventory over time (holding or carrying cost). These costs were discussed in the previous section.

6. Stockouts (shortages) can be completely avoided if orders are placed at the right time.

With these assumptions, the graph of inventory usage over time has a sawtooth shape, as in Figure 3. In Figure 3, Q represents the amount that is ordered. If this amount is 500 dresses, all 500 dresses arrive at one time (when an order is received). Thus, the inventory level jumps from 0 to 500 dresses. In general, an inventory level increases from 0 to Q units when an order arrives.

Because demand is constant over time, inventory drops at a uniform rate over time. (Refer to the sloped lines in Figure 3.) Each time the inventory level reaches 0, the new order is placed and received, and the inventory level again jumps to Q units (represented by the vertical lines). This process continues indefinitely over time.

Learning Objective

3. Explain and use the EOQ model for independent inventory demand

Minimizing Costs

The objective of most inventory models is to minimize total costs. With the assumptions just given, significant costs are setup (or ordering) cost and holding (or carrying) cost. All other costs, such as the cost of the inventory itself, are constant. Thus, if we minimize the sum of setup and holding costs, we will also be minimizing total costs. To help you visualize this, in Figure 4 we graph total costs as a function of the order quantity, Q. The optimal order size, Q^*, will be the quantity that minimizes the total costs. As the quantity ordered increases, the total number of orders placed per year will decrease. Thus, as the quantity ordered increases, the annual setup or ordering cost will decrease. But as the order quantity increases, the holding cost will increase due to the larger average inventories that are maintained.

As we can see in Figure 4, a reduction in either holding or setup cost will reduce the total cost curve. A reduction in setup cost curve also reduces the optimal order quantity (lot size). In addi-

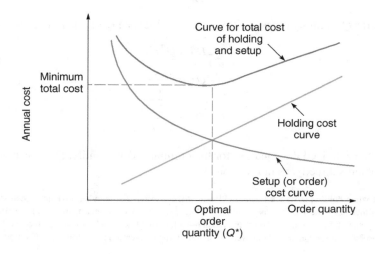

◄ **Figure 4**

Total Cost as a Function of Order Quantity

tion, smaller lot sizes have a positive impact on quality and production flexibility. At Toshiba, the $40 billion Japanese conglomerate, workers can make as few as 10 laptop computers before changing models. This lot-size flexibility has allowed Toshiba to move toward a "build-to-order" mass customization system, an important ability in an industry that has product life cycles measured in months, not years.

You should note that in Figure 4, the optimal order quantity occurs at the point where the ordering-cost curve and the carrying-cost curve intersect. This was not by chance. With the EOQ model, the optimal order quantity will occur at a point where the total setup cost is equal to the total holding cost.[4] We use this fact to develop equations that solve directly for Q^*. The necessary steps are:

1. Develop an expression for setup or ordering cost.
2. Develop an expression for holding cost.
3. Set setup cost equal to holding cost.
4. Solve the equation for the optimal order quantity.

Using the following variables, we can determine setup and holding costs and solve for Q^*:

$$Q = \text{Number of units per order}$$
$$Q^* = \text{Optimum number of units per order (EOQ)}$$
$$D = \text{Annual demand in units for the inventory item}$$
$$S = \text{Setup or ordering cost for each order}$$
$$H = \text{Holding or carrying cost per unit per year}$$

1. Annual set up cost = (Number of orders placed per year) × (Setup or order cost per order)

$$= \left(\frac{\text{Annual demand}}{\text{Number of units in each order}} \right)(\text{Setup or order cost per order})$$

$$= \left(\frac{D}{Q} \right)(S) = \frac{D}{Q}S$$

2. Annual holding cost = (Average inventory level) × (Holding cost per unit per year)

$$= \left(\frac{\text{Order quantity}}{2} \right)(\text{Holding cost per unit per year})$$

$$= \left(\frac{Q}{2} \right)(H) = \frac{Q}{2}H$$

3. Optimal order quantity is found when annual setup cost equals annual holding cost, namely:

$$\frac{D}{Q}S = \frac{Q}{2}H$$

4. To solve for Q^*, simply cross-multiply terms and isolate Q on the left of the equal sign:

$$2DS = Q^2 H$$

$$Q^2 = \frac{2DS}{H}$$

$$Q^* = \sqrt{\frac{2DS}{H}} \qquad\qquad (1)$$

Now that we have derived the equation for the optimal order quantity, Q^*, it is possible to solve inventory problems directly, as in Example 3.

---

[4]This is the case when holding costs are linear and begin at the origin—that is, when inventory costs do not decline (or they increase) as inventory volume increases and all holding costs are in small increments. Additionally, there is probably some learning each time a setup (or order) is executed—a fact that lowers subsequent setup costs. Consequently, the EOQ model is probably a special case. However, we abide by the conventional wisdom that this model is a reasonable approximation.

EXAMPLE 3

Finding the optimal order size at Sharp, Inc.

Sharp, Inc., a company that markets painless hypodermic needles to hospitals, would like to reduce its inventory cost by determining the optimal number of hypodermic needles to obtain per order.

Approach: The annual demand is 1,000 units; the setup or ordering cost is $10 per order; and the holding cost per unit per year is $.50.

Solution: Using these figures, we can calculate the optimal number of units per order:

$$Q^* = \sqrt{\frac{2DS}{H}}$$

$$Q^* = \sqrt{\frac{2(1,000)(10)}{0.50}} = \sqrt{40,000} = 200 \text{ units}$$

Insight: Sharp, Inc., now knows how many needles to order per order. The firm also has a basis for determining ordering and holding costs for this item, as well as the number of orders to be processed by the receiving and inventory departments.

Learning exercise: If D increases to 1,200 units, what is the new Q^*? [Answer: $Q^* = 219$ units.]

Related problems: 5, 6, 7, 8, 9, 12, 13, 15, 36, 38

Excel OM Data File Ch12Ex3.xls

We can also determine the expected number of orders placed during the year (N) and the expected time between orders (T), as follows:

$$\text{Expected number of orders} = N = \frac{\text{Demand}}{\text{Order quantity}} = \frac{D}{Q^*} \qquad (2)$$

$$\text{Expected time between orders} = T = \frac{\text{Number of working days per year}}{N} \qquad (3)$$

Example 4 illustrates this concept.

EXAMPLE 4

Computing number of orders and time between orders at Sharp, Inc.

Sharp, Inc. (in Example 3), has a 250-day working year and wants to find the number of orders (N) and the expected time between orders (T).

Approach: Using Equations (2) and (3), Sharp enters the data given in Example 3.

Solution:

$$N = \frac{\text{Demand}}{\text{Order quantity}}$$

$$= \frac{1,000}{200} = 5 \text{ orders per year}$$

$$T = \frac{\text{Number of working days per year}}{\text{Expected number of orders}}$$

$$= \frac{250 \text{ working days per year}}{5 \text{ orders}} = 50 \text{ days between orders}$$

Insight: The company now knows not only how many needles to order per order but that the time between orders is 50 days and that there are five orders per year.

Learning exercise: If D = 1,200 units instead of 1,000, find N and T. [Answer: $N \cong 5.48$, $T = 45.62$.]

Related problems: 12, 13, 15

As mentioned earlier in this section, the total annual variable inventory cost is the sum of setup and holding costs:

$$\text{Total annual cost} = \text{Setup (order) cost} + \text{Holding cost} \qquad (4)$$

In terms of the variables in the model, we can express the total cost TC as:

$$TC = \frac{D}{Q} S + \frac{Q}{2} H \qquad (5)$$

Example 5 shows how to use this formula.

Active Model 12.1

Examples 3, 4, and 5 are further illustrated in Active Model 12.1 on your CD-ROM.

▶ *This store takes 4 weeks to get an order for Levis 501 jeans filled by the manufacturer. If the store sells 10 pairs of size 30–32 Levis a week, the store manager could set up two containers, keep 40 pairs of jeans in the second container, and place an order whenever the first container is empty. This would be a fixed-quantity reordering system. It is also called a "two-bin" system and is an example of a very elementary, but effective, approach to inventory management*

AP Wide World Photos

EXAMPLE 5

Computing combined cost of ordering and holding

Sharp, Inc. (from Examples 3 and 4), wants to determine the combined annual ordering and holding costs.

Approach: Apply Equation (5), using the data in Example 3.

Solution:

$$TC = \frac{D}{Q}S + \frac{Q}{2}H$$
$$= \frac{1,000}{200}(\$10) + \frac{200}{2}(\$.50)$$
$$= (5)(\$10) + (100)(\$.50)$$
$$= \$50 + \$50 = \$100$$

Insight: These are the annual setup and holding costs. The $100 total does not include the actual cost of goods. Notice that in the EOQ model, holding costs always equal setup (order) costs.

Learning exercise: Find the total annual cost if $D = 1,200$ units in Example 3. [Answer: $109.54.]

Related problems: 9, 12, 13, 14, 38b,c

Inventory costs may also be expressed to include the actual cost of the material purchased. If we assume that the annual demand and the price per hypodermic needle are known values (e.g., 1,000 hypodermics per year at $P = \$10$) and total annual cost should include purchase cost, then Equation (5) becomes:

$$TC = \frac{D}{Q}S + \frac{Q}{2}H + PD$$

Because material cost does not depend on the particular order policy, we still incur an annual material cost of $D \times P = (1,000)(\$10) = \$10,000$. (Later in this chapter we will discuss the case in which this may not be true—namely, when a quantity discount is available.)[5]

[5]The formula for the economic order quantity (Q^*) can also be determined by finding where the total cost curve is at a minimum (i.e., where the slope of the total cost curve is zero). Using calculus, we set the derivative of the total cost with respect to Q^* equal to 0.

The calculations for finding the minimum of $TC = \frac{D}{Q}S + \frac{Q}{2}H + PD$

are Expected number of ord

Thus, $Q^* = \sqrt{\frac{2DS}{H}}$.

Robust Model   A benefit of the EOQ model is that it is robust. By **robust** we mean that it gives satisfactory answers even with substantial variation in its parameters. As we have observed, determining accurate ordering costs and holding costs for inventory is often difficult. Consequently, a robust model is advantageous. Total cost of the EOQ changes little in the neighborhood of the minimum. The curve is very shallow. This means that variations in setup costs, holding costs, demand, or even EOQ make relatively modest differences in total cost. Example 6 shows the robustness of EOQ.

Robust
Giving satisfactory answers even with substantial variation in the parameters.

EXAMPLE 6

EOQ is a robust model

Management in the Sharp, Inc., examples underestimates total annual demand by 50% (say demand is actually 1,500 needles rather than 1,000 needles) while using the same Q. How will the annual inventory cost be impacted?

Approach: We will solve for annual costs twice. First, we will apply the wrong EOQ; then we will recompute costs with the correct EOQ.

Solution: The annual inventory cost increases only $25 ($100 vs. $125), or 25%. Here is why: If demand in Example 5 is actually 1,500 needles rather than 1,000, but management uses an order quantity of $Q = 200$ (when it should be $Q = 244.9$ based on $D = 1,500$), the sum of holding and ordering cost increases 25%:

$$\text{Annual cost} = \frac{D}{Q}S + \frac{Q}{2}H$$

$$= \frac{1,500}{200}(\$10) + \frac{200}{2}(\$.50)$$

$$= \$75 + \$50 = \$125$$

However, had we known that the demand was for 1,500 with an EOQ of 244.9 units, we would have spent $122.47, as shown:

$$\text{Annual cost} = \frac{1,500}{244.9}(\$10) + \frac{244.9}{2}(\$.50)$$

$$= 6.125(\$10) + 122.45(\$.50)$$

$$= \$61.25 + \$61.22 = \$122.47$$

Insight: Note that the expenditure of $125.00, made with an estimate of demand that was substantially wrong, is only 2% ($2.52/$122.47) higher than we would have paid had we known the actual demand and ordered accordingly. Note also, that were if not due to rounding, the annual holding costs and ordering costs would be exactly equal.

Learning exercise: Demand at Sharp remains at 1,000, H is still $.50, and we order 200 needles at a time (as in Example 5). But if the true order cost = S = $15 (rather than $10), what is the annual cost? [Answer: Annual order cost increases to $75, and annual holding cost stays at $50. So the total cost = $125.]

Related problems: 8b, 14

We may conclude that the EOQ is indeed robust and that significant errors do not cost us very much. This attribute of the EOQ model is most convenient because our ability to accurately forecast demand, holding cost, and ordering cost is limited.

Reorder Points

Now that we have decided *how much* to order, we will look at the second inventory question, *when* to order. Simple inventory models assume that receipt of an order is instantaneous. In other words, they assume (1) that a firm will place an order when the inventory level for that particular item reaches zero and (2) that it will receive the ordered items immediately. However, the time between placement and receipt of an order, called **lead time**, or delivery time, can be as short as a few

Lead time
In purchasing systems, the time between placing an order and receiving it; in production systems, the wait, move, queue, setup, and run times for each component produced.

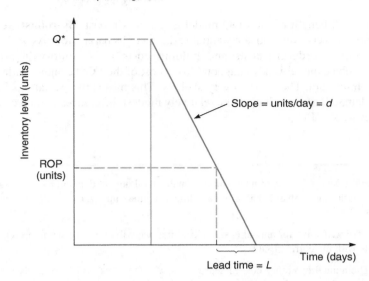

► **Figure 5**

The Reorder Point (ROP)

$Q*$ is the optimum order quantity, and lead time represents the time between placing and receiving an order.

hours or as long as months. Thus, the when-to-order decision is usually expressed in terms of a **reorder point (ROP)**—the inventory level at which an order should be placed (see Figure 5).

Reorder point (ROP)

The inventory level (point) at which action is taken to replenish the stocked item.

The reorder point (ROP) is given as:

$$ROP = (\text{Demand per day}) \times (\text{Lead time for a new order in days})$$
$$= d \times L \tag{6}$$

This equation for ROP *assumes that demand during lead time and lead time itself are constant.* When this is not the case, extra stock, often called **safety stock**, should be added.

Safety stock

Extra stock to allow for uneven demand; a buffer.

The demand per day, d, is found by dividing the annual demand, D, by the number of working days in a year:

$$d = \frac{D}{\text{Number of working days in a year}}$$

Computing the reorder point is demonstrated in Example 7.

EXAMPLE 7

Computing reorder points (ROP) for iPods

An Apple distributor has a demand for 8,000 iPods per year. The firm operates a 250-day working year. On average, delivery of an order takes 3 working days. It wants to calculate the reorder point.

Approach: Compute the daily demand and then apply Equation (6).

Solution:

$$d = \frac{D}{\text{Number of working days in a year}} = \frac{8,000}{250}$$
$$= 32 \text{ units}$$
$$ROP = \text{Reorder point} = d \times L = 32 \text{ units per day} \times 3 \text{ days}$$
$$= 96 \text{ units}$$

Insight: Thus, when iPod inventory stock drops to 96 units, an order should be placed. The order will arrive 3 days later, just as the distributor's stock is depleted.

Learning exercise: If there are only 200 working days per year, what is the correct ROP? [Answer: 120 iPods.]

Related problems: 9d, 10, 11, 13f

Learning Objective

4. Compute a reorder point and explain safety stock

Safety stock is especially important in firms whose raw material deliveries may be uniquely unreliable. For example, San Miguel Corp. in the Philippines uses cheese curd imported from Europe. Because the normal mode of delivery is lengthy and variable, safety stock may be substantial.

Production Order Quantity Model

5. Apply the production order quantity model

In the previous inventory model, we assumed that the entire inventory order was received at one time. There are times, however, when the firm may receive its inventory over a period of time. Such cases require a different model, one that does not require the instantaneous-receipt assumption. This model is applicable under two situations: (1) when inventory continuously flows or builds up over a period of time after an order has been placed or (2) when units are produced and sold simultaneously. Under these circumstances, we take into account daily production (or inventory-flow) rate and daily demand rate. Figure 6 shows inventory levels as a function of time.

Because this model is especially suitable for the production environment, it is commonly called the **production order quantity model**. It is useful when inventory continuously builds up over time, and traditional economic order quantity assumptions are valid. We derive this model by setting ordering or setup costs equal to holding costs and solving for optimal order size, Q^*. Using the following symbols, we can determine the expression for annual inventory holding cost for the production order quantity model:

Production order quantity model

An economic order quantity technique applied to production orders.

$Q =$ Number of units per order

$H =$ Holding cost per unit per year

$p =$ Daily production rate

$d =$ Daily demand rate, or usage rate

$t =$ Length of the production run in days

1. $\left(\begin{array}{c}\text{Annual inventory}\\\text{holding cost}\end{array}\right) = (\text{Average inventory level}) \times \left(\begin{array}{c}\text{Holding cost}\\\text{per unit per year}\end{array}\right)$

2. $\left(\begin{array}{c}\text{Average inventory}\\\text{level}\end{array}\right) = (\text{Maximum inventory level})/2$

3. $\left(\begin{array}{c}\text{Maximum}\\\text{inventory level}\end{array}\right) = \left(\begin{array}{c}\text{Total production during}\\\text{the production run}\end{array}\right) - \left(\begin{array}{c}\text{Total used during}\\\text{the production run}\end{array}\right)$

$= pt - dt$

However, $Q =$ total produced $= pt$, and thus $t = Q/p$. Therefore:

$$\text{Maximum inventory level} = p\left(\frac{Q}{p}\right) - d\left(\frac{Q}{p}\right) = Q - \frac{d}{p}Q$$

$$= Q\left(1 - \frac{d}{p}\right)$$

4. Annual inventory holding cost (or simply holding cost) =

$$\frac{\text{Maximum inventory level}}{2}(H) = \frac{Q}{2}\left[1 - \left(\frac{d}{p}\right)\right]H$$

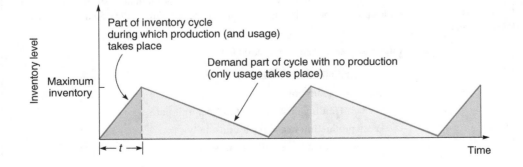

◄ **Figure 6**

Change in Inventory Levels over Time for the Production Model

▶ *Each order may require a change in the way a machine or process is set up. Reducing setup time usually means a reduction in setup cost; and reductions in setup costs make smaller batches (lots) economical to produce. Increasingly, set up (and operation) is performed by computer-controlled machines, such as this one, operating from previously written programs.*

Using this expression for holding cost and the expression for setup cost developed in the basic EOQ model, we solve for the optimal number of pieces per order by equating setup cost and holding cost:

$$\text{Setup cost} = (D/Q)S$$

$$\text{Holding cost} = \tfrac{1}{2}HQ[1-(d/p)]$$

Set ordering cost equal to holding cost to obtain Q_p^*:

$$\frac{D}{Q}S = \tfrac{1}{2}HQ[1-(d/p)]$$

$$Q^2 = \frac{2DS}{H[1-(d/p)]}$$

$$Q_p^* = \sqrt{\frac{2DS}{H[1-(d/p)]}} \tag{7}$$

In Example 8, we use the above equation, Q_p^*, to solve for the optimum order or production quantity when inventory is consumed as it is produced.

EXAMPLE 8

A production order quantity model

Excel Data OM File Ch12Ex8.xls

Nathan Manufacturing, Inc., makes and sells specialty hubcaps for the retail automobile aftermarket. Nathan's forecast for its wire-wheel hubcap is 1,000 units next year, with an average daily demand of 4 units. However, the production process is most efficient at 8 units per day. So the company produces 8 per day but uses only 4 per day. The company wants to solve for the optimum number of units per order. (*Note:* This plant schedules production of this hubcap only as needed, during the 250 days per year the shop operates.)

Approach: Gather the cost data and apply Equation (7):

$$\text{Annual demand} = D = 1,000 \text{ units}$$

$$\text{Setup costs} = S = \$10$$

$$\text{Holding cost} = H = \$0.50 \text{ per unit per year}$$

$$\text{Daily production rate} = p = 8 \text{ units daily}$$

$$\text{Daily demand rate} = d = 4 \text{ units daily}$$

solution:

$$Q_p^* = \sqrt{\frac{2DS}{H[1-(d/p)]}}$$

$$Q_p^* = \sqrt{\frac{2(1,000)(10)}{0.50[1-(4/8)]}}$$

$$= \sqrt{\frac{20,000}{0.50(1/2)}} = \sqrt{80,000}$$

$$= 282.8 \text{ hubcaps, or } 283 \text{ hubcaps}$$

Active Model 12.2

Example 8 is further illustrated in Active Model 12.2 on the CD-ROM.

Insight: The difference between the production order quantity model and the basic EOQ model is the annual holding cost, which is reduced in the production order quantity model.

Learning exercise: If Nathan can increase its daily production rate from 8 to 10, how does TC change? [Answer: $Q_p^* = 258$.]

Related problems: 16, 17, 18, 37

You may want to compare this solution with the answer in Example 3, which had identical D, S, and H values. Eliminating the instantaneous-receipt assumption, where $p = 8$ and $d = 4$, resulted in an increase in Q^* from 200 in Example 3 to 283 in Example 8. This increase in Q^* occurred because holding cost dropped from \$.50 to (\$.50 × $\frac{1}{2}$), making a larger order quantity optimal. Also note that:

$$d = 4 = \frac{D}{\text{Number of days the plant is in operation}} = \frac{1,000}{250}$$

We can also calculate Q_p^* when *annual* data are available. When annual data are used, we can express Q_p^* as:

$$Q_p^* = \sqrt{\frac{2DS}{H\left(1 - \dfrac{\text{Annual demand rate}}{\text{Annual production rate}}\right)}} \tag{8}$$

OM in Action Inventory Accuracy at Milton Bradley

Milton Bradley, a division of Hasbro, Inc., has been manufacturing toys for more than 100 years. Founded by Milton Bradley in 1860, the company started by making a lithograph of Abraham Lincoln. Using his printing skills, Bradley developed games, including the Game of Life, Chutes and Ladders, Candy Land, Scrabble, and Lite Brite. Today, the company produces hundreds of games, requiring billions of plastic parts.

Once Milton Bradley has determined the optimal quantities for each production run, it must make them and assemble them as a part of the proper game. Some games require literally hundreds of plastic parts, including spinners, hotels, people, animals, cars, and so on. According to Gary Brennan, director of manufacturing, getting the right number of pieces to the right toys and production lines is the most important issue for the credibility of the company. Some orders can require 20,000 or more perfectly assembled games delivered to their warehouses in a matter of days.

Games with the incorrect number of parts and pieces can result in some very unhappy customers. It is also

Anthony Labbe Photography

time-consuming and expensive for Milton Bradley to supply the extra parts or to have toys or games returned. When shortages are found during the assembly stage, the entire production run is stopped until the problem is corrected. Counting parts by hand or machine is not always accurate. As a result, Milton Bradley now weighs pieces and completed games to determine if the correct number of parts have been included. If the weight is not exact, there is a problem that is resolved before shipment. Using highly accurate digital scales, Milton Bradley is now able to get the right parts in the right game at the right time. Without this simple innovation, the most sophisticated production schedule is meaningless.

Sources: The Wall Street Journal (April 15, 1999): B1; *Plastics World* (March 1997): 22–26; and *Modern Materials Handling* (September 1997): 55–57.

Quantity Discount Models

Quantity discount
A reduced price for items purchased in large quantities.

To increase sales, many companies offer quantity discounts to their customers. A **quantity discount** is simply a reduced price (P) for an item when it is purchased in larger quantities. Discount schedules with several discounts for large orders are common. A typical quantity discount schedule appears in Table 2. As can be seen in the table, the normal price of the item is $5. When 1,000 to 1,999 units are ordered at one time, the price per unit drops to $4.80; when the quantity ordered at one time is 2,000 units or more, the price is $4.75 per unit. As always, management must decide when and how much to order. However, with an opportunity to save money on quantity discounts, how does the operations manager make these decisions?

As with other inventory models discussed so far, the overall objective is to minimize total cost. Because the unit cost for the third discount in Table 2 is the lowest, you may be tempted to order 2,000 units or more merely to take advantage of the lower product cost. Placing an order for that quantity, however, even with the greatest discount price, may not minimize total inventory cost. Granted, as discount quantity goes up, the product cost goes down. However, holding cost increases because orders are larger. Thus the major trade-off when considering quantity discounts is between *reduced product cost* and *increased holding cost*. When we include the cost of the product, the equation for the total annual inventory cost can be calculated as follows:

$$\text{Total cost} = \text{Setup cost} + \text{Holding cost} + \text{Product cost}$$

6. Explain and use the quarterly discount model

or

$$TC = \frac{D}{Q}S + \frac{Q}{2}H + PD \tag{9}$$

where Q = Quantity ordered
D = Annual demand in units
S = Ordering or setup cost per order or per setup
P = Price per unit
H = Holding cost per unit per year

Now, we have to determine the quantity that will minimize the total annual inventory cost. Because there are several discounts, this process involves four steps:

Step 1: For each discount, calculate a value for optimal order size Q^*, using the following equation:

$$Q^* = \sqrt{\frac{2DS}{IP}} \tag{10}$$

Note that the holding cost is IP instead of H. Because the price of the item is a factor in annual holding cost, we cannot assume that the holding cost is a constant when the price per unit changes for each quantity discount. Thus, it is common to express the holding cost as a percent (I) of unit price (P) instead of as a constant cost per unit per year, H.

Don't forget to adjust order quantity upward if the quantity is too low to qualify for the discount.

Step 2: For any discount, if the order quantity is too low to qualify for the discount, adjust the order quantity upward to the *lowest* quantity that will qualify for the discount. For example, if Q^* for discount 2 in Table 2 were 500 units, you would adjust this value up to 1,000 units. Look at the second discount in Table 2. Order quantities between 1,000 and 1,999 will qualify for the 4% discount. Thus, if Q^* is below 1,000 units, we will adjust the order quantity up to 1,000 units.

▶ **Table 2**

A Quantity Discount Schedule

Discount Number	Discount Quantity	Discount (%)	Discount Price (P)
1	0 to 999	no discount	$5.00
2	1,000 to 1,999	4	$4.80
3	2,000 and over	5	$4.75

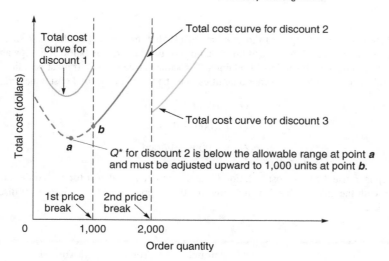

◄ **Figure 7**

Total Cost Curve for the Quantity Discount Model

The reasoning for step 2 may not be obvious. If the order quantity, Q^*, is below the range that will qualify for a discount, a quantity within this range may still result in the lowest total cost.

As shown in Figure 7, the total cost curve is broken into three different total cost curves. There is a total cost curve for the first ($0 \leq Q \leq 999$), second ($1,000 \leq Q \leq 1,999$), and third ($Q \geq 2,000$) discount. Look at the total cost (TC) curve for discount 2. Q^* for discount 2 is less than the allowable discount range, which is from 1,000 to 1,999 units. As the figure shows, the lowest allowable quantity in this range, which is 1,000 units, is the quantity that minimizes total cost. Thus, the second step is needed to ensure that we do not discard an order quantity that may indeed produce the minimum cost. Note that an order quantity computed in step 1 that is *greater* than the range that would qualify it for a discount may be discarded.

Step 3: Using the preceding total cost equation, compute a total cost for every Q^* determined in steps 1 and 2. If you had to adjust Q^* upward because it was below the allowable quantity range, be sure to use the adjusted value for Q^*.

Step 4: Select the Q^* that has the lowest total cost, as computed in step 3. It will be the quantity that will minimize the total inventory cost.

Let us see how this procedure can be applied with an example.

EXAMPLE 9

Quantity discount model

Excel OM Data File Ch12Ex9.xls

Wohl's Discount Store stocks toy race cars. Recently, the store has been given a quantity discount schedule for these cars. This quantity schedule was shown in Table 2. Thus, the normal cost for the toy race cars is $5.00. For orders between 1,000 and 1,999 units, the unit cost drops to $4.80; for orders of 2,000 or more units, the unit cost is only $4.75. Furthermore, ordering cost is $49.00 per order, annual demand is 5,000 race cars, and inventory carrying charge, as a percent of cost, I, is 20%, or .2. What order quantity will minimize the total inventory cost?

Approach: We will follow the four steps just outlined for a quantity discount model.

Solution: The first step is to compute Q^* for every discount in Table 2. This is done as follows:

$$Q_1^* = \sqrt{\frac{2(5,000)(49)}{(.2)(5.00)}} = 700 \text{ cars per order}$$

$$Q_2^* = \sqrt{\frac{2(5,000)(49)}{(.2)(4.80)}} = 714 \text{ cars per order}$$

$$Q_3^* = \sqrt{\frac{2(5,000)(49)}{(.2)(4.75)}} = 718 \text{ cars per order}$$

The second step is to adjust upward those values of Q^* that are below the allowable discount range. Since Q_1^* is between 0 and 999, it need not be adjusted. Because Q_2^* is below the allowable range of 1,000 to 1,999, it must be adjusted to 1,000 units. The same is true for Q_3^*: It must be adjusted to 2,000 units. After this step, the following order quantities must be tested in the total cost equation:

$$Q_1^* = 700$$
$$Q_2^* = 1{,}000\text{—adjusted}$$
$$Q_3^* = 2{,}000\text{—adjusted}$$

The third step is to use the total cost equation (9) and compute a total cost for each order quantity. This step is taken with the aid of Table 3, which presents the computations for each level of discount introduced in Table 2.

▶ **Table 3**

Total Cost Computations for Wohl's Discount Store

Discount Number	Unit Price	Order Quantity	Annual Product Cost	Annual Ordering Cost	Annual Holding Cost	Total
1	$5.00	700	$25,000	$350	$350	$25,700
2	$4.80	1,000	$24,000	$245	$480	$24,725
3	$4.75	2,000	$23,750	$122.50	$950	$24,822.50

The fourth step is to select that order quantity with the lowest total cost. Looking at Table 3, you can see that an order quantity of 1,000 toy race cars will minimize the total cost. You should see, however, that the total cost for ordering 2,000 cars is only slightly greater than the total cost for ordering 1,000 cars. Thus, if the third discount cost is lowered to $4.65, for example, then this quantity might be the one that minimizes total inventory cost.

Insight: The quantity discount model's third cost factor, annual product cost, is now a major variable with impact on the final cost and decision. It takes substantial increases in order and holding costs to compensate for a large quantity price break.

Learning exercise: Wohl's has just been offered a third price break. If it orders 2,500 or more cars at a time, the unit cost drops to $4.60. What is the optimal order quantity now? [Answer: $Q_4^* = 2{,}500$, for a total cost of $24,248.]

Related problems: 19, 20, 21, 22, 23, 24, 25

PROBABILISTIC MODELS AND SAFETY STOCK

All the inventory models we have discussed so far make the assumption that demand for a product is constant and certain. We now relax this assumption. The following inventory models apply when product demand is not known but can be specified by means of a probability distribution. These types of models are called **probabilistic models**.

Probabilistic model

A statistical model applicable when product demand or any other variable is not known but can be specified by means of a probability distribution.

Service level

The complement of the probability of a stockout.

An important concern of management is maintaining an adequate service level in the face of uncertain demand. The **service level** is the *complement* of the probability of a stockout. For instance, if the probability of a stockout is 0.05, then the service level is .95. Uncertain demand raises the possibility of a stockout. One method of reducing stockouts is to hold extra units in inventory. As we noted, such inventory is usually referred to as safety stock. It involves adding a number of units as a buffer to the reorder point. As you recall from our previous discussion:

$$\text{Reorder point} = \text{ROP} = d \times L$$

where d = Daily demand
L = Order lead time, or number of working days it takes to deliver an order

The inclusion of safety stock (ss) changes the expression to:

$$\text{ROP} = d \times L + ss \tag{11}$$

The amount of safety stock maintained depends on the cost of incurring a stockout and the cost of holding the extra inventory. Annual stockout cost is computed as follows:

Annual stockout costs = The sum of the units short for each demand level
× The probability of that demand level × The stockout cost/unit
× The number of orders per year   (12)

Example 10 illustrates this concept.

EXAMPLE 10

Determining safety stock with probabilistic demand and constant lead time

David Rivera Optical has determined that its reorder point for eyeglass frames is 50 ($d \times L$) units. Its carrying cost per frame per year is $5, and stockout (or lost sale) cost is $40 per frame. The store has experienced the following probability distribution for inventory demand during the reorder period. The optimum number of orders per year is six.

	Number of Units	Probability
	30	.2
	40	.2
ROP →	50	.3
	60	.2
	70	.1
		1.0

How much safety stock should David Rivera keep on hand?

Approach: The objective is to find the amount of safety stock that minimizes the sum of the additional inventory holding costs and stockout costs. The annual holding cost is simply the holding cost per unit multiplied by the units added to the ROP. For example, a safety stock of 20 frames, which implies that the new ROP, with safety stock, is 70 (= 50 + 20), raises the annual carrying cost by $5(20) = $100.

However, computing annual stockout cost is more interesting. For any level of safety stock, stockout cost is the expected cost of stocking out. We can compute it, as in Equation (12), by multiplying the number of frames short (Demand – ROP) by the probability of demand at that level, by the stockout cost, by the number of times per year the stockout can occur (which in our case is the number of orders per year). Then we add stockout costs for each possible stockout level for a given ROP.

Solution: We begin by looking at zero safety stock. For this safety stock, a shortage of 10 frames will occur if demand is 60, and a shortage of 20 frames will occur if the demand is 70. Thus the stockout costs for zero safety stock are:

(10 frames short) (.2) ($40 per stockout) (6 possible stockouts per year)
+ (20 frames short) (.1) ($40) (6) = $960

The following table summarizes the total costs for each of the three alternatives:

Safety Stock	Additional Holding Cost	Stockout Cost		Total Cost
20	(20) ($5) = $100		$ 0	$100
10	(10) ($5) = $ 50	(10) (.1) ($40) (6)	= $240	$290
0	$ 0	(10) (.2) ($40) (6) + (20) (.1) ($40) (6) = $960		$960

The safety stock with the lowest total cost is 20 frames. Therefore, this safety stock changes the reorder point to 50 + 20 = 70 frames.

Insight: The optical company now knows that a safety stock of 20 frames will be the most economical decision.

Learning exercise: David Rivera's holding cost per frame is now estimated to be $20, while the stockout cost is $30 per frame. Does the reorder point change? [Answer: Safety stock = 10 now, with a total cost of $380, which is the lowest of the three. ROP = 60 frames.]

Related problems: 29, 30, 31

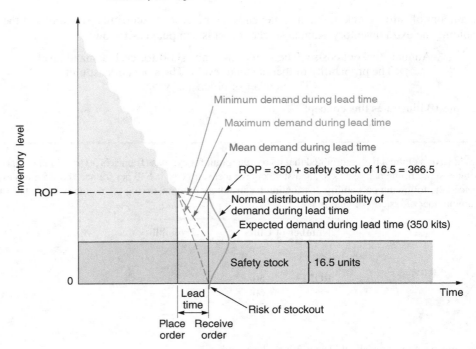

► **Figure 8**

**Probabilistic Demand
for a Hospital Item**

Expected number of kits
needed during lead time is
350, but for a 95% service
level, the reorder point
should be raised to 366.5.

When it is difficult or impossible to determine the cost of being out of stock, a manager may decide to follow a policy of keeping enough safety stock on hand to meet a prescribed customer service level. For instance, Figure 8 shows the use of safety stock when demand (for hospital resuscitation kits) is probabilistic. We see that the safety stock in Figure 8 is 16.5 units, and the reorder point is also increased by 16.5.

The manager may want to define the service level as meeting 95% of the demand (or, conversely, having stockouts only 5% of the time). Assuming that demand during lead time (the reorder period) follows a normal curve, only the mean and standard deviation are needed to define the inventory requirements for any given service level. Sales data are usually adequate for computing the mean and standard deviation. In the following example we use a normal curve with a known mean (μ) and standard deviation (σ) to determine the reorder point and safety stock necessary for a 95% service level. We use the following formula:

$$\text{ROP} = \text{Expected demand during lead time} + Z\sigma_{dLT} \qquad \text{(13)}$$

where
Z = Number of standard deviations
σ_{dLT} = Standard deviation of demand during lead time

EXAMPLE 11

Safety stock with
probabilistic demand

Memphis Regional Hospital stocks a "code blue" resuscitation kit that has a normally distributed demand during the reorder period. The mean (average) demand during the reorder period is 350 kits, and the standard deviation is 10 kits. The hospital administrator wants to follow a policy that results in stockouts only 5% of the time.

(a) What is the appropriate value of Z? (b) How much safety stock should the hospital maintain? (c) What reorder point should be used?

Approach: The hospital determines how much inventory is needed to meet the demand 95% of the time. The figure in this example may help you visualize the approach. The data are as follows:

μ = Mean demand = 350 kits

σ_{dLT} = Standard deviation of demand during lead time = 10 kits

Z = Number of standard normal deviations

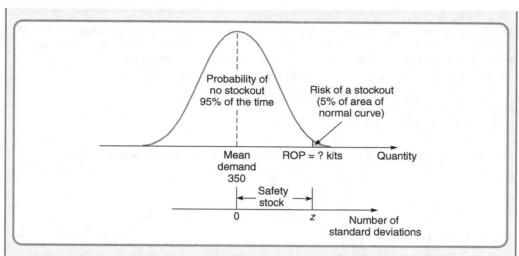

Solution:

a. We use the properties of a standardized normal curve to get a Z-value for an area under the normal curve of .95 (or $1 - .05$). Using a normal table (see Appendix I), we find a Z-value of 1.65 standard deviations from the mean.

b. Because: Safety stock $= x - \mu$

And: $Z = \dfrac{x - \mu}{\sigma_{dLT}}$

Then: Safety stock $= Z\sigma_{dLT}$ **(14)**

Solving for safety stock, as in Equation (14), gives:

Safety stock $= 1.65(10) = 16.5$ kits

This is the situation illustrated in Figure 8.

c. The reorder point is:

ROP $=$ Expected demand during lead time $+$ Safety stock

$= 350$ kits $+ 16.5$ kits of safety stock $= 366.5$, or 367 kits

Insight: The cost of the inventory policy increases dramatically (exponentially) with an increase in service levels.

Learning exercise: What policy results in stockouts 10% of the time? [Answer: $Z = 1.28$; safety stock $= 12.8$; ROP $= 363$ kits.]

Related problems: 27, 28, 38

Other Probabilistic Models

Equations (13) and (14) assume that both an estimate of expected demand during lead times and its standard deviation are available. When data on lead time demand are *not* at hand, these formulas cannot be applied. However, three other models are available. We need to determine which model to use for three situations:

1. Demand is variable and lead time is constant

2. Lead time is variable, and demand is constant

3. Both demand and lead time are variable

All three models assume that demand and lead time are independent variables. Note that our examples use days, but weeks can also be used. Let us examine these three situations separately, because a different formula for the ROP is needed for each.

Learning Objective

7. Understand service levels and probabilistic inventory models

Demand Is Variable and Lead Time Is Constant   When *only the demand is variable*, then:

$$\text{ROP} = (Average \text{ daily demand} \times \text{Lead time in days}) + Z\sigma_{dLT} \qquad \textbf{(15)}$$

where $\sigma_{dLT} = $ Standard deviation of demand during lead time $= \sigma_d \sqrt{\text{Lead time}}$

and $\sigma_d = $ Standard deviation of demand per day

351

EXAMPLE 12

ROP for variable demand and constant lead time

The *average* daily demand for Apple iPods at a Circuit Town store is 15, with a standard deviation of 5 units. The lead time is constant at 2 days. Find the reorder point if management wants a 90% service level (i.e., risk stockouts only 10% of the time). How much of this is safety stock?

Approach: Apply Equation (15) to the following data:

Average daily demand (normally distributed) = 15
Lead time in days (constant) = 2
Standard deviation of daily demand = σ_d = 5
Service level = 90%

Solution: From the normal table (Appendix I), we derive a Z-value for 90% of 1.28. Then:

$$ROP = (15 \text{ units} \times 2 \text{ days}) + Z\sigma_d \sqrt{\text{Lead time}}$$
$$= 30 + 1.28(5)(\sqrt{2})$$
$$= 30 + 1.28(5)(1.41) = 30 + 9.02 = 39.02 \cong 39$$

Thus, safety stock is about 9 iPods.

Insight: The value of Z depends on the manager's stockout risk level. The smaller the risk, the higher the Z.

Learning exercise: If the Circuit Town manager wants a 95% service level, what is the new ROP? [Answer: ROP = 41.63, or 42.]

Related problem: 32

Lead Time Is Variable and Demand is Constant When the demand is constant and *only the lead time is variable*, then:

$$ROP = (\text{Daily demand} \times \textit{Average} \text{ lead time in days}) + Z(\text{Daily demand}) \times \sigma_{LT} \qquad (16)$$

where σ_{LT} = Standard deviation of lead time in days

EXAMPLE 13

ROP for constant demand and variable lead time

The Circuit Town store in Example 12 sells about 10 digital cameras a day (almost a constant quantity). Lead time for camera delivery is normally distributed with a mean time of 6 days and a standard deviation of 3 days. A 98% service level is set. Find the ROP.

Approach: Apply Equation (16) to the following data:

Daily demand = 10
Average lead time = 6 days
Standard deviation of lead time = σ_{LT} = 3 days
Service level = 98%, so Z (from Appendix I) = 2.055

Solution: From the equation we get:

$$ROP = (10 \text{ units} \times 6 \text{ days}) + 2.055(10 \text{ units})(3)$$
$$= 60 + 61.65 = 121.65$$

The reorder point is about 122 cameras.

Insight: Note how the very high service level of 98% drives the ROP up.

Learning exercise: If a 90% service level is applied, what does the ROP drop to? [Answer: ROP = 60 + (1.28)(10)(3) = 60 + 38.4 = 98.4, since the Z-value is only 1.28.]

Related problem: 33

Both Demand and Lead Time Are Variable When both the demand and lead time are variable, the formula for reorder point becomes more complex[6]:

$$ROP = (\text{Average daily demand} \times \text{Average lead time}) + Z\sigma_{dLT} \qquad (17)$$

where
$$\sigma_d = \text{Standard deviation of demand per day}$$
$$\sigma_{LT} = \text{Standard deviation of lead time in days}$$

and
$$\sigma_{dLT} = \sqrt{(\text{Average lead time} \times \sigma_d^2) + (\text{Average daily demand})^2 \sigma_{LT}^2}$$

[6]Refer to S. Narasimhan, D. W. McLeavey, and P. Billington, *Production Planning and Inventory Control*, 2nd ed. (Upper Saddle River, NJ: Prentice Hall, 1995), Chap. 6, for details. Note that Equation (17) can also be expressed as
$$ROP = \text{Average daily demand} \times \text{Average lead time} + Z\sqrt{(\text{Average lead time} \times \sigma_d^2) + \bar{d}^2 \sigma_{LT}^2}$$

EXAMPLE 14

ROP for variable demand and variable lead time

The Circuit Town store's most popular item is six-packs of 9-volt batteries. About 150 packs are sold per day, following a normal distribution with a standard deviation of 16 packs. Batteries are ordered from an out-of-state distributor; lead time is normally distributed with an average of 5 days and a standard deviation of 1 day. To maintain a 95% service level, what ROP is appropriate?

Approach: Determine a quantity at which to reorder by applying Equation (17) to the following data:

Average daily demand = 150 packs
Standard deviation of demand = σ_d = 16 packs
Average lead time = 5 days
Standard deviation of lead time = σ_{LT} = 1 day
Service level = 95%, so Z = 1.65 (from Appendix I)

Solution: From the equation we compute:

$$\text{ROP} = (150 \text{ packs} \times 5 \text{ days}) + 1.65\,\sigma_{dLT}$$

$$\text{where} \quad \sigma_{dLT} = \sqrt{(5 \text{ days} \times 16^2) + (150^2 \times 1^2)}$$

$$= \sqrt{(5 \times 256) + (22{,}500 \times 1)}$$

$$= \sqrt{1{,}280 + 22{,}500} = \sqrt{23{,}780} \cong 154$$

So $\text{ROP} = (150 \times 5) + 1.65(154) \cong 750 + 254 = 1{,}004$ packs

Insight: When both demand and lead time are variable, the formula looks quite complex. But it is just the result of squaring the standard deviations in Equations (15) and (16) to get their variances, then summing them, and finally taking the square root.

Learning exercise: For an 80% service level, what is the ROP? [Answer: Z = .84 and ROP = 879 packs.]

Related problem: 34

FIXED-PERIOD (P) SYSTEMS

The inventory models that we have considered so far are **fixed-quantity**, or **Q**, **systems**. That is, the same fixed amount is added to inventory every time an order for an item is placed. We saw that orders are event triggered. When inventory decreases to the reorder point (ROP), a new order for Q units is placed.

To use the fixed-quantity model, inventory must be continuously monitored. This is called a **perpetual inventory system**. Every time an item is added to or withdrawn from inventory, records must be updated to make sure the ROP has not been reached.

In a **fixed-period**, or **P**, **system**, on the other hand, inventory is ordered at the end of a given period. Then, and only then, is on-hand inventory counted. Only the amount necessary to bring total inventory up to a prespecified target level is ordered. Figure 9 illustrates this concept.

Fixed-quantity (Q) system
An EOQ ordering system with the same order amount each time.

Perpetual inventory system
A system that keeps track of each withdrawal or addition to inventory continuously, so records are always current.

Fixed-period (P) system
A system in which inventory orders are made at regular time intervals.

◀ **Figure 9**

Inventory Level in a Fixed-Period (P) System

Various amounts (Q_1, Q_2, Q_3, etc.) are ordered at regular time intervals (P) based on the quantity necessary to bring inventory up to the target quantity (T).

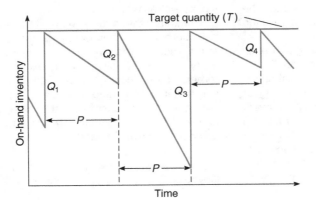

Fixed-period systems have several of the same assumptions as the basic EOQ fixed-quantity system:

- The only relevant costs are the ordering and holding costs.
- Lead times are known and constant.
- Items are independent of one another.

The downward-sloped line in Figure 9 again represents on-hand inventory. But now, when the time between orders (P) passes, we place an order to raise inventory up to the target quantity (T). The amount ordered during the first period may be Q_1, the second period Q_2, and so on. The Q_i value is the difference between current on-hand inventory and the target inventory level. Example 15 illustrates how much to reorder in a simple P system.

EXAMPLE 15

P-system ordering

Hard Rock London has a back order for three leather bomber jackets in its retail shop. There are no jackets in stock, none are expected from earlier orders, and it is time to place an order. The target value is 50 jackets. How many bomber jackets should be ordered?

Approach: Consider the four variables: the target quantity, on-hand inventory, earlier orders en route, and back orders.

Solution: Order amount (Q) = Target quantity (T) – On-hand inventory – Earlier orders not yet received + Back orders = 50 – 0 – 0 + 3 = 53 jackets

Insight: Because demand in a P system is variable, some orders will be larger than the EOQ and some will be smaller.

Learning exercise: Hard Rock has a back order of 5 London T-shirts, no on-hand inventory, a target quantity of 400, and no orders not yet received. What is Q? [Answer: 405 T-shirts.]

Related problem: 35

The advantage of the fixed-period system is that there is no physical count of inventory items after an item is withdrawn—this occurs only when the time for the next review comes up. This procedure is also convenient administratively, especially if inventory control is only one of several duties of an employee.

A fixed-period system is appropriate when vendors make routine (i.e., at fixed-time interval) visits to customers to take fresh orders or when purchasers want to combine orders to save ordering and transportation costs (therefore, they will have the same review period for similar inventory items). For example, a vending machine company may come to refill its machines every Tuesday. This is also the case at Anheuser-Busch, whose sales reps may visit a store every 5 days (see the *OM in Action* box "66,207,896 Bottles of Beer on the Wall").

OM in Action   66,207,896 Bottles of Beer on the Wall

When Dereck Gurden pulls up at one of his customers' stores—7-Eleven, Buy N Save, or one of dozens of liquor marts and restaurants in the 800-square-mile territory he covers in California's Central Valley—managers usually stop what they're doing and grab a note pad. This is because, as Gurden claims, "I know more about these guys' businesses than they do . . . at least in the beer section."

What makes Gurden and other sales reps for Anheuser-Busch distributors so smart? It's BudNet, the King of Beer's top-secret crown jewel—a nationwide data network through which drivers and reps report, in excruciating detail, on sales, shelf space, inventory, and displays at thousands of stores. How does it work? As Gurden walks a store, he inputs what he sees to his handheld PC, then plugs into a cell phone and fires off new orders, along with

the data he has gathered. Anheuser has made a deadly accurate science of finding out what beer lovers are buying, as well as when, where, and why.

Matching these data with U.S. census figures of neighborhoods, Anheuser mines data down to the sales at individual stores. The company can pinpoint age, ethnicity, education, political, and sexual orientation of customers at your local 7-Eleven. BudNet is the primary reason Anheuser's share of the $75 billion U.S. beer market continues to increase, and the company has posted double-digit profit gains for 20 straight quarters while its competitors have flat-lined.

Sources: Business 2.0 (January/February 2001): 47–49; *Beverage Industry* (May 2004): 20–23; and *The Wall Street Journal* (March 23, 2004): C3.

The disadvantage of the P system is that because there is no tally of inventory during the review period, there is the possibility of a stockout during this time. This scenario is possible if a large order draws the inventory level down to zero right after an order is placed. Therefore, a higher level of safety stock (as compared to a fixed-quantity system) needs to be maintained to provide protection against stockout during both the time between reviews and the lead time.

Summary

Inventory represents a major investment for many firms. This investment is often larger than it should be because firms find it easier to have "just-in-case" inventory rather than "just-in-time" inventory. Inventories are of four types:

1. Raw material and purchased components
2. Work-in-process
3. Maintenance, repair, and operating (MRO)
4. Finished goods

In this chapter, we discussed independent inventory, ABC analysis, record accuracy, cycle counting, and inventory models used to control independent demands. The EOQ model, production order quantity model, and quantity discount model can all be solved using Excel, Excel OM, or POM for Windows software. A summary of the inventory models presented in this chapter is shown in Table 4.

◄ **Table 4**

Models for Independent Demand Summarized

Q = Number of units per order	P = Price
EOQ = Optimum order quantity (Q^*)	I = Annual inventory carrying cost as a percent
D = Annual demand in units	μ = Mean demand
S = Setup or ordering cost for each order	σ_{dLT} = Standard deviation of demand during lead-time
H = Holding or carrying cost per unit per year in dollars	σ_{LT} = Standard deviation of lead time
p = Daily production rate	Z = Standardized value under the normal curve
d = Daily demand rate	

EOQ:

$$Q^* = \sqrt{\frac{2DS}{H}} \qquad (1)$$

EOQ production order quantity model:

$$Q_p^* = \sqrt{\frac{2DS}{H[1-(d/p)]}} \qquad (7)$$

Total cost for the EOQ and quantity discount EOQ models:

$$
\begin{aligned}
TC =\ & \text{Total cost} \\
=\ & \text{Setup cost} + \text{Holding cost} + \text{Product cost} \\
=\ & \frac{D}{Q}S + \frac{Q}{2}H + PD \qquad (9)
\end{aligned}
$$

Quantity discount EOQ model:

$$Q^* = \sqrt{\frac{2DS}{IP}} \qquad (10)$$

Probability model with expected lead time demand known:

$$\text{ROP} = \text{Expected demand during lead time} + Z\sigma_{dLT} \qquad (13)$$

$$\text{Safety stock} = Z\sigma_{dLT} \qquad (14)$$

Probability model with variable demand and constant lead time:

$$\text{ROP} = (\text{Average daily demand} \times \text{Lead time in days}) + Z\sigma_{dLT} \qquad (15)$$

Probability model with constant demand and variable lead time:

$$\text{ROP} = (\text{Daily demand} \times \text{Average lead time in days}) + Z(\text{Daily demand})\,\sigma_{LT} \qquad (16)$$

Probability model with both demand and lead time variable:

$$\text{ROP} = (\text{Average daily demand} \times \text{Average lead time in days}) + Z\sigma_{dLT} \qquad (17)$$

Key Terms

Raw material inventory	Ordering cost	Quantity discount
Work-in-process (WIP) inventory	Setup cost	Probabilistic model
MRO	Setup time	Service level
Finished-goods inventory	Economic order quantity (EOQ) model	Fixed-quantity (Q) system
ABC analysis	Robust	Perpetual inventory system
Cycle counting	Lead time	Fixed-period (P) system
Shrinkage	Reorder point (ROP)	
Pilferage	Safety stock	
Holding cost	Production order quantity model	

Using Software to Solve Inventory Problems

This section presents three ways to solve inventory problems with computer software. First, you can create your own Excel spreadsheets. Second, you can use the Excel OM software that comes with this text and is found on the student CD. Third, POM for Windows, also on your CD, can solve all problems marked with a **P**.

Creating Your Own Excel Spreadsheets

Program 1 illustrates how you can make an Excel model to solve Example 8. This is a production order quantity model. Below Program 1 is a listing of the formulas needed to create the spreadsheet.

▶ **Program 1**

Using Excel for a Production Model, with Data from Example 8

	A	B
1	**Nathan Manufacturing, Inc.**	
2		
3	Demand rate, D	1000
4	Setup cost, S	$ 10.00
5	Holding cost, H	$ 0.50
6	Daily production rate, p	8
7	Daily demand rate, d	4
8	Days per year	250
9	Unit price, P	$ 200.00
10		
11		
12	Optimal production quantity, Q*	282.84
13	Maximum Inventory	141.42
14	Average Inventory	70.71
15	Number of Setups	3.54
16	Time (days) between production runs	70.71
17		
18	Holding cost	$ 35.36
19	Setup cost	$ 35.36
20		
21	Unit costs	$ 200,000
22		
23	Total cost, Tc	$ 200,071
24		

Computations

Value	Cell	Excel Formula
Optimal production quantity, Q*	B12	=SQRT(2*B3*B4/B5)*SQRT(B6/(B6-B7))
Maximum Inventory	B13	=B12*(B6-B7)/B6
Average Inventory	B14	=B13/2
Number of Setups	B15	=B3/B12
Time (days) between production runs	B16	=B8/B15
Holding cost	B18	=B14*B5
Setup cost	B19	=B15*B4
Unit costs	B21	=B9*B3
Total cost, Tc	B22	=B18+B19+B21

Using Excel OM

Excel OM allows us to easily model inventory problems ranging from ABC analysis, to the basic EOQ model, to the production model, to quantity discount situations.

Program 2 shows the input data, selected formulas, and results for an ABC analysis, using data from Example 1. After the data are entered, we use the *Data* and *Sort* Excel commands to rank the items from largest to smallest dollar volumes.

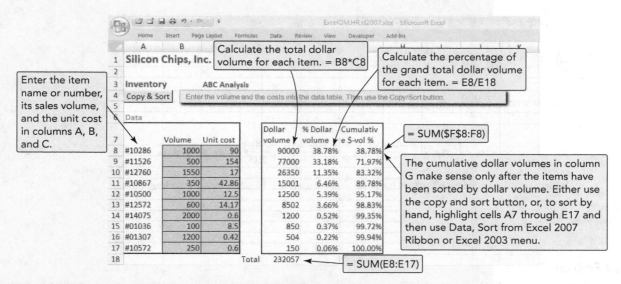

▲ **Program 2** Using Excel OM for an ABC Analysis, with Data from Example 1

Using POM for Windows

The POM for Windows Inventory module can also solve the entire EOQ family of problems.

Solved Problems

 Virtual Office help is available on Student DVD.

Solved Problem 1

David Alexander has compiled the following table of six items in inventory at Angelo Products, along with the unit cost and the annual demand in units:

Identification Code	Unit Cost ($)	Annual Demand (units)
XX1	5.84	1,200
B66	5.40	1,110
3CPO	1.12	896
33CP	74.54	1,104
R2D2	2.00	1,110
RMS	2.08	961

Use ABC analysis to determine which item(s) should be carefully controlled using a quantitative inventory technique and which item(s) should not be closely controlled.

Solution

The item that needs strict control is 33CP, so it is an A item. Items that do not need to be strictly controlled are 3CPO, R2D2, and RMS; these are C items. The B items will be XX1 and B66.

Code	Annual dollar volume = Unit Cost × Demand
XX1	$ 7,008.00
B66	$ 5,994.00
3CPO	$ 1,003.52
33CP	$82,292.16
R2D2	$ 2,220.00
RMS	$ 1,998.88

Total cost = $100,516.56
70% of total cost = $70,347.92

Solved Problem 2

The Warren W. Fisher Computer Corporation purchases 8,000 transistors each year as components in minicomputers. The unit cost of each transistor is $10, and the cost of carrying one transistor in inventory for a year is $3. Ordering cost is $30 per order.

What are (a) the optimal order quantity, (b) the expected number of orders placed each year, and (c) the expected time between orders? Assume that Fisher operates on a 200-day working year.

solution

(a) $Q^* = \sqrt{\dfrac{2DS}{H}} = \sqrt{\dfrac{2(8,000)(30)}{3}} = 400$ units

(b) $N = \dfrac{D}{Q^*} = \dfrac{8,000}{400} = 20$ orders

(c) Time between orders $= T = \dfrac{\text{Number of working days}}{N} = \dfrac{200}{20} = 10$ working days

With 20 orders placed each year, an order for 400 transistors is placed every 10 working days.

Solved Problem 3

Annual demand for notebook binders at Meyer's Stationery Shop is 10,000 units. Brad Meyer operates his business 300 days per year and finds that deliveries from his supplier generally take 5 working days. Calculate the reorder point for the notebook binders.

solution

$$L = 5 \text{ days}$$

$$d = \frac{10,000}{300} = 33.3 \text{ units per day}$$

$$\text{ROP} = d \times L = (33.3 \text{ units per day})(5 \text{ days})$$
$$= 166.7 \text{ units}$$

Thus, Brad should reorder when his stock reaches 167 units.

Solved Problem 4

Leonard Presby, Inc., has an annual demand rate of 1,000 units but can produce at an average production rate of 2,000 units. Setup cost is $10; carrying cost is $1. What is the optimal number of units to be produced each time?

solution

$$Q_p^* = \sqrt{\dfrac{2DS}{H\left(1 - \dfrac{\text{Annual demand rate}}{\text{Annual production rate}}\right)}} = \sqrt{\dfrac{2(1,000)(10)}{1[1 - (1,000/2,000)]}}$$

$$= \sqrt{\dfrac{20,000}{1/2}} = \sqrt{40,000} = 200 \text{ units}$$

Solved Problem 5

Whole Nature Foods sells a gluten-free product for which the annual demand is 5,000 boxes. At the moment it is paying $6.40 for each box; carrying cost is 25% of the unit cost; ordering costs are $25. A new supplier has offered to sell the same item for $6.00 if Whole Nature Foods buys at least 3,000 boxes per order. Should the firm stick with the old supplier, or take advantage of the new quantity discount?

solution

Under present price of $6.40 per box:

Economic order quantity, using Equation (10):

$$Q^* = \sqrt{\frac{2DS}{IP}}$$

$$Q^* = \sqrt{\frac{2(5,000)(25)}{(0.25)(6.40)}}$$

$$= 395.3, \text{ or } 395 \text{ boxes}$$

where
D = period demand
S = order cost
P = price per box
I = holding cost as percent
H = holding cost = IP

Total cost = Order cost + Holding cost + Purchase cost

$$= \frac{DS}{Q} + \frac{Q}{2}H + PD$$

$$= \frac{(5,000)(25)}{395} + \frac{(395)(0.25)(6.40)}{2} + (6.40)(6,000)$$

$$= 316 + 316 + 32,000$$

$$= \$32,632$$

Note: Order and carrying costs are rounded.

Under the quantity discount price of $6.00 per box:

Total cost = Order cost + Holding cost + Purchase cost

$$= \frac{DS}{Q} + \frac{Q}{2}H + PD$$

$$= \frac{(5,000)(25)}{3000} + \frac{(5,000)(0.25)(6.00)}{2} + (6.00)(5,000)$$

$$= 42 + 3,750 + 30,000$$

$$= \$33,792$$

Therefore, the old supplier with whom Whole Nature Foods would incur a total cost of $32,632 is preferable.

Solved Problem 6

Children's art sets are ordered once each year by Ashok Kumar, Inc., and the reorder point, without safety stock (dL) is 100 art sets. Inventory carrying cost is $10 per set per year, and the cost of a stockout is $50 per set per year. Given the following demand probabilities during the reorder period, how much safety stock should be carried?

Demand during Reorder Period	Probability
0	.1
50	.2
ROP → 100	.4
150	.2
200	.1
	1.0

solution

		Incremental Costs	
Safety Stock	Carrying Cost	Stockout Cost	Total Cost
0	0	50 × (50 × 0.2 + 100 × 0.1) = 1,000	$1,000
50	50 × 10 = 500	50 × (0.1 × 50) = 250	750
100	100 × 10 = 1,000	0	1,000

The safety stock that minimizes total incremental cost is 50 sets. The reorder point then becomes 100 sets + 50 sets, or 150 sets.

Solved Problem 7

What safety stock should Ron Satterfield Corporation maintain if mean sales are 80 during the reorder period, the standard deviation is 7, and Ron can tolerate stockouts 10% of the time?

solution

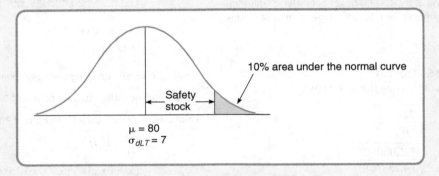

From Appendix I, Z at an area of .9 (or $1 - .10$) = 1.28, and Equation (14):

$$\text{Safety stock} = Z\sigma_{dLT}$$
$$= 1.28(7) = 8.96 \text{ units, or } 9 \text{ units}$$

Solved Problem 8

The daily demand for 52″ plasma TVs at Sarah's Discount Emporium is normally distributed, with an average of 5 and a standard deviation of 2 units. The lead time for receiving a shipment of new TVs is 10 days and is fairly constant. Determine the reorder point and safety stock for a 95% service level.

solution

The ROP for this variable demand and constant lead time model uses Equation (15):

$$\text{ROP} = (\text{Average daily demand} \times \text{Lead time in days}) + Z\sigma_{dLT}$$

where $\sigma_{dLT} = \sigma_d \sqrt{\text{Lead time}}$

So, with $Z = 1.65$,

$$\text{ROP} = (5 \times 10) + 1.65(2)\sqrt{10}$$
$$= 50 + 10.4 = 60.4 \cong 60 \text{ TVs}$$

The safety stock is 10.4, or about 10 TVs.

Solved Problem 9

The demand at Arnold Palmer Hospital for a specialized surgery pack is 60 per week, virtually every week. The lead time from McKesson, its main supplier, is normally distributed, with a mean of 6 weeks for this product and a standard deviation of 2 weeks. A 90% weekly service level is desired. Find the ROP.

solution

Here the demand is constant and lead time is variable, with data given in weeks, not days. We apply Equation (16):

$$\text{ROP} = (\text{Weekly demand} \times \text{Average lead time in weeks}) + Z(\text{Weekly demand})\sigma_{LT}$$

where σ_{LT} = standard deviation of lead time in weeks = 2

So, with $Z = 1.28$, for a 90% service level:

$$\text{ROP} = (60 \times 6) + 1.28(60)(2)$$
$$= 360 + 153.6 = 513.6 \cong 514 \text{ surgery packs}$$

Self-Test

- **Before taking the self-test,** *refer to the learning objectives listed at the beginning of the selection and the key terms listed at the end of the selection.*
- *Use the key at the back of the selection to* **correct** *your answers.*
- **Restudy** *pages that correspond to any questions you answered incorrectly or material you feel uncertain about.*

1. ABC analysis divides on-hand inventory into three classes based upon:
   a) unit price
   b) the number of units on hand
   c) annual demand
   d) annual dollar values

2. Cycle counting:
   a) provides a measure of inventory turnover
   b) assumes that all inventory records must be verified with the same frequency
   c) is a process by which inventory records are periodically verified
   d) all of the above

3. The service industry is improving inventory management through a number of methods. These include:
   a) shrinkage and pilferage
   b) good personnel selection
   c) bar coding of incoming and outgoing merchandise
   d) a and b above
   e) b and c above

4. Annual holding costs are usually:
   a) under 6% of inventory value
   b) 6% to 9% of inventory value
   c) 9% to 12% of inventory value
   d) 12% to 15% of inventory value
   e) over 15% of inventory value

5. The difference(s) between the basic EOQ model and the production order quantity model is(are) that:
   a) the production order quantity model does not require the assumption of known, constant demand
   b) the EOQ model does not require the assumption of negligible lead time
   c) the production order quantity model does not require the assumption of instantaneous delivery
   d) all of the above

6. Extra units held in inventory to reduce stockouts are called:
   a) reorder point
   b) safety stock
   c) just-in-time inventory
   d) all of the above

7. The two most important inventory-based questions answered by the typical inventory model are:
   a) when to place an order and the cost of the order
   b) when to place an order and how much of an item to order
   c) how much of an item to order and the cost of the order
   d) how much of an item to order and with whom the order should be placed

8. The appropriate level of safety stock is typically determined by:
   a) minimizing an expected stockout cost
   b) choosing the level of safety stock that assures a given service level
   c) carrying sufficient safety stock so as to eliminate all stockouts

9. Inventory record accuracy can be improved through:
   a) cycle counting
   b) reorder points
   c) ABC analysis
   d) all of the above

Active Model Exercise

This active model explores the basics of a typical inventory decision and the sensitivity of the model to changes in demand and costs. It uses the data from Examples 3, 4, and 5.

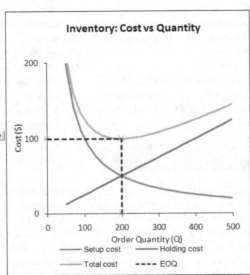

◀ **Active Model 12.1**

An EOQ Analysis of the Data in Examples 3, 4, and 5 for Sharp, Inc.

Questions

1. What is the EOQ and what is the lowest total cost?

2. What is the annual cost of *carrying* inventory at the EOQ and the annual cost of *ordering* inventory at the EOQ of 200 units?

3. From the graph, what can you conclude about the relationship between the lowest total cost and the costs of ordering and carrying inventory?

4. How much does the total cost increase if the store manager orders 50 more hypodermics than the EOQ? 50 fewer hypodermics?

5. What happens to the EOQ and total cost when demand is doubled? When carrying cost is doubled?

6. Scroll through lower setup cost values and describe the changes to the graph. What happens to the EOQ?

7. Comment on the sensitivity of the EOQ model to errors in demand or cost estimates.

Internet and Student CD-ROM Exercises

Visit our Companion Web site or use your student CD-ROM/DVD to help with material in this chapter.

 On Our Companion Web Site,
    www.prenhall.com/heizer
- Self-Study Quizzes
- Practice Problems
- Virtual Company Tour
- Internet Cases
- PowerPoint Lecture

 On Your Student CD-ROM
- Practice Problems
- Active Model Exercises
- Excel OM
- Excel OM Example Data Files
- POM for Windows

 On Your Student DVD
- Video Clip and Video Case
- Virtual Office Hours for Solved Problems

Discussion Questions

1. Describe the four types of inventory.
2. With the advent of low-cost computing, do you see alternatives to the popular ABC classifications?
3. What is the purpose of the ABC classification system?
4. Identify and explain the types of costs that are involved in an inventory system.
5. Explain the major assumptions of the basic EOQ model.
6. What is the relationship of the economic order quantity to demand? To the holding cost? To the setup cost?
7. Explain why it is not necessary to include product cost (price or price times quantity) in the EOQ model, but the quantity discount model requires this information.
8. What are the advantages of cycle counting?
9. What impact does a decrease in setup time have on EOQ?
10. When quantity discounts are offered, why is it not necessary to check discount points that are below the EOQ or points above the EOQ that are not discount points?
11. What is meant by *service level*?
12. Explain the following: All things being equal, the production inventory quantity will be larger than the economic order quantity.
13. Describe the difference between a fixed-quantity (Q) and a fixed-period (P) inventory system.
14. Explain what is meant by the expression "robust model." Specifically, what would you tell a manager who exclaimed, "Uh-oh, we're in trouble! The calculated EOQ is wrong, Actual demand is 10% greater than estimated."
15. What is "safety stock"? What does safety stock provide safety against?
16. When demand is not constant, the reorder point is a function of what four parameters?
17. How are inventory levels monitored in retail stores?
18. State a major advantage, and a major disadvantage, of a fixed-period (P) system.

Ethical Dilemma

Wayne Hills Hospital in tiny Wayne, Nebraska, faces a problem common to large, urban hospitals as well as to small, remote ones like itself. That problem is deciding how much of each type of whole blood to keep in stock. Because blood is expensive and has a limited shelf life (up to 5 weeks under 1–6°C refrigeration), Wayne Hills naturally wants to keep its stock as low as possible. Unfortunately, past disasters such as a major tornado and a train wreck demonstrated that lives would be lost when not enough blood was available to handle massive needs. The hospital administrator wants to set an 85% service level based on demand over the past decade. Discuss the implications of this decision. What is the hospital's responsibility with regard to stocking lifesaving medicines with short shelf lives? How would you set the inventory level for a commodity such as blood?

Problems*

•• **1** L. Houts Plastics is a large manufacturer of injection-molded plastics in North Carolina. An investigation of the company's manufacturing facility in Charlotte yields the information presented in the table below. How would the plant classify these items according to an ABC classification system?

L. Houts Plastics Charlotte Inventory Levels

Item Code #	Average Inventory (units)	Value ($/unit)
1289	400	3.75
2347	300	4.00
2349	120	2.50
2363	75	1.50
2394	60	1.75
2395	30	2.00
6782	20	1.15
7844	12	2.05
8210	8	1.80
8310	7	2.00
9111	6	3.00 Px

• **2** Boreki Enterprise has the following 10 items in inventory. Theodore Boreki asks you, a recent OM graduate, to divide these items into ABC classifications. What do you report back?

Item	Annual Demand	Cost/Unit
A2	3,000	$ 50
B8	4,000	12
C7	1,500	45
D1	6,000	10
E9	1,000	20
F3	500	500
G2	300	1,500
H2	600	20
I5	1,750	10
J8	2,500	5 Px

•• **3** Jean-Marie Bourjolly's restaurant has the following inventory items that it orders on a weekly basis:

Inventory Item	$ Value/Case	# Ordered/Week
Rib eye steak	135	3
Lobster tail	245	3
Pasta	23	12
Salt	3	2
Napkins	12	2
Tomato sauce	23	11
French fries	43	32
Pepper	3	3
Garlic powder	11	3
Trash can liners	12	3
Table cloths	32	5
Fish filets	143	10
Prime rib roasts	166	6
Oil	28	2

Inventory Item	$ Value/Case	# Ordered/Week
Lettuce (case)	35	24
Chickens	75	14
Order pads	12	2
Eggs (case)	22	7
Bacon	56	5
Sugar	4	2

a) Which is the most expensive item, using annual dollar volume?
b) Which are C items?
c) What is the annual dollar volume for all 20 items? Px

• **4** Howard Electronics, a small manufacturer of electronic research equipment, has approximately 7,000 items in its inventory and has hired Joan Blasco-Paul to manage its inventory. Joan has determined that 10% of the items in inventory are A items, 35% are B items, and 55% are C items. She would like to set up a system in which all A items are counted monthly (every 20 working days), all B items are counted quarterly (every 60 working days), and all C items are counted semiannually (every 120 working days). How many items need to be counted each day?

• **5** William Beville's computer training school, in Richmond, stocks workbooks with the following characteristics:

$$\text{Demand } D = 19,500 \text{ units/year}$$
$$\text{Ordering cost } S = \$25/\text{order}$$
$$\text{Holding cost } H = \$4/\text{unit/year}$$

a) Calculate the EOQ for the workbooks.
b) What are the annual holding costs for the workbooks?
c) What are the annual ordering costs? Px

• **6** If $D = 8,000$ per month, $S = \$45$ per order, and $H = \$2$ per unit per month, what is the economic order quantity? Px

•• **7** Henry Crouch's law office has traditionally ordered ink refills 60 units at a time. The firm estimates that carrying cost is 40% of the $10 unit cost and that annual demand is about 240 units per year. The assumptions of the basic EOQ model are thought to apply. For what value of ordering cost would its action be optimal?

• **8** Madeline Thimmes's Dream Store sells water beds and assorted supplies. Her best-selling bed has an annual demand of 400 units. Ordering cost is $40; holding cost is $5 per unit per year.
a) To minimize the total cost, how many units should be ordered each time an order is placed?
b) If the holding cost per unit was $6 instead of $5, what would the optimal order quantity be? Px

• **9** Southeastern Bell stocks a certain switch connector at its central warehouse for supplying field service offices. The yearly demand for these connectors is 15,000 units. Southeastern estimates its annual holding cost for this item to be $25 per unit. The cost to place and process an order from the supplier is $75. The company operates 300 days per year, and the lead time to receive an order from the supplier is 2 working days.
a) Find the economic order quantity.
b) Find the annual holding costs.
c) Find the annual ordering costs.
d) What is the reorder point? Px

*Note: Px means the problem may be solved with POM for Windows and/or Excel OM.

• **10** Lead time for one of your fastest-moving products is 21 days. Demand during this period averages 100 units per day. What would be an appropriate reorder point?

• **11** Annual demand for the notebook binders at Duncan's Stationery Shop is 10,000 units. Dana Duncan operates her business 300 days per year and finds that deliveries from her supplier generally take 5 working days. Calculate the reorder point for the notebook binders that she stocks.

•• **12** Thomas Kratzer is the purchasing manager for the headquarters of a large insurance company chain with a central inventory operation. Thomas's fastest-moving inventory item has a demand of 6,000 units per year. The cost of each unit is $100, and the inventory carrying cost is $10 per unit per year. The average ordering cost is $30 per order. It takes about 5 days for an order to arrive, and the demand for 1 week is 120 units. (This is a corporate operation, and there are 250 working days per year.)
a) What is the EOQ?
b) What is the average inventory if the EOQ is used?
c) What is the optimal number of orders per year?
d) What is the optimal number of days in between any two orders?
e) What is the annual cost of ordering and holding inventory?
f) What is the total annual inventory cost, including cost of the 6,000 units? **Px**

•• **13** Joe Henry's machine shop uses 2,500 brackets during the course of a year. These brackets are purchased from a supplier 90 miles away. The following information is known about the brackets:

Annual demand:	2,500
Holding cost per bracket per year:	$1.50
Order cost per order:	$18.75
Lead time:	2 days
Working days per year:	250

a) Given the above information, what would be the economic order quantity (EOQ)?
b) Given the EOQ, what would be the average inventory? What would be the annual inventory holding cost?
c) Given the EOQ, how many orders would be made each year? What would be the annual order cost?
d) Given the EOQ, what is the total annual cost of managing the inventory?
e) What is the time between orders?
f) What is the reorder point (ROP)? **Px**

•• **14** Myriah Fitzgibbon, of L.A. Plumbing, uses 1,200 of a certain spare part that costs $25 for each order, with an annual holding cost of $24.
a) Calculate the total cost for order sizes of 25, 40, 50, 60, and 100.
b) Identify the economic order quantity and consider the implications for making an error in calculating economic order quantity. **Px**

••• **15** M. Cotteleer Electronics supplies microcomputer circuitry to a company that incorporates microprocessors into refrigerators and other home appliances. One of the components has an annual demand of 250 units, and this is constant throughout the year. Carrying cost is estimated to be $1 per unit per year, and the ordering cost is $20 per order.
a) To minimize cost, how many units should be ordered each time an order is placed?
b) How many orders per year are needed with the optimal policy?

c) What is the average inventory if costs are minimized?
d) Suppose that the ordering cost is not $20, and Cotteleer has been ordering 150 units each time an order is placed. For this order policy (of $Q = 150$) to be optimal, determine what the ordering cost would have to be. **Px**

•• **16** Race One Motors is an Indonesian car manufacturer. At its largest manufacturing facility, in Jakarta, the company produces subcomponents at a rate of 300 per day, and it uses these subcomponents at a rate of 12,500 per year (of 250 working days). Holding costs are $2 per item per year, and ordering costs are $30 per order.
a) What is the economic production quantity?
b) How many production runs per year will be made?
c) What will be the maximum inventory level?
d) What percentage of time will the facility be producing components?
e) What is the annual cost of ordering and holding inventory? **Px**

•• **17** Radovilsky Manufacturing Company, in Hayward, California, makes flashing lights for toys. The company operates its production facility 300 days per year. It has orders for about 12,000 flashing lights per year and has the capability of producing 100 per day. Setting up the light production costs $50. The cost of each light is $1. The holding cost is $0.10 per light per year.
a) What is the optimal size of the production run?
b) What is the average holding cost per year?
c) What is the average setup cost per year?
d) What is the total cost per year, including the cost of the lights? **Px**

•• **18** Arthur Meiners is the production manager of Wheel-Rite, a small producer of metal parts. Wheel-Rite supplies Cal-Tex, a larger assembly company, with 10,000 wheel bearings each year. This order has been stable for some time. Setup cost for Wheel-Rite is $40, and holding cost is $.60 per wheel bearing per year. Wheel-Rite can produce 500 wheel bearings per day. Cal-Tex is a just-in-time manufacturer and requires that 50 bearings be shipped to it each business day.
a) What is the optimum production quantity?
b) What is the maximum number of wheel bearings that will be in inventory at Wheel-Rite?
c) How many production runs of wheel bearings will Wheel-Rite have in a year?
d) What is the total setup + holding cost for Wheel-Rite? **Px**

•• **19** Cesar Rogo Computers, a Mississippi chain of computer hardware and software retail outlets, supplies both educational and commercial customers with memory and storage devices. It currently faces the following ordering decision relating to purchases of CD-ROMs:

$$D = 36,000 \text{ disks}$$
$$S = \$25$$
$$H = \$0.45$$
$$\text{Purchase price} = \$0.85$$
$$\text{Discount price} = \$0.82$$
$$\text{Quantity needed to qualify for the discount} = 6,000 \text{ disks}$$

Should the discount be taken? **Px**

•• **20** Bell Computers purchases integrated chips at $350 per chip. The holding cost is $35 per unit per year, the ordering cost is $120 per order, and sales are steady, at 400 per month. The company's supplier, Rich Blue Chip Manufacturing, Inc., decides to offer price concessions in order to attract larger orders. The price structure is shown below.

a) What is the optimal order quantity and the minimum cost for Bell Computers to order, purchase, and hold these integrated chips?

Rich Blue Chip's Price Structure

Quantity Purchased	Price/Unit
1–99 units	$350
100–199 units	$325
200 or more units	$300

b) Bell Computers wishes to use a 10% holding cost rather than the fixed $35 holding cost in part a. What is the optimal order quantity, and what is the optimal cost? **Px**

•• **21** Wang Distributors has an annual demand for an airport metal detector of 1,400 units. The cost of a typical detector to Wang is $400. Carrying cost is estimated to be 20% of the unit cost, and the ordering cost is $25 per order. If Ping Wang, the owner, orders in quantities of 300 or more, he can get a 5% discount on the cost of the detectors. Should Wang take the quantity discount? **Px**

•• **22** The catering manager of LaVista Hotel, Lisa Ferguson, is disturbed by the amount of silverware she is losing every week. Last Friday night, when her crew tried to set up for a banquet for 500 people, they did not have enough knives. She decides she needs to order some more silverware, but wants to take advantage of any quantity discounts her vendor will offer.

For a small order (2,000 pieces or less) her vendor quotes a price of $1.80/piece.

If she orders 2,001–5,000 pieces, the price drops to $1.60/piece. 5,001–10,000 pieces brings the price to $1.40/piece, and 10,001 and above reduces the price to $1.25.

Lisa's order costs are $200 per order, her annual holding costs are 5%, and the annual demand is 45,000 pieces. For the best option:
a) What is the optimal order quantity?
b) What is the annual holding cost?
c) What is the annual ordering (setup) cost?
d) What are the annual costs of the silverware itself with an optimal order quantity?
e) What is the total annual cost, including ordering, holding, and purchasing the silverware? **Px**

•• **23** Rocky Mountain Tire Center sells 20,000 go-cart tires per year. The ordering cost for each order is $40, and the holding cost is 20% of the purchase price of the tires per year. The purchase price is $20 per tire if fewer than 500 tires are ordered, $18 per tire if 500 or more—but fewer than 1,000—tires are ordered, and $17 per tire if 1,000 or more tires are ordered. How many tires should Rocky Mountain order each time it places an order? **Px**

•• **24** M. P. VanOyen Manufacturing has gone out on bid for a regulator component. Expected demand is 700 units per month. The item can be purchased from either Allen Manufacturing or Baker Manufacturing. Their price lists are shown in the table. Ordering cost is $50, and annual holding cost per unit is $5.

Allen Mfg.		Baker Mfg.	
Quantity	Unit Price	Quantity	Unit Price
1–499	$16.00	1–399	$16.10
500–999	15.50	400–799	15.60
1,000+	15.00	800+	15.10

a) What is the economic order quantity?
b) Which supplier should be used? Why?
c) What is the optimal order quantity and total annual cost of ordering, purchasing, and holding the component? **Px**

••• **25** Chris Sandvig Irrigation, Inc., has summarized the price list from four potential suppliers of an underground control valve. See the table below. Annual usage is 2,400 valves; order cost is $10 per order; and annual inventory holding costs are $3.33 per unit.

Which vendor should be selected and what order quantity is best if Sandvig Irrigation wants to minimize total cost?

Vendor A		Vendor B	
Quantity	Price	Quantity	Price
1–49	$35.00	1–74	$34.75
50–74	34.75	75–149	34.00
75–149	33.55	150–299	32.80
150–299	32.35	300–499	31.60
300–499	31.15	500+	30.50
500+	30.75		

Vendor C		Vendor D	
Quantity	Price	Quantity	Price
1–99	$34.50	1–199	$34.25
100–199	33.75	200–399	33.00
200–399	32.50	400+	31.00
400+	31.10		**Px**

••• **26** Emery Pharmaceutical uses an unstable chemical compound that must be kept in an environment where both temperature and humidity can be controlled. Emery uses 800 pounds per month of the chemical, estimates the holding cost to be 50% of the purchase price (because of spoilage), and estimates order costs to be $50 per order. The cost schedules of two suppliers are as follows:

Vendor 1		Vendor 2	
Quantity	Price/lb	Quantity	Price/lb
1–499	$17.00	1–399	$17.10
500–999	16.75	400–799	16.85
1,000+	16.50	800–1,199	16.60
		1,200+	16.25

a) What is the economic order quantity for both suppliers?
b) What quantity should be ordered and which supplier should be used?
c) What is the total cost for the most economic order size?
d) What factor(s) should be considered besides total cost? **Px**

•• **27** Barbara Flynn is in charge of maintaining hospital supplies at General Hospital. During the past year, the mean lead time demand for bandage BX-5 was 60 (and was normally distributed). Furthermore, the standard deviation for BX-5 was 7. Ms. Flynn would like to maintain a 90% service level.
a) What safety stock level do you recommend for BX-5?
b) What is the appropriate reorder point? **Px**

•• **28** Based on available information, lead time demand for PC jump drives averages 50 units (normally distributed), with a standard deviation of 5 drives. Management wants a 97% service level.
a) What value of Z should be applied?
b) How many drives should be carried as safety stock?
c) What is the appropriate reorder point? **Px**

••• 29   Authentic Thai rattan chairs (shown in the photo) are delivered to Gary Schwartz's chain of retail stores, called The Kathmandu Shop, once a year. The reorder point, without safety stock, is 200 chairs. Carrying cost is $30 per unit per year, and the cost of a stockout is $70 per chair per year. Given the following demand probabilities during the reorder period, how much safety stock should be carried?

Demand during Reorder Period	Probability
0	0.2
100	0.2
200	0.2
300	0.2
400	0.2 **Px**

•• 30   Tobacco is shipped from North Carolina to a cigarette manufacturer in Cambodia once a year. The reorder point, without safety stock, is 200 kilos. The carrying cost is $15 per kilo per year, and the cost of a stockout is $70 per kilo per year. Given the following demand probabilities during the reorder period, how much safety stock should be carried?

Demand During Reorder Period (kilos)	Probability
0	0.1
100	0.1
200	0.2
300	0.4
400	0.2 **Px**

••• 31   Mr. Beautiful, an organization that sells weight training sets, has an ordering cost of $40 for the BB-1 set. (BB-1 stands for Body Beautiful Number 1.) The carrying cost for BB-1 is $5 per set per year. To meet demand, Mr. Beautiful orders large quantities of BB-1 seven times a year. The stockout cost for BB-1 is estimated to be $50 per set. Over the past several years, Mr. Beautiful has observed the following demand during the lead time for BB-1:

Demand during Lead Time	Probability
40	.1
50	.2
60	.2
70	.2
80	.2
90	.1
	1.0

The reorder point for BB-1 is 60 sets. What level of safety stock should be maintained for BB-1? **Px**

•• 32   Chicago's Hard Rock Hotel distributes a mean of 1,000 bath towels per day to guests at the pool and in their rooms. This demand is normally distributed with a standard deviation of 100 towels per day, based on occupancy. The laundry firm that has the linen contract requires a 2-day lead time. The hotel expects a 98% service level to satisfy high guest expectations.
a) What is the ROP?
b) What is the safety stock? **Px**

•• 33   First Printing has contracts with legal firms in San Francisco to copy their court documents. Daily demand is almost constant at 12,500 pages of documents. The lead time for paper delivery is normally distributed with a mean of 4 days and a standard deviation of 1 day. A 97% service level is expected. Compute First's ROP. **Px**

••• 34   Gainesville Cigar stocks Cuban cigars that have variable lead times because of the difficulty in importing the product: Lead time is normally distributed with an average of 6 weeks and a standard deviation of 2 weeks. Demand is also a variable and normally distributed with a mean of 200 cigars per week and a standard deviation of 25 cigars. For a 90% service level, what is the ROP? **Px**

• 35   Louisiana Power and Light orders utility poles on the first business day of each month from its supplier in Oregon. The target value is 40 poles in this fixed-period system (P-system). It is time to order and there are 5 poles on hand. Because of a delayed shipment last month, 18 poles ordered earlier should arrive shortly. How many poles should be ordered now?

••• 36   Kim Clark has asked you to help him determine the best ordering policy for a new product. The demand for the new product has been forecasted to be about 1,000 units annually. To help you get a handle on the carrying and ordering costs, Kim has given you the list of last year's costs. He thought that these costs might be appropriate for the new product.

Cost Factor	Cost ($)	Cost Factor	Cost ($)
Taxes for the warehouse	2,000	Warehouse supplies	280
Receiving and incoming inspection	1,500	Research and development	2,750
New product development	2,500	Purchasing salaries & wages	30,000
Acct. Dept. costs to pay invoices	500	Warehouse salaries & wages	12,800
Inventory insurance	600	Pilferage of inventory	800
Product advertising	800	Purchase order supplies	500
Spoilage	750	Inventory obsolescence	300
Sending purchasing orders	800	Purchasing Dept. overhead	1,000

He also told you that these data were compiled for 10,000 inventory items that were carried or held during the year. You have also determined that 200 orders were placed last year. Your job as a new operations management graduate is to help Kim determine the economic order quantity for the new product.

•••• 37 Emarpy Appliance is a company that produces all kinds of major appliances. Bud Banis, the president of Emarpy, is concerned about the production policy for the company's best-selling refrigerator. The annual demand for this has been about 8,000 units each year, and this demand has been constant throughout the year. The production capacity is 200 units per day. Each time production starts, it costs the company $120 to move materials into place, reset the assembly line, and clean the equipment. The holding cost of a refrigerator is $50 per year. The current production plan calls for 400 refrigerators to be produced in each production run. Assume there are 250 working days per year.

a) What is the daily demand of this product?
b) If the company were to continue to produce 400 units each time production starts, how many days would production continue?
c) Under the current policy, how many production runs per year would be required? What would the annual setup cost be?
d) If the current policy continues, how many refrigerators would be in inventory when production stops? What would the average inventory level be?
e) If the company produces 400 refrigerators at a time, what would the total annual setup cost and holding cost be?

f) If Bud Banis wants to minimize the total annual inventory cost, how many refrigerators should be produced in each production run? How much would this save the company in inventory costs compared to the current policy of producing 400 in each production run? **Px**

•••• 38 A gourmet coffee shop in downtown San Francisco is open 200 days a year and sells an average of 75 pounds of Kona coffee beans a day. (Demand can be assumed to be distributed normally with a standard deviation of 15 pounds per day). After ordering (fixed cost = $16 per order), beans are always shipped from Hawaii within exactly 4 days. Per-pound annual holding costs for the beans are $3.

a) What is the economic order quantity (EOQ) for Kona coffee beans?
b) What are the total annual holding costs of stock for Kona coffee beans?
c) What are the total annual ordering costs for Kona coffee beans?
d) Assume that management has specified that no more than a 1% risk during stockout is acceptable. What should the reorder point (ROP) be?
e) What is the safety stock needed to attain a 1% risk of stockout during lead time?
f) What is the annual holding cost of maintaining the level of safety stock needed to support a 1% risk?
g) If management specified that a 2% risk of stockout during lead time would be acceptable, would the safety stock holding costs decrease or increase?

Case Studies

Zhou Bicycle Company

Zhou Bicycle Company (ZBC), located in Seattle, is a wholesale distributor of bicycles and bicycle parts. Formed in 1981, by University of Washington Professor Yong-Pin Zhou, the firm's primary retail outlets are located within a 400-mile radius of the distribution center. These retail outlets receive the order from ZBC within 2 days after notifying the distribution center, provided that the stock is available. However, if an order is not fulfilled by the company, no backorder is placed; the retailers arrange to get their shipment from other distributors, and ZBC loses that amount of business.

The company distributes a wide variety of bicycles. The most popular model, and the major source of revenue to the company, is the AirWing. ZBC receives all the models from a single manufacturer in China, and shipment takes as long as 4 weeks from the time an order is placed. With the cost of communication, paperwork, and customs clearance included, ZBC estimates that each time an order is placed, it incurs a cost of $65. The purchase price paid by ZBC, per bicycle, is roughly 60% of the suggested retail price for all the styles available, and the inventory carrying cost is 1% per month (12% per year) of the purchase price paid by ZBC. The retail price (paid by the customers) for the AirWing is $170 per bicycle.

ZBC is interested in making an inventory plan for 2008. The firm wants to maintain a 95% service level with its customers to minimize the losses on the lost orders. The data collected for the past 2 years are summarized in the following table. A forecast for AirWing model sales in 2008 has been developed and will be used to make an inventory plan for ZBC.

Demands for AirWing Model

Month	2006	2007	Forecast for 2008
January	6	7	8
February	12	14	15
March	24	27	31
April	46	53	59
May	75	86	97
June	47	54	60
July	30	34	39
August	18	21	24
September	13	15	16
October	12	13	15
November	22	25	28
December	38	42	47
Total	343	391	439

Discussion Questions

1. Develop an inventory plan to help ZBC.
2. Discuss ROPs and total costs.
3. How can you address demand that is not at the level of the planning horizon?

Source: Professor Kala Chand Seal, Loyola Marymount University.

Sturdivant Sound Systems

Sturdivant Sound Systems manufactures and sells sound systems for both home and auto. All parts of the sound systems, with the exception of DVD players, are produced in the Rochester, New York, plant. DVD players used in the assembly of Sturdivant systems are purchased from Morris Electronics of Concord, New Hampshire.

Sturdivant purchasing agent Mary Kim submits a purchase requisition for DVD players once every 4 weeks. The company's annual requirements total 5,000 units (20 per working day), and the cost per unit is $60. (Sturdivant does not purchase in greater quantities because Morris Electronics does not offer quantity discounts.) Because Morris promises delivery within 1 week following receipt of a purchase requisition, rarely is there a shortage of DVD players. (Total time between date of order and date of receipt is 5 days.)

Associated with the purchase of each shipment are procurement costs. These costs, which amount to $20 per order, include the costs of preparing the requisition, inspecting and storing the delivered goods, updating inventory records, and issuing a voucher and a check for payment. In addition to procurement costs, Sturdivant incurs inventory carrying costs that include insurance, storage, handling, taxes, and so forth. These costs equal $6 per unit per year.

Beginning in August of this year, Sturdivant management will embark on a companywide cost-control program in an attempt to improve its profits. One area to be closely scrutinized for possible cost savings is inventory procurement.

Discussion Questions

1. Compute the optimal order quantity of DVD players.
2. Determine the appropriate reorder point (in units).
3. Compute the cost savings that the company will realize if it implements the optimal inventory procurement decision.
4. Should procurement costs be considered a linear function of the number of orders?

Source: Reprinted by permission of Professor Jerry Kinard, Western Carolina University.

Inventory Control at Wheeled Coach

Video Case

Controlling inventory is one of Wheeled Coach's toughest problems. Operating according to a strategy of mass customization and responsiveness, management knows that success is dependent on tight inventory control. Anything else results in an inability to deliver promptly, chaos on the assembly line, and a huge inventory investment. Wheeled Coach finds that almost 50% of the $40,000 to $100,000 cost of every ambulance it manufactures is purchased materials. A large proportion of that 50% is in chassis (purchased from Ford), aluminum (from Reynolds Metal), and plywood used for flooring and cabinetry construction (from local suppliers). Wheeled Coach tracks these A inventory items quite carefully, maintaining tight security/control and ordering carefully so as to maximize quantity discounts while minimizing on-hand stock. Because of long lead times and scheduling needs at Reynolds, aluminum must actually be ordered as much as 8 months in advance.

In a crowded ambulance industry in which it is the only giant, its 45 competitors don't have the purchasing power to draw the same discounts as Wheeled Coach. But this competitive cost advantage cannot be taken lightly, according to President Bob Collins.

"Cycle counting in our stockrooms is critical. No part can leave the locked stockrooms without appearing on a bill of materials."

Accurate bills of material (BOM) are a requirement if products are going to be built on time. Additionally, because of the custom nature of each vehicle, most orders are won only after a bidding process. Accurate BOMs are critical to cost estimation and the resulting bid. For these reasons, Collins was emphatic that Wheeled Coach maintain outstanding inventory control. The *Global Company Profile* featuring Wheeled Coach provides further details about the ambulance inventory control and production process.

Discussion Questions*

1. Explain how Wheeled Coach implements ABC analysis.
2. If you were to take over as inventory control manager at Wheeled Coach, what additional policies and techniques would you initiate to ensure accurate inventory records?
3. How would you go about implementing these suggestions?

*You may wish to view this case on your DVD before answering these questions.

Additional Case Studies

Internet case studies: Visit our Companion Web site at www.prenhall.com/heizer for these free case studies:

- **Southwestern University F:** The university must decide how many football day programs to order, and from whom.
- **LaPlace Power and Light:** This utility company is evaluating its current inventory policies.

Harvard has selected these Harvard Business School cases to accompany this chapter:

harvardbusinessonline.hbsp.harvard.edu

- **Pioneer Hi-Bred International, Inc.** (#898-238): Deals with the challenges in managing inventory in a large, complex agribusiness firm.
- **L.L. Bean, Inc.: Item Forecasting and Inventory** (#893-003): The firm must balance costs of understocking and overstocking when demand for catalog items is uncertain.
- **Blanchard Importing and Distribution Co., Inc.** (#673-033): Illustrates two main types of errors resulting from the use of EOQ models.

Bibliography

Abernathy, Frederick H., et al. "Control Your Inventory in a World of Lean Retailing." *Harvard Business Review* 78, no. 6 (November–December 2000): 169–176.

Arnold, David. "Seven Rules of International Distribution." *Harvard Business Review* 78, no. 6 (November–December 2000): 131–137.

Arnold, J. R., and S. Chapman. *Introduction to Materials Management*, 5th ed. Upper Saddle River, NJ: Prentice Hall (2004).

Balakrishnan, R., B. Render, and R. M. Stair. *Managerial Decision Modeling with Spreadsheets*, 2nd ed. Upper Saddle River, NJ: Prentice Hall (2007).

Bradley, James R., and Richard W. Conway. "Managing Cyclic Inventories." *Production and Operations Management* 12, no. 4 (winter 2003): 464–479.

Cannon, Alan R., and Richard E. Crandall, "The Way Things Never Were." *APICS—The Performance Advantage* (January 2004): 32–35.

Chapmas, Stephen. *Fundamentals of Production Planning and Control*. Upper Saddle River, NJ: Prentice Hall (2006).

Chopra, Sunil, Gilles Reinhardt, and Maqbool Dada. "The Effect of Lead Time Uncertainty on Safety Stocks." *Decision Sciences* 35, no. 1 (winter 2004): 1–24.

Coleman, B. Jay. "Determining the Correct Service Level Target." *Production and Inventory Management Journal* 41, no. 1 (1st quarter 2000): 19–23.

Corsten, Daniel, and Nirmalya Kumar. "Profits in the Pie of the Beholder." *Harvard Business Review* (May 2003): 22–23.

Landvater, D. V. *World Class Production and Inventory Management*. Newburg, NH: Oliver Wight Publications (1997).

Noblitt, James M. "The Economic Order Quantity Model: Panacea or Plague?" *APICS—The Performance Advantage* (February 2001): 53–57.

Robison, James A. "Inventory Profile Analysis." *Production and Inventory Management Journal* 42, no. 2 (2nd quarter 2001): 8–13.

Rubin, Paul A., and W. C. Benton. "A Generalized Framework for Quantity Discount Pricing Schedules." *Decision Sciences* 34, no. 1 (winter 2003): 173–188.

Sell, William H. "Recovering Value from I.O.$." *APICS—The Performance Advantage* (November/December 2003): 50–53.

Vollmann, T. E., W. L. Berry, D. C. Whybark, and F. R. Jacobs. *Manufacturing Planning and Control for Supply Chain Management*, 5th ed. Burr Ridge, IL: Irwin/McGraw (2005).

Witt, Clyde E. "Mobile Warehouse Supplies U.S. Marines in Iraq." *Material Handling Management* 60, no. 8 (August 2005): 24–25.

Zipkin, Paul. *Foundations of Inventory Management*. New York: Irwin/McGraw-Hill (2000).

Internet Resources

APICS: The Educational Society for Resource Management: **www.apics.org**

Center for Inventory Management: **www.inventorymanagement.com**

Institute of Industrial Engineers: **www.iienet.org**

Inventory Control Forum: **www.cris.com/~kthill/sites.htm**

Solutions to Even Numbered Problems

2 A items are G2 and F3; B items are A2, C7, and D1; all others are C.

4 108 items

6 600 units

8 (a) 80 units
   (b) 73 units

10 2,100 units

12 (a) 189.74 units
   (b) 94.87
   (c) 31.62
   (d) 7.91
   (e) $1,897.30
   (f) $601,897

14 (a) Order quantity variations have limited impact on total cost.
   (b) EOQ = 50

16 (a) 671 units
   (b) 18.63
   (c) 559 = max. inventory
   (d) 16.7%
   (e) $1,117.90

18 (a) 1,217 units
   (b) 1,095 = max. inventory
   (c) 8.22 production runs
   (d) $657.30

20 (a) EOQ = 200, total cost = $1,446,380
   (b) EOQ = 200, total cost = $1,445,880

22 (a) 16,971 units
   (b) $530.33
   (c) $530.33
   (d) $56,250
   (e) $57,310.66

24 (a) EOQ = 410
   (b) Vendor Allen has slightly lower cost.
   (c) Optimal order quantity = 1,000 @ total cost of $128,920

26 (a) EOQ (1) = 336; EOQ (2) = 335
   (b) Order 1,200 from Vendor 2.
   (c) At 1,200 lb., total cost = $161,275.
   (d) Storage space and perishability.

28 **(a)** Z = 1.88

(b) Safety stock = Zσ = 1.88(5) = 9.4 drives

(c) ROP = 59.4 drives

30 100 kilos of safety stock

32 **(a)** 2,291 towels

(b) 291 towels

34 ROP = 1,718 cigars

36 EOQ = 442

38 **(a)** Q = 400 lbs

(b) $600

(c) $600

(d) ROP = 369.99

(e) 69.99

(f) $209.97

(g) Safety stock = 61.61

Solutions to Self Test

1. d; **2.** c; **3.** e; **4.** e; **5.** c; **6.** b; **7.** b; **8.** b; **9.** d.

Aggregate Planning

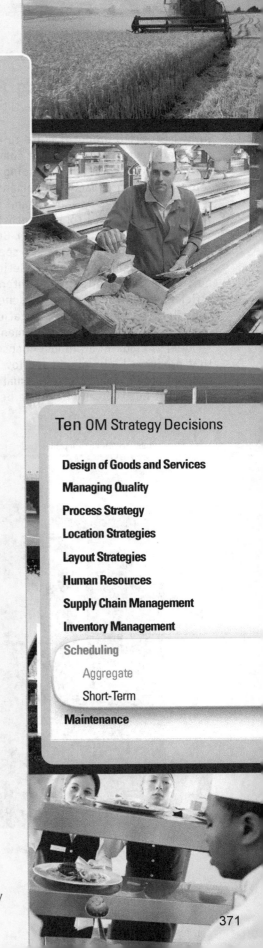

Outline

Ten OM Strategy Decisions

Design of Goods and Services

Managing Quality

Process Strategy

Location Strategies

Layout Strategies

Human Resources

Supply Chain Management

Inventory Management

Scheduling
  Aggregate
  Short-Term

Maintenance

Learning Objectives

When you complete this selection you should be able to

1. Define aggregate planning
2. Identify optional strategies for developing an aggregate plan
3. Prepare a graphical aggregate plan
4. Solve an aggregate plan via the transportation method of linear programming
5. Understand and solve a yield management problem

Global Company Profile: Anheuser-Busch

Aggregate Planning Provides a Competitive Advantage at Anheuser-Busch

Anheuser-Busch produces close to 40% of the beer consumed in the U.S. The company achieves efficiency at such volume by doing an excellent job of matching capacity to demand.

Matching capacity and demand in the intermediate term (3 to 18 months) is the heart of aggregate planning. Anheuser-Busch matches fluctuating demand by brand to specific plant, labor, and inventory capacity. Meticulous cleaning between batches, effective maintenance, and efficient employee and facility scheduling contribute to high facility utilization, a major factor in all high capital investment facilities.

Beer is made in a product-focused facility—one that produces high volume and low variety. Product-focused production processes usually require high fixed cost but typically have the benefit of low variable costs. Maintaining high use of such facilities is critical because high capital costs require high use to be competitive. Performance above the break-even point requires high use, and downtime is disastrous.

Beer production can be divided into four stages. The first stage is the selection and assurance of raw material delivery and quality. The second stage is the actual brewing process from milling to aging. The third stage is packaging into the wide variety of containers desired by the market.

The fourth and final stage is distribution, which includes temperature-controlled delivery and storage. Each stage has its resource limitations. Developing the aggregate plan to make it all work is demanding. Effective aggregate planning is a major ingredient in competitive advantage at Anheuser-Busch.

Anheuser-Busch Companies, Inc.

▲ *Shown are brew kettles in which wort, later to become beer, is boiled and hops are added for the flavor and bitter character they impart.*

◄ *In the brewhouse control room, process control uses computers to monitor the starting-cellar process, where wort is in its final stage of preparation before being fermented into beer.*

► *The canning line imprints on each can a code that identifies the day, year, and 15-minute period of production; the plant at which the product was brewed and packaged; and the production line used. This system allows any quality-control problems to be tracked and corrected.*

◄ *A critical ingredient, hops, is being added to give the beer "character."*

Manufacturers like Anheuser-Busch, GE, and Yamaha face tough decisions when trying to schedule products like beer, air conditioners, and jet skis, the demand for which is heavily dependent on seasonal variation. If the firms increase output and a summer is warmer than usual, they stand to increase sales and market share. However, if the summer is cool, they may be stuck with expensive unsold product. Developing plans that minimize costs connected with such forecasts is one of the main functions of an operations manager.

Aggregate planning (also known as **aggregate scheduling**) is concerned with determining the quantity and timing of production for the intermediate future, often from 3 to 18 months ahead. Operations managers try to determine the best way to meet forecasted demand by adjusting production rates, labor levels, inventory levels, overtime work, subcontracting rates, and other controllable variables. Usually, *the objective of aggregate planning is to meet forecasted demand while minimizing cost over the planning period*. However, other strategic issues may be more important than low cost. These strategies may be to smooth employment levels, to drive down inventory levels, or to meet a high level of service.

For manufacturers, the aggregate schedule ties the firm's strategic goals to production plans, but for service organizations, the aggregate schedule ties strategic goals to workforce schedules.

Four things are needed for aggregate planning:

- A logical overall unit for measuring sales and output, such as air-conditioning units at GE or cases of beer at Anheuser-Busch
- A forecast of demand for a reasonable intermediate planning period in these aggregate terms
- A method for determining the costs that we discuss in this chapter
- A model that combines forecasts and costs so that scheduling decisions can be made for the planning period

In this selection we describe the aggregate planning decision, show how the aggregate plan fits into the overall planning process, and describe several techniques that managers use when developing an aggregate plan. We stress both manufacturing and service-sector firms.

THE PLANNING PROCESS

Demand forecasting can address short-, medium-, and long-range problems. Long-range forecasts help managers deal with capacity and strategic issues and are the responsibility of top management (see Figure 1). Top management formulates policy-related questions, such as facility location and expansion, new product development, research funding, and investment over a period of several years.

Medium-range planning begins once long-term capacity decisions are made. This is the job of the operations manager. **Scheduling decisions** address the problem of matching productivity to fluctuating demands. These plans need to be consistent with top management's long-range strategy and work within the resources allocated by earlier strategic decisions. Medium- (or "intermediate-") range planning is accomplished by building an aggregate production plan.

Short-range planning may extend up to a year but is usually less than 3 months. This plan is also the responsibility of operations personnel, who work with supervisors and foremen to "disaggregate" the intermediate plan into weekly, daily, and hourly schedules. Tactics for dealing with short-term planning involve loading, sequencing, expediting, and dispatching.

Figure 1 illustrates the time horizons and features for short-, intermediate-, and long-range planning.

THE NATURE OF AGGREGATE PLANNING

As the term *aggregate* implies, an aggregate plan means combining appropriate resources into general, or overall, terms. Given demand forecast, facility capacity, inventory levels, workforce size, and related inputs, the planner has to select the rate of output for a facility over the next 3 to 18 months. The plan can be for manufacturing firms such as Anheuser-Busch and Whirlpool, hospitals, colleges, or Prentice Hall, the company that published this textbook.

Take, for a manufacturing example, Snapper, which produces many different models of lawn mowers. It makes walk-behind mowers, rear-engine riding mowers, garden tractors, and many

---

Aggregate planning (or aggregate scheduling)
An approach to determine the quantity and timing of production for the intermediate future (usually 3 to 18 months ahead).

1. Define aggregate planning

Scheduling decisions
Plans that match production to changes in demand.

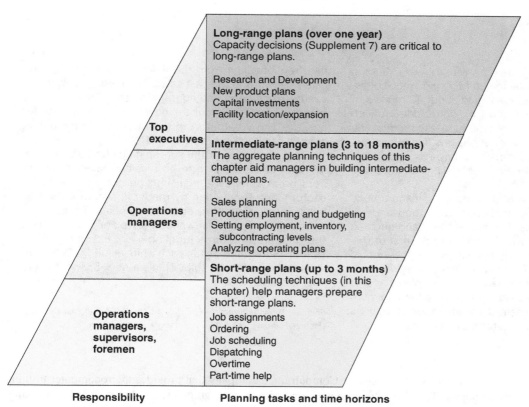

*If top management does
a poor or inconsistent job
of long-term planning,
problems will develop
that make the aggregate
planner's job very tough.*

more, for a total of 145 models. For each month in the upcoming 3 quarters, the aggregate plan
for Snapper might have the following output (in units of production) for Snapper's "family" of
mowers:

Quarter 1			Quarter 2			Quarter 3		
Jan.	Feb.	March	April	May	June	July	Aug.	Sept.
150,000	120,000	110,000	100,000	130,000	150,000	180,000	150,000	140,000

Note that the plan looks at production *in the aggregate* (the family of mowers), not as a product-
by-product breakdown. Likewise, an aggregate plan for BMW tells the auto manufacturer how
many cars to make, but not how many should be two-door versus four-door or red versus green.[1]
It tells Nucor Steel how many tons of steel to produce but does not differentiate grades of steel.
(We extend the discussion of planning at Snapper in the *OM in Action* box "Building the Plan at
Snapper.")

Briggs & Stratton Power Products Marketing

▲ *Operations personnel build an aggregate plan using the total expected demand for all of the family products, such as
145 models at Snapper (a few of which are shown above). Only when the forecasts are assembled in the aggregate plan
does the company decide how to meet the total requirement with the available resources. These resource constraints
include facility capacity, workforce size, supply chain limitations, inventory issues, and financial resources.*

[1]For detailed discussion on BMW's planning, see B. Fleishman, S. Ferber, and P. Henrich, "Strategic Planning of BMW's
Global Production Network," *Interfaces* 36, no. 3 (May–June 2006): 194–208.

OM in Action — Building the Plan at Snapper

Every bright red Snapper lawn mower sold anywhere in the world comes from a factory in McDonough, Georgia. Ten years ago, the Snapper line had about 40 models of mowers, leaf blowers, and snow blowers. Today, reflecting the demands of mass customization, the product line is much more complex. Snapper designs, manufactures, and sells 145 models. This means that aggregate planning and the related short-term scheduling have become more complex, too.

In the past, Snapper met demand by carrying a huge inventory for 52 regional distributors and thousands of independent dealerships. It manufactured and shipped tens of thousands of lawn mowers, worth tens of millions of dollars, without quite knowing when they would be sold—a very expensive approach to meeting demand. Some changes were necessary. The new plan's goal is for each distribution center to receive only the minimum inventory necessary to meet demand. Today, operations managers at Snapper evaluate production capacity and

use frequent data from the field as inputs to sophisticated software to forecast sales. The new system tracks customer demand and aggregates forecasts for every model in every region of the country. It even adjusts for holidays and weather. And the number of distribution centers has been cut from 52 to 4.

Once evaluation of the aggregate plan against capacity determines the plan to be feasible, Snapper's planners break down the plan into production needs for each model. Production by model is accomplished by building rolling monthly and weekly plans. These plans track the pace at which various units are selling. Then, the final step requires juggling work assignments to various work centers for each shift, such as 265 lawn mowers in an 8-hour shift. That's a new Snapper every 109 seconds.

Sources: The Wall Street Journal (July 14, 2006): B1, B6; *Fast Company* (January/February 2006): 67–71; and **www.snapper.com**.

In the service sector, consider Computrain, a company that provides microcomputer training for managers. The firm offers courses on spreadsheets, graphics, databases, word processing, and writing Web pages, and employs several instructors to meet the demand for its services from business and government. Demand for training tends to be very low near holiday seasons and during summer, when many people take their vacations. To meet the fluctuating needs for courses, the company can hire and lay off instructors, advertise to increase demand in slow seasons, or subcontract its work to other training agencies during peak periods. Again, aggregate planning makes decisions about intermediate-range capacity, not specific courses or instructors.

Aggregate planning is part of a larger production planning system. Therefore, understanding the interfaces between the plan and several internal and external factors is useful. Figure 2 shows that the operations manager not only receives input from the marketing department's demand forecast, but must also deal with financial data, personnel, capacity, and availability of raw materials. In a manufacturing environment, the process of breaking the aggregate plan down into greater detail is called **disaggregation**. Disaggregation results in a **master production schedule**, which provides input to material requirements planning (MRP) systems. The master production schedule addresses the purchasing or production of parts or components needed to make final products. Detailed work schedules for people and priority scheduling for products result as the final step of the production planning system.

Disaggregation
The process of breaking an aggregate plan into greater detail.

Master production schedule
A timetable that specifies what is to be made and when.

AGGREGATE PLANNING STRATEGIES

When generating an aggregate plan, the operations manager must answer several questions:

Learning Objective

2. Identify optional strategies for developing an aggregate plan

1. Should inventories be used to absorb changes in demand during the planning period?
2. Should changes be accommodated by varying the size of the workforce?
3. Should part-timers be used, or should overtime and idle time absorb fluctuations?
4. Should subcontractors be used on fluctuating orders so a stable workforce can be maintained?
5. Should prices or other factors be changed to influence demand?

All of these are legitimate planning strategies. They involve the manipulation of inventory, production rates, labor levels, capacity, and other controllable variables. We will now examine eight options in more detail. The first five are called *capacity options* because they do not try to change demand but attempt to absorb the fluctuations in it. The last three are *demand options* through which firms try to smooth out changes in the demand pattern over the planning period.

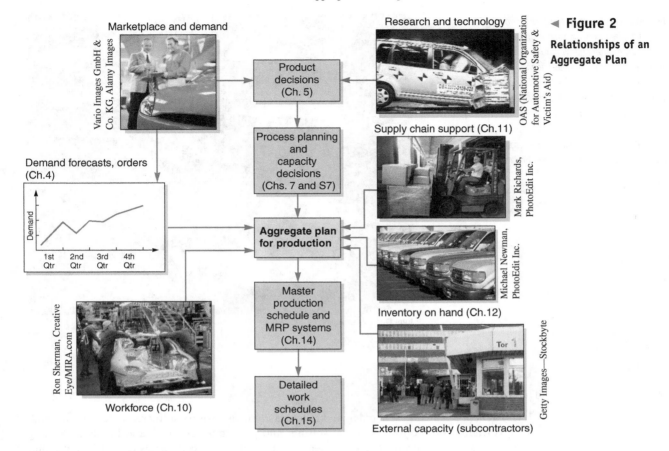

Vario Images GmbH & Co. KG, Alamy Images

Marketplace and demand

Research and technology

OAS (National Organization for Automotive Safety & Victim's Aid)

◄ **Figure 2**

Relationships of an Aggregate Plan

Product decisions (Ch. 5)

Supply chain support (Ch.11)

Mark Richards, PhotoEdit Inc.

Demand forecasts, orders (Ch.4)

Process planning and capacity decisions (Chs. 7 and S7)

Aggregate plan for production

Inventory on hand (Ch.12)

Michael Newman, PhotoEdit Inc.

Demand

1st Qtr | 2nd Qtr | 3rd Qtr | 4th Qtr

Ron Sherman, Creative Eye/MIRA.com

Master production schedule and MRP systems (Ch.14)

Detailed work schedules (Ch.15)

Workforce (Ch.10)

External capacity (subcontractors)

Getty Images—Stockbyte

Capacity Options

A firm can choose from the following basic capacity (production) options:

Aggregate planning in the real world involves a lot of trial and error.

1. *Changing inventory levels:* Managers can increase inventory during periods of low demand to meet high demand in future periods. If this strategy is selected, costs associated with storage, insurance, handling, obsolescence, pilferage, and capital invested will increase. (These costs typically range from 15% to 40% of the value of an item annually.) On the other hand, when the firm enters a period of increasing demand, shortages can result in lost sales due to potentially longer lead times and poorer customer service.

2. *Varying workforce size by hiring or layoffs:* One way to meet demand is to hire or lay off production workers to match production rates. However, often new employees need to be trained, and the average productivity drops temporarily as they are absorbed into the firm. Layoffs or firings, of course, lower the morale of all workers and can lead to lower productivity.

3. *Varying production rates through overtime or idle time:* It is sometimes possible to keep a constant workforce while varying working hours, cutting back the number of hours worked when demand is low and increasing them when it rises. Yet when demand is on a large upswing, there is a limit on how much overtime is realistic. Overtime pay requires more money, and too much overtime can wear workers down to the point that overall productivity drops off. Overtime also implies the increased overhead needed to keep a facility open. On the other hand, when there is a period of decreased demand, the company must somehow absorb workers' idle time—usually a difficult process.

4. *Subcontracting:* A firm can acquire temporary capacity by subcontracting work during peak demand periods. Subcontracting, however, has several pitfalls. First, it may be costly; second, it risks opening the client's door to a competitor. Third, it is often hard to find the perfect subcontract supplier, one who always delivers the quality product on time.

5. *Using part-time workers:* Especially in the service sector, part-time workers can fill unskilled labor needs. This practice is common in restaurants, retail stores, and supermarkets.

▶ *John Deere and Company, the "granddaddy" of farm equipment manufacturers, uses sales incentives to smooth demand. During the fall and winter off-seasons, sales are boosted with price cuts and other incentives. About 70% of Deere's big machines are ordered in advance of seasonal use—about double the industry rate. Incentives hurt margins, but Deere keeps its market share and controls costs by producing more steadily all year long. Similarly, in service businesses like L.L. Bean, some customers are offered free shipping on orders placed before the Christmas rush.*

John Deere & Company

Demand Options

The basic demand options are:

1. *Influencing demand:* When demand is low, a company can try to increase demand through advertising, promotion, personal selling, and price cuts. Airlines and hotels have long offered weekend discounts and off-season rates; telephone companies charge less at night; some colleges give discounts to senior citizens; and air conditioners are least expensive in winter. However, even special advertising, promotions, selling, and pricing are not always able to balance demand with production capacity.

2. *Back ordering during high-demand periods:* Back orders are orders for goods or services that a firm accepts but is unable (either on purpose or by chance) to fill at the moment. If customers are willing to wait without loss of their goodwill or order, back ordering is a possible strategy. Many firms back order, but the approach often results in lost sales.

3. *Counterseasonal product and service mixing:* A widely used active smoothing technique among manufacturers is to develop a product mix of counterseasonal items. Examples include companies that make both furnaces and air conditioners or lawn mowers and snowblowers. However, companies that follow this approach may find themselves involved in products or services beyond their area of expertise or beyond their target market.

> *Negative inventory means a company owes units to customers. It either loses sales or back orders to make it up.*

These eight options, along with their advantages and disadvantages, are summarized in Table 1.

Mixing Options to Develop a Plan

Although each of the five capacity options and three demand options may produce an effective aggregate schedule, some combination of capacity options and demand options may be better.

Many manufacturers assume that the use of the demand options has been fully explored by the marketing department and those reasonable options incorporated into the demand forecast. The operations manager then builds the aggregate plan based on that forecast. However, using the five capacity options at his command, the operations manager still has a multitude of possible plans. These plans can embody, at one extreme, a *chase strategy* and, at the other, a *level-scheduling strategy*. They may, of course, fall somewhere in between.

Chase strategy

A planning strategy that sets production equal to forecasted demand.

Chase Strategy A **chase strategy** attempts to achieve output rates for each period that match the demand forecast for that period. This strategy can be accomplished in a variety of ways. For example, the operations manager can vary workforce levels by hiring or laying off or

▼ **Table 1 Aggregate Planning Options: Advantages and Disadvantages**

Option	Advantages	Disadvantages	Some Comments
Changing inventory levels	Changes in human resources are gradual or none; no abrupt production changes.	Inventory holding costs may increase. Shortages may result in lost sales.	Applies mainly to production, not service, operations.
Varying workforce size by hiring or layoffs	Avoids the costs of other alternatives.	Hiring, layoff, and training costs may be significant.	Used where size of labor pool is large.
Varying production rates through overtime or idle time	Matches seasonal fluctuations without hiring/training costs.	Overtime premiums; tired workers; may not meet demand.	Allows flexibility within the aggregate plan.
Subcontracting	Permits flexibility and smoothing of the firm's output.	Loss of quality control; reduced profits; loss of future business.	Applies mainly in production settings.
Using part-time workers	Is less costly and more flexible than full-time workers.	High turnover/training costs; quality suffers; scheduling difficult.	Good for unskilled jobs in areas with large temporary labor pools.
Influencing demand	Tries to use excess capacity. Discounts draw new customers.	Uncertainty in demand. Hard to match demand to supply exactly.	Creates marketing ideas. Overbooking used in some businesses.
Back ordering during high-demand periods	May avoid overtime. Keeps capacity constant.	Customer must be willing to wait, but goodwill is lost.	Many companies back order.
Counterseasonal product and service mixing	Fully utilizes resources; allows stable workforce.	May require skills or equipment outside firm's areas of expertise.	Risky finding products or services with opposite demand patterns.

can vary production by means of overtime, idle time, part-time employees, or subcontracting. Many service organizations favor the chase strategy because the inventory option is difficult or impossible to adopt. Industries that have moved toward a chase strategy include education, hospitality, and construction.

Level Strategy   A level strategy (or **level scheduling**) is an aggregate plan in which production is uniform from period to period. Firms like Toyota and Nissan keep production at uniform levels and may (1) let the finished-goods inventory go up or down to buffer the difference between demand and production or (2) find alternative work for employees. Their philosophy is that a stable workforce leads to a better-quality product, less turnover and absenteeism, and more employee commitment to corporate goals. Other hidden savings include employees who are more experienced, easier scheduling and supervision, and fewer dramatic startups and shutdowns. Level scheduling works well when demand is reasonably stable.

Level scheduling
Maintaining a constant output rate, production rate, or workforce level over the planning horizon.

METHODS FOR AGGREGATE PLANNING

For most firms, neither a chase strategy nor a level strategy is likely to prove ideal, so a combination of the eight options (called a **mixed strategy**) must be investigated to achieve minimum cost. However, because there are a huge number of possible mixed strategies, managers find that aggregate planning can be a challenging task. Finding the one "optimal" plan is not always possible. Indeed, some companies have no formal aggregate planning process: They use the same plan from year to year, making adjustments up or down just enough to fit the new annual demand. This method certainly does not provide much flexibility, and if the original plan was suboptimal, the entire production process will be locked into suboptimal performance.

Mixed strategy
A planning strategy that uses two or more controllable variables to set a feasible production plan.

In this section, we introduce several techniques that operations managers use to develop more useful and appropriate aggregate plans. They range from the widely used graphical method to a series of more formal mathematical approaches, including the transportation method of linear programming.

Mixed plans are more complex than single, or "pure," ones but typically yield a better strategy.

Graphical Methods

Graphical techniques
Aggregate planning techniques that work with a few variables at a time to allow planners to compare projected demand with existing capacity.

Graphical techniques are popular because they are easy to understand and use. Basically, these plans work with a few variables at a time to allow planners to compare projected demand with existing capacity. They are trial-and-error approaches that do not guarantee an optimal production plan, but they require only limited computations and can be performed by clerical staff. Following are the five steps in the graphical method:

1. Determine the demand in each period.
2. Determine capacity for regular time, overtime, and subcontracting each period.
3. Find labor costs, hiring and layoff costs, and inventory holding costs.
4. Consider company policy that may apply to the workers or to stock levels.
5. Develop alternative plans and examine their total costs.

These steps are illustrated in Examples 1 to 4.

Learning Objective

3. Prepare a graphical aggregate plan

EXAMPLE 1

Graphical approach to aggregate planning for a roofing supplier

A Juarez, Mexico, manufacturer of roofing supplies has developed monthly forecasts for a family of products. Data for the 6-month period January to June are presented in Table 2. The firm would like to begin development of an aggregate plan.

Month	Expected Demand	Production Days	Demand per Day (computed)
Jan.	900	22	41
Feb.	700	18	39
Mar.	800	21	38
Apr.	1,200	21	57
May	1,500	22	68
June	1,100	20	55
	6,200	124	

▶ **Table 2**

Monthly Forecasts

Approach: Plot daily and average demand to illustrate the nature of the aggregate planning problem.

Solution: First, compute demand per day by dividing the expected monthly demand by the number of production days (working days) each month and drawing a graph of those forecasted demands (Figure 3). Second, draw a dotted line across the chart that represents the production rate required to meet average demand over the 6-month period. The chart is computed as follows:

$$\text{Average requirement} = \frac{\text{Total expected demand}}{\text{Number of production days}} = \frac{6,200}{124} = 50 \text{ units per day}$$

▶ **Figure 3**

Graph of Forecast and Average Forecast Demand

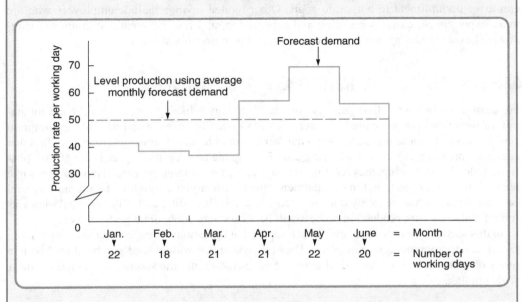

Insight: Changes in the production rate become obvious when the data are graphed. Note that in the first 3 months, expected demand is lower than average, while expected demand in April, May, and June is above average.

Learning exercise: If demand for June increases to 1,200 (from 1,100), what is the impact on Figure 3? [Answer: The daily rate for June will go up to 60, and average production will increase to 50.8 (6,300/124).]

Related problem: 1

The graph in Figure 3 illustrates how the forecast differs from the average demand. Some strategies for meeting the forecast were listed earlier. The firm, for example, might staff in order to yield a production rate that meets *average* demand (as indicated by the dashed line). Or it might produce a steady rate of, say, 30 units and then subcontract excess demand to other roofing suppliers. Other plans might combine overtime work with subcontracting to absorb demand. Examples 2 to 4 illustrate three possible strategies.

EXAMPLE 2

Plan 1 for the roofing supplier—a constant workforce

Excel OM Data File Ch13Ex2.xls

◄ **Table 3**

Cost Information

One possible strategy (call it plan 1) for the manufacturer described in Example 1 is to maintain a constant workforce throughout the 6-month period. A second (plan 2) is to maintain a constant workforce at a level necessary to meet the lowest demand month (March) and to meet all demand above this level by subcontracting. Both plan 1 and plan 2 have level production and are, therefore, called *level strategies*. Plan 3 is to hire and lay off workers as needed to produce exact monthly requirements—*a chase strategy*. Table 3 provides cost information necessary for analyzing these three alternatives:

Inventory carrying cost	$ 5 per unit per month
Subcontracting cost per unit	$ 10 per unit
Average pay rate	$ 5 per hour ($40 per day)
Overtime pay rate	$ 7 per hour (above 8 hours per day)
Labor-hours to produce a unit	1.6 hours per unit
Cost of increasing daily production rate (hiring and training)	$300 per unit
Cost of decreasing daily production rate (layoffs)	$600 per unit

Analysis of Plan 1. Approach: Here we assume that 50 units are produced per day and that we have a constant workforce, no overtime or idle time, no safety stock, and no subcontractors. The firm accumulates inventory during the slack period of demand, January through March, and depletes it during the higher-demand warm season, April through June. We assume beginning inventory = 0 and planned ending inventory = 0:

Solution: We construct the table below and accumulate the costs:

Month	Production at 50 Units per Day	Demand Forecast	Monthly Inventory Change	Ending Inventory
Jan.	1,100	900	+200	200
Feb.	900	700	+200	400
Mar.	1,050	800	+250	650
Apr.	1,050	1,200	−150	500
May	1,100	1,500	−400	100
June	1,000	1,100	−100	0
				1,850

Total units of inventory carried over from one month to the next month = 1,850 units

Workforce required to produce 50 units per day = 10 workers

Because each unit requires 1.6 labor-hours to produce, each worker can make 5 units in an 8-hour day. Thus to produce 50 units, 10 workers are needed.

Active Model 13.1

Example 2 is further illustrated in Active Model 13.1 on the CD-ROM.

Finally, the costs of plan 1 are computed as follows:

Costs		Calculations
Inventory carrying	$ 9,250	(= 1,850 units carried × $5 per unit)
Regular-time labor	49,600	(= 10 workers × $40 per day × 124 days)
Other costs (overtime, hiring, layoffs, subcontracting)	0	
Total cost	$58,850	

Insight: Note the significant cost of carrying the inventory.

Learning exercise: If demand for June decreases to 1,000 (from 1,100), what is the change in cost? [Answer: Total inventory carried will increase to 1,950 at $5, for an inventory cost of $9,750 and total cost of $59,350.]

Related problems: 2, 3, 4, 5, 6, 7, 8, 9, 10, 11, 12, 19

The graph for Example 2 was shown in Figure 3. Some planners prefer a *cumulative* graph to display visually how the forecast deviates from the average requirements. Note that both the level production line and the forecast line produce the same total production. Such a graph is provided in Figure 4.

▶ **Figure 4**

Cumulative Graph for Plan 1

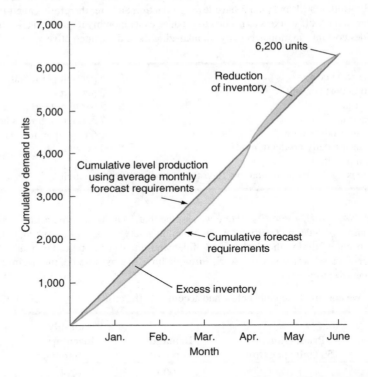

EXAMPLE 3

Plan 2 for the roofing supplier—use of subcontractors within a constant workforce

Analysis of Plan 2. Approach: Although a constant workforce is also maintained in plan 2, it is set low enough to meet demand only in March, the lowest demand-per-day month. To produce 38 units per day in-house, 7.6 workers are needed. (You can think of this as 7 full-time workers and 1 part-timer.) *All* other demand is met by subcontracting. Subcontracting is thus required in every other month. No inventory holding costs are incurred in plan 2.

Solution: Because 6,200 units are required during the aggregate plan period, we must compute how many can be made by the firm and how many must be subcontracted:

$$\text{In-house production} = 38 \text{ units per day} \times 124 \text{ production days}$$

$$= 4,712 \text{ units}$$

$$\text{Subcontract units} = 6,200 - 4,712 = 1,488 \text{ units}$$

The costs of plan 2 are computed as follows:

Costs		Calculations
Regular-time labor	$37,696	(= 7.6 workers × $40 per day × 124 days)
Subcontracting	14,880	(= 1,488 units × $10 per unit)
Total cost	$52,576	

Insight: Note the lower cost of regular labor but the added subcontracting cost.

Learning exercise: If demand for June increases to 1,200 (from 1,100), what is the change in cost? [Answer: Subcontracting requirements increase to 1,588 at $10 per unit, for a subcontracting cost of $15,880 and a total cost of $53,576.]

Related problems: 2, 3, 4, 5, 6, 7, 8, 9, 10, 11, 12, 19

Analysis of Plan 3. Approach: The final strategy, plan 3, involves varying the workforce size by hiring and firing as necessary. The production rate will equal the demand, and there is no change in production from the previous month, December.

Solution: Table 4 shows the calculations and the total cost of plan 3. Recall that it costs $600 per unit produced to reduce production from the previous month's daily level and $300 per unit change to increase the daily rate of production through hirings.

EXAMPLE 4

Plan 3 for the roofing supplier—hiring and firing

◄ **Table 4**

Cost Computations for Plan 3

Month	Forecast (units)	Daily Production Rate	Basic Production Cost (demand × 1.6 hr per unit × $5 per hr)	Extra Cost of Increasing Production (hiring cost)	Extra Cost of Decreasing Production (layoff cost)	Total Cost
Jan.	900	41	$ 7,200	—	—	$ 7,200
Feb.	700	39	5,600	—	$1,200 (= 2 × $600)	6,800
Mar.	800	38	6,400	—	$ 600 (= 1 × $600)	7,000
Apr.	1,200	57	9,600	$5,700 (= 19 × $300)	—	15,300
May	1,500	68	12,000	$3,300 (= 11 × $300)	—	15,300
June	1,100	55	8,800	—	$7,800 (= 13 × $600)	$16,600
			$49,600	$9,000	$9,600	$68,200

Thus, the total cost, including production, hiring, and layoff, for plan 3 is $68,200.

Insight: Note the substantial cost associated with changing (both increasing and decreasing) the production levels.

Learning exercise: If demand for June increases to 1,200 (from 1,100), what is the change in cost? [Answer: Daily production for June is 60 units, which is a decrease of 8 units in the daily production rate from May's 68 units, so the new layoff cost is $4,800 (= 8 × $600), with a total cost of $65,200.]

Related problems: 2, 3, 4, 5, 6, 7, 8, 9, 10, 11, 12, 19

The final step in the graphical method is to compare the costs of each proposed plan and to select the approach with the least total cost. A summary analysis is provided in Table 5. We see that because plan 2 has the lowest cost, it is the best of the three options.

Of course, many other feasible strategies can be considered in a problem like this, including combinations that use some overtime. Although graphing is a popular management tool, its help is in evaluating strategies, not generating them. To generate strategies, a systematic approach that considers all costs and produces an effective solution is needed.

► **Table 5**

Comparison of the
Three Plans

Cost	Plan 1 (constant workforce of 10 workers)	Plan 2 (workforce of 7.6 workers plus subcontract)	Plan 3 (hiring and layoffs to meet demand)
Inventory carrying	$ 9,250	$ 0	$ 0
Regular labor	49,600	37,696	49,600
Overtime labor	0	0	0
Hiring	0	0	9,000
Layoffs	0	0	9,600
Subcontracting	0	14,880	0
Total cost	$58,850	$52,576	$68,200

Mathematical Approaches

This section briefly describes some of the mathematical approaches to aggregate planning that have been developed over the past 50 years.

The Transportation Method of Linear Programming When an aggregate planning problem is viewed as one of allocating operating capacity to meet forecasted demand, it can be formulated in a linear programming format. The **transportation method of linear programming** is not a trial-and-error approach like graphing but rather produces an optimal plan for minimizing costs. It is also flexible in that it can specify regular and overtime production in each time period, the number of units to be subcontracted, extra shifts, and the inventory carryover from period to period.

In Example 5, the supply consists of on-hand inventory and units produced by regular time, overtime, and subcontracting. Costs per unit, in the upper-right corner of each cell of the matrix in Table 7, relate to units produced in a given period or units carried in inventory from an earlier period.

Transportation method of linear programming
A way of solving for the optimal solution to an aggregate planning problem.

EXAMPLE 5

Aggregate planning
with the transportation
method

Excel OM Data File
Ch13Ex5.xls

Farnsworth Tire Company would like to develop an aggregate plan via the transportation method. Data that relate to production, demand, capacity, and cost at its West Virginia plant are shown in Table 6.

▼ **Table 6** Farnsworth's Production, Demand, Capacity, and Cost Data

	Sales Period		
	Mar.	**Apr.**	**May**
Demand	800	1,000	750
Capacity:			
Regular	700	700	700
Overtime	50	50	50
Subcontracting	150	150	130
Beginning inventory	100 tires		

Costs	
Regular time	$40 per tire
Overtime	$50 per tire
Subcontract	$70 per tire
Carrying cost	$ 2 per tire per month

Approach: Solve the aggregate planning problem by minimizing the costs of matching production in various periods to future demands.

solution: Table 7 illustrates the structure of the transportation table and an initial feasible solution.

◄ **Table 7**

Farnsworth's Transportation Table[a]

SUPPLY FROM	DEMAND FOR				TOTAL CAPACITY AVAILABLE (supply)
	Period 1 (Mar.)	Period 2 (Apr.)	Period 3 (May)	Unused Capacity (dummy)	
Beginning inventory	0 100	2	4	0	100
Period 1 — Regular time	40 700	42	44	0	700
Period 1 — Overtime	50	52 50	54	0	50
Period 1 — Subcontract	70	72 150	74	0	150
Period 2 — Regular time	✕	40 700	42	0	700
Period 2 — Overtime	✕	50 50	52	0	50
Period 2 — Subcontract	✕	70 50	72	0 100	150
Period 3 — Regular time	✕	✕	40 700	0	700
Period 3 — Overtime	✕	✕	50 50	0	50
Period 3 — Subcontract	✕	✕	70	0 130	130
TOTAL DEMAND	800	1,000	750	230	2,780

[a]Cells with an x indicate that back orders are not used at Farnsworth. When using Excel OM or POM for Windows to solve, you must insert a *very* high cost (e.g., 9999) in each cell that is not used for production.

Learning Objective

4. Solve an aggregate plan via the transportation method of linear programming

When setting up and analyzing this table, you should note the following:

1. Carrying costs are $2/tire per month. Tires produced in 1 period and held for 1 month will have a $2 higher cost. Because holding cost is linear, 2 months' holdover costs $4. So when you move across a row from left to right, regular time, overtime, and subcontracting costs are lowest when output is used the same period it is produced. If goods are made in one period and carried over to the next, holding costs are incurred. Beginning inventory, however, is generally given a unit cost of 0 if it is used to satisfy demand in period 1.

2. Transportation problems require that supply equals demand; so, a dummy column called "unused capacity" has been added. Costs of not using capacity are zero.

3. Because back ordering is not a viable alternative for this particular company, no production is possible in those cells that represent production in a period to satisfy demand in a past period (i.e., those periods with an "X"). If back ordering *is* allowed, costs of expediting, loss of goodwill, and loss of sales revenues are summed to estimate backorder cost.

4. Quantities in red in each column of Table 7 designate the levels of inventory needed to meet demand requirements (shown in the bottom row of the table). Demand of 800 tires in March is met by using 100 tires from beginning inventory and 700 tires from regular time.

5. In general, to complete the table, allocate as much production as you can to a cell with the smallest cost without exceeding the unused capacity in that row or demand in that column. If there is still some demand left in that row, allocate as much as you can to the next-lowest-cost cell. You then repeat this process for periods 2 and 3 (and beyond, if necessary). When you are finished, the sum of

all your entries in a row must equal the total row capacity, and the sum of all entries in a column must equal the demand for that period. (This step can be accomplished by the transportation method or by using POM for Windows or Excel OM software.)

Try to confirm that the cost of this initial solution is $105,900. The initial solution is not optimal, however. See if you can find the production schedule that yields the least cost (which turns out to be $105,700) using software or by hand.

Insight: The transportation method is flexible when costs are linear but does not work when costs are nonlinear.

Learning example: What is the impact on this problem if there is no beginning inventory? [Answer: Total capacity (units) available is reduced by 100 units and the need to subcontract increases by 100 units.]

Related problems: 13, 14, 15, 16, 17, 18

The transportation method of linear programming described in the above example was originally formulated by E. H. Bowman in 1956. Although it works well in analyzing the effects of holding inventories, using overtime, and subcontracting, it does not work when nonlinear or negative factors are introduced. Thus, when other factors such as hiring and layoffs are introduced, the more general method of linear programming must be used.

Management coefficients model

A formal planning model built around a manager's experience and performance.

Management Coefficients Model Bowman's **management coefficients model**[2] builds a formal decision model around a manager's experience and performance. The assumption is that the manager's past performance is pretty good, so it can be used as a basis for future decisions. The technique uses a regression analysis of past production decisions made by managers. The regression line provides the relationship between variables (such as demand and labor) for future decisions. According to Bowman, managers' deficiencies are mostly inconsistencies in decision making.

Other Models Two additional aggregate planning models are the linear decision rule and simulation. The *linear decision rule (LDR)* attempts to specify an optimum production rate and workforce level over a specific period. It minimizes the total costs of payroll, hiring, layoffs, overtime, and inventory through a series of quadratic cost curves.[3]

A computer model called *scheduling by simulation* uses a search procedure to look for the minimum-cost combination of values for workforce size and production rate.

Comparison of Aggregate Planning Methods

Although these mathematical models have been found by researchers to work well under certain conditions, and linear programming has found some acceptance in industry, the fact is that most sophisticated planning models are not widely used. Why? Perhaps it reflects the average manager's attitude about what he or she views as overly complex models. Like all of us, planners like to understand how and why the models on which they are basing important decisions work. Additionally, operations managers need to make decisions quickly based on the changing dynamics of the workplace—and building good models is time-consuming. This may explain why the simpler graphical approach is more generally accepted.

Table 8 highlights some of the main features of graphing, transportation, management coefficients, and simulation planning models.

[2]E. H. Bowman, "Consistency and Optimality in Managerial Decision Making," *Management Science* 9, no. 2 (January 1963): 310–321.
[3]Because LDR was developed by Charles C. Holt, Franco Modigliani, John F. Muth, and Herbert Simon, it is popularly known as the HMMS rule. For details, see Martin K. Starr, *Production and Operations Management* (Cincinnati, OH: Atomic Dog Publishing, 2004): 490–493.

◄ **Table 8**

Summary of Four Major Aggregate Planning Methods

Technique	Solution Approaches	Important Aspects
Graphical methods	Trial and error	Simple to understand and easy to use. Many solutions; one chosen may not be optimal.
Transportation method of linear programming	Optimization	LP software available; permits sensitivity analysis and new constraints; linear functions may not be realistic.
Management coefficients model	Heuristic	Simple, easy to implement; tries to mimic manager's decision process; uses regression.
Simulation	Change parameters	Complex; model may be difficult to build and for managers to understand.

AGGREGATE PLANNING IN SERVICES

Some service organizations conduct aggregate planning in exactly the same way as we did in Examples 1 through 5 in this chapter, but with demand management taking a more active role. Because most services pursue *combinations* of the eight capacity and demand options discussed earlier, they usually formulate mixed aggregate planning strategies. In industries such as banking, trucking, and fast foods, aggregate planning may be easier than in manufacturing.

Controlling the cost of labor in service firms is critical. Successful techniques include:

1. Accurate scheduling of labor-hours to assure quick response to customer demand
2. An on-call labor resource that can be added or deleted to meet unexpected demand
3. Flexibility of individual worker skills that permits reallocation of available labor
4. Flexibility in rate of output or hours of work to meet changing demand

These options may seem demanding, but they are not unusual in service industries, in which labor is the primary aggregate planning vehicle. For instance:

- Excess capacity is used to provide study and planning time by real estate and auto salespersons.
- Police and fire departments have provisions for calling in off-duty personnel for major emergencies. Where the emergency is extended, police or fire personnel may work longer hours and extra shifts.
- When business is unexpectedly light, restaurants and retail stores send personnel home early.
- Supermarket stock clerks work cash registers when checkout lines become too lengthy.
- Experienced waitresses increase their pace and efficiency of service as crowds of customers arrive.

Approaches to aggregate planning differ by the type of service provided. Here we discuss five service scenarios.

◄ *The heavy demands of the December holiday season place a special burden on aggregate planning at UPS. UPS maximizes truck and plane resource availability for the season, as well as overtime and temporary workers to match capacity to demand.*

Greg Foster, Gregory Foster, Inc.

Restaurants

In a business with a highly variable demand, such as a restaurant, aggregate scheduling is directed toward (1) smoothing the production rate and (2) finding the optimal size of the workforce. The general approach usually requires building very modest levels of inventory during slack periods and depleting inventory during peak periods, but using labor to accommodate most of the changes in demand. Because this situation is very similar to those found in manufacturing, traditional aggregate planning methods may be applied to services as well. One difference that should be noted is that even modest amounts of inventory may be perishable. In addition, the relevant units of time may be much smaller than in manufacturing. For example, in fast-food restaurants, peak and slack periods may be measured in fractions of an hour and the "product" may be inventoried for as little as 10 minutes.

Hospitals

Hospitals face aggregate planning problems in allocating money, staff, and supplies to meet the demands of patients. Michigan's Henry Ford Hospital, for example, plans for bed capacity and personnel needs in light of a patient-load forecast developed by moving averages. The necessary labor focus of its aggregate plan has led to the creation of a new floating staff pool serving each nursing pod.

National Chains of Small Service Firms

With the advent of national chains of small service businesses such as funeral homes, oil change outlets, and photocopy/printing centers, the question of aggregate planning versus independent planning at each business establishment becomes an issue. Both purchases and production capacity may be centrally planned when demand can be influenced through special promotions. This approach to aggregate scheduling is often advantageous because it reduces costs and helps manage cash flow at independent sites.

Miscellaneous Services

Most "miscellaneous" services—financial, transportation, and many communication and recreation services—provide intangible output. Aggregate planning for these services deals mainly with planning for human resource requirements and managing demand. The twofold goal is to level demand peaks and to design methods for fully utilizing labor resources during low-demand periods. Example 6 illustrates such a plan for a legal firm.

EXAMPLE 6

Aggregate planning in a law firm

► **Table 9**

Labor Allocation at Klasson and Avalon, Forecasts for Coming Quarter (1 lawyer = 500 hours of labor)

Klasson and Avalon, a medium-size Tampa law firm of 32 legal professionals, wants to develop an aggregate plan for the next quarter. The firm has developed 3 forecasts of billable hours for the next quarter for each of 5 categories of legal business it performs (column 1, Table 9). The 3 forecasts (best, likely, and worst) are shown in columns 2, 3, and 4 of Table 9.

	Labor-Hours Required			Capacity Constraints	
	(2)	(3)	(4)	(5)	(6)
(1)		Forecasts		Maximum	Number of
Category of Legal Business	Best (hours)	Likely (hours)	Worst (hours)	Demand in People	Qualified Personnel
Trial work	1,800	1,500	1,200	3.6	4
Legal research	4,500	4,000	3,500	9.0	32
Corporate law	8,000	7,000	6,500	16.0	15
Real estate law	1,700	1,500	1,300	3.4	6
Criminal law	3,500	3,000	2,500	7.0	12
Total hours	19,500	17,000	15,000		
Lawyers needed	39	34	30		

Approach: If we make some assumptions about the workweek and skills, we can provide an aggregate plan for the firm. Assuming a 40-hour workweek and that 100% of each lawyer's hours are billed, about 500 billable hours are available from each lawyer this fiscal quarter.

Solution: We divide hours of billable time (which is the demand) by 500 to provide a count of lawyers needed (lawyers represent the capacity) to cover the estimated demand. Capacity then is shown to be 39, 34, and 30 for the three forecasts, best, likely, and worst, respectively. For example, the best-case scenario of 19,500 total hours, divided by 500 hours per lawyer, equals 39 lawyers needed. Because all 32 lawyers at Klasson and Avalon are qualified to perform basic legal research, this skill has maximum scheduling flexibility (column 6). The most highly skilled (and capacity-constrained) categories are trial work and corporate law. The firm's best-case forecast just barely covers trial work, with 3.6 lawyers needed (see column 5) and 4 qualified (column 6). And corporate law is short 1 full person.

Overtime may be used to cover the excess this quarter, but as business expands, it may be necessary to hire or develop talent in both of these areas. Available staff adequately covers real estate and criminal practice, as long as other needs do not use their excess capacity. With its current legal staff of 32, Klasson and Avalon's best-case forecast will increase the workload by $[(39 - 32)/32 =]$ 22% (assuming no new hires). This represents 1 extra day of work per lawyer per week. The worst-case scenario will result in about a 6% underutilization of talent. For both of these scenarios, the firm has determined that available staff will provide adequate service.

Insight: While our definitions of demand and capacity are different than for a manufacturing firm, aggregate planning is as appropriate, useful, and necessary in a service environment as in manufacturing.

Learning exercise: If the criminal law best-case forecast increases to 4,500 hours, what happens to the number of lawyers needed? [Answer: The demand for lawyers increases to 41.]

Related problems: 20, 21

Source: Adapted from Glenn Bassett, *Operations Management for Service Industries* (Westport, CT: Quorum Books, 1992): 110.

Airline Industry

Airlines and auto-rental firms also have unique aggregate scheduling problems. Consider an airline that has its headquarters in New York, two hub sites in cities such as Atlanta and Dallas, and 150 offices in airports throughout the country. This planning is considerably more complex than aggregate planning for a single site or even for a number of independent sites.

Aggregate planning consists of tables or schedules for (1) number of flights in and out of each hub; (2) number of flights on all routes; (3) number of passengers to be serviced on all flights; (4) number of air personnel and ground personnel required at each hub and airport; and (5) determining the seats to be allocated to various fare classes. Techniques for determining seat allocation are called yield, or revenue, management, our next topic.

YIELD MANAGEMENT

Most operations models, like most business models, assume that firms charge all customers the same price for a product. In fact, many firms work hard at charging different prices. The idea is to match the demand curve by charging based on differences in the customer's willingness to pay. The management challenge is to identify those differences and price accordingly. The technique for multiple price points is called yield management.

Yield (or **revenue**) **management** is the aggregate planning process of allocating the company's scarce resources to customers at prices that will maximize yield or revenue. Popular use of the technique dates to the 1980s, when American Airlines's reservation system (called SABRE) allowed the airline to alter ticket prices, in real time and on any route, based on demand information. If it looked like demand for expensive seats was low, more discounted seats were offered. If demand for full-fare seats was high, the number of discounted seats was reduced.

Yield (or **revenue**) **management**
Capacity decisions that determine the allocation of resources to maximize profit or yield.

OM in Action   Yield Management at Hertz

For over 90 years, Hertz has been renting standard cars for a fixed amount per day. During the past two decades, however, a significant increase in demand has derived from airline travelers flying for business purposes. As the auto-rental market has changed and matured, Hertz has offered more options, including allowing customers to pick up and drop off in different locations. This option has resulted in excess capacity in some cities and shortages in others.

These shortages and overages alerted Hertz to the need for a yield management system similar to those used in the airline industry. The system is used to set prices, regulate the movement, and ultimately determine the availability of cars at each location. Through research, Hertz

found that different city locations peak on different days of the week. So cars are moved to peak-demand locations from locations where the demand is low. By altering both the price and quantity of cars at various locations, Hertz has been able to increase "yield" and boost revenue.

The yield management system is primarily used by regional and local managers to better deal with changes in demand in the U.S. market. Hertz's plan to go global with the system, however, faces major challenges in foreign countries, where restrictions against moving empty cars across national borders are common.

Sources: The Wall Street Journal (December 30, 2003): D1 and (March 3, 2000): W-4; and *Cornell Hotel and Restaurant Quarterly* (December 2001): 33–46.

Learning Objective

5. Understand and solve a yield management problem

American Airlines's success in yield management spawned many other companies and industries to adopt the concept. Yield management in the hotel industry began in the late 1980s at Marriott International, which now claims an additional $400 million a year in profit from its management of revenue. The competing Omni hotel chain uses software that performs more than 100,000 calculations every night at each facility. The Dallas Omni, for example, charges its highest rates (about $279) on weekdays but heavily discounts (to as low as $99) on weekends. Its sister hotel in San Antonio, which is in a more tourist-oriented destination, reverses this rating scheme, with better deals for its consumers on weekdays. Similarly, Walt Disney World has multiple prices: an annual admission pass for an adult was recently quoted at $421; but for a Florida resident, $318; for a member of the AAA, $307; and for active-duty military, $385. The *OM in Action* box "Yield Management at Hertz," describes this practice in the rental car industry.

Organizations that have *perishable inventory*, such as airlines, hotels, car rental agencies, cruise lines, and even electrical utilities, have the following shared characteristics that make yield management of interest[4]:

1. Service or product can be sold in advance of consumption.
2. Demand fluctuates.
3. The resource (capacity) is relatively fixed.
4. Demand can be segmented.
5. Variable costs are low and fixed costs are high.

Example 7 illustrates how yield management works in a hotel.

EXAMPLE 7

Yield management

The Cleveland Downtown Inn is a 100-room hotel that has historically charged one set price for its rooms, $150 per night. The variable cost of a room being occupied is low. Management believes the cleaning, air-conditioning, and incidental costs of soap, shampoo, and so forth, are $15 per room per night. Sales average 50 rooms per night. Figure 5 illustrates the current pricing scheme. Net sales are $6,750 per night with a single price point.

Approach: Analyze pricing from the perspective of yield management. We note in Figure 5 that some guests would have been willing to spend more than $150 per room—"money left on the table." Others would be willing to pay more than the variable cost of $15 but less than $150—"passed-up contribution."

---

[4]R. Oberwetter, "Revenue Management," *OR/MS Today* (June 2001): 41–44.

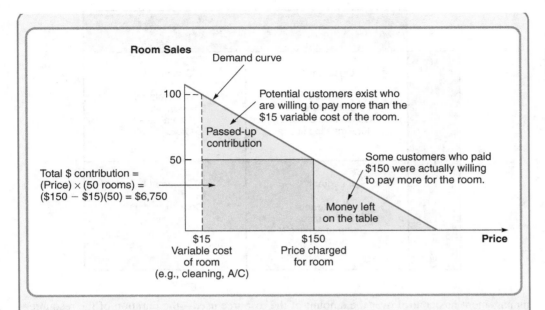

► **Figure 5**

Hotel Sets Only One Price Level

Solution: In Figure 6, the inn decides to set *two* price levels. It estimates that 30 rooms per night can be sold at $100 and another 30 rooms at $200, using yield management software that is widely available.

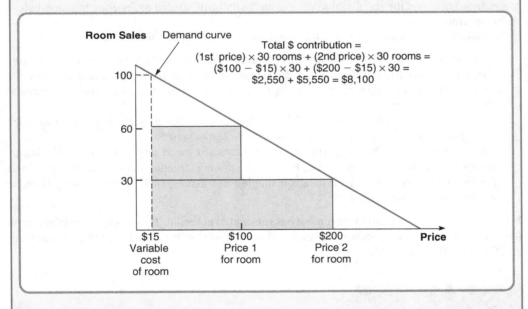

► **Figure 6**

Hotel with Two Price Levels

Insight: Yield management has increased total contribution to $8,100 ($2,550 from $100 rooms and $5,550 from $200 rooms). It may be that even more price levels are called for at Cleveland Downtown Inn.

Learning exercise: If the hotel develops a third price of $150 and can sell half of the $100 rooms at the increased rate, what is the contribution? [Answer: $8,850 = (15 × $85) + (15 × $135) + (30 × $185).]

Related problem: 22

Industries traditionally associated with revenue management operate in quadrant 2 of Figure 7. They are able to apply variable pricing for their product and control product use or availability (number of airline seats or hotel rooms sold at economy rate). On the other hand, movie theaters, arenas, or performing arts centers (quadrant 1) have less pricing flexibility but still use time (evening or matinee) and location (orchestra, side, or balcony) to manage revenue. In both cases,

► **Figure 7**

Yield Management Matrix

Industries in quadrant 2 are traditionally associated with revenue management.

Source: Adapted from S. Kimes and K. McGuire, "Function Space Revenue Management," *Cornell Hotel and Restaurant Administration Quarterly* 42, no. 6 (December 2001): 33–46.

	Price	
	Tend to be fixed	**Tend to be variable**
Predictable use	**Quadrant 1:** Movies Stadiums/arenas Convention centers Hotel meeting space	**Quadrant 2:** Hotels Airlines Rental cars Cruise lines
Unpredictable use	**Quadrant 3:** Restaurants Golf courses Internet service providers	**Quadrant 4:** Continuing care hospitals

Duration of use

management has control over the amount of the resource used—the duration of the resource—such as a seat for 2 hours.

In the lower half of Figure 7, the manager's job is more difficult because the duration of the use of the resource is less controllable. However, with imagination, managers are using excess capacity even for these industries. For instance, the golf course may sell less desirable tee times at a reduced rate, and the restaurant may have an "early bird" special to generate business before the usual dinner hour.

To make yield management work, the company needs to manage three issues:

1. Multiple pricing structures: These structure must be feasible and appear logical (and preferably fair) to the customer. Such justification may take various forms, for example, first-class seats on an airline or the preferred starting time at a golf course. (See the Ethical Dilemma at the end of this chapter).
2. Forecasts of the use and duration of the use: How many economy seats should be available? How much will customers pay for a room with an ocean view?
3. Changes in demand: This means managing the increased use as more capacity is sold. It also means dealing with issues that occur because the pricing structure may not seem logical and fair to all customers. Finally, it means managing new issues, such as overbooking because the forecast was not perfect.

Precise pricing through yield management has substantial potential. Therefore, several firms now have software available to address the issue. These include NCR's Teradata, SPS, DemandTec, and Oracle with Profit Logic.

Summary

Aggregate planning provides companies with a necessary weapon to help capture market shares in the global economy. The aggregate plan provides both manufacturing and service firms the ability to respond to changing customer demands while still producing at low-cost and high-quality levels.

The aggregate schedule sets levels of inventory, production, subcontracting, and employment over an intermediate time range, usually 3 to 18 months. This chapter describes several aggregate planning techniques, ranging from the popular graphical approach to a variety of mathematical models such as linear programming.

The aggregate plan is an important responsibility of an operations manager and a key to efficient production. Output from the aggregate schedule leads to a more detailed master production schedule, which is the basis for disaggregation, job scheduling, and MRP systems.

Aggregate plans for manufacturing firms and service systems are similar. Restaurants, airlines, and hotels are all service systems that employ aggregate plans, and have an opportunity to implement yield management. But regardless of the industry or planning method, the most important issue is the implementation of the plan. In this respect, managers appear to be more comfortable with faster, less complex, and less mathematical approaches to planning.

Key Terms

Aggregate planning (or aggregate scheduling)
Scheduling decisions
Disaggregation
Master production schedule

Chase strategy
Level scheduling
Mixed strategy
Graphical techniques

Transportation method of linear programming
Management coefficients model
Yield (or revenue) management

Using Software for Aggregate Planning

This section illustrates the use of Excel OM and POM for Windows in aggregate planning.

X Using Excel OM

Excel OM's Aggregate Planning module is demonstrated in Program 1. Again using data from Example 2, Program 1 provides input and some of the formulas used to compute the costs of regular time, overtime, subcontracting, holding, shortage, and increase or decrease in production. The user must provide the production plan for Excel OM to analyze.

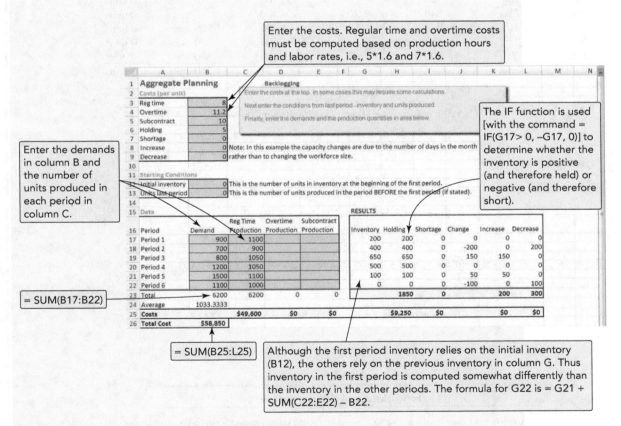

Enter the costs. Regular time and overtime costs must be computed based on production hours and labor rates, i.e., 5*1.6 and 7*1.6.

The IF function is used [with the command = IF(G17> 0, –G17, 0)] to determine whether the inventory is positive (and therefore held) or negative (and therefore short).

Enter the demands in column B and the number of units produced in each period in column C.

= SUM(B17:B22)

= SUM(B25:L25)

Although the first period inventory relies on the initial inventory (B12), the others rely on the previous inventory in column G. Thus inventory in the first period is computed somewhat differently than the inventory in the other periods. The formula for G22 is = G21 + SUM(C22:E22) – B22.

▲ **Program 1** Using Excel OM for Aggregate Planning, with Example 2 Data

P Using POM for Windows

The POM for Windows Aggregate Planning module performs aggregate or production planning for up to 90 time periods. Given a set of demands for future periods, you can try various plans to determine the lowest-cost plan based on holding, shortage, production, and changeover costs. Four methods are available for planning. More help is available on each after you choose the method.

Solved Problems

Solved Problem 1

The roofing manufacturer described in Examples 1 to 4 of this chapter wishes to consider yet a fourth planning strategy (plan 4). This one maintains a constant workforce of eight people and uses overtime whenever necessary to meet demand. Use the information found in Table 3. Again, assume beginning and ending inventories are equal to zero.

solution

Employ eight workers and use overtime when necessary. Note that carrying costs will be encountered in this plan.

Month	Production Days	Production at 40 Units per Day	Beginning-of-Month Inventory	Forecast Demand This Month	Overtime Production Needed	Ending Inventory
Jan.	22	880	—	900	20 units	0 units
Feb.	18	720	0	700	0 units	20 units
Mar.	21	840	20	800	0 units	60 units
Apr.	21	840	60	1,200	300 units	0 units
May	22	880	0	1,500	620 units	0 units
June	20	800	0	1,100	300 units	0 units
					1,240 units	80 units

Carrying cost totals = 80 units × $5/unit/month = $400

Regular pay:

$$8 \text{ workers} \times \$40/\text{day} \times 124 \text{ days} = \$39,680$$

To produce 1,240 units at overtime rate (of $7/hour) requires (1,240 × 1.6 =) 1,984 hours.

$$\text{Overtime pay} = \$7/\text{hour} \times 1,984 \text{ hours} = \$13,888$$

Plan 4

Costs (workforce of 8 plus overtime)

Carrying cost	$ 400	(80 units carried × $5/unit)
Regular labor	39,680	(8 workers × $40/day × 124 days)
Overtime	13,888	(1,984 hours × $7/hour)
Hiring or firing	0	
Subcontracting	0	
Total costs	$53,968	

Plan 2 is still preferable at $52,576.

Solved Problem 2

A Dover, Delaware, plant has developed the accompanying supply, demand, cost, and inventory data. The firm has a constant workforce and meets all its demand. Allocate production capacity to satisfy demand at a minimum cost. What is the cost of this plan?

Demand Forecast

Period	Demand (units)
1	450
2	550
3	750

Supply Capacity Available (units)

Period	Regular Time	Overtime	Subcontract
1	300	50	200
2	400	50	200
3	450	50	200

Other Data

Initial inventory	50 units
Regular-time cost per unit	$50
Overtime cost per unit	$65
Subcontract cost per unit	$80
Carrying cost per unit per period	$ 1
Back order cost per unit per period	$ 4

Solution

		DEMAND FOR				
SUPPLY FROM		Period 1	Period 2	Period 3	Unused Capacity (dummy)	TOTAL CAPACITY AVAILABLE (supply)
Beginning inventory		0 50	1	2	0	50
Period 1	Regular time	50 300	51	52	0	300
	Overtime	65 50	66	67	0	50
	Subcontract	80 50	81	82	0 150	200
Period 2	Regular time	54	50 400	51	0	400
	Overtime	69	65 50	66	0	50
	Subcontract	84	80 100	81 50	0 50	200
Period 3	Regular time	58	54	50 450	0	450
	Overtime	73	69	65 50	0	50
	Subcontract	88	84	80 200	0	200
TOTAL DEMAND		450	550	750	200	1,950

Cost of plan:

Period 1: $50(\$0) + 300(\$50) + 50(\$65) + 50(\$80) = \$22,250$

Period 2: $400(\$50) + 50(\$65) + 100(\$80) = \$31,250$

Period 3: $50(\$81) + 450(\$50) + 50(\$65) + 200(\$80) = \$45,800\,*$

Total cost $\$99,300$

*Includes 50 units of subcontract and carrying cost.

Self-Test

- **Before taking the self-test**, refer to the learning objectives listed at the beginning of the selection and the key terms listed at the end of the selection.
- Use the key at the end of the chapter to **correct** your answers.
- **Restudy** pages that correspond to any questions you answered incorrectly or material you feel uncertain about.

1. Aggregate planning is concerned with determining the quantity and timing of production in the:
   a) short term
   b) intermediate term
   c) long term
   d) all of the above

2. Aggregate planning deals with a number of constraints. These typically are:
   a) job assignments, job ordering, dispatching, and overtime help
   b) part-time help, weekly scheduling, and SKU production scheduling
   c) subcontracting, employment levels, inventory levels, and capacity
   d) capital investment, expansion or contracting capacity, and R&D
   e) facility location, production budgeting, overtime, and R&D

3. Aggregate planning may require:
   a) back ordering
   b) influencing demand
   c) counterseasonal product mixing
   d) subcontracting
   e) all of the above

4. An aggregate planning model is the:
   a) transportation method
   b) linear decision rule
   c) management coefficients model
   d) graphic method
   e) all of the above

5. The critical element in aggregate planning for most services is:
   a) capital investment
   b) labor flexibility

   c) inventory management
   d) subcontracting
   e) all of the above

6. Which of the following aggregate planning strategies requires employing relatively unskilled personnel to be most effective?
   a) varying production rates through overtime or idle time
   b) using part-time workers
   c) back ordering during high-demand periods
   d) subcontracting

7. Which of the following aggregate planning strategies is likely to have the least impact on quality in the service industry?
   a) using part-time workers
   b) changing inventory level
   c) subcontracting
   d) varying production rates through overtime or idle time

8. Managers typically do not use sophisticated planning models because:
   a) these models do not provide information pertinent to the decision at hand
   b) they view these models as overly complex and do not fully understand them
   c) research has demonstrated that such models seldom work well
   d) the time periods addressed by such models are too long

9. Level scheduling usually results in _____ than other strategies.
   a) higher costs
   b) better quality
   c) more subcontracting
   d) more employee turnover

10. Yield management requires that management deals with:
    a) multiple pricing structures
    b) changes in demand
    c) forecasts of use
    d) forecasts of duration of use
    e) all of the above

Active Model Exercise

This active model contains a 6-month aggregate planning problem using a leveling strategy. You can use the scrollbars to adjust the base level of daily production during the month, the amount of daily overtime, and the amount of subcontracting. Note that the formulas are set up such that subcontracting is chosen before overtime since in the example the subcontracting cost per unit is less than the overtime cost per unit.

Questions

1. Each worker makes five units per day. If the number of workers is reduced from 10 to 9, dropping the daily capacity, what happens to the cost?

2. What regular time level minimizes the total cost?

3. How low can the regular daily capacity get before overtime will be required?

4. How low can the regular daily capacity get before there will not be enough capacity to meet the demand?

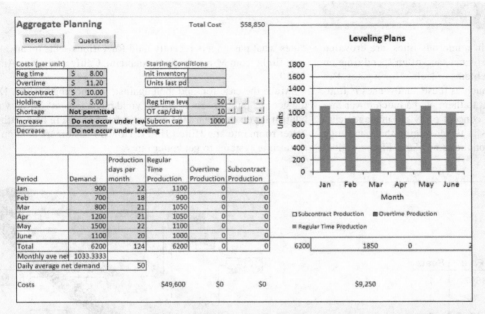

▲ **Active Model 13.1** Analysis of Aggregate Plan 1 Using the Roofing Manufacturer Data in Example 2

Internet and Student CD-ROM/DVD Exercises

Visit our Companion Web site or use your student CD-ROM/DVD to help with material in this chapter.

On Our Companion Web Site,
www.prenhall.com/heizer
- Self-Study Quizzes
- Practice Problems
- Virtual Company Tour
- Internet Case
- PowerPoint Lecture

On Your Student CD-ROM
- Practice Problems
- Active Model Exercise
- ExcelOM
- Excel OM Example Data File
- POM for Windows

On Your Student DVD
- Virtual Office Hours for Solved Problems

Discussion Questions

1. Define aggregate planning.
2. Explain what the term *aggregate* in "aggregate planning" means.
3. List the strategic objectives of aggregate planning. Which one of these is most often addressed by the quantitative techniques of aggregate planning? Which one of these is generally the most important?
4. Define chase strategy.
5. What is a pure strategy? Provide a few examples.
6. What is level scheduling? What is the basic philosophy underlying it?
7. Define mixed strategy. Why would a firm use a mixed strategy instead of a simple pure strategy?

8. What are the advantages and disadvantages of varying the size of the workforce to meet demand requirements each period?
9. Why are mathematical models not more widely used in aggregate planning?
10. How does aggregate planning in service differ from aggregate planning in manufacturing?
11. What is the relationship between the aggregate plan and the master production schedule?
12. Why are graphical aggregate planning methods useful?
13. What are major limitations of using the transportation method for aggregate planning?
14. How does yield management impact an aggregate plan?

Ethical Dilemma

Airline passengers today stand in numerous lines, are crowded into small seats on mostly full airplanes, and often spend time on taxiways because of air-traffic problems or lack of open gates. But what gripes travelers almost as much as these annoyances is finding out that the person sitting next to them paid a much lower fare than they did for their seat. This concept of "yield management" or "revenue management" results in ticket pricing that can range from free to thousands of dollars on the same plane. Figure 8 illus-

trates what passengers recently paid for various seats on an 11:35 A.M. flight from Minneapolis to Anaheim, California, on an Airbus A320.

Make the case for, and then against, this pricing system. Does the general public seem to accept yield management? What would happen if you overheard the person in front of you in line getting a better room rate at a Hilton Hotel? How do customers manipulate the airline systems to get better fares?

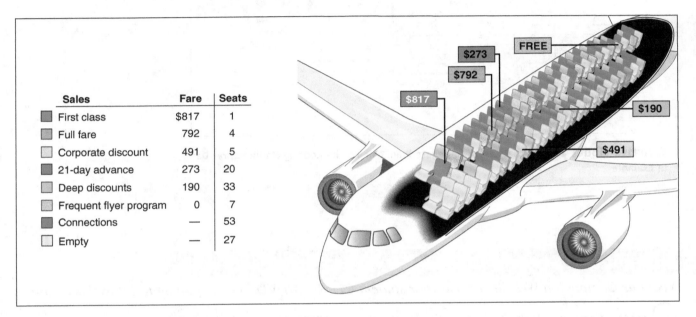

Sales	Fare	Seats
First class	$817	1
Full fare	792	4
Corporate discount	491	5
21-day advance	273	20
Deep discounts	190	33
Frequent flyer program	0	7
Connections	—	53
Empty	—	27

▲ **Figure 8**   Yield Management Seat Costs on a Typical Flight

Problems*

•   **1**   Prepare a graph of the monthly forecasts and average forecasted demand for Industrial Air Corp., a manufacturer of a variety of large air conditioners for commercial applications.

Month	Production Days	Demand Forecast
January	22	1,000
February	18	1,100
March	22	1,200
April	21	1,300
May	22	1,350
June	21	1,350
July	21	1,300
August	22	1,200
September	21	1,100
October	22	1,100
November	20	1,050
December	20	900

Note: **Px** means the problem may be solved with POM for Windows and/or Excel OM.

••   **2**   a) Develop another plan for the Mexican roofing manufacturer described in Examples 1 to 4 and Solved Problem 1. For this plan, plan 5, the firm wishes to maintain a constant workforce of six, using subcontracting to meet remaining demand. Is this plan preferable?

b) The same roofing manufacturer in Examples 1 to 4 and Solved Problem 1 has yet a sixth plan. A constant workforce of seven is selected, with the remainder of demand filled by subcontracting. Is this better than plans 1–5? **Px**

•••   **3**   The president of Hill Enterprises, Terri Hill, projects the firm's aggregate demand requirements over the next 8 months as follows:

Jan.	1,400	May	2,200
Feb.	1,600	June	2,200
Mar.	1,800	July	1,800
Apr.	1,800	Aug.	1,400

Her operations manager is considering a new plan, which begins in January with 200 units on hand and ends with zero inventory. Stockout cost of lost sales is $100 per unit. Inventory holding cost is $20 per unit per month. Ignore any idle-time costs. The plan is called plan A.

Plan A: Vary the workforce level to execute a "chase" strategy by producing the quantity demanded in the *prior* month. The December demand and rate of production are both 1,600 units per month. The cost of hiring additional workers is $5,000 per 100 units. The cost of laying off workers is $7,500 per 100 units. Evaluate this plan. **Px**

•• **4** Using the information in Problem 3, develop plan B. Produce at a constant rate of 1,400 units per month, which will meet minimum demands. Then use subcontracting, with additional units at a premium price of $75 per unit. Evaluate this plan by computing the costs for January through August. **Px**

••• **5** Hill is now considering plan C. Beginning inventory, stockout costs, and holding costs are provided in Problem 3:
a) Plan C: Keep a stable workforce by maintaining a constant production rate equal to the average requirements and allow varying inventory levels.
b) Plot the demand with a graph that also shows average requirements. Conduct your analysis for January through August. **Px**

••• **6** Hill's operations manager (see Problems 3 through 5) is also considering two mixed strategies for January–August:
a) Plan D: Keep the current workforce stable at producing 1,600 units per month. Permit a maximum of 20% overtime at an additional cost of $50 per unit. A warehouse now constrains the maximum allowable inventory on hand to 400 units or less.
b) Plan E: Keep the current workforce, which is producing 1,600 units per month, and subcontract to meet the rest of the demand. Evaluate plans D and E. **Px**

••• **7** Michael Carrigg, Inc., is a DVD manufacturer in need of an aggregate plan for July through December. The company has gathered the following data:

Costs	
Holding cost	$8/DVD/month
Subcontracting	$80/DVD
Regular-time labor	$12/hour
Overtime labor	$18/hour for hours above 8 hours/worker/day
Hiring cost	$40/worker
Layoff cost	$80/worker

Demand	
July	400
Aug.	500
Sept.	550
Oct.	700
Nov.	800
Dec.	700

Other Data	
Current workforce (June)	8 people
Labor-hours/DVD	4 hours
Workdays/month	20 days
Beginning inventory	150 DVDs*
Ending inventory	0 DVDs

*Note that there is no holding cost for June.

Corbis Royalty Free

What will each of the two following strategies cost?
a) Vary the workforce so that production meets demand. Carrigg had eight workers on board in June.
b) Vary overtime only and use a constant workforce of eight. **Px**

•• **8** You manage a consulting firm down the street from Michael Carrigg, Inc., and to get your foot in the door, you have told Mr. Carrigg (see Problem 7) that you can do a better job at aggregate planning than his current staff. He said, "Fine. You do that, and you have a 1-year contract." You now have to make good on your boast using the data in Problem 7. If you develop a plan with back orders, which Mr. Carrigg doesn't like, be sure to include a $16-per-DVD-per-month cost.

••• **9** Mary Rhodes, operations manager at Kansas Furniture, has received the following estimates of demand requirements:

July	Aug.	Sept.	Oct.	Nov.	Dec.
1,000	1,200	1,400	1,800	1,800	1,600

Assuming stockout costs for lost sales of $100 per unit, inventory carrying costs of $25 per unit per month, and zero beginning and ending inventory, evaluate these two plans on an *incremental* cost basis:
- Plan A: Produce at a steady rate (equal to minimum requirements) of 1,000 units per month and subcontract additional units at a $60 per unit premium cost.
- Plan B: Vary the workforce, which performs at a current production level of 1,300 units per month. The cost of hiring additional workers is $3,000 per 100 units produced. The cost of layoffs is $6,000 per 100 units cut back. **Px**

••• **10** Mary Rhodes (see Problem 9) is considering two more mixed strategies. Using the data in Problem 9, compare plans C and D with plans A and B and make a recommendation.
- Plan C: Keep the current workforce steady at a level producing 1,300 units per month. Subcontract the remainder to meet demand. Assume that 300 units remaining from June are available in July.
- Plan D: Keep the current workforce at a level capable of producing 1,300 units per month. Permit a maximum of 20% overtime at a premium of $40 per unit. Assume that warehouse

limitations permit no more than a 180-unit carryover from month to month. This plan means that any time inventories reach 180, the plant is kept idle. Idle time per unit is $60. Any additional needs are subcontracted at a cost of $60 per incremental unit.

••• 11 Liz Perry Health and Beauty Products has developed a new shampoo and you need to develop its aggregate schedule. The cost accounting department has supplied you the cost relevant to the aggregate plan and the marketing department has provided a four-quarter forecast. All are shown as follows:

Quarter	Forecast
1	1,400
2	1,200
3	1,500
4	1,300

Costs	
Previous quarter's output	1,500 units
Beginning inventory	0 units
Stockout cost for back orders	$50 per unit
Inventory holding cost	$10 per unit for every unit held at the end of the quarter
Hiring workers	$40 per unit
Layoff workers	$80 per unit
Unit cost	$30 per unit
Overtime	$15 extra per unit
Subcontracting	Not available

Your job is to develop an aggregate plan for the next four quarters.
a) First, try a chase plan by hiring and layoffs (to meet the forecast) as necessary.
b) Then try a plan that holds employment steady.
c) Which is the more economical plan for Liz Perry Health and Beauty Products? Px

••• 12 Missouri's Soda Pop, Inc., has a new fruit drink for which it has high hopes. Steve Allen, the production planner, has assembled the following cost data and demand forecast:

Quarter	Forecast
1	1,800
2	1,100
3	1,600
4	900

Costs/Other Data
Previous quarter's output = 1,300 cases
Beginning inventory = 0 cases
Stockout cost = $150 per case
Inventory holding cost = $40 per case at end of quarter
Hiring employees = $40 per case
Terminating employees = $80 per case
Subcontracting cost = $60 per case
Unit cost on regular time = $30 per case
Overtime cost = $15 extra per case
Capacity on regular time = 1,800 cases per quarter

Steve's job is to develop an aggregate plan. The three initial options he wants to evaluate are:
• Plan A: a chase strategy that hires and fires personnel as necessary to meet the forecast.
• Plan B: a level strategy.
• Plan C: a level strategy that produces 1,200 cases per quarter and meets the forecasted demand with inventory and subcontracting.
a) Which strategy is the lowest-cost plan?
b) If you are Steve's boss, the VP for operations, which plan do you implement and why? Px

•• 13 Josie Gall's firm has developed the following supply, demand, cost, and inventory data. Allocate production capacity to meet demand at a minimum cost using the transportation method. What is the cost? Assume that the initial inventory has no holding cost in the first period and backorders are not permitted.

Supply Available

Period	Regular Time	Overtime	Subcontract	Demand Forecast
1	30	10	5	40
2	35	12	5	50
3	30	10	5	40

Initial inventory	20 units
Regular-time cost per unit	$100
Overtime cost per unit	$150
Subcontract cost per unit	$200
Carrying cost per unit per month	$ 4

•• 14 Haifa Instruments, an Israeli producer of portable kidney dialysis units and other medical products, develops a 4-month aggregate plan. Demand and capacity (in units) are forecast as follows:

Capacity Source	Month 1	Month 2	Month 3	Month 4
Labor				
Regular time	235	255	290	300
Overtime	20	24	26	24
Subcontract	12	15	15	17
Demand	255	294	321	301

The cost of producing each dialysis unit is $985 on regular time, $1,310 on overtime, and $1,500 on a subcontract. Inventory carrying cost is $100 per unit per month. There is to be no beginning or ending inventory in stock and backorders are not permitted. Set up a production plan that minimizes cost using the transportation method. Px

•• 15 The production planning period for flat-screen monitors at Georgia's Fernandez Electronics, Inc., is 4 months. Cost data are as follows:

Regular-time cost per monitor	$ 70
Overtime cost per monitor	$110
Subcontract cost per monitor	$120
Carrying cost per monitor per month	$ 4

For each of the next 4 months, capacity and demand for flat-screen monitors are as follows:

	Period			
	Month 1	**Month 2**	**Month 3ª**	**Month 4**
Demand	2,000	2,500	1,500	2,100
Capacity				
Regular time	1,500	1,600	750	1,600
Overtime	400	400	200	400
Subcontract	600	600	600	600

ªFactory closes for 2 weeks of vacation.

Fernandez Electronics expects to enter the planning period with 500 monitors in stock. Back ordering is not permitted (meaning, for example, that monitors produced in the second month cannot be used in the first month). Develop a production plan that minimizes costs using the transportation method. **Px**

••• 16 A large Omaha feed mill, B. Swart Processing, prepares its 6-month aggregate plan by forecasting demand for 50-pound bags of cattle feed as follows: January, 1,000 bags; February, 1,200; March, 1,250; April, 1,450; May, 1,400; and June, 1,400. The feed mill plans to begin the new year with no inventory left over from the previous year and backorders are not permitted. It projects that capacity (during regular hours) for producing bags of feed will remain constant at 800 until the end of April, and then increase to 1,100 bags per month when a planned expansion is completed on May 1. Overtime capacity is set at 300 bags per month until the expansion, at which time it will increase to 400 bags per month. A friendly competitor in Sioux City, Iowa, is also available as a backup source to meet demand—but can provide only 500 bags total during the 6-month period. Develop a 6-month production plan for the feed mill using the transportation method.

Cost data are as follows:

Regular-time cost per bag (until April 30)	$12.00
Regular-time cost per bag (after May 1)	$11.00
Overtime cost per bag (during entire period)	$16.00
Cost of outside purchase per bag	$18.50
Carrying cost per bag per month	$ 1.00

Px

•• 17 Lon Min has developed a specialized airtight vacuum bag to extend the freshness of seafood shipped to restaurants. He has put together the following demand cost data:

Quarter	Forecast (units)	Regular Time	Over-time	Sub-contract
1	500	400	80	100
2	750	400	80	100
3	900	800	160	100
4	450	400	80	100

Initial inventory = 250 units	
Regular time cost = $1.00/unit	
Overtime cost = $1.50/unit	
Subcontracting cost = $2.00/unit	
Carrying cost = $0.20/unit/quarter	
Back-order cost = $0.50/unit/quarter	

Min decides that the initial inventory of 250 units will incur the 20¢/unit cost from each prior quarter (unlike the situation in most companies, where a 0 unit cost is assigned).

a) Find the optimal plan using the transportation method.
b) What is the cost of the plan?
c) Does any regular time capacity go unused? If so, how much in which periods?
d) What is the extent of back ordering in units and dollars? **Px**

••• 18 José Martinez of El Paso has developed polished stainless steel parts for his tortilla machine that makes it more of a "showpiece" for display in Mexican restaurants. He needs to develop a 5-month aggregate plan. His forecast of capacity and demand follows:

	Month				
	1	**2**	**3**	**4**	**5**
Demand	150	160	130	200	210
Capacity					
Regular	150	150	150	150	150
Overtime	20	20	10	10	10

Subcontracting: 100 units available over the 5-month period
Beginning inventory: 0 units
Ending inventory required: 20 units

Costs	
Regular-time cost per unit	$100
Overtime cost per unit	$125
Subcontract cost per unit	$135
Inventory cost per unit per month	$ 3

Assume that back orders are not permitted. Using the transportation method, what is the total cost of the optimal plan? **Px**

Fernando Sanchez

••••19 Chris Fisher, owner of an Ohio firm that manufactures display cabinets, develops an 8-month aggregate plan. Demand and capacity (in units) are forecast as follows:

Capacity Source (units)	Jan.	Feb.	Mar.	Apr.	May	June	July	Aug.
Regular time	235	255	290	300	300	290	300	290
Overtime	20	24	26	24	30	28	30	30
Subcontract	12	16	15	17	17	19	19	20
Demand	255	294	321	301	330	320	345	340

The cost of producing each unit is $1,000 on regular time, $1,300 on overtime, and $1,800 on a subcontract. Inventory carrying cost is $200 per unit per month. There is no beginning or ending inventory in stock, and no back orders are permitted from period to period.

a) Set up a production plan that minimizes cost by producing exactly what the demand is each month. Let the workforce vary by using regular time first, then overtime, and then subcontracting. This plan allows no backorders or inventory. What is this plan's cost?

b) Through better planning, regular-time production can be set at exactly the same amount, 275 units, per month. Does this alter the solution?

c) If overtime costs rise from $1,300 to $1,400, will your answer to part (a) change? What if overtime costs then fall to $1,200? **Px**

••• **20** Forrester and Cohen is a small accounting firm, managed by Joseph Cohen since the retirement in 2005 of his partner Brad Forrester. Cohen and his 3 CPAs can together bill 640 hours per month. When Cohen or another accountant bills more than 160 hours per month, he or she gets an additional "overtime" pay of $62.50 for each of the extra hours: This is above and beyond the $5,000 salary each draws during the month. (Cohen draws the same base pay as his employees.) Cohen strongly discourages any CPA from working (billing) more than 240 hours in any given month. The demand for billable hours for the firm over the next 6 months is estimated below:

Month	Estimate of Billable Hours
Jan.	600
Feb.	500
Mar.	1,000
Apr.	1,200
May	650
June	590

Cohen has an agreement with his former partner that Brad Forrester will help out during the busy tax season, if needed, for an hourly fee of $125. Cohen will not even consider laying off one of his colleagues in the case of a slow economy. He could, however, hire another CPA at the same salary, as business dictates.

a) Develop an aggregate plan for the 6-month period.
b) Compute the cost of Cohen's plan of using overtime and Forrester.
c) Should the firm remain as is, with a total of 4 CPAs?

•• **21** Refer to the CPA firm in Problem 20. In planning for next year, Cohen estimates that billable hours will increase by 10% in each of the 6 months. He therefore proceeds to hire a fifth CPA. The same regular time, overtime, and outside consultant (i.e., Forrester) costs still apply.

a) Develop the new aggregate plan and compute its costs.
b) Comment on the staffing level with five accountants. Was it a good decision to hire the additional accountant?

•• **22** Southeastern Airlines's daily flight from Atlanta to Charlotte uses a Boeing 737, with all-coach seating for 120 people. In the past, the airline has priced every seat at $140 for the one-way flight. An average of 80 passengers are on each flight. The variable cost of a filled seat is $25. Katie Morgan, the new operations manager, has decided to try a yield revenue approach, with seats priced at $80 for early bookings and at $190 for bookings within 1 week of the flight. She estimates that the airline will sell 65 seats at the lower price and 35 at the higher price. Variable cost will not change. Which approach is preferable to Ms. Morgan?

Case Studies

Southwestern University: (G)*

With the rising demands of a successful football program, the campus police chief at Southwestern University, John Swearingen, wants to develop a 2-year plan that involves a request for additional resources.

The SWU department currently has 26 sworn officers. The size of the force has not changed over the past 15 years, but the following changes have prompted the chief to seek more resources:

- The size of the athletic program, especially football, has increased.
- The college has expanded geographically, with some new research facilities and laboratories now miles away from the main campus.
- Traffic and parking problems have increased.
- More portable, expensive computers with high theft potential are dispersed across the campus.
- Alcohol and drug problems have increased.
- The size of the surrounding community has doubled.
- The police need to spend more time on education and prevention programs.

The college is located in Stephenville, Texas, a small town about 30 miles southwest of the Dallas/Forth Worth metroplex. During the summer months, the student population is around 5,000. This number swells to 20,000 during fall and spring semesters. Thus demand

for police and other services is significantly lower during the summer months. Demand for police services also varies by:

- Time of day (peak time is between 10 P.M. and 2 A.M.).
- Day of the week (weekends are the busiest).
- Weekend of the year (on football weekends, 50,000 extra people come to campus).
- Special events (check-in, checkout, commencement).

Football weekends are especially difficult to staff. Extra police services are typically needed from 8 A.M. to 5 P.M. on five football Saturdays. All 26 officers are called in to work double shifts. More than 40 law enforcement officers from surrounding locations are paid to come in on their own time, and a dozen state police lend a hand free of charge (when available). Twenty-five students and local residents are paid to work traffic and parking. During the last academic year (a 9-month period), overtime payments to campus police officers totaled over $120,000.

Other relevant data include the following:

- The average starting salary for a police officer is $28,000.
- Work-study and part-time students and local residents who help with traffic and parking are paid $9.00 an hour.

- Overtime is paid to police officers who work over 40 hours a week at the rate of $18.00 an hour. Extra officers who are hired part time from outside agencies also earn $18.00 an hour.
- There seems to be an unlimited supply of officers who will work for the college when needed for special events.
- With days off, vacations, and average sick leave considered, it takes five persons to cover one 24-hour, 7-day-a-week position.

The schedule of officers during fall and spring semesters is:

	Weekdays	Weekend
First shift (7 A.M.–3 P.M.)	5	4
Second shift (3 P.M.–11 P.M.)	5	6
Third shift (11 P.M.–7 A.M.)	6	8

Staffing for football weekends and special events is *in addition to* the preceding schedule. Summer staffing is, on average, half that shown.

Swearingen thinks that his present staff is stretched to the limit. Fatigued officers are potential problems for the department and the community. In addition, neither time nor personnel has been set aside for crime prevention, safety, or health programs. Interactions of police officers with students, faculty, and staff are minimal and usually negative in nature. In light of these problems, the chief would like to request funding for four additional officers, two assigned to new programs and two to alleviate the overload on his current staff. He would also like to begin limiting overtime to 10 hours per week for each officer.

Discussion Questions

1. Which variations in demand for police services should be considered in an aggregate plan for resources? Which variations can be accomplished with short-term scheduling adjustments?
2. Evaluate the current staffing plan. What does it cost? Are 26 officers sufficient to handle the normal workload?
3. What would be the additional cost of the chief's proposal? How would you suggest that he justify his request?
4. How much does it currently cost the college to provide police services for football games? What would be the pros and cons of completely subcontracting this work to outside law enforcement agencies?
5. Propose other alternatives.

*This integrated case study runs throughout the text. Other issues facing Southwestern's football stadium include: (A) Managing the renovation project; (B) Forecasting game attendance; (C) Quality of facilities; (D) Break-even analysis of food services; (E) Locating the new stadium; (F) Inventory palnning of football programs; and (G) Scheduling of campus security officers/staff for game days.

Source: Adapted from C. Haksever, B. Render, and R. Russell, *Service Management and Operations*, 2nd ed. (Upper Saddle River, NJ: Prentice Hall, 2000), 308–309. Reprinted by permission of Prentice Hall, Inc.

Andrew-Carter, Inc.

Andrew-Carter, Inc. (A-C), is a major Canadian producer and distributor of outdoor lighting fixtures. Its products are distributed throughout South and North America and have been in high demand for several years. The company operates three plants to manufacture fixtures and distribute them to five distribution centers (warehouses).

During the present global slowdown, A-C has seen a major drop in demand for its products, largely because the housing market has declined. Based on the forecast of interest rates, the head of operations feels that demand for housing and thus for A-C's products will remain depressed for the foreseeable future. A-C is considering closing one of its plants, as it is now operating with a forecast excess capacity of 34,000 units per week. The forecast weekly demands for the coming year are as follows:

Warehouse 1	9,000 units
Warehouse 2	13,000
Warehouse 3	11,000
Warehouse 4	15,000
Warehouse 5	8,000

Plant capacities, in units per week, are as follows:

Plant 1, regular time	27,000 units
Plant 1, on overtime	7,000
Plant 2, regular time	20,000
Plant 2, on overtime	5,000
Plant 3, regular time	25,000
Plant 3, on overtime	6,000

If A-C shuts down any plants, its weekly costs will change, because fixed costs will be lower for a nonoperating plant. Table 1 shows production costs at each plant, both variable at regular time and overtime, and fixed when operating and shut down. Table 2 shows distribution costs from each plant to each distribution center.

▼ **Table 1** Andrew-Carter, Inc., Variable Costs and Fixed Production Costs per Week

Plant	Variable Cost (per unit)	Fixed Cost per Week	
		Operating	Not Operating
1, regular time	$2.80	$14,000	$6,000
1, overtime	3.52		
2, regular time	2.78	12,000	5,000
2, overtime	3.48		
3, regular time	2.72	15,000	7,500
3, overtime	3.42		

▼ **Table 2** Andrew-Carter, Inc., Distribution Costs per Unit

From Plants	To Distribution Centers				
	W1	W2	W3	W4	W5
1	$.50	$.44	$.49	$.46	$.56
2	.40	.52	.50	.56	.57
3	.56	.53	.51	.54	.35

Discussion Questions

1. Evaluate the various configurations of operating and closed plants that will meet weekly demand. Determine which configuration minimizes total costs.
2. Discuss the implications of closing a plant.

Source: Reprinted by permission of Professor Michael Ballot, University of the Pacific, Stockton, CA.

Additional Case Studies

Internet Case Studies: Visit our Companion Web site at **www.prenhall.com/heizer** *for this free case study:*

- **Cornwell Glass:** Involves setting a production schedule for an auto glass producer.

Harvard has selected these Harvard Business School cases to accompany this chapter:

harvardbusinessonline.hbsp.harvard.edu

- **MacPherson Refrigeration Ltd.** (#93-D021): Students need to evaluate three aggregate production plans for the company's products.
- **Sport Obermeyer Ltd.** (#695-022): This Asian skiwear company has to match supply with demand for products with uncertain demand and a globally dispersed supply chain.
- **Chaircraft Corp.** (#689-082): Illustrates effective production planning in a multistage process affected by seasonal demand.

Bibliography

Chen, Fangruo. "Salesforce Initiative, Market Information, and Production/Inventory Planning." *Management Science* 51, no. 1 (January 2005): 60–75.

Fisher, M. L., J. H. Hammond, W. R. Obermeyer, and A. Raman. "Making Supply Meet Demand in an Uncertain World." *Harvard Business Review* 72, no. 3 (1994): 83–93.

Gunasekaran, A., and H. B. Marri. "Application of Aggregate Planning Models in Developing Countries." *International Journal of Computed Applications in Technology* 20, no. 4 (2004): 172.

Hopp, Wallace J., and Mark L. Spearman. *Factory Physics*, 3rd ed. New York: Irwin/McGraw-Hill (2008).

Hurtubise, S., and C. Olivier. "Planning Tools for Managing the Supply Chain." *Computers & Industrial Engineering* 46, no. 4 (June 2004): 763.

Kimes, S. E., and G. M. Thompson. "Restaurant Revenue Management at Chevy's." *Decision Sciences* 35, no. 3 (summer 2004): 371–393.

Metters, R., K. King-Metters, M. Pullman, and S. Walton. *Successful Service Operations Management.* 2nd ed. Mason, OH: Thompson-South-Western (2006).

Mukhopadhyay, S., S. Samaddar, and G. Colville. "Improving Revenue Management Decision Making for Airlines." *Decision Science* 38, no. 2 (May 2007): 309–327.

Plambeck, Erica L., and Terry A. Taylor. "Sell the Plant? The Impact of Contract Manufacturing on Innovation, Capacity, and Profitability." *Management Science* 51, no. 1 (January 2005): 133–150.

Ryan, D. M. "Optimization Earns Its Wings." *OR/MS Today* 27, no. 2 (2000): 26–30.

Sasser, W. E. "Match Supply and Demand in Service Industries." *Harvard Business Review* 54, no. 6 (November–December 1976): 133–140.

Silver, E. A., D. F. Pyke, and R. Peterson. *Inventory Management and Production Planning and Scheduling.* New York: Wiley (1998).

Vollmann, T. E., W. L. Berry, D. C. Whybark, and F. R. Jacobs. *Manufacturing Planning and Control for Supply Chain Management,* 5th ed. Burr Ridge, IL: Irwin (2005).

Internet Resource

APICS courses: **www.apics.org**

Solutions to Even Numbered Problems

2 (a) $54,560 = total cost
(b) $53,320 = total cost
No, plan 2 is better than either of these.

4 Cost = $214,000 for plan B

6 (a) Plan D, $122,000; (b) plan E is $129,000

8 Each answer you develop will differ.

10 (a) Plan C, $92,000; (b) plan D, $82,300, assuming initial inventory = 0

12 (a) Cost is $314,000.
(b) Cost is $329,000 (but an alternative approach yields $259,500).

(c) Cost is $222,000.
(d) Plan C.
(e) Plan C, with lowest cost and steady employment.

14 $1,186,810

16 $100,750

18 $90,850

20 (a, b) Cost using O.T. and Forrester = $198,125.
(c) A case could be made for either position.

22 Current model = $9,200 in sales; proposed model yields $9,350, which is only slightly better.

Solutions to Self Test

1. b; **2.** c; **3.** e; **4.** e; **5.** b; **6.** b; **7.** a; **8.** b; **9.** b; **10.** e.

Material Requirements Planning (MRP) and ERP

Outline

Ten OM Strategy Decisions

Design of Goods and Services

Managing Quality

Process Strategy

Location Strategies

Layout Strategies

Human Resources

Supply Chain Management

Inventory Management

　Independent Demand

　Dependent Demand

　JIT and Lean Operations

Scheduling

　Aggregate

　Short-Term

Maintenance

Learning Objectives

When you complete this selection you should be able to

1. Develop a product structure
2. Build a gross requirements plan
3. Build a net requirements plan
4. Determine lot sizes for lot-for-lot, EOQ, and PPB

5. Describe MRP II
6. Describe closed-loop MRP
7. Describe ERP

MRP Provides a Competitive Advantage for Wheeled Coach

Wheeled Coach, headquartered in Winter Park, Florida, is the largest manufacturer of ambulances in the world. The $200 million firm is an international competitor that sells more than 25% of its vehicles to markets outside the U.S. Twelve major ambulance designs are produced on assembly lines (i.e., a repetitive process) at the Florida plant, using 18,000 different inventory items, of which 6,000 are manufactured and 12,000 purchased. Most of the product line is custom designed and

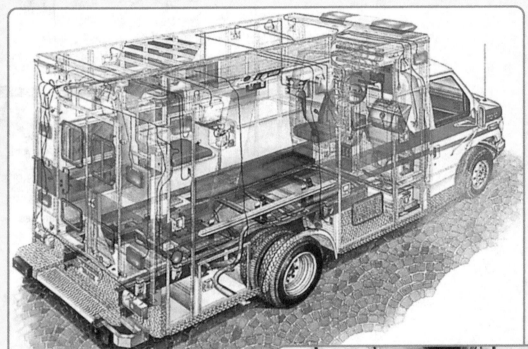

Collins Industries, Inc.

◀ *This cutaway of one ambulance interior indicates the complexity of the product, which for some rural locations may be the equivalent of a hospital emergency room in miniature. To complicate production, virtually every ambulance is custom-ordered. This customization necessitates precise orders, excellent bills of materials, exceptional inventory control from supplier to assembly, and an MRP system that works.*

▶ *Wheeled Coach uses work cells to feed the assembly line. It maintains a complete carpentry shop (to provide interior cabinetry), a paint shop (to prepare, paint, and detail each vehicle), an electrical shop (to provide for the complex electronics in a modern ambulance), an upholstery shop (to make interior seats and benches), and as shown here, a metal fabrication shop (to construct the shell of the ambulance).*

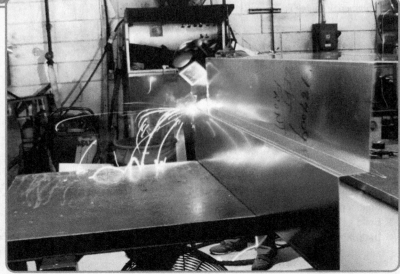

Wheeled Coach Industries, Incorporated

assembled to meet the specific and often unique requirements demanded by the ambulance's application and customer preferences.

This variety of products and the nature of the process demand good material requirements planning. Effective use of an MRP system requires accurate bills of material and inventory records. The Wheeled Coach system, which uses MAPICS DB software, provides daily updates and has reduced inventory by more than 30% in just 2 years.

Wheeled Coach insists that four key tasks be performed properly. First, the material plan must meet both the requirements of the master schedule and the capabilities of the production facility.

Second, the plan must be executed as designed. Third, inventory investment must be minimized through effective "time-phased" material deliveries, consignment inventories, and a constant review of purchase methods. Finally, excellent record integrity must be maintained. Record accuracy is recognized as a fundamental ingredient of Wheeled Coach's successful MRP program. Its cycle counters are charged with material audits that not only correct errors but also investigate and correct problems.

Wheeled Coach Industries uses MRP as the catalyst for low inventory, high quality, tight schedules, and accurate records. Wheeled Coach has found competitive advantage via MRP.

Wheeled Coach Industries, Incorporated

◀ *On six parallel lines, ambulances move forward each day to the next workstation. The MRP system makes certain that just the materials needed at each station arrive overnight for assembly the next day.*

 Video 14.1

MRP at Wheeled Coach Ambulances

▶ *Here an employee is installing the wiring for an ambulance. There are an average of 15 miles of wire in a Wheeled Coach vehicle. This compares to 17 miles of wire in a sophisticated F-16 fighter jet.*

Collins Industries, Inc.

Wheeled Coach and many other firms have found important benefits in MRP. These benefits include (1) better response to customer orders as the result of improved adherence to schedules, (2) faster response to market changes, (3) improved utilization of facilities and labor, and (4) reduced inventory levels. Better response to customer orders and to the market wins orders and market share. Better utilization of facilities and labor yields higher productivity and return on investment. Less inventory frees up capital and floor space for other uses. These benefits are the result of a strategic decision to use a *dependent* inventory scheduling system. Demand for every component of an ambulance is dependent.

DEPENDENT DEMAND

Dependent demand means that the demand for one item is related to the demand for another item. Consider a Ford F-150 truck. Ford's demand for tires and radiators depends on the production of F-150's. Five tires and one radiator go into each finished F-150 truck. Demand for items is *dependent* when the relationship between the items can be determined. Therefore, once management receives an order or makes a forecast of the demand for the final product, quantities required for all components can be computed, because all components are dependent items. The Boeing Aircraft operations manager who schedules production of one plane per week, for example, knows the requirements down to the last rivet. For any product, all components of that product are dependent demand items. *More generally, for any item for which a schedule can be established, dependent techniques should be used.*

When the requirements of MRP are met, dependent models are preferable to the EOQ models.[1] Dependency exists for all component parts, subassemblies, and supplies once a master schedule is known. Dependent models are better not only for manufacturers and distributors but also for a wide variety of firms from restaurants to hospitals. The dependent technique used in a production environment is called **material requirements planning (MRP)**.

Because MRP provides such a clean structure for dependent demand, it has evolved as the basis for Enterprise Resource Planning (ERP). ERP is an information system for identifying and planning the enterprise-wide resources needed to take, make, ship, and account for customer orders. We will discuss ERP in the latter part of this selection.

DEPENDENT INVENTORY MODEL REQUIREMENTS

Effective use of dependent inventory models requires that the operations manager know the following:

1. Master production schedule (what is to be made and when)
2. Specifications or bill of material (materials and parts required to make the product)
3. Inventory availability (what is in stock)
4. Purchase orders outstanding (what is on order, also called expected receipts)
5. Lead times (how long it takes to get various components)

We now discuss each of these requirements in the context of material requirements planning (MRP).

Master Production Schedule

A **master production schedule (MPS)** specifies what is to be made (i.e., the number of finished products or items) and when. The schedule must be in accordance with a production plan. The production plan sets the overall level of output in broad terms (e.g., product families, standard hours, or dollar volume). The plan also includes a variety of inputs, including financial plans, customer demand, engineering capabilities, labor availability, inventory fluctuations, supplier performance, and other considerations. Each of these inputs contributes in its own way to the production plan, as shown in Figure 1.

As the planning process moves from the production plan to execution, each of the lower-level plans must be feasible. When one is not, feedback to the next higher level is used to make the

---

Material requirements planning (MRP)

A dependent demand technique that uses a bill-of-material, inventory, expected receipts, and a master production schedule to determine material requirements.

Master production schedule (MPS)

A timetable that specifies what is to be made and when.

---

[1]The inventory models (EOQ) assume that the demand for one item is independent of the demand for another item. For example, EOQ assumes the demand for refrigerator parts is *independent* of the demand for refrigerators and that demand for parts is constant.

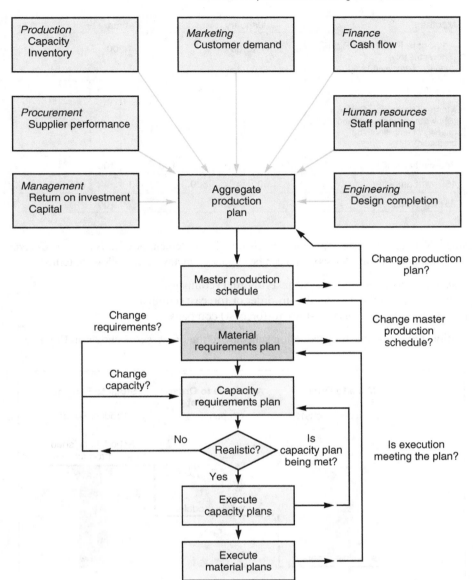

Regardless of the complexity of the planning process, the aggregate production plan and its derivative, the master production schedule, must be developed.

necessary adjustment. One of the major strengths of MRP is its ability to determine precisely the feasibility of a schedule within aggregate capacity constraints. This planning process can yield excellent results. The production plan sets the upper and lower bounds on the master production schedule. The result of this production planning process is the master production schedule.

The master production schedule tells us what is required to satisfy demand and meet the production plan. This schedule establishes what items to make and when: It *disaggregates* the aggregate production plan. While the *aggregate production plan* (as discussed in previous chapter) is established in gross terms such as families of products or tons of steel, the *master production schedule* is established in terms of specific products. Figure 2 shows the master production schedules for three stereo models that flow from the aggregate production plan for a family of stereo amplifiers.

Managers must adhere to the schedule for a reasonable length of time (usually a major portion of the production cycle—the time it takes to produce a product). Many organizations establish a master production schedule and establish a policy of not changing ("fixing") the near-term portion of the plan. This near-term portion of the plan is then referred to as the "fixed," "firm," or "frozen" schedule. Wheeled Coach, the subject of the *Global Company Profile* for this chapter, fixes the last 14 days of its schedule. Only changes farther out, beyond the fixed schedule are permitted. The master production schedule is a "rolling" production schedule. For example, a fixed 7-week plan has an additional week added to it as each week is completed, so a 7-week fixed schedule is

The master production schedule is derived from the aggregate schedule.

▶ **Figure 2**

The Aggregate Production Plan Provides the Basis for Development of the Detailed Master Production Schedule

Months	January				February			
Aggregate Production Plan (Shows the total quantity of amplifiers)	1,500				1,200			
Weeks	1	2	3	4	5	6	7	8
Master Production Schedule (Shows the specific type and quantity of amplifier to be produced)								
240-watt amplifier	100		100		100		100	
150-watt amplifier		500		500		450		450
75-watt amplifier			300			100		

maintained. Note that the master production schedule is a statement of *what is to be produced*, not a forecast of demand. The master schedule can be expressed in any of the following terms:

1. A *customer order in a job shop* (make-to-order) company
2. *Modules in a repetitive* (assemble-to-order or forecast) company
3. An *end item in a continuous* (stock-to-forecast) company

This relationship of the master production schedule to the processes is shown in Figure 3.

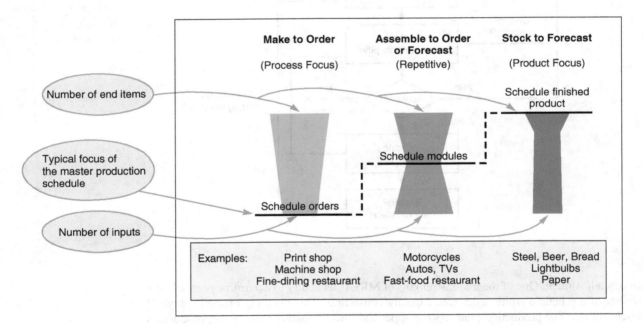

▲ **Figure 3**   Typical Focus of the Master Production Schedule in Three Process Strategies

A master production schedule for two of Nancy's Specialty Foods' products, crabmeat quiche and spinach quiche, might look like Table 1.

▶ **Table 1**

Master Production Schedule for Crabmeat Quiche and Spinach Quiche at Nancy's Specialty Foods

	Gross Requirements for Crabmeat Quiche									
Day	6	7	8	9	10	11	12	13	14	and so on
Amount	50		100	47	60		110	75		

	Gross Requirements for Spinach Quiche									
Day	7	8	9	10	11	12	13	14	15	16	and so on
Amount	100	200	150			60	75		100		

Bills of Material

Defining what goes into a product may seem simple, but it can be difficult in practice. To aid this process, manufactured items are defined via a bill of material. A **bill of material (BOM)** is a list of quantities of components, ingredients, and materials required to make a product. Individual drawings describe not only physical dimensions but also any special processing as well as the raw material from which each part is made. Nancy's Specialty Foods has a recipe for quiche, specifying ingredients and quantities, just as Wheeled Coach has a full set of drawings for an ambulance. Both are bills of material (although we call one a recipe, and they do vary somewhat in scope).

Because there is often a rush to get a new product to market, however, drawings and bills of material may be incomplete or even nonexistent. Moreover, complete drawings and BOMs (as well as other forms of specifications) often contain errors in dimensions, quantities, or countless other areas. When errors are identified, engineering change notices (ECNs) are created, further complicating the process. An *engineering change notice* is a change or correction to an engineering drawing or bill of material.

One way a bill of material defines a product is by providing a product structure. Example 1 shows how to develop the product structure and "explode" it to reveal the requirements for each component. A bill of material for item A in Example 1 consists of items B and C. Items above any level are called *parents*; items below any level are called *components* or *children*. By convention, the top level in a BOM is the 0 level.

> **Bill of material (BOM)**
> A listing of the components, their description, and the quantity of each required to make one unit of a product.

EXAMPLE 1

Developing a product structure and gross requirements

Speaker Kits, Inc., packages high-fidelity components for mail order. Components for the top-of-the-line speaker kit, "Awesome" (A), include 2 standard 12-inch speaker kits (Bs) and 3 speaker kits with amp-boosters (Cs).

Each B consists of 2 speakers (Ds) and 2 shipping boxes each with an installation kit (E). Each of the three 300-watt speaker kits (Cs) has 2 speaker boosters (Fs) and 2 installation kits (Es). Each speaker booster (F) includes 2 speakers (Ds) and 1 amp-booster (G). The total for each Awesome is 4 standard 12-inch speakers and twelve 12-inch speakers with the amp-booster. (Most purchasers require hearing aids within 3 years, and at least one court case is pending because of structural damage to a men's dormitory.) As we can see, the demand for B, C, D, E, F, and G is completely dependent on the master production schedule for A—the Awesome speaker kits.

Approach: Given the above information, we construct a product structure and "explode" the requirements.

Solution: This structure has four levels: 0, 1, 2, and 3. There are four parents: A, B, C, and F. Each parent item has at least one level below it. Items B, C, D, E, F, and G are components because each item has at least one level above it. In this structure, B, C, and F are both parents and components. The number in parentheses indicates how many units of that particular item are needed to make the item immediately above it. Thus, $B_{(2)}$ means that it takes two units of B for every unit of A, and $F_{(2)}$ means that it takes two units of F for every unit of C.

Learning Objective

1. Develop a product structure

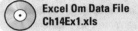

Excel Om Data File
Ch14Ex1.xls

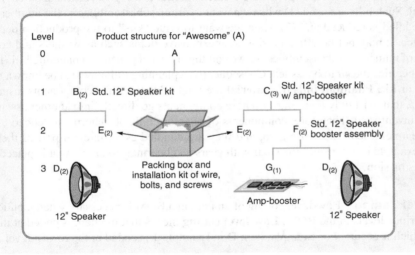

Once we have developed the product structure, we can determine the number of units of each item required to satisfy demand for a new order of 50 Awesome speaker kits. We "explode" the requirements as shown:

Part B:	$2 \times$ number of As =	(2)(50) =	100
Part C:	$3 \times$ number of As =	(3)(50) =	150
Part D:	$2 \times$ number of Bs + $2 \times$ number of Fs =	(2)(100) + (2)(300) =	800
Part E:	$2 \times$ number of Bs + $2 \times$ number of Cs =	(2)(100) + (2)(150) =	500
Part F:	$2 \times$ number of Cs =	(2)(150) =	300
Part G:	$1 \times$ number of Fs =	(1)(300) =	300

Insight: We now have a visual picture of the Awesome speaker kit requirements and knowledge of the quantities required. Thus, for 50 units of A, we will need 100 units of B, 150 units of C, 800 units of D, 500 units of E, 300 units of F, and 300 units of G.

Learning exercise: If there are 100 Fs in stock, how many Ds do you need? [Answer: 600.]

Related problems: 1, 3a, 13a, 25a

Bills of material not only specify requirements but also are useful for costing, and they can serve as a list of items to be issued to production or assembly personnel. When bills of material are used in this way, they are usually called *pick lists*.

Modular bills

Bills of material organized by major subassemblies or by product options.

Modular Bills   Bills of material may be organized around product modules (see previous chapter). *Modules* are not final products to be sold but are components that can be produced and assembled into units. They are often major components of the final product or product options. Bills of material for modules are called **modular bills**. Bills of material are sometimes organized as modules (rather than as part of a final product) because production scheduling and production are often facilitated by organizing around relatively few modules rather than a multitude of final assemblies. For instance, a firm may make 138,000 different final products but may have only 40 modules that are mixed and matched to produce those 138,000 final products. The firm builds an aggregate production plan and prepares its master production schedule for the 40 modules, not the 138,000 configurations of the final product. This approach allows the MPS to be prepared for a reasonable number of items (the narrow portion of the middle graphic in Figure 3) and to postpone assembly. The 40 modules can then be configured for specific orders at final assembly.

Planning bills (or kits)

A material grouping created in order to assign an artificial parent to a bill of material; also called "pseudo" bills.

Phantom bills of material

Bills of material for components, usually assemblies, that exist only temporarily; they are never inventoried.

Planning Bills and Phantom Bills   Two other special kinds of bills of material are planning bills and phantom bills. **Planning bills** are created in order to assign an artificial parent to the bill of material. Such bills are used (1) when we want to group subassemblies so the number of items to be scheduled is reduced and (2) when we want to issue "kits" to the production department. For instance, it may not be efficient to issue inexpensive items such as washers and cotter pins with each of numerous subassemblies, so we call this a *kit* and generate a planning bill. The planning bill specifies the *kit* to be issued. Consequently, a planning bill may also be known as **kitted material**, or **kit**. **Phantom bills of material** are bills of material for components, usually subassemblies, that exist only temporarily. These components go directly into another assembly and are never inventoried. Therefore, components of phantom bills of material are coded to receive special treatment; lead times are zero, and they are handled as an integral part of their parent item. An example is a transmission shaft with gears and bearings assembly that is placed directly into a transmission.

Low-level coding

A number that identifies items at the lowest level at which they occur.

Low-Level Coding   Low-level coding of an item in a BOM is necessary when identical items exist at various levels in the BOM. **Low-level coding** means that the item is coded at the lowest level at which it occurs. For example, item D in Example 1 is coded at the lowest level at which

◀ *For manufacturers like Harley-Davidson, which produces a large number of end products from a relatively small number of options, modular bills of material provide an effective solution.*

Dave Bartruff, Stock Boston

it is used. Item D could be coded as part of B and occur at level 2. However, because D is also part of F, and F is level 2, item D becomes a level-3 item. Low-level coding is a convention to allow easy computing of the requirements of an item. When the BOM has thousands of items or when requirements are frequently recomputed, the ease and speed of computation become a major concern.

Low-level coding ensures that an item is always at the lowest level of usage.

Accurate Inventory Records

Knowledge of what is in stock is the result of good inventory management. Good inventory management is an absolute necessity for an MRP system to work. If the firm has not achieved at least 99% record accuracy, then material requirements planning will not work.[2]

Purchase Orders Outstanding

Knowledge of outstanding orders should exist as a by-product of well-managed purchasing and inventory-control departments. When purchase orders are executed, records of those orders and their scheduled delivery dates must be available to production personnel. Only with good purchasing data can managers prepare good production plans and effectively execute an MRP system.

Lead Times for Components

Once managers determine when products are needed, they determine when to acquire them. The time required to acquire (that is, purchase, produce, or assemble) an item is known as **lead time**. Lead time for a manufactured item consists of *move*, *setup*, and *assembly* or *run times* for each component. For a purchased item, the lead time includes the time between recognition of need for an order and when it is available for production.

When the bill of material for Awesome speaker kits (As), in Example 1, is turned on its side and modified by adding lead times for each component (see Table 2), we then have a *time-phased product structure*. Time in this structure is shown on the horizontal axis of Figure 4 with item A due for completion in week 8. Each component is then offset to accommodate lead times.

Lead time
In purchasing systems, the time between recognition of the need for an order and receiving it; in production systems, it is the order, wait, move, queue, setup, and run times for each component.

---

[2]Record accuracy of 99% may sound good, but note that even when each component has an availability of 99% and a product has only seven components, the likelihood of a product being completed is only .932 (since $.99^7 = .932$).

► **Figure 4**

Time-Phased Product Structure

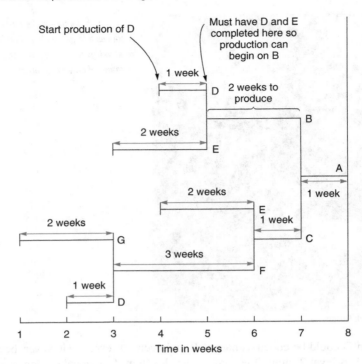

Start production of D

Must have D and E completed here so production can begin on B

1 week — D — 2 weeks to produce — B

2 weeks — E

A — 1 week

2 weeks — E — 1 week — C

2 weeks — G

3 weeks — F

1 week — D

Time in weeks

▼ **Table 2**

Lead Times for Awesome Speaker Kits (As)

Component	Lead Time
A	1 week
B	2 weeks
C	1 week
D	1 week
E	2 weeks
F	3 weeks
G	2 weeks

Gross material requirements plan

A schedule that shows the total demand for an item (prior to subtraction of on-hand inventory and scheduled receipts) and (1) when it must be ordered from suppliers, or (2) when production must be started to meet its demand by a particular date.

MRP STRUCTURE

Although most MRP systems are computerized, the MRP procedure is straightforward and can be done by hand. A master production schedule, a bill of material, inventory and purchase records, and lead times for each item are the ingredients of a material requirements planning system (see Figure 5).

Once these ingredients are available and accurate, the next step is to construct a gross material requirements plan. The **gross material requirements plan** is a schedule, as shown in Example 2. It combines a master production schedule (that requires one unit of A in week 8) and the time-phased schedule (Figure 4). It shows when an item must be ordered from suppliers if there is no inventory on hand or when the production of an item must be started to satisfy demand for the finished product by a particular date.

MRP software programs are popular because many organizations face dependent demand situations.

► **Figure 5**

Structure of the MRP System

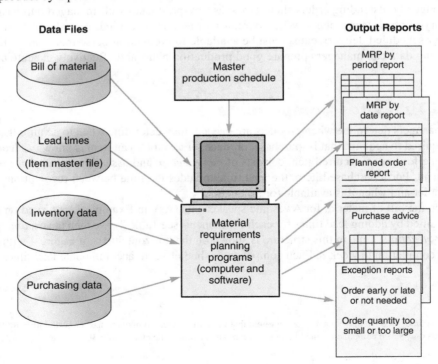

Data Files

Bill of material

Lead times (Item master file)

Inventory data

Purchasing data

Master production schedule

Material requirements planning programs (computer and software)

Output Reports

MRP by period report

MRP by date report

Planned order report

Purchase advice

Exception reports

Order early or late or not needed

Order quantity too small or too large

EXAMPLE 2

Building a gross requirements plan

Each Awesome speaker kit (item A of Example 1) requires all the items in the product structure for A. Lead times are shown in Table 2.

Approach: Using the information in Example 1 and Table 2, we construct the gross material requirements plan with a production schedule that will satisfy the demand of 50 units of A by week 8.

Solution: We prepare a schedule as shown in Table 3.

◄ **Table 3**

Gross Material Requirements Plan for 50 Awesome Speaker Kits (As)

				Week					Lead Time
	1	2	3	4	5	6	7	8	
A. Required date								50	
Order release date							50		1 week
B. Required date							100		
Order release date					100				2 weeks
C. Required date							150		
Order release date						150			1 week
E. Required date					200	300			
Order release date			200	300					2 weeks
F. Required date						300			
Order release date			300						3 weeks
D. Required date			600		200				
Order release date		600		200					1 week
G. Required date			300						
Order release date	300								2 weeks

You can interpret the gross material requirements shown in Table 3 as follows: If you want 50 units of A at week 8, you must start assembling A in week 7. Thus, in week 7, you will need 100 units of B and 150 units of C. These two items take 2 weeks and 1 week, respectively, to produce. Production of B, therefore, should start in week 5, and production of C should start in week 6 (lead time subtracted from the required date for these items). Working backward, we can perform the same computations for all of the other items. Because D and E are used in two different places in Awesome speaker kits, there are two entries in each data record.

Insight: The gross material requirements plan shows when production of each item should begin and end in order to have 50 units of A at week 8. Management now has an initial plan.

Learning exercise: If the lead time for G decreases from 2 weeks to 1 week, what is the new order release date for G? [Answer: 300 in week 2.]

Related problems: 2, 4, 6, 8b, 9, 10a, 11a, 13b, 25b

Learning Objective

2. Build a gross requirements plan

So far, we have considered *gross material requirements*, which assumes that there is no inventory on hand. When there is inventory on hand, we prepare a **net requirements plan**. When considering on-hand inventory, we must realize that many items in inventory contain subassemblies or parts. If the gross requirement for Awesome speaker kits (As) is 100 and there are 20 of those speakers on hand, the net requirement for Awesome speaker kits (As) is 80 (that is, 100 − 20). However, each Awesome speaker kit on hand contains 2 Bs. As a result, the requirement for Bs drops by 40 Bs (20 A kits on hand × 2 Bs per A). Therefore, if inventory is on hand for a parent item, the requirements for the parent item and all its components decrease because each Awesome kit contains the components for lower-level items. Example 3 shows how to create a net requirements plan.

Net material requirements
The result of adjusting gross requirements for inventory on hand and scheduled receipts.

EXAMPLE 3

Determining net requirements

Speaker Kits, Inc., developed a product structure from a bill of material in Example 1. Example 2 developed a gross requirements plan. Given the following on-hand inventory, Speaker Kits, Inc., now wants to construct a net requirements plan.

Active Model 14.1

Examples 1–3 are further illustrated in Active Model 14.1 on the CD-ROM.

Item	On Hand	Item	On Hand
A	10	E	10
B	15	F	5
C	20	G	0
D	10		

Approach: A net material requirements plan includes gross requirements, on-hand inventory, net requirements, planned order receipt, and planned order release for each item. We begin with A and work backward through the components.

Solution: Shown in the chart below is the net material requirements plan for product A.

Lot Size	Lead Time (weeks)	On Hand	Safety Stock	Allo-cated	Low-Level Code	Item Identi-fication		Week								
								1	2	3	4	5	6	7	8	
Lot-for-Lot	1	10	—	—	0	A	Gross Requirements								50	
							Scheduled Receipts									
							Projected On Hand	10	10	10	10	10	10	10	10	10
							Net Requirements								40	
							Planned Order Receipts								40	
							Planned Order Releases							40		
Lot-for-Lot	2	15	—	—	1	B	Gross Requirements							80ᴬ		
							Scheduled Receipts									
							Projected On Hand	15	15	15	15	15	15	15	15	
							Net Requirements							65		
							Planned Order Receipts							65		
							Planned Order Releases						65			
Lot-for-Lot	1	20	—	—	1	C	Gross Requirements							120ᴬ		
							Scheduled Receipts									
							Projected On Hand	20	20	20	20	20	20	20	20	
							Net Requirements							100		
							Planned Order Receipts							100		
							Planned Order Releases						100			
Lot-for-Lot	2	10	—	—	2	E	Gross Requirements						130ᴮ	200ᶜ		
							Scheduled Receipts									
							Projected On Hand	10	10	10	10	10	10			
							Net Requirements						120	200		
							Planned Order Receipts						120	200		
							Planned Order Releases				120	200				
Lot-for-Lot	3	5	—	—	2	F	Gross Requirements							200ᶜ		
							Scheduled Receipts									
							Projected On Hand	5	5	5	5	5	5	5		
							Net Requirements							195		
							Planned Order Receipts							195		
							Planned Order Releases				195					
Lot-for-Lot	1	10	—	—	3	D	Gross Requirements				390ᶠ		130ᴮ			
							Scheduled Receipts									
							Projected On Hand	10	10	10	10					
							Net Requirements				380		130			
							Planned Order Receipts				380		130			
							Planned Order Releases			380		130				
Lot-for-Lot	2	0	—	—	3	G	Gross Requirements				195ᶠ					
							Scheduled Receipts									
							Projected On Hand				0					
							Net Requirements				195					
							Planned Order Receipts				195					
							Planned Order Releases		195							

Net Material Requirements Plan for Product A *Note that the superscript is the source of the demand.*

Constructing a net requirements plan is similar to constructing a gross requirements plan. Starting with item A, we work backward to determine net requirements for all items. To do these computations, we refer to the product structure, on-hand inventory, and lead times. The gross requirement for A is 50 units in week 8. Ten items are on hand; therefore, the net requirements and the scheduled **planned order receipt** are both 40 items in week 8. Because of the 1-week lead time, the **planned order release** is 40 items in week 7 (see the arrow connecting the order receipt and order release). Referring to week 7 and the product structure in Example 1, we can see that 80 (2×40) items of B and 120 (3×40) items of C are required in week 7 to have a total for 50 items of A in week 8. The letter superscripted A to the right of the gross figure for items B and C was generated as a result of the demand for the parent, A. Performing the same type of analysis for B and C yields the net requirements for D, E, F, and G. Note the on-hand inventory in row E in week 6 is zero. It is zero because the on-hand inventory (10 units) was used to make B in week 5. By the same token, the inventory for D was used to make F in week 3.

Insight: Once a net requirement plan is completed, management knows the quantities needed, an ordering schedule, and a production schedule for each component.

Learning exercise: If the on-hand inventory quantity of component F is 95 rather than 5, how many units of G will need to be ordered in week 1? [Answer: 105 units.]

Related problems: 5, 7, 8c, 10b, 11b, 12, 13c, 14, 15, 16a, 25, 27

Examples 2 and 3 considered only product A, the Awesome speaker kit, and its completion only in week 8. Fifty units of A were required in week 8. Normally, however, there is a demand for many products over time. For each product, management must prepare a master production schedule (as we saw earlier in Table 1). Scheduled production of each product is added to the master schedule and ultimately to the net material requirements plan. Figure 6 shows how several product schedules, including requirements for components sold directly, can contribute to one gross material requirements plan.

Most inventory systems also note the number of units in inventory that have been assigned to specific future production but not yet used or issued from the stockroom. Such items are often referred to as *allocated* items. Allocated items increase requirements and may then be included in an MRP planning sheet, as shown in Figure 7.

The allocated quantity has the effect of increasing the requirements (or, alternatively, reducing the quantity on hand). The logic, then, of a net requirements MRP is:

$$\underbrace{\left[\left(\begin{array}{c}\text{Gross}\\\text{requirements}\end{array}\right)+\left(\text{Allocations}\right)\right]}_{\text{Total requirements}}-\underbrace{\left[\left(\begin{array}{c}\text{On}\\\text{hand}\end{array}\right)+\left(\begin{array}{c}\text{Scheduled}\\\text{receipts}\end{array}\right)\right]}_{\text{Available inventory}}=\begin{array}{c}\text{Net}\\\text{requirements}\end{array}$$

Learning Objective

3. Build a net requirements plan

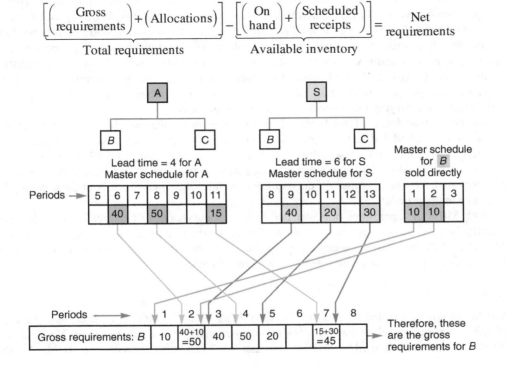

◄ Figure 6

Several Schedules Contributing to a Gross Requirements Schedule for B

One B is in each A, and one B is in each S; additionally, 10 Bs sold directly are scheduled in week 1, and 10 more that are sold directly are scheduled in week 2.

Lot Size	Lead Time	On Hand	Safety Stock	Allocated	Low-Level Code	Item ID		Period							
								1	2	3	4	5	6	7	8
Lot For Lot	1	0	0	10	0	Z	Gross Requirements								80 90
							Scheduled Receipts								0
							Projected On Hand	0	0	0	0	0	0	0	0	0
							Net Requirements								90
							Planned Order Receipts								90
							Planned Order Releases							90	

▲ **Figure 7** Sample MRP Planning Sheet for Item Z

Safety Stock The continuing task of operations managers is to remove variability. This is the case in MRP systems as in other operations systems. Realistically, however, managers need to realize that bills of material and inventory records, like purchase and production quantities, as well as lead times, may not be perfect. This means that some consideration of safety stock may be prudent. Because of the significant domino effect of any change in requirements, safety stock should be minimized, with a goal of ultimate elimination. When safety stock is deemed absolutely necessary, the usual policy is to build it into the projected on-hand inventory of the MRP logic. Distortion can be minimized when safety stock is held at the finished goods level and at the purchased component or raw material level.

MRP MANAGEMENT

The material requirements plan is not static. And since MRP systems increasingly are integrated with just-in-time (JIT) techniques, we now discuss these two issues.

MRP Dynamics

Bills of material and material requirements plans are altered as changes in design, schedules, and production processes occur. Additionally, changes occur in material requirements whenever the master production schedule is modified. Regardless of the cause of any changes, the MRP model can be manipulated to reflect them. In this manner, an up-to-date requirements schedule is possible.

Due to the changes that occur in MRP data, it is not uncommon to recompute MRP requirements about once a week. Conveniently, a central strength of MRP is its timely and accurate *replanning* capability. However, many firms find they do not want to respond to minor scheduling or quantity changes even if they are aware of them. These frequent changes generate what is called **system nervousness** and can create havoc in purchasing and production departments if implemented. Consequently, OM personnel reduce such nervousness by evaluating the need and impact of changes prior to disseminating requests to other departments. Two tools are particularly helpful when trying to reduce MRP system nervousness.

The first is time fences. **Time fences** allow a segment of the master schedule to be designated as "not to be rescheduled." This segment of the master schedule is therefore not changed during the periodic regeneration of schedules. The second tool is pegging. **Pegging** means tracing upward in the BOM from the component to the parent item. By pegging upward, the production planner can determine the cause for the requirement and make a judgment about the necessity for a change in the schedule.

With MRP, the operations manager *can* react to the dynamics of the real world. How frequently the manager wishes to impose those changes on the firm requires professional judgment. Moreover, if the nervousness is caused by legitimate changes, then the proper response may be to investigate the production environment—not adjust via MRP.

MRP and JIT

MRP does not do detailed scheduling—it plans. MRP will tell you that a job needs to be completed on a certain week or day but does not tell you that Job X needs to run on Machine A at 10:30 A.M. and be completed by 11:30 A.M. so that Job X can then run on machine B. MRP is also

System nervousness
Frequent changes in an MRP system.

Time fences
A means for allowing a segment of the master schedule to be designated as "not to be rescheduled."

Pegging
In material requirements planning systems, tracing upward in the bill of material from the component to the parent item.

a planning technique with *fixed* lead times. Fixed lead times can be a limitation. For instance, the lead time to produce 50 units may vary substantially from the lead time to produce 5 units. These limitations complicate the marriage of MRP and just-in-time (JIT). What is needed is a way to make MRP more responsive to moving material rapidly in small batches. An MRP system combined with JIT can provide the best of both worlds. MRP provides the plan and an accurate picture of requirements; then JIT rapidly moves material in small batches, reducing work-in-process inventory. Let's look at four approaches for integrating MRP and JIT: finite capacity scheduling, small buckets, balanced flow, and supermarkets.

Finite Capacity Scheduling (FCS) Most MRP software loads work into infinite size "buckets." The **buckets** are time units, usually one week. Traditionally, when work is to be done in a given week, MRP puts the work there without regard to capacity. Consequently, MRP is considered an *infinite* scheduling technique. Frequently, as you might suspect, this is not realistic. Finite capacity scheduling (FCS) considers department and machine capacity, which is *finite*, hence the name. FCS provides the precise scheduling needed for rapid material movement. We are now witnessing a convergence of FCS and MRP. Sophisticated FCS systems modify the output from MRP systems to provide a finite schedule.

Buckets
Time units in a material requirements planning system.

Small Bucket Approach MRP is an excellent tool for resource and scheduling management in process-focused facilities, that is, in job shops. Such facilities include machine shops, hospitals, and restaurants, where lead times are relatively stable and poor balance between work centers is expected. Schedules are often driven by work orders, and lot sizes are the exploded bill-of-material size. In these enterprises, MRP can be integrated with JIT through the following steps.

Step 1: Reduce MRP "buckets" from weekly to daily to perhaps hourly. Buckets are time units in an MRP system. Although the examples in this chapter have used weekly *time buckets*, many firms now use daily or even fraction-of-a-day time buckets. Some systems use a **bucketless system** in which all time-phased data have dates attached rather than defined time periods or buckets.

Bucketless system
Time-phased data are referenced using dated records rather than defined time periods, or buckets.

Step 2: The planned receipts that are part of a firm's planned orders in an MRP system are communicated to the work areas for production purposes and used to sequence production.

Step 3: Inventory is moved through the plant on a JIT basis.

Step 4: As products are completed, they are moved into inventory (typically finished-goods inventory) in the normal way. Receipt of these products into inventory reduces the quantities required for subsequent planned orders in the MRP system.

Step 5: A system known as *back flush* is used to reduce inventory balances. **Back flushing** uses the bill of material to deduct component quantities from inventory as each unit is completed.

Back flush
A system to reduce inventory balances by deducting everything in the bill of material on completion of the unit.

The focus in these facilities becomes one of maintaining schedules. Nissan achieves success with this approach by computer communication links to suppliers. These schedules are confirmed, updated, or changed every 15 to 20 minutes. Suppliers provide deliveries 4 to 16 times per day. Master schedule performance is 99% on time, as measured every hour. On-time delivery from suppliers is 99.9% and for manufactured piece parts, 99.5%.

Balanced Flow Approach MRP supports the planning and scheduling necessary for repetitive operations, such as the assembly lines at Harley-Davidson, Whirlpool, and a thousand other places. In these environments, the planning portion of MRP is combined with JIT execution. The JIT portion uses kanbans, visual signals, and reliable suppliers to pull the material through the facility. In these systems, execution is achieved by maintaining a carefully balanced flow of material to assembly areas with small lot sizes.

Supermarket Another technique that joins MRP and JIT is the use of a "supermarket." In many firms, subassemblies, their components, and hardware items are common to a variety of products. In such cases, releasing orders for these common items with traditional lead-time offset, as is done in an MRP system, is not necessary. The subassemblies, components, and hardware items can be maintained in a common area, sometimes called a **supermarket**, adjacent to the production areas where they are used. Items in the supermarket are replenished by a JIT/kanban system.

Supermarket
An inventory area that holds common items that are replenished by a kanban system.

LOT-SIZING TECHNIQUES

Lot-sizing decision

The process of, or techniques used in, determining lot size.

Lot-for-lot

A lot-sizing technique that generates exactly what is required to meet the plan.

An MRP system is an excellent way to determine production schedules and net requirements. However, whenever we have a net requirement, a decision must be made about *how much* to order. This decision is called a **lot-sizing decision**. There are a variety of ways to determine lot sizes in an MRP system; commercial MRP software usually includes the choice of several lot-sizing techniques. We now review a few of them.

Lot-for-Lot   In Example 3, we used a lot-sizing technique known as **lot-for-lot**, which produced exactly what was required. This decision is consistent with the objective of an MRP system, which is to meet the requirements of *dependent* demand. Thus, an MRP system should produce units only as needed, with no safety stock and no anticipation of further orders. When frequent orders are economical and just-in-time inventory techniques implemented, lot-for-lot can be very efficient. However, when setup costs are significant or management has been unable to implement JIT, lot-for-lot can be expensive. Example 4 uses the lot-for-lot criteria and determines cost for 10 weeks of demand.

EXAMPLE 4

Lot sizing with lot-for-lot

Learning Objective

4. Determine lot sizes for lot-for-lot, EOQ, and PPB

Speaker Kits, Inc., wants to compute its ordering and carrying cost of inventory on lot-for-lot criteria.

Approach: With lot-for-lot, we order material only as it is needed. Once we have the cost of ordering (setting up), the cost of holding each unit for a given time period, and the production schedule, we can assign orders to our net requirements plan.

Solution: Speaker Kits has determined that, for the 12-inch speaker unit, setup cost is $100 and holding cost is $1 per period. The production schedule, as reflected in net requirements for assemblies, is as follows:

MRP Lot Sizing: Lot-for-Lot Technique*

		1	2	3	4	5	6	7	8	9	10
Gross requirements		35	30	40	0	10	40	30	0	30	55
Scheduled receipts											
Projected on hand	35	35	0	0	0	0	0	0	0	0	0
Net requirements		0	30	40	0	10	40	30	0	30	55
Planned order receipts			30	40		10	40	30		30	55
Planned order releases		30	40		10	40	30		30	55	

*Holding costs = $1/unit/week; setup cost = $100; gross requirements average per week = 27; lead time = 1 week.

The lot-sizing solution using the lot-for-lot technique is shown in the table. The holding cost is zero as there is never any inventory; but seven separate setups (one associated with each order) yield a total cost of $700.

Insight: When supply is reliable and frequent orders are inexpensive, but holding cost or obsolescence is high, lot-for-lot ordering can be very efficient.

Learning exercise: What is the impact on total cost if holding cost is $2 per period rather than $1? [Answer: Total holding cost remains zero, as no units are held from one period to the next with lot-for-lot.]

Related problems: 17, 20, 21, 22

MRP is preferable when demand is dependent. Statistical techniques such as EOQ may be preferable when demand is independent.

Economic Order Quantity   EOQ can be used as a lot-sizing technique. But as we indicated there, EOQ is preferable when *relatively constant* independent demand exists, not when we *know* the demand. EOQ is a statistical technique using averages (such as average demand for a year), whereas the MRP procedure assumes *known* (dependent) demand reflected in a master production schedule. Operations managers should take advantage of demand information when it is known, rather than assuming a constant demand. EOQ is examined in Example 5.

◄ *This Nissan line in Smyrna, Tennessee, has little inventory because Nissan schedules to a razor's edge. At Nissan, MRP helps reduce inventory to world-class standards. World-class automobile assembly requires that purchased parts have a turnover of slightly more than once a day and that overall turnover approaches 150 times per year.*

John Russell, AP Wide World Photos

per week of $1, Speaker Kits, Inc., wants to examine its cost with lot sizes based on an EOQ criteria.

Approach: Using the same cost and production schedule as in Example 4, we determine net requirements and EOQ lot sizes.

Solution: Ten-week usage equals a gross requirement of 270 units; therefore, weekly usage equals 27, and 52 weeks (annual usage) equals 1,404 units. The EOQ model is:

$$Q^* = \sqrt{\frac{2DS}{H}}$$

where D = annual usage = 1,404
            S = setup cost = $100
            H = holding (carrying) cost, on an annual basis per unit
              = $1 × 52 weeks = $52

$$Q^* = 73 \text{ units}$$

MRP Lot Sizing: EOQ Technique*

		1	2	3	4	5	6	7	8	9	10
Gross requirements		35	30	40	0	10	40	30	0	30	55
Scheduled receipts											
Projected on hand	35	35	0	43	3	3	66	26	69	69	39
Net requirements		0	30	0	0	7	0	4	0	0	16
Planned order receipts			73			73		73			73
Planned order releases		73			73		73		73		

*Holding costs = $1/unit/week; setup cost = $100; gross requirements average per week = 27; lead time = 1 week.

$$\text{Setups} = 1,404 / 73 = 19 \text{ per year}$$
$$\text{Setup cost} = 19 \times \$100 = \$1,900$$
$$\text{Holding cost} = \frac{73}{2} \times (\$1 \times 52 \text{ weeks}) = \$1,898$$
$$\text{Setup cost} + \text{Holding cost} = \$1,900 + 1,898 = \$3,798$$

The EOQ solution yields a computed 10-week cost of $730 [$3,798 × (10 weeks/52 weeks) = $730].

Lot sizing with EOQ

With a setup cost of $100 and a holding cost

Insight: EOQ can be an effective lot-sizing technique when demand is relatively constant. However, notice that actual holding cost will vary from the computed $730, depending on the rate of actual usage. From the preceding table, we can see that in our 10-week example, costs really are $400 for four setups, plus a holding cost of 318 units at $1 per week for a total of $718. Because usage was not constant, the actual computed cost was in fact less than the theoretical EOQ ($730), but more than the lot-for-lot rule ($700). If any stockouts had occurred, these costs too would need to be added to our actual EOQ cost of $718.

Learning exercise: What is the impact on total cost if holding cost is $2 per period rather than $1? [Answer: The EOQ quantity becomes 52, the theoretical annual total cost becomes $5,404, and the 10-week cost is $1,039 ($5,404 × (10/52).]

Related problems: 18, 20, 21, 22

Part period balancing (PPB)
An inventory ordering technique that balances setup and holding costs by changing the lot size to reflect requirements of the next lot size in the future.

Economic part period (EPP)
A period of time when the ratio of setup cost to holding cost is equal.

Part Period Balancing **Part period balancing (PPB)** is a more dynamic approach to balance setup and holding cost.[3] PPB uses additional information by changing the lot size to reflect requirements of the next lot size in the future. PPB attempts to balance setup and holding cost for known demands. Part period balancing develops an **economic part period (EPP)**, which is the ratio of setup cost to holding cost. For our Speaker Kits example, EPP = $100/$1 = 100 units. Therefore, holding 100 units for one period would cost $100, exactly the cost of one setup. Similarly, holding 50 units for two periods also costs $100 (2 periods × $1 × 50 units). PPB merely adds requirements until the number of part periods approximates the EPP—in this case, 100. Example 6 shows the application of part period balancing.

EXAMPLE 6

Lot sizing with part period balancing

Speaker Kits, Inc., wants to compute the costs associated with lot sizing using part period balancing. It will use a setup cost of $100 and a $1 holding cost.

Approach: Using the same costs and production schedule as Examples 3 and 4, we develop a format that helps us compute the PPB quantity and apply that to our net requirements plan.

Solution: The procedure for computing the order releases of 80, 100, and 55 is shown in the following PPB calculation. In the second table, we apply the PPB order quantities to the net requirements plan.

PPB Calculations

Periods Combined	Trial Lot Size (cumulative net requirements)	Part Periods	Costs Setup	Holding	Total
2	30	0	40 units held for 1 period = $40		
2, 3	70	$40 = 40 \times 1$	10 units held for 3 periods = $30		
2, 3, 4	70	40			
2, 3, 4, 5	80	$70 = 40 \times 1 + 10 \times 3$	100 +	70	= 170
2, 3, 4, 5, 6	120	$230 = 40 \times 1 + 10 \times 3 + 40 \times 4$			
(Therefore, combine periods 2 through 5; 70 is as close to our EPP of 100 as we are going to get.)					
6	40	0			
6, 7	70	$30 = 30 \times 1$			
6, 7, 8	70	$30 = 30 \times 1 + 0 \times 2$			
6, 7, 8, 9	100	$120 = 30 \times 1 + 30 \times 3$	100 +	120	= 220
(Therefore, combine periods 6 through 9; 120 is as close to our EPP of 100 as we are going to get.)					
10	55	0	100 +	0	= 100
			300 +	190	= 490

[3]J. J. DeMatteis, "An Economic Lot-Sizing Technique: The Part-Period Algorithms," *IBM Systems Journal* 7 (1968): 30–38.

MRP Lot Sizing: PPB Technique*

		1	2	3	4	5	6	7	8	9	10
Gross requirements		35	30	40	0	10	40	30	0	30	55
Scheduled receipts											
Projected on hand	35	35	0	50	10	10	0	60	30	30	0
Net requirements		0	30	0	0	0	40	0	0	0	55
Planned order receipts			80				100				55
Planned order releases		80				100				55	

*Holding costs = $1/unit/week; setup cost = $100; gross requirements average per week = 27; lead time = 1 week.

EPP is 100 (setup cost divided by holding cost = $100/$1). The first lot is to cover periods 1, 2, 3, 4, and 5 and is 80.

The total costs are $490, with setup costs totaling $300 and holding costs totaling $190.

Insight: Both the EOQ and PPB approaches to lot sizing balance holding cost and ordering cost. But PPB places an order each time holding cost equals ordering cost, while EOQ takes a longer averaging approach.

Learning exercise: What is the impact on total cost if holding cost is $2 per period rather than $1? [Answer: With higher holding costs, reorder points become more frequent, with orders now being placed for 70 units in period 1, 50 in period 4, 60 in period 6, and 55 in period 9.]

Related problems: 19, 20, 21, 22

Wagner-Whitin Algorithm The **Wagner-Whitin procedure** is a dynamic programming model that adds some complexity to the lot-size computation. It assumes a finite time horizon beyond which there are no additional net requirements. It does, however, provide good results.[4]

Wagner-Whitin procedure
A technique for lot-size computation that assumes a finite time horizon beyond which there are no additional net requirements to arrive at an ordering strategy.

Lot-Sizing Summary In the three Speaker Kits lot-sizing examples, we found the following costs:

Lot-for-lot	$700
EOQ	$730
Part period balancing	$490

These examples should not, however, lead operations personnel to hasty conclusions about the preferred lot-sizing technique. In theory, new lot sizes should be computed whenever there is a schedule or lot-size change anywhere in the MRP hierarchy. However, in practice, such changes cause the instability and system nervousness referred to earlier in this chapter. Consequently, such frequent changes are not made. This means that all lot sizes are wrong because the production system cannot respond to frequent changes.

In general, the lot-for-lot approach should be used whenever low-cost deliveries can be achieved. Lot-for-lot is the goal. Lots can be modified as necessary for scrap allowances, process constraints (for example, a heat-treating process may require a lot of a given size), or raw material purchase lots (for example, a truckload of chemicals may be available in only one lot size). However, caution should be exercised prior to any modification of lot size because the modification can cause substantial distortion of actual requirements at lower levels in the MRP hierarchy. When setup costs are significant and demand is reasonably smooth, part period balancing (PPB), Wagner-Whitin, or even EOQ should provide satisfactory results. Too much concern with lot sizing yields false accuracy because of MRP dynamics. A correct lot size can be determined only after the fact, based on what actually happened in terms of requirements.

---

[4]We leave discussion of the algorithm to mathematical programming texts. The Wagner-Whitin algorithm yields a cost of $455 for the data in Examples 4, 5, and 6.

User Solutions, Inc.

► Many MRP programs, such as Resource Manager for Excel and DB, are commercially available. Resource Manager's initial menu screen is shown here.

A demo program is available for student use at **www.usersolutions.com**.

EXTENSIONS OF MRP

In this section, we review three extensions of MRP.

Material Requirements Planning II (MRP II)

Material requirements planning II
A system that allows, with MRP in place, inventory data to be augmented by other resource variables; in this case, MRP becomes *material resource planning*.

Material requirements planning II is an extremely powerful technique. Once a firm has MRP in place, inventory data can be augmented by labor-hours, by material cost (rather than material quantity), by capital cost, or by virtually any other resource. When MRP is used this way, it is usually referred to as **MRP II**, and *resource* is usually substituted for *requirements*. MRP then stands for material *resource* planning.

For instance, so far in our discussion of MRP, we have scheduled units (quantities). However, each of these units requires resources in addition to its components. Those additional resources include labor-hours, machine-hours, and accounts payable (cash). Each of these resources can be used in an MRP format just as we used quantities. Table 4 shows how to determine the labor-hours, machine-hours, and cash that a sample master production schedule will require in each period. These requirements are then compared with the respective capacity (that is, labor-hours, machine-hours, cash, etc.), so operations managers can make schedules that will work.

To aid the functioning of MRP II, most MRP II computer programs are tied into other computer files that provide data to the MRP system or receive data from the MRP system. Purchasing, production scheduling, capacity planning, and warehouse management are a few examples of this data integration.

Learning Objective

5. Describe MRP II

► **Table 4**

Material Resource Planning (MRP II)

By utilizing the logic of MRP, resources such as labor, machine-hours, and cost can be accurately determined and scheduled. Weekly demand for labor, machine-hours, and payables for 100 units are shown.

			Week	
	5	**6**	**7**	**8**
A. Units (lead time 1 week)				100
Labor: 10 hours each				1,000
Machine: 2 hours each				200
Payable: $0 each				$ 0
B. Units (lead time 2 weeks, 2 each required)			200	
Labor: 10 hours each			2,000	
Machine: 2 hours each			400	
Payable: Raw material at $5 each			$1,000	
C. Units (lead time 4 weeks, 3 each required)	300			
Labor: 2 hours each	600			
Machine: 1 hour each	300			
Payable: Raw material at $10 each	$3,000			

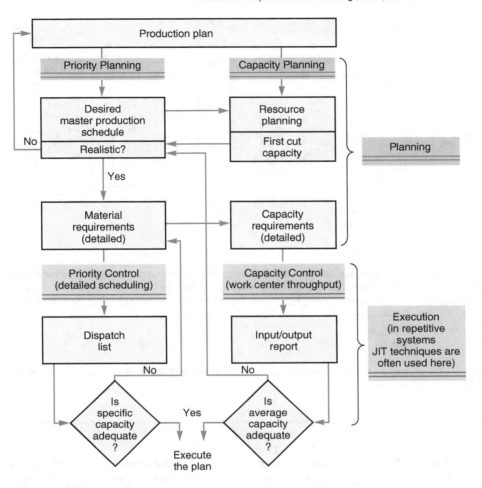

◄ **Figure 8**

Closed-Loop Material Requirements Planning

Source: Adapted from *Capacity Planning and Control Study Guide* (Alexandria, VA: American Production and Inventory Control Society). Reprinted by permission.

Learning Objective

6. Describe closed-loop MRP

Closed-Loop MRP

Closed-loop material requirements planning implies an MRP system that provides feedback to scheduling from the inventory control system. Specifically, a **closed-loop MRP system** provides information to the capacity plan, master production schedule, and ultimately to the production plan (as shown in Figure 8). Virtually all commercial MRP systems are closed-loop.

Closed-loop MRP system
A system that provides feedback to the capacity plan, master production schedule, and production plan so planning can be kept valid at all times.

Capacity Planning

In keeping with the definition of closed-loop MRP, feedback about workload is obtained from each work center. **Load reports** show the resource requirements in a work center for all work currently assigned to the work center, all work planned, and expected orders. Figure 9(a) shows that the initial load in the milling center exceeds capacity in weeks 4 and 6. Closed-loop MRP systems allow production planners to move the work between time periods to smooth the load or at least bring it within capacity. (This is the "capacity planning" side of Figure 8.) The closed-loop MRP system can then reschedule all items in the net requirements plan (see Figure 9[b]).

Load report
A report for showing the resource requirements in a work center for all work currently assigned there as well as all planned and expected orders.

Tactics for smoothing the load and minimizing the impact of changed lead time include the following:

1. *Overlapping,* which reduces the lead time, sends pieces to the second operation before the entire lot is completed on the first operation.
2. *Operations splitting* sends the lot to two different machines for the same operation. This involves an additional setup, but results in shorter throughput times, because only part of the lot is processed on each machine.
3. *Order,* or, *lot splitting* involves breaking up the order and running part of it ahead of schedule.

Example 7 shows a brief detailed capacity scheduling example using order splitting to improve utilization.

► **Figure 9**

(a) Initial Resource
Requirements Profile
for a Milling Center
(b) Smoothed Resource
Requirements Profile
for a Milling Center

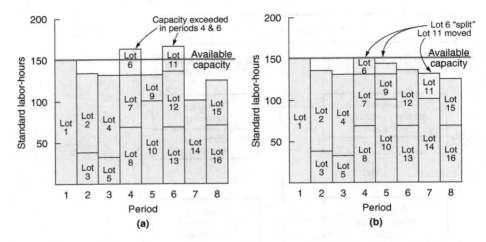

(a)

(b)

EXAMPLE 7

Order splitting

Kevin Watson, the production planner at Wiz Products, needs to develop a capacity plan for the direct numeric control (DNC) work cell. He has the production orders shown below for the next 5 days and 440 minutes available in the work center each day. The parts being produced require 20 minutes each.

Day	1	2	3	4	5
Orders	20	24	23	20	24

Approach: Compute the time available in the work center and the time necessary to complete the production requirements.

Solution:

Day	Units Ordered	Capacity Required (minutes)	Capacity Available (minutes)	Utilization: Over/ (Under) (minutes)	Production Planner's Action	New Production Schedule
1	20	400	440	(40)		22
2	24	480	440	40	Split order: move 2 units to day 1	22
3	23	460	440	20	Split order: move 1 unit to day 4	22
4	20	400	440	(40)		22
5	24	480	440	40	Split order: move 1 unit to day 4 and 1 unit to day 6 or request overtime.	22
	111					

Insight: By splitting the order, the production planner is able to utilize capacity more effectively and still meet the order requirements.

Learning exercise: If the units ordered for day 5 increase to 26, what are the production planner's options? [Answer: In addition to moving 1 unit to day 4, move the 3 units of production to day 6, or request overtime.]

Related problems: 23, 24

When the workload consistently exceeds work-center capacity, the tactics just discussed are not adequate. This may mean adding capacity. Options include adding capacity via personnel, machinery, overtime, or subcontracting.

MRP IN SERVICES

The demand for many services or service items is classified as dependent demand when it is directly related to or derived from the demand for other services. Such services often require product-structure trees, bills-of-material and labor, and scheduling. MRP can make a major contribution to operational performance in such services. Examples from restaurants, hospitals, and hotels follow.

Restaurants In restaurants, ingredients and side dishes (bread, vegetables, and condiments) are typically meal components. These components are dependent on the demand for meals. The meal is an end item in the master schedule. Figure 10 shows (a) a product-structure tree and (b) a bill of material for veal picante, a top-selling entrée in a New Orleans restaurant. Note that the various components of veal picante (that is, veal, sauce, and linguini) are prepared by different kitchen personnel (see part [a] of Figure 10). These preparations also require different amounts of time to complete. Figure 10(c) shows a bill-of-labor for the veal dish. It lists the operations to be performed, the order of operations, and the labor requirements for each operation (types of labor and labor-hours).

Hospitals MRP is also applied in hospitals, especially when dealing with surgeries that require known equipment, materials, and supplies. Houston's Park Plaza Hospital and many hospital suppliers, for example, use the technique to improve the scheduling and management of expensive surgical inventory.

Hotels Marriott develops a bill-of-material (BOM) and a bill-of-labor when it renovates each of its hotel rooms. Marriott managers explode the BOM to compute requirements for materials, furniture, and decorations. MRP then provides net requirements and a schedule for use by purchasing and contractors.

Distribution Resource Planning (DRP)

When dependent techniques are used in the supply chain, they are called distribution resource planning (DRP). **Distribution resource planning (DRP)** is a time-phased stock-replenishment plan for all levels of the supply chain.

Distribution resource planning (DRP)
A time-phased stock-replenishment plan for all levels of a distribution network.

(a) PRODUCT STRUCTURE TREE

(b) BILL OF MATERIALS

Part Number	Description	Quantity	Unit of Measure	Unit Cost
10001	Veal picante	1	Serving	—
20002	Cooked linguini	1	Serving	—
20003	Prepared veal and sauce	1	Serving	—
20004	Spinach	0.1	Bag	0.94
30004	Uncooked linguini	0.5	Pound	—
30005	Veal	1	Serving	2.15
30006	Sauce	1	Serving	0.80

(c) BILL OF LABOR FOR VEAL PICANTE

Work Center	Operation	Labor Type	Setup Time	Run Time
1	Assemble dish	Chef	.0069	.0041
2	Cook linguini	Helper one	.0005	.0022
3	Cook veal and sauce	Assistant chef	.0125	.0500

◄ **Figure 10**

Product Structure Tree, Bill-of-Material, and Bill-of-Labor for Veal Picante

Source: Adapted from John G. Wacker, "Effective Planning and Cost Control for Restaurants," *Production and Inventory Management* (1st quarter 1985): 60. Reprinted by permission of American Production and Inventory Control Society.

DRP procedures and logic are analogous to MRP. With DRP, expected demand becomes gross requirements. Net requirements are determined by allocating available inventory to gross requirements. The DRP procedure starts with the forecast at the retail level (or the most distant point of the distribution network being supplied). All other levels are computed. As is the case with MRP, inventory is then reviewed with an aim to satisfying demand. So that stock will arrive when it is needed, net requirements are offset by the necessary lead time. A planned order release quantity becomes the gross requirement at the next level down the distribution chain.

DRP *pulls* inventory through the system. Pulls are initiated when the top or retail level orders more stock. Allocations are made to the top level from available inventory and production after being adjusted to obtain shipping economies. Effective use of DRP requires an integrated information system to rapidly convey planned order releases from one level to the next. The goal of the DRP system is small and frequent replenishment within the bounds of economical ordering and shipping.

ENTERPRISE RESOURCE PLANNING (ERP)

Enterprise resource planning (ERP)

An information system for identifying and planning the enterprise-wide resources needed to take, make, ship, and account for customer orders.

Advances in MRP II systems that tie customers and suppliers to MRP II have led to the development of enterprise resource planning (ERP) systems. **Enterprise resource planning (ERP)** is software that allows companies to (1) automate and integrate many of their business processes, (2) share a common database and business practices throughout the enterprise, and (3) produce information in real time. A schematic showing some of these relationships for a manufacturing firm appears in Figure 11.

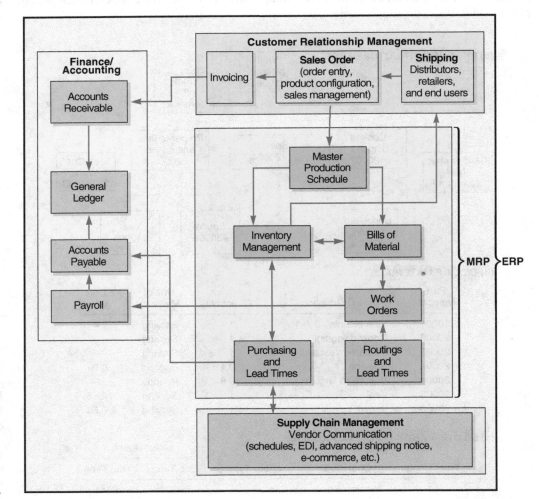

► **Figure 11**

MRP and ERP Information Flows, Showing Customer Relationship Management (CRM), Supply Chain Management (SCM), and Finance/Accounting

Other functions such as human resources are often also included in ERP systems.

The objective of an ERP system is to coordinate a firm's whole business, from supplier evaluation to customer invoicing. This objective is seldom achieved, but ERP systems are evolving as umbrella systems that tie together a variety of specialized systems. This is accomplished by using a centralized database to assist the flow of information among business functions. Exactly what is tied together, and how, varies on a case-by-case basis. In addition to the traditional components of MRP, ERP systems usually provide financial and human resource (HR) management information. ERP systems also include:

- *Supply chain management (SCM)* software to support sophisticated vendor communication, e-commerce, and those activities necessary for efficient warehousing and logistics. The idea is to tie operations (MRP) to procurement, to materials management, and to suppliers, providing the tools necessary for effective management of all four areas.
- *Customer relationship management (CRM)* software for the incoming side of the business. CRM is designed to aid analysis of sales, target the most profitable customers, and manage the sales force.

Besides these five modules (MRP, finance, HR, SCM, and CRM), many other options are usually available from vendors of ERP software. These vendors have built modules to provide a variety of "solution" packages that are mixed and matched to individual company needs. Indeed, the trick to these large database and integrated ERP systems is to develop interfaces that allow file access to the databases. SAP, a large ERP vendor, has developed about a thousand *business application-programming interfaces* (BAPIs) to access its database. Similarly, other ERP vendors have designed the systems to facilitate integration with third-party software. The demand for interfaces to ERP systems is so large that a new software industry has developed to write the interfaces. This new category of programs is sometimes called *middleware* or *enterprise application integration* (EAI) software. These interfaces allow the expansion of ERP systems so they can integrate with other systems, such as warehouse management, logistics exchanges, electronic catalogs, quality management, and product life cycle management. It is this potential for integration with other systems, including the rich supply of third-party software offerings, that makes ERP so enticing.

In addition to data integration, ERP software promises reduced transaction costs and fast, accurate information. A strategic emphasis on just-in-time systems and supply chain integration drives the desire for enterprise-wide software. The *OM in Action* box "Managing Benetton with ERP Software," provides an example of how ERP software helps integrate company operations.

OM in Action   Managing Benetton with ERP Software

Thanks to ERP, the Italian sportswear company Benetton can probably claim to have the world's fastest factory and the most efficient distribution in the garment industry. Located in Ponzano, Italy, Benetton makes and ships 50 million pieces of clothing each year. That is 30,000 boxes every day—boxes that must be filled with exactly the items ordered going to the correct store of the 5,000 Benetton outlets in 60 countries. This highly automated distribution center uses only 19 people. Without ERP, hundreds of people would be needed.

Here is how ERP software works:

1. *Ordering:* A salesperson in the south Boston store finds that she is running out of a best-selling blue sweater. Using a laptop PC, her local Benetton sales agent taps into the ERP sales module.
2. *Availability:* ERP's inventory software simultaneously forwards the order to the mainframe in Italy and finds that half the order can be filled immediately from the Italian warehouse. The rest will be manufactured and shipped in 4 weeks.

3. *Production:* Because the blue sweater was originally created by computer-aided design (CAD), ERP manufacturing software passes the specifications to a knitting machine. The knitting machine makes the sweaters.
4. *Warehousing:* The blue sweaters are boxed with a radio frequency ID (RFID) tag addressed to the Boston store and placed in one of the 300,000 slots in the Italian warehouse. A robot flies by, reading RFID tags, picks out any and all boxes ready for the Boston store, and loads them for shipment.
5. *Order tracking:* The Boston salesperson logs onto the ERP system through the Internet and sees that the sweater (and other items) are completed and being shipped.
6. *Planning:* Based on data from ERP's forecasting and financial modules, Benetton's chief buyer decides that blue sweaters are in high demand and quite profitable. She decides to add three new hues.

Sources: The Wall Street Journal (April 10, 2007): B1; *Frontline Solutions* (April 2003): 54; and *MIT Sloan Management Review* (fall 2001): 46–53.

In an ERP system, data are entered only once into a common, complete, and consistent database shared by all applications. For example, when a Nike salesperson enters an order into his ERP system for 20,000 pairs of sneakers for Foot Locker, the data are instantly available on the manufacturing floor. Production crews start filling the order if it is not in stock, accounting prints Foot Locker's invoice, and shipping notifies the Foot Locker of the future delivery date. The salesperson, or even the customer, can check the progress of the order at any point. This is all accomplished using the same data and common applications. To reach this consistency, however, the data fields must be defined identically across the entire enterprise. In Nike's case, this means integrating operations at production sites from Vietnam to China to Mexico, at business units across the globe, in many currencies, and with reports in a variety of languages.

Each ERP vendor produces unique products. The major vendors, SAP AG (a German firm), BEA (Canada), SSAGlobal, American Software, PeopleSoft/Oracle, CMS Software (all of the U.S.), sell software or modules designed for specific industries (a set of SAP's modules is shown in Figure 12). However, companies must determine if their way of doing business will fit the standard ERP module. If they determine that the product will not fit the standard ERP product, they can change the way they do business to accommodate the software. But such a change can have an adverse impact on their business process, reducing a competitive advantage. Alternatively, ERP software can be customized to meet their specific process requirements. Although the vendors build the software to keep the customization process simple, many companies spend up to five times the cost of the software to customize it. In addition to the expense, the major downside of customization is that when ERP vendors provide an upgrade or enhancement to the software, the customized part of the code must be rewritten to fit into the new version. ERP programs cost from a minimum of $300,000 for a small company to hundreds of millions of dollars for global giants like General Motors and Coca-Cola. It is easy to see, then, that ERP systems

▼ **Figure 12** SAP's Modules for ERP

Cash to Cash
Covers all financial related activity:

| Accounts receivable | General ledger | Cash management |
| Accounts payable | Treasury | Asset management |

Promote to Deliver
Covers front-end customer-oriented activities:

Marketing

Quote and order processing

Transportation

Documentation and labeling

After sales service

Warranty and guarantees

Design to Manufacture
Covers internal production activities:

Design engineering	Shop floor reporting
Production engineering	Contract/project management
Plant maintenance	
	Subcontractor management

Recruit to Retire
Covers all HR- and payroll-oriented activity:

| Time and attendance | Payroll |
| Travel and expenses | |

Procure to Pay
Covers sourcing activities:

Vendor sourcing

Purchase requisitioning

Purchase ordering

Purchase contracts

Inbound logistics

Supplier invoicing/matching

Supplier payment/settlement

Supplier performance

Dock to Dispatch
Covers internal inventory management:

| Warehousing | Forecasting | Physical inventory |
| Distribution planning | Replenishment planning | Material handling |

Source: www.sap.com.

OM in Action   There Is Nothing Easy about ERP

In 2000, the Switzerland-based consumer food giant Nestlé SA signed a $200 million contract with SAP for an ERP system. To this $200 million, Nestlé added $80 million for consulting and maintenance. And this was in addition to $500 million for hardware and software as part of a data center overhaul. Jeri Dunn, CIO of Nestlé USA, counsels that successful implementation is dependent on changing business processes and achieving universal "buy-in." Then, and only then, can an organization focus on installing the software. With many autonomous divisions and 200 operating companies and subsidiaries in 80 countries, the challenge of changing the processes and obtaining buy-in was substantial.

Standardizing processes is difficult, fraught with dead ends and costly mistakes. Nestlé had 28 points of customer order entry, multiple purchasing systems, and no idea how much volume was being done with a particular vendor; every factory did purchasing on its own with its own specifications. Nestlé USA was paying 29 different prices for vanilla—to the same vendor!

The newly established common databases and business processes led to consistent data and more trustworthy demand forecasts for the many Nestlé products. Nestlé now forecasts down to the level of the distribution center. This improved forecasting allows the company to reduce inventory and the related transportation expenses that occur when too much of a product is sent to one place while there is a shortage in another. The supply chain improvements accounted for much of Nestlé's $325 million in savings.

ERP projects are notorious for taking a long time and a lot of money, and this one was no exception, but after 3 years, the last modules of Nestlé's system were installed—and Nestlé thinks this installation is a success.

Sources: Materials Management and Distribution (March 2003): 27; *Businessline* (March 12, 2004): 1; and CIO (May 15, 2002): 62–70.

are expensive, full of hidden issues, and time consuming to install. As the *OM in Action* box "There Is Nothing Easy about ERP" notes, Nestlé, too, found nothing easy about ERP.

Advantages and Disadvantages of ERP Systems

We have alluded to some of the pluses and minuses of ERP. Here is a more complete list of both.

Advantages:
1. Provides integration of the supply chain, production, and administrative process.
2. Creates commonality of databases.
3. Can incorporate improved, reengineered, "best processes."
4. Increases communication and collaboration among business units and sites.
5. Has a software database that is off-the-shelf coding.
6. May provide a strategic advantage over competitors.

Disadvantages:
1. Is very expensive to purchase, and even more costly to customize.
2. Implementation may require major changes in the company and its processes.
3. Is so complex that many companies cannot adjust to it.
4. Involves an ongoing process for implementation, which may never be completed.
5. Expertise in ERP is limited, with staffing an ongoing problem.

ERP in the Service Sector

ERP vendors have developed a series of service modules for such markets as health care, government, retail stores, and financial services. Springer-Miller Systems, for example, has created an ERP package for the hotel market with software that handles all front- and back-office functions. This system integrates tasks such as maintaining guest histories, booking room and dinner reservations, scheduling golf tee times, and managing multiple properties in a chain. PeopleSoft/Oracle combines ERP with supply chain management to coordinate airline meal preparation. In the grocery industry, these supply chain systems are known as *efficient consumer response* (ECR) systems. As is the case in manufacturing, **efficient consumer response** systems tie sales to buying, to inventory, to logistics, and to production.

Efficient consumer response (ECR)
Supply chain management systems in the grocery industry that tie sales to buying, to inventory, to logistics, and to production.

Summary

Material requirements planning (MRP) is the preferred way to schedule production and inventory when demand is dependent. For MRP to work, management must have a master schedule, precise requirements for all components, accurate inventory and purchasing records, and accurate lead times.

Production should often be lot-for-lot in an MRP system. When properly implemented, MRP can contribute in a major way to reduction in inventory while improving customer-service levels. MRP techniques allow the operations manager to schedule and replenish stock on a "need-to-order" basis rather than simply a "time-to-order" basis.

The continuing development of MRP systems has led to the integration of production data with a variety of other activities, including the supply chain and sales. As a result, we now have integrated database-oriented enterprise resource planning (ERP) systems. These expensive and difficult-to-install ERP systems, when successful, support strategies of differentiation, response, and cost leadership.

Key Terms

Material requirements planning (MRP)
Master production schedule (MPS)
Bill of material (BOM)
Modular bills
Planning bills (or kits)
Phantom bills of material
Low-level coding
Lead time
Gross material requirements plan
Net material requirements

Planned order receipt
Planned order release
System nervousness
Time fences
Pegging
Buckets
Bucketless system
Back flush
Supermarket
Lot-sizing decision

Lot-for-lot
Part period balancing (PPB)
Economic part period (EPP)
Wagner-Whitin procedure
Material requirements planning II (MRP II)
Closed-loop MRP system
Load report
Distribution resource planning (DRP)
Enterprise resource planning (ERP)
Efficient consumer response (ECR)

Using Software to Solve MRP Problems

There are many commercial MRP software packages, for companies of all sizes. MRP software for small and medium-size companies includes User Solutions, Inc., a demo of which is available at **www.usersolutions.com**, and MAX, from Exact Software North America, Inc. Software for larger systems is available from SAP, CMS, BEA, Oracle, i2 Technologies, and many others. The Excel OM software that accompanies this text includes an MRP module, as does POM for Windows. The use of both is explained in the following sections.

✗ Using Excel OM

Using Excel OM's MRP module requires the careful entry of several pieces of data. The initial MRP screen is where we enter (1) the total number of occurrences of items in the BOM (including the top item), (2) what we want the BOM items to be called (i.e., Item no., Part), (3) total number of periods to be scheduled, and (4) what we want the periods called (i.e., days, weeks).

Excel OM's second MRP screen provides the data entry for an indented bill of material. Here we enter (1) the name of each item in the BOM, (2) the quantity of that item in the assembly, and (3) the correct indent (i.e., parent/child relationship) for each item. The indentations are critical as they provide the logic for the BOM explosion. The indentations should follow the logic of the product structure tree with indents for each assembly item in that assembly.

Excel OM's third MRP screen repeats the indented BOM and provides the standard MRP tableau for entries. This is shown in Program 1 using the data from Examples 1, 2, and 3.

P Using POM for Windows

The POM for Windows MRP module can also solve Examples 1 to 3. Up to 18 periods can be analyzed. Here are the inputs required:

1. *Item names:* The item names are entered in the left column. The same item name will appear in more than one row if the item is used by two parent items. Each item must follow its parents.
2. *Item level:* The level in the indented BOM must be given here. The item *cannot* be placed at a level more than one below the item immediately above.
3. *Lead-time:* The lead time for an item is entered here. The default is 1 week.
4. *Number per parent:* The number of units of this subassembly needed for its parent is entered here. The default is 1.
5. *On hand:* List current inventory on hand once, even if the subassembly is listed twice.

The data in columns A, B, C, D (down to row 15) are entered on the second screen and automatically transferred here.

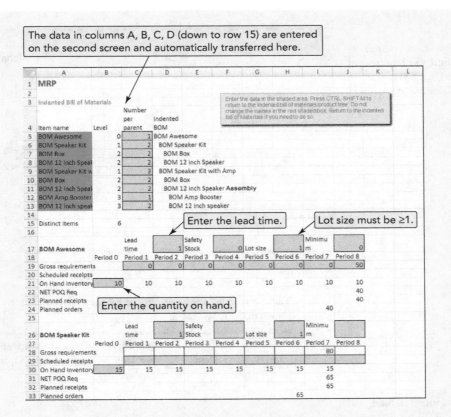

◀ **Program 1**

Using Excel OM's MRP Module to Solve Examples 1, 2, and 3

6. *Lot size:* The lot size can be specified here. A 0 or 1 will perform lot-for-lot ordering. If another number is placed here, then all orders for that item will be in integer multiples of that number.
7. *Demands:* The demands are entered in the end item row in the period in which the items are demanded.
8. *Scheduled receipts:* If units are scheduled to be received in the future, they should be listed in the appropriate time period (column) and item (row). (An entry here in level 1 is a demand; all other levels are receipts.)

Solved Problems

Virtual Office Hours help is available on Student DVD.

Solved Problem 1

Determine the low-level coding and the quantity of each component necessary to produce 10 units of an assembly we will call Alpha. The product structure and quantities of each component needed for each assembly are noted in parenthesis.

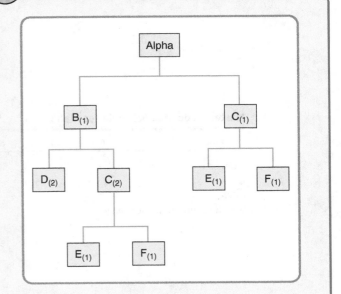

Solution

Redraw the product structure with low-level coding. Then multiply down the structure until the requirements of each branch are determined. Then add across the structure until the total for each is determined.

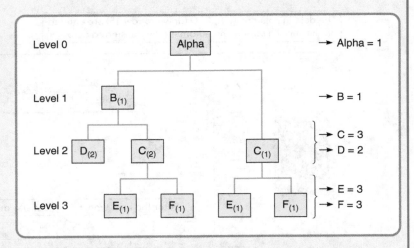

Es required for left branch:

$$(1_{alpha} \times 1_B \times 2_C \times 1_E) = 2$$

and Es required for right branch:

$$(1_{alpha} \times 1_C \times 1_E) = \frac{1}{3} \text{ Es required in total}$$

Then "explode" the requirement by multiplying each by 10, as shown in the following table:

Level	Item	Quantity per Unit	Total Requirements for 10 Alpha
0	Alpha	1	10
1	B	1	10
2	C	3	30
2	D	2	20
3	E	3	30
3	F	3	30

Solved Problem 2

Using the product structure for Alpha in Solved Problem 1, and the following lead times, quantity on hand, and master production schedule, prepare a net MRP table for Alphas.

Item	Lead Time	Qty On Hand
Alpha	1	10
B	2	20
C	3	0
D	1	100
E	1	10
F	1	50

Master Production Schedule for Alpha

Period	6	7	8	9	10	11	12	13
Gross requirements			50			50		100

Solution

See the chart on the next page.

Lot Size	Lead Time (# of Periods)	On Hand	Safety Stock	Allo-cated	Low-Level Code	Item ID		Period (week, day)												
								1	2	3	4	5	6	7	8	9	10	11	12	13
Lot-for-Lot	1	10	—	—	0	Alpha (A)	Gross Requirements								50			50		100
							Scheduled Receipts													
							Projected On Hand 10								10					
							Net Requirements								40			50		100
							Planned Order Receipts								40			50		100
							Planned Order Releases							40			50		100	
Lot-for-Lot	2	20	—	—	1	B	Gross Requirements							40(A)			50(A)		100(A)	
							Scheduled Receipts													
							Projected On Hand 20							20						
							Net Requirements							20			50		100	
							Planned Order Receipts							20			50		100	
							Planned Order Releases					20			50		100			
Lot-for-Lot	3	0	—	—	2	C	Gross Requirements					40(B)		40(A)	100(B)		200(B) + 50(A)		100(A)	
							Scheduled Receipts													
							Projected On Hand 0													
							Net Requirements					40		40	100		250		100	
							Planned Order Receipts					40		40	100		250		100	
							Planned Order Releases		40		40	100		250		100				
Lot-for-Lot	1	100	—	—	2	D	Gross Requirements					40(B)			100(B)		200(B)			
							Scheduled Receipts													
							Projected On Hand 100					100			60					
							Net Requirements								40		200			
							Planned Order Receipts								40		200			
							Planned Order Releases							40		200				
Lot-for-Lot	1	10	—	—	3	E	Gross Requirements		40(C)		40(C)	100(C)		250(C)		100(C)				
							Scheduled Receipts													
							Projected On Hand 10		10											
							Net Requirements		30		40	100		250		100				
							Planned Order Receipts		30		40	100		250		100				
							Planned Order Releases	30		40	100		250		100					
Lot-for-Lot	1	50	—	—	3	F	Gross Requirements		40(C)		40(C)	100(C)		250(C)		100(C)				
							Scheduled Receipts													
							Projected On Hand 50		50		10					—				
							Net Requirements				30	100		250		100				
							Planned Order Receipts				30	100		250		100				
							Planned Order Releases			30	100		250		100					

Net Material Requirements Planning Sheet for Alpha

The letter in parentheses (A) is the source of the demand.

Self-Test

- **Before taking the self-test,** refer to the learning objectives listed at the beginning of the selection and the key terms listed at the end of the selection.
- Use the key at the back of the text to **correct** your answers.
- **Restudy** pages that correspond to any questions you answered incorrectly or material you feel uncertain about.

1. The list of quantities of components, ingredients, and materials required to produce a product is the:
   a) bill-of-material
   b) engineering change notice
   c) purchase order
   d) all of the above

2. _____ allows a segment of the master schedule to be designated as "not to be rescheduled."
   a) Regenerative MRP
   b) System nervousness
   c) Pegging
   d) DRP
   e) None of the above

3. A lot-sizing procedure that assumes a finite time horizon beyond which there are no additional net requirements is:
   a) Wagner-Whitin algorithm
   b) part period balancing
   c) economic order quantity
   d) all of the above

4. Breaking up the order and running part of it ahead of schedule is known as:
   a) overlapping
   b) operations splitting
   c) order, or lot, splitting
   d) pegging

5. In a product structure diagram:
   a) parents are found only at the top level of the diagram
   b) parents are found at every level in the diagram
   c) children are found at every level of the diagram except the top level
   d) all items in the diagrams are both parents and children
   e) all of the above are true

6. The difference between a gross material requirements plan (gross MRP) and a net materials requirements plan (net MRP) is:
   a) the gross MRP may not be computerized, but the net MRP must be computerized
   b) the gross MRP includes consideration of the inventory on hand, whereas the net MRP doesn't include the inventory consideration
   c) the net MRP includes consideration of the inventory on hand, whereas the gross MRP doesn't include the inventory consideration
   d) the gross MRP doesn't take taxes into account, whereas the net MRP includes the tax considerations
   e) the net MRP is only an estimate, whereas the gross MRP is used for actual production scheduling

7. To effectively use dependent inventory models, the operations manager needs to know:
   a) the master production schedule (which tells what is to be made and when)
   b) the specifications or bill-of-material (which tells how to make the product)
   c) the purchase orders outstanding (which tell what is on order)
   d) the lead times (or how long it takes to get various components)
   e) all of the above

8. A phantom bill-of-material is a bill-of-material developed for:
   a) a final product for which production is to be discontinued
   b) a subassembly that exists only temporarily
   c) a module that is a major component of a final product
   d) the purpose of grouping subassemblies when we wish to issue "kits" for later use

9. When a bill-of-material is used in order to assign an artificial parent to a bill-of-material, it is usually called a:
   a) modular bill-of-material
   b) pick list
   c) phantom bill-of-material
   d) planning bill-of-material

Active Model Exercise

We use Active Model 14.1 to demonstrate the effects of lot sizes (multiples) and minimum lot sizes.

Questions

1. Suppose that item B must be ordered in multiples of dozens. Which items are affected by this change?

2. Suppose that the minimum order quantity for item C is 200 units. Which items are affected by this change?

Order Releases

[Reset Data] [Questions]

Master Production Schedule

	Week							
	1	2	3	4	5	6	7	8
Item A	0	0	0	0	0	0	0	50

Item Master File

	Lead time	On hand	Lot size multiple	Minimum lot size
A	1	10	1	0
B	2	15	1	0
C	1	20	1	0
D	1	10	1	0
E	2	10	1	0
F	3	5	1	0
G	2	0	1	0

Planned Order Releases

	Week							
	1	2	3	4	5	6	7	8
A							40	
B					65			
C						100		
D		380		130				
E			120	200				
F			195					
G	195							

◄ **Active Model 14.1**

An Analysis of the MRP Model Used by Speaker Kits, Inc., in Examples 1–3

Internet and Student CD-ROM/DVD Exercises

Visit our Companion Web site or use your student CD-ROM/DVD to help with material in this chapter.

On Our Companion Web Site, www.prenhall.com/heizer
- Self-Study Quizzes
- Practice Problems
- Virtual Company Tour
- Internet Cases
- PowerPoint Lecture

On Your Student CD-ROM
- Practice Problems
- Active Model Exercise
- Excel OM
- Excel OM Example Data File
- POM for Windows

On Your Student DVD
- Video Clip and Video Case
- Virtual Office Hours for Solved Problems

Discussion Questions

1. What is the difference between a *gross* requirements plan and a *net* requirements plan?
2. Once a material requirements plan (MRP) has been established, what other managerial applications might be found for the technique?
3. What are the similarities between MRP and DRP?
4. How does MRP II differ from MRP?
5. Which is the best lot-sizing policy for manufacturing organizations?
6. What impact does ignoring carrying cost in the allocation of stock in a DRP system have on lot sizes?
7. MRP is more than an inventory system; what additional capabilities does MRP possess?
8. What are the options for the production planner who has:
   (a) scheduled more than capacity in a work center next week?
   (b) a consistent lack of capacity in that work center?
9. Master schedules are expressed in three different ways depending on whether the process is continuous, a job shop, or repetitive. What are these three ways?
10. What functions of the firm affect an MRP system? How?
11. What is the rationale for (a) a phantom bill of material, (b) a planning bill of material, and (c) a pseudo bill of material?
12. Identify five specific requirements of an effective MRP system.
13. What are the typical benefits of ERP?
14. What are the distinctions between MRP, DRP, and ERP?
15. What are the disadvantages of ERP?
16. Use the Web or other sources to:
    (a) Find stories that highlight the advantages of an ERP system.
    (b) Find stories that highlight the difficulties of purchasing, installing, or failure of an ERP system.
17. Use the Web or other sources to identify what an ERP vendor (SAP, PeopleSoft/Oracle, American Software, etc.) includes in these software modules:
    (a) Customer relationship management.
    (b) Supply chain management.
    (c) Product life cycle management.
18. The very structure of MRP systems suggests fixed lead times. However, many firms have moved toward JIT and kanban techniques. What are the techniques, issues, and impact of adding JIT inventory and purchasing techniques to an organization that has MRP?

Ethical Dilemma

For many months your prospective ERP customer has been analyzing the hundreds of assumptions built into the $800,000 ERP software you are selling. So far, you have knocked yourself out to try to make this sale. If the sale goes through, you will reach your yearly quota and get a nice bonus. On the other hand, loss of this sale may mean you start looking for other employment.

The accounting, human resource, supply chain, and marketing teams put together by the client have reviewed the specifications and finally recommended purchase of the software. However, as you looked over their shoulders and helped them through the evaluation process, you began to realize that their purchasing procedures—with much of the purchasing being done at hundreds of regional stores—were not a good fit for the software. At the very least, the customizing will add $250,000 to the implementation and training cost. The team is not aware of the issue, and you know that the necessary $250,000 is not in the budget.

What do you do?

Problems*

•   **1**   You have developed the following simple product structure of items needed for your gift bag for a rush party for prospective pledges in your organization. You forecast 200 attendees. Assume that there is no inventory on hand of any of the items. Explode the bill of material. (Subscripts indicate the number of units required.)

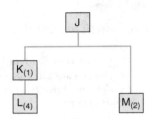

••   **2**   You are expected to have the gift bags in Problem 1 ready at 5 P.M.. However, you need to personalize the items (monogrammed pens, note pads, literature from the printer, etc.). The lead time is 1 hour to assemble 200 Js once the other items are prepared. The other items will take a while as well. Given the volunteers you have, the other time estimates are item K (2 hours), item L (1 hour), and item M (4 hours). Develop a time-phased assembly plan to prepare the gift bags.

••   **3**   The demand for subassembly S is 100 units in week 7. Each unit of S requires 1 unit of T and 2 units of U. Each unit of T requires 1 unit of V, 2 units of W, and 1 unit of X. Finally, each unit of U requires 2 units of Y and 3 units of Z. One firm manufactures all items. It takes 2 weeks to make S, 1 week to make T, 2 weeks to make U, 2 weeks to make V, 3 weeks to make W, 1 week to make X, 2 weeks to make Y, and 1 week to make Z.
a) Construct a product structure. Identify all levels, parents, and components.
b) Prepare a time-phased product structure.

••   **4**   Using the information in Problem 3, construct a gross material requirements plan. Px

••   **5**   Using the information in Problem 3, construct a net material requirements plan using the following on-hand inventory.

Item	On-Hand Inventory	Item	On-Hand Inventory
S	20	W	30
T	20	X	25
U	40	Y	240
V	30	Z	40 Px

••   **6**   Refer again to Problems 3 and 4. In addition to 100 units of S, there is also a demand for 20 units of U, which is a component of S. The 20 units of U are needed for maintenance purposes. These units are needed in week 6. Modify the *gross material requirements plan* to reflect this change. Px

••   **7**   Refer again to Problems 3 and 5. In addition to 100 units of S, there is also a demand for 20 units of U, which is a component of S. The 20 units of U are needed for maintenance purposes. These units are needed in week 6. Modify the *net material requirements plan* to reflect this change. Px

••   **8**   As the production planner for Adams-Ebert Products, Inc., you have been given a bill of material for a bracket that is made up of a base, two springs, and four clamps. The base is assembled from one clamp and two housings. Each clamp has one handle and one casting. Each housing has two bearings and one shaft. There is no inventory on hand.
a) Design a product structure noting the quantities for each item and show the low-level coding.
b) Determine the gross quantities needed of each item if you are to assemble 50 brackets.
c) Compute the net quantities needed if there are 25 of the base and 100 of the clamp in stock. Px

••   **9**   Your boss at Adams-Ebert Products, Inc., has just provided you with the schedule and lead times for the bracket in Problem 8. The unit is to be prepared in week 10. The lead times for the components are bracket (1 week), base (1 week), spring (1 week), clamp (1 week), housing (2 weeks), handle (1 week), casting (3 weeks), bearing (1 week), and shaft (1 week).
a) Prepare the time-phased product structure for the bracket.
b) In what week do you need to start the castings? Px

••• **10**   a) Given the product structure and master production schedule (Figure 14 on the next page), develop a gross requirements plan for all items.
b) Given the preceding product structure, master production schedule, and inventory status (Figure 14), develop a net materials requirements (planned order release) for all items. Px

Note: Px means the problem may be solved with POM for Windows and/or Excel OM. Many of the exercises in this selection (1 through 16 and 23 through 27) can be done on *Resource Manager for Excel*, a commercial system made available by User Solutions, Inc. Access to a trial version of the software and a set of notes for the user is available at **www.usersolutions.com**.

Lot Size	Lead Time (# of periods)	On Hand	Safety Stock	Allo-cated	Low-Level Code	Item ID		Period (week, day)							
								1	2	3	4	5	6	7	8
							Gross Requirements								
							Scheduled Receipts								
							Projected On Hand								
							Net Requirements								
							Planned Order Receipts								
							Planned Order Releases								
							Gross Requirements								
							Scheduled Receipts								
							Projected On Hand								
							Net Requirements								
							Planned Order Receipts								
							Planned Order Releases								
							Gross Requirements								
							Scheduled Receipts								
							Projected On Hand								
							Net Requirements								
							Planned Order Receipts								
							Planned Order Releases								
							Gross Requirements								
							Scheduled Receipts								
							Projected On Hand								
							Net Requirements								
							Planned Order Receipts								
							Planned Order Releases								
							Gross Requirements								
							Scheduled Receipts								
							Projected On Hand								
							Net Requirements								
							Planned Order Receipts								
							Planned Order Releases								

▲ **Figure 13** MRP Form for Homework Problems in this chapter

For several problems in this chapter, a copy of this form may be helpful.

••• **11** Given the following product structure, master production schedule, and inventory status (Figure 15) and assuming the requirements for each BOM item is 1: (a) develop a gross requirements plan for Item C; (b) develop a net requirements plan for Item C. **Px**

•••• **12** Based on the following data (see Figure 15), complete a net material requirements schedule for:
a) All items (10 schedules in all), assuming the requirement for each BOM item is 1.

b) All 10 items, assuming the requirement for all items is 1, except B, C, and F, which require *2 each*. **Px**

••• **13** Electro Fans has just received an order for one thousand 20-inch fans due week 7. Each fan consists of a housing assembly, two grills, a fan assembly, and an electrical unit. The housing assembly consists of a frame, two supports, and a handle. The fan assembly consists of a hub and five blades. The electrical unit consists of a motor, a switch, and a knob. The

▼ **Figure 14** Information for Problem 10

Master Production Schedule for X1

PERIOD	7	8	9	10	11	12
Gross requirements		50		20		100

ITEM	LEAD TIME	ON HAND		ITEM	LEAD TIME	ON HAND
X1	1	50		C	1	0
B1	2	20		D	1	0
B2	2	20		E	3	10
A1	1	5				

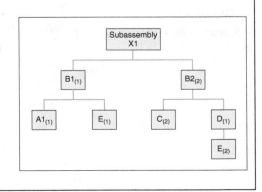

► Figure 15

Information for Problems 11 and 12

PERIOD		8	9	10	11	12
Gross requirements: A		100		50		150
Gross requirements: H			100		50	

ITEM	ON HAND	LEAD TIME	ITEM	ON HAND	LEAD TIME
A	0	1	F	75	2
B	100	2	G	75	1
C	50	2	H	0	1
D	50	1	J	100	2
E	75	2	K	100	2

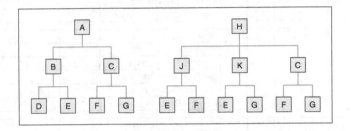

following table gives lead times, on-hand inventory, and scheduled receipts.
a) Construct a product structure.
b) Construct a time-phased product structure.
c) Prepare a net material requirements plan. **Px**

Data Table for Problem 13

Component	Lead Time	On Hand Inventory	Lot Size	Scheduled Receipt
20″ Fan	1	100	—	
Housing	1	100	—	
Frame	2	—	—	
Supports (2)	1	50	100	
Handle	1	400	500	
Grills (2)	2	200	500	
Fan Assembly	3	150	—	
Hub	1	—	—	
Blades (5)	2	—	100	
Electrical Unit	1	—	—	
Motor	1	—	—	
Switch	1	20	12	
Knob	1	—	25	200 knobs in week 2

••• 14 A part structure, lead time (weeks), and on-hand quantities for product A are shown in Figure 16. From the information shown, generate
a) An indented bill of material for product A.
b) Net requirements for each part to produce 10 As in week 8 using lot-for-lot. **Px**

••• 15 You are product planner for product A (in Problem 14 and Figure 16). The field service manager, Al Trostel, has just called and told you that the requirements for B and F should each be increased by 10 units for his repair requirements in the field.
a) Prepare a list showing the quantity of each part required to produce the requirements for the service manager *and* the production request of 10.
b) Prepare a net requirement plan by date for the new requirements (for both production and field service), assuming that the field service manager wants his 10 units of B and F in week 6 and the 10 production units in week 8. **Px**

••• 16 You have just been notified via fax that the lead time for component G of product A (Problem 15 and Figure 16) has been increased to 4 weeks.
a) Which items have changed and why?

► Figure 16

Information for Problems 14, 15 and 16

PART	INVENTORY ON HAND
A	0
B	2
C	10
D	5
E	4
F	5
G	1
H	10

PART STRUCTURE TREE

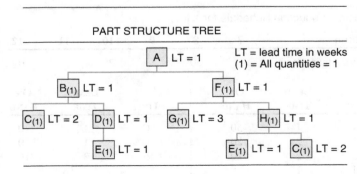

b) What are the implications for the production plan?

c) As production planner, what can you do? **Px**

Data Table for Problems 17 through 19*

Period	1	2	3	4	5	6	7	8	9	10	11	12
Gross requirements	30		40		30	70	20		10	80		50

*Holding cost = $2.50/unit/week; setup cost = $150; lead time = 1 week; beginning inventory = 40.

••• **17** Develop a lot-for-lot solution and calculate total relevant costs for the data in the preceding table. **Px**

••• **18** Develop an EOQ solution and calculate total relevant costs for the data in the preceding table. Stockout costs equal $10 per unit. **Px**

••• **19** Develop a PPB solution and calculate total relevant costs for the data in the preceding table. **Px**

••• **20** Using the gross requirements schedule in Examples 4, 5, and 6 in the text, prepare an alternative ordering system that always orders 100 units the week prior to a shortage (a fixed order quantity of 100) with the same costs as in the example (setup at $100 each, holding at $1 per unit per period). What is the cost of this ordering system? **Px**

••• **21** Using the gross requirements schedule in Examples 4, 5, and 6 in the text, prepare an alternative ordering system that orders every 3 weeks for 3 weeks ahead (a periodic order quantity). Use the same costs as in the example (setup at $100 each, holding at $1 per unit per period). What is the cost of this ordering system? **Px**

••• **22** Using the gross requirements schedule in Examples 4, 5, and 6 in the text, prepare an alternative ordering system of your own design that uses the same cost as in the example (setup at $100 each, holding at $1 per unit per period). Can you do better than the costs shown in the text? What is the cost of your ordering system? **Px**

••• **23** Katherine Hepburn, Inc., has received the following orders:

Period	1	2	3	4	5	6	7	8	9	10
Order size	0	40	30	40	10	70	40	10	30	60

The entire fabrication for these units is scheduled on one machine. There are 2,250 usable minutes in a week, and each unit will take 65 minutes to complete. Develop a capacity plan, using lot splitting, for the 10-week time period.

••• **24** David Jurman, Ltd., has received the following orders:

Period	1	2	3	4	5	6	7	8	9	10
Order size	60	30	10	40	70	10	40	30	40	0

The entire fabrication for these units is scheduled on one machine. There are 2,250 usable minutes in a week, and each unit will take 65 minutes to complete. Develop a capacity plan, using lot splitting, for the 10-week time period.

•• **25** Heather Adams, production manager for a Colorado exercise equipment manufacturer, needs to schedule an order for 50 UltimaSteppers, which are to be shipped in week 8. Subscripts indicate quantity required for each parent. Assume lot-for-lot ordering. Below is information about the steppers:

Item	Lead Time	On-Hand Inventory	Components
Stepper	2	20	$A_{(1)}, B_{(3)}, C_{(2)}$
A	1	10	$D_{(1)}, F_{(2)}$
B	2	30	$E_{(1)}, F_{(3)}$
C	3	10	$D_{(2)}, E_{(3)}$
D	1	15	
E	2	5	
F	2	20	

a) Develop a product structure for Heather.

b) Develop a time-phased structure.

c) Develop a net material requirements plan for F. **Px**

•••• **26** You are scheduling production of your popular Rustic Coffee Table. The table requires a top, four legs, $\frac{1}{8}$ gallon of stain, $\frac{1}{16}$ gallon of glue, 2 short braces between the legs and 2 long braces between the legs, and a brass cap that goes on the bottom of each leg. You have 100 gallons of glue in inventory, but none of the other components. All items except the brass caps, stain, and glue are ordered on a lot-for-lot basis. The caps are purchased in quantities of 1,000, stain and glue by the gallon. Lead time is 1 day for each item. Schedule the order releases necessary to produce 640 coffee tables on days 5 and 6, and 128 on days 7 and 8. **Px**

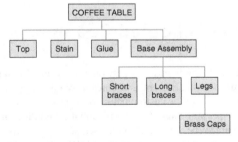

•••• **27** Using the data for the coffee table in Problem 26, build a labor schedule when the labor standard for each top is 2 labor hours; each leg including brass cap installation requires $\frac{1}{4}$ hour, as does each cross brace. Base assembly requires 1 labor-hour, and final assembly requires 2 labor-hours. What is the total number of labor-hours required each day, and how many employees are needed each day at 8 hours per day?

Case Studies

Ikon's Attempt at ERP

Ikon Office Solutions is the world's largest independent office technology company, with revenues approaching $5 billion and operations in the U.S., Canada, Mexico, the United Kingdom, France, Germany, and Denmark. Ikon is pursing a growth strategy to move from what was more than 80 individually operating copier dealers to an integrated solutions company. Its goal is to provide total office technology solutions, ranging from copiers, digital printers, and document management services to systems integration, training, and other network technology services. The company has rapidly expanded its service capability with an aggressive acquisition effort that has included technology services and document management companies.

Given these objectives, the company seemed to need ERP software. A few years ago, it began a pilot project in the Northern California district to assess the possibility of using SAP's enterprise software applications companywide. Chief Information Officer David Gadra, who joined Ikon about a month after the pilot system was turned on, however, decided not to roll it out. Ikon will take a $25 million write-off on the cost of the pilot.

"There were a number of factors that made us decide this project was more challenging than beneficial for us," says Gadra. "When we added everything up—human factors, functionality gaps, and costs incurred—we decided our environment is ill defined for SAP." Instead, Ikon is bringing all 13 of its regional operations onto a home-grown application system.

"I don't blame the consultants or SAP," he says. "We made errors on our side in estimating the amount of business change we'd have to make as part of this implementation."

The vast majority of the $25 million loss represents consultant fees; less than 10% went to pay for the software itself. At any given point in the project, Ikon was paying 40 to 50 outside consultants $300 an hour.

Ikon budgeted $12 million to get the system running. That cost came in at over $14 million, including $8 million paid to IBM for consulting.

A major reason the company decided to drop SAP was its conclusion that the software didn't sufficiently address the needs of a service company like Ikon, as opposed to those of manufacturers. For example, SAP didn't have an adequate feature for tracking service calls. Ikon also had great difficulty assembling an internal team of SAP experts. Ikon's costs were high because the firm relied heavily on consultants.

"I am extremely disappointed by Ikon's announcement," says SAP America president Jeremy Coote, describing Ikon's earlier pilot as on time and "extremely successful." Coote calls Ikon's decision to scrap the project "an example of what happens when you don't sell at the corporate level" as well as the divisional level. A newer version of SAP is to include a service management module.

Discussion Questions

1. What are the information needs at Ikon and what alternatives does Ikon have to meet these needs?
2. What are the advantages and disadvantages of ERP software in meeting these needs?
3. What risks did the company take in selecting SAP software for evaluation?
4. Why did Ikon cancel the SAP project?

Sources: Ikon Annual Reports; *Information Week* (April 1997): 25; and J. R. Gordon and S. R. Gordon, *Information Systems: A Management Approach*, 3rd ed. (New York: Wiley, 2003).

MRP at Wheeled Coach

Video Case

Wheeled Coach, the world's largest manufacturer of ambulances, builds thousands of different and constantly changing configurations of its products. The custom nature of its business means lots of options and special designs—and a potential scheduling and inventory nightmare. Wheeled Coach addressed such problems, and succeeded in solving a lot of them, with an MRP system (described in the *Global Company Profile* that opens this chapter). As with most MRP installations, however, solving one set of problems uncovers a new set.

One of the new issues that had to be addressed by plant manager Lynn Whalen was newly discovered excess inventory. Managers discovered a substantial amount of inventory that was not called for in any finished products. Excess inventory was evident because of the new level of inventory accuracy required by the MRP system. The other reason was a new series of inventory reports generated by the IBM MAPICS MRP system purchased by Wheeled Coach. One of those reports indicates where items are used and is known as the "Where Used" report. Interestingly, many inventory items were not called out on bills-of-material (BOMs) for any current products. In some cases, the reason some parts were in the stockroom remained a mystery.

The discovery of this excess inventory led to renewed efforts to ensure that the BOMs were accurate. With substantial work, BOM accuracy increased and the number of engineering change notices

(ECNs) decreased. Similarly, purchase-order accuracy, with regard to both part numbers and quantities ordered, was improved. Additionally, receiving department and stockroom accuracy went up, all helping to maintain schedule, costs, and ultimately, shipping dates and quality.

Eventually, Lynn Whalen concluded that the residual amounts of excess inventory were the result, at least in part, of rapid changes in ambulance design and technology. Another source was customer changes made after specifications had been determined and materials ordered. This latter excess occurs because, even though Wheeled Coach's own throughput time is only 17 days, many of the items that it purchases require much longer lead times.

Discussion Questions*

1. Why is accurate inventory such an important issue at Wheeled Coach?
2. Why does Wheeled Coach have excess inventory, and what kind of a plan would you suggest for dealing with it?
3. Be specific in your suggestions for reducing inventory and how to implement them.

*You may wish to view this case on your DVD before answering the questions.

Additional Case Studies

Internet Case Study: Visit our Companion Web site at www.prenhall.com/heizer for this free case study:

- **Auto Parts, Inc.:** Distributor of automobile replacement parts has major MRP problems.

Harvard has selected these Harvard Business School cases to accompany this chapter:

harvardbusinessonline.hbsp.harvard.edu

- **Digital Equipment Corp.: The Endpoint Model** (#688-059): Describes implementation of an MRP II system to reduce cycle time of orders.
- **Tektronix, Inc.: Global ERP Implementation** (#699-043): Examines Tektronix's implementation of an ERP system in its three global business divisions.
- **Vardelay Industries, Inc.** (#697-037): Discusses ERP and related issues of process reengineering, standardization, and change management.
- **Moore Medical Corp.** (#601-142): Examines Moore's ERP investment and further investment in additional modules.

Bibliography

Anussornnitisarn, P., and S. F. Nof. "e-Work: The Challenge of the Next Generation ERP Systems." *Production Planning & Control* 14, no. 8 (December 2003): 753–765.

Bell, Steve. "Time Fence Secrets." *APICS* 16, no. 4 (April 2006): 44–48.

Bolander, Steven F., and Sam G. Taylor. "Scheduling Techniques: A Comparison of Logic." *Production and Inventory Management Journal* 41, no. 1 (1st quarter 2000): 1–5.

Crandall, Richard E. "The Epic Life of ERP." *APICS* 16, no. 2 (February 2006): 17–19.

Gattiker, Thomas F. "Anatomy of an ERP Implementation Gone Awry." *Production and Inventory Management* 43, nos. 3–4 (3rd/4th quarter 2002): 96–105.

Kanet, J., and V. Sridharan. "The Value of Using Scheduling Information in Planning Material Requirements." *Decision Sciences* 29, no. 2 (spring 1998): 479–498.

Koh, S. C. L., and S. M. Saad. "Managing Uncertainty in ERP-controlled Manufacturing Environments." *International Journal of Production Economics* 101, no. 1 (May 2006): 109.

Krupp, James A. G. "Integrating Kanban and MRP to Reduce Lead Time." *Production and Inventory Management Journal* 43, nos. 3–4 (3rd/4th quarter 2002): 78–82.

Lawrence, Barry F., Daniel F. Jennings, and Brian E. Reynolds. *ERP in Distribution*. Florence, KY: Thomson South-Western, (2005).

Moncrief, Stephen. "Push and Pull." *APICS—The Performance Advantage* (June 2003): 46–51.

Norris, G. *E-Business & ERP*. New York: Wiley (2005).

Olson, D. L. *Managerial Issues of Enterprise Resource Planning*. New York: McGraw-Hill (2004).

Segerstedt, A. "Master Production Scheduling and a Comparison of MRP and Cover-Time Planning." *International Journal of Production Research* 44, no. 18–19 (September 2006): 3585.

Summer, M. *Enterprise Resource Planning*. Upper Saddle River, NJ: Prentice Hall (2005).

Wacker, John G., and Malcolm Miller. "Configure-to-Order Planning Bills of Material: Simplifying a Complex Product Structure for Manufacturing Planning and Control." *Production and Inventory Management Journal* 41, no. 2 (2nd quarter 2000): 21–26.

Wagner, H. M., and T. M. Whitin. "Dynamic Version of the Economic Lot Size Model." *Management Science* 5, no. 1 (1958): 89–96.

Internet Resources

American Software: **www.amsoftware.com**
APICS magazine online edition:
   www.apics.org/resources/magazine
Armstrong Management Group: **www.armstrongmg.com**
Business Research in Information and Technology: **www.brint.com**
CMS Software, Inc.: **www.cmssoftware.com**

i2 Technologies: **www.i2.com**
Intelligent Enterprise Software: **www.iqms.com**
Oracle/Peoplesoft: **www.oracle.com**
SAP America: **www.sap.com**
Software evaluation: **www.technologyevaluation.com**
SSA Global: **www.ssaglobal.com**

Solutions to Even Numbered Problems

2 The time-phased plan for the gift bags is:

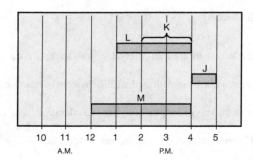

Someone should start on item M by noon.

4 Gross material requirements plan:

Item		Week								Lead Time (wk.)
		1	2	3	4	5	6	7	8	
S	Gross req.							100		
	Order release					100				2
T	Gross req.						100			
	Order release				100					1
U	Gross req.						200			
	Order release			200						2
V	Gross req.					100				
	Order release		100							2
W	Gross req.					200				
	Order release	200								3
X	Gross req.					100				
	Order release			100						1
Y	Gross req.				400					
	Order release		400							2
Z	Gross req.				600					
	Order release		600							1

6 Gross material requirements plan, modified to include the 20 units of U required for maintenance purposes:

Item		Week								Lead Time (wk.)
		1	2	3	4	5	6	7	8	
S	Gross req.							100		
	Order release					100				2
T	Gross req.						100			
	Order release				100					1
U	Gross req.						200	20		
	Order release			200	20					2
V	Gross req.					100				
	Order release		100							2
W	Gross req.					200				
	Order release	200								3
X	Gross req.					100				
	Order release		100							1
Y	Gross req.				400	40				
	Order release	400	40							2
Z	Gross req.			600	60					
	Order release	600	60							1

8 (a)

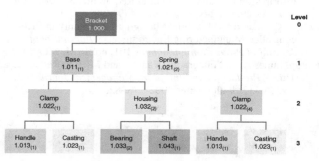

(b) For 50 brackets, the gross requirements are for 50 bases, 100 springs, 250 clamps, 250 handles, 250 castings, 100 housings, 200 bearings, and 100 shafts.

(c) For 50 brackets, net requirements are 25 bases, 100 springs, 125 clamps, 125 handles, 125 castings, 50 housings, 100 bearings, and 50 shafts.

10 (a) Gross material requirements plan for the first three items:

Item		Week											
		1	2	3	4	5	6	7	8	9	10	11	12
X1	Gross req.								50		20		100
	Order release							50		20		100	
B1	Gross req.								50		20		100
	Order release						50		20		100		
B2	Gross req.								100		40		200
	Order release						100		40		200		

(b) The net materials requirement plan for the first two items:

Level: 0 Item: X1	Parent: Lead Time:								Quantity: Lot Size: L4L			
Week No.	1	2	3	4	5	6	7	8	9	10	11	12
Gross Requirement								50		20		100
Scheduled Receipt												
On-Hand Inventory								50		0		0
Net Requirement								0		20		100
Planned Order Receipt										20		100
Planned Order Release									20		100	

Level: 1 Item: B1	Parent: X1 Lead Time: 2								Quantity: 1X Lot Size: L4L			
Week No.	1	2	3	4	5	6	7	8	9	10	11	12
Gross Requirement									20		100	
Scheduled Receipt												
On-Hand Inventory									20		0	
Net Requirement									0		100	
Planned Order Receipt											100	
Planned Order Release									100			

12 (a) Net material requirements schedule (only items A and H are shown):

	Week											
	1	2	3	4	5	6	7	8	9	10	11	12
A Gross required								100		50		150
On hand								0		0		0
Net required								100		50		150
Order receipt								100		50		150
Order release							100		50		150	
H Gross required									100		50	
On hand									0		0	
Net required									100		50	
Order receipt									100		50	
Order release								100		50			

(b) Net material requirements schedule (only items B and C are shown; schedule for items A and H remains the same as in part a.)

	Week												
	1	2	3	4	5	6	7	8	9	10	11	12	13
B Gross Requirements							200		100		300		
Scheduled Receipts													
Projected On Hand	100						100		0		0		
Net Requirements							100		100		300		
Planned Order Receipts							100		100		300		
Planned Order Releases						100		100		300			
C Gross Requirements							200	200	100	100	300		
Scheduled Receipts													
Projected On Hand	50						50						
Net Requirements							150	200	100	100	300		
Planned Order Receipts							150	200	100	100	300		
Planned Order Releases						150	200	100	100	300			

14 (a)

Level	Description	Qty
0	A	1
1	B	1
2	C	1
2	D	1
3	E	1
1	F	1
2	G	1
2	H	1
3	E	1
3	C	1

Note: with low-level coding, "C" would be a level-3 code.

(b) Solution for Items A, B, F (on next page):

14 (b)

Lot Size	Lead Time	On Hand	Safety Stock	Allo-cated	Low-Level Code	Item ID		Period (week) 1	2	3	4	5	6	7	8
Lot for Lot	1	0	—	—	1	A	Gross Requirement								10
							Scheduled Receipt								
							Projected On Hand								0
							Net Requirement								10
							Planned Receipt								10
							Planned Release							10	
Lot for Lot	1	2	—	—	1	B	Gross Requirement								10
							Scheduled Receipt								
							Projected On Hand	2	2	2	2	2	2	2	0
							Net Requirement							8	
							Planned Receipt							8	
							Planned Release						8		
Lot for Lot	1	5	—	—	1	F	Gross Requirement								10
							Scheduled Receipt								
							Projected On Hand	5	5	5	5	5	5	5	0
							Net Requirement							5	
							Planned Receipt							5	
							Planned Release						5		

16 (a) Only item G changes.

    (b) Component F and 4 units of A will be delayed one week.

    (c) Options include: delaying 4 units of A for 1 week; asking supplier of G to expedite production.

18 EOQ = 57; Total cost = $1,630

20 $650

22 $455

24 Selection for first 5 weeks:

Week	Units	Capacity Required (time)	Capacity Available (time)	Over/ (Under)	Production Scheduler's Action
1	60	3,900	2,250	1650	Lot split. Move 300 minutes (4.3 units) to week 2 and 1,350 minutes to week 3.
2	30	1,950	2,250	(300)	
3	10	650	2,250	(1,600)	
4	40	2,600	2,250	350	Lot split. Move 250 minutes to week 3. Operations split. Move 100 minutes to another machine, overtime, or subcontract.
5	70	4,550	2,250	2,300	Lot split. Move 1,600 minutes to week 6. Overlap operations to get product out door. Operations split. Move 700 minutes to another machine, overtime, or subcontract.

26 Here are the order releases for the table and the top:

Lot Size	Lead Time (# of periods)	On Hand	Safety Stock	Allo-cated	Low-Level Code	Item ID		Period (day) 1	2	3	4	5	6	7	8
Lot for Lot	1	—	—	—	0	Table	Gross Requirements					640	640	128	128
							Scheduled Receipts								
							Projected on Hand								
							Net Requirements					640	640	128	128
							Planned Order Receipts					640	640	128	128
							Planned Order Releases				640	640	128	128	
Lot for Lot	1	—	—	—	1	Top	Gross Requirements					640	640	128	128
							Scheduled Receipts								
							Projected on Hand								
							Net Requirements					640	640	128	128
							Planned Order Receipts					640	640	128	128
							Planned Order Releases				640	640	128	128	

Solutions to Self Test

1. a; **2.** e; **3.** a; **4.** c; **5.** c; **6.** c; **7.** e; **8.** b; **9.** d.

JIT and Lean Operations

Outline

Ten OM Strategy Decisions

Design of Goods and Services

Managing Quality

Process Strategy

Location Strategies

Layout Strategies

Human Resources

Supply Chain Management

Inventory Management
  Independent Demand
  Dependent Demand
  JIT and Lean Operations

Scheduling

Maintenance

Learning Objectives

When you complete this selection you should be able to

1. Define just-in-time, TPS, and lean operations
2. Define the seven wastes and the 5Ss
3. Explain JIT partnerships
4. Determine optimal setup time
5. Define kanban
6. Compute the required number of kanbans
7. Explain the principles of the Toyota Production System

Global Company Profile:
Toyota Motor Corporation

Achieving Competitive Advantage with Lean Operations at Toyota Motor Corporation

Toyota Motor Corporation, with annual sales of over 9 million cars and trucks, is the largest vehicle manufacturer in the world. Two techniques, just-in-time (JIT) and the Toyota Production System (TPS), have been instrumental in this post-WWII growth. Toyota, with a wide range of vehicles, competes head-to-head with successful long-established companies in Europe and the U.S. Taiichi Ohno, a former vice president of Toyota, created the basic framework for the world's most discussed systems for improving productivity, JIT and TPS. These two concepts provide much of the foundation for lean operations:

- Central to JIT is a philosophy of continued problem solving. In practice, JIT means making only what is needed, when it is needed. JIT provides an excellent vehicle for finding and eliminating problems because problems are easy to find in a system that has no slack. When excess inventory is eliminated, quality, layout, scheduling, and supplier issues become immediately evident—as does excess production.

- Central to TPS is a continuing effort to create and produce products under ideal conditions. Ideal conditions exist only when facilities, machines, and people are brought together, adding value without waste. Waste undermines productivity by diverting resources to excess inventory, unnecessary processing, and poor quality. Respect for people, extensive training, cross-training, and standard work practices of empowered employees focusing on driving out waste are fundamental to TPS.

Toyota's latest implementation of TPS and JIT are present at its new San Antonio plant,

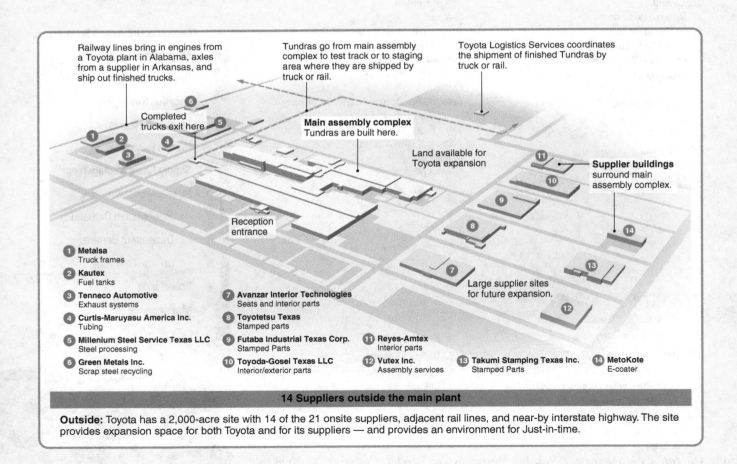

Railway lines bring in engines from a Toyota plant in Alabama, axles from a supplier in Arkansas, and ship out finished trucks.

Tundras go from main assembly complex to test track or to staging area where they are shipped by truck or rail.

Toyota Logistics Services coordinates the shipment of finished Tundras by truck or rail.

Completed trucks exit here

Main assembly complex
Tundras are built here.

Land available for Toyota expansion

Supplier buildings surround main assembly complex.

Reception entrance

Large supplier sites for future expansion.

1. **Metalsa** Truck frames
2. **Kautex** Fuel tanks
3. **Tenneco Automotive** Exhaust systems
4. **Curtis-Maruyasu America Inc.** Tubing
5. **Millenium Steel Service Texas LLC** Steel processing
6. **Green Metals Inc.** Scrap steel recycling
7. **Avanzar Interior Technologies** Seats and interior parts
8. **Toyotetsu Texas** Stamped parts
9. **Futaba Industrial Texas Corp.** Stamped Parts
10. **Toyoda-Gosei Texas LLC** Interior/exterior parts
11. **Reyes-Amtex** Interior parts
12. **Vutex Inc.** Assembly services
13. **Takumi Stamping Texas Inc.** Stamped Parts
14. **MetoKote** E-coater

14 Suppliers outside the main plant

Outside: Toyota has a 2,000-acre site with 14 of the 21 onsite suppliers, adjacent rail lines, and near-by interstate highway. The site provides expansion space for both Toyota and for its suppliers — and provides an environment for Just-in-time.

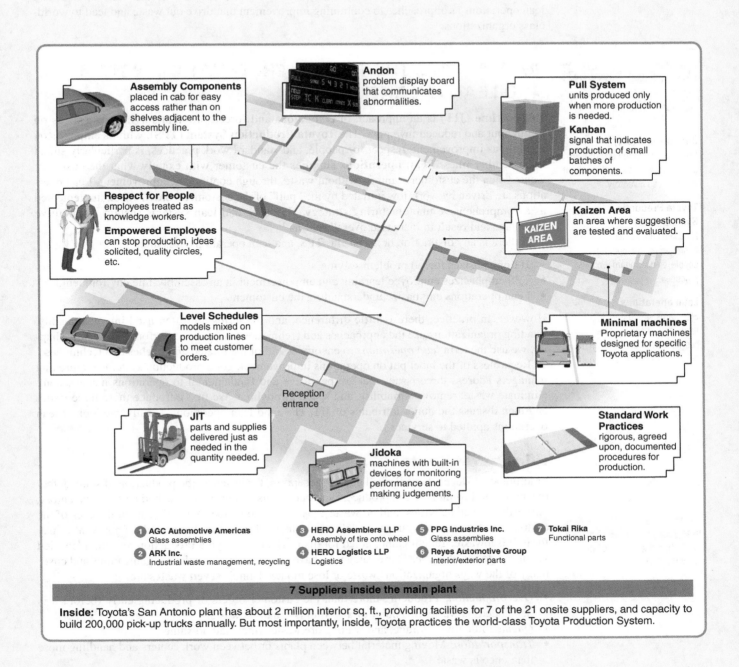

Assembly Components placed in cab for easy access rather than on shelves adjacent to the assembly line.

Andon problem display board that communicates abnormalities.

Pull System units produced only when more production is needed.

Kanban signal that indicates production of small batches of components.

Respect for People employees treated as knowledge workers.

Empowered Employees can stop production, ideas solicited, quality circles, etc.

Kaizen Area an area where suggestions are tested and evaluated.

KAIZEN AREA

Level Schedules models mixed on production lines to meet customer orders.

Minimal machines Proprietary machines designed for specific Toyota applications.

Reception entrance

JIT parts and supplies delivered just as needed in the quantity needed.

Jidoka machines with built-in devices for monitoring performance and making judgements.

Standard Work Practices rigorous, agreed upon, documented procedures for production.

1. **AGC Automotive Americas** Glass assemblies
2. **ARK Inc.** Industrial waste management, recycling
3. **HERO Assemblers LLP** Assembly of tire onto wheel
4. **HERO Logistics LLP** Logistics
5. **PPG Industries Inc.** Glass assemblies
6. **Reyes Automotive Group** Interior/exterior parts
7. **Tokai Rika** Functional parts

7 Suppliers inside the main plant

Inside: Toyota's San Antonio plant has about 2 million interior sq. ft., providing facilities for 7 of the 21 onsite suppliers, and capacity to build 200,000 pick-up trucks annually. But most importantly, inside, Toyota practices the world-class Toyota Production System.

the largest Toyota land site for an automobile assembly plant in the U.S. Interestingly, despite its annual production of 200,000 Tundra pick-up trucks, the building itself is one of the smallest in the industry. Modern automobiles have 30,000 parts, but at Toyota, independent suppliers combine many of these parts into sub-assemblies. Twenty-one of these suppliers are on site at the San

Antonio facility and transfer components to the assembly line on a JIT basis.

Operations such as these taking place in the new San Antonio plant are why Toyota continues to perform near the top in quality and maintain the lowest labor-hour assembly time in the industry. JIT, TPS, and lean operations work—and they provide a competitive advantage at Toyota Motor Corporation.

As shown in the *Global Company Profile*, the Toyota Production System (TPS) contributes to a world-class operation at Toyota Motor Corporation. In this chapter, we discuss JIT, TPS, and lean operations as approaches to continuing improvement that drive out waste and lead to world-class organizations.

JUST-IN-TIME, THE TOYOTA PRODUCTION SYSTEM, AND LEAN OPERATIONS

Just-in-time (JIT)
Continuous and forced problem solving via a focus on throughput and reduced inventory.

Toyota Production System (TPS)
Focus on continuous improvement, respect for people, and standard work practices.

Lean operations
Eliminates waste through a focus on exactly what the customer wants.

Just-in-time (JIT) is an approach of continuous and forced problem solving via a focus on throughput and reduced inventory. The **Toyota Production System** (TPS), with its emphasis on continuous improvement, respect for people, and standard work practices, is particularly suited for assembly lines. **Lean operations** supplies the customer with exactly what the customer wants when the customer wants it, without waste, through continuous improvement. Lean operations are driven by workflow initiated by the "pull" of the customer's order. When implemented as a comprehensive manufacturing strategy, JIT, TPS, and lean systems sustain competitive advantage and result in increased overall returns.[1]

If there is any distinction between JIT, TPS, and lean operations, it is that:

- JIT emphasizes forced problem solving.
- TPS emphasizes employee learning and empowerment in an assembly-line environment.
- Lean operations emphasize understanding the customer.

However, in practice, there is little difference, and the terms are often used interchangeably. Leading organizations use the approaches and techniques that make sense for them. In this chapter, we use the term *lean operations* to encompass all of the related approaches and techniques.

Regardless of the label put on operations improvement, good production systems require that managers address three issues that are pervasive and fundamental to operations management: eliminate waste, remove variability, and speed throughput. We first introduce these three issues and then discuss the major attributes of JIT, TPS, and lean operations. Finally, we look at lean operations applied to services.

Eliminate Waste

Traditional producers have limited goals—accepting, for instance, the production of some defective parts and inventory. Lean producers set their sights on perfection; no bad parts, no inventory, only value-added activities, and no waste. Any activity that does not add value in the eyes of the customer is a waste. The customer defines product value. If the customer does not want to pay for it, it is a waste. Taiichi Ohno, noted for his work on the Toyota Production System, identified seven categories of waste. These categories have become popular in lean organizations and cover many of the ways organizations waste or lose money. Ohno's **seven wastes** are:

Seven wastes
Overproduction
Queues
Transportation
Inventory
Motion
Overprocessing
Defective product

- *Overproduction:* Producing more than the customer orders or producing early (before it is demanded) is waste. Inventory of any kind is usually a waste.
- *Queues:* Idle time, storage, and waiting are wastes (they add no value).
- *Transportation:* Moving material between plants or between work centers and handling more than once is waste.
- *Inventory:* Unnecessary raw material, work-in-process (WIP), finished goods, and excess operating supplies add no value and are wastes.
- *Motion:* Movement of equipment or people that adds no value is waste.
- *Overprocessing:* Work performed on the product that adds no value is waste.
- *Defective product:* Returns, warranty claims, rework, and scrap are a waste.

A broader perspective—one that goes beyond immediate production—suggests that other resources, such as energy, water, and air, are often wasted but should not be. Efficient, ethical, socially responsible production minimizes inputs and maximizes outputs, wasting nothing.

---

[1]Research suggests that the more JIT is comprehensive in breadth and depth, the greater overall returns will be. See Rosemary R. Fullerton and Cheryl S. McWatters, "The Production Performance Benefits from JIT Implementation," *Journal of Operations Management* 19, no. 1 (January 2001): 81–96.

For over a century, managers have used "housekeeping" for a neat, orderly, and efficient workplace and as a means of reducing waste. Operations managers have embellished "housekeeping" to include a checklist—now known as the 5Ss.[2] The Japanese developed the initial 5Ss. Not only are the 5Ss a good checklist for lean operations, they also provide an easy vehicle with which to assist the culture change that is often necessary to bring about lean operations. The **5Ss** follow:

5Ss

A lean production checklist:
Sort
Simplify
Shine
Standardize
Sustain

- *Sort/segregate:* Keep what is needed and remove everything else from the work area; when in doubt, throw it out. Identify non-value items and remove them. Getting rid of these items makes space available and usually improves work flow.
- *Simplify/straighten:* Arrange and use methods analysis tools to improve work flow and reduce wasted motion. Consider long-run and short-run ergonomic issues. Label and display for easy use only what is needed in the immediate work area.
- *Shine/sweep:* Clean daily; eliminate all forms of dirt, contamination, and clutter from the work area.
- *Standardize:* Remove variations from the process by developing standard operating procedures and checklists; good standards make the abnormal obvious. Standardize equipment and tooling so that cross-training time and cost are reduced. Train and retrain the work team so that when deviations occur, they are readily apparent to all.
- *Sustain/self-discipline:* Review periodically to recognize efforts and to motivate to sustain progress. Use visuals wherever possible to communicate and sustain progress.

U.S. managers often add two additional Ss that contribute to establishing and maintaining a lean workplace:

- *Safety:* Build good safety practices into the above five activities.
- *Support/maintenance:* Reduce variability, unplanned downtime, and costs. Integrate daily shine tasks with preventive maintenance.

The Ss provide a vehicle for continuous improvement with which all employees can identify. Operations managers need think only of the examples set by a well-run hospital emergency room or the spit-and-polish of a fire department for a benchmark. Offices and retail stores, as well as manufacturers, have also successfully used the 5Ss in their respective efforts to eliminate waste and move to lean operations.[3] Operations managers reduce waste any way possible so assets are released for other, more productive, purposes.

Remove Variability

Managers seek to remove variability caused by both internal and external factors. **Variability** is any deviation from the optimum process that delivers perfect product on time, every time. Variability is a polite word for problems. The less variability in a system, the less waste in the system. Most variability is caused by tolerating waste or by poor management. Among the many sources of variability are:

Variability

Any deviation from the optimum process that delivers perfect product on time, every time.

- Incomplete or inaccurate drawings or specifications
- Poor production processes that allow employees and suppliers to produce improper quantities or late or non-conforming units
- Unknown customer demands

Both JIT and inventory reduction are effective tools for identifying causes of variability. The precise timing of JIT makes variability evident, just as inventory hides variability. The removal of variability allows managers to move good materials on schedule and add value at each step of the production process.

---

[2]The term 5S comes from the Japanese words seiri (*sort* and clear out), seiton (*straighten* and configure), seiso (*scrub* and cleanup), seiketsu (maintain *sanitation* and cleanliness of self and workplace), and shitsuke (*self-discipline and standardization* of these practices).

[3]Jeff Arnold and Christy Bures, "Revisiting a Retail Challenge," *Industrial Engineer* 35, no. 12 (December 2003): 38–41; and Lea A. P. Tonkin, "Elgin Sweeper Company Employees Clear a Path Toward Lean Operations with Their Lean Enterprise System," *Target* 20, no. 2 (2004): 46–52.

Improve Throughput

Throughput
The time required to move orders through the production process, from receipt to delivery.

Manufacturing cycle time
The time between the arrival of raw materials and the shipping of finished products.

Pull system
A concept that results in material being produced only when requested and moved to where it is needed just as it is needed.

Throughput is a measure (in units or time) that it takes to move an order from receipt to delivery. Each minute products remain on the books, costs accumulate and competitive advantage is lost. The time that an order is in the shop is called **manufacturing cycle time**. This is the time between the arrival of raw materials and the shipping of finished product. For example, phone-system manufacturer Northern Telecom now has materials pulled directly from qualified suppliers to the assembly line. This effort has reduced a segment of Northern's manufacturing cycle time from 3 weeks to just 4 hours, the incoming inspection staff from 47 to 24, and problems on the shop floor caused by defective materials by 97%. Driving down manufacturing cycle time can make a major improvement in throughput.

A technique for increasing throughput is a pull system. A **pull system** *pulls a* unit to where it is needed just as it is needed. Pull systems are a standard tool of JIT systems. Pull systems use signals to request production and delivery from supplying stations to stations that have production capacity available. The pull concept is used both within the immediate production process and with suppliers. By *pulling* material through the system in very small lots—just as it is needed—waste and inventory are removed. As inventory is removed, problems become evident, and continuous improvement is emphasized. Removing the cushion of inventory also reduces both investment in inventory and manufacturing cycle time. A push system dumps orders on the next downstream workstation, regardless of timeliness and resource availability. Push systems are the antithesis of JIT. Pulling material through a production process as it is needed rather than in a "push" mode typically lowers cost and improves schedule performance, enhancing customer satisfaction.

JUST-IN-TIME (JIT)

With its forced problem solving via a focus on rapid throughput and reduced inventory, JIT provides a powerful strategy for improving operations. With JIT, materials arrive *where* they are needed only *when* they are needed. When good units do not arrive just as needed, a "problem" has been identified. By driving out waste and delay in this manner, JIT reduces costs associated with excess inventory, cuts variability and waste, and improves throughput. JIT is a key ingredient of lean operations and is particularly helpful in supporting strategies of rapid response and low cost. Every moment material is held, an activity that adds value should be occurring. Consequently, as Figure 1 suggests, JIT often yields a competitive advantage.

Effective JIT requires a meaningful buyer–supplier partnership.

▶ *Many services have adopted JIT techniques as a normal part of their business. Restaurants like Olive Garden and Red Lobster expect and receive JIT deliveries. Both buyer and supplier expect fresh, high-quality produce delivered without fail just when it is needed. The system doesn't work any other way.*

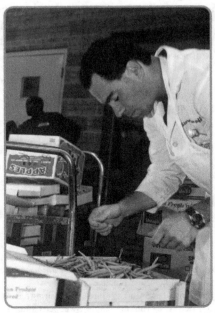

Culinary Institute of America

JIT TECHNIQUES:

Suppliers:	Few vendors; Supportive supplier relationships; Quality deliveries on time, directly to work areas.
Layout:	Work-cells; Group technology; Flexible machinery; Organized workplace; Reduced space for inventory.
Inventory:	Small lot sizes; Low setup time; Specialized parts bins
Scheduling:	Zero deviation from schedules; Level schedules; Suppliers informed of schedules; Kanban techniques
Preventive maintenance:	Scheduled; Daily routine; Operator involvement
Quality production:	Statistical process control; Quality suppliers; Quality within the firm
Employee empowerment:	Empowered and cross-trained employees; Training support; Few job classifications to ensure flexibility of employees
Commitment:	Support of management, employees, and suppliers

WHICH RESULTS IN:

Rapid throughput frees assets

Quality improvement reduces waste

Cost reduction adds pricing flexibility

Variability reduction

Rework reduction

WHICH WINS ORDERS BY:

Faster response to the customer at lower cost and higher quality—

A Competitive Advantage

◄ **Figure 1**

JIT Contributes to Competitive Advantage

JIT Partnerships

A **JIT partnership** exists when a supplier and a purchaser work together with open communication and a goal of removing waste and driving down costs. Close relationships and trust are critical to the success of JIT. Figure 2 shows the characteristics of JIT partnerships. Some specific goals of JIT partnerships are:

- *Removal of unnecessary activities*, such as receiving, incoming inspection, and paperwork related to bidding, invoicing, and payment.
- *Removal of in-plant inventory* by delivery in small lots directly to the using department as needed.
- *Removal of in-transit inventory* by encouraging suppliers to locate nearby and provide frequent small shipments. The shorter the flow of material in the resource pipeline, the less inventory. Inventory can also be reduced through a technique known as *consignment*. **Consignment inventory** (see the *OM in Action* box "Lean Production at Cessna Aircraft"), a variation of vendor-managed inventory, means the supplier maintains the title to the inventory until it is used. For instance, an assembly plant may find a hardware supplier that is willing to locate its warehouse where the user currently has its stockroom. In this manner, when hardware is needed, it is no farther than the stockroom, and the supplier can ship to other, perhaps smaller, purchasers from the "stockroom."
- *Obtain improved quality and reliability* through long-term commitments, communication, and cooperation.

Leading organizations view suppliers as extensions of their own organizations and expect suppliers to be fully committed to improvement. Such relationships require a high degree of respect by both supplier and purchaser. Supplier concerns can be significant; Harley-Davidson, for example, initially had difficulty implementing JIT because supplier issues outweighed the perceived benefits.

JIT partnerships

Partnerships of suppliers and purchasers that remove waste and drive down costs for mutual benefits.

Consignment inventory

An arrangement in which the supplier maintains title to the inventory until it is used.

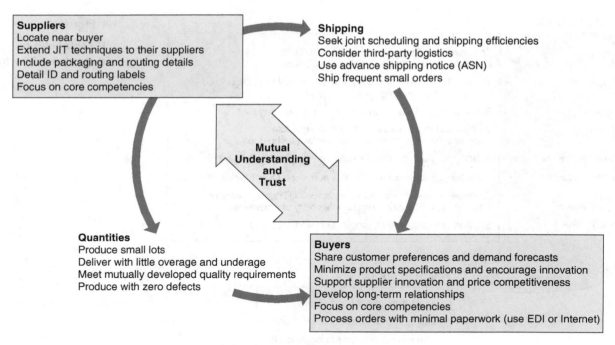

Suppliers
Locate near buyer
Extend JIT techniques to their suppliers
Include packaging and routing details
Detail ID and routing labels
Focus on core competencies

Shipping
Seek joint scheduling and shipping efficiencies
Consider third-party logistics
Use advance shipping notice (ASN)
Ship frequent small orders

Mutual Understanding and Trust

Quantities
Produce small lots
Deliver with little overage and underage
Meet mutually developed quality requirements
Produce with zero defects

Buyers
Share customer preferences and demand forecasts
Minimize product specifications and encourage innovation
Support supplier innovation and price competitiveness
Develop long-term relationships
Focus on core competencies
Process orders with minimal paperwork (use EDI or Internet)

▲ **Figure 2** Characteristics of JIT Partnerships

Concerns of Suppliers

Learning Objective

3. Explain JIT partnerships

Successful JIT partnerships require that supplier concerns be addressed. These concerns include:

1. *Diversification:* Suppliers may not want to tie themselves to long-term contracts with one customer. The suppliers' perception is that they reduce their risk if they have a variety of customers.
2. *Scheduling:* Many suppliers have little faith in the purchaser's ability to produce orders to a smooth, coordinated schedule.
3. *Changes:* Engineering or specification changes can play havoc with JIT because of inadequate lead time for suppliers to implement the necessary changes.
4. *Quality:* Capital budgets, processes, or technology may limit quality.
5. *Lot sizes:* Suppliers may see frequent delivery in small lots as a way to transfer buyer's holding costs to suppliers.

OM in Action   Lean Production at Cessna Aircraft

When Cessna Aircraft opened its new plant in Independence, Kansas, it saw the opportunity to switch from a craftwork mentality producing small single-engine planes to a lean manufacturing system. In doing so, Cessna adopted three lean practices.

First, Cessna set up consignment- and vendor-managed inventories with several of its suppliers. Blanket purchase orders allow Honeywell, for example, to maintain a 30-day supply of avionic parts onsite. Other vendors were encouraged to use a nearby warehouse to keep parts that could then be delivered daily to the production line.

Second, Cessna managers committed to cross-training, in which team members learn the duties of other team members and can shift across assembly lines as needed. To develop these technical skills, Cessna brought in 60 retired assembly-line workers to mentor and teach new employees. Employees were taught to work as a team and to assume responsibility for their team's quality.

Third, the company used group technology and manufacturing cells to move away from a batch process that resulted in large inventories and unsold planes. Now, Cessna pulls product through its plant only when a specific order is placed.

These commitments to manufacturing efficiency are part of the lean operations that has made Cessna the world's largest manufacturer of single-engine aircraft.

Sources: **www.cessna.com** (2007); *Strategic Finance* (November 2002): 32; *Purchasing* (September 4, 2003): 25–30; and *Fortune* (May 1, 2000): 1222B.

JIT LAYOUT

JIT layouts reduce another kind of waste—movement. The movement of material on a factory floor (or paper in an office) does not add value. Consequently, managers want flexible layouts that reduce the movement of both people and material. JIT layouts place material directly in the location where needed. For instance, an assembly line should be designed with delivery points next to the line so material need not be delivered first to a receiving department and then moved again. This is what VF Corporation's Wrangler Division in Greensboro, North Carolina, did; denim is now delivered directly to the line. Toyota has gone one step farther and places hardware and components in the chassis of each vehicle moving down the assembly line. This is not only convenient, but it allows Toyota to save space and opens areas adjacent to the assembly line previously occupied by shelves. When a layout reduces distance, firms often save labor and space and may have the added bonus of eliminating potential areas for accumulation of unwanted inventory. Table 1 provides a list of layout tactics.

▼ **Table 1**

JIT Layout Tactics

Build work cells for families of products

Include a large number of operations in a small area

Minimize distance

Design little space for inventory

Improve employee communication

Use poka-yoke devices

Build flexible or movable equipment

Cross-train workers to add flexibility

Distance Reduction

Reducing distance is a major contribution of work cells, work centers, and focused factories. The days of long production lines and huge economic lots, with goods passing through monumental, single-operation machines, are gone. Now firms use work cells, often arranged in a U shape, containing several machines performing different operations. These work cells are often based on group technology codes. Group technology codes help identify components with similar characteristics so we can group them into families. Once families are identified, work cells are built for them. The result can be thought of as a small product-oriented facility where the "product" is actually a group of similar products—a family of products. The cells produce one good unit at a time, and ideally they produce the units *only* after a customer orders them.

Increased Flexibility

Modern work cells are designed so they can be easily rearranged to adapt to changes in volume, product improvements, or even new designs. Almost nothing in these new departments is bolted down. This same concept of layout flexibility applies to office environments. Not only is most office furniture and equipment movable, but so are office walls, computer connections, and telecommunications. Equipment is modular. Layout flexibility aids the changes that result from product *and* process improvements that are inevitable with a philosophy of continuous improvement.

Impact on Employees

Employees working together are cross trained so they can bring flexibility and efficiency to the work cell. JIT layouts allow employees to work together so they can tell each other about problems and opportunities for improvement. When layouts provide for sequential operations, feedback can be immediate. Defects are waste. When workers produce units one at a time, they test each product or component at each subsequent production stage. Machines in work cells with self-testing poka-yoke functions detect defects and stop automatically when they occur. Before JIT, defective products were replaced from inventory. Because surplus inventory is not kept in JIT facilities, there are no such buffers. Getting it right the first time is critical.

In a JIT system, each worker inspects the arriving part, knowing that the part must be good before it goes on to the next "customer."

Reduced Space and Inventory

Because JIT layouts reduce travel distance, they also reduce inventory by removing space for inventory. When there is little space, inventory must be moved in very small lots or even single units. Units are always moving because there is no storage. For instance, each month Security Pacific Corporation's focused facility sorts 7 million checks, processes 5 million statements, and mails 190,000 customer statements. With a JIT layout, mail processing time has been reduced by 33%, salary costs by tens of thousands of dollars per year, floor space by 50%, and in-process waiting lines by 75% to 90%. Storage, including shelves and drawers, has been removed.

OM in Action Let's Try Zero Inventory

Just-in-time tactics are being incorporated in manufacturing to improve quality, drive down inventory investment, and reduce other costs. However, JIT is also established practice in restaurants, where customers expect it, and a necessity in the produce business, where there is little choice. Pacific Pre-Cut Produce, a $14 million fruit and vegetable processing company in Tracy, California, holds inventory to zero. Buyers are in action in the wee hours of the morning. At 6 A.M., produce production crews show up. Orders for very specific cuts and mixtures of fruit and vegetable salads and stir-fry ingredients for supermarkets, restaurants, and institutional kitchens pour in from 8 A.M. until 4 P.M. Shipping begins at 10 P.M. and continues until the last order is filled and loaded at 5 A.M. the next morning. Inventories are once again zero, and things are relatively quiet for an hour or so; then the routine starts

again. Pacific Pre-Cut Produce has accomplished a complete cycle of purchase, manufacture, and shipping in about 24 hours.

VP Bob Borzone calls the process the ultimate in mass customization. "We buy everything as a bulk commodity, then slice and dice it to fit the exact requirements of the end user. There are 20 different stir-fry mixes. Some customers want the snow peas clipped on both ends, some just on one. Some want only red bell peppers in the mix, some only yellow. You tailor the product to the customer's requirements. You're trying to satisfy the need of a lot of end users, and each restaurant and retailer wants to look different."

Sources: Supermarket News (September 27, 2004): 31; *Inbound Logistics* (August 1997): 26–32; and *Progressive Grocer* (January 1998): 51–56.

JIT INVENTORY

Inventories in production and distribution systems often exist "just in case" something goes wrong. That is, they are used just in case some variation from the production plan occurs. The "extra" inventory is then used to cover variations or problems. Effective inventory tactics require "just in time," not "just in case." **Just-in-time inventory** is the minimum inventory necessary to keep a perfect system running. With just-in-time inventory, the exact amount of goods arrives at the moment it is needed, not a minute before or a minute after. The *OM in Action* box "Let's Try Zero Inventory" suggests that it can be done. Some useful JIT inventory tactics are shown in Table 2 and discussed in more detail in the following sections.

Just-in-time inventory

The minimum inventory necessary to keep a perfect system running.

Reduce Variability

The idea behind JIT is to eliminate inventory that hides variability in the production system. This concept is illustrated in Figure 3, which shows a lake full of rocks. The water in the lake represents inventory flow, and the rocks represent problems such as late deliveries, machine breakdowns, and poor personnel performance. The water level in the lake hides variability and problems. Because inventory hides problems, they are hard to find.

► **Figure 3**

Inventory Has Two Costs, One for Holding the Inventory and One for the Problems It Hides— Just as Water in a Lake Hides the Rocks

Video 16.1

Sailing through the Problems of Excess Inventory

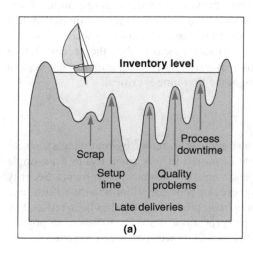

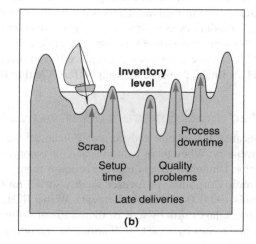

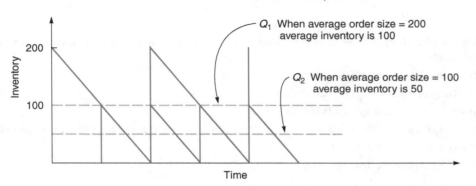

◀ **Figure 4**

Frequent Orders Reduce Average Inventory

A lower order size increases the number of orders and total ordering cost but reduces average inventory and total holding cost.

Reduce Inventory

Operations managers move toward JIT by first removing inventory. Reducing inventory uncovers the "rocks" in Figure 3(a) that represent the variability and problems currently being tolerated. With reduced inventory, management chips away at the exposed problems until the lake is clear. After the lake is clear, managers make additional cuts in inventory and continue to chip away at the next level of exposed problems (see Figure 3[b]). Ultimately, there will be virtually no inventory and no problems (variability).

Dell estimates that the rapid changes in technology costs $\frac{1}{2}\%$ to 2% of its inventory's value *each week*. Shigeo Shingo, co-developer of the Toyota JIT system, says, "Inventory is evil." He is not far from the truth. If inventory itself is not evil, it hides evil at great cost.

"Inventory is evil."
Shigeo Shingo

Reduce Lot Sizes

Just-in-time has also come to mean elimination of waste by reducing investment in inventory. The key to JIT is producing good product in small lot sizes. Reducing the size of batches can be a major help in reducing inventory and inventory costs. When inventory usage is constant, the average inventory level is the sum of the maximum inventory plus the minimum inventory divided by 2. Figure 4 shows that lowering the order size increases the number of orders but drops inventory levels.

Ideally, in a JIT environment, order size is one and single units are being pulled from one adjacent process to another. More realistically, analysis of the process, transportation time, and containers used for transport are considered when determining lot size. Such analysis typically results in a small lot size but a lot size larger than one. Once a lot size has been determined, the EOQ production order quantity model can be modified to determine the desired setup time. The production order quantity model takes the form:

$$Q^* = \sqrt{\frac{2DS}{H[1-(d/p)]}} \tag{1}$$

where
- D = Annual demand
- S = Setup cost
- H = Holding cost
- d = Daily demand
- p = Daily production

Example 1 shows how to determine the desired setup time.

▼ **Table 2**

JIT Inventory Tactics

Use a pull system to
  move inventory
Reduce lot size
Develop just-in-time
  delivery systems
  with suppliers
Deliver directly to the
  point of use
Perform to schedule
Reduce setup time
Use group technology

EXAMPLE 1

Determining optimal setup time

Crate Furniture, Inc., a firm that produces rustic furniture, desires to move toward a reduced lot size. Crate Furniture's production analyst, Aleda Roth, determined that a 2-hour production cycle would be acceptable between two departments. Further, she concluded that a setup time that would accommodate the 2-hour cycle time should be achieved.

Approach: Roth developed the following data and procedure to determine optimum setup time analytically:

D = Annual demand = 400,000 units

d = Daily demand = 400,000 per 250 days = 1,600 units per day

p = Daily production rate = 4,000 units per day

Q = EOQ desired = 400 (which is the 2-hour demand; that is, 1,600 per day per four 2-hour periods)

H = Holding cost = $20 per unit per year

S = Setup cost (to be determined)

Solution: Roth determines that the cost, on an hourly basis, of setting up equipment is $30. Further, she computes that the setup cost per setup should be:

$$Q = \sqrt{\frac{2DS}{H(1-d/p)}}$$

$$Q^2 = \frac{2DS}{H(1-d/p)}$$

$$S = \frac{(Q^2)(H)(1-d/p)}{2D}$$

$$S = \frac{(400)^2(20)(1-1,600/4,000)}{2(400,000)}$$

$$= \frac{(3,200,000)(0.6)}{800,000} = \$2.40$$

Setup time = $2.40/(hourly labor rate)

= $2.40/($30 per hour)

= 0.08 hour, or 4.8 minutes

Insight: Now, rather than produce components in large lots, Crate Furniture can produce in a 2-hour cycle with the advantage of an inventory turnover of four *per day*.

Learning exercise: If labor cost goes to $40 per hour, what should be the setup time? [Answer: .06 hour, or 3.6 minutes.]

Related problems: 8, 9, 10

Learning Objective

4. Determine optimal set-up time

Only two changes need to be made for small-lot material flow to work. First, material handling and work flow need to be improved. With short production cycles, there can be very little wait time. Improving material handling is usually easy and straightforward. The second change is more challenging, and that is a radical reduction in setup times. We discuss setup reduction next.

Reduce Setup Costs

Both inventory and the cost of holding it go down as the inventory-reorder quantity and the maximum inventory level drop. However, because inventory requires incurring an ordering or setup cost that must be applied to the units produced, managers tend to purchase (or produce) large orders. With large orders, each unit purchased or ordered absorbs only a small part of the setup cost. Consequently, the way to drive down lot sizes *and* reduce average inventory is to reduce setup cost, which in turn lowers the optimum order size.

The effect of reduced setup costs on total cost and lot size is shown in Figure 5. Moreover, smaller lot sizes hide fewer problems. In many environments, setup cost is highly correlated with setup time. In a manufacturing facility, setups usually require a substantial amount of preparation. Much of the preparation required by a setup can be done prior to shutting down the machine or process. Setup times can be reduced substantially, as shown in Figure 6. For instance, in Kodak's Guadalajara, Mexico, plant a team reduced the setup time to change a bearing from 12 hours to 6 minutes![4] This is the kind of progress that is typical of world-class manufacturers.

Reduced lot sizes must be accompanied by reduced setup times; otherwise, the setup cost is assigned to fewer units.

[4]Frank Carguello and Marty Levin, "Excellence at Work in Guadalajara, Mexico, Operation," *Target* 15, no. 3 (3rd quarter 1999): 51–53.

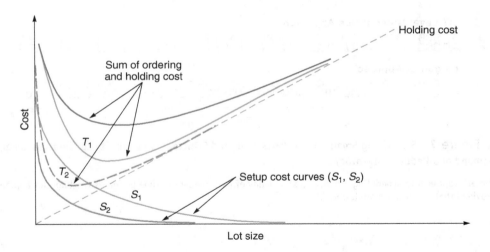

Just as setup costs can be reduced at a machine in a factory, setup time can also be reduced during the process of getting the order ready. It does little good to drive down factory setup time from hours to minutes if orders are going to take 2 weeks to process or "set up" in the office. This is exactly what happens in organizations that forget that JIT concepts have applications in offices as well as in the factory. Reducing setup time (and cost) is an excellent way to reduce inventory investment and to improve productivity.

JIT SCHEDULING

Effective schedules, communicated both within the organization and to outside suppliers, support JIT. Better scheduling also improves the ability to meet customer orders, drives down inventory by allowing smaller lot sizes, and reduces work-in-process. For instance, Ford Motor Company now ties some suppliers to its final assembly schedule. Ford communicates its schedules to bumper manufacturer Polycon Industries from the Ford Oakville production control system. The scheduling system describes the style and color of the bumper needed for each vehicle moving down the final assembly line. The scheduling system transmits the information to portable terminals carried by Polycon warehouse personnel who load the bumpers onto conveyors leading to the loading dock. The bumpers are then trucked 50 miles to the Ford plant. Total time is 4 hours. Table 3 suggests several items that can contribute to achieving these goals, but two techniques (in addition to communicating schedules) are paramount. They are *level schedules* and *kanban*.

▼ **Table 3**

JIT Scheduling Tactics

Communicate schedules to suppliers
Make level schedules
Freeze part of the schedule
Perform to schedule
Seek one-piece-make and one-piece-move
Eliminate waste
Produce in small lots
Use kanbans
Make each operation produce a perfect part

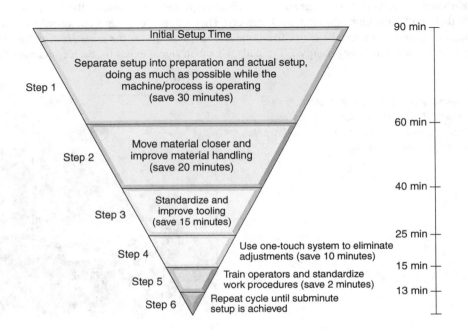

◀ **Figure 6**

Steps for Reducing Setup Times

Reduced setup times are a major JIT component.

JIT Level Material-Use Approach

AA BBB C AA BBB C AA BBB C AA BBB C AA BBB C AA BBB C AA BBB C AA BBB C

Large-Lot Approach

AAAAAA BBBBBBBBB CCC AAAAAA BBBBBBBBB CCC AAAAAA BBBBBBBBB CCC

→ Time

▲ **Figure 7** **Scheduling Small Lots of Parts A, B, and C Increases Flexibility to Meet Customer Demand and Reduces Inventory**

The JIT approach to scheduling produces just as many of each model per time period as the large-lot approach, provided that setup times are lowered.

Level Schedules

Level schedules process frequent small batches rather than a few large batches. Because this technique schedules many small lots that are always changing, it has on occasion been called "jelly bean" scheduling. Figure 7 contrasts a traditional large-lot approach using large batches with a JIT level schedule using many small batches. The operations manager's task is to make and move small lots so the level schedule is economical. This requires success with the issues discussed in this chapter that allow small lots. As lots get smaller, the constraints may change and become increasingly challenging. At some point, processing a unit or two may not be feasible. The constraint may be the way units are sold and shipped (four to a carton), or an expensive paint changeover (on an automobile assembly line), or the proper number of units in a sterilizer (for a food-canning line).

The scheduler may find that *freezing* the portion of the schedule closest to due dates allows the production system to function and the schedule to be met. Freezing means not allowing changes to be part of the schedule. Operations managers expect the schedule to be achieved with no deviations from the schedule.

Kanban

One way to achieve small lot sizes is to move inventory through the shop only as needed rather than *pushing* it on to the next workstation whether or not the personnel there are ready for it. As noted earlier, when inventory is moved only as needed, it is referred to as a *pull* system, and the ideal lot size is one. The Japanese call this system *kanban*. Kanbans allow arrivals at a work center to match (or nearly match) the processing time.

Kanban is a Japanese word for *card*. In their effort to reduce inventory, the Japanese use systems that "pull" inventory through work centers. They often use a "card" to signal the need for another container of material—hence the name *kanban*. *The card is the authorization for the next container of material to be produced.* Typically, a kanban signal exists for each container of items

▶ *A kanban need not be as formal as signal lights or empty carts. The cook in a fast-food restaurant knows that when six cars are in line, eight meat patties and six orders of french fries should be cooking.*

Donna Shader

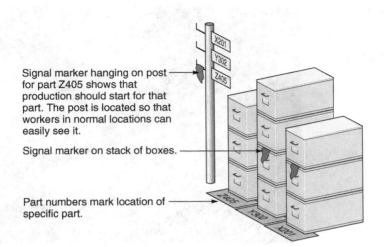

◄ Figure 8

Diagram of Outbound Stockpoint with Warning-Signal Marker

Signal marker hanging on post for part Z405 shows that production should start for that part. The post is located so that workers in normal locations can easily see it.

Signal marker on stack of boxes.

Part numbers mark location of specific part.

X201
Y302
Z405

to be obtained. An order for the container is then initiated by each kanban and "pulled" from the producing department or supplier. A sequence of kanbans "pulls" the material through the plant.

The system has been modified in many facilities so that even though it is called a *kanban*, the card itself does not exist. In some cases, an empty position on the floor is sufficient indication that the next container is needed. In other cases, some sort of signal, such as a flag or rag (Figure 8) alerts that it is time for the next container.

When there is visual contact between producer and user, the process works like this:

1. The user removes a standard-size container of parts from a small storage area, as shown in Figure 8.
2. The signal at the storage area is seen by the producing department as authorization to replenish the using department or storage area. Because there is an optimum lot size, the producing department may make several containers at a time.

Learning Objective

5. Define kanban

Figure 9 shows how a kanban works, pulling units as needed from production. This system is similar to the resupply that occurs in your neighborhood supermarket: The customer buys; the stock clerk observes the shelf or receives notice from the end-of-day sales list and restocks. When the limited supply, if any, in the store's storage is depleted, a "pull" signal is sent to the warehouse, distributor, or manufacturer for resupply, usually that night. The complicating factor in a manufacturing firm is the time needed for actual manufacturing (production) to take place.

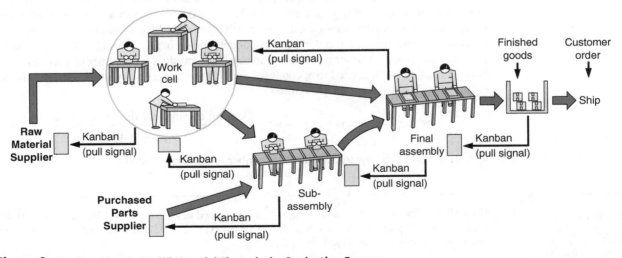

▲ Figure 9 **Kanban Signals "Pull" Material Through the Production Process**

As a customer "pulls" an order from finished goods, a signal (card) is sent to the final assembly area. The final assembly area produces and resupplies finished goods. When final assembly needs components, it sends a signal to its suppliers, a subassembly area and a work cell. These areas supply final assembly. The work cell, in turn, sends a signal to the raw material supplier, and the subassembly area notifies the work cell and purchased parts supplier of a requirement.

▶ *Kanban containers at Harley-Davidson are specially made for individual parts, and many feature padding to protect the finish. These containers serve an important role in inventory reduction: Because they are the only place inventory is stored, they serve as a signal to supply new parts to the line. After all the pieces have been removed, the container is returned to its originating cell, signaling the worker there to build more.*

Video 16.2

JIT at Harley-Davidson

Several additional points regarding kanbans may be helpful:

- When the producer and user are not in visual contact, a card can be used; otherwise, a light or flag or empty spot on the floor may be adequate.
- Because a pull station may require several resupply components, several kanban pull techniques can be used for different products at the same pull station.
- Usually, each card controls a specific quantity or parts, although multiple card systems are used if the producing work cell produces several components or if the lot size is different from the move size.
- In an MRP system, the schedule can be thought of as a "build" authorization and the kanban as a type of "pull" system that initiates the actual production.
- The kanban cards provide a direct control (limit) on the amount of work-in-process between cells.
- If there is an immediate storage area, a two-card system may be used—one card circulates between user and storage area, and the other circulates between the storage area and the producing area.

Determining the Number of Kanban Cards or Containers   The number of kanban cards, or containers, in a JIT system sets the amount of authorized inventory. To determine the number of containers moving back and forth between the using area and the producing areas, management first sets the size of each container. This is done by computing the lot size, using a model such as the production order quantity model (shown in Equation 11). Setting the number of containers involves knowing (1) lead time needed to produce a container of parts and (2) the amount of safety stock needed to account for variability or uncertainty in the system. The number of kanban cards is computed as follows:

$$\text{Number of kanbans (containers)} = \frac{\text{Demand during lead time} + \text{Safety stock}}{\text{Size of container}}$$

Example 2 illustrates how to calculate the number of kanbans needed.

EXAMPLE 2

Determining the number of kanban containers

Hobbs Bakery produces short runs of cakes that are shipped to grocery stores. The owner, Ken Hobbs, wants to try to reduce inventory by changing to a kanban system. He has developed the following data and asked you to finish the project.

Daily demand = 500 cakes

Production lead time = Wait time + Material handling time + Processing time = 2 days

Safety stock = $\frac{1}{2}$ day

Container size (determined on a production order size EOQ basis) = 250 cakes

Approach: Having determined that the EOQ size is 250, we then determine the number of kanbans (containers) needed.

Solution: Demand during lead time (= Lead time × Daily demand = 2 days × 500 cakes =) 1,000

Safety stock = 250

Number of kanbans (containers) needed =

$$\frac{\text{Demand during lead time} + \text{Safety stock}}{\text{Container size}} = \frac{1,000 + 250}{250} = 5$$

Insight: Once the reorder point is hit, five containers should be released.

Learning exercise: If lead time drops to 1 day, how many containers are needed? [Answer: 3.]

Related problems: 1, 2, 3, 4, 5, 6

Learning Objective

6. Compute the required number of kanbans

Advantages of Kanban Containers are typically very small, usually a matter of a few hours' worth of production. Such a system requires tight schedules. Small quantities must be produced several times a day. The process must run smoothly with little variability in quality of lead time because any shortage has an almost immediate impact on the entire system. Kanban places added emphasis on meeting schedules, reducing the time and cost required by setups, and economical material handling.

Whether it is called kanban or something else, the advantages of small inventory and *pulling* material through the plant only when needed are significant. For instance, small batches allow only a very limited amount of faulty or delayed material. Problems are immediately evident. Numerous aspects of inventory are bad; only one aspect—availability—is good. Among the bad aspects are poor quality, obsolescence, damage, occupied space, committed assets, increased insurance, increased material handling, and increased accidents. Kanban systems put downward pressure on all these negative aspects of inventory.

In-plant kanban systems often use standardized, reusable containers that protect the specific quantities to be moved. Such containers are also desirable in the supply chain. Standardized containers reduce weight and disposal costs, generate less wasted space in trailers, and require less labor to pack, unpack, and prepare items.

The manufacturing inventory to sales ratio continues to drop, thanks in large part to JIT.

JIT QUALITY

The relationship between JIT and quality is a strong one. They are related in three ways. First, JIT cuts the cost of obtaining good quality. This saving occurs because scrap, rework, inventory investment, and damage costs are buried in inventory. JIT forces down inventory; therefore, fewer bad units are produced and fewer units must be reworked. In short, whereas inventory *hides* bad quality, JIT immediately *exposes* it.

New United Motor Manufacturing, Inc. (NUMMI)

◄ *The New United Motor Manufacturing (NUMMI) plant in Fremont, California, is a joint venture between Toyota and General Motors and builds cars for both companies. The plant was, of course, designed as a Toyota Production System (TPS), using just-in-time (JIT). Management even moved a water tower to ensure that new loading docks would facilitate JIT arrivals and JIT movement of parts within the plant. This plant, like most JIT facilities, also empowers employees so they can stop the entire production line by pulling the overhead cord if any quality problems are spotted.*

Second, JIT improves quality. As JIT shrinks queues and lead time, it keeps evidence of errors fresh and limits the number of potential sources of error. In effect, JIT creates an early warning system for quality problems so that fewer bad units are produced and feedback is immediate. This advantage can accrue both within the firm and with goods received from outside vendors.

Finally, better quality means fewer buffers are needed and, therefore, a better, easier-to-employ JIT system can exist. Often the purpose of keeping inventory is to protect against unreliable quality. If consistent quality exists, JIT allows firms to reduce all costs associated with inventory. Table 4 suggests some requirements for quality in a JIT environment.

TOYOTA PRODUCTION SYSTEM

Toyota Motor's Eiji Toyoda and Taiichi Ohno are given credit for the Toyota Production System (TPS) (see the *Global Company Profile* that opens this chapter). Three core components of TPS are continuous improvement, respect for people, and standard work practice.

Learning Objective

7. Explain the principles of
the Toyota Production System

Continuous Improvement

Continuous improvement under TPS means building an organizational culture and instilling in its people a value system stressing that processes can be improved—indeed, that improvement is an integral part of every employee's job. Instilling these values begins at recruiting and continues through extensive and continuing training. One of the reasons continuous improvement works at Toyota, we should note, is because of another core value at Toyota, Toyota's respect for people.

Respect for People

At Toyota, people are recruited, trained, and treated as knowledge workers. Aided by aggressive cross-training and few job classifications, TPS engages the mental as well as physical capacities of employees in the challenging task of improving operations. Employees are empowered. They are empowered to make improvements. They are empowered to stop machines and processes when quality problems exist. Indeed, empowered employees are a necessary part of TPS. This means that those tasks that have traditionally been assigned to staff are moved to employees. Toyota recognizes that employees know more about their jobs than anyone else. TPS respects employees by giving them the opportunity to enrich both their jobs and their lives.

Standard Work Practice

Standard work practice at Toyota includes these underlying principles:

- Work is completely specified as to content, sequence, timing, and outcome.
- Internal and external customer–supplier connections are direct, specifying personnel, methods, timing, and quantity.
- Product and service flows are to be simple and direct. Goods and services are directed to a specific person or machine.
- Improvements in the system must be made in accordance with the "scientific method," at the lowest possible level in the organization.[5]

TPS requires that activities, connections, and flows include built-in tests to automatically signal problems. Any gap between what is expected and what occurs becomes immediately evident. The education and training of Toyota's employees and the responsiveness of the system to problems make the seemingly rigid system flexible and adaptable to changing circumstances. The result is ongoing improvements in reliability, flexibility, safety, and efficiency.

---

[5]Adopted from Steven J. Spear, "Learning to Lead at Toyota," *Harvard Business Review* 82, no. 5 (May 2004): 78–86; Steven Spear and H. Kent Bowen, "Decoding the DNA of the Toyota Production System," *Harvard Business Review* 77, no. 5 (September–October 1999): 97–106.

LEAN OPERATIONS

Lean production can be thought of as the end result of a well-run OM function. While JIT and TPS tend to have an *internal* focus, lean production begins *externally* with a focus on the customer. Understanding what the customer wants and ensuring customer input and feedback are starting points for lean production. Lean operations means identifying customer value by analyzing all the activities required to produce the product and then optimizing the entire process from the customer's perspective. The manager identifies what creates value for the customer and what does not.

Building a Lean Organization

The transition to lean production is difficult. Building an organizational culture where learning, empowerment, and continuous improvement are the norm is a challenge. However, organizations that focus on JIT, quality, and employee empowerment are often lean producers. Such firms drive out activities that do not add value in the eyes of the customer: they include leaders like United Parcel Service, Harley-Davidson, and, of course, Toyota. Even traditionally craft-oriented organizations such as Louis Vuitton (see the *OM in Action* box) find improved productivity with lean operations. Lean operations adopt a philosophy of minimizing waste by striving for perfection through continuous learning, creativity, and teamwork. They tend to share the following attributes:

- *Use JIT techniques* to eliminate virtually all inventory.
- *Build systems that help employees* produce a perfect part every time.
- *Reduce space requirements* by minimizing travel distance.
- *Develop partnerships with suppliers*, helping them to understand the needs of the ultimate customer.
- *Educate suppliers* to accept responsibility for satisfying end customer needs.
- *Eliminate all but value-added activities.* Material handling, inspection, inventory, and rework are the likely targets because these do not add value to the product.
- *Develop employees* by constantly improving job design, training, employee commitment, teamwork, and empowerment.
- *Make jobs challenging*, pushing responsibility to the lowest level possible.
- *Build worker flexibility* through cross-training and reducing job classifications.

Success requires the full commitment and involvement of managers, employees, and suppliers. The rewards that lean producers reap are spectacular. Lean producers often become benchmark performers.

OM in Action Going Lean at Louis Vuitton

LVMH Moet Hennessy Louis Vuitton is the world's largest luxury-goods company. Its Louis Vuitton unit, responsible for half of the company's profit, makes very upscale handbags and enjoys a rich markup on sales of about $5 billion. The return-on-investment is excellent, but sales could be even better: the firm often can't match production with the sales pace of a successful new product. In the high fashion business that is all about speed-to-market, this is bad news; a massive overhaul was in order.

Changes on the factory floor were key to the overhaul. The traditional approach to manufacturing at Louis Vuitton was batch production: craftsmen, working on partially completed handbags, performed specialized tasks such as cutting, gluing, sewing, and assembly. Carts moved batches of semi-finished handbags on to the next workstation. It took 20 to 30 workers 8 days to make a handbag. And defects were high. Lean manufacturing looked like the way to go.

Craftsmen were retrained to do multiple tasks in small U-shaped work cells. Each work cell now contains 6 to 12

Colin Young-Wolff, PhotoEdit Inc.

cross-trained workers and the necessary sewing machines and work tables. Consistent with one-piece flow, the work is passed through the cell from worker to worker. The system reduces inventory and allows workers to detect flaws earlier. Rework under the old system was sometimes as high as 50% and internal losses as high as 4%. Returns are down by two-thirds. The system has not only improved productivity and quality, it also allows Louis Vuitton to respond to the market faster—with daily scheduling as opposed to weekly scheduling.

Sources: The Wall Street Journal (October 9, 2006): A1, A15 and (January 31, 2006): A1, A13.

LEAN OPERATIONS IN SERVICES

The features of lean operations apply to services just as they do in other sectors. Here are some examples applied to suppliers, layout, inventory, and scheduling in the service sector.

Suppliers   As we have noted, virtually every restaurant deals with its suppliers on a JIT basis. Those that do not are usually unsuccessful. The waste is too evident—food spoils and customers complain or get sick.

Layouts   Lean layouts are required in restaurant kitchens, where cold food must be served cold and hot food hot. McDonald's, for example, has reconfigured its kitchen layout at great expense to drive seconds out of the production process, thereby speeding delivery to customers. With the new process, McDonald's can produce made-to-order hamburgers in 45 seconds. Layouts also make a difference in airline baggage claim, where customers expect their bags just-in-time.

Inventory   Stockbrokers drive inventory down to nearly zero every day. Most sell and buy orders occur on an immediate basis because an unexecuted sell or buy order is not acceptable to most clients. A broker may be in serious trouble if left holding an unexecuted trade. Similarly, McDonald's reduces inventory waste by maintaining a finished-goods inventory of only 10 minutes; after that, it is thrown away. Hospitals, such as Arnold Palmer (described in this chapter's Video Case Study), manage JIT inventory and low safety stocks for many items. Even critical supplies such as pharmaceuticals may be held to low levels by developing community networks as backup systems. In this manner, if one pharmacy runs out of a needed drug, another member of the network can supply it until the next day's shipment arrives.

 Video 16.3

JIT at Arnold Palmer Hospital

Scheduling   At airline ticket counters, the focus of the system is customer demand, but rather than being satisfied by inventory availability, demand is satisfied by personnel. Through elaborate scheduling, ticket counter personnel show up just-in-time to cover peaks in customer demand. In other words, rather than "things" inventoried, personnel are scheduled. At a salon, the focus is only slightly different: the *customer* is scheduled to assure prompt service. At McDonald's and Wal-Mart, scheduling of personnel is down to 15-minute increments, based on precise forecasting of demand. Additionally, at McDonald's, production is done in small lots to ensure that fresh, hot hamburgers are delivered just-in-time. In short, both personnel and production are scheduled to meet specific demand. Notice that in all three of these lean organizations—the airline ticket counter, the salon, and McDonald's—scheduling is a key ingredient. Excellent forecasts drive those schedules. Those forecasts may be very elaborate, with seasonal, daily, and even hourly components in the case of the airline ticket counter (holiday sales, flight time, etc.), seasonal and weekly components at the salon (holidays and Fridays create special problems), or down to a few minutes at McDonald's.

▶ *Lean operations take on an unusual form in an operating room. McKesson-General, Baxter International, and many other hospital suppliers provide surgical supplies for hospitals on a JIT basis. (1) They deliver prepackaged surgical supplies based on hospital operating schedules, and (2) the surgical packages themselves are prepared so supplies are available in the sequence in which they will be used during surgery.*

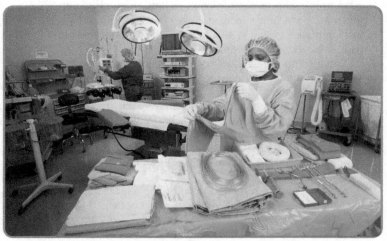

Cardinal Health, Medical Products & Services

To deliver goods and services to customers under continuously changing demand, suppliers need to be reliable, inventories lean, cycle times short, and schedules nimble. A lean focus engages and empowers employees to create and deliver the customer's perception of value, eliminating whatever does not contribute to this goal. Lean operations are currently being developed with great success in many firms, regardless of their products. Lean techniques are widely used in both goods-producing and service-producing firms; they just look different.

Summary

JIT, TPS, and lean operations are philosophies of continuous improvement. Lean operations focus on customer desires, TPS focuses on respect for people and standard work practices, and JIT focuses on driving out waste by reducing inventory. But all three approaches reduce waste in the production process. And because waste is found in anything that does not add value, organizations that implement these techniques are adding value more efficiently than other firms. The expectation of these systems is that empowered employees work with committed management to build systems that respond to customers with ever-lower cost and higher quality.

Key Terms

Just-in-time (JIT)
Toyota Production System (TPS)
Lean operations
Seven wastes
5Ss

Variability
Throughput
Manufacturing cycle time
Pull system
JIT partnerships

Consignment inventory
Just-in-time inventory
Level schedules
Kanban

Solved Problem

 Virtual Office Hours help is available on Student DVD.

Solved Problem 1

Krupp Refrigeration, Inc., is trying to reduce inventory and wants you to install a kanban system for compressors on one of its assembly lines. Determine the size of the kanban and the number of kanbans (containers) needed.

Setup cost = $10

Annual holding cost per compressor = $100

Daily production = 200 compressors

Annual usage = 25,000 (50 weeks × 5 days each × daily usage of 100 compressors)

Lead time = 3 days

Safety stock = $\frac{1}{2}$ day's production of compressors

Solution

First, we must determine kanban container size. To do this, we determine the production order quantity (see Equation [1]), which determines the kanban size:

$$Q_p = \sqrt{\frac{2DS}{H\left(1 - \frac{d}{p}\right)}} = \sqrt{\frac{2(25,000)(10)}{H\left(1 - \frac{d}{p}\right)}} = \sqrt{\frac{500,000}{100\left(1 - \frac{100}{200}\right)}} = \sqrt{\frac{500,000}{50}}$$

$= \sqrt{10,000} = 100$ compressors. So the production order size and the size of the kanban container = 100.

Then we determine the number of kanbans:

Demand during lead time = 300 (= 3 days × daily usage of 100)

Safety stock = 100 (= $\frac{1}{2}$ day's production × 200)

$$\text{Number of kanbans} = \frac{\text{Demand during lead time} + \text{Safety stock}}{\text{Size of container}}$$

$$= \frac{300 + 100}{100} = \frac{400}{100} = 4 \text{ containers}$$

Self-Test

- *Before taking the self-test*, refer to the learning objectives listed at the beginning of the selection and the key terms listed at the end of the selection.
- Use the key at the end of the chapter to **correct** your answers.
- *Restudy* pages that correspond to any questions you answered incorrectly or material you feel uncertain about.

1. Continuous improvement and forced problem solving is a reasonable definition of:
   a) lean operations
   b) expedited management
   c) the 5Ss of housekeeping
   d) just-in-time
   e) Toyota Production System

2. Supplying the customer needs without waste best describes:
   a) lean operations
   b) expedited management
   c) the 5Ss of housekeeping
   d) just-in-time
   e) Toyota Production System

3. Employee empowerment and standard work practices best describes:
   a) lean operations
   b) expedited management
   c) the 5Ss of housekeeping
   d) just-in-time
   e) Toyota Production System

4. Taiichi Ohno's seven wastes are _____, _____, _____, _____, _____, _____, and _____.

5. The 5Ss for lean production are _____, _____, _____, _____, and _____.

6. A "pull" system:
   a) dumps orders on the next downstream workstation
   b) defines the time between arrival and shipping
   c) is the time it takes to move an order from receipt to delivery
   d) produces material only when requested
   e) all of the above

7. Concerns of suppliers when moving to JIT include:
   a) small lots may seem economically prohibitive
   b) realistic quality demands
   c) changes without adequate lead time
   d) erratic schedules
   e) all of the above

8. TPS's standard work practices include:
   a) completely specified work
   b) "pull" systems
   c) level scheduling
   d) kanbans
   e) JIT techniques

9. Lean producers remove waste by:
   a) focusing on inventory reduction
   b) using JIT techniques
   c) reducing space requirements
   d) developing partnerships with suppliers
   e) all of the above

10. Manufacturing cycle time is:
    a) time to push an order through a facility
    b) time from order receipt to delivery
    c) time between arrival of raw material and shipping of finished product
    d) time between placing an order with a supplier and receipt

Internet and Student CD-ROM/DVD Exercises

Visit our Companion Web site or use your student CD-ROM/DVD to help with material in this chapter.

 On Our Companion Web Site,
www.prenhall.com/heizer
- Self-Study Quizzes
- Practice Problems
- Virtual Company Tour
- PowerPoint Lecture

On Your Student CD-ROM
- Practice Problems
- Excel OM
- POM for Windows

 On Your Student DVD
- Video Clips and Video Case
- Virtual Office Hours for Solved Problem

Discussion Questions

1. What is JIT?
2. What is a lean producer?
3. What is TPS?
4. What is level scheduling?
5. JIT attempts to remove delays, which do not add value. How then does JIT cope with weather and its impact on crop harvest and transportation times?

6. What are three ways in which JIT and quality are related?
7. How does TPS contribute to competitive advantage?
8. What are the characteristics of just-in-time partnerships with respect to suppliers?
9. Discuss how the Japanese word for *card* has application in the study of JIT.

10. Standardized, reusable containers have fairly obvious benefits for shipping. What is the purpose of these devices within the plant?

11. Does lean production work in the service sector? Provide an illustration.

12. Which lean techniques work in both the manufacturing *and* service sectors?

Ethical Dilemma

In this lean operations world, in an effort to lower handling costs, speed delivery, and reduce inventory, retailers are forcing their suppliers to do more and more in the way of preparing their merchandise for their cross-docking warehouses, shipment to specific stores, and shelf presentation. Your company, a small manufacturer of aquarium decorations, is in a tough position. First, Mega-Mart wanted you to develop bar-code technology, then special packaging, then small individual shipments bar coded for each store (this way when the merchandise hits the warehouse it is cross-docked immediately to the correct truck and store and is ready for shelf placement). And now Mega-Mart wants you to develop RFID—immediately. Mega-Mart has made it clear that suppliers that cannot keep up with the technology will be dropped.

Earlier, when you didn't have the expertise for bar codes, you had to borrow money and hire an outside firm to do the development, purchase the technology, and train your shipping clerk. Then, meeting the special packaging requirement drove you into negative income for several months, resulting in a loss for last year. Now it appears that the RFID request is impossible. Your business, under the best of conditions, is marginally profitable, and the bank may not be willing to bail you out again. Over the years, Mega-Mart has slowly become your major customer and without them, you are probably out of business. What are the ethical issues and what do you do?

Problems*

•   **1**   Leblanc Electronics, Inc., in Nashville, produces short runs of custom airwave scanners for the defense industry. You have been asked by the owner, Larry Leblanc, to reduce inventory by introducing a kanban system. After several hours of analysis, you develop the following data for scanner connectors used in one work cell. How many kanbans do you need for this connector?

Daily demand	1,000 connectors
Lead time	2 days
Safety stock	$\frac{1}{2}$ day
Kanban size	500 connectors

•   **2**   Chip Gillikin's company wants to establish kanbans to feed a newly established work cell. The following data have been provided. How many kanbans are needed?

Daily demand	250 units
Production lead time	$\frac{1}{2}$ day
Safety stock	$\frac{1}{4}$ day
Kanban size	50 units

••   **3**   Chris Millikan Manufacturing, Inc., is moving to kanbans to support its telephone switching-board assembly lines. Determine the size of the kanban for subassemblies and the number of kanbans needed.

Setup cost = $30

Annual holding
          cost = $120 per subassembly

Daily production = 20 subassemblies

Annual usage = 2,500 (50 weeks × 5 days each
                      × daily usage of 10 subassemblies)

Lead time = 16 days

Safety stock = 4 days' production of subassemblies. **Px**

••   **4**   Maggie Moylan Motorcycle Corp. uses kanbans to support its transmission assembly line. Determine the size of the kanban for the mainshaft assembly and the number of kanbans needed.

Setup cost = $20

Annual holding cost
of mainshaft assembly = $250 per unit

Daily production = 300 mainshafts

Annual usage = 20,000 (= 50 weeks × 5 days each
                      × daily usage of 80 mainshafts)

Lead time = 3 days

Safety stock = $\frac{1}{2}$ day's production of mainshafts

Green Gear Cycling, Inc.

Note: **Px** means the problem may be solved with POM for Windows and/or Excel OM.

• **5** Discount-Mart, a major East Coast retailer, wants to determine the economic order quantity for its halogen lamps. It currently buys all halogen lamps from Specialty Lighting Manufacturers, in Atlanta. Annual demand is 2,000 lamps, ordering cost per order is $30, carrying cost per lamp is $12.

a) What is the EOQ?

b) What are the total annual costs of holding and ordering (managing) this inventory?

c) How many orders should Discount-Mart place with Specialty Lighting per year? **Px**

• • • **6** Discount-Mart (see Problem 5), as part of its new JIT program, has signed a long-term contract with Specialty Lighting and will place orders electronically for its halogen lamps. Ordering costs will drop to $.50 per order, but Discount-Mart also reassessed its carrying costs and raised them to $20 per lamp.

a) What is the new economic order quantity?

b) How many orders will now be placed?

c) What is the total annual cost of managing the inventory with this policy? **Px**

• • **7** How do your answers to Problems 5 and 6 provide insight into a JIT purchasing strategy?

• • • **8** Bill Penny has a repetitive manufacturing plant producing trailer hitches in Arlington, Texas. The plant has an average inventory turnover of only 12 times per year. He has therefore determined that he will reduce his component lot sizes. He has developed the following data for one component, the safety chain clip:

Annual demand = 31,200 units

Daily demand = 120 units

Daily production (in 8 hours) = 960 units

Desired lot size (1 hour of production) = 120 units

Holding cost per unit per year = $12

Setup labor cost per hour = $20

How many minutes of setup time should he have his plant manager aim for regarding this component?

• • • **9** Given the following information about a product, at Phyllis Simon's firm, what is the appropriate setup time?

Annual demand = 39,000 units

Daily demand = 150 units

Daily production = 1,000 units

Desired lot size = 150 units

Holding cost per unit per year = $10

Setup labor cost per hour = $40

• • • **10** Rick Wing has a repetitive manufacturing plant producing automobile steering wheels. Use the following data to prepare for a reduced lot size. The firm uses a work year of 305 days.

Annual demand for steering wheels	30,500
Daily demand	100
Daily production (8 hours)	800
Desired lot size (2 hours of production)	200
Holding cost per unit per year	$10

a) What is the setup cost, based on the desired lot size?

b) What is the setup time, based on $40 per hour setup labor?

Case Studies

Mutual Insurance Company of Iowa

Mutual Insurance Company of Iowa (MICI) has a major insurance office facility located in Des Moines, Iowa. The Des Moines office is responsible for processing all of MICI's insurance claims for the entire nation. The company's sales have experienced rapid growth during the last year, and as expected, record levels in claims followed. Over 2,500 forms for claims a day are now flowing into the office for processing. Unfortunately, fewer than 2,500 forms a day are flowing out. The total time to process a claim, from the time it arrives to the time a check is mailed, has increased from 10 days to 10 weeks. As a result, some customers are threatening legal action. Sally Cook, the manager of Claims Processing, is particularly distressed, as she knows that a claim seldom requires more than 3 hours of actual work. Under the current administrative procedures, human resources limitations, and facility constraints, there appear to be no easy fixes for the problem. But clearly, something must be done, as the workload has overwhelmed the existing system.

MICI management wants aggressive, but economical, action taken to fix the problem. Ms. Cook has decided to try a JIT approach to claim processing. With support from her bosses, and as a temporary fix, Cook has brought in part-time personnel from MICI sales divisions across the country to help. They are to work down the claims backlog while a new JIT system is installed.

Meanwhile, Claims Processing managers and employees are to be trained in JIT principles. With JIT principles firmly in mind, managers will redesign jobs to move responsibilities for quality control activities to each employee, holding them responsible for quality work and any necessary corrections. Cook will also initiate worker-training programs that explain the entire claim processing flow, as well as provide comprehensive training on each step in the process. Data-entry skills will also be taught to both employees and managers in an effort to fix responsibility for data accuracy on the processor rather than on data entry clerks. Additionally, cross training will be emphasized to enable workers within departments to process a variety of customer claim applications in their entirety.

Cook and her supervisors are also reexamining the insurance and claim forms currently in use. They want to see if standardization of forms will cut processing time, reduce data-entry time, and cut work-in-process.

They hope the changes will also save training time. Making changes in work methods and worker skills leads logically to a need for change in the layout of the Claims Processing Department. This potential change represents a major move from the departmental layout of the past, and will be a costly step. To help ensure the successful implementation of this phase of the changeover, Cook estab-

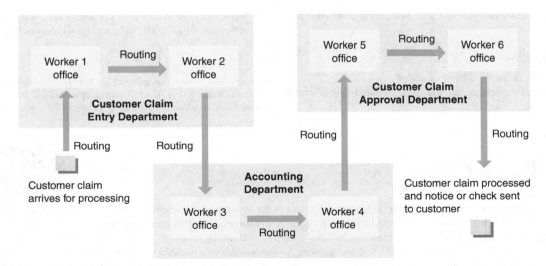

▲ **Figure 10**   **Claims Processing Department Layout**

lished a team made up of supervisors, employees, and an outside office layout consultant. She also had the team visit the Kawasaki motorcycle plant in Lincoln, Nebraska, to observe their use of work cells to aid JIT.

The team concluded that a change in the office facilities was necessary to successfully implement and integrate JIT concepts at MICI. The team believes it should revise the layout of the operation and work methods to bring them in line with "group technology cell" layouts. An example of the current departmental layout and claim processing flow pattern is presented in Figure 10. As can be seen in this figure, customer claims arrive for processing at the facility and flow through a series of offices and departments to eventually complete the claim process. Although the arrangement of the offices and workers in Figure 10 is typical, the entire facility actually operates 20 additional flows, each consisting of the same three departments. However, not all of the 20 flows are configured the same. The number of employees, for example, varies depending on the claim form requirements (larger claims have to be approved by more people). So while all forms must pass through the same three departments (Customer Claim Entry,

Accounting, and Customer Claim Approval), the number of workers for each claim may vary from two to four. For this reason, the MICI facility currently maintains a staff of over 180 office workers just to process and route claims. All these people work for Ms. Cook.

Discussion Questions

1. Identify the attributes you would expect the Claims Processing Department at MICI to have once the new JIT system is in place.
2. What will the restructured cell layout for claim processing in Figure 10 look like? Draw it.
3. What assumptions are you making about personnel and equipment in the new group technology cell layout?
4. How will the new JIT oriented system benefit the MICI operation? Explain.

Source: Adapted from Marc J. Schniederjans, *Topics in Just-in-Time Management*, pp. 283–285. Reprinted by permission of Prentice Hall, Inc., Upper Saddle River, NJ.

JIT after the Fire

World-renowned Toyota Motor Corporation has a worldwide presence, with Toyota's investment in North America alone exceeding $13 billion in 11 manufacturing plants. Toyota is at the forefront of lean firms and a showcase of JIT. Executives from all over the world make the journey to Toyota to see how JIT works.

But early one Saturday morning in February, a fire roared through the huge Aisin Seiki plant in Kariya, Japan. The fire incinerated the main source of crucial brake valves that Toyota buys from Aisin and uses in most of its cars. Aisin has long been a supplier of the critical brake-fluid-proportioning valves (P-valves), supplying 99% of Toyota's requirement for the valve. About 80% of Aisin's total output goes to Toyota. As the smoke cleared, the extent of the disaster was clear—most of the 506 special machines used to manufacture the P-valves were useless. A few might be repaired in 2 weeks, but most would need to be replaced—and the

lead time was 6 weeks. Both Aisin and Toyota had been operating at full capacity.

Consistent with JIT practices, Toyota maintained only a 4-hour supply of the valve. And there were few of the valves in the closely knit network that constituted Toyota's supply chain. Depending on a single source and holding little inventory is a risk, but it also keeps Toyota lean and its costs low. The Toyota plants in Japan build 14,000 cars a day. Without that valve, production would come to a rapid halt. Moreover, Toyota production managers were dismayed to find they needed 200 variations of the P-valve.

Consistent with the *keiretsu* networks that are typical of Japan's manufacturing sector, Toyota holds 23% of Aisin's stock, and Aisin's president is Kanshiro Toyoda of the Toyoda family that founded the automaker. Kosuke Ikebuchi, a Toyota senior managing director, was tracked down at 8 A.M. at a golf course clubhouse and given the bad news.

Discussion Questions

1. If you are Mr. Ikebuchi, what do you do?
2. What does this experience tell you (and Aisin and Toyota) about just-in-time?

3. If you had been in charge of Chrysler's JIT supplies the morning of September 11, 2001, what actions would you have taken?

Sources: Case is based on material in: *The Wall Street Journal* (July 20, 2007): B1, (May 8, 1997): A1, A5 and (September 24, 2001): B1, B4; and *Harvard Business Review* (September–October 1999): 97–106.

JIT at Arnold Palmer Hospital

Video Case

Orlando's Arnold Palmer Hospital, founded in 1989, specializes in treatment of women and children and is renowned for its high-quality rankings (top 10% of 2000 benchmarked hospitals), its labor and delivery volume (more than 13,000 births per year, and growing), and its neonatal intensive care unit (one of the highest survival rates in the nation). But quality medical practices and high patient satisfaction require costly inventory—some $30 million per year and thousands of SKUs.* With pressure on medical care to manage and reduce costs, Arnold Palmer Hospital has turned toward controlling its inventory with just-in-time (JIT) techniques.

Within the hospital, for example, drugs are now distributed at nursing workstations via dispensing machines (almost like vending machines) that electronically track patient usage and post the related charge to each patient. The dispensing stations are refilled each night, based on patient demand and prescriptions written by doctors.

To address JIT issues externally, Arnold Palmer Hospital turned toward a major distribution partner, McKesson General Medical, which as a first-tier supplier provides the hospital with about one quarter of all its medical/surgical inventory. McKesson supplies sponges, basins, towels, mayo stand covers, syringes, and hundreds of other medical/surgical items. To ensure coordinated daily delivery of inventory purchased from McKesson, an account executive has been assigned to the hospital on a full-time basis, as well as two other individuals who address customer service and product issues. The result has been a drop in Central Supply average daily inventory from $400,000 to $114,000 since JIT.

JIT success has also been achieved in the area of *custom surgical packs*. Custom surgical packs are the sterile coverings, disposable plastic trays, gauze, and the like, specialized to each type of surgical procedure. Arnold Palmer Hospital uses 10 different custom packs for various surgical procedures. "Over 50,000 packs are used each year, for a total cost of about $1.5 million," says George DeLong, head of Supply Chain Management.

The packs are not only delivered in a JIT manner but packed that way as well. That is, they are packed in the reverse order they are used so each item comes out of the pack in the sequence it is needed. The packs are bulky, expensive, and must remain sterile. Reducing the inventory and handling while maintaining an assured sterile supply for scheduled surgeries presents a challenge to hospitals.

Here is how the supply chain works: Custom packs are *assembled* by a packing company with *components supplied* primarily from manufacturers selected by the hospital, and *delivered* by McKesson from its local warehouse. Arnold Palmer Hospital works with its own surgical staff (through the Medical Economics Outcome Committee) to identify and standardize the custom packs to reduce the number of custom pack SKUs. With this integrated system, pack safety stock inventory has been cut to one day.

The procedure to drive the custom surgical pack JIT system begins with a "pull" from the doctor's daily surgical schedule. Then, Arnold Palmer Hospital initiates an electronic order to McKesson between 1:00 and 2:00 P.M. daily. At 4:00 A.M. the next morning McKesson delivers the packs. Hospital personnel arrive at 7:00 A.M. and stock the shelves for scheduled surgeries. McKesson then reorders from the packing company, which in turn "pulls" necessary inventory for the quantity of packs needed from the manufacturers.

Arnold Palmer Hospital's JIT system reduces inventory investment, expensive traditional ordering, and bulky storage, and supports quality with a sterile delivery.

Discussion Questions**

1. What do you recommend be done when an error is found in a pack as it is opened for an operation?
2. How might the procedure for custom surgical packs described here be improved?
3. When discussing JIT in services, the text notes that suppliers, layout, inventory, and scheduling are all used. Provide an example of each of these at Arnold Palmer Hospital.
4. When a doctor proposes a new surgical procedure, how do you recommend the SKU for a new custom pack be entered into the hospital's supply chain system?

*SKU = stock keeping unit

**You may wish to view this video case on your student DVD before answering these questions.

Additional Case Studies

Harvard has selected these Harvard Business School cases to accompany this text:

harvardbusinessonline.hbsp.harvard.edu

- **Johnson Controls Automotive Systems Group: The Georgetown, Kentucky, Plant** (#693-086): Examines the challenge of JIT with growing variation and a change from JIT delivery to JIT assembly.
- **Injex Industries** (#697-003): Examines supplier concerns as Injex provides components to a single, demanding customer on a JIT basis.

Bibliography

Ahls, Bill. "Advanced Memory and Lean Change," *IIE Solutions* 33, no. 1 (January 2001): 40–42.

Bacheldor, Beth, and Laurie Sullivan. "Never Too Lean." *Information Week* 985 (April 19, 2004): 36–42.

Bruun, Peter, and Robert N. Mefford. "Lean Production and the Internet." *International Journal of Production Economics* 89, no. 3 (June 18, 2004): 247.

Burke, Robert, and Gregg Messel. "From Simulation to Implementation: Cardinal Health's Lean Journey." *Target: Innovation at Work* 19, no. 2 (2nd quarter 2003): 27–32.

Hall, Robert W. "'Lean' and the Toyota Production System." *Target* 20, no. 3 (3rd issue 2004): 22–27.

Keyte, Beau, and Drew Locher. *The Complete Lean Enterprise.* University Park, IL: Productivity Press, 2004.

King, Andrew A., and Michael J. Lenox. "Lean and Green? An Empirical Examination of the Relationship Between Lean Production and Environmental Performance." *Production and Operations Management* 10, no. 3 (fall 2001): 244–256.

Klassen, Robert D. "Just-in-Time Manufacturing and Pollution Prevention Generate Mutual Benefits in the Furniture Industry." *Interfaces* 30, no. 3 (May–June 2000): 95–106.

Morgan, James M., and Jeffrey K. Liker. *The Toyota Product Development System.* New York: Productivity Press, 2007.

Parks, Charles M. "The Bare Necessities of Lean." *Industrial Engineer* 35, no. 8 (August 2003): 39.

Schonberger, Richard J. "Lean Extended." *Industrial Engineer* (December 2005): 26–31.

van Veen-Dirks, Paula. "Management Control and the Production Environment." *International Journal of Production Economics* 93 (January 8, 2005): 263.

Womack, James P., and Daniel T. Jones. "Lean Consumption." *Harvard Business Review* (March 2005): 58–68.

Womack, James P., and Daniel T. Jones. *Lean Solutions: How Companies and Customers Can Create Value and Wealth Together.* New York: The Free Press, 2005.

Internet Resources

Business Open Learning Archive: **www.bola.biz/index.html**

Gemba Research: **www.gemba.com**

Kanban—and the environment:
www.epa.gov/lean/thinking/kanban.htm

Kanban—explanation:
www.graphicproducts.com/tutorials/kanban/

Manufacturing Engineering: **www.mfgeng.com**

Mid-America Manufacturing Technology Center:
www.mamtc.com

Toyota Motor Corp.:
www.toyota.co.jp/en/vision/production_system

Solutions to Even Numbered Problems

2 3.75, or 4 kanbans

4 Size of kanban = 66; number of kanbans = 5.9, or 6

6 (a) EOQ = 10 lamps
   (b) 200 orders/yr.
   (c) $200

8 7.26 min.

10 (a) Setup cost = $5.74
   (b) Setup time = 8.61 min.

Solutions to Self test

1. d; **2.** a; **3.** e; **4.** overproduction, queues, transportation, inventory, motion, overprocessing, defective product; **5.** sort; simplify; shine; standardize; sustain; **6.** d; **7.** e; **8.** a; **9.** e; **10.** c.

476

Index

481

485